TROPICAL &
SUBTROPICAL TREES

AN ENCYCLOPEDIA

MARGARET BARWICK

TROPICAL & SUBTROPICAL TREES

AN ENCYCLOPEDIA

Chief Editor: Anton van der Schans

Foreword by Larry M. Schokman   Illustrations by Jan Barwick Claudy

With 2,305 illustrations, 1,981 in color

TIMBER PRESS

PORTLAND, OREGON

This book is dedicated to
David for his love and steadfast support,
Paulina for her generosity,
Eleanor for her enlightment
and to Jo, Amy and Jack
who promise to continue to cherish our planet.

First published in the United Kingdom in 2004 by Thames & Hudson Ltd

Published in North America in 2004 by
Timber Press, Inc.
The Haseltine Building
133 S.W. Second Avenue, Suite 450
Portland, Oregon 97204-3527, U.S.A.

www.timberpress.com

ISBN 0-88192-661-2

A catalog record for this book is available from the Library of Congress

Printed and bound in Singapore by Tien Wah Press Pte Ltd

CONTENTS

FOREWORD

As we begin the new millennium, we tend to be mesmerized by technological advances, usually, and unfortunately, at the expense of our links with nature. We reach for the stars but tend to forget the ground upon which we stand. Computers, concrete and cars have an insidious way of lulling humanity into a short-sighted slumber that will have horrendous repercussions unless we participate in, and not prey on, our planet. Society is rapidly moving away from nature and we are destroying and/or consuming resources critical to our survival. Unless we change this philosophy, we can look forward to diminished lifestyles, despite rising expectations. The ultimate victory in our battle against environmental decay and pollution depends to a large extent on how we protect and preserve the plant life around us.

From time immemorial, traders, explorers, buccaneers and colonial powers have been fascinated by tropical islands. Their interest has taken an inevitable toll on these islands' respective ecosystems. In this age of quick and relatively inexpensive travel, a new wave of ecological invaders leave their cities and gravitate to these idyllic surroundings. To accommodate affluent tourists, the natural wealth of the islands is rapidly disappearing because hotels, resorts and an exploding population eventually replace the natural habitat.

One of every eight plant species is threatened with extinction, according to the first comprehensive worldwide assessment of plant endangerment. This analysis took over twenty years of diligent work by conservationists and horticulturalists around the globe.

Margaret Barwick was born in New Zealand. In 1986, her late husband, David, retired as Governor of the British Virgin Islands in Tortola, where she designed and planted the first botanical garden in that country. They moved to live in the Cayman Islands, where she was involved in the founding of the Queen Elizabeth II Botanic Park, creating the Nature Trail and planting some of the first horticultural areas.

Margaret has woven a compendium of facts about trees for our gardens that are collectively a part of the larger landscape of nature. Gardening and horticulture are interrelated and connected by ideas, activities, spaces and cultural constraints. We do not need a formal English garden or an Italian Renaissance garden to feel that we are in vogue. Margaret emphasizes the importance of preserving threatened environmental resources, respecting and incorporating the indigenous flora, but not at the expense of biodiversity. Cultivation of the garden ethic must begin with a healthy respect for nature.

Tropical & Subtropical Trees is truly a labour of love, containing a great deal of botanical and horticultural information not found in similar publications. Margaret also shares a lifetime of gardening experience that she acquired as the wife of a British civil servant during their peregrinations around the world.

Larry M. Schokman
The Kampong of the National Tropical Botanical Garden,
Coconut Grove, Miami,
Florida, USA.

PROLOGUE

'For all its mass, a tree is a remarkable thing. All of its internal life exists within three paper-thin layers of tissue – the phloem, xylem and cambium – just beneath the bark, which together form a moist sleeve around the dead heartwood. However tall it grows, a tree is just a few pounds of living cells thinly spread between roots and leaves. These three diligent layers of cells perform all the intricate science and engineering needed to keep a tree alive, and the efficiency with which they do it is one of the wonders of life. Without noise or fuss, every tree in a forest lifts massive volumes of water – several hundred gallons in the case of a large tree on a hot day – from its roots to its leaves, where it is returned to the atmosphere. Imagine the din and commotion, the clutter of machinery that would be needed for a fire department to raise a similar volume of water.

And lifting water is just one of the many jobs that the phloem, xylem and cambium perform. They also manufacture lignin and cellulose; regulate the storage and production of tannin, sap, gum, oils and resins; dole out minerals and nutrients; convert starches into sugars for future growth (which is where maple syrup comes into the picture); and goodness knows what else. But because all this is happening in such a thin layer, it also leaves the tree terribly vulnerable to invasive organisms. To combat this, trees have formed elaborate defence mechanisms. The reason a rubber tree seeps latex when cut is that this is its way of saying to insects and other organisms, "Not tasty. Nothing here for you. Go away." Trees can also deter destructive creatures like caterpillars by flooding their leaves with tannin, which makes the leaves less tasty and so inclines the caterpillar to look elsewhere. When infestations are particularly severe, some trees can even communicate the fact. Some species of oaks release a chemical that tells other oaks in the vicinity that an attack is under way. In response, the neighbouring oaks step up their tannin production, the better to withstand the coming onslaught.

By such means, of course, does nature tick along. The problem arises when a tree encounters an attacker for which evolution has left it unprepared, and seldom has a tree been more helpless against an invader than the American Chestnut against *Endothia parasitica*. It enters a Chestnut effortlessly, devours the cambium cells and positions itself for attack on the next tree before the tree has the faintest idea, chemically speaking, what hit it. It spreads by means of spores, which are produced in the hundreds of millions in each canker. A single woodpecker can transfer a billion spores on one flight between trees. At the height of the American Chestnut blight, every woodland breeze would lose spores in uncountable trillions to drift in a pretty lethal haze on to neighbouring hillsides. The mortality rate was 100 per cent. In just over thirty years the American Chestnut became a memory. The Appalachians alone lost four billion trees, a quarter of its cover, in a generation.

A great tragedy, of course. But how lucky, when you think about it, that these diseases are at least species specific. Instead of a Chestnut blight or Dutch Elm disease or Dogwood anthracnose, what if there was just a tree blight – something indiscriminate and unstoppable that swept through whole forests? In fact, there is. It's called acid rain.'

> Bill Bryson,
> reproduced by his kind permission
> from his book *A Walk in the Woods,*
> Broadway Books, New York, 1998,
> a story of his adventures walking the Appalachian Trail
> in the eastern United States.

ACKNOWLEDGMENTS

We wish to acknowledge the following friends and colleagues who graciously and enthusiastically contributed to this work:

George Craig of Scotland and Cayman, friend and benefactor, who believed in this book and made it happen. Also:

Rosemary Sandberg for her gentle guidance and determination,

Mark Lane of Thames & Hudson Ltd, a wise counsellor and partisan; and especially:

Anton van der Schans of Cairns, N Queensland, Australia; biologist, landscaper and dedicated dendrologist, who patiently navigated me through the labyrinth of Australia's tropical flora and tracked down and photographed so many of the trees.

Larry Schokman, plantsman extraordinaire, Director of The Kampong of the National Tropical Botanical Garden, Miami, USA, for his friendship, common sense and encouragement.

Chuck Hubbuch, old friend and Past Director of Plant Collections at Fairchild Tropical Garden, Coral Gables, Florida, USA; as well as:

Don Evans, Benoit Jonckheere and other staff members for their encouragement and for ensuring the scientific integrity of this book.

To my wonderful, talented family:

Simon and **Babbity Barwick** of Cayman, designers par excellence, for their professional advice and superb layouts,

Jan Barwick Claudy for her exquisite illustrations, and

Miranda Barwick Philbin for her support, photographic skills and wit.

Ian Turner, Assistant Director, Singapore Botanic Gardens, and:

Andrea Kee Heng Choon, Research Officer, for their great kindness and invaluable advice during my visit.

Ali Ibrahim, conservationist and superb photographer, of the National Parks Board, Singapore, who introduced me to the inner magic of the island of Pulau Ubin, as well as providing information and photographs, and

Tan Jiew Hoe whose gracious hospitality made my visit to Singapore especially memorable.

Harriet Veitch, journalist of Sydney, Australia, for her dedicated, untiring, long-distance proof-reading, and her father and lifelong friend,

Jock Veitch, for taking up his pencil when needed.

Jerry Rogers of Sydney and Queensland, Australia, who was important in keeping me up to date on rare fruits and for faithfully recording them on film, and:

Dr. Wyn Courtney for her enduring friendship, geographical guidance and Baobab research.

Dr. Angela Leiva Sanchez and the staff of the Jardin Botanico Nacional of Cuba, as well as,

Dr. Laziro and staff of the Jardin Botanico de Cienfuegos, Cuba, for their gracious reception and scientific help, particularly my dear friends:

Hermes Rodriguez Sanchez and **Duany**, for ongoing help, advice and superb photographs.

Timothy R. Phillips, Superintendent, and

Dr. Jim Bauml, Senior Biologist, The Arboretum of Los Angeles, USA, for making my visit so fulfilling.

Brian Cooney of Mt. Coot-tha Botanic Gardens in Brisbane, Australia, for his participation and

David Warmington, Curator, along with:

Norma Coley, Keith English and Peter Shanahan of Flecker Botanic Gardens, Cairns, N Queensland, Australia,

Alan and **Susie Carle** at the Botanical Ark in Mossman, N Queensland, who inspire so many with their knowledge and achievements, as do the dedicated plantspeople:

Ross Hunter of Mt. Molloy, Queensland, who cheerfully shared his knowledge and photographs, and

John and **Chris Farrington** whose support and valuable reviews are greatly appreciated.

David Orr and **Erin Purple** of the Waimea Arboretum are remembered for their patience and generous help, as are:

Indre Furlong-Kelly, Director, and

Vishnu Ramsawak, Horticulturalist, of the Royal Botanic Gardens, Trinidad,

Steve Maximay of the University of the West Indies, Trinidad, and

Narisa Abdool, the dedicated guardian of the Wild Fowl Trust in Trinidad, all of whom made my visit to their glorious country so special.

Chris Rollins and **Susan Barnwell** of the Fruit and Spice Park in Homestead, Florida, are remembered for their cheerful and enthusiastic participation, and

Dr. Terence Walters of Montgomery Botanical Center, Miami, USA, who assisted me during my visits there.

Special thanks also to many eminent Australians who assisted Anton in his research, including:
Dr. Betsy Jackes, of James Cook University, Townsville, Queensland,
Hugh Clelland of Northern Territory University Darwin, and
Joseph Corbin of Darwin and Qatar, all of whom gave freely of their advice.
Dave Griffiths, Curator, and **Sharon Wilson**, Horticulturalist, of the George Brown Darwin Botanic Gardens, and their fellow Northern Territory plantspeople:
Darryl South, Kerry and **Sandra Byrnes, Joe** and **Karen Perner.**
Glenn Thomas of Queensland University of Technology, and Horticulturists:
John Popham, Matt O'Riley, **Rigel Jensen, Dr. Geoff Stocker, Dr. Tony Irvine**, and **Maarten Buijs** of Siteplan, Cairns, and
Julie Lake, Horticulturalist and author of Brisbane.
Michael Ferrero of Nong-Nooch Botanic Gardens in Thailand. Without their expert collaboration the integrity of this work would be diminished.

We also wish to acknowledge the generous help of
John Leach of Andromeda Gardens, Barbados, a garden full of old memories,
Mike Winterstein of the United States Dept. Agriculture Research Service, in Miami, USA,
Willy Ingram and **Robbie Binder**, exemplary nurserypeople and treasured friends, of Homestead, Florida, USA, for the many plant-hunting and photographic safaris we took together, and
Ernesto Rodriguez and **Dimitrius Petropoulos**, passionate plantspeople of Ernesto's Good Earth Nursery, Miami, Florida, USA.
Sandy Urquhart of Grand Cayman, nurseryperson, landscape designer and lifelong friend, who tested the theory, and
Patricia Bradley of Cayman, an ornithologist who offered scientific guidance.
Louise Gross of Coconut Grove, Miami, USA, who sheltered, nourished and encouraged, while
Jane Brown of Irian Jaya searched the Indonesian jungles with her camera, and

Jocelyn Fauvet, neighbour and friend of SW France, enthusiastically recorded the flora of West and East Africa, as well as Madagascar.

Grateful thanks also to:
Terry Barnard of Dubai and France for her local research, photography and proof-reading, and
Sue and **Andy Grieff, Maureen Emmet** and **Sue Rowat** of Costa Blanca, Spain, for pursuing and capturing Mediterranean species with their cameras, as well as checking the integrity.

Appreciation to:
Gil Appleton,writer and journalist, for sage advice and guidance,
Beryl Giles writer, journalist and publisher of Sydney, Australia, for her last-minute input,
Mary Moody and her daughter, **Miriam Hannay**, of Yetholme, E Australia, for adding their experience and professionalism to the project.
David and **Lucie Glenn** of Havanna, Cuba, are saluted for their continued kindness and hospitality. Also:
Sarah Bailey of London, UK, for her countless acts of salvage, and
Shabnam Alibai of Fort Lauderdale, Florida, USA, for her typically generous participation.
Dr. Joe Jackman of Cayman for sharing his knowledge.

We are indebted to:
Edward Fletcher of Cheltenham, UK, for generously loaning his precious Baobab slides,
Dennis McGlade of Olin Partnership, Philadelphia, USA, and
Raymond Jungles of Key West, Florida, USA, eminent landscape architects, for their endorsements; also,
Andy Vernon of the Royal Botanic Gardens at Kew, London, UK, for his wicked wit and early research.
Philippe Timsit of Paris, France, a computer wizard who introduced me to my initial database, and
Shirley Lauer of Cayman, who took me through the first, faltering steps into the realms of computerdom.

Finally, many, many thanks to,
Jan Wikborg of Oslo, Norway, film producer and gentleman, who patiently guided me through the labyrinth of photographic theory.

HOW TO USE THIS BOOK

The definition of a tree is based on the loose scientific description of species that have a columnar, woody stem supporting branches, and whose height varies according to the species, the environment and other factors. Although the term 'tree' is normally applied to woody plants that reach a height of 6 m (20 ft), in certain cases some spp. (i.e. Tabebuia spp., a few of which are more shrub-like) have been included for expediency.

TREE SIZES
Tall = over 16 m (50 ft)   Medium = 8–16 m (26–50 ft)   Small = under 8 m (26 ft)

SCIENTIFIC DATA
Scientific data generally follows *The Plant Book*, by D. J. Mabberly, Cambridge University Press, 1997, as well as taxonomic advice from botanists and horticulturalists at the Royal Botanic Gardens at Kew, in London, UK, Fairchild Tropical Gardens, Miami, Florida, USA, Singapore Botanic Gardens and Flecker Gardens, Cairns, Queensland, Australia, as well as many associates and colleagues. Other guidance has been drawn from *The New Royal Horticultural Society Dictionary of Gardening*, Macmillan Press Co. Ltd. and up-to-date flora of relevant regions.

LAYOUT OF THE BOOK
Plants are listed in alphabetical order of their genus. Each genus is represented by one species, which is the most relevant or common of its genus in its region. It is listed by its common name, origin, growth habits, cultural requirements, morphology and landscape use. A general description of its historic, economic and medicinal importance is also included. In a case where more than one species of a genus is described, the data is reduced to the essential characteristics of the species.

The book is divided into 2 major parts:

PART 1 This describes trees that are grown for their flowers and foliage, edible fruit, spices or timber. It also includes information on species that have traditionally provided an essential element to the lives of their communities.

PART 2 This consists of cross-reference tables that show the significant characteristics of major flowering and foliage trees for quick reference.

EXPLANATION OF TERMS

Each genus is represented by a type species, usually chosen as the most typical and well known of the genus.
The type species is illustrated by photographs of the overall form, the flowers, fruit, bark and, if possible, the natural habitat.
Information includes:

Genus: the Latin name of the group of plants to which the tree belongs

Species: the Latin name of the specific plant within the genus

Author: the botanist who named the species: (L.) Willd., etc.

No. of species: the total number of species in the genus

Common name: the most universally popular common name or the common name in its native region

Synonyms: previous Latin names given to this species

Family: the family to which the genus (and species) belongs

Silhouette : showing the architectural growth habit and the average size of the species in cultivation, allowing that many trees do not reach their natural height when cultivated. The maximum height shown is 30m (100 ft)

Origin: where the plant is native or endemic

Height: the optimum known height to which the tree grows in its natural habitat

(Plant) type: the most important characteristics of the tree

Status: whether or not the species is threatened or endangered

Habitat: a broad description of the native habitat of the species

Growth: the average speed of growth

Flowering: the season during which the tree normally blooms

Dry tol: the tolerance of the tree to prolonged dry conditions

Salt tol: the tolerance of the tree to salt-laden winds

Light: the optimum amount of light needed for good growth

Soil: specific soil requirements

Nutrition: suggested supplementary nourishment required for good growth

Hazards: elements of hazard to humans: spines, toxins, etc.

Problems: general problems associated with the tree

Environment: the role the tree plays in its environment

Propagation: how the tree is bred or reproduced from parent stock

Leaves: description of the normal, mature leaf characteristics
Flowers: description of the normal flower characteristics
Fruit: description of the normal, mature fruit characteristics
Use: the general use of the tree for planting: for seaside or arid sites; evergreen foliage for shade; for seasonal colour display; small fruit tree planted in a backyard (for household consumption); large specimens suitable for parks and public open spaces; for street planting because of their non-aggressive roots and sturdy, non-brittle framework; evergreens suitable for hedging, screening, barriers or windbreaks; small to moderately sized specimens for their architectural form, foliage or trunk; suitable for planters or confined spaces; suited for planting in a heated conservatory or for use as a bonsai specimen.
General: a description of the tree together with its social and economic uses
Cultivars: a short list of the most important cultivars generally available
Blue note bar: used to warn of the invasiveness of the species or a change in nomenclature

ABBREVIATIONS

The following abbreviations have been used in the captions of Parts 1 and 2 of this book.

Arch.	Archipelago	**f.**	form	**Malesia**	region of Malaysia and Indonesia	**salt tol.**	salt tolerance
auctt.	of authors	**fl.**	flower			**sd**	seed
C	Central	**fls**	flowers			**sds**	seeds
cm	centimetres	**flowg**	flowering	**m**	metres	**sp.**	species
cv.	cultivar	**fr.**	fruit	**mm**	millimetres	**spp.**	more than one species
coast.	coastal	**fruitg**	fruiting	**N. Guinea**	New Guinea		
cvs	cultivars	**ft**	feet	**N**	North	**subsp.**	subspecies
decid.	deciduous	**in.**	inches	**NT**	Northern Territory	**syn.**	synonym
diam.	diameter	**infl.**	inflorescence			**USA**	United States of America
dioec.	dioecious	**Is**	Islands	**NSW**	New South Wales		
dry tol.	dry tolerance	**KZN**	KwaZuluNatal			**var.**	variety
E	East	**lf**	leaf	**nutrit.**	nutrition	**vars**	varieties
everg.	evergreen	**lflt**	leaflet	**pr**	pair	**yrs**	years
Eng.	English	**lvs**	leaves	**propag.**	propagation	**W**	West
environ.	environment	**Malay Pen.**	Malay Peninsula	**Qld**	Queensland	**Trop.**	tropical

COLOUR KEY
FOR SUMMARY BOXES

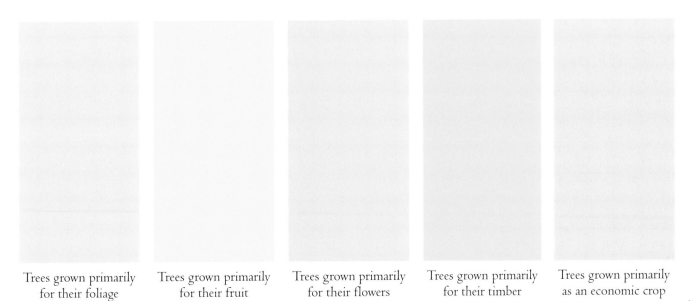

| Trees grown primarily for their foliage | Trees grown primarily for their fruit | Trees grown primarily for their flowers | Trees grown primarily for their timber | Trees grown primarily as an economic crop |

PLANT HARDINESS ZONES

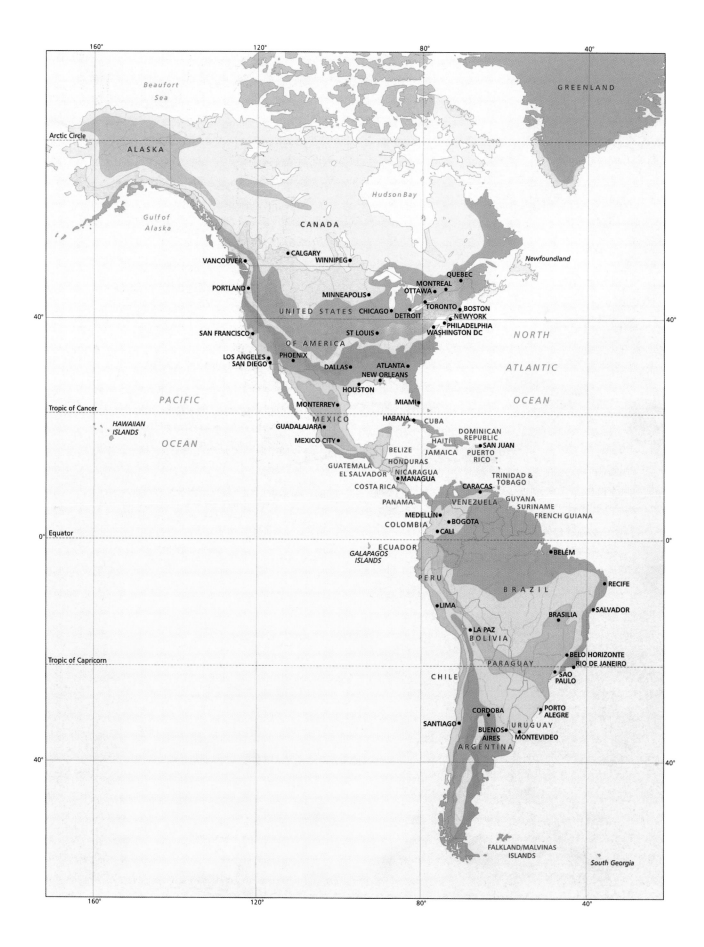

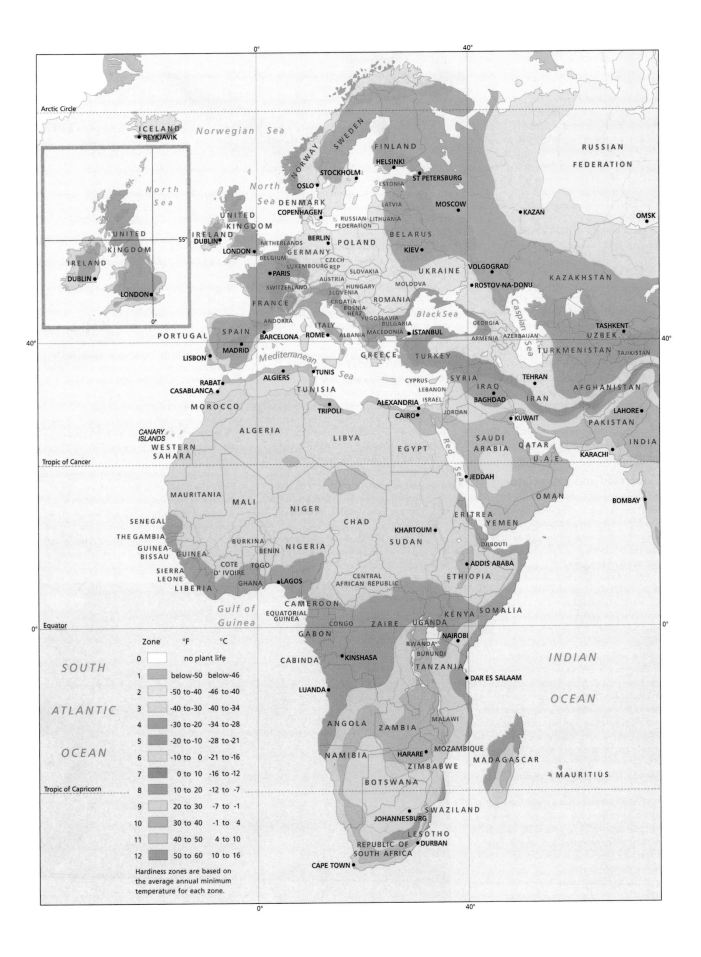

Zone legend:

Zone	°F	°C
0	no plant life	
1	below -50	below -46
2	-50 to -40	-46 to -40
3	-40 to -30	-40 to -34
4	-30 to -20	-34 to -28
5	-20 to -10	-28 to -21
6	-10 to 0	-21 to -16
7	0 to 10	-16 to -12
8	10 to 20	-12 to -7
9	20 to 30	-7 to -1
10	30 to 40	-1 to 4
11	40 to 50	4 to 10
12	50 to 60	10 to 16

Hardiness zones are based on the average annual minimum temperature for each zone.

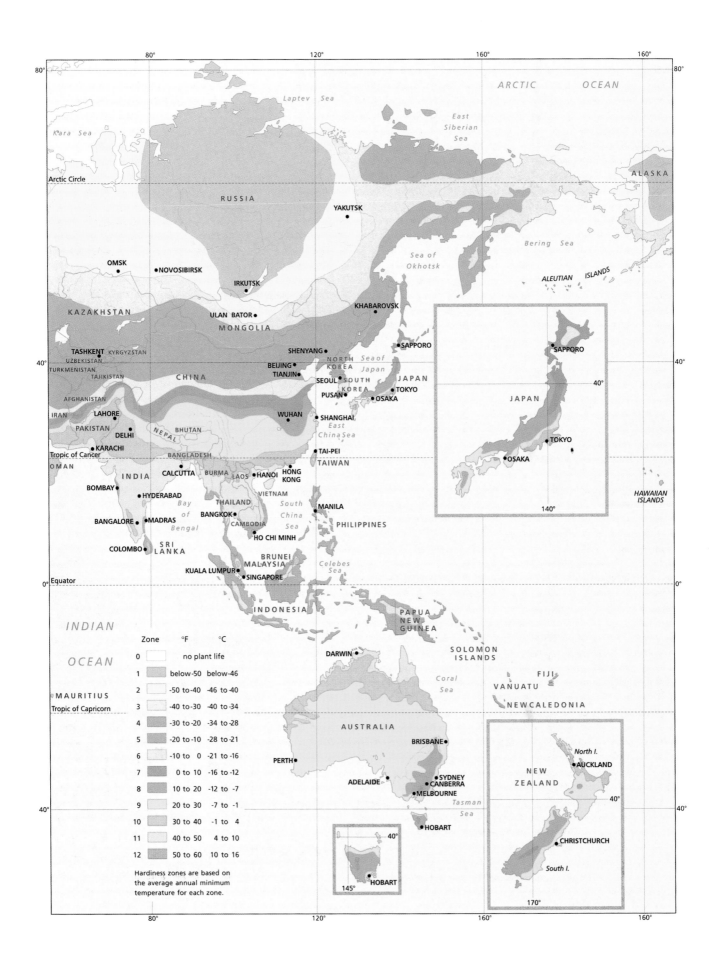

Zone	°F	°C
0	no plant life
1	below -50	below -46
2	-50 to -40	-46 to -40
3	-40 to -30	-40 to -34
4	-30 to -20	-34 to -28
5	-20 to -10	-28 to -21
6	-10 to 0	-21 to -16
7	0 to 10	-16 to -12
8	10 to 20	-12 to -7
9	20 to 30	-7 to -1
10	30 to 40	-1 to 4
11	40 to 50	4 to 10
12	50 to 60	10 to 16

Hardiness zones are based on
the average annual minimum
temperature for each zone.

THE ORIGINS OF TREES

The story begins with algae, primitive plants without leaves and stems that were the only living matter for two or three billion years before plants with leaves and stems began to appear. It is no surprise that the earth's colonization by plants should have proceeded so slowly. The first real plants not only had to create tissues capable of producing thick, cellular walls that could resist air and wind, but also to develop those complex adaptations that made metabolism and reproduction possible through roots and breathing systems. It was these thick, cellular walls that were later to evolve as the wood of trees.

During the early stages, reproductive methods changed rapidly. These primeval plants were spore-bearing. They could no longer rely on water for the mobile, male gametes to reach the stationary, female gametes, but were forced to rely on their spores for propagation, as flowers did not exist. They evolved during the Carboniferous period, so called because, as they died, the plants laid down the fossil coal carbons used today as fuel. Immense forests gradually evolved, composed of mainly *Equisetem* (horsetails) and ferns. This flora is mainly extinct, although descendants of the tree ferns and equisetums still exist in some regions. For tens of millions of years, these primeval forests acted as highly efficient purifying agents for the atmosphere, which then contained much more carbon dioxide than it does today. By fixing carbon and giving off oxygen, they permitted the evolution of animals and vegetables, which require large quantities of oxygen. At the same time, this process created cleaner, purer air that allowed more solar energy to reach the earth's surface. It was during this era that the large group of plants that we call gymnosperms first evolved. The early Cretaceous period, some 120 million years ago, saw the emergence of plants with true flowers and fruits with seeds.

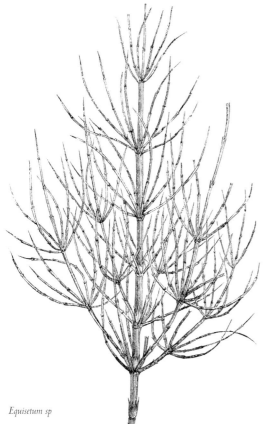

Equisetum sp

Throughout the comparatively recent Tertiary period, trees began to appear. They resembled the trees of today, and many of them still survive. But by the time primitive man appeared, the surface of the earth had been swept by at least four ice ages and plants had to fight for survival. The second ice age was the most severe, although it was separated from the first ice age by a relatively temperate period of some 50,000 years. During the first period, the poles were covered by ice caps that still exist today. With each era of cooling and warming, only the most well-established or adaptable plants survived. Gradually, evolutionary processes increased the diversity of plant families in different continents and climate zones, leading to a series of astonishing mutations and adaptations. Particularly influential were the high mountain ranges that checked plant migrations and gave some protection to the flora that had already enjoyed a more favourable environment during the warmer, Tertiary period. Thus plants became more and more specialized, and this evolutionary process still continues, even if plants seem to be unchanging.

During the planet's cataclysmic periods of warming and cooling, its environment changed dramatically, but the flora went on gradually adapting itself to the new conditions. During this process of interaction and modification, the biological communities adapted to the changing biosphere, gradually creating ecosystems. These are biological systems of interacting species that are dependent on their physical environment and on each other. Each ecosystem is bound up not only with the climate and other environmental factors, but with every form of life that develops within it, fauna as well as flora. There are many influences on these ecosystems. They include latitude, height above sea level and continental, coastal or island situations. Atmospheric factors such as light, temperature, humidity, rain, wind and carbon dioxide are all essential, as are the physical and chemical properties of the soil. Within this complex system, the stability of each element is important to the equilibrium of the whole; insects and animals obtain nourishment from the plants and, in turn, they help in their pollination and distribution. Human intervention can alter this equilibrium and lead to its destruction. Thoughtless actions could destroy the miracle that nature has taken three billion years to create.

FACTORS AFFECTING THE GROWTH OF TROPICAL AND SUBTROPICAL TREES

THE TROPICS lies north and south of the equator (o°) between the tropics of Cancer in the north (23°N) and Capricorn in the south (23°S). The equatorial region is at, or near, the equator, where temperatures and humidity are constantly high and daylight hours are equal in length. The subtropics lie adjacent to, or border on, the tropics.

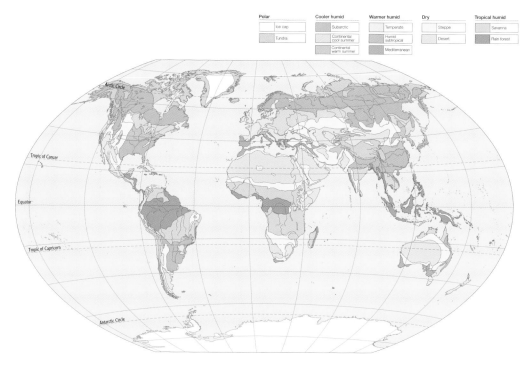

Map showing major climatic regions

The map above shows that the tropical and subtropical regions lie across vast reaches of the Pacific, Indian and Atlantic Oceans, with relatively little actual land mass; there are large areas of desert and many isolated islands. Tropical regions encompass many climatic and geographical features that affect the environment and thus the living conditions of their flora. Each of these factors determines the plants' design, as well as the mechanisms of their growth and reproduction. Each distinct plant community, or ecosystem, is formed of a great number of coexistent plant species that exhibit uniformity in certain characteristics. Dominant, and most important, are the tall-trunked, woody trees that originally formed communities, or forests. A simplified subdivision has been adopted that divides these forest communities into a few principal types:

RAINFORESTS are remarkable ecosystems that cover roughly 7 per cent of the land surface of our planet, yet are estimated to contain nearly 60 per cent of all earthly species. These vast forests are found in the permanently wet tropics in equatorial regions. They are composed of a continuous canopy of evergreen species, with many trees at least 30m (100 ft) tall, the largest reaching 60m (200 ft) or more. This 'jungle' is rich in thick-stemmed lianas, and in woody as well as herbaceous epiphytes and rhizomatous plants. Because of the lack of exploration and development, some forests of South East Asia, Asia-Pacific, Africa and the Amazon Basin have enjoyed continuous existence for millions of years and, because of their isolation, have been able to develop their rich and diverse composition to provide food, medicines and new energy sources. Norman Meyers, the English conservationist and leading expert on the environment, has described them as 'green machines' that 'perform the alchemy of sunlight, water and nutrients...through their watershed effects they act as a "sponge," soaking up rainfall before releasing it slowly and steadily into rivers.'

Rainforest in Barron Gorge, N Qld, Australia.>

Dry Eucalypt woodland on the Bismark Pange, N Qld, Australia.

TROPICAL, DRY, MONSOON or SEASONAL FORESTS are the most endangered of all major tropical ecosystems. They comprise 42 per cent of all tropical forests and encompass large areas of northern Australia, Africa, South East Asia, major parts of South America and many tropical islands. These forests are regulated by the seasonal rains and are often deciduous during the dry season, which is 4–7 months long. They lack the diversity of the rainforest, being up to 50 per cent less rich in species and having fewer epiphytes, ferns, vines and understorey flora. Nonetheless, dry forests are the parental climate for many major tropical food crops such as corn, rice, beans, sweet potatoes, sorghum and pasture grasses, and for cattle and other animals. Traditionally, in many regions, tropical, dry, forest land has been cleared for farming and grazing. Tree species with showy flowers are more abundant in these regions, with blooming often triggered when dry periods are followed by heavy rain.

TROPICAL, COASTAL REGIONS and ISLANDS, with their sandy beaches, coral reefs and palm-fringed shores, are now synonymous with tourism and are a year-round playground for those who wish to escape the rigours of the temperate winters. Tropical coastlines have become the most valuable property in the tropics, resulting in widespread clearing for development. This has had a marked effect on coastal regions, with the erosion and degradation of the coastal ridge, swamps and wetlands and the loss of sand beaches, leaving the land prey to hurricanes and flooding. Because of their isolation, many island species are endemic to that particular environment and, with the relatively small size and restricted genetic diversity of the habitats, they are naturally vulnerable.

< Coastal scrub and woodland of many islands, like this beach ridge in Little Cayman in the W Indies, are particularly vulnerable due to their desirability for development.

MANGROVE FORESTS, both marine and riverine, are essential to the climatic health of coastal regions, especially low-lying islands that lack mountains, rivers or lakes, geographical features necessary to the process of creating rainfall. With their high humidity and evaporation, mangrove ecosystems may literally create rain and, through their complicated filtering system, replenish water tables. Mangroves, which are linked to seagrass beds and coral reefs by tidal and animal movement, prevent coastal erosion, afford protected habitats for birds and other fauna, and provide a constant source of nutrients. The landside regions of mangrove forests are a habitat for many species of terrestrial fauna, while seaside fringes provide an important nursery for young fish and other marine life and a larder for larger, ocean fish. With the draining or filling in of mangrove swamps and associated wetlands, rainfall is decreased, water tables diminished, habitats lost and nearby reefs, so often the most important commercial asset of coastal regions, have their marine life seriously degraded.

Mangrove swamp on the island of Palau Ubin, off the coast of Singapore. This island is a protected reserve and is managed by the National Parks Board of Singapore. >

CLIMATE: temperature variations, diurnal and seasonal, which are determined by the latitude (distance from the equator, resulting in equatorial, tropical and subtropical zones) and the relief (continental and oceanic, mountains, plateaux, plains and river valleys), rainfall (amount and season) and prevailing winds.

SOILS: mineral and chemical content, humus, water content and drainage.

FIRE: though the role of fire is not understood thoroughly, it appears to override the other factors given above.

The implications of seasonal growth rhythms can be observed in cultivation. In Australia, for instance, subtropical plants from SE Queensland, which typically produce maximum shoot growth in spring and autumn, may be successfully cultivated in cooler, southern Australia. There they can grow through the summer months, provided adequate water is available, and survive the winter, if frosts do not exceed a species' lowest tolerance. Similarly, many tropical species from NE Queensland will grow well in cooler, subtropical, SE Queensland.

A fuller, yet simplified range of tropical and subtropical vegetation types is presented in this table:

1. RAINFOREST TYPES PRIMARILY AFFECTED BY TEMPERATURE, AND BY LATITUDE AND ALTITUDE (rainfall deficiency is not a significant factor)
    Equatorial lowland rainforest
    Tropical (subequatorial) rainforest
    Subtropical rainforest (including Araucanian rainforest)
    Upland rainforest
    Montane cloud forest
    Mountain meadows in the equatorial tropics

2. VEGETATION TYPES PRIMARILY AFFECTED BY THE SEASONAL DISTRIBUTION AND AMOUNT OF RAINFALL, WITH FIRE-SENSITIVE OR FIRE-ADAPTED COMMUNITIES
    Fire-sensitive communities
    Monsoon rainforest
    Vine thicket
    Thorn scrub

    Fire-adapted communities
    Secondary and transitional rainforests
    Open forests
    Woodlands
    Savannahs
    Semi-desert and desert vegetation

3. HEATHLANDS AFFECTED PRIMARILY BY THE SOIL
    Rainforest heath
    Sclerophyll heath

4. LITTORAL VEGETATION
    Aquatic littoral forests
    Gallery forests
    Forested wetlands
    Marine littoral vegetation
    Mangroves
    Beaches

PLANT CLASSIFICATION

This is the system of arranging all plants in groups with a name that is understood internationally. Latin is the universally accepted language for the precise specification and naming of these groups. The system is divided and subdivided and can become complicated. The following is a simplified version.

The Plant Kingdom is separated into four

DIVISIONS:

THALOPHYTES are the simplest plant forms, algae and fungi, which are not differentiated into roots, stems or leaves.

BRYOPHYTES comprise mosses and liverworts. These plants may be differentiated into stems and leaves but they lack true roots and conducting tissue.

PTERIDOPHYTES comprise ferns and their relatives, which are reproduced by spores.

SPERMATOPHYTES describe plants reproduced by means of seeds. Spermatophytes include most of our familiar cultivated plants.

Spermatophytes are divided into two main

CLASSES:

GYMNOSPERMS, which are not flowering plants, have ovules and seeds borne on the surface of a sporophyll, such as a cone scale. Included in this group are cycads and conifers, which in the broad sense include familiar cone-bearing pines, *Agathis* and *Araucaria*, as well as trees such as *Podocarpus* with fleshy fruit. These species are amongst the most primitive and ancient of vascular plants and many are considered living fossils.

ANGIOSPERMS, which have ovules and seeds enclosed within an ovary, borne in a flower that mostly includes sepals, petals and stamens. Angiosperms form the largest group of vascular plants that is estimated to contain more than 250,000 species. They are the most sophisticated of plant forms and are best adapted to survive in a wide range of climates and situations. Without the angiosperms, which are the major source of food, fibre, timber and medicine, human beings would not have been able to survive on this planet.

Podocarpus is a Gymnosperm

Archidendron is an Angiosperm

Angiosperms are further divided into two main

SUBCLASSES:

MONOCOTYLEDON: plants bearing only one cotyledon, or seed leaf.
Grasses, lilies, bromeliads, orchids, ferns and palms are monocotyledons, shortened to monocots.
DICOTYLEDON: plants bearing two cotyledons, or seed leaves.
Perennial and annual herbs, shrubs and trees are dicotyledons, shortened to dicots.
This book deals mostly with dicotyledons and includes some gymnosperms.

Dicotyledons are classified taxonomically, but can also be categorized by organisms as follows:

1. HERBACEOUS: perennials and annuals.
2. SUBSHRUBS: plants smaller than shrubs that produce abundant growth with wood only at the base; they die back at the end of the growing season.
3. SHRUBS: woody plants that divide into branches below or near ground level into several main stems.
4. TREES: arboreal perennials or woody plants with a single main, woody stem or trunk that is usually unbranched near the ground but has branches growing from it, height varying according to species, environment and other factors. Generally, the term 'tree' is applied to woody species measuring more than 6m (20 ft). Trees often form communities with a continuous canopy, known as a forest, or more open woodland or scrubland.

Both monocotyledons and dicotyledons are separated into

SUPERORDERS:

These are groups of families thought to possess a degree of evolutionary unity. These superorders have the suffix -**idae**.
There are 21 superorders within the dicotyledons, such as MAGNOLIIDAE and ROSIDAE.
There are 6 superorders within the monocotyledons.

Classes comprise

ORDERS:

the names of which often terminate in -**ales**, as in
Magnoli**ales** and Laur**ales**, which are orders of the superorder, MAGNOLIIDAE.
Fab**ales**, Myrt**ales**, Euphorbi**ales** and Sapind**ales**, which are all included in the largest superorder, ROSIDAE.

And each order is subdivided into

FAMILIES:

A family is the highest unit of the taxonomic hierarchy described in this book. Family names have the suffix -**aceae**. For instance, the order of Myrtales includes such families as Lythr**aceae**, Punic**aceae**, Myrt**aceae** and Combret**aceae**. The Fabales order encompasses the huge pea family, Fab**aceae** (or Leguminosae). Each family is composed of plants that share certain characteristics of flower, fruit and, sometimes, leaf, but they differ among themselves in ways that set them apart so that they can be recognized as lesser units or genera.

Large families are sometimes divided into

SUBFAMILIES:

Subfamilies have a suffix -**oideae**. The amorphous Fabaceae (or Leguminosae) family is divided into 3 subfamilies, Mimos**oideae**, (with many-stamened flowers that resemble *Mimosa*), Caesalpini**oideae** (including *Cassia*, *Bauhinia* and *Delonix*) and Papilion**oideae** (with pea-like flowers such as *Bolusanthus speciosus* or *Lonchocarpus latifolius*).

Mimosoideae

Caesalpinioideae

Papilionoideae

SUBFAMILIES OF FABACEAE

Within Families of plants we have units known as

GENERA (singular form, genus)

A genus consists of one or more species and is the smallest natural group containing related, but distinct, species. For example, in the Myrtaceae family, there are 129 genera; Fabaceae includes 642 genera, while the Euphorbiaceae encompasses 313 genera. The genus is always given a capital letter. Within the Bignoniaceae family, for example, we find the genera Catalpa, Tabebuia and Crescentia.

A genus comprises one or more

SPECIES (sp.; plural form, spp.)

Species are a group of plants with common characteristics, distinct from others of the same genus. They have the ability to breed among themselves but not usually with members of another group. The word 'species' is both plural and singular, but its abbreviations, sp. for singular, spp. for plural, define which is which. In the Myrtaceae family is found the genus *Eugenia* ,which has 550 species (spp.), while included in the Fabaceae is the genus *Cassia*, with thirty species (spp.) However, the genus *Amherstia*, (also Fabaceae) has only one species (sp.) and is termed a monotypic genus. The name of a species is always written with a lower case rather than a capital letter. Both the genus and the species are usually shown in italics, as in *Amherstia nobilis*.

Brownea coccinea

Brownea coccinea subsp. *capitella*

Within a species, plants may exhibit considerable natural variation. Finer degrees of classification often use somewhat ambiguously defined ranks, in decreasing order, as follows:

SUBSPECIES (subsp. or ssp.)

describes a form of a species that shares geographic or ecological distinction, for instance, *Brownea coccinea* subsp. *capitella* and *Brownea coccinea* subsp. *coccinea* are both distinct forms of *Brownea coccinea* of Venezuela.

VARIETY (var.)

refers to a group of plants sharing morphological similarities and restricted geographical range, maintaining their distinction from other plants of the same species; *Conocarpus erectus* var. *sericeus*, for example, is a naturally occurring, silver-leafed form of *Conocarpus erectus*.

FORM (forma or f.)

denotes plants exhibiting repeated aberration from the typical form, usually involving a single character, e.g. leaf colour.

'CULTIVAR' (cv.)

is a compound word derived from CULTIvated VARiety, now officially and widely used in horticulture. The correct usage is variety for natural varieties and cultivar for those of cultivated origin; the former may have Latinized names and the latter vernacular names. Thus is found *Plumeria rubra* cv. 'Jean Moragne'. The cultivar is abbreviated to the letters cv. and the names of cultivars are given quotation marks and are not italicized.

SYNONYMS (syn.)

is a systematic name to which another is preferred, or an earlier name now replaced, or, in some cases, a name in common use but misapplied.

COMMON NAMES

are the most confusing of all elements of nomenclature as the same plant may be called different names in different regions or countries. They do, however, form an important part of our horticultural heritage. It must be remembered that the botanical name is the truest common name because it remains standard through all languages.

AUTHOR (or AUTHORS)

In taxonomy, the author, or authors, is the person, or persons, who published the first valid name of a taxon (biological category or group). A botanical name is followed by that of its author or authors, one or more names or abbreviations of names that indicate who published that name of a taxon. For example, in *Chrysophyllum cainito* (L.), L. is the abbreviation for Carolus Linnaeus, the inventor of the binomial system, who even adapted this Latinized pseudonym from his real name, Carl von Linné (1707–1778), and in *Cordia subcordata* (Lam.), Lam. is short for Jean Baptiste de Lamarck (1744–1829). Names of joint authors are connected as in the following example: *Casimiroa edulis* (Llave. & Lex.) has as authors Pablo de la Llave (1773–1833) and Juan Joseé Martinez de Lexarza (1785–1824). If one botanist published a name proposed by another, their names are connected by ex as in *Pterocarpus dalbergioides* (Roxb. ex DC), Roxburgh having published a name proposed by de Candolle.

Classification breakdown of:

GOLDEN SHOWER CASSIA (*CASSIA FISTULA*). *See page 92 for how it relates to a plant profile:*

KINGDOM	:	Plantae
DIVISION	:	Spermatophyta
CLASS	:	Angiospermae
SUBCLASS	:	Dicotyledon
SUPERORDER	:	Rosidae
ORDER	:	Fabales
FAMILY	:	Fabaceae (or Leguminosae)
SUBFAMILY	:	Caesalpinioideae
GENUS	:	*Cassia*
SPECIES (author)	:	*fistula* (L.)
SYNONYM	:	(*C. excelsa*)
COMMON NAMES	:	GOLDEN SHOWER CASSIA
		INDIAN LABURNUM

This, then, is the phylogenetic system of arranging all plants in groups with a name that is understood internationally. Botanists divide and subdivide the classes into a systematic hierarchy. Latin is the universally accepted language for the precise specification and naming of these groups. With the advance of technology and research, there has been a series of systems published in the latter decades of the 20th century, but as yet none has been universally selected as definitive. In this book, the system followed is that described in *Flowering Plants of the World*, edited by V.H. Heywood, published by Oxford University Press, 1993. This work follows, in the main, the sequence of families and order given by G.L. Stebbins, published 1974, and Cronquist, published 1968.

Other guidance has come from D.J. Mabberley's *The Plant Book*, 2nd edition, 1997, in which he largely builds on this system, incorporating updated naming. As it provides an accessible, compact, but quite comprehensive, reference for many readers, whether botanists or keen plantspeople, its nomenclature has been followed in most cases.

With the modern advancement in DNA and its implications in taxonomic classification, traditional systems are constantly being challenged, resulting in many changes that are confusing to the average plantsperson. This book endeavours to indicate the most recent modifications in genera and species and, in most cases, to implement these changes, although in some instances the old name is retained (as in *Chorisia*, for example, which is now officially in the genus *Ceiba*); others, like *Pongamia*, are included in its new genus, *Millettia*. These are minor taxonomic transgressions included to arrange the content in the most useful way.

HOW TO IDENTIFY TREES

It is usually easy to identify trees in a botanic garden or arboretum because they are normally labelled correctly, but in the wild, or even in urban gardens, it is more difficult. The information given in this book for each tree is designed to help in identification, with simple descriptions of each of the following elements of the genus or species. The only sure method of identification is to use a scientific flora, but for the amateur, these checklists, although seemingly daunting, can help to develop observational skills. Of course, it may be the dry season and the tree naked of all clues, but even with no flowers or fruit, information can often be picked up by using good observational work. Always search under the tree for old leaves or fruit, or pick a mature leaf or fallen fruit for later identification. If you collect seeds from an unknown tree for propagation, hoping to identify it later, it is important to note as much as possible about the mother tree – location, leaves, flowers and entire fruit – as seeds alone will not provide sufficient information. Above all, try to learn the Latin names and families of plants. It may seem difficult, but in no time the pattern of their characteristics will become obvious.

1. HABITAT: *many trees are habitat-specific and adapted to the conditions it provides. However, species distribution is often limited by seed dispersal. In cultivation, however, many show wider adaptability.*
Assess the habitat: is it humid, dry, arid or windy and exposed? Is it coastal, mountainous, in a valley or swamp or by a riverside? Is it savannah, brushland, dry woodland or rainforest? Does the tree grow in full sun or shade? Is the soil rocky or rich?

2. THE TREE: *each basic tree shape is genetically determined; each species has specific, arboreal architecture, although this may be modified by competition such as crowding, cultivation or adverse environmental factors.*
HEIGHT: assess the approximate height of the mature tree; compared with other trees, is it very tall, medium or small?
GROWTH PATTERN: define the shape of the tree; is it wide-canopied, narrow, rounded, oval, vase-shaped or flat-topped?
FOLIAGE: is it fine- or coarse-textured, dense or open, even or clumped into distinct 'clouds' or layers?
DECIDUOUS or EVERGREEN: is the tree without leaves? Is there evidence of seasonal leaf-drop, or does it keep its leaves throughout the year?

3. THE TRUNK AND BRANCHES: *much of the character of a tree is contained in its skeleton.*
TRUNK: how tall is it before the branches begin? Is it straight or curved? Does it divide into several trunks? How does it enter the ground – with buttresses and/or large surface roots? Are there aerial or stilt roots?
BARK: is it smooth or rough, spiny, cracked or channelled, flaking or stripping off? (This is valid only on mature trees.)
BRANCHES: notice the manner in which the branches grow. Are they few or many? Are they held erect, sweeping downwards or spreading horizontally ? How do they divide, regularly or irregularly?
TWIGS: are they hairy or smooth? Are they rounded, flattened, square or hollow in cross section?
STIPULES: are they present at leaf nodes? Check near actively growing tips.
SPINES: are there any spines, thorns or prickles? What is their arrangement?
LATEX: break off a healthy leaf and look at the base of its petiole. Is sap or latex oozing out, and what is its consistency – watery, milky or sticky?

smooth and peeling   spiny

cracked or channelled   flaking and stripping off

simple (heart-shaped)

compound (pinnate)

simple (needle-like)

simple (coloured)

4. THE LEAVES: *these manufacture food for the tree by photosynthesis.*

TYPE: are they simple or compound? Always look at mature leaves; is there a difference between juvenile and mature leaves (as in Proteaceae)?

ARRANGEMENT: are they held opposite (many Rubiaceae), alternately (Euphorbiaceae) or in whorls (*Alstonia*) on the main stems?

SHAPE: is each leaf needle-like (*Pinus*), a tiny scale (*Casuarina*), heart-shaped (*Quararibea cordata*), narrow, scythe-like (*Eucalyptus*), rounded (*Greyia*), with an elongated tip (*Ficus benjamina*)?

TEXTURE: is it thin (*Dalbergia sissoo*), thick and leathery (*Clusia*), furry or hairy (*Calotropis*), or velvety plush below (*Chrysophyllum oliviforme*)?

COLOUR: is the leaf greyish green (*Conocarpus erectus* subsp. *sericeus*), bluish green (*Ficus racemosa*), dark green (*Canella winterana*), mid green (*Senna*) or light green (*Leptospermum madidum* subsp. *sativum*)? Is it variegated (*Erythrina variegata* var. *variegata*)?

WHAT COLOUR IS IT BELOW: are the emergent leaves reddish (*Mesua*) or paler (*Maniltoa*)?

PETIOLE: is it long (*Cecropia*) or short (*Brunfelsia*)? Are the petioles 'winged' (*Filicium* or *Inga paterno*)?

MARGINS: are the edges scalloped (*Greyia*), serrated (*Azadirachta*), rolled under (*Jacquinia*) or undulate (*Coccoloba*)?

VEINS: are the veins clearly visible on the upper or lower surface? What pattern do they make? Are they deeply indented or 'quilted' (*Dillenia indica*)? Are the veins pale (*Quararibea*) or reddish (*Quassia amara*)?

ODOUR: when crushed, does the leaf have an odour (*Citrus* or *Murraya koenigii*)?

STIPULES: does it have a little leaf-like appendage where the base of its petiole attaches to the stem?

5. THE FLOWERS: *it is said that you can never tell a book by its cover; likewise, beware of judging a tree from its flowers.*
The four blooms shown (right) belong to four quite different genera and yet, superficially, they appear similar.

TYPE: are they inconspicuous (*Chrysophyllum*) or showy (*Brownea* or *Delonix*)?

SIZE: what size are they? Are they few or many?

POSITION: are they held terminally (*Coccoloba*), are they axillary, in the crotch of the leaves (*Coffea*) or directly on the trunk and/or branches (*Theobroma cacao*)?

STALKS (or rachis): are they long (*Senna alata*), short (*Oncoba*) or non-existent (*Mesua* and *Mammea*)?

COMPOSITION: using the diagrams in the Appendix, check their floristic composition: solitary (*Magnolia*), panicle (*Nuxia*), thyrse (*Lophanthera lactescens*) or spike (*Vitex agnus-castus*). What shape is the flower: funnelform (*Brugmansia*), tubular (*Ixora*) or salverform (*Tabebuia*)?

PETALS: what type of petals do they have and how many are there? Are they fused together (*Kigelia africana*) or do they have no petals, only sepals (*Ceratopetalum*)? Are the petals aborted early (*Barringtonia*)?

STAMENS: are there many of them (more than ten) (*Syzygium*), or few (less than four) (some *Bauhinia*)? Are they united (*Clusia*)?

COLOUR: what colour are the petals? Do they change as they age (*Hibiscus tiliaceus*)? Are both the upper and lower surfaces of the petals the same colour (*Kigelia africana*)? Is there a different-coloured 'throat' or 'eye' (*Tabebuia*)? Are there spots, blotches or stripes (*Monodora myristica*)?

Mesua ferrea

Oncoba spinosa

Mammea americana

Camellia sinensis

SEPALS: what shape are they? Are they salverform, tubular, pea-like, campanulate? Do they persist after the petals have fallen?

ODOUR: are the flowers pungent or fragrant? Is the scent nocturnal (*Brugmansia*) or diurnal (*Cestrum diurnum*)?

POLLINATORS: are there signs of any insects, such as bees visiting *Acacia* flowers, or of nectar-loving birds visiting *Callistemon*?

SEASON: the season of blooming is often specific to a species or genus and may be crucial to the final identification. This may, however, vary in cultivation outside its native range.

| legume | follicle | berry | drupe |

5. THE FRUIT: *the fruit is composed from the embryo of the flower and its position on the tree and basic composition will reflect that.*

FORM: what type of fruit is it – a legume (*Adenanthera, Bauhinia, Delonix*), a follicle (*Sterculia, Tabebuia, Plumeria*), a berry (*Psidium* or *Antidesma*), a drupe (*Mangifera*) or an aggregate fruit (*Annona*), a cone (*Araucaria*) or capsule (*Swietenia*)? Is it rounded, elongated or flat? Is it ripe and still intact (*Hymenaea*) or split open (*Adenanthera*)?

SIZE: Check the size of a mature fruit.

COLOUR: the fruit may be young and green. Search for signs of the colour on ripening fruit.

POSITION: where is the fruit held on the tree? Is it held terminally (*Litchi*), axillary (*Morus*) or caulescent, that is, directly on the limbs and trunk (*Lansium, Artocarpus*)?

OUTER SURFACE: is it smooth (*Persea americana*), furry (*Pachira aquatica*), prickly (*Durio*), woody (*Aegle marmelos*)?

PULP: if possible, open up a ripe fruit. Is there soft pulp (*Diospyros*)? Does it have an odour? What colour is it? Is it sticky or does it have latex (*Chrysophyllum*)?

ARIL: is there an aril around the seed (*Inga, Blighia, Litchi, Aphanamixis*)? What colour is it?

ODOUR: is there a strong odour? If so, how would you describe it?

SEEDS: do not confuse fruit with seeds. Remember, seeds are usually contained within the fruit (exceptions are *Anacardium* or *Podocarpus*). Are there many or few? Study the seed and determine its structure. Is it winged (*Tabebuia* or *Moringa*)? Does it have 'silk parachutes' (*Ceiba* or *Calotropis*)?

This little blooming Bauhinia was found growing wild in dry woodland in Cuba, but it was difficult to identify at a distance and without the security of a label. Unfortunately, it was not possible to get closer to it as it was on private land.

PART I

A–Z Listing of Tropical & Subtropical Trees

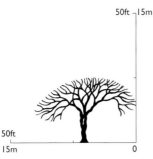

50ft ⌐15m

50ft
15m   0

Acacia farnesiana

SWEET ACACIA

(L.) Willd.   1,200 spp.

Mimosa farnesiana

FABACEAE (Mimosoideae)

ORIGIN	Trop. America
HEIGHT	up to 7 m (23 ft)
TYPE	deciduous, small, spiny flowering tree
STATUS	not threatened
HABITAT	dry coastal lowland; wasteland
GROWTH	fast
FLOWG	intermittently, year-round
DRY TOL.	high
SALT TOL.	high
LIGHT	full sun
SOIL	widely tolerant; well-drained
NUTRIT.	normally not necessary
HAZARDS	spiny
PROBLEMS	none
ENVIRON.	bee nectar
PROPAG.	seeds
LEAVES	2-pinnate, bluish green, crowded on short spur twigs; to 5 cm (2 in.); 2–6 pinnae, with 25 tiny leaflets
FLWS	showy; deep yellow; long-stalked, with tiny balls of stamens; very fragrant
FRUIT	a legume, to 8 × 1 cm (3 × 0.4 in.); straight or curved pod, dark brown; persistent
USE	seaside; living barrier; specimen; large planter; median strip; civic centre; xerophytic
ZONE	9–12

THE ACACIA CLAN comprises 1,200 species, 900 of which are found in Australia, where they are generally known as Wattle. *Acacia farnesiana* is a Trop. American species which, typical of its genus, grows in a much-branched, shrubby, spreading fashion. It has a brittle trunk and limbs, dark brown, smooth, skin-like bark and slender, white thorns. Little, 2-pinnate leaves are crowded on short spur twigs. Long-stalked, deep yellow, sweetly fragrant pompom flowers are borne intermittently throughout the year and are followed by pea-like pods that continue for many months. This thorny, little tree has many uses in its regions. For some Trop. American villagers, the flowers are important in their everyday lives, for both therapeutic and other purposes. The flowers are used to make concoctions for headaches and an infusion for dyspepsia. On a lighter note, fresh blooms are dried and then placed under pillows or used to perfume household linen, with a supposedly erotic effect. In the south of France, *A. farnesiana* is cultivated for the perfume industry, although harvesting the blooms is hazardous because of the tree's vicious thorns. A violet-scented perfume, known commercially as Cassie Ancienne, is distilled from the essential oil secreted by the little flowers and is used to fortify Violet oil. This, in turn, is used in confectionery and soaps, as well as for fragrance. The leaves and pods, which are valuable as animal fodder, are high in tannins and have been employed traditionally in the tanning industry, as well as for making dye. Mucilage from the bark resembles gum arabic, which is used as a glue and in incense, and all parts of the tree have a medicinal use. Heartwood of *A. farnesiana* is reddish brown, hard and heavy and, because of its small calliper, is used mainly for tool handles. Bees are attracted to the blooms and the resulting Sweet Acacia honey is highly regarded.

NOTE: *A. farnesiana* **has proved invasive in many dry, sandy or coastal regions.**

A. farnesiana; fragrant pompom fls are used to make a violet-scented perfume.

A. farnesiana; mucilage from the bark resembles gum arabic and all parts of the tree have a medicinal use.

A. farnesiana; pairs of long, slender, white spines make harvesting fls for the perfume industry a hazardous task.

A. farnesiana; Sweet Acacia is found in fields and on wasteland in many parts of the tropics and is cultivated for the essential oil of its fls. Photographed at Huntingdon Gardens, Los Angeles, USA.

Acacia acuifera; (Benth.), Bahamas endemic, to 6 m (20 ft). Known as PORK AND DOUGHBOY, CASSIPE or BAHAMAS ROSEWOOD, this is a charming, glabrous, fine-textured, much-branched shrub or small tree found in dry, sandy scrublands. The lvs comprise a single pr of diminutive lflts, while the abundant, long-lasting, globose yellow fls are equally small and compact. This rare, non-spiny xerophyte is particularly good for landscape use. (9–12)

Acacia auriculaeformis; (Cunne & Benth.), N Australia to New Guinea, to 30 m (100 ft). The willow-like lvs of EARLEAF ACACIA or BLACK WATTLE are actually expanded petioles known as phyllodes, which act as lf blades. Fls are spike-like, while the fr. is coiled and shaped like an ear. This fast-growing, invasive sp. with weak, brittle growth is valued regionally for fuel or fodder. (10–12) NOTE: considered an invasive pest in many regions.

Acacia baileyana; (F. Meull.), Australia, to 8 m (26 ft). COOTAMUNDRA WATTLE or BAILEY'S ACACIA is a fast-growing, spring-blooming sp. that develops a dense, arching habit. This sp. is popular throughout the warm subtropics for its attractive, finely divided, frosted, bipinnate foliage and its abundant, narrow clusters of golden yellow, globose blooms. The sd pods are silvery. Also purple and golden-tipped foliage forms. (9–11)

Acacia confusa; (Merr.), Taiwan and Philippines, to 15 m (50 ft), known in Hawaii as FALSE KOA because of its strong resemblance to the endemic *A. koa*; it differs in its narrower, straighter phyllodes and shorter, narrower pods. Fls are globose. *A. confusa* is popular as an ornamental in Hawaii; it was introduced by the Board of Agriculture & Forestry about 1915. (9–12) NOTE: this sp. has escaped cultivation in Hawaii.

Acacia cornigera; ([L.] Willd.), (syn. *A. sphaerocephala*), C America, to 6 m. (20 ft). BULL'S THORN or BARBED WIRE ACACIA is native to arid regions. Gargantuan, treacherous thorns are hollow and provide homes for tiny stinging ants that enter by a small entry hole at the base of each thorn. Ants extract sweet liquid from the extra-floral nectaries on lf petioles and protect the tree. Lvs are bipinnate; and inflorescence is an elongated, yellow spike. (10–12)

Acacia dunnii; ([Maiden] Turrill), Australia endemic, to 7 m (23 ft). ELEPHANT EAR WATTLE, a single-stemmed, ornamental small tree of dry, open woodland. Stems and lvs covered with a whitish bloom. This sp. is distinguished by its large, broad, blue-grey, phylloidal lvs and bright yellow, spherical fls held in abundant panicles. Fr. to 13 cm (5 in.), whitish grey when ripe. Fast growing; needs humidity. Blooms in flushes year-round. (9–11)

Acacia karroo; (Hayne), S Africa endemic, to 15 m (50 ft). SWEET THORN is one of the most common trees in S Africa, Namibia and Zimbabwe and is adapted to a variety of soils in low-lying areas with clay soils and near water courses. Grows as a smallish tree with a short trunk and spreading crown or or as a tall, slender tree. With dark green, 2-pinnate lvs, deep yellow fls in spherical heads and sickle-shaped fr. that persists on the tree for a year. (9–11)

Acacia leptocarpa; (Cunn. ex Benth.) endemic of trop. north east of Australia, to 10 m (33 ft). This graceful, opulent, coastal sp. forms an airy, open crown of glossy, scythe-like, deep green phylloidal lvs. In early spring, it glows with its abundant golden spikes of blooms. They are followed by a profusion of stringy, coiled, brown fr. This sp. is found on sandy soils in open coastal bushland and along swampy lowlands. (10–12)

Acacia longifolia; ([Andrews] Willd.), E Australia, to 8 m (26 ft). SYDNEY GOLDEN WATTLE or SALLOW WATTLE, this spring-flowg sp. has phylloidal lvs and narrow spikes of fls. It is lime-tolerant and often used as rootstock for more acid-loving sp. This sp. hybridizes freely with *A. retinodes*. **NOTE: although widely planted as an ornamental in many subtrop. regions, it has become a pest in some parts, particularly in S Africa.** (9–11)

Acacia nilotica subsp. *tomentosa*; ([Benth] Bren.), (syn. *A. arabica; A. scorpioides*), Trop. Africa and India, to 10 m (33 ft). GUM ARABIC TREE, BABUL or EGYPTIAN MIMOSA has bipinnate lvs and globose fls. It is distinguished by its grey-white, felty fr. and black-skinned bark, which cracks to expose a rusty red layer and exudes a sticky, reddish resin. It is known as Indian Gum Arabic and is collected commercially. Bark and fr. are high in tannin. (10–12)

Acacia podalyriifolia; (G. Don.) NE Australia endemic, to 5 m (16 ft). QLD SILVER WATTLE is a large shrub or small tree with smooth, grey-brown bark. Its branches are glaucous and its young shoots densely white-pubescent. The phyllodes are blue-green, white-tomentose, ovate to elliptic and often undulate. The Infl. is held in branched racemes, to 30 cm (12 in), globose, bright yellow. Fr. to 1.2 × 2 cm (4.7 × 0.8 in.), much compressed, softly hairy. (9–11)

Acacia saligna; ([Labill.] H.L. Wendl.), (syn. *A. cyanophylla*), W Australia endemic, to 7 m (23 ft). WEEPING- or GOLDEN-WREATH WATTLE is a small sp., popular for its tumble of wiry limbs and chains of golden spring blooms. In S Africa and Libya, it is used to rehabilitate coastal sand dunes and for fodder and tan bark. It is planted as a fast-growing ornamental in many subtrop. regions. **NOTE: this sp. has become a pest in S Africa.** (9–11)

Acacia seyal; (Delile.), in drier parts from Egypt to Kenya, to 10 m (33 ft). WHISTLING- or THIRTY-THORN or SHITTUMWOOD, well-known, thorny, flat-topped. Like *A. xanthophloea*, its trunk and limbs are covered in mealy powder. *A. seyal*, powder is bright, rusty red and rubs off to reveal thin, green, chlorophyll-producing bark below. Fragrant, bright yellow, globose, spring fls attract honeybees. Bark yields an edible gum. (10–12)

Acacia xanthophloea; (Benth.), E and S Africa endemic, to 25 m (82 ft). FEVER TREE or NAIVASHA THORN, of humid riverbanks and thought to mark malaria- infested areas. The trunks and limbs are covered with vivid, chartreuse-yellow powder that, when rubbed off, reveals bright green bark, which continues to produce chlorophyll when the tree is leafless. The twigs have slender, white spines; the fls are globose and bright yellow. The trees are browsed by game. (9–12)

Acacia tortilis: (Haynes), widespread in Africa, to 20 m (66 ft). UMBRELLA THORN, with its familiar flat, parasol crown, is ubiquitous to dry African savannahs. This sp. is adapted to a broad range of climatic conditions and thus varies considerably from region to region and has been divided into several subspp. Shown here is *A tortilis* subsp. *heterantha* that grows to 10 m (33 ft), of S Africa. It is an elderly tree that has finally developed its sturdy framework and distinctive, mature canopy. A feature of this subsp. is its 2 types of very sharp spines, which are short, blackish and hooked, as well as straight and needle-like. The bi pinnate lvs are probably the smallest of all *Acacia*. Fls are white, globose and the abundant small fr. pods are flattened and spirally coiled (like *A. auriculaeformis*). (9–12)

Acokanthera oppositifolia

ORDEAL POISONWOOD

(Lam.) Codd.   5 spp.

A. venenata; A. longiflora

APOCYNACEAE

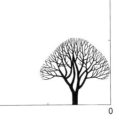

ORIGIN	Trop. E and S Africa
HEIGHT	up to 7 m (23 ft)
TYPE	semi-deciduous, flowering, toxic tree
STATUS	not threatened
HABITAT	scrub woodlands; along watercourses; coastal scrub
GROWTH	moderate
FLOWG	autumn, winter, spring
DRY TOL.	high
SALT TOL.	moderate
LIGHT	full sun
SOIL	fertile, well-drained
NUTRIT.	balanced fertilizer annually; deep, organic mulch
HAZARDS	highly toxic sap
PROBLEMS	scale, mealy bugs
ENVIRON.	insect and Hawk Moth nectar; fruit for birds
PROPAG.	seeds; semi-ripe cuttings
LEAVES	simple; deep green; oblong-lanceolate; mucronate, opposite; thick, leathery, with spine-like point
FLOWERS	showy; white or pink; long-tubed; stalkless; sweetly fragrant
FRUIT	a berry, to 20 mm (0.8 in.); fleshy, red, then purplish black
USE	specimen; container; winter-flowering small tree; accent; large container; conservatory; xerophytic
ZONE	9–12

ON HIGH HILL-SLOPES and dry plateaux from E Africa to S Africa, *Acokanthera oppositifolia* grows as a small, heavily foliaged tree, but at lower elevations and under cultivation it is more often diffusely shrub-like. Its thick, leathery leaves are tipped with a sharp, spine-like point and are crowded in whorls along the stems. Its stalkless, long-tubed, white or pinkish flowers are held in dense, axillary clusters. They resemble those of the shrub Daphne and are sweetly fragrant. The ornamental fruit is plum-like and bright red, ripening black. This infamously toxic genus, found from Arabia to S Africa, is very closely related to the African genus *Carissa*, and includes species that were previously designated as such. *A. oppositifolia* contains cardiac glycosides, including the powerful ouabain, which has the effect of digitalin. If ouabain is absorbed through the skin and into the blood system, death can follow within 20 minutes. Traditionally, the potently toxic sap has been used by African tribes as an ordeal poison, a decoction from the bark and wood being mixed with a local *Euphorbia* latex and *Acacia* gum and applied to arrow tips. Another method is to coat the spiny, woody fruit of the herb *Tribulus terrestris* with this mixture and then scatter it in the path of the intended barefooted victims. Curiously, ripe fruit is deemed edible in some regions, although generally in S Africa all parts of the plant are considered highly toxic — even meat grilled on a fire using the wood has proved fatal.

*** *A. oblongifolia*; ([Hochst.] Codd.), (syn. *A. spectabilis*), from Mozambique to S Africa, to 6 m (20 ft). DUNE POISONBUSH or DUINEGIFBOOM occurs on coastal dunes and bushland. It is distinguished by its more rounded leaves that have hair-like tips. Its abundant, white, strongly fragrant, early-spring blooms make it popular as a garden ornamental in subtropical regions, but the sap of this species is toxic. (9–12)

A. oblongifolia; its lovely fragrant blooms are held in dense clusters.

A. oppositifolia; a popular ornamental for its delightful, fragrant, winter fls, despite the fact that it contains lethal sap that has been used traditionally in Africa as an ordeal poison.

A. oppositifolia; plum-like, ornamental fr. is bright red, ripening black.

A. oppositifolia; a small tree of the high plateaux of E and S Africa. Photographed in Durban, KZN, S Africa.

100ft ┐ 30m

75ft
22.5m   0

Acrocarpus fraxinifolius

SHINGLE TREE

Arn.   1 sp.

FABACEAE (Caesalpinioideae)

ORIGIN	India to Java
HEIGHT	up to 60 m (197 ft)
TYPE	deciduous, large flowering tree
STATUS	not threatened
HABITAT	wet evergreen rainforest; deciduous monsoon forest
GROWTH	extremely fast
FLOWG	early spring
DRY TOL.	moderate to low
SALT TOL.	low
LIGHT	full sun to part shade
SOIL	fertile, humid
NUTRIT.	balanced fertilizer annually
HAZARDS	none
PROBLEMS	subject to termite attack
ENVIRON.	bird and insect nectar
PROPAG.	ripe seeds, but may be slow to germinate
LEAVES	2-pinnate; deep green, paler below; leaflets oblique-oblong; new leaves, coral red
FLOWERS	showy; vivid, pinkish scarlet; held in erect, dense, spike-like racemes
FRUIT	legume, linear; to 16 × 2 cm (6 × 0.8 in.); compressed, dehiscent; winged along ventrical suture
USE	large flowering tree; public open space; timber tree
ZONE	10—12

IN ITS NATIVE, MOUNTAINOUS rainforest habitats of Trop. Asia, the giant ***Acrocarpus fraxinifolius*** may develop a splendid, lofty trunk with a clean, straight bole to two-thirds of its height, with massive buttresses in old age. In lower, dryer regions, it may not attain the same stature and is often found with a much shorter trunk and a fairly sparse crown of long, upwardly sweeping, slender limbs. Ash-like (hence *fraxinifolius*), the 2-pinnate, enormous, frond-like leaves have large, glabrous, oblique-oblong leaflets that are briefly shed during cold or dry seasons. In early spring, when leafless, the canopy ignites in a blaze of vivid, pinkish scarlet blooms that are borne in dense, darting, bottlebrush spikes at the tips of sturdy, naked twigs. Each tiny flower is set in a green calyx and is composed of 5 narrow petals that enclose perky, long, red stamens and a green style. As the blooms fade, they are replaced by a sumptuous, if fleeting, display of coral-red, new foliage. Many tiny, flat seeds are contained in a thin, compressed, strap-like pod that has a ridged wing along one side. *A. fraxinifolius* is an important timber tree, particularly in India and Burma, and has been introduced also into Africa and C America for timber plantations. The sapwood is pinkish white, while the heartwood is hard and dark red and is variously known as Pink or Red Cedar. It is popular in S India for furniture-making and general building. Because it splits easily and regularly, it also makes excellent roof shingles and it is this property that explains the derivation of its common name there. The Shingle Tree is fast growing and is recorded as growing up to 3 m (10 ft) per year. Regionally, it is commonly planted as shade for smaller coffee trees, while in the tea plantations of Darjeeling, its timber has long been used for making tea chests. When young, *A. fraxinifolius* has been observed to behave as a climber and strangler of other trees.

A. fraxinifolius; with darting, bottlebrush spikes that attract birds and insects.

A. fraxinifolius; valued for its timber that is known as Pink or Red Cedar and is used to make tea chests.

A. fraxinifolius; has large, leguminous pods filled with black sds that may be slow to germinate.

A. fraxinifolius; young trees growing at Yungaburra in N Qld, Australia. They will grow even taller and become massively buttressed in old age.

7

Adansonia digitata

BAOBAB

L.   8 spp.

MALVACEAE (formerly Bombacaeae)

OF THE EIGHT SPECIES of this genus, *Adansonia digitata* is the most renowned and the only one found on the African continent. Slow growing and deciduous, it forms a monumentally swollen trunk with relatively few, short branches and palmate leaves. Great, pendulous, creamy white, pungently fragrant flowers, each with a massive staminal column tipped with stamens, are borne nocturnally and pollinated by bats. Hefty, velvety fruit pods contain angular, woody seeds surrounded by astringent, whitish powder, rich in vitamin C, as well as citric and tartaric acids. It is used locally, particularly in W Africa, to make a porridge and also a refreshing drink that is reputed to reduce fever. African folklore is filled with tales of the bewitched Baobab, which is thought by many Africans to possess the souls or spirits of ancestors. In Malawi, legend has it that the gods became angry with the Baobab so, as a punishment, they drew it out of the ground and then thrust it back upside down. This is easy to believe when the mammoth tree is seen rising from the bleached, grassy infinity of the plains, its colossal, pock-marked trunk topped with massive, naked, root-like, stubby limbs. Only in the spring, during the rains, when it becomes cloaked in new foliage, does the Baobab become truly tree-like. The trunk may measure up to 10 m (33 ft) in girth, but often it decays with age and becomes hollow at its centre, creating a storage cavity that fills with rainwater. Baobabs are said to be amongst the longest-lived trees in the world and are reported to survive for 2,000 years, but, as the wood is soft and spongy in texture and provides no age rings, it is impossible to verify this. When it dies, the tree slowly collapses into an undignified, soft mass. Fibre stripped from the inner bark is woven into rope, or it can be pounded and stretched to create a primitive cloth. Other items provided by *A. digitata* are soap, dye, glue, fodder and local medicine.

ORIGIN	Sub-Saharan Africa
HEIGHT	up to 20 m (66 ft)
TYPE	deciduous, large flowering tree
STATUS	not threatened
HABITAT	dry savannah; coastal woodland, up to 500 m (1,600 ft)
GROWTH	slow
FLOWG	spring and summer
DRY TOL.	high
SALT TOL.	moderate
LIGHT	full sun
SOIL	widely tolerant; well-drained
NUTRIT.	general fertilizer annually
HAZARDS	none
PROBLEMS	requires winter dormancy
ENVIRON.	bat and bird nectar
PROPAG.	fresh seeds, but slow to germinate
LEAVES	digitate; olive-green, leaflets white below; to 7.5 cm (3 in.)
FLOWERS	showy; white; large, pendulous, with massive staminal column; nocturnally, pungently fragrant
FRUIT	capsule, to 30 cm (12 in.); woody, velvety; filled with powdery, astringent pulp; large, woody seeds
USE	public open space; botanic collection; curiosity; bonsai subject; xerophytic
ZONE	10—12

A. digitata; a dramatic bloom still open at dawn, having been open all night.

A. digitata; this mammoth tree rises from the bleached, grassy infinity of the plains of the Zambezi Valley, its colossal, pock-marked trunk topped with massive, root-like, stubby limbs.

A. digitata; huge, woody, velvety fr. with large, angular sds set in woody fibres and covered in whitish powder.

A. digitata; this young specimen has a trunk that looks like an elephant's foot.

Adansonia grandidieri; (Baillon), Madagascar endemic, to 30 m (100 ft). RENIALA (Queen of the Forest) is rare and endangered; it is the tallest tree on the west coast of the island. *A. grandidieri* is notable for its massive, pole-like trunk and few, very short, stubby limbs. Typical of this genus, this sp. is bare of lvs for most of the year, with foliage briefly during rains. Fls are small, erect and white, with pinkish sepals. Large, oily sds are eaten and the bark is stripped for making ropes. (**10–12**)

Adansonia gregori; (F. Muell.), (*A. gibbosa*), Australia, to 16 m (52 ft). BOAB, BOTTLE- or DEAD RAT-TREE of sandy soils in low rainfall areas, mainly beside drainage lines and creeks. It is distinguished by its globular shape in maturity, to 3 m (10 ft) diam., found to contain up to 300 litres (79 gals) of water. Fls (white) are visited by honeyeating birds. Aborigines eat the sds raw or roasted and the lvs as a vegetable and make stout twine from the young bark. (**10–12**)

Adansonia rubrostipa; (Jum. & Perrier), (syn. *A. fony*), Madagascar endemic, to 13 m (43 ft) in forests, but only 6 m (20 ft) or less in dense bush. This small sp. is known locally as RINGY, ZAMENA or BORINGY and is distinguished by its red-barked, strongly bottle-shaped trunk. Lvs are long-petioled, lflts have dentate margins; fls are pale yellow or red. This sp. is frequent on the west coast and in the south-west of the island, to 300 m (984 ft). (**10–12**)

Adansonia za; (Baillon), (syn *A. alba*), Madagascar endemic, to 30 m (100 ft). This sp. is also a very large tree that is frequent on sedimentary or crystalline rocks in the Morondava region, from sea level to 600 m (1,969 ft). The trunk is thick, narrowing towards the crown. Lflts are oblanceolate with long petioles. Fls are bright yellow with a somewhat reddish base. This sp. is considered to be closely related to *A. madagascariensis*. (**10–12**)

Adenanthera pavonina

RED SANDALWOOD

L.   12 spp.

FABACEAE (Mimosoideae)

100ft — 30m

75ft

22.5m — 0

ORIGIN	Trop. Asia to the Solomon Is
HEIGHT	up to 17 m (56 ft)
TYPE	deciduous or semi-deciduous foliage tree
STATUS	not threatened
HABITAT	dry or humid, coastal deciduous woodland
GROWTH	fast
FLOWG	winter and early spring
DRY TOL.	high
SALT TOL.	moderate
LIGHT	full sun
SOIL	widely tolerant; well-drained
NUTRIT.	normally not necessary
HAZARDS	none
PROBLEMS	invasive; messy leaves
ENVIRON.	bee nectar
PROPAG.	seeds (soak first)
LEAVES	pinnate; bright green; to 40 cm (16 in.); leaflets, elliptic to ovate
FLOWERS	showy; creamy yellow, in dense, slender racemes; fragrant
FRUIT	a legume, to 22 cm (9 in.); coils on opening to expel hard, bright red, lustrous seeds
USE	seaside; shade tree; agricultural shade tree; street tree; land reclamation; xerophytic
ZONE	10–12

ADENANTHERA PAVONINA is a slender, very fast-growing, coastal tree that is undemanding of soil or moisture. It has erect, arching growth and a wide-spreading, buoyant crown of bright green, pinnate foliage. During winter and early spring, highly scented, creamy yellow flowers are held on stiff, slender, slightly drooping, compact spikes. It is the fruit, however, that is the most remarkable feature of this common, small tree. As the narrow, thin-shelled, leguminous pods mature, they twist and burst open, assuming many contorted shapes and displaying the hard, ceramic-like, lustrous, brilliant red seeds contained within. These seeds, which have a high oil content (24%), are roasted and eaten in some regions of Asia. They are also famously used in tropical tourist venues for local bead-craft. Adenanthera means 'goldsmith' in Arabic and the seeds, which are known in the trade as Madatiya or Circassian seeds, were used traditionally by apothecaries and goldsmiths as weights, each seed being equal to nearly 4 grains (0.25 g). The smooth, pale grey bark of *A. pavonina* is rich in saponin, used in the manufacture of both detergents and medicines, while the shredded bark yields a red dye. In India, Brahmins rub bark shavings against a wet stone to make a red paste and use it for religious, facial marks. A decoction of the leaves is taken to help alleviate rheumatism and gout. The reddish purple heartwood is hard, heavy, strong and durable, a valued timber in many countries, where it is used for cabinetry or construction and for making articles of fine art. It is an important honey plant.

***A. microsperma*; (Teism. & Binn.), (syn. *A. pavonina* var. *microsperma*) Burma to Indonesia, to 20 m (66 ft). The leaves are finer than *A. pavonina*; the flowers are creamy yellow, turning orange with age; the fruit is twisted into a very tight coil. (10–12)

NOTE: *A. pavonina* may prove to be invasive in lowland regions.

A. pavonina; is a weed tree in the Cayman Is, where it is known as Curly Bean. Arabic goldsmiths traditionally used the lacquered sds as apothecary and goldsmiths' weights.

A. pavonina; slender spikes of tiny star-like, fragrant fls.

A. pavonina; a fast-growing tree with erect, arching growth and a spreading crown of fresh, green foliage.

A. microsperma; with finer foliage and larger fls, at the USDA Arboretum in Miami, Florida, USA.

ORIGIN	Arabia and E Africa
HEIGHT	up to 6 m (20 ft)
TYPE	deciduous, succulent shrub or small tree
STATUS	specially protected
HABITAT	savannahs, lowland coast and dry valleys
GROWTH	slow
FLOWG	dry season
DRY TOL.	high
SALT TOL.	moderate
LIGHT	full sun
SOIL	fertile; very well-drained
NUTRIT.	slow-release, low-nitrogen fertilizer before flowering
HAZARDS	toxic sap and seeds
PROBLEMS	will rot in poor drainage
ENVIRON.	insect nectar
PROPAG.	seeds; cuttings; layers
LEAVES	simple; deep green; spathulate, leathery, glossy, in terminal whorls
FLOWERS	showy; pink or red, rarely white, with dark or pale eye; not fragrant
FRUIT	a follicle, to 10 cm (4 in.); seeds brown with hairy tufts at each end
USE	accent; specimen; large container; bonsai subject; conservatory; xerophytic
ZONE	9–11

50ft ⌐15m

50ft
15m   0

Adenium obesum

DESERT ROSE

(Forssk.) Roemer & Schultes   5 spp.

APOCYNACEAE

THE CELEBRATED African *Adenium* and the Trop. American *Plumeria* are both members of the Apocynaceae family and share many of the same characteristics. Foliage of both genera is whorled towards the stem ends and their non-fragrant, funnel-shaped blooms share many similarities. *Adenium* are pachycauls, adapted for life in the harsh semi-deserts and savannahs of their regions by thick, unarmed, swollen trunks and a few, short, stumpy limbs. Some species have subterranean stems for more water-retention, for instance, *Adenium swazicum* [Stapf.] of E Africa. There has been much confusion about the widespread *Adenium* genus. At one point, it was thought to be monospecific, with many subspecies, but, as there is great variation in its composition from region to region, taxonomists lately divided it into 5 distinct species, with several subspecies. ***Adenium obesum*** is the most widespread and commonly grown species. Although mainly found as a small shrub, this slow-growing species may attain tree-like heights under special circumstances. It holds its showy, red (sometimes with a white eye), pink or, rarely, white blooms in small, terminal corymbs. All parts of *Adenium* are charged with milky latex and the seeds contain cardiac glycosides, making them extremely toxic. They were used traditionally in Africa as an ordeal poison, for arming spearheads and as a means of stunning and catching fish. Despite this, its leaves and stems are browsed by kudu, an African antelope, and other game. The plant also has medical applications. ***Adenium obesum*** is best grown from large, well-callused cuttings or, better still, because it is so slow growing, from the layering of large branches.

*** *A. multiflorum*; (Klotzsch.), (syn. *A. obesum* var. *multiflorum*) S Africa, to 6 m (20 ft), IMPALA LILY is a succulent shrub or small tree of lowland bushveld. It is distinguished by its pale, pinkish white blooms with frilled, bright crimson margins. (9–11)

A. multiflorum; with stunning pink and red frilly-edged fls.

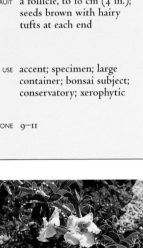

A. swazicum; (Stapf.) has enlarged caudex (or stem), dwarfed habit, tomentose new growth and undulate lvs.

A. obesum; a small specimen in full bloom after early spring rains.

A. obesum; despite its alluring, vibrant, pink blooms, this is a robust xerophyte, built to withstand challenging, desert conditions.

Aegle marmelos

BAEL FRUIT

(L.) Corr. Serr.   3 spp.

Feronia pellucida; Crateva marmelos

RUTACEAE

50ft ⌐15m

50ft
15m   0

ORIGIN	Himalayas, India, Burma
HEIGHT	up to 13 m (40 ft)
TYPE	deciduous, small fruiting tree
STATUS	not threatened
HABITAT	dry and humid lowland woodlands
GROWTH	moderate
FLOWG	intermittently, all year
DRY TOL.	moderate
SALT TOL.	low
LIGHT	full sun
SOIL	fertile, water-retentive
NUTRIT.	organic mulch; nitrogen-rich, citrus fertilizer
HAZARDS	spiny limbs
PROBLEMS	none
ENVIRON.	bee nectar
PROPAG.	seeds; division of suckers
LEAVES	3-foliate; bright green, to 7.5 cm (3 in.); ovate, crenate; long-petioled, pungent
FLOWERS	showy; greenish white; with narrow petals; held in axillary panicles; fragrant
FRUIT	a berry, to 15 cm (6 in.) diam.; globose to pear-shaped; with smooth, hard, brittle rind
USE	living barrier; small fruiting tree; large planter; xerophytic
ZONE	10—12

AEGLE MARMELOS, a spiny member of the citrus family, with 3-foliate, long- petioled, pungent leaves, has widely arching or drooping growth, forming a dishevelled, small suckering tree. The trunk and branches are smooth or finely fissured and flaking. If cut, they ooze a slimy sap that is used locally as a glue. The many-stamened, waxy, sweet-smelling, citrus-like blooms are quite showy, being greenish white and held in axillary panicles. They are followed by the green, tough-skinned, globose, gourd-like fruit, which bounces like a ball when thrown to the ground. As it matures, its astringent rind hardens and turns greyish green or yellow. There are many seeds embedded in its sweet, orange-coloured, slimy pulp. This is aromatic, mucilaginous, somewhat doughy in consistency and, to some, reminiscent of marmalade. In India, where the Bael Fruit is sacred to Hindus and consequently it is forbidden to uproot it, *A. marmelos* (or Bengal Quince, as it is also known) is a generous and varied provider. Sweet, nutritious drinks, sherbets and preserves are made from the pulp of the fruit. A pungent, essential oil (mycotoxic) is extracted from the rind and is used in the making of perfume and soap. In some areas, before the fruit has completely ripened, it is boiled, strained and sweetened and is then administered as a specific for dysentery, haemorrhoids or diarrhoea. It is also used as an aphrodisiac and its reputation is such that it has been described as the Viagra of the plant world. Specifically, a concoction made from the fruit is given to Filipino bridegrooms on their honeymoon night. Once the fruit is ripe, it is considered to have a tonic effect and is used particularly as a laxative. Decorative boxes are fashioned from the hard, dried shells of the fruit, and the rind provides a yellow dye. The wood is fine-grained and is used to make small objects, while the roots, bark and pulp have medicinal value. This is an important honey plant.

A. marmelos; these arching, rather dishevelled trees line a walk at the Jardin Botanico Nationale in Cuba. This sp. is a great domestic provider in its native regions.

A. marmelos; in India, the pungent fr is renowned for its medicinal qualities.

A. marmelos; the fr matures with a hard, shell-like rind and decorated boxes are fashioned from them.

A. marmelos; with 3-foliate lvs and sharp, slender spines that make this sp. an excellent choice as a living barrier.

ORIGIN	Subtrop. E Africa
HEIGHT	up to 33 m (108 ft)
TYPE	evergreen, dioecious conifer-type tree
STATUS	restricted distribution
HABITAT	dry highland forest, from 1,200–3,000 m (4,000–10,000 ft)
GROWTH	moderately fast
FLOWG	summer
DRY TOL.	moderate
SALT TOL.	moderate
LIGHT	full sun to bright shade
SOIL	fertile, slightly acid
NUTRIT.	high-nitrogen fertilizer
HAZARDS	none
PROBLEMS	none
ENVIRON.	seeds for monkeys and birds
PROPAG.	seeds; cuttings; layers
LEAVES	linear; bluish green; spirally arranged on wiry, weeping stems; apex, tapered
FLOWERS	dioecious; staminate males, in slender catkins; females, ovulate scales, drupe-like
FRUIT	to 2.5 cm (1 in.); drupe-like structure of ovulate scales fused together; ovoid, pruinose
USE	small shade tree; accent; screening; street tree; public open space; large planter; conservatory
ZONE	9–11

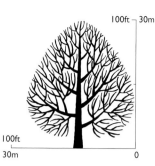

100ft — 30m
100ft
30m — 0

Afrocarpus gracilior

WEEPING PODOCARPUS

(Pilger.) Page 3 spp.

Podocarpus gracilior

PODOCARPACEAE

UNTIL RECENTLY, this elegant and popular tree was *Podocarpus gracilior*, but taxonimists have relocated it in the genus *Afrocarpus*. It is a member of a prehistoric clan of gymnosperms (comprising 17 plant families) that are differentiated from normal seed-bearing plants, angiosperms, in having seeds that are not protected by enclosure in an ovary, as in conifers, yew and cycads. Like *Podocarpus*, *Afrocarpus* species are evergreen, with linear rather than scale-like leaves; the staminate male cones are slender and catkin-like, while the drupe-like, unprotected, fused, ovulate scales of the females are strikingly pruinose and thinly fleshy. (Female seeds of the *Podocarpus* are held on the top of a fleshy 'receptacle'.) **Afrocarpus gracilior** is found growing on forest soils or riverbanks in moderately dry or moist districts situated from 1,200–3,000 m (4,000–10,000 ft) and is important as a timber tree in E Africa, where it is considered to be one of the most handsome of the native species. Horticulturally, the **A. gracilior** is popular for its graceful habit of growth, as its Latin name *gracilior* suggests. It has a straight, smooth, brown bole that becomes tinged with purple and supports a filmy, often columnar, crown. The arching, pendulous branches are clad in fine, needle-like, light green foliage that tumbles in soft, ballooning masses, with periodic flushes of frosty, pale green, new growth. The tree is known in the trade by the diminutive Podo, and is valued particularly for its soft, durable wood, which is considered superior to that of either cedar or pine. In its habitat, it is recorded as growing up to 60 cm (24 in.) a year, but in cultivation its growth is slower and the tree is usually much smaller than in its natural environment. Although **A. gracilior** has enjoyed great horticultural popularity in the tropics in recent years, it does not thrive in the heat of the tropical lowlands, preferring instead the higher elevations or the cooler subtropics.

A. gracilior; the male fls are held in slender catkins and have copious, powdery pollen.

A. gracilior; the drupe-like, unprotected, fused, ovulate scales of the females, are strikingly pruinose and thinly fleshy.

A. gracilior; arching, pendulous limbs are clad in fine, needle-like lvs.

A. gracilior; a young specimen demonstrating the affinity of these gymnosperms with conifers. This everg. sp. is popular as an accent or shade tree.

Agathis robusta

QLD KAURI

(Moore & Meull.) Bail.   20 spp.

ARAUCARIACEAE

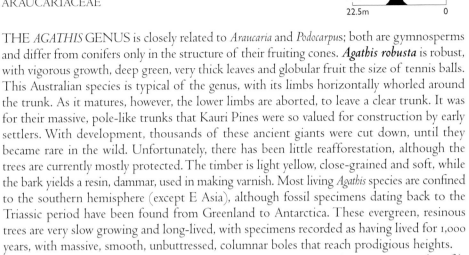

THE *AGATHIS* GENUS is closely related to *Araucaria* and *Podocarpus*; both are gymnosperms and differ from conifers only in the structure of their fruiting cones. *Agathis robusta* is robust, with vigorous growth, deep green, very thick leaves and globular fruit the size of tennis balls. This Australian species is typical of the genus, with its limbs horizontally whorled around the trunk. As it matures, however, the lower limbs are aborted, to leave a clear trunk. It was for their massive, pole-like trunks that Kauri Pines were so valued for construction by early settlers. With development, thousands of these ancient giants were cut down, until they became rare in the wild. Unfortunately, there has been little reafforestation, although the trees are currently mostly protected. The timber is light yellow, close-grained and soft, while the bark yields a resin, dammar, used in making varnish. Most living *Agathis* species are confined to the southern hemisphere (except E Asia), although fossil specimens dating back to the Triassic period have been found from Greenland to Antarctica. These evergreen, resinous trees are very slow growing and long-lived, with specimens recorded as having lived for 1,000 years, with massive, smooth, unbuttressed, columnar boles that reach prodigious heights.
***A. dammara*; ([Lamb.] Rich), (syn. *A. alba*), SE Asia to New Guinea, to 50 m (164 ft). AMBOINA PINE or PITCH TREE is one of the most massive trees of the mountain forests of Malaysia. It has thick, resinous, scaly-grey bark tinged red, and pendent branches. It is easily recognized in its habitat by its great size and its tapering, conical shape. It is renowned for its copious resin, known as Manila Copal, Bendang or Damar Minyak. The scaly, fibrous bark is burnt to deter mosquitoes. (10–12)
*** *A. microstachya*; (J.F. Bail. & C.T. White), N Qld, Australia, to 50 m (164 ft). ATHERTON or BULL-KAURI has smallish, narrow leaves and a spreading crown. (9–12)

ORIGIN	E Qld, Australia, endemic
HEIGHT	up to 50 m (164 ft)
TYPE	evergreen, very large resinous conifer
STATUS	threatened
HABITAT	drier rainforest, from near sea level to 1,500 m (5,000 ft)
GROWTH	slow
FLOWG	spring
DRY TOL.	moderate
SALT TOL.	moderate
LIGHT	full sun or bright shade
SOIL	deep, fertile, well-drained
NUTRIT.	high-nitrogen fertilizer annually
HAZARDS	none
PROBLEMS	none
ENVIRON.	wind-pollinated; fruit for wild animals
PROPAG.	seeds; cuttings of leading shoot
LEAVES	simple; dark green; to 12 cm (4.7 in.); new leaves tinged red, stalk elliptic, apex blunt
FLOWERS	cones; monoecious; scaly; females, larger, red-brown; males, stiff, cylindrical
FRUIT	a cone; males, subsessile; females, ovoid, stalked; seeds, solitary, winged
USE	specimen; public open space; botanic collection; large avenue tree
ZONE	9–11

A. microstachya; with developing bluish green, cone-like, female fr.

A. robusta; planted in a public open space in Innisfall, northern Qld, Australia, this endemic young tree demonstrates its typically upwardly stretching structure and massive pole-like trunk.

A. microstachya; with finer foliage and a billowing crown.

A. robusta; the massive trunks have distinctively colourful, flaking bark.

(1) ***Agathis borneensis***; (Warb.), Malaysia, Sumatra and Borneo, to 50 m (164 ft) or more. The bark is grey to very dark grey. (2) This sp. is easily recognized by its very large, ovate to elliptic lvs measuring from 9 × 4 cm (3.5 × 1.6 in.); they are pale green below with incurved margins. Male cones are oblong, short-stalked to 7 × 2.5 cm (2.8 × 1 in.), obtuse; peduncle to 1 cm (.4 in.). Female cones globose to ovoid, to 10 cm (4 in.), scales triangular, tips spreading. (10–12) (3) ***Agathis macrophylla***; ([Lindley] Masters), (syn. *A. vitensis*), Solomon Is, Vanuatu and Fiji, to 30 m (99 ft) or more. This sp. is known as Dakua or Fijian Kauri. It resembles *A. dammara* but the lvs are larger, being ovate to lanceolate, thick, to 18 × 5 cm (7 × 2 in.), leathery, dark green above, apex tapered and margins inrolled. The limbs of this sp. are massive and widespreading; the bark is white and scaly. The male cones are globose, cylindric, erect, to 2.5 × 1.0 cm (1 × 0.4 in.); the female cones are erect, ovoid to globose, to 10 × 10 cm (4 × 4 in.); the fertile scales acuminate, glaucous. Traditionally, this Kauri has been used to construct superior canoes. This specimen was photographed at Foster Botanic Gardens in Honolulu, Hawaii. (4) *A. macrophylla*, showing the lvs and trunk. (10–12)

***Agathis australis*; ([D. Don] Salisb.), New Zealand; up to 50 m (164 ft). KAURI PINE develops a narrow-conic crown and bark is grey, suffused purple. Lvs are glaucous-green, ovate to lanceolate, 10 × 1 cm (4 × 0.4 in.); female cones are subglobose, to 6 × 8 cm (2.4 × 3 in.) on mature trees. *A. australis* is a warm-temperate to subtrop. sp., being native to the northern, frost-free region of the North Island. This monumental old Kauri Pine, with its massive bole, is preserved at the Warkworth Kauri Park north of Auckland in New Zealand and demonstrates clearly the value of this majestic genus as a timber tree. This is an endangered sp. now because of its exploitation during the early days of logging. The search for Kauri timber was said to be the original reason for the colonization of these remote, southern Pacific islands at a timee when the British Navy was desperately in need of timber to make the masts of their ships. (9–10)**

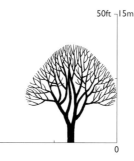

50ft ⌐15m

50ft
15m   0

Alberta magna

NATAL FLAME BUSH

E. Meyer   1 sp.

RUBIACEAE

NATIVE OF COASTAL RAVINES AND EVERGREEN FORESTS of the Transkei and of Natal in S Africa, **Alberta magna** is a small forest tree, so slow growing that it is mostly encountered as a large shrub. *Alberta* is a monospecific genus, consisting only of the species **A. magna**. As befits its local common name, the Natal Flame Bush has a neat, erect, wide-spreading habit and branches close to the ground. It is multi-stemmed, and the bark on the younger, main stems is grey-brown, fairly smooth and has transverse grooves. It becomes rougher with age. The dark green, leathery, elliptic, opposite leaves are glossy above and pale below, with distinctive, yellowish midribs. In S Africa, the blooms appear in early summer and continue until late autumn. The striking, tubular flowers are either a luminous, dark red or intense, orange crimson and are borne in dense, axillary or terminal heads that are similar to those of the closely related *Hamelia*. Each slender, fiery tube is enlivened by perky, exserted stamens. After the flowers have faded, the embryo swells into a simple shuttlecock, with 2 of the persistent sepals enlarging into papery, petal-like wings that are attached to its apex. They turn a glowing, deep scarlet, with the bracts persisting for several months before finally turning brown. As soon as the fruit is fully ripe, it detaches itself and is dispersed on the wind by means of its propeller-like wings. The bark has been found to have medicinal properties and is used locally. **A. magna**, shown below, was photographed in the Huntingdon Gardens in Pasadena, south of Los Angeles, California, USA, where the horticultural staff described the great difficulties that can be encountered in propagating and raising this extremely rare, slow-growing species. One theory is that fruit requires 1 full year to mature before seeds are viable. Such are its circumstances that **A. magna** has been listed as threatened and was celebrated in S Africa as Tree of the Year for 2002/2003.

ORIGIN	Eastern S Africa
HEIGHT	up to 10 m (33 ft)
TYPE	evergreen, small flowering tree
STATUS	threatened
HABITAT	humid ravines and evergreen forests in coastal regions
GROWTH	very slow
FLOWG	early summer to autumn
DRY TOL.	low
SALT TOL.	moderate to high
LIGHT	sheltered sun; bright shade
SOIL	fertile; water-retentive
NUTRIT.	balanced fertilizer annually; deep, organic mulch
HAZARDS	none
PROBLEMS	difficult to propagate
ENVIRON.	nectar for birds
PROPAG.	seeds (fresh); cuttings; layers
LEAVES	simple; dark green; elliptic, leathery, paler below; with yellow midribs
FLOWERS	showy; dark red to orange-crimson; tubular; held in crowded clusters
FRUIT	a nut, with 2 bright red, papery wings (enlarged calyx lobes)
USE	specimen; collection; large planter; courtyard; conservatory
ZONE	9–11

A. magna; with showy, red winged fr. that persist for several months.

A. magna; bark on young, main stems is fairly smooth with transverse grooves, becomes rougher with age.

A. magna; in a quiet corner of the fabled Huntingdon Gardens in Pasadena, California, USA.

A. magna; a rare, celebrated, S African native of everg. forests. It is known there as the Natal Flame Bush.

Albizia lebbeck

WOMAN'S TONGUE

[L.] Benth.   117 spp.

Mimosa lebbeck

FABACEAE (Mimosoideae)

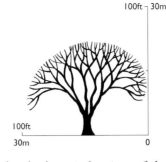

ALBIZIA LEBBECK is native to most parts of the tropical and subtropical regions of the Old World. It has, however, found its way to most warm corners of the New World. *A. lebbeck* shares many of the same genes as *Samanea saman*, which has been included in the *Albizia* genus by some taxonimists. Although it appears remarkably like the Saman Tree, *A. lebbeck* has a much more compact growth. While the crown is relatively wide spreading, it is less umbrella-shaped, with possibly distorted or disorganized growth. In spring, short-lived, fragrant, greenish white, powder-puff flowers are held stiffly, either singly or in groups, at twig ends; they deepen to a creamy ochre with age. The flowers are followed rapidly by abundant, thin, flat beans that are marked with the dark contours of the seeds within. The fruit gradually mature to become pale, straw-coloured, papery pods that persist on the leafless tree for many months, clattering in the wind and earning them one of their common names, Woman's Tongue. *A. lebbeck* is extremely fast growing and tolerant of degraded or nutritionally poor soils and has been widely planted in the drier parts of the tropics for agro-forestry. Unfortunately, the root system of this tree is shallow, though wide, and the trees are easily blown over in storms. Furthermore, it has brittle limbs that are liable to crack in heavy gales, making this species unsuitable for planting near buildings, pathways or roadsides. *A. lebbeck* has proved valuable as shade for coffee and cocoa, as well as for providing fodder and fuel wood in difficult, arid areas. Its excellent dark brown timber is likened to Black Walnut.

*** *A. anthelmintica*; (Brongn.) Trop. and S Africa, to 10 m (33 ft). WORM-BARK FALSE THORN is a multi-stemmed, slightly spiny species of dry, sandy bushland. A preparation of its bark and shoots is effective against intestinal parasites, especially tapeworm. A honey plant. (9–11)

NOTE: *A. lebbeck* has proved invasive in many lowland regions.

ORIGIN	N Africa to N Australia
HEIGHT	up to 30 m (100 ft)
TYPE	deciduous foliage tree
STATUS	not threatened
HABITAT	tropical to subtropical sandy river beds and savannahs
GROWTH	fast
FLOWG	spring
DRY TOL.	high
SALT TOL.	high
LIGHT	full sun
SOIL	widely tolerant, well-drained
NUTRIT.	normally not necessary
HAZARDS	brittle limbs
PROBLEMS	scale; possibly nematodes
ENVIRON.	bee nectar
PROPAG.	seeds (soaked); semi-ripe cuttings
LEAVES	2-pinnate; bright green; leaflets asymmetrical, blunt-tipped; glaucous below
FLOWERS	showy; greenish white, fading to creamy ochre with age; fragrant
FRUIT	legume, to 15 cm, (6 in.); flat, dehiscent, pale tan, papery, persistent
USE	seaside; summer shade; agricultural shade; land reclamation; fodder and firewood; xerophytic
ZONE	10–12

A. lebbeck: with its feet in the water, in Grand Cayman, this usually decid. sp. may keep its floppy mop of lvs most of the year, providing welcome shade for tourists.

A. lebbeck; powder-puff, white fls fade cream and collapse after pollination.

A. lebbeck; fls are followed quickly by thin, flat beans marked with dark bumps by the sds within.

A. lebbeck; straw-coloured, papery pods persist on the bare tree for many months, clattering in the wind.

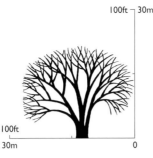

100ft — 30m

100ft
30m   0

Aleurites moluccana

CANDLENUT

(L.) Wild.   5 spp.

A. triloba

EUPHORBIACEAE (Crotonoideae)

ORIGIN	SE Asia to Pacific
HEIGHT	up to 20 m (66 ft)
TYPE	evergreen foliage (fruiting) tree
STATUS	not threatened
HABITAT	moist, lowland limestone forest
GROWTH	moderate
FLOWG	intermittently, year-round
DRY TOL.	moderate to high
SALT TOL.	moderate
LIGHT	full sun
SOIL	widely tolerant, water-retentive
NUTRIT.	normally not necessary
HAZARDS	all parts of the tree are poisonous
PROBLEMS	messy fruit drop; invasive
ENVIRON.	insect nectar
PROPAG.	seeds; hardwood cuttings
LEAVES	palmate; yellowish green; to 20 cm (8 in.); long, stout petioles; frosted below
FLOWERS	showy; floury white; held in erect, branched cymes
FRUIT	a drupe, to 6 cm (2.4 in.) diam.; stoutly stalked, ball-like; yielding oil
USE	street tree; public open space; specimen; xerophytic
ZONE	10–12

ALEURITES MOLUCCANA belongs to the Euphorbia family and is found in the humid lowlands of SE Asia and in parts of the Pacific. It is easily distinguished because, even from a great distance, the tree may be identified by its glinting, silvery, maple-like foliage. The lobed leaves are deeply dusted with a frosty, mealy tomen, especially when young, and are held on long, hinged petioles that allow them to sway and glitter in the slightest breeze. Little, floury white flowers are held stiffly erect, accentuating and complementing the silvery leaves. The flowers are followed by an abundant crop of large, fleshy fruit that contain 1 or 2 very oily, hard-shelled seeds. These resemble walnuts to some degree and traditionally they were strung together on the midrib of coconut leaves to be lit and used as candles. *A. moluccana* is the State Tree of Hawaii, where it is probably non-native, and is known as Kukui. It grows abundantly in the gullies of the lower mountain slopes, where it dominates the natural flora. It was chosen for its diverse domestic uses, for making costume jewellery and for its useful oils, known variously as China Wood-, Candle-nut- or Lumbang- oil, all of which have many medicinal applications. The oil has also been used in tanning and as a drying oil for varnishes and artists' paints. Soot from the burnt oil or nuts is used in India to make kohl and, in the Pacific, for tattooing. It also provides an important, copper-red dye that is used for decorating tapa bark cloth. In Indonesia and Malaysia, the nuts are used in local cooking to thicken curries and other dishes. The timber is soft and not durable but in parts of Asia it is used to make plywood.

✱✱✱ *A. montana*; ([Lour.] E. Wilson), S China. Like *A. fordii* (Hems.), the seeds yield Tung oil, a drying oil that is used in the manufacture of paints and varnishes. (10–12)

NOTE: *A. moluccana* has proved very invasive in many regions.

A. moluccana; new growth and lvs are frosty-white tomentose.

A. montana; sds yield a drying oil (Tung oil) used in the manufacture of paints and varnishes.

A. moluccana; oil-rich candle-nuts are held on sturdy stalks. In the Philippines, oil is extracted commercially.

A. moluccana; this famous, fast-growing sp. signals its presence by flashing the glittering white tops of its large, palmate, emergent lvs.

Alloxylon flammeum

TREE WARATAH

(Hill & Meull.) Weston & Crisp   4 spp.

Oreocallis wickhamii: (misapplied name), O. sp. nova

PROTEACEAE (Grevilleoidea–Embothrieae)

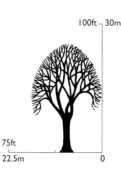

IN LATE SPRING, in the highland or coastal rainforests of Australia's eastern coast, from Qld to northern NSW , the ***Alloxylon flammeum*** can be found signalling its presence with its bright red, spidery blooms. In full flower, it is considered to be one of Australia's most spectacular trees. Under cultivation, *A. flammeum* forms a single, short, cylindrical trunk and a slender, ovoid crown, with rusty hairy new growth, while its young limbs are a chocolate-brown colour. Like some other species in this large family, the elegant, glossy, dark green leaves have distinct juvenile and mature stages and vary greatly in shape from linear to broadly ovate. Mature leaves are often deeply lobed toward their tips, with rusty hairy petioles. Blooms comprise a dense, terminal cluster of erect, slender, bright crimson tubes that resemble a many-tentacled sea anemone. In autumn or early winter, oblong, brown, woody follicles follow the flowers; they are closely packed with winged seeds. *A. flammeum* is a member of the illustrious Proteaceae of the southern hemisphere, which includes so many of S Africa's and Australia's most outstanding species. Here, they thrive in the rich, acid soils and the mild, temperate climates. Until recently, this species has been known as *Oreocallis wickhamii*. Although *A. flammeum* may be propagated by cuttings, to attain the best root growth it is recommended that it be raised from fresh seed. It must be grown in full sun in order to achieve maximum flowering, but needs protection from desiccating winds. It also requires high humidity for successful results.

*** ***A. wickhamii***; ([W. Hill & F. Meull.]Weston & Crisp), (syn. *Ebothrium wickhamii*, *Oreocallis wickhamii*), NE Qld, Australia, to 20 m (66 ft). PINK SILKY OAK has a dense, erect habit with bluish green, entire (unlobed) foliage. The flowers differ in being pinkish red, axillary and partially hidden in the leaves. (**10–12**)

ORIGIN	Australia, endemic
HEIGHT	8–30 m (26–100 ft)
TYPE	evergreen flowering tree
STATUS	not threatened
HABITAT	highland and coastal rainforest fringes
GROWTH	moderate
FLOWG	late spring, early summer
DRY TOL.	low
SALT TOL.	moderate
LIGHT	full sun
SOIL	humid, acid loam
NUTRIT.	balanced fertilizer annually; deep, organic mulch
HAZARDS	none
PROBLEMS	allergic to phosphates
ENVIRON.	nectar for birds
PROPAG.	seeds; cuttings; layers
LEAVES	simple; dark green, paler below; variable, possibly lobed at maturity
FLOWERS	showy; bright scarlet; held in dense heads; with slender, tubular petals
FRUIT	a follicle, to 10 cm (4 in.); woody; packed with winged seeds
USE	specimen; large planter; courtyard; accent; street tree; civic centre; conservatory
ZONE	9–11

A. flammeum; demonstrates the distinctive floral design of the Proteaceae clan.

A. flammeum; with very variable, fern-like, juvenile foliage.

A. flammeum; a fine example in Qld, Australia, with its tubular fls, resembling many-tentacled sea anemone.

A. wickhamii; the fls differ in being pinkish red, axillary and somewhat hidden in the lvs.

100ft ⌐ 30m
75ft
22.5m   0

Alstonia scholaris

DEVIL TREE

(L.) R. Br.   43 spp.

APOCYNACEAE

ORIGIN	from Africa to Asia, and Australia
HEIGHT	up to 20 m (65 ft)
TYPE	evergreen foliage and flowering tree
STATUS	not threatened
HABITAT	humid evergreen forests
GROWTH	fast
FLOW'G	spring to late autumn
DRY TOL.	moderate
SALT TOL.	low
LIGHT	full sun or part shade
SOIL	rich, water-retentive
NUTRIT.	balanced fertilizer annually; deep, organic mulch
HAZARDS	none
PROBLEMS	none
ENVIRON.	butterfly nectar
PROPAG.	seeds; hardwood cuttings
LEAVES	simple; rich green; to 20 cm (8 in.); spathulate, whorled, leathery
FLOWERS	showy; greenish white; slender-tubed; held in compact, downy cymes
FRUIT	a follicle, to 60 cm (24 in.); held in untidy, pendent bundles; seeds, hairy
USE	shade tree; street tree; specimen; public open space
ZONE	10—12

ALSTONIA SCHOLARIS is a stately tree of dense, erect growth. The trunk is often fluted and buttressed, and the bark is dark grey, rough and saturated with bitter, milky sap. All its parts – limbs, leaves and flowers – have a whorled arrangement. When young, the tree develops in layers, with the branches held in horizontal, whorled planes to form a narrow, oval crown; as it matures, the tree takes on a more open, irregular form. The shiny, tough, leathery leaves are silvery downy, with numerous, parallel lateral veins. In spring, and again in autumn, the deep green canopy is elegantly upholstered with large posies of greenish white, slender-tubed blooms that are held rigidly erect in downy, long-stemmed, compact, spoked heads that come from the axils of the leaves. Pairs of long, flattened, sinuous, string-like pods follow the flowers and dangle untidily from the twigs. They are sought after by mynah birds, which use them to make their nests. In certain parts of India, particularly Bombay, it was believed that each leaf of the Devil Tree was the domain of a particular spirit and that once a year all the trees of the forest assembled to pay homage. Local people tap the bark for its sticky, bitter sap, which is known as Dita and is well regarded as a powerful tonic, vermifuge and, ostensibly, as an anti-malarial drug. *A. scholaris* has soft wood, known regionally as Milk- or Cheese-wood, which is white and exceedingly lightweight. In India, it is used traditionally to make coffins and chalkboards and, after being coated with pipeclay, for school slates, hence its Latin name, *scholaris*. A pen made from the Arenga palm is used to write on them. The soft wood is also popular in Sri Lanka for hand-carved masks.

*** *Alstonia macrophylla*; (Wallich.), SE Asia, to 20 m (66 ft). Pulai, a lean, stretching species, differs in having a less compact habit and much smaller flowers. (10—12)

NOTE: these species may be invasive in some regions.

A. macrophylla; smaller, less compact infl.

A. scholaris; a stately native in the countryside near Cairns, N Qld, Australia.

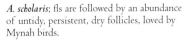

A. scholaris; fls are followed by an abundance of untidy, persistent, dry follicles, loved by Mynah birds.

A. scholaris; with stoutly stemmed, spoked heads of slender, tubed fls that are held rigidly erect. They have copious nectar that is particularly attractive to butterflies.

Amherstia nobilis

QUEEN OF FLOWERING TREES

Wallich   1 sp.

FABACEAE (Caesalpinioideae)

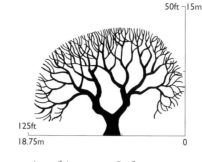

50ft ⌐15m

125ft
18.75m   0

AMHERSTIA NOBILIS is monospecific, a solitary species of its genus. It forms a stout, heavily barked trunk and robust, widely spreading limbs, which support a luxuriant, lustrous crown of huge, cascading foliage. Like *Brownea* and *Saraca*, *A. nobilis* is a 'handkerchief' tree with limp, pendulous, new growth that emerges silvery pink and expands coppery maroon. The satiny flowers are arranged in grand, graceful, red-branched candelabra, and are up to 1 m (3.3 ft) in length. These unique, slender, crimson blooms are splashed white and yellow, reminiscent of those of *Delonix regia*. They hang and dangle on slender stems and look like silken, mythological insects that have long, curving, filament feelers and are arched and suspended in mid-flight. Even the elegantly curved fruit is decorative, being variegated crimson and yellow when young. Because it seldom sets seed or, if it does, the seeds are rarely viable, the Burmese eventually established a method of propagation by layering the young limbs. This tree deserves its title of Queen of Flowering Trees because it is probably the most desirable and sought-after of tropical trees. This is partly because of its rarity, due to the scarcity of seeds and propagative material, but overwhelmingly because of its singular elegance. It was discovered in 1826 by the botanist Nathaniel Wallich (1786–1854) in a Burmese monastery garden at Kogun, on the Saluen River, in the province of Martaban. Wallich, who was the director of the Calcutta Botanic Gardens, named it for Lady Sarah Amherst, who collected plants in Asia in the early 19th century. Since then, this species has been found only twice in the wild, making it extremely rare and endangered. Its young leaves and flowers are eaten by the local people. *A. nobilis* is native to the monsoonal, teak-forest regions of Burma, where there is a distinct dry season, needed to trigger blooming, and where the soil is calcareous — neutral, but rich and deep.

ORIGIN	Burma, endemic
HEIGHT	up to 12 m (40 ft)
TYPE	evergreen flowering tree
STATUS	highly endangered
HABITAT	lowland, monsoon teak forest on calcareous soil
GROWTH	slow
FLOWG	after rain breaks a dry spell
DRY TOL.	low
SALT TOL.	low
LIGHT	sheltered, in full sun
SOIL	rich; water-retentive
NUTRIT.	organic fertilizer; deep, organic mulch
HAZARDS	none
PROBLEMS	difficult to propagate
ENVIRON.	bird nectar
PROPAG.	seeds; air layers; greenwood cuttings
LEAVES	pinnate; dark green; to 1 m (3.2 ft); leaflets oblong, to 20 cm (8 in.)
FLOWERS	showy; scarlet and white; held in large, branched, pendent racemes
FRUIT	a legume, to 15 cm (6 in.); broad pods; with 3–4 seeds; viable fruit rarely seen
USE	humid, shade garden; courtyard; specimen; botanic collection; conservatory
ZONE	11–12

A. nobils; with a limp, pendulous 'handkerchief' of new lvs.

A. nobilis; the blooms of this exotic sp. perhaps recall an exotic insect arched and suspended in mid-flight, with long, curving, filament feelers. Burmese villagers eat the young fls and lvs.

A. nobilis; despite the elegant fr., this sp. seldom sets sd outside its natural habitat as it lacks its pollinators.

A. nobilis; with robust, widely spreading limbs, that support a luxuriant, lustrous crown of cascading foliage.

ORIGIN	Ecuador to Costa Rica
HEIGHT	6–10 m (20–33 ft)
TYPE	evergreen, small foliage tree
STATUS	not threatened
HABITAT	coastal swamps and woodlands
GROWTH	moderate
FLOWG	year-round
DRY TOL.	moderate to high
SALT TOL.	high
LIGHT	full sun; bright shade
SOIL	fertile; preferably humid
NUTRIT.	high-nitrogen fertilizer; deep, organic mulch
HAZARDS	none
PROBLEMS	possibly invasive roots
ENVIRON.	bat nectar
PROPAG.	seeds; layers; root cuttings
LEAVES	simple; very dark green; to 19 cm (7.5 in.); leathery, glossy
FLOWERS	inconspicuous; greenish pink without, yellow within; tubular-campanulate
FRUIT	a pepo, to 9 cm (3.5 in.); small, hard-skinned, egg-shaped gourd; containing many flat seeds
USE	seaside; small shade tree; wind barrier; specimen; courtyard; conservatory; xerophytic
ZONE	9–11

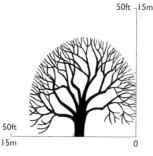

50ft ⌐15m
50ft
15m 0

Amphitecna latifolia

BLACK CALABASH

(Mill.) A. Gentry   18 spp.

Enellagma latifolia

BIGNONIACEAE

IN CULTIVATION, this small, tropical American tree, with a sinewy trunk and 3–4 angulate branches, forms a globular, densely foliaged crown of the darkest, glossiest green. In its natural, swampy, coastal habitats, the ***Amphitecna latifolia*** establishes dense thickets, rooting as its branches settle in the brackish mud. It will flourish equally well, however, in a dry habitat, where it forms a sturdy trunk and a wide, diffusely limbed crown. The roots, in their relentless search for water, may prove invasive. Curious, little, waxy, cauliflorous flowers remain hidden, either on the trunk itself or amongst the leaves. Clasped in a fleshy, bright green tubular calyx, the inflated, bell-shaped, pinkish yellow or dull, rosy green flowers are slightly folded to begin with; as they emerge, their frilly lips and 4 stout stamens are revealed, recalling the blooms of the closely related *Crescentia cujete* or *Parmentiera cerifera*. The fruit is a small, smooth, thin, hard-walled, ovoid gourd, which takes up to a year to fully mature. It is filled with whitish pulp and many glossy, black, heart-shaped seeds that are edible and are reported to have been used as a cocoa substitute on the W Indian island of Puerto Rico. *A. latifolia* is an excellent small tree for coastal gardens, particularly because it is tolerant of sandy or brackish, alkaline soils. However, because the flowers of this species do not self-pollinate, they may require cross-pollination with another plant nearby, or hand-pollination. *** *A. macrophylla*; ([Seem.] Miers ex Baill.), Mexico, to 7 m (23 ft). Branchlets angular, leathery leaves are clustered at tips. Flowers are white and held in clusters. (9–11) ****A. regalis*; ([Lind.] A. Gentry), Mexico, to 12 m (40 ft). This shrub or small tree is renowned for its magnificent, leathery, glabrous leaves (up to 1 m [3.3 ft] in length), which are clustered towards the tips of the branches (9–11)

A. latifolia; charming fls are mostly hidden deep in the lvs.

A. latifolia; a sprawling thicket of trees growing in a small swamp at Fairchild Tropical Gardens in Miami, USA.

A. latifolia; thin-walled, calabash-like fr. contain many flat, heart-shaped sds that may be sterile.

A. latifolia; an everg. sp. of coast. swamp, Black Calabash forms a dense, rounded crown of superb, dark green foliage. This makes it particularly effective as a coast. screen.

Anacardium occidentale

CASHEW

L.   11 spp.

Acajou occidentale

ANACARDIACEAE

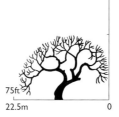

ANACARDIUM OCCIDENTALE is an awkward, knobbly, little desert tree, with dull green, long-petioled, leathery leaves and stiffly branched panicles of little, fragrant, whitish flowers that deepen to red. This member of the infamously toxic Anacardiaceae clan (which includes delicious tropical fruit such as mango, otaheiti apple and purple mombin) provides both a nut and a fruit. The fruit is curiously arranged, with its large embryo, or nut, exposed and attached to the base of the fleshy 'fruit' (the receptacle) like a baby developed outside the womb. The receptacle resembles a red or yellow apple and although its resinous, spongy flesh is rather astringent, it is nevertheless pleasantly acid. The red 'apple' is considered superior to the yellow form. A kidney-shaped nut hangs from the base of the 'apple' and is the true fruit; its oily kernel is toxic and must be roasted before being eaten. Care must be taken in handling raw nuts as the inside of the shell contains an irritant, which may burn the skin. In Brazil, a drink, Cajuado, is prepared from fermented fruit, while in India an intoxicating beverage, known as Kajus or Feni, is distilled from the nut. Most parts of *A. occidentale* are useful. Thick, black oil is extracted from the nuts and known commercially as Cardol oil. It is employed medicinally and is also used as an insecticide to preserve bookbindings and wooden carvings against insect attack. Cashew-nut shells yield a liquid, known by its initials CNSL, which is used in brake linings and clutches and in plastic resins. Indelible ink is made from the sap, which is also considered to have contraceptive properties. Although xerophytic, *A. occidentale* will tolerate swampy, seasonally flooded or poorly drained land. The seeds, however, often germinate poorly, but can easily be tested for fertility by being put in a sugar solution; those that float usually prove to be fertile.

ORIGIN	Trop. America
HEIGHT	up to 12 m (40 ft)
TYPE	semi-deciduous fruiting tree
STATUS	vulnerable
HABITAT	arid thickets on poor soil
GROWTH	slow
FLOWG	intermittently, year-round
DRY TOL.	high
SALT TOL.	moderate
LIGHT	full sun
SOIL	fertile, water-retentive
NUTRIT.	balanced fertilizer annually
HAZARDS	nut toxic unless roasted
PROBLEMS	anthracnose fungus
ENVIRON.	bee nectar; wild fruit for birds
PROPAG.	seeds; cuttings; layers
LEAVES	simple; dull green, obovate, stiff, rough and leathery
FLOWERS	showy; yellowish white, deepening to dark red; held in small panicles; fragrant
FRUIT	a drupe, to 3 cm (1.2 in.); with a single seed, held at the base of a large, edible, fleshy receptacle
USE	backyard tree; courtyard; large planter; xerophytic
ZONE	10–12

A. occidentale; little whitish and brick-red fls in wide-spreading panicles.

A. occidentale; produces fls and fr. intermittently all year. The fr., with its large embryo, or nut, exposed, is attached to the base of the fleshy 'fr.', which is known as the receptacle.

A. occidentale; the red 'apple' form, which is considered to be more tasty than the yellow variety.

A. occidentale; in Brazil, an intoxicating drink, knwon as Cajuado, is made from the fermented fr.

ORIGIN	Trop. America; W Africa
HEIGHT	up to 30 m (100 ft)
TYPE	evergreen, large foliage tree
STATUS	not threatened
HABITAT	humid or dry coastal woodland, swamp and savannahs
GROWTH	moderate
FLOWG	spring to summer
DRY TOL.	moderate to high
SALT TOL.	moderate
LIGHT	full sun to partial shade
SOIL	fertile; water-retentive
NUTRIT.	balanced fertilizer annually; organic mulch
HAZARDS	poisonous fruit and bark
PROBLEMS	none
ENVIRON.	bee nectar; wild fruit for bats
PROPAG.	seeds
LEAVES	pinnate; rich green; to 40 cm (16 in.); leaflets 7–13, oblong or elliptic, slightly shiny
FLOWERS	showy; pink or light purple; held in long panicles; fragrant
FRUIT	a legume, to 4 cm (1.5 in.); fleshy, ovoid; with a single seed
USE	shade tree; street tree; public open space; specimen; wind barrier; xerophytic
ZONE	10–12

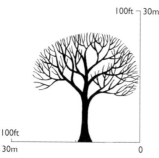

100ft ⌐ 30m
100ft
30m
0

Andira inermis

CABBAGE BARK

(Wright) HBK ex D.C.   30 spp.

Geoffroea jamaicensis; A. jamaicensis

FABACEAE (Papilionoideae)

WITH AGE, THIS EXCELLENT TREE develops a tall, buttressed bole and a buoyant crown of glossy, rich green, large pinnate leaves. Although not flamboyant, the erect inflorescences of *Andira inermis* carry masses of little, stalkless, purplish pink, sweetly fragrant, pea-like flowers, which are very decorative and, being rich in nectar, attract many pollinators. When growing in dry woodland habitats, it flowers twice a year, but in more humid areas it tends to bloom less often. The hard, ovoid, thick, fleshy fruit is indehiscent and contains 1 poisonous seed. Known as Cabbage Bark in the W Indies, *A. inermis* earned its undistinguished nickname from the fact that the bark smells of foetid cabbage. Despite this, the tree, with its luxuriant, densely foliaged, evergreen crown, sturdy form and exceptional adaptability, lends itself to many landscape uses. Even in the driest and dustiest season it always manages to give an impression of flourishing. In the rainforests of C and S America, where *A. inermis* reaches lofty heights, it is renowned for its timber, which is known as Kuraru or Partridge Wood. The sapwood is light brown, but the heartwood is highly figured and decorative, varying from yellowish brown to dark, reddish brown, with sharply contrasting bands of light and dark colour. Despite its vulnerability to attack by dry-wood termites, it was very popular in parts of Trop. America for high-grade furniture before large calliper trees became scarce. Locally, the bark is used medicinally, while a preparation of the seeds is employed as an emetic, despite the fact that both the bark and the fruit are considered toxic and are said to cause blindness if smoke from burning the wood gets into the eyes. This is an important honey plant.

*** *A. araroba*; (Aguiar), (syn. *Vataireopsis araroba*), Trop. America, to 35 m (115 ft). ARAROBA has erect panicles of pale purple flowers. Source of Goa powder, used for skin ailments. (10-12)

A. inermis; fls vary from deep, rose-pink to light purple.

A. inermis; because of these pebbly, toxic sds, this sp. is known, as Pig's Turd in British Virgin Is, W Indies.

A. inermis; long panicles of little rosy pink, pea-like fls are carried intermittently year-round and attract many pollinators.

A. inermis; an old, hurricane-battered specimen at Jardin Botanico de Cienfuegos, Cuba, demonstrating how tall the bole can grow and which makes it so desirable for cutting into timber.

Annona muricata

SOURSOP

L.

137 spp.

ANONNACEAE

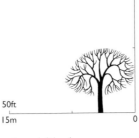

50ft — 15m

50ft
15m 0

WITH A DENSE CROWN of spicily aromatic, rich green, laurel-like leaves, compact, erect growth and a high tolerance of alkaline soils and drought conditions, *Annona muricata* is the most handsome and easiest to grow of its genus. Typical of the Annonaceae family, the blooms comprise 3 fleshy, triangular petals that abort once the flower is pollinated. They have an unpleasant, pungent odour that attracts flies and other insects, which are their pollinators. The fruit of *A. muricata*, like the flowers, is cauliflorous, forming on the trunk and major stems. It is a football-sized syncarp – a multiple fruit composed of many united pistils, each ending in a fleshy spine, which grows from the old style. Each of its white, sweetly aromatic segments of flesh contains a single, black, shiny seed. Light or bright green and irregularly heart- or kidney-shaped, the large, thin-skinned fruit may weigh 3 kg (6.5 lb). In texture and taste, it has been compared to cotton wool saturated with sour juice, but there are many devotees who would stoutly come to the fruit's defence and who are addicted to Soursop juice, ice cream or sorbet. Others consider the taste to be overpoweringly aromatic and even to contain a lurking hint of turpentine. *A. muricata* is the only species of *Annona* that lends itself to processing and preservation. It is high in vitamins B and C and is an important fruit in SE Asia, where it is cooked green with coconut milk. The pungent leaves are well known for their sleep-inducing properties; a potion is brewed from them or they are simply placed fresh under a pillow. The pulp and leaves are used to treat fever, diarrhoea and scurvy. The green fruit, seeds and leaves of the *Annona* species are said to have insecticidal properties. *A. muricata* is an excellent subject for the garden, providing screening or a backdrop for colourful plantings. It also makes a handsome accent tree.

ORIGIN	W Indies; C America
HEIGHT	up to 7 m (23 ft)
TYPE	evergreen, small fruiting tree
STATUS	not threatened
HABITAT	coastal limestone; lowland woodland
GROWTH	fast
FLOWG	spring to summer
DRY TOL.	high
SALT TOL.	moderate
LIGHT	full sun or bright shade
SOIL.	fertile, well-drained
NUTRIT.	balanced fertilizer, early spring; deep, organic mulch
HAZARDS	toxic seeds; eye irritant
PROBLEMS	seed borer; scale; mealy bugs
ENVIRON.	nectar for insects
PROPAG.	seeds; semi-ripe cuttings
LEAVES	simple; rich green, to 25 cm (10 in.); obovate, lustrous; paler below; very pungent
FLOWERS	inconspicuous; yellow-green; 3-petalled; fleshy; foetid; cauliflorous
FRUIT	a syncarp, to 35 cm (14 in.); with white, aromatic flesh; skin softly spiny; seeds black, shiny
USE	seaside; backyard tree; screening; large container; courtyard; conservatory; xerophytic
ZONE	10—12

A. muricata; with large, softly spiny, multiple fr. This fast-growing, everg. sp has glossy foliage that is strongly pungent and used to make a sleeping potion.

A. muricata; has a typical 3-petalled, fleshy, *Annona* fl. with a foetid odour.

A. muricata; shiny, black sds are set in cottony, white, aromatic flesh that is popular for juices and ice cream.

A. muricata; with a dense crown of spicily aromatic, rich green, laurel-like lvs and compact, erect growth.

Annona cherimola; (Mill.), S America, to 9 m (30 ft). CHERIMOYA or GRAVEOLA, the doyen of the *Annona* clan, is considered superior to a ripe pear. It is grown commercially in California and Spain but does not thrive in the true tropics. It is smooth like *A. reticulata*, but green-skinned and much fleshier. Typical of this genus, male and female fl. parts do not mature at the same time, necessitating hand-pollination in some regions. (8–10)

Annona glabra; (L.), (syn. *A. palustris*; *A. laurifolia*), Trop. America, W Africa, to 12 m (39 ft). MONKEY-, POND- or DOG-APPLE, is a sp. of humid lowlands and coastal mangrove swamps. The abundant, sweetly scented fr. is edible but unpalatable and not usually eaten by humans. (10–12) **NOTE: this sp. has become seriously invasive in NE Qld, Australia, forming pure thickets. It was introduced to be used as rootstock for other spp.**

Annona reticulata; (L.), W Indies and C America, to 8 m (26 ft). CUSTARD APPLE, BULLOCK HEART or CORAZON is a most handsome *Anonna* with rich green foliage over an expanded canopy. However, the stout-stemmed fr. of *A. reticulata* is the least esteemed of this popular clan, the pulp being unpleasantly grainy with large sds. In Barbados, it is unkindly known as 'Suck-and-Spit' and Sri Lankans consider it a cause of leprosy. (10–12)

Annona squamosa; (L.), Trop. America, to 6 m (20 ft). SUGAR APPLE, SWEET-SOP or CACHIMAN has a sparse, rounded, greyish green foliage. Fr., however, has delicious sweet, custardy, fragrant pulp. Insert shows mummified fr. caused by seed-boring insects, which is a common problem of this sp. Sds of *A. squamosa* contain an insecticide, acetogin. In Australia and other regions, this sp. is grafted onto *A. glabra* stock. (10–12)

Antidesma bunius

BIGNAY

(L.) Spreng.   170 spp.

A. dallachyanum

EUPHORBIACEAE (Amanoeae)

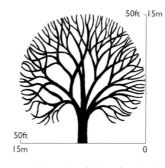

ORIGIN	Himalayas to Australia
HEIGHT	up to 14 m (46 ft)
TYPE	evergreen, fruiting dioecious tree
STATUS	not threatened
HABITAT	humid lowland forest
GROWTH	moderate
FLOWG	spring
DRY TOL.	moderate
SALT TOL.	low
LIGHT	full sun or part shade
SOIL	fertile, water-retentive
NUTRIT.	high-potassium fertilizer; deep, organic mulch
HAZARDS	none
PROBLEMS	none
ENVIRON.	nectar for insects; wild fruit for birds
PROPAG.	seeds; cuttings; grafts; layers
LEAVES	simple; dark green; to 17.5 cm (7 in.); glossy, elliptic to oblong
FLOWERS	inconspicuous; greenish yellow; borne in narrow spikes, to 18 cm (8 in.); male flowers, foetid
FRUIT	a berry, to 1 cm (0.4 in.); red, ripening black; currant-like, juicy, in abundant clusters
USE	screening; windbreak; public open space; small street tree; backyard tree
ZONE	10–12

THE *ANTIDESMA* GENUS belongs to the great Euphorbiaceae. Typical of that family, it is dioecious, that is, it bears pollen and fruit on separate trees. This should necessitate at least 1 male tree in the vicinity, although, in fact, most females may bear profusely without male pollen. Both male and female flowers are held in abundant spikes; male flowers have an unpleasant odour of powdered fish that appeals to flies and other insects that pollinate the blooms. Borne in dense, currant- or grape-like clusters, the yellowish green fruit turns red, then purple or black on ripening. It has a succulent, purple flesh, which may be sweet or slightly bitter, and is often likened to cranberries and is eaten fresh or made into preserves or juice. Throughout its large, natural range, which boasts such a plethora of delicious fruit, *A. bunius* is valued for its domestic uses. In Indonesia, Bignay fruit is included in fish dishes, while in the Philippines the young leaves are eaten raw in salads, stewed with rice or mixed with vegetables. In some regions, an excellent, light table wine is made from the ripe fruit. The bark is stripped to provide a tough fibre and the hard, reddish timber is valued for general building. Australian forms of *A. bunius*, found in the rainforests of NE Qld, have evolved a shrubby habit, with broader leaves and shorter bunches of larger fruit. These Antipodean trees tend to retain their lower branches, making them desirable for planting as screening and windbreaks. Both there and in other parts of the tropics *A. bunius* has enjoyed popularity as an undemanding, evergreen ornamental.

*** *A. platyphyllum*; (H. Mann), Hawaii, endemic, to 15 m (50 ft). HAME is found in wet forests. Its hard, red-brown wood is resistant to shipworms and excellent for boatbuilding, while the ripe fruit is used to colour tapa, a paper-like cloth made from the bark. (10–12)

A. platyphyllum; an endemic sp. of Hawaii, where it is known as Hame and is renowned for its hard, red heartwood.

A. bunius; Bignay is a dioec. sp. and only a female tree will bear these luscious berries in early to late autumn. In some regions, an excellent wine is made from them.

A. bunius; has enjoyed popularity as an undemanding ornamental and for its hard, reddish timber.

A. bunius; a dioec. sp. bearing fruit and pollen on separate trees.

ORIGIN	from India to Malesia and Solomon Is
HEIGHT	up to 15 m (50 ft)
TYPE	evergreen, fruiting foliage tree
STATUS	not threatened
HABITAT	rainforests to humid thickets
GROWTH	moderate
FLOWG	summer
DRY TOL.	moderate
SALT TOL.	low
LIGHT	full sun to part shade
SOIL	rich, humid, water-retentive
NUTRIT.	balanced fertilizer annually; deep, organic mulch
HAZARDS	all parts poisonous
PROBLEMS	none
ENVIRON.	insect nectar
PROPAG.	seeds; semi-ripe cuttings
LEAVES	odd-pinnate; deep green; to 1 m (3.3 ft); leaflets, up to 7 pairs, oblique base
FLOWERS	showy; pale yellow; males, in dangling, branched clusters; females, unbranched
FRUIT	a capsule, to 5 cm (2 in.); globose, leathery; yellow, fleshy; seeds with red aril; dehiscent
USE	small shade tree; street tree; specimen; public open space
ZONE	10–12

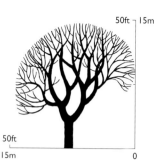

50ft ⌐ 15m

50ft
15m   0

Aphanamixis polystachya

AMOORA

(Wallich.) R. Parker   3 spp.

A. rohituka; Amoora rohituka

MELIACEAE

GROWN FOR ITS HANDSOME FOLIAGE and ornamental fruit, this distinguished species has smooth, thin, dark grey, strongly astringent bark. *Aphanamixis polystachya* forms a heavily rounded crown and has purplish crimson new growth. Superficially, it resembles *Cedrela odorata*, and has enormous, glossy, dark green, leathery leaves that are 1 m (3.3 ft) long. These are clustered near the ends of the flexuous, drooping branches and are divided feather-fashion with obliquely oval leaflets. Little, staminate, globose, pale yellow male flowers are arranged in sturdy, branched clusters and dangled from the leaf bases, while the female flowers are unbranched; although quite showy, these blooms tend to be hidden in the leaves. They are followed by ornamental, leathery, fleshy, rounded, golden yellow or pink-flushed fruit that split into 3 valves to reveal oval, chestnut-coloured seeds, which are enclosed in thin, bright scarlet arils. Like those of the related chinaberry or neem of the Meliaceae family, the luscious-looking fruit of **A. polystachya** are not edible. Seeds yield a semi-drying, oily latex, which is toxic but important in India and Sri Lanka, where it is used as a rubbing liniment for rheumatism, a dressing for sores, a cure for certain blood diseases and as a domestic lighting fuel. The bark has been used in some parts of its region to treat enlarged spleens. The reddish heartwood, which is known commercially as Tasua, is hard and evenly grained, with many uses.

✱✱✱ **A. grandifolia**; ([Bl.] C. DC.) (*Amoora grandifolia*), to 13 m (43 ft), E India. Also known as AMOORA, it is popular in Hawaii as an elegant shade tree and for its decorative fruit, which hang in spikes that are 60 cm (24 in.) long. They are very ornamental, being bright pink or red, with black seeds set in fleshy orange-red arils. (10–12)

NOTE: in some areas of its natural region, **A. polystachya** has a tendency to harbour ants in its hollow shoots.

A. grandifolia; bright, pinkish red, ornamental fr.

A. polystachya; with rugged bark and hard, reddish heartwood, known commercially as Tasua.

A. polystachya; has a rounded crown with purplish crimson, new growth; this sp. superficially resembles *Cedrela odorata*.

A. polystachya; with little pale yellow fls in long, dangling clusters and pinkish yellow fr. splitting to reveal their red arils. Sds contain valuable oils.

Araucaria heterophylla

NORFOLK PINE

(Salisb.) Franco   18–19 spp.

A. excelsa

ARAUCARIACEAE

ARAUCARIA HETEROPHYLLA is a popular columnar tree endemic to the small island of Norfolk, which lies between New Zealand and the island of New Caledonia in the South Pacific. *A. heterophylla* is a superbly structured species, with stout limbs whorled in horizontal planes around a mast-like axis. The stiff, leathery leaves are held spirally on the main axis and oppositely or alternately on lateral shoots. *A. heterophylla* is a gymnosperm, closely related to the *Agathis* genus, and bears both male and female cones. In some regions, this stately, coastal tree has earned a bad reputation, particularly in some parts of Trop. America, where it is often planted singly as an accent in small, suburban gardens and, decorated with lights, used as a Christmas tree during the festive season. In urban areas, however, *A. heterophylla* suffers from pollution, which strips its protective wax coating, making the foliage susceptible to salt damage. Nevertheless, this magnificent, seaworthy giant is extensively planted in Hawaii and Australia along coastal regions and is the signature of many of Australia's celebrated surfing beaches, where it provides shade and stabilizes the sandy shoreline. *A. heterophylla* has been cultivated commercially on Ascension Island, in the S Atlantic, to make masts for sailing ships. Contrary to popular theory, it is not necessary for this *Araucaria* to be left to grow with a single trunk; an excellent shape may be formed if the leader is cut away when it is young, causing the tree to develop a multiple crown, which encourages sturdier, fuller and shorter growth. *Araucaria* species may be propagated by layering lateral limbs, but the resulting young plant will never produce a leader, but continue a plagiotropic growth. Several cultivars of *A. heterophylla* are available, including those with variegated, striped or glaucous foliage, and others with compact or dwarf forms.

ORIGIN	Norfolk Is, endemic
HEIGHT	up to 60 m (197 ft)
TYPE	evergreen, dioecious, very large foliage tree
STATUS	threatened
HABITAT	coastal lowlands; along strand
GROWTH	fast
FLOWG	spring
DRY TOL.	high
SALT TOL.	high
LIGHT	full sun
SOIL	tolerant, very well-drained
NUTRIT.	high-nitrogen fertilizer, annually
HAZARDS	spiny
PROBLEMS	scale; fungus
ENVIRON.	seeds for birds
PROPAG.	seeds; layers
LEAVES	linear; dark green; stiff, leathery; spiralled around stems
FLOWERS	male cones, catkin-like, dense, cylindrical; female cones, much larger, with spiralled scales
FRUIT	female cones to 8.5 cm (3.5 in.); solitary; seeds winged for dispersal
USE	seaside; accent; wind barrier; public open space; large container; conservatory; xerophytic
ZONE	9–11

A. heterophylla; when the leader is cut, the tree develops a multiple crown.

A. heterophylla; Norfolk Island Pine is popular for seaside shade along the coasts of Australia. Apart from providing shade, this sp. binds and stabilizes the beach sand.

A. heterophylla; often planted as a living Christmas tree in the W Indies. Here it adorns a small cottage by the sea.

A. bidwillii; huge, pineapple-like cones with edible sds; cones have a tendency to drop without warning.

Araucaria columnaris; ([Forst.] Hook.), (syn. A. cookii), New Caledonia, up to 60 m (197 ft). Known as COOK PINE, as Capt. Cook discovered it on the famous Isle of Pines, New Caledonia. In its natural habitat, this sp. often masses in monocultural forests. Distinguished by its very narrow, column-like crown, the numerous, scale-like, narrowly triangular lvs are sharp-pointed, to 1.5 cm (0.59 in). Female cones are ovoid, to 10 cm (4 in.). Photographed at the Royal Botanic Gardens in Sydney, Australia. (9–11)

Araucaria cunninghamii; (D. Don.), endemic of E. Australia, up to 60 m (197 ft). HOOP PINE is found on mountain slopes, river banks and coast. forests of E Australia. *A cunninghamii* has stiffly erect, sturdy limbs with an asymmetrically, rounded crown. Foliage is compact at the tips of its limbs; it is dense and lvs are needle-like, not scaly. Fr. are smaller than *A. bidwillii*, up to 10 cm (4 in.). Shown here in Qld, where this sp. is popular for highway and seaside planting. (9–11)

Araucaria bidwillii; (Hook.), Qld, Australia endemic, to 50 m (164 ft). BUNYA-BUNYA PINE, native of coast. and upland rainforests, loses its conical apex with maturity, forming a rounded crown. Its shiny, prickly foliage is tasselled towards the ends of slender, descending limbs. The fr. has overlapping scales of up to 30 cm (12 in) long, pineapple-like cones weighing up to 4.5 kg. (10 lbs) with edible sds. Timber is very desirable, being hard and lightweight. (9–11)

Archidendron lucyi

SCARLET BEAN

F. Muell.   94 SPP.

FABACEAE (Mimosoideae)

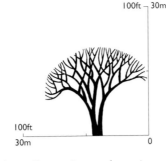

THIS LARGE, LEGUMINOUS GENUS of shrubs and small trees is mostly native to Indo-Malesia and Australia. *Archidendron lucyi* is a worthy species found in the humid, lowland monsoonal forests of eastern Malesia and the Solomon Islands to N Qld's Wet Tropics World Heritage Area (WTWHA). Typical of its genus, *A. lucyi* is fast growing, forming a relaxed, rounded crown of broad, coarsely 2-pinnate leaves with somewhat triangular leaflets. The smoothish, grey bark has a singular smell of rotten tomatoes when cut. Honeysuckle-scented flowers, which superficially resemble those of the *Inga* genus, are arranged in globular heads, with narrow, tube-like blooms containing delicate bundles of fine, white, silky stamens forming small 'powder puffs'. They are cauliflorous and short-lived, lasting only a day, but are produced profusely over a period of several months, attracting bees and nectar-loving birds, such as the native Honeyeaters. Gradually, the flowers are replaced by spectacular fruit, which particularly distinguishes this genus. The bright scarlet pods are thick, woody, spirally curved and, on opening, contort and coil, revealing pruinose, black seeds dangled on short stalks from the glowing, orange walls of the carpel. *Archidendron* species, native of lowland rainforests, require shelter and a certain degree of shade and humidity to thrive and to protect their delicate, cauliflorous blooms. Pruning the trees has been shown to improve their shape.

*** *A. grandiflorum*, ([Sol. ex Benth.] I.C. Neilsen), Qld and Northern NSW, Australia, to 16 m (52 ft). Known as FAIRY PAINTBRUSH or PINK LACE FLOWER, this rare species is also a rainforest tree. It develops an irregular, slightly fluted trunk and spreading crown. The large, stunning flowers are lightly scented, borne terminally and are extremely attractive to butterflies. Both these species are honey plants (9–11)

ORIGIN	E. Malesia to Solomon Is and Qld, Australia
HEIGHT	up to 18 m (59 ft)
TYPE	evergreen, small flowering (fruiting) tree
STATUS	limited distribution
HABITAT	humid lowland rainforest and monsoonal forests
GROWTH	moderate
FLOWG	spring and summer
DRY TOL.	moderate
SALT TOL.	low
LIGHT	semi-shade or sheltered sun
SOIL	fertile, water-retentive
NUTRIT.	low-nitrogen fertilizer; deep, organic mulch
HAZARDS	none
PROBLEMS	none
ENVIRON.	bee nectar and wild seeds for birds
PROPAG.	fresh seeds
LEAVES	2-pinnate; rich green, with leathery leaflets
FLOWERS	showy; white; held in globular heads of narrow, tubular blooms with many stamens
FRUIT	a legume, to 10 cm, (4 in.); bright scarlet, spiralled; with pruinose, black seeds
USE	shade garden; specimen; courtyard; large planter; civic centre; conservatory
ZONE	9–11

A. lucyi; the heads of the fluffy white blooms are held for only 1 day.

A. lucyi; this small Australian, leguminous, rainforest tree is mostly popular for its lacquered, bright scarlet, gold-lined pods and large, black sds covered in blue 'bloom'.

A. lucyi; delicate, starry, sweetly-fragrant, 'powder puff' blooms are followed by decorative bright scarlet fr.

A. grandiflorum; called Fairy Paint Brush because its white stamens appear to be dipped into crimson paint.

ORIGIN	Madagascar to Indian and Pacific Oceans and Australia
HEIGHT	up to 8 m (26 ft)
TYPE	evergreen, dioecious, small foliage tree
STATUS	not threatened
HABITAT	coastal strand
GROWTH	slow
FLOWG	year-round
DRY TOL.	moderate
SALT TOL.	very high
LIGHT	full sun
SOIL	tolerant; very well-drained
NUTRIT.	generally not necessary
HAZARDS	none
PROBLEMS	none
ENVIRON.	insect nectar
PROPAG.	seeds; cuttings
LEAVES	simple; greenish grey; silky-pubescent, ovate, crispy, succulent
FLOWERS	showy; whitish; dioecious; held in widely branched panicles, with 1-sided, coiled spikes
FRUIT	a capsule, to 5 cm (2 in.); 2-parted, corky, pea-like, held in large bundles
USE	seaside; accent; specimen; screening; courtyard; coastal median strip
ZONE	10–12

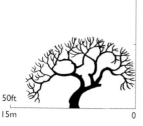

50ft ⌐15m

50ft
15m   0

Argusia argentea

TREE HELIOTPROPE

Boehmer   4 spp.

Messerschmidia argentea; Tournefortia argentea

BORAGINACEAE

ARGUSIA ARGENTEA is a species frequently found on coasts from E Africa to the Pacific and is particularly common on coral islands. Along with scaevola, pandanus, coconuts and casuarinas, it is often the most common vegetation along the coral strand of many atolls of the Pacific and Indian Oceans. *A. argentea* is distinguished by its softly woody, zigzagged limbs and large, oblanceolate leaves that are covered in silvery, silky tomen and held in bold, floppy, terminal rosettes. Most of the year, stiffly erect, octopus-like flower panicles bear abundant, small, milky white flowers, reminiscent of heliotrope. They are held in one-sided, coiled (scorpioid) cymes. As they fade, bundles of little, yellowish or whitish, pea-like, 2-celled, globose drupes develop, eventually becoming brown and corky. *A. argentea* is a slow-growing species, forming, as it does, many flexible limbs, possibly a thick, soft-barked, knobbly trunk and a wide parasol canopy. It is only with constant pruning that this so-called heliotrope develops a single, sturdy trunk and finally earns its status as a tree. As such, this is a totally salt-resistant species and is popular as a small beach tree for resort landscaping in Hawaii, where it is known as Tahinu; it is, in fact, not native here, but was introduced many years ago. Although *A. argentea* has little economic value, in the Pacific various medicinal uses have been found for the leaves. In New Caledonia, they have been used against illness caused by eating toxic fish and also to relieve itching. In Kiribati (previously Gilbert Is), juice is extracted from the leaves and used to reduce fever. In Fiji, the plant is believed to be effective against various stomach troubles. In India, the young leaves are eaten raw for their parsley-like flavour and, in some areas there, they are dried and smoked as a substitute for tobacco.

NOTE: some authors still regard *Argusia argentea* as *Tournefortia argentea*.

A argentea; softly-pubescent, light, grey-green lvs held in large rosettes.

A. argentea; with many flexible limbs and possibly a thick, soft-barked, knobbly trunk.

A. argentea; the abundant pea-like fr. are held on many-branched, terminal panicles on the female trees.

A. argentea; is known as Tahinu in Hawaii, where it is cultivated as a beach tree at resorts. Although not large, it does provide a little welcome shade.

33

Artocarpus altilis

BREADFRUIT

(L.) Fosb.   50 spp.

A. communis; A. incisus

MORACEAE

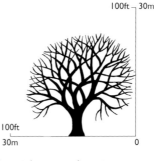

100ft — 30m

100ft

30m   0

ALL FIFTY SPECIES OF *ARTOCARPUS* are native to Indo-Malaysia and are important to village life, providing fruit, edible seeds, timber and bark-fibre. The true origins of ***Artocarpus altilis*** are obscure, although it has been cultivated in Malaya and the Pacific since prehistory; with its huge, decorative, deeply cut leaves, it is one of the most handsome of species. It was introduced into the W Indies by Captain William Bligh, the British naval officer famous for his part in the mutiny on HMS *Bounty* in 1789, but who carried plants from Tahiti to St Vincent and Jamaica in 1793. The genus *Artocarpus* is of the fig family, Moraceae, and male and female flowers are carried separately on the same tree. Male flowers become long, yellowish green and club-shaped, while the globose, multiple female embryo is composed of many individual fruit containing a dense, whitish, starchy, pulp formed of an enlarged receptacle, or stalk. Football-sized, pale green and warty skinned, the fruit exists in 2 forms, 1 seedless and the other having large, brown, chestnut-like seeds. The seedless form is the most common and is an important source of carbohydrate and vitamins, especially A and B. Its mealy flesh is usually white or yellowish and is eaten like potatoes, boiled, fried or baked. The seeded variety is covered in stubbly spines like a jakfruit (jackfruit) and is known as breadnut, Pana de Pepitas or Chataignier. Its plump, starchy seeds are boiled and eaten like chestnuts. *A. altilis* bears its main crop in summer, but also fruits briefly in winter. While Breadnut may be grown from seed, the seedless type must be propagated from root suckers or layers. Breadfruit do not keep for long and must be eaten quickly; in Samoa, excess fruit is buried in sand to preserve it. The lightweight wood was used in Hawaii to make canoe hulls or surfboards, while the sticky, milky sap served to fill their seams and, in some regions, was used as a type of chewing gum or as a means of trapping small birds.

ORIGIN	SE Asia
HEIGHT	up to 20 m (66 ft)
TYPE	evergreen fruiting tree
STATUS	rare in the wild
HABITAT	lowland humid tropics
GROWTH	fast
FLOWG	summer (also winter)
DRY TOL.	low to moderate
SALT TOL.	moderate
LIGHT	full sun
SOIL	fertile, water-retentive
NUTRIT.	complete fertilizer in spring; deep, organic mulch
HAZARDS	none
PROBLEMS	aborts fruit in dry conditions
ENVIRON.	insect nectar
PROPAG.	root cuttings; layers
LEAVES	pinnately lobed; rich green; to 60 cm (24 in.); ovate; thick; heavy
FLOWERS	inconspicuous; male flowers, in elongated, velvety tube, they abort early; females, in globose, multiple head
FRUIT	a syncarp, to 20 cm (8 in.); light green; a multiple fruit with starchy flesh
USE	seaside; shade tree; backyard tree; specimen
ZONE	10—12

A. altilis; dense, potato-like, white flesh is boiled, baked or roasted.

A. altilis; this sp. was brought to the W Indies from Tahiti in the Pacific by Captain Bligh. Above shows fr. (female embryo) developing alongside the mature male fl.

A. altilis; Breadnut (Kamansi in the Philippines), a spiny form with large, chestnut-like sds.

A. altilis var. *samoensis*; with simple, unlobed lvs., at Lyon Arboretum, Honolulu, Hawaii.

(1) ***Artocarpus heterophyllus***; (Lam.), (syn. *A. integrifolia*); poss. India; to 21 m (69 ft), JAKFRUIT (or JACKFRUIT). Of the 50 *Artocarpus* spp., this is the only other widely cultivated sp. *A. heterophyllus* has simple lvs only lobed on seedlings. Fast-growing, (mostly from sd), it forms a lush, dark green, everg. canopy. Jakfruit thrives in both moist and semi-dry areas but demands richer soil and more shelter than Breadfruit. (2) Perhaps the world's largest edible fr., it is borne on the trunk and limbs. It resembles the Durian, but the skin is blunt-spined. (3) Composed of fleshy segments known as 'pegs', containing a large, whitish, edible sd and interspersed with fibrous 'rags', rich in pectin. Seedlings vary in fruit quality, from those with inferior, mushy flesh, to superior, crisp flesh. These fr. are a good source of carbohydrates, calcium and phosphorus. Fr. can be eaten when ripe (with a strong odour) or unripe, when it is boiled in water or coconut milk, fried or curried. When ripe, flesh is sweet, aromatic and eaten out-of-hand or prepared as a dessert. Ripe pulp is fermented and distilled for alcohol and large kernels are eaten boiled or roasted. Wood chips yield yellow dye used to colour Buddhists' robes. (10–12)

(4) A plantation of ***Artocarpus altilis*** in George Town, Grand Cayman, where this fr. is a very important staple in the local diet. This distinctive, sumptuously foliaged tree surely rivals the coconut as a symbol of the topics.

(1) *Artocarpus elastica*; (Reinw. ex Blume), W Malesia, to 50 m (164 ft). This sp. is known as TERAP in Malaysia, where it is common in the drier, eastern regions. Juvenile lvs are extraordinarily large – well over 1 m (3.23 ft) in length and deeply incised; they become simple and much smaller in mature trees. Male fls are finger-like, furrowed and ridged; ripe female fr. (2) have a nauseatingly, rancid smell. In his *Wayside Trees of Malaya*, E. J. H. Corner describes the tree 'Terap bark is tough and strips readily into big sheets. It is used for clothing, lining baskets and bins, for house walls and for string. The latex is most tenacious and used for bird-lime: trunks of the trees are tapped for this reason. Fruit is eaten by monkeys and squirrels.' Photographed at Flecker Botanic Gardens in Cairns, N Qld, Australia. (10–12) (3) *Artocarpus* sp. (possibly *A. fulvicortex*); to 24 m (79 ft). This handsome, ornamental sp. is typical of a large number of *Artocarpus* that grow wild in the equatorial forests of Indo-malaysia. This tree has a luxuriant canopy of large, simple, leathery lvs that are oval to broadly-ovate, or obovate with a slightly heart-shaped base and prominent veins. New growth is densely red-brown hairy. (4) Small fr. often have pink or red, finely warty, spongy flesh.

ORIGIN	Qld, Australia, endemic
HEIGHT	10–30 m (33–100 ft)
TYPE	evergreen flowering and fruiting tree
STATUS	rare and threatened
HABITAT	mostly in upland wet rainforest, up to 1,200 m (4,000 ft)
GROWTH	fairly slow
FLOWG	summer
DRY TOL.	low
SALT TOL.	low
LIGHT	best in full, sheltered sun
SOIL	fertile, water-retentive
NUTRIT.	organic fertilizer; deep, organic mulch
HAZARDS	none
PROBLEMS	allergic to phosphates
ENVIRON.	butterfly nectar; wild fruit for birds and bats
PROPAG.	seeds (scarified); cuttings
LEAVES	simple or lobed; dark green above, rusty hairy below; heavily veined
FLOWERS	showy; creamy white or brownish; held in slender, drooping, compact racemes
FRUIT	a drupe, to 2.5 cm (1 in.); blue-purple, fleshy; with a large, edible kernel
USE	specimen; large planter; courtyard; small street tree; civic centre; large conservatory
ZONE	9–11

100ft – 30m
75ft
22.5m   0

Athertonia diversifolia

ATHERTON OAK

Johnson & B. Briggs   1 sp.

PROTEACEAE (Grevilleoideae – Macadamieae)

WITH A STRONGLY ERECT HABIT OF GROWTH, *Athertonia diversifolia* is distinguished in all its elements, but is particularly celebrated for its arresting foliage, especially when young. This rare, monotypic species is another remarkable Proteacee, endemic to the wet rainforests in N Qld, Australia, mainly at 700–1,200 m (2,300–4,000 ft) elevations on the volcanic soils of the Atherton Tableland. However, it is also found near sea level. In cultivation, it will grow as far south as Sydney. The juvenile growth emerges covered in a golden, rusty velour and then develops magnificent, strongly fiddle-shaped leaves. The mature foliage is smaller and more variable, glossy dark green above, paler green and heavily veined below, where the prominent venation is accentuated by bright, golden rusty hairs. In summer, hidden below the leaves, slender, crowded bottlebrush racemes of tiny, curling, creamy white or yellowish flowers, with little whiskery white stamens, are dangled on long, rusty hairy rachis, echoing those of Macadamia. The fruit is equally desirable, consisting of bluish purple, fleshy, plum-like berries that contain delicious, edible, sweet, crispy kernels. This species is therefore both a desirable ornamental and a provider. In autumn, as a bonus, the mature foliage turns glorious reds and oranges before fading to a glossy black and falling. *A. diversifolia* is most striking when planted in strong light, though it dislikes exposure to hot winds. For the best results, it requires protection, well-prepared soil, adequate water and a deep mulch. Although relatively slow growing, this is a steady developer and should flower and fruit when 7–8 years old. Even without its attractive flowers and fruit, *A. diversifolia* has a distinguished appearance and has been used as a container plant with success. The seeds are slow to germinate unless they are first scarified.

A. diversifolia; fls are dangled below the foliage and are thus protected from the sun.

A. diversifolia; the town of Atherton lies on the Atherton Tableland region, where this rare sp. is found.

A. diversifolia; has splendidly ornamental, juvenile foliage that has accentuated veins.

A. diversifolia; with bluish purple, fleshy, plum-like berries that contain edible, sweet, crispy kernels.

37

Averrhoa carambola

STAR FRUIT

L.   2 (poss. 3) spp.

OXALIDACEAE

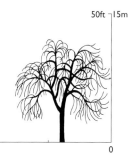

50ft ⌐15m

50ft
15m   0

AVERROHA CARAMBOLA, a popular, oriental fruit tree and a member of the oxalis family, was named in honour of an Arabian physician called Averrhoes. It is an elegant, densely limbed, arching and spreading small tree, with bright green, lustrous foliage, which is glaucous below. *A. carambola* in full, vibrant bloom is very decorative, with each slender limb smothered in sprightly, little, cauliflorous or axillary, pinkish red or purplish blooms; it has several cycles of flowers and fruit during the year. It is a vigorous tree and may produce prodigious harvests, with the interior of its diffusely branched crown seemingly illuminated by a profusion of translucent, amber, lantern-like fruit. These are waxy, golden and longitudinally deeply 5-ribbed. They slice into attractive star shapes that are popular as a novel food garnish, particularly for desserts. The fruit varies greatly in taste from very sweet to very sour. To ensure sweetness, the trees are best grafted with the scion of a selected cultivar. Sweet varieties are the most popular for eating raw or to use as a dessert, but the sour form is used widely in the commercial production of drinks and preserves. *A. carambola* provides an excellent source of vitamin C and, because its taste is neither too strong nor too overpowering, it has proved popular in the USA for use in tropical-flavour juice blends. Like *A. bilimbi*, the fresh juice is an effective stain-remover, from hands, clothes and even weapons. In SE Asia, *A. carambola* has always been valued by the Chinese communities as an antidote to high blood pressure. In Thailand, it is used to reduce blood sugar levels in diabetics. In Indonesia, it is used to alleviate hypertension, gingivitis and acne, while locally the flowers are used to relieve coughs and the leaves to relieve rheumatism. *A. carambola* is slightly frost hardy, given a warm, sunny spot. *Averrhoa* species are excellent honey plants.

ORIGIN	Malaysia to Melanesia
HEIGHT	up to 10 m (33 ft)
TYPE	evergreen, small fruiting (flowering) tree
STATUS	not common in the wild
HABITAT	humid forests and woodlands on sandy loam
GROWTH	slow
FLOWG	intermittently, all year
DRY TOL.	moderate
SALT TOL.	low
LIGHT	sun to very bright shade
SOIL	rich, well-drained
NUTRIT.	well rotted compost; deep, organic mulch
HAZARDS	none
PROBLEMS	fruit fly; fungus
ENVIRON.	bee and butterfly nectar
PROPAG.	seeds; layers; cuttings; grafting
LEAVES	pinnate; rich green; spirally arranged; leaflets 5–11, ovate to elliptic
FLOWERS	showy; pinkish red or purplish (or whitish); cauliflorous or axillary along upper surface of limbs
FRUIT	a berry, to 12 × 5.6 cm (4.7 × 2.2 in.); deep yellow, fleshy; star-shaped in cross section
USE	backyard tree; small flowering tree; large container; accent; courtyard; large conservatory
ZONE	10–12

A. carambola; with masses of little bright pink, ornamental fls.

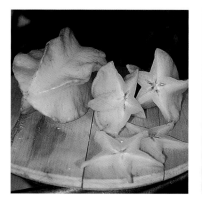

A. carambola; a virile young tree at the Fruit and Spice Park in Homestead, Florida, USA, which produces abundant flushes of fr. all-year-round.

A. carambola; has become very popular for its deeply ridged fr. that forms a star when cut in cross-section.

A. carambola; a vigorous tree may produce prodigious harvests several times a year.

(1) ***Averrhoa bilimbi***; (L.), Moluccas of the Philippines, to 11 m (36 ft). BILIMBI, BELIMBING or CUCUMBER TREE, is a slow-growing, sparsely branched sp. with an open, somewhat irregular crown of light green lvs. This sp. prefers a trop., monsoon climate with a definite dry season. *A. bilimbi* thrives up to medium elevations and enjoys well-drained or sandy soil; it is easily identified by its thin, bright green, pinnate lvs that dangle their lflts in a limp fashion, giving the tree an exhausted air. (2) Tiny, deep red fls are held in finely tomentose, slender, stalked clusters that sprout directly from the trunk and main branches. (3) As they are pollinated, fr. develops and is dangled on stout stems; it will turn yellowish as it matures. The fr. is much smaller than the *A. carambola*, resembling little gherkin cucumbers. (The French call it Cornichon.) They are very juicy, unlike Carambola, but extremely sour, with a high oxalic acid content. In Malaysia, where this fr. is highly esteemed, it is usually stewed with sugar, made into pickles or added to curries. Juice from the fr. is used for removing stains from linen. (10–12)

The homestead, 'Bend-in-the-River', in southern Qld, Australia, where, like many local enthusiasts, the owner has established a comprehensive collection of rare fruits from all over the tropics. Included of course, is *A. bilimbi.*

Azadirachta indica

NEEM TREE

A. Juss.
2 spp.

Melia azadirachta

MELIACEAE

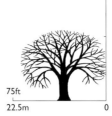

100ft – 30m

75ft
22.5m

0

IN THE 1920S, a German Entomologist, Heinrich Schumtterer, working in the Sudan, noticed that *Azadirachta indica* were the only green plants left untouched by a plague of locusts. Farmers in India have known for centuries that their native *A. indica* had amazing medicinal properties and could also withstand attacks by insects, but it was not until the last decade of the 20th century that this remarkable species was much studied and promoted for biological insect control. *A. indica*, closely related to mahogany, is a fast-growing evergreen, which is very drought-resistant and has a wide tolerance of soils, as long as it is well drained. Neem (or Nim) is a classic tree, with a sturdy, rough-barked trunk and limbs supporting a well-developed, rounded canopy of bright green, saw-toothed, pinnate leaves. In spring, it bears sprightly, branched panicles of tiny, white flowers, which are followed by bundles of berry-like, bitter-fleshed fruit. Extracts of Neem have been found to cause sterility in insects and to inhibit their egg laying. Its seeds provide Azadirachtin, which disrupts the metamorphosis of insect larvae; by inhibiting moulting, it prevents the larvae from developing into pupae. To humans, however, it is non-toxic and it has proved to be a useful, powerful pesticide, capable of destroying bacteria and over 200 insect species. In India, *A. indica* was traditionally valued for its antiseptic resin, which was added to toothpastes, soaps and lotions. Extracts from the leaves and fruit are also used as a vermifuge. An aromatic oil extracted from the seeds is known as Margosa oil and has long been used to relieve leprosy and shows anti-carcinogenic properties. From Somalia to Mauritania, this species is widely cultivated and has been planted to contain the southward encroachment of the Sahara Desert. It is an important honey plant.

NOTE: this species is considered invasive in some regions.

ORIGIN	SE Asia
HEIGHT	up to 16 m (53 ft)
TYPE	evergreen foliage tree
STATUS	not threatened
HABITAT	evergreen lowland forests
GROWTH	fast
FLOWG	spring
DRY TOL.	high
SALT TOL.	high
LIGHT	full sun
SOIL	widely tolerant, well-drained
NUTRIT.	balanced fertilizer annually
HAZARDS	none
PROBLEMS	may be invasive
ENVIRON.	bee nectar; wild fruit for birds
PROPAG.	fresh seeds
LEAVES	pinnate; dark green; to 4.5 cm (18 in.); leaflets deeply toothed, curved
FLOWERS	fairly showy; greenish white; held in large, airy panicles; fragrant
FRUIT	a drupe, to 1.5 cm (6 in.); yellowish, fleshy, inflated; with very hard seeds
USE	seaside; shade tree; small street tree; specimen; desert reclamation; coastal screening; xerophytic
ZONE	10—12

A. indica; has airy sprays of fragrant fls that are adored by honeybees.

A. indica; popular for its shade and drought tol., this superb sp. provides a welcome dense, dark, rich green canopy for shade in the most hostile of environs.

A. indica; fr. is loved by bats and birds and it is sometimes difficult to find sds.

A. indica; the smoothish grey bark splits and cracks as it ages.

LEMON-SCENTED MYRTLE

7 spp.   F. Meull.

MYRTACEAE

ORIGIN	E Qld, Australia, endemic
HEIGHT	3–20 m (10–66 ft)
TYPE	evergreen, flowering aromatic tree
STATUS	not threatened
HABITAT	coastal forests and rain-forests
GROWTH	moderately fast
FLOWG	summer and autumn
DRY TOL.	moderate
SALT TOL.	moderate
LIGHT	full sun
SOIL	humid, fertile, well-drained
NUTRIT.	balanced fertilizer annually; deep, organic mulch
HAZARDS	none
PROBLEMS	none
ENVIRON.	nectar for bees and insects
PROPAG.	seeds; cuttings (slow); layers
LEAVES	simple; rich green; broad lanceolate to narrow ovate; lemon-scented
FLOWERS	showy; pale green to creamy-white; bell-shaped sepals; many stamened; held in axillary clusters
FRUIT	a capsule. to 2 mm (0.08 in.); 2-celled; held in persistent lobes of the calyx
USE	specimen tree; courtyard; background shrub; street tree; large planter; civic centre; bonsai subject
ZONE	9–11

100ft — 30m
75ft
22.5m   0

BACKHOUSIA CITRIODORA, a native of the coastal forests and rainforests of Qld, Australia, has long been popular as a garden specimen. In cultivation, this myrtle is often found as a large shrub and may be controlled as such. In the wild, it can reach to 20 m (66 ft). *B. citriodora* is relatively slow growing and has a light brown bark that is rough and scaly and flakes off to reveal a light orange or yellowish epidermis. It forms a bushy, low-branching crown, with reddish new growth, and blooms when quite young. As the flowers fade, the stamens are aborted and fruit capsules form in the centre of the persistent, cupped, pale green sepals. Although a subtropical species, *B. citriodora* can tolerate frost-free temperate regions, provided it is given a sheltered, sunny position. Australia is extremely rich in Myrtaceae species, including Eucalyptus and Syzygium. The Myrtle family is distinguished by its ornamental, fluffy, many-stamened blooms and often by aromatic foliage that is rich in oil glands; *B. citriodora* is typical of the genus. Of the 7 *Backhousia* species all, except 1 from New Guinea, are endemic to Australia. All contain essential oils and are scented to varying degrees. *B. citriodora* is rich in citral, which gives a lemon aroma when the leaves are crushed, and has culinary and other commercial applications. To replicate high-yielding clones, cuttings are the preferred propagation method, but they may be slow to 'strike'. Another non de plume for this species, Lemon Ironwood, aptly conveys that the timber is very hard and heavy.

*** *B. bancroftii*; (Bailey), NE Qld, to 25 m (82 ft). JOHNSTONE RIVER HARDWOOD is a dominant canopy tree in some areas of lowland, wet, tropical rainforest, south of Cairns. It is distinguished by its glossy foliage, red tip growth and white flowers. This species also has hard wood. *Backhousia* are important honey plants. (10–11)

B. citriodora; with large-stamened fls, typical of the Myrtle family.

B. citriodora; famous for its wood, which is very hard and heavy.

B. citriodora; the pale green, cupped calyxes persist after the petals have fallen.

B. citriodora; a sumptuous, autumn display of developing fr. by an old specimen in the Royal Botanic Garden in Sydney, Australia.

Banksia dentata

TROPICAL BANKSIA

L. f.   73 spp.

PROTEACEAE (Banksieae)

50ft ⌐15m

50ft
⌐15m   0

THE *BANKSIA* GENUS was named for Sir Joseph Banks, a botanist who sailed with Captain Cook to the South Seas in his ship, the *Endeavour*, on its voyage of discovery in 1768. *Banksia* are one of the most celebrated Australian species, perhaps ranking with the S African *Protea* in popularity with florists, and are widely cultivated for this trade. Of the 73 species, all but one are endemic to Australia, with one tropical species, **Banksia dentata**, found also in New Guinea. This tropical *Banksia* is a sparsely branched, small tree, which develops a gnarled, scraggy appearance, with its trunk and main limbs being covered in rough, dark grey bark. The inner bark is blood red. The mature leaves are wedge-shaped with deeply toothed margins and are dull green above, silvery hairy below. Typical of many Proteaceae, the erect inflorescence of **B. dentata** is composed of a dense spike of up to 1,000 tiny, bracted, yellow flowers with extended, straight, wiry stigmas and shorter stamens. These are adapted to accommodate their pollinators, honey-sucking birds or possums. The fruit is a compressed, cylindrical cone with a number of resinous seed capsules attached that resemble little cockleshells. A phenomenon of this genus is that most species require fire to ignite the resin and dehisce the seed capsule before it can release its winged seeds. The resin of **B. dentata** is chemically different and the fruit opens without fire.

*** **B. integrifolia**, (L. F.) var. *integrifolia*; SE Qld to E Vic., Australia, to 25 m (82 ft). COAST BANKSIA, or WHITE HONEYSUCKLE, is a coastal forest species, often found on sand dunes. It is slow growing and often becomes stunted and gnarled, remaining quite small but with great character. **B. integrifolia** has whorls of simple, stiff leaves, dark green above and silvery white below. The pale yellow flowers are held most of the year in cylindrical, erect, terminal spikes. This species is widespread and popular as a street tree. (8–11)

ORIGIN	N Australia to New Guinea
HEIGHT	up to 7 m (23 ft)
TYPE	evergreen, small flowering tree
STATUS	not threatened
HABITAT	open savannah woodland or heathland; on wet sandy soils
GROWTH	slow
FLOWG	all year (mostly summer)
DRY TOL.	moderate
SALT TOL.	low
LIGHT	full sun
SOIL	acid, fertile, well-drained
NUTRIT.	fertilizer with sequestered iron; organic mulch
HAZARDS	none
PROBLEMS	root fungus
ENVIRON.	nectar for birds and insects
PROPAG.	seeds (rot and may need fungicide); grafting
LEAVES	simple; dull green, silvery hairy below; whorled, leathery; with dentate margins
FLOWERS	showy; light yellow; held in erect, terminal, dense spikes, to 15 cm (6 in.)
FRUIT	a 'cone', to 13 cm (5.1 in.), with follicles attached; seeds winged
USE	specimen; courtyard; large planter; accent; conservatory
ZONE	10–12

B. **dentata**; composed of a dense spike of tiny, bracted fls with extended, wiry stigmas and shorter stamens, adapted for their pollinators – honey-sucking birds or possums.

B. **integrifolia**; a pristine, unopened bloom and stiff, silvery, cardboard-like lvs.

B. **dentata**; barnacled, resinous fr. capsules containing unripe, winged sds leave gaping holes in the fr. when they fall.

B. **dentata**; this trop. *Banksia* is a sparsely branched small tree that develops a gnarled, scraggy appearance.

ORIGIN	Madagascar to Pacific
HEIGHT	up to 20 m (66 ft)
TYPE	evergreen foliage (flowering) tree
STATUS	not threatened
HABITAT	coastal forest; lagoon shores; river estuaries; swamps
GROWTH	moderate
FLOWG	year-round
DRY TOL.	moderate to high
SALT TOL.	very high
LIGHT	full sun or bright shade
SOIL	fertile, humid, well-drained
NUTRIT.	balanced fertilizer annually; deep, organic mulch
HAZARDS	poisonous seeds
PROBLEMS	messy flower and leaf litter
ENVIRON.	bat nectar
PROPAG.	seeds (entire ripe fruit set near top of soil); semi-ripe cuttings
LEAVES	simple; deep green; to 38 × 8 cm (15 × 3 in.); spathulate, crowded at stem ends
FLOWERS	showy; white, with mass of crimson-tipped, white stamens; nocturnally fragrant
FRUIT	a drupe, to 10 cm (4 in.); a square, heart-shaped cube, with persistent calyx at tip; 1 toxic seed
USE	seaside; large shade tree; public open space; large planter; large conservatory
ZONE	10–12

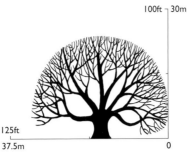

100ft ┐ 30m
125ft
37.5m
0

BARRINGTONIA

(L.) Kurtz. 39 spp.

Mammea asiatica; B. speciosa

LECYTHIDACEAE

BARRINGTONIA IS A GENUS of 39 species largely found in tropical Africa. The most renowned of them is **Barringtonia asiatica**, a noble native of Trop. Asia and the Pacific. Magnolia-like, it is crowned by a dense, billowing canopy of lacquered, dark green, spathulate leaves clustered towards the ends of long, downward-sweeping, languid limbs. **B. asiatica** thrives with its roots dabbling in the brackish waters of lagoons, inlets, estuaries and seasonally flooded coastal regions. Barringtonias are nocturnal bloomers; at dusk, 4 thick, inflated sepals unfold to release 4 small, white, lightly fragrant petals, and a great 'brush' of silky, white, crimson-tipped filaments; they are charged with pollen to tempt bats and flying foxes, its nocturnal pollinators. Come the dawn, the spent, limp tassels fall and carpet the ground. (This mechanism can be seen in detail by cutting a flowering twig with a mature bud during the day and watching as it opens during the evening.) Outsized, fibrous, spongy fruit are formed that resemble small coconuts and with a similar wrapping of smooth, water-proof skin. They have a 4-cornered, heart-shaped base and conical apex that is crowned with 2 persistent calyxes. The Portuguese aptly named them Boneto de Arzobisipo, or Archbishop's Cap, to reflect their shape. The fruit is light and buoyant and designed to float from island to inlet, which explains why this species is so widely distributed around the world. The dry fruit are used as fishing floats in Tahiti, where *B. asiatica* is known as Hotu or Hutu, meaning 'heart'. The fruit contains 1 large, toxic seed that is sometimes grated and used as bait to stun and catch fish, particularly in Polynesia. Because of its tolerance of seaside conditions, **B. astiatica** has been widely planted throughout the littoral regions of the tropics as a large shade tree for the beach.

NOTE: B. asiatica may become invasive in coastal areas, particularly in sandy soils.

B. asiatica; fragrant blooms are aborted at dawn after being pollinated by bats.

B. asiatica; a giant specimen grows in pure sand on the coast of the Cayman Is in the W Indies.

B. asiatica; the square-based, heart-shaped fr. becomes very light when ripe and dry. It is waterproof and designed to float.

B. asiatica; an ample, wide-spreading sp. with a sumptuous, Magnolia-like, everg. canopy of slightly folded, leathery, waxy lvs. *Barringtonia* thrives in a humid, coast. environ.

43

Barringtonia

(1 and 2) *Barringtonia acutangula*; ([L.] Gaertn.), from Afghanistan to Australia, to 13 m (43 ft). Known as INDIAN OAK or STREAM BARRINGTONIA, this sp. may grow as a small tree or shrub, with a dense, spreading crown. Native of riverbanks, swampy sites or rocky or sandy shores, this is a versatile sp., particularly suited to humid, shady situations. The beautiful chains of bright pink to white, staminous fls are nocturnal, opening at sunset and aborting at daybreak. *B. acutangula* is briefly decid. in spring when it has bright, coppery red new growth. Fr. is an angular, winged capsule to 6 cm (2.5 in). (9–12) (3 and 4) *Barringtonia calyptrata*; (Benth.). New Guinea to NE Qld, Australia, to 30 m (100 ft). MANGO- or CASSOWARY-PINE. In drier

areas this sp. is a small, open tree but in rainforests it may be densely foliaged and much taller. In summer, it is liberally adorned with sumptuous, musky, honey-fragrant cylinders of creamy blooms, rich in nectar, which attract lorikeets, insects and bats. Typical of its family, the large, glossy lvs are whorled around the tips of the branchlets. Normally decid., the old lvs turn deep red before falling. Large and fleshy, with a single sd, the blue-bloomed, toxic fr. smells of mangoes and is a preferred food of Cassowary birds. The white timber is soft and pine-like. Aborigines used this sp. as a source for medicine, bark-fibre and fish poison. *B. calyptrata* is planted successfully as a street tree in Cairns, N Qld, Australia. (10–12)

(1) ***Barringtonia edulis***; (A. Gray). (syn. *B. samoensis*), from SE Celebes to New Guinea, Micronesia and Polynesia, to 12 m (39 ft). This sparsely branched sp. of humid sites has gargantuan, short-petioled, long, narrow, polished lvs that are whorled towards the ends of the limbs; they have crenate to serrate, inrolled margins measuring to 100 × 24 cm (39 × 9 in.). Emerging from within the enormous lvs is a robust infl. — a compact cone of red buds that will split into 3–4 calyx lobes to release the 4-petalled, cream or red fls to form a luxuriant, fluffy tube. (1) This pendulous infl. measure to 55 cm (22 in.) and holds up to 150 fls; it is nocturnally fragrant and specifically evolved for bat pollination. (2) Shown is the developing fl. spike, that begins as a reddish purple 'corn cob' of buds. The fr. that follows the blooms is purplish blue, ovoid, 6-ribbed, to 7 cm (3 in.); a few remain on the their stout axis, having already been nibbled by flying foxes. The lightweight wood of this sp. is used for outrigger canoe floats. (10–12) (3 and 4) ***Barringtonia racemosa***; ([L.] Spreng.), from Africa, Asia, Pacific Is. and Australia, to 20 m (66 ft). Kenyans call this sp. MTOKO; in Qld, Australia, it is known as FRESHWATER MANGROVE. It is found at river estuaries and mangrove swamps. Typical of the genus, the many-stamened fls are nocturnal and fragrant. They open as the sun sets, aborting as it rises; these delightful blooms have 4 petals; stamens may be pink or white. (10–12)

Bauhinia variegata

POOR MAN'S ORCHID

L.   300 spp.

Phanera variegata

FABACEAE (Caesalpinioideae)

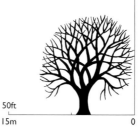

50ft ⌐15m

50ft
15m   0

THE *BAUHINIA* GENUS was chosen to commemorate the famous French botanists and brothers, Johannes Bauhin (1541–1613) and Caspar Bauhin (1560–1624), because of its twin-lobed leaves. ***Bauhinia variegata*** grows wild in China and is held sacred by Buddhists, who grow it near their temples. It is also found across Burma and India, up to the foothills of the Himalayas. Until the discovery of the wondrous, natural hybrid *B. × blakeana* in southern China, ***B. variegata*** was considered a choice flowering tree. In fact, the 2 species are very alike, with flowers of a similar lavender or rosy purple colour, although the petals of the hybrid are considerably wider and more vivid. Both species are fragrant, have 5 stamens and 1 superior petal that is larger and sturdier, with a brilliant splashing of deep magenta or violet, hence *variegata*. Currently, ***B. variegata*** is considered inferior to *B. × blakeana* because of its habit of producing masses of long, woody pods as soon as the flowering has finished and which persist for months. *Bauhinia* tend to have a disorganized habit of growth, with limbs criss-crossing inwards into the centre of the crown. They respond well to pruning and shaping, which should be done as soon as the flowering has ceased, to promote new growth for next season's blooming. At the same time, the unsightly pods should be removed. Like so many tropical trees, ***B. variegata*** has many domestic uses: the juvenile leaves and the seed pods are edible, and the young, green bark, which detaches easily, is used for cordage and as a source of tannin. The wood, which is known as Mountain Ebony, is dark, hard and heavy, with an attractive grain.

*** ***B. variegata*** var. 'Alba', known commonly as the WHITE ORCHID TREE. This variety is not as floriferous as the type but is, nevertheless, a worthy small tree

NOTE: *B. variegata* is considered invasive in many regions.

ORIGIN	India to China
HEIGHT	up to 12 m (39 ft)
TYPE	deciduous, small flowering tree
STATUS	not threatened
HABITAT	common in deciduous bamboo forests and open areas, especially on limestone
GROWTH	fast
FLOWG	winter to spring
DRY TOL.	high
SALT TOL.	moderate
LIGHT	full sun
SOIL	fertile, well-drained
NUTRIT.	high-potassium fertilizer; organic mulch
HAZARDS	none
PROBLEMS	potassium deficiency
ENVIRON.	bird and insect nectar
PROPAG.	seeds; cuttings
LEAVES	2-lobed; dull green; to 20 cm (8 in.); leathery, strongly veined
FLOWERS	showy; pale magenta and rosy purple; with 5 stamens; fragrant
FRUIT	a legume, to 20 cm (8 in.); woody, flattened; when ripe, it splits open with great force
USE	specimen; small street tree; small flowering tree; large planter; large conservatory
ZONE	10–12

B. variegata var. *rubra*; with greyish green lvs, deep crimson fls and reddish fr.

B. variegata; this charming, winter-blooming sp. grows wild in China and is held sacred by Buddhists, who grow it near their temples so that the fls may be used for votive offerings.

B. variegata; splendidly colourful in winter, but is black-listed in S Florida, USA, because of its invasive tendencies.

B. variegata var. 'Alba'; although not as floriferous as the pink form, this white var. is nevertheless most elegant.

Bauhinia binata; (Blanco.), (syn. *B. hookeri*; *Lysiphyllum hookeri*), Insular SE Asia, up to 10 m (33 ft). ALIBANGBANG or PEGUNNY is a sp. of coast. regions and may grow as a multi-trunked tree or develop tendrils and become vinelike. This sp. is distinguished by its 10 red stamens and reflexed petals; it is spring-blooming and naturally salt-resistant. (10–12) **NOTE: some authors still regard this sp. as** *Lysiphyllum hookeri.*

Bauhinia × blakeana; (Dunn.), endemic of China, to 12 m (39 ft). HONG KONG ORCHID. In the 19th century, this form of *Bauhinia* was discovered in the Ghangou province of China and named for the wife of the governor of Hong Kong. A cross between *B. purpurea* and *B. variegata*, *B.* × *blakeana* must be propagated by cuttings and layers. Fls have 5 stamens; they are fragrant and vary from deep lavender to deep magenta-red. This sp. does not bear fr. (10–12)

Bauhinia divaricata; (L.), of Jamaica, Cayman Is and Honduras, to 6 m (20 ft). Known as BULL-HOOF BAUHINIA for its little cloven lvs, this charming small sp. has a bushy, arching habit with long, slender, flexible limbs. White, narrowly-petalled, spidery blooms have only 1 stamen; they mostly turn rosy pink as they fade. Native of dry woodlands, this xerophytic sp. is fairly slow growing and blooms year-round. Excellent for tub culture. (10–12)

Bauhinia forficata; (Link.), (syn. *B. candicans*; *B. grandiflora*), S America, to 15 m (50 ft). SPINY BULL-HOOF or CASCAO-DE-VACA is a spiny sp. native of coastal rainforests. The nocturnally fragrant fls are moth-pollinated and fade with the morning sun. *B. forficata* may tolerate temperatures to -5 C degrees (23 F) for short periods in warm temperate climates. It has 10 stamens and is summer blooming. Excellent for tub culture. (10–12)

Bauhinia malabarica; (Roxb.), (syn. *Lysiphyllum malabarica*), SE Asia, to 15 m (50 ft). Malabar Orchid Tree is fairly fast growing, forming a sturdy, open-crowned tree with fissured bark. Lvs thick and leathery, green above and glaucous silvery below; eaten as relish in some regions. Fls are pubescent and nectar-rich; bell-shaped calyxes do not split open; petals pinkish or white, in dense, pendent, pinkish-stemmed clusters. Stamens 10. (10–12)

Bauhinia monandra; (Kurz.), (syn. *B. kappler*), Burma, to 10 m (33 ft). Butterfly Bauhinia or Mariposa blooms late spring and early autumn with pale pink, red-freckled, waxy 'butterfly' blooms with a single fertile stamen. Small and compact in stature, with layered branching, this sp. is ideal for small spaces. Ripe sds explode and are flung far from their thick-walled pods. Decid. in winter. (10–12) **NOTE: this sp. may become invasive.**

Bauhinia petersiana; (Bolle.), E Africa, to 7 m (23 ft). White African Bauhinia or Zambezi Coffee is normally a small, spreading tree or large shrub; it may become vine-like or a scrambler. Valued for its medical qualities: lvs boiled and steam inhaled for common colds and infected eyes treated by washing with an infusion of bark. Ground sds are sometimes used locally as a coffee substitute. Stamens 5. Blooming in early summer. (9–12)

Bauhinia purpurea; (L. non Hort.), (syn. *B. triandra; B. kurzii; B. violacea*), India to Malaya, to 12 m (39 ft). Australian- or Fall-Orchid Tree. This sp. is easily confused with *B. variegata*, but the fls are usually deeper, reddish purple (occasionally pink or white), with narrower, strap-like petals and 3 stamens. *B. purpurea* forms a very bushy crown and blooms when lvs are still on the tree. Autumn blooming, with fragrant fls. (10–12)

Bauhinia semla; (Wunderlin), (syn. *B.emarginata*; *B. retusa*; *B. roxburghiana*), SE Asia, to 10 m (33 ft). This small, cold-tolerant sp. of high regions has a somewhat erratic habit of growth with leathery, bi-lobed lvs to 13 cm (5.12 in). Blooming from autumn to winter, it has a compound, corymbose infl. composed of small fls to 2 cm (0.8 in.), which are either creamy white or yellowish; each bloom is spotted purplish red like those of *B. tarapotensis*. Stamens 3. An important honey tree. (**10–12**)

Bauhinia rufescens; (Lam.), Trop. Africa, to 10 m (33 ft). The Silver Butterfly Tree has evolved to meet the exigencies of xerophytic life. With a stocky build and very tough, leathery, silvery lvs, this sp. begins life with a neat, distinctly layered form, its blackish, willowy stems contrasting with the foliage and the small, white, folded fls set in large calyxes. The fls are followed by curling, explosive pods. Stamens 10. A honey tree. (**9–12**)

Bauhinia tarapotensis; (Benth.), Peru to Ecuador, to 15 m (50 ft). This Tarapot Orchid Tree was photographed at Fairchild Tropical Gardens in Miami, Florida, in late autumn when it was garlanded with abundant, branched panicles of minute, creamy white blooms and many honey bees. The centres of the fls are finely speckled rosy mauve. This is an important honey tree. (**10–12**)

Bauhinia tomentosa; (L.), (syn. *B. picta* ; *B. taitensis*), Old World Trops, to 9 m (30 ft). St Thomas Tree or Bell Bauhinia is a slow-growing, tall shrub or small tree. The pendent, bell-like blooms are either wholly pale yellow or have a dark blotch at their throats, fading to deep rosy lavender with age. This blotch is likened to the blood of the martyred St Thomas and gives this sp. its common name. Stamens 10. (**10–12**)

Bertholettia excelsa

BRAZIL NUT

Bonpl.   1 sp.

LECYTHIDACEAE

THE SURVIVAL OF THE NOBLE ***BERTHOLETTIA EXCELSA*** is threatened by the disappearance of Amazonian rainforest. Native of the great Amazon and Orinoco river basins, it is often the tallest tree, with its clear, pole-like bole soaring up to hold its cauliflower-like crown above the forest canopy. From the forest floor, ***B. excelsa*** is easily distinguished by its rich red or grey, deeply fissured bark. During the dry season, large panicles of white flowers, which closely resemble those of the *Lecythis* species, are held erect above its gigantic canopy. Following the flowers, the legendary Brazil nuts slowly develop. Typical of the Lecythidaceae family, the thick, woody fruit has a small lid-like structure (operculum) at its tip that is designed to open and release the ripe seeds. Trees grow for 10–26 years before beginning to produce fruit, which then may take 14 months to mature. Each fruit weighs up to 2 kg (4.5 lb) and may drop 50 m (164 ft) from the treetops, making this a dangerous occupation for the harvesters, who are known as Castanheiros. There are 12–24 creamy, oily nuts arranged inside the hard, brown shell like segments of an orange. Agoutis, large, burrowing rodents, are the only wild creatures small or strong enough to remove the nuts and it is they who distribute them. Brazil nuts form a significant part of the diet of the region, being high in protein (14–17%) and oil (63–69%). The kernels are sometimes grated and mixed with cassava (manioc) flour to make unleavened bread. The nuts burn like mini candles and the oil is used for cooking and for lamps, in soap and as a livestock feed. In some regions, a brew from the bark is used to treat liver disease. ***B. excelsa*** is self-sterile and must grow in a group to ensure cross-pollination. Although it is illegal to fell these trees, large specimens are still cut down for their fine, weather-resistant timber and to make way for urban expansion.

ORIGIN	Amazonian rainforest
HEIGHT	to 50 m (164 ft)
TYPE	evergreen, large fruiting tree
STATUS	threatened
HABITAT	rainforests of Orinoco and Amazon Basins
GROWTH	moderate
FLOWG	year-round
DRY TOL.	low
SALT TOL.	low
LIGHT	full sun
SOIL	humid, fertile, deep
NUTRIT.	balanced fertilizer yearly; deep, organic mulch
HAZARDS	falling heavy fruit
PROBLEMS	none
ENVIRON.	wild bee nectar; fruit for agoutis
PROPAG.	scarified seeds
LEAVES	simple; dark green; to 36 × 15 cm (14 × 6 in.); wavy-edged; glabrous, leathery
FLOWERS	showy; creamy white; to 2.5 cm (1 in.); in large, erect panicles
FRUIT	a capsule, to 16 cm (6.3 in.) diam.; globose, thick, woody; seeds 12–14
USE	large nut tree; public open space; botanic collection
ZONE	10–12

B. excelsa; this specimen, at the historic Royal Botanic Gardens in Trinidad, is much smaller than those in the rainforest. It has not had to push its way up through the forest canopy.

B. excelsa; heavy, impenetrable packaging make these nuts treacherous to harvest.

B. excelsa; creamy, oily, white kernels are protected by woody, pebble-like shells, which are very difficult to crack open.

B. excelsa; with deeply fissured bark, makes this sp. easily distinguished, below on the forest floor.

ORIGIN	Trop. Asia to Australia and Polynesia
HEIGHT	up to 20 m (66 ft)
TYPE	semi-deciduous, dioecious foliage tree
STATUS	not threatened
HABITAT	moist lowland forest and along riverbanks
GROWTH	very fast
FLOWG	spring
DRY TOL.	moderate
SALT TOL.	moderate
LIGHT	full sun
SOIL	fertile, well-drained
NUTRIT.	balanced fertilizer annually
HAZARDS	brittle wood
PROBLEMS	scales; weak-wooded
ENVIRON.	insect nectar; wild bird fruit
PROPAG.	seeds
LEAVES	3-foliate; deep, rich green; slightly cupped; margins with serrated edges
FLOWERS	showy; greenish yellow, petal-less; dioecious; held in compact panicles
FRUIT	a berry, to 1 cm (0.4 in.); abundant; green, ripening pinkish red
USE	large shade tree; public open space; screening; street tree
ZONE	10—12

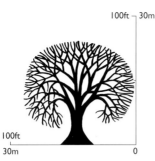

100ft — 30m
100ft
30m

Blume.   2 spp.

B. trifoliata

EUPHORBIACEAE (Bischofieae)

BISCHOFIA JAVANICA, a handsome, if melancholy, heavy-limbed, spreading tree, was very fashionable in Florida, USA, a few years ago. Now it is rarely propagated, having been officially banned there because it is considered weak-wooded. Strangely, however, it was one of the few large trees left standing in some areas after the disastrous Hurricane Andrew of 1992. *B. javanica* is very fast growing, developing a stout, sturdy trunk and a bulky, symmetrically rounded crown. The bark is reddish brown, smooth in young trees, but flaky in age, when the outer layer may be easily rubbed off. In its native regions, the soft bark, which exudes a slightly sticky red sap, is said to be used by Bengal tigers for cleaning their claws. A very dense, dark canopy is formed by its 3-foliate, glossy, blackish green foliage and, like many *Euphorbia* species, the leaves turn deep red before they are shed. The narrow, branched clusters of flowers are dioecious, with males and females on separate trees. When the male tree is in full, spring bloom, its mossy, greenish white posies of petal-less, pollen-laden blooms recall the avocado. As they are pollinated, female flowers form masses of small berries, which turn pinkish red with age. The timber, known in the trade as Bishopwood or Java cedar, has dark crimson heartwood and a strong odour of vinegar. Despite being fast growing, it is fairly durable and particularly valued for use under water, often being used for harbour piles or for bridges. Apart from growing wild in many parts of Polynesia, *B. javanica* is also cultivated there for its wood, often in small plantations where, apart from other uses, it makes excellent charcoal. In Samoa and Tonga, a brown dye is extracted from the inner bark and used to decorate tapa bark cloth.

NOTE: *B. javanica* **has proved seriously invasive in some regions.**

B. javanica; little, mossy green, male fls greatly resemble those of Avocado.

B. javanica; has dark crimson heartwood and a strong odour of vinegar. Despite being fast-growing, it is fairly durable.

B. javanica; each tiny fl. transforms into a berry, such is the fecundity of this sp. Green fruit ripen coral-pink.

B. javanica; this fast-growing sp. requires ample space to develop its sombre, bulky crown. Here, it is shown on the rainforest edge in N Qld, Australia, concealing its massive trunk and hefty limbs.

Bixa orellana

ANATTO

L.   1 sp.

B. americana; B. urucurana

BIXACEAE

IN THE EARLY DAYS of the botanic exploration of the Amazon and other humid regions of Trop. C and S America, **Bixa orellana** was recognized not only as a desirable ornamental, but also for its importance to everyday village life. It forms a loose, shrubby canopy of large, heart-shaped leaves and rusty red, new growth, with terminal, sturdily branched panicles of pale pink blooms that mimic the way single wild roses cup their boss of pink stamens. As the flowers fade, they are replaced by brilliant red, soft-spined, young fruit that persist until they mature to a deep brown. Seeds were swiftly distributed to all parts of the tropical world, particularly to Ceylon (now Sri Lanka) and other parts of SE Asia, and by the early 1800s this species was widely cultivated as a quick-growing cash crop for export, especially to America and England. *B. orellana* is grown primarily for its decorative, red, spiny fruit that are packed with small, angular, woody seeds covered in a powdery, sealing wax red powder. This substance, bixin (a carotenoid), provides a tasteless and non-toxic, orange-red dye that has found use as a food colouring for rice, margarine, butter, cheese — the red wax crust covering Edam cheese, for example — chocolate and confectionery, as well as for making soaps and skin products. Since the banning of synthetic colourants, the consumption of bixin has doubled. Bixa powder was once used as a fabric dye, Congo red, but has been replaced by synthetic dye. Traditionally, Amerindians obtained fire by friction from its soft, white wood, while they used the red, powdery aril of the seeds for body paint and as an insect deterrent, dissolved in castor oil and then applied to the body. The fibrous bark provided cordage and the yellow sap yielded a gum similar to gum arabic, known as Kesum. 'Albino' varieties exist, with pure white flowers and pale yellowish fruit. These are honey plants.

ORIGIN	Mexico to S America
HEIGHT	up to 7 m (23 ft)
TYPE	evergreen, small flowering and fruiting tree
STATUS	not threatened
HABITAT	coastal and inland thickets
GROWTH	fast
FLOWG	year-round (summer)
DRY TOL.	moderate
SALT TOL.	low; hates brackish water
LIGHT	full sun
SOIL	rich, slightly acid
NUTRIT.	rich, organic fertilizer; deep, organic mulch
HAZARDS	none
PROBLEMS	chlorosis
ENVIRON.	bee nectar
PROPAG.	seeds; cuttings
LEAVES	simple; ruddy green; ovate cordate, long-petioled, thin-textured
FLOWERS	showy; pale pink, white or lavender; rose-like, simple; with many pink stamens
FRUIT	a capsule, to 6 cm (2.4 in.); reddish to rich brown; densely, softly spiny; seeds have a red, powdery coating
USE	small flowering tree; dye plant; planter; accent; flower border; screening; conservatory
ZONE	10–12

B. orellana; rose-like, with many pink stamens, this bloom attracts bees.

B. orellana; a young fr. revealing its precious contents of small, wooden, angular sds that are covered in red powder. This powder is used in commerce as food colouring.

B. orellana; a worthy garden ornamental, grown as much for its charming blooms as for its decorative fr.

B. orellana; an 'albino' form with white fls and rounded, pale yellowish fr. grows at the Fruit and Spice Park, Florida, USA.

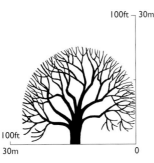

100ft — 30m

100ft
30m

0

ORIGIN	Trop. W Africa
HEIGHT	up to 20 m (66 ft)
TYPE	evergreen fruiting tree
STATUS	not threatened
HABITAT	seasonally dry lowland woodland
GROWTH	fast
FLOWG	intermittently, all-year
DRY TOL.	high
SALT TOL.	moderate
LIGHT	full sun
SOIL	fertile, well-drained
NUTRIT.	balanced fertilizer annually; organic mulch
HAZARDS	fruit parts extremely toxic
PROBLEMS	may be invasive
ENVIRON.	wild fruit for birds and bats; nectar for bees
PROPAG.	seeds; greenwood cuttings
LEAVES	simple; bright green; glabrous, elliptic, slightly stiff; to 30 cm (12 in.)
FLOWERS	showy; creamy white; held in long, unbranched, terminal clusters; fragrant
FRUIT	a capsule, to 8 cm (3 in.); 4-celled; red to yellow-ochre; seeds black, set in fleshy, cream aril
USE	small shade tree; small fruiting tree; specimen; xerophytic
ZONE	10–12

Blighia sapida

AKEE

Konig.   4 spp.

Cupania sapida

SAPINDACEAE

BLIGHIA WAS NAMED in honour of Captain William Bligh of the *Bounty* mutiny. He is recorded as having brought *Blighia sapida* seeds from Guinea in W Africa to Jamaica in the W Indies, in 1793. Slaves there were doubtless familiar with this curious fruit and would have known how to eat it, vitally important because if it is eaten before it is completely ripe, it is deadly poisonous. *B. sapida* is a very decorative, vigorous species with a billowing crown of large, bright green, coarsely pinnate leaves. Irregularly throughout the year, the canopy is showered with arching spikes of creamy white, fragrant flowers, which give way to large, polished, brilliant red or rosy ochre, 4-parted, ornamental fruit, dangled on long, sturdy stalks from the tips of the limbs. The fruit are safe to eat only when they are fully ripe and have split open naturally, exposing 4 large, glossy black seeds embedded in spongy, cream-coloured, buttery arils. Great care must be taken in the preparation of this fruit as a peptide, hypoglycine A, is contained in the unripe arils, and the pink raphe that attaches the aril to its seed is deadly toxic. The arils must be detached carefully, without any coloured membrane of the raphe attached. They are eaten raw or, more often, sautéed, when they resemble scrambled eggs. In Jamaica, along with mango and breadfruit, *B. sapida* (known as Akee), is the most commonly planted backyard tree. Akee and dried codfish is Jamaica's national dish. The fruit lather in warm water and are used in Ghana for washing. The timber, which is reddish brown, hard and durable, with an open, coarse grain, is used in Nigeria for building. The dried husks are rich in potash. This is a honey plant.

*** *B. unijugata*; (Bak.) Trop. Africa, to 18 m (60 ft). The flowers are white and very fragrant. The fruit is pinkish red and contain 3 black, shiny seeds, set in large, yellow arils. (10–12)

NOTE: *B. sapida* may escape cultivation in sandy soils.

B. sapida; abundant, spikes of sweetly fragrant, cream fls, adored by honeybees.

B. sapida; Akee is a small, ornamental tree with large, glossy foliage enlightened by the red globes of the ripe fr.

B. sapida; safe to eat only when split open naturally; glossy, black seeds embedded in spongy, buttery, cream-coloured arils.

B. sapida; the large, rosy red, ornamental fr. that forms several times a year is dangled on sturdy 'cords' to accommodate bats, which adore the ripe fr.

53

Bolusanthus speciosus

TREE WISTERIA

(Bol.) Harms.   1 sp.

FABACEAE (Papilionoideae)

THIS SMALL, DECIDUOUS, multi-stemmed, monospecific African tree is found on heavy, alkaline soils of bushveld and high savannahs. *Bolusanthus speciosus* is a sturdy, shapely, elegant tree with deeply striated, dark brown, rugged bark, erectly arching branches and drooping foliage. The glossy, leathery, pinnate, silvery hairy, asymmetric leaves hang downwards on slim, terminal twigs, as do Wisteria-like, deep or pale violet-blue, fragrant blooms. It is for these exquisite flowers that this rugged xerophyte has become one of the most sought-after flowering trees of the tropics and subtropics. Sadly, the blooming period is only about 4 weeks, but worth waiting for. Although *B. speciosa* may attain 21 m (69 ft) or more in height, it is often much smaller in cultivation. Replacing the flowers are tawny cream pods, borne in untidy clusters. They ripen slowly, persisting on the tree for up to a year. It is easy to understand why this E African native, which is closely related to the Trop. American *Lonchocarpus*, was formerly included in that genus. *Bolusanthus* wood is highly esteemed in E Africa, where it is considered one of the best and hardest of the region, but is limited by the small pieces available. It is resistant to ants and borers and, for this reason, is widely used for fence posts. It has been so extensively cut for domestic use that it is in danger of becoming rare in the wild, although it is popular as an ornamental. The bark is used medicinally.

B. speciosus may do better in the subtropics or in the true tropics over 300 m (1,000 ft) because it comes from high savannah plateaux, which have dry, cool winters. In Los Angeles, USA, and Qld, Australia, it has not thrived because of voracious attacks from caterpillars. It flourishes in Mareeba, N Qld, at 400 m (1,300 ft), with a rainfall of 914 mm (36 in.) and average temperatures between 29C–16.4C (84F–62F).

ORIGIN	Mozambique, E Africa
HEIGHT	up to 21 m (69 ft)
TYPE	deciduous flowering tree
STATUS	threatened
HABITAT	grassland thickets; high savannahs
GROWTH	moderate
FLOWG	spring
DRY TOL.	high
SALT TOL.	low
LIGHT	full sun
SOIL	fertile, slightly acid
NUTRIT.	magnesium-rich fertilizer; organic mulch
HAZARDS	none
PROBLEMS	caterpillars
ENVIRON.	insect nectar
PROPAG.	seeds (easy)
LEAVES	pinnate; dark green; to 25 cm (10 in.); leaflets oblong, glossy, leathery
FLOWERS	showy; blue-violet; to 30 cm (12 in.); crowded, held in pendent racemes; fragrant
FRUIT	a legume, to 8 cm (3 in.); tawny cream when ripe; flat, indehiscent, persistent
USE	large flowering tree; specimen; street tree; public open space; bonsai subject; xerophytic
ZONE	9–12

B. speciosus; abundant, leguminous fr. hangs on the tree for up to a year.

B. speciosus; the unusual deep, blue-violet of the Wisteria-like blooms makes this small African tree most desirable for ornamental planting. It is becoming scarce in its native region.

B. speciosus; a superb specimen in Mareeba, N Qld, Australia, at 400 m (1,300 ft), and rainfall 914 mm (35 in.) a year.

B. speciosus; deeply striated, rugged bark that has has been found to have medicinal uses in its native Africa.

Bombax ceiba

RED SILK COTTON TREE

L.   20 spp.

B. malabaricum

MALVACEAE (formerly Bombacaceae)

100ft ┐ 30m

75ft
22.5m   0

ORIGIN	Trop. Asia to Australia
HEIGHT	up to 25 m (82 ft)
TYPE	deciduous, large flowering tree
STATUS	not threatened
HABITAT	humid, lowland deciduous forests
GROWTH	moderate
FLOWG	winter to early spring
DRY TOL.	moderate to high
SALT TOL.	low
LIGHT	full sun
SOIL	rich, deep, well-drained
NUTRIT.	balanced fertilizer annually
HAZARDS	conical spines on trunk
PROBLEMS	none
ENVIRON.	insect nectar
PROPAG.	seeds; semi-ripe cuttings
LEAVES	digitate; bright green; leaflets to 25 cm (10 in.), long-petioled
FLOWERS	showy; deep to light red (rarely orange or yellow); large, blunt-tipped; heavy, waxy petals
FRUIT	a capsule, to 15 cm (6 in.); woody, oblong ovoid, 5-celled; velvety dark brown
USE	large flowering tree; public open space; specimen; xerophytic
ZONE	10–12

BOMBAX CEIBA IS AN IMPOSING TREE: tall, deciduous, with rigidly upthrusting limbs arranged in whorls around a mast-like trunk that is usually undivided and generally supported by large buttresses. The grey bark is covered with sharp, conical spines when young but becomes increasingly smooth with age. Digitate leaves are long-petioled and tend to be leathery. In early spring, when the tree is leafless, swollen buds appear clustered towards the branch ends. The flowers develop and swell, enclosed in heavy, silky hairy, cup-shaped calyxes. These burst open with dramatic effect to release their magnificent contents. The legendary blooms have 5 heavily waxy, recurved, deep or light red petals centred with a 2-layered coronet of pink filaments tipped with purple. The flowers are short-lived but secrete a reservoir of sweet, intoxicating nectar that is irresistible to the birds, squirrels and bees that act as its pollinators. As the blooms are pollinated, they abort to bring brilliant colour to the ground below. In Burma and other Asian regions, they are harvested because they are much relished as a curry vegetable. The large, oblong, velvety brown fruit contain many seeds which, like kapok, are attached to fine, silky hairs that are often used as a filling for cushions and pillows. The greyish, dark-streaked wood is soft and pithy, and large trunks are often hollowed out to make native canoes. A transparent gum exudes from the bark and the sapling roots and is used in traditional medicine.

*** **B. buonopozense**; (P. Beauv.); W and C Africa, to 40 m (130 ft). GOLD COAST BOMBAX is a much bigger tree. The trunk and young limbs are covered with enormous, conical spines. The flowers are bright orange, pink or red. (10–12)

B. ceiba; with sparse, rigid, upthrusting limbs around a sturdy, buttressed trunk.

B. buonopozense; chess set carved from the gigantic spines of the trunk. See a single spine set in the centre of the board.

B. buonopozense; fls are orange, pink or red. The trunk and young limbs are covered with enormous, conical spines.

B. ceiba; fls are short-lived but secrete a reservoir of sweet, intoxicating nectar, irresistible to birds, squirrels and bees, which collectively, act as pollinators.

Brachychiton acerifolius

ILLAWARRA FLAME TREE

F. Meull.   31 spp.

MALVACEAE (formerly Sterculiaceae)

AUSTRALIA IS FAMOUS for the unique and often bizarre character of its flora and fauna and ***Brachychiton acerifolius*** is no exception. It is a member of the illustrious Sterculiaceae (or cocoa) family that includes many of the most spectacular, flowering tropical trees. There are many forms of this superb genus in Australia, with ***B. acerifolius***, native to subtropical, moist rainforests and the coastal scrubs of NSW and Qld, the most common. Characteristically, it forms a massive trunk that has the capacity to retain water as a reserve against drought, while stiff and obliquely pointing upwards, the branches create a dense, pyramidal crown. Tough, glossy, deep green leaves form a dense canopy. They are variable from simple to palmately lobed, resembling a maple. During the winter months, ***B. acerifolius*** sheds its foliage and in late spring the greenish grey skeleton becomes aflame with minute, iridescent, rosy scarlet blooms that have no petals but are composed of tiny, inflated, flaring, bell-shaped, waxy calyxes held on widely branched, scarlet stems. As they fade, new foliage is formed; emerging leaves are flushed a fiery rose, then deepen to green as they mature. The boat-shaped fruit contains bristly seeds. When these are shed, they leave an outer coat that forms a honeycomb structure within the follicles. In the wild, ***B. acerifolius*** may reach 40 m (130 ft) but in cultivation, like most rainforest trees, it is much smaller. Gum is exuded from the bark, which also yields a useful fibre.

*** ***B. rupestris***; ([Mitch. ex Lindl.] Schum.), Qld, Australia, endemic. QLD BOTTLETREE or NARROW-LEAFED BOTTLETREE is a large, very slow-growing tree, with a trunk that becomes bottle-shaped with age. The leaves are simple on mature trees, digitately 3–9 divided on young trees. The flowers are short-stalked, softly pubescent, campanulate and creamy white, with red splashed and striped throats. (9–11)

ORIGIN	N. Australia
HEIGHT	up to 40 m (130 ft)
TYPE	deciduous, large flowering tree
STATUS	not threatened
HABITAT	moist coastal forests and scrubland, to 1,800 m (6,000 ft)
GROWTH	moderate
FLOWG	late spring to summer
DRY TOL.	moderate to high
SALT TOL.	low
LIGHT	full sun
SOIL	moderately fertile, acid
NUTRIT.	high-potassium fertilizer; organic mulch
HAZARDS	none
PROBLEMS	none
ENVIRON.	insect nectar
PROPAG.	seeds; ripe-wood cuttings
LEAVES	palmate; rich green; to 20 cm (8 in.); emergent foliage red
FLOWERS	showy; rosy scarlet; minute, flaring, bell-shaped calyxes; held in dense, widely branched, red-stalked panicles
FRUIT	a follicle, to 20 × 5 cm (5 × 2 in.); pubescent, long-beaked and long-stalked; hairy seeds
USE	large flowering tree; street tree; public open space; accent; large planter; civic centre; bonsai subject
ZONE	9–11

B. acerifolius; long-stalked, inflated, bell-shaped fls on rigid, red stalks.

B. acerifolius; this sturdy, flaming specimen was photographed in Mosman, in Sydney, where it is very popular as a street tree.

B. acerifolius; boat-shaped fr. follicles are packed with plump, deep yellow, bristly sds that are edible.

B. rupestris; native of drier rainforests of central Qld. This slow-growing, bottle-shaped sp. can tolerate light frosts.

(1) ***Brachychiton australe***; ([Schott. & Endl.] A. Terrace), N. Qld, Australia endemic, to 10 m, (33 ft). BROAD-LEAVED BOTTLE TREE is found in dry scrub and vine thickets, and has a bottle-shaped trunk and smooth, pointed, maple-like lvs. The white fls are scented. Sds have irritant hairs. (2) ***Brachychiton bidwillii***; (Hook), Qld, Australia, to 6 m (20 ft), LITTLE KURRAJONG is a large shrub of rocky slopes and dry vine thickets, and blooms when very young. It has decid., maple-like lvs and reddish tomentose new growth. (3) ***Brachychiton discolor***; (F. Meull.), (syn. *B. luridus*), NSW to N Australia endemic, to 30 m (100 ft). QLD LACEBARK is a decid., spreading sp., native to dry rainforests and coast. scrub. The heart-shaped lvs are deeply, 3–7-lobed, dark green above and densely downy below. The large, felty, bell-shaped blooms are borne in axillary clusters before the new lvs, and are dense, softly bristly and velvety, rose-pink or red. Fr. follicles measure to 20 × 5 cm (8 × 2 in.) and are heavily pubescent inside and out. Like *B. acerifolius*, this sp. has a fibrous trunk, emitting a hollow sound when tapped. (10–12) (4) ***Brachychiton diversifolius***; (R. Br.), Australia endemic, to 15 m (50 ft). KURRAJONG is a sturdy, semi-decid. tree with a well-formed crown. Lvs are smooth, ovate to elongated, heart-shaped, to 15 × 5 cm (6 × 2 in.) with long, pointed tips. Fls are bell-shaped, hairy and greenish yellow on the outside, spotted red-brown on the inside, to 1.5 cm (0.6 in.). Fr. follicles are smooth, oblong to ovoid and woody, with a short, pointed tip, and split open when ripe; with prickly hairs inside and many bristly yellow sds. (10–12)

57

(1) ***Brachychiton populneus***; ([Schott. & Endl.] R. Br.), (syn. *B. diversifolius* var. *muelleri*), E Australia endemic, to 20 m (66 ft). KURRAJONG is a pyramidal crowned, everg. (or semi-decid.) sp., native to drier, lowland woodlands, rocky hillsides and widely distributed from Victoria in the south to Eucalypt woodlands to the north (Atherton Tableland, in N Qld.). Lvs are variable: ovate and long-pointed and Poplar-like (lobed when young) – used as fodder in times of drought. Fls are bell-shaped with strongly reflexed 'petals', creamy white or greenish, with yellow or purplish red-lined throats. (8–11) (2) ***Brachychiton × rosea***; (Hort.), from 10–20 m (33–66 ft). A horticultural hybrid of *B. acerifolius* and *B. populneus* with a cylindrical trunk and grey, finely fissured bark. Shiny lvs are lanceolate to ovate, paler below. In summer, each much-branched infl. has up to 100 little deep rose, bell-shaped calyxes. Fr. follicles are ellipsoid, to 11 cm (4.3 in), glabrous, stellate hairy within. (3 and 4) ***Brachychiton velutinosus***; (Koster.), N Qld, Australia, New Guinea, to 20 m (66 ft) WARRO of coast. lowlands, vine thickets and woodlands to 500 m (1,641 ft). Closely related to *B. discolor*, this sp. is distinguished by its shallowly 3-lobed lvs, the colour of its fls and their stellate-pubescent stamens. Young trees have smooth, lime-green bark on limbs, becoming slightly fissured with age. This sp. adapts to any reasonably well-drained soil. Propagation by sd., grafting or possibly cuttings. (10–12)

ORIGIN	C and S America; Cuba
HEIGHT	up to 18 m (60 ft)
TYPE	evergreen flowering tree or tall shrub
STATUS	not threatened
HABITAT	wet, wooded lowland regions
GROWTH	moderate
FLOWG	winter
DRY TOL.	low
SALT TOL.	low
LIGHT	full sun
SOIL	fertile, water-retentive
NUTRIT.	balanced fertilizer annually
HAZARDS	none
PROBLEMS	none
ENVIRON.	insect nectar
PROPAG.	seed; cuttings
LEAVES	simple; deep green; to 20 × 8 cm (8 × 3 in.); with lateral veins
FLOWERS	showy; white (occasionally yellow), with a purple spot at throat; tubular, persistent; turning brown with age
FRUIT	a capsule, to 2 cm (0.8 in.); oblong, exploding on ripening; with 4 seeds
USE	small flowering tree; pond or riverside; large planter; courtyard
ZONE	10–12

100ft – 30m
75ft
22.5m — 0

Bravaisia integerrima

JIGGER-WOOD

(Spreng.) Standl.   3 spp.

B. floribunda

ACANTHACEAE

BRAVAISIA INTEGERRIMA is one of the few actual trees included in the large Acanthaceae clan that includes many of the tropical world's most colourful flowering shrubs and herbs. *B. integerrima* forms a densely billowing, erect crown of finely pubescent, twiggy, squarish branchlets (characteristic of its group) and variable, broadly ovate leaves. It flowers in late winter or early spring, when the blooms are held in branched, showy, terminal panicles. Individually, these fragile, little, tubular blooms are expanded at the mouth with 5 large, reflexed lobes. They are milky white or, occasionally, a yellowish colour, and have a deep purple stain at the base of their inflated throats. As the flowers fade, they turn brownish and persist on the tree for some time. Held as they are in abundant cymes at the tips of the sturdy, erect branch tips, they create an effect of foaming spring blossom. At a distance, this is reminiscent of apple or pear trees and the canopy swirling and swaying in the breeze creates a very romantic impression. The small, oblong fruit capsules are 4-seeded and explode on ripening. The *Bravaisia* genus is comprised of 3 species, 2 of which are found in mangrove swamps. The most ornamental, **B. integerrima**, is a native of humid habitats and is found on the seasonally flooded plains of the Pacific coast of C America, in association with *Haema-toxylum campechianum*, *Diospyros dignya*, *Pachira aquatica* and *Salix chilensis*. Those specimens of **B. integerrima** that actually grow in the water develop stilt roots to hold the bole above the water mark and to help keep it from rotting. This species varies greatly; in Mexico it is found as a small, multi-trunked tree, while in S America it may reach up to 25 m (82 ft) and have a single trunk. The wood is creamy reddish and slightly fragrant but does not appear to have any commercial use.

B. integerrima; white, tubular, persistent blooms dry brown as they age.

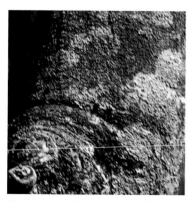

B. integerrima; with deeply furrowed bark, the wood is creamy reddish and slightly fragrant.

B. integerrima; with abundant, blossom-like, winter blooms held on sturdy, pale grey stems.

B. integerrima; on a sunny, early spring day at Fairchild Tropical Gardens in Miami, Florida, the Jigger-wood trees are foaming with their abundant, milky white blooms.

59

Brosimum alicastrum

MAYAN BREADNUT

Swartz.   13 spp.

MORACEAE

ORIGIN	Trop. America
HEIGHT	up to 30 m (100 ft)
TYPE	evergreen, large, fruiting foliage tree
STATUS	not threatened
HABITAT	seasonally flooded or dry limestone woodland
GROWTH	moderate
FLOWG	intermittently, all year
DRY TOL.	high
SALT TOL.	moderate
LIGHT	full sun or bright shade
SOIL	fertile, water-retentive
NUTRIT.	high-nitrogen fertilizer; deep, organic mulch
HAZARDS	none
PROBLEMS	none
ENVIRON.	bee nectar
PROPAG.	seeds; greenwood cuttings
LEAVES	simple; dark green; to 17 × 6 cm (7 × 2.4 in.); margins possibly serrated or wavy-edged
FLOWERS	inconspicuous; 1 female surrounded by many males, held in a compact, spherical head
FRUIT	a syncarp, to 2.5 cm (1 in.); yellow or orange; with sweet, edible, thin flesh; mealy seed with a large, nutty kernel
USE	large shade tree; street tree; public open space; xerophytic
ZONE	10–12

LIKE BREADFRUIT AND JAKFRUIT, the Mayan Breadnut is a member of the great fig family and an important tree for the Mayans of C America. Pure stands of these trees still dominate Mayan ruins. **Brosimum alicastrum** is an imposing species with a broad, dense, deep green crown and a narrowly buttressed, grey-barked trunk, making it particularly suitable for street planting. The bloom is composed of a spherical head of many male flowers, with a single female set in the centre. The small, spherical or ellipsoid fruit is golden orange, with sweet, edible pulp and 1 large seed containing a nutty kernel. Along with the Guiana chestnut, jakfruit and breadnut, **B. alicastrum** is popular for these mealy seeds, which are said to resemble potatoes in flavour. They are either boiled or roasted like chestnuts, ground into a flour or roasted as a coffee substitute. **B. alicastrum** is of easy culture, being very tolerant of shallow, calcareous soils – even seasonal flooding – and is one of the most important trees of the Yucatan because of its value as a forage plant for domestic animals. The leaves and young branches are cut as fodder for horses and mules, or sometimes slashed low for browsing. During the dry season, it is often the only fodder available. The hard, pale wood is used by carpenters and cabinetmakers.

*** **B. utile**; ([Kunth.] Oken), Venezuela to Costa Rica, where it is known as COW TREE or PALO DE VACA. Regionally, this extraordinary species is a prodigious provider. When an incision is made in the bark, a nutritious, milky sap flows out. This slightly viscous, resinous but nourishing white liquid is consumed like milk or is used to create a 'cheese' made from the thread-like curds that form on the surface of the liqiuid when it is exposed to the air. (10–12)

B. alicastrum; carries many small, spherical heads of male fls.

B. alicastrum; a specimen at Fairchild Tropical Gardens in Miami, Florida. In Cuba, where this sp. is native and important agriculturally, the roasted, chestnut-like fr. are known as Guamaro.

B. utile; a young Cow Tree at Fairchild Tropical Gardens. It earned its name for its nutritious, copious, milky sap.

B. utile; with this sp., there is no need for a cow: when an incision is made in the bark, a nutritious milky sap flows out.

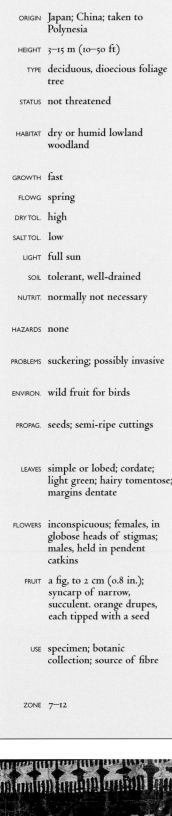

ORIGIN	Japan; China; taken to Polynesia
HEIGHT	3–15 m (10–50 ft)
TYPE	deciduous, dioecious foliage tree
STATUS	not threatened
HABITAT	dry or humid lowland woodland
GROWTH	fast
FLOWG	spring
DRY TOL.	high
SALT TOL.	low
LIGHT	full sun
SOIL	tolerant, well-drained
NUTRIT.	normally not necessary
HAZARDS	none
PROBLEMS	suckering; possibly invasive
ENVIRON.	wild fruit for birds
PROPAG.	seeds; semi-ripe cuttings
LEAVES	simple or lobed; cordate; light green; hairy tomentose; margins dentate
FLOWERS	inconspicuous; females, in globose heads of stigmas; males, held in pendent catkins
FRUIT	a fig, to 2 cm (0.8 in.); syncarp of narrow, succulent. orange drupes, each tipped with a seed
USE	specimen; botanic collection; source of fibre
ZONE	7–12

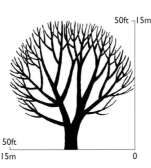

50ft — 15m
50ft
15m
0

Broussonetia papyrifera

PAPER MULBERRY

(L.) Vent.   8 spp.

MORACEAE

BROUSSONETIA PAPYRIFERA, originally from E Asia, was taken to Polynesia very early in its history. It has played a very important role in the Pacific for its papery bark, which is used to make traditional bark cloth. In Hawaii, where it is known as Wauke, this species was already widely established before colonial times. Depending upon climate and habitat, it is either found as a multi-stemmed shrub or a as a medium-sized tree. Its trunk and branches are greyish red, thick, rigid and pithy, with softly pubescent skin. The leaves are heart-shaped and possibly lobed, rough on the upper surface and woolly below. This is a dioecious species, males being pendulous, staminate catkins, while females form a fuzzy, round head composed of stigmas which, when pollinated, form curious, succulent, orange-red 'tentacles' that are tipped with a single seed. The most important feature of *B. papyrifera* is, however, its bark, which is used to make tough, durable, papery material. This may serve as fabric, leather or paper, depending on its preparation. Traditionally, this species has been coppiced in order to obtain young, long, clean shoots from which the young bark is stripped into ribbons. After scraping, soaking and beating, it yields a fine, white, fibrous 'cloth', known as tapa. The narrow strips are joined with an arrowroot paste and then beaten together to form the tapa, which is warm, flexible, resistant to water and is used to fashion all types of clothing and bedding that last for many years. Wauke trees are now rare in Hawaii, but in Samoa, where the species is known as U'a, the tradition has survived longer and tapa (or Siapo) is made there in the same manner.
*** Cvs: 'Cucullata': leaves large, unlobed, irregular. 'Lacinata': weak shrublet, with tiny remnants of leaves. 'Leucocarpa': fruit white. 'Variegata': leaves white and yellow.

NOTE: *B. papyrifera* is seriously invasive in some regions.

B. papyrifera; a fast-growing, multi-stemmed sp. with hairy tomentose lvs.

B. papyrifera; the bark is used to make the famous Polynesian bark cloth known as Tapa. Patterns are stencilled onto it.

B. papyrifera; the trunk and branches are greyish red, thick, rigid and pithy, with a softly pubescent, fibrous skin.

B. papyrifera; has succulently tentacled, female fr. Because of its fibrous bark, this is a sp. that has played an important role in the everyday life of the Polynesians of the Pacific.

Brownea macrophylla

PANAMA FLAME

Linden.   12 spp.

FABACEAE (Caesalpinioideae)

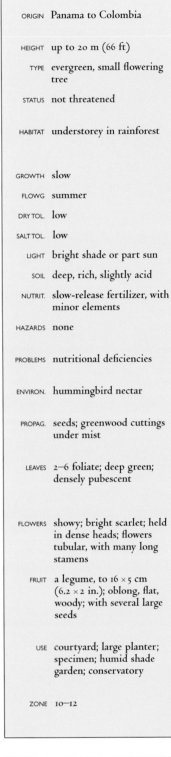

ORIGIN	Panama to Colombia
HEIGHT	up to 20 m (66 ft)
TYPE	evergreen, small flowering tree
STATUS	not threatened
HABITAT	understorey in rainforest
GROWTH	slow
FLOWG	summer
DRY TOL.	low
SALT TOL.	low
LIGHT	bright shade or part sun
SOIL	deep, rich, slightly acid
NUTRIT.	slow-release fertilizer, with minor elements
HAZARDS	none
PROBLEMS	nutritional deficiencies
ENVIRON.	hummingbird nectar
PROPAG.	seeds; greenwood cuttings under mist
LEAVES	2–6 foliate; deep green; densely pubescent
FLOWERS	showy; bright scarlet; held in dense heads; flowers tubular, with many long stamens
FRUIT	a legume, to 16 × 5 cm (6.2 × 2 in.); oblong, flat, woody; with several large seeds
USE	courtyard; large planter; specimen; humid shade garden; conservatory
ZONE	10–12

THIS GLAMOUROUS GENUS is a member of the handkerchief trees, so called for their curious, limp tassels of new leaves. All 12 species of *Brownea* are native of S American rainforests, which are home to so many outstanding, flowering, tropical trees. *Brownea* was named for Dr Patrick Browne, an Irish medical doctor and pioneer naturalist who wrote the *Natural History of Jamaica* in 1756. *Brownea macrophylla* is a typically sumptuous, if blowsy, species that begins its life with low-spreading, ungainly limbs that frequently sweep the ground. With age, it develops a short trunk, angular branchlets and a widely domed crown of large, pendulous, rich green, pinnate leaves that, on emergence, appear almost bloom-like as they form soft, limp, pinkish 'handkerchiefs'. This phenomena is caused by the elongation of the large, terminal leaf bud that contains a downward curving 'tube' of alternating scale-leaves of gradually increasing size. The buds split to spill out their tassels of new leaves, which remain flaccid for several days before gradually stiffening and deepening to green. Flowers and fruit are cauliflorous, developing directly on the trunk and older branches and are consequently hidden from view. With the new leaves, tightly packed, claw-like fists of flower buds emerge. They gradually open, beginning at their outermost edge, and transform into rich scarlet bells, each of which spouts several long, whiskery, red stamens, to form a luxuriant posy reminiscent of a rhododendron. Each bloom contains copious nectar with which to quench the thirst of the little hummingbirds that are its pollinators. During the day, the leaves act as a protective shield for the flowers, drooping over them and shading them from the hot sun. In the cool of evening, the leaves then reflex a little, to reveal the glowing blooms.

B. macrophylla; legume with very large, irregular-shaped sds.

B. macrophylla; buds emerge and gradually open into rich scarlet bells, each spouting long, whiskery, red stamens to form a luxuriant posy reminiscent of a Rhododendron.

B. rosa-del-monte; a flaccid pink tassel of young lvs. on emergence. They will deepen to green as they mature.

B. macrophylla; with a somewhat disorganized, low, spreading, dome-like canopy.

Brownea coccinea subsp. ***capitella***; (Jacq.), (syn. *B. capitella*), Venezuela, known as the LANTERN BROWNEA for the way in which the fl. hangs on the tree and also for the distinctive, inflated sepals. The stamens of this sp. are joined in 1 bundle for half their length. This specimen was photographed at Fairchild Tropical Gardens in Miami, Florida. Some forms are pinkish red. (**10–12**)

Brownea coccinea subsp. ***coccinea***; (Jacq.), (syn. *B. latifolia*), Venezuela. SCARLET FLAME BEAN is a very floriferous and rather carefree sp., with fairly open and weeping growth. Its 'handkerchief' of new lvs. is waxy, dull pink with no spots. This specimen was photographed at the Singapore Botanic Gardens, where they have an important collection of this genus. (**10–12**)

Brownea grandiceps; (Jacq.), Venezuela. This is the famous ROSE OF VENEZUELA, which resembles *B. ariza* in its compactness and pale, frosted buds. The stamens are short and recessed, and the fls. very tightly packed. The 'handkerchief' of new lvs. is large and speckled with browny pink. Photographed at Fairchild Tropical Gardens, Miami, Florida. (**10–12**)

Brownea rosa-del-monte; (Bergius), (syn. *B. ariza*); Colombia. FLORA DE ROSA, CLAVELLINO or PALO DE CRUZ. These sumptuous fls. have their buds covered in a pinkish grey 'bloom'. Gradually the large, tightly packed buds open from the outer rim, slowly progressing to the centre. The 'handkerchief' of new lvs. is pink and unmarked. (**10–12**). **Note: some authors consider this sp. as *B. ariza*.**

Brugmansia suaveolens

ANGEL'S TRUMPET

(Willd.) Bercht. & Presl.   5 spp.

Datura suaveolens

SOLANACEAE

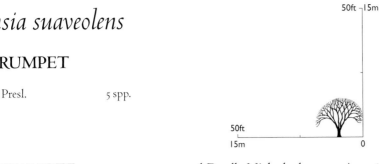

50ft ⌐15m

50ft

15m   0

ORIGIN	Andes. Ecuador
HEIGHT	up to 5 m (16 ft)
TYPE	evergreen, small flowering tree or tall shrub
STATUS	not threatened
HABITAT	frost-free, highland scrubland and banks of streams
GROWTH	moderately fast
FLOWG	in flushes, all year
DRY TOL.	moderate
SALT TOL.	low
LIGHT	bright shade or part sun
SOIL	rich, moisture-retentive
NUTRIT.	organic fertilizer; deep, organic mulch
HAZARDS	poisonous parts
PROBLEMS	nematodes; spider mite
ENVIRON.	moth nectar
PROPAG.	seeds; large cuttings; layers
LEAVES	simple; rich green; oblong-elliptic; possibly coarsely toothed, pubescent
FLOWERS	showy; white; possibly pink-tinged; trumpet-shaped; fragrant
FRUIT	a berry, to 15 cm (6 in.); cylindric to fusiform; fleshy, 2-chambered
USE	specimen; humid shade garden; large planter; accent; courtyard; conservatory
ZONE	9–12

THE SOLANACEAE TRIBE, potatoes, tomatoes, and Deadly Nightshade, comprises 56 genera, almost all of which are found in the Americas. Three family members, *Brugmansia*, *Brunfelsia* and *Cestrum*, each include popular, ornamental trees and shrubs that are nocturnally fragrant, have poisonous, narcotic and medically significant parts and are mostly from the cooler, higher regions of Trop. America. *Brugmansia suaveolens* (previously known as Datura) is a moderately fast-growing, short-lived, softly pubescent, brittle and herbaceous plant that does attain tree status but is more often shrub-like. Funnelform blooms emerge in yellowish, tightly pleated buds that unfold to form white- or pink-tinged trumpets that are characterized by their synchronicity in flowering – all individuals in proximity flower in unison. Nocturnally fragrant to attract moths, they hang half-closed during the day, but in the evening reflex and spread open, only to collapse and fall with the sun, leaving behind their inflated, bell-shaped calyxes, along with the stamens and style. It is known, like most *Brugmansia*, as Angel's Trumpet for its splendid, pendent, flaring blooms, but the name belies the diabolical properties of the leaves, which are used in the formulation of the arrow-poison, curare, as well as being one of the additives used in the preparation of the hallucinogenic drink, Ayahuasca, or Yagé. Its foliage plays an important medicinal role regionally. An infusion of the leaves is prepared for use as a calmative to relieve tension and is also used as a treatment for various aches and pains. The leaves are also combined with the seeds to concoct a narcotic.

*** *B. aurea*; (Lagerh.), S America, to 10 m (33 ft). Flowers are white to deep yellow.

*** *B. sanguinea*; ([Ruiz. & Pav.] D. Don.), Colombia to Chile, to 11 m (36 ft). RED ANGEL'S TRUMPET has narrowly tubular, yellow and red, fluted flowers. (8–10)

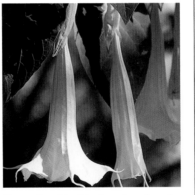

B. suaveolens; this white form shows how the fl. closes and hangs down in daylight.

B. suaveolens; the pink-tipped cultivar. 'Frost-Pink', in full, spectacular bloom at Queen Elizabeth II Botanic Park in Grand Cayman, W Indies.

B. aurea; as the day fades, fls are reflexed and become fragrant, ready to receive their nocturnal pollinators.

B. sanguinea; this sp., with fluted, yellow and red fls, is native to high elevations and is more cold-tolerant than the other spp.

ORIGIN	W Indies
HEIGHT	up to 5 m (16 ft)
TYPE	evergreen, small flowering tree or tall shrub
STATUS	uncommon in the wild
HABITAT	dry coastal woodland and scrub of lower mountain slopes
GROWTH	slow to moderate
FLOWG	intermittently, after rain
DRY TOL.	high
SALT TOL.	moderate
LIGHT	bright shade to full sun
SOIL	fertile, well-drained
NUTRIT.	organic fertilizer; organic mulch
HAZARDS	poisonous fruit
PROBLEMS	none
ENVIRON.	moth nectar; wild fruit for birds
PROPAG.	seeds; cuttings; layers
LEAVES	simple; dullish green; elliptic to ovate, slightly thickened
FLOWERS	showy; white then yellow; solitary, salver-shaped, 5-lobed; very fragrant
FRUIT	a capsule, to 2 cm (0.8 in.); orange-yellow, filled with many seeds
USE	large planter; specimen; hedge; flowering border; accent; xerophytic; conservatory
ZONE	10–12

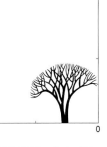

50ft ⌐15m
50ft
15m   0

Brunfelsia americana

LADY-OF-THE-NIGHT

L.   40 spp.

SOLANACEAE

BRUNFELSIAS, of the Tomato, Potato and Deadly Nightshade family, are mostly native of dry, alkaline regions. **Brunfelsia americana** is an evergreen, fairly slow-growing shrub or small tree found in moist or dry limestone woodland and coastal scrub. It develops a slender, fairly sparse, vase-shaped form, with its elliptic to obovate, slightly thickened leaves crowded on short side twigs. One of the distinguishing features of this genus is the way in which the flowers, which are triggered into bloom by a sudden shower of rain, change colour as they age. A mature tree in full bloom may be sprinkled with 3 different coloured blooms. Although *B. americana* is one of the easiest *Brunfelsia* to cultivate, it may not compare with some of the more showy, purple-flowered species. *B. americana* is known as Lady-of-the Night for its powerful, nocturnal fragrance. It has long-tubed, moth-pollinated blooms with puckered petals that gradually deepen in hue over a period of days, from pearly white (when they are at their most attractive to their nocturnal pollinators) to deep cream and finally rich ochre. This is an easily cultivated species that may be propagated from the abundant seeds contained in its thin-skinned, little, orange-yellow, tomato-like (toxic) fruit, grown from green or mature wood cuttings or, for quickest results, layered. Brunfelsias will tolerate light shade and prefer to be sheltered from strong winds.

*** **B. grandiflora**; (D. Don.), Venezuela to Bolivia, to 3.5 m (11.5 ft). YESTERDAY-TODAY-AND-TOMORROW is a beguiling shrub or small tree with slender, arching, spreading branches. It is named for its changing, fragrant, deep purple flowers with a white eye; each day, the colour fades until it is pale violet. (9–11)

B. americana; with golden, tomato-like fr., which attract fruit-eating birds.

B. grandiflora; known as Yesterday-Today-and-Tomorrow for its changing purple, fragrant blooms.

B. americana; a slender, multi-trunked sp. of dry, coast. limestone woodlands and scrub of the W Indies.

B. americana; triggered into sumptuous, fragrant bloom by a shower of rain after a dry spell. Fr. will quickly form; as it ripens, it is shed and the tree is ready for another display.

Brya ebenus

JAMAICAN EBONY

(L.) DC.   12 spp.

Asplanthus ebenus

FABACEAE (Papilionoideae)

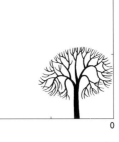

THIS SMALL NATIVE OF JAMAICA AND CUBA is spindly, bony to begin with, its long, woody, wand-like limbs bearing the tiniest olive-green, pinnate leaves and minute, rich yellow pea flowers clustered evenly along their length. Slowly, the tree develops into a slender beauty, with gracefully arching stems, and periodically transforms itself into a fountain of gold. The pale, fibrous bark flakes in strips and the wood is very dense and hard. **Brya ebenus** is famous for its fine-grained, dense heartwood that blackens with maturity to resemble ebony and has been used to make musical instruments and other small objects. This rugged, little W Indian native is known in Jamaica as Coccos-wood. **B. ebenus** is thought to act as a rain gauge, foretelling its onset by suddenly flowering. There is also a theory that its blooming coincides with a full moon. While the moon's influence is doubtful, this species does burst into glorious bloom with the first spots of rain. **B. ebenus** has enormous value as a landscape subject, particularly as a xerophyte, although it performs very well as a small cultivated tree in almost any setting except humid shade, where it will grow but not bloom well. Because of its stiff, twiggy, finely foliaged nature, this species is a favourite nesting tree for small, vulnerable birds, especially hummingbirds. It also attracts butterflies. This is a honey plant.

*** **B. microphylla**; (Bisse) Cuban endemic, to 10 m (33 ft). GRANADILLO is a rare, xerophytic species of dry, coastal and mountain forests. It is often small and shrubby. The leaves are leathery and very small, to 5 × 3 mm (0.2 × 0.1 in.); the little, pea-like flowers resemble those of **B. ebenus** and are also bright yellow.

ORIGIN	Jamaica and Cuba
HEIGHT	up to 8 m (26 ft)
TYPE	semi-deciduous, small flowering tree
STATUS	limited distribution
HABITAT	dry lowland woodland; coastal scrub
GROWTH	slow
FLOWG	year-round, after rain
DRY TOL.	high
SALT TOL.	high
LIGHT	full sun
SOIL	fertile, very well-drained
NUTRIT.	balanced fertilizer annually
HAZARDS	none
PROBLEMS	none
ENVIRON.	nectar for bees and butterflies
PROPAG.	seeds
LEAVES	pinnate; rich green; tiny, clustered along length of stem
FLOWERS	showy; deep yellow; clustered in leaf axils
FRUIT	a legume, to 1 cm (0.4 in.); a circular samara; containing a single seed
USE	seaside; small flowering tree; accent; courtyard; large planter; median strip; bonsai subject; xerophytic
ZONE	10–12

B. ebenus; a young, vigorous specimen blooming after a summer shower and demonstrating its arching growth with its precocious, butter-yellow fls set along the length of its wiry limbs.

B. ebenus; with arching wands of tiny, pea-like blooms after a sudden shower.

B. ebenus; the fls transform into little circular sd pods with a single wing surrounding the solitary sd.

B. ebenus; has very shaggy, peeling bark. The heartwood is fine-grained, dense, and known as 'Ebony' in Jamaica.

ORIGIN	Trop. America
HEIGHT	up to 25 m (82 ft)
TYPE	evergreen or deciduous, large foliage tree
STATUS	not threatened
HABITAT	moist and coastal forests; lowland thickets
GROWTH	moderate
FLOWG	intermittently, all year
DRY TOL.	high
SALT TOL.	moderate
LIGHT	full sun
SOIL	fertile, deep
NUTRIT.	high-nitrogen fertilizer; deep, organic mulch
HAZARDS	spiny; staining sap
PROBLEMS	eriophyd mites
ENVIRON.	bee nectar
PROPAG.	seeds; layers
LEAVES	simple; rich green; 3–9 cm (1.2–3.5 in.); spathulate, whorled; very varied in size and shape
FLOWERS	fairly showy; pale yellow; held in dense, slender spikes
FRUIT	a drupe, to 8 mm (0.3 in.); ovoid-conic, 5-angled; with persistent calyx
USE	large shade tree; street tree; public open space; specimen; screening; xerophytic
ZONE	10–12

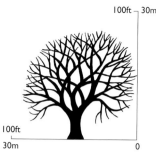

100ft – 30m
100ft
30m
0

Bucida buceras

BLACK OLIVE

L.   8 spp.

Buceras bucida; Terminalia buceras

COMBRETACEAE

TYPICAL OF ITS COMBRETACEAE FAMILY, which includes *Terminalia catappa*, the ***Bucida buceras*** begins life with the strong, horizontally layered growth of its sympodial-type branches dividing evenly again and again to form twiggy fans at the stem ends. Sometimes, its axillary buds are modified into spines. ***B. burceras***, anchored by a brown, fissured, sturdy trunk, develops a superb, spreading crown of typically spathulate, rounded leaves that are wider at their tips, tapered at their base and grouped or whorled towards the ends of the twigs to form attractive, regular planes of fresh green. Although the yellowish, bisexual flowers are minute, they are so abundant that they are look quite showy. The little spikes of flowers are also laden with pollen and attract swarms of bees. A bizarre feature of this genus is that if its minute fruit drupes are bitten by a mite, they develop slender, horn-like galls and grow to resemble long, deformed haricot beans. ***B. buceras*** is a noble species of classic form and texture reminiscent of an oak, and it certainly plays a similar role in the tropical landscape. Because the leaves of this species are so extremely varied, with the small, fine type possibly the most desirable, those planning to plant an avenue or large grouping should carefully select the young trees to ensure matching foliage. The sapwood is a yellowish or light brown and the heartwood a dark, greenish brown, with longitudinal stripes. It is very hard, heavy, strong, tough and relatively fine-grained, but difficult to work because of its high density. However, the bark has been found useful in tanning. This is an important honey plant.

NOTE: *B. buceras* is regionally native to Florida, USA, but it is officially listed as undesirable there because its sap stains masonry.

B. buceras; bees love the nectar-rich fls that are held erect on stout stalks.

B. buceras; the fr. appears to form bean-like capsules – but they are, in fact, enlarged by galls caused by a mite.

B. spinosa; with small spindle-shaped fr., showing that they have not been infected by gall mites.

B. buceras; this Trop. American sp. forms an enchanting, classic, everg. canopy of (mostly) finely textured foliage and is considered by many to play the role of an oak tree in the tropics.

(1) ***Bucida buceras*** var. 'Shady Lady'; (Hort.), to 8 m (26 ft). This young specimen demonstrates the characteristics of this superb, small-leafed, slow-growing form of Black Olive, which has a most agreeable, compact, often weeping form. It is a particularly desirable sp. for small spaces and specimen planting. Both 'Shady Lady' and *B. spinosa* (below) make excellent subjects for Bonsai culture. Shady Lady does not bear fr. and is therefore propagated vegetatively. (10–12)

(2) ***Bucida macrostachya***; (Standl.), from Mexico to Honduras. This sp. has much larger parts than those other family members. (3) This close-up of the foliage demonstrates its sympodial, twiggy growth and the whorled arrangement of the spathulate lvs. It also shows the close link between the *Bucida* and *Terminalia* genera, both members of the Combretaceae family. (10–12)

Bucida spinosa; ([North.] Jenn.), to 7 m (23 ft), of Cuba (where it is called Jucarillo) and the Bahamas (where it is Spiny Black Olive). This spiny sp. is native of marshy areas, coast. and savannah scrublands. It is semi-decid. and the trees depicted here, in winter, are in the process of losing their old lvs and revealing the delicate, feathered tracery of their finely twiggy limbs. This group of trees was photographed at Fairchild Tropical Gardens in Miami, Florida, where tourists know it as the Ming Tree, the name it enjoys as a Bonsai plant. This spiny, diminutive, xerophytic sp. is very slow growing and reasonably (but not totally) salt-tolerant. It is an excellent subject for a large container or planter. (10–12)

ORIGIN	N Qld, Australia
HEIGHT	8–30 m (26–100 ft)
TYPE	evergreen, small or large flowering tree
STATUS	common, within a limited range
HABITAT	very wet rainforest
GROWTH	fast
FLOWG	summer
DRY TOL.	low
SALT TOL.	low
LIGHT	full sun
SOIL	rich, acid loam
NUTRIT.	organic fertilizer; deep, organic mulch
HAZARDS	none
PROBLEMS	allergic to phosphates
ENVIRON.	nectar for butterflies
PROPAG.	seeds
LEAVES	simple or lobed; dark green, paler and silvery hairy below
FLOWERS	showy; white; held in slender racemes; curling, tubular flowers
FRUIT	a follicle, to 30 cm (12 in.); brown, woody, beaked; with winged seeds
USE	specimen; large planter; accent; street tree; courtyard; civic centre; conservatory
ZONE	9–11

100ft – 30m
75ft
22.5m – 0

Buckinghamia celsissima

IVORY CURL TREE

F. Muell.   2 spp.

PROTEACEAE (Grevilleoideae – Embrothrieae)

BUCKINGHAMIA CELCISSIMA was named in honour of Richard Grenville (1823–80), third Duke of Buckingham, and the tree is another member of the renowned Protea family that is endemic to the southern hemisphere. In its northern Qld rainforest habitats, *B. celsissima* soars to a great height, holding its tufted crown high above the forest to reach the sunlight. It is for this reason that the species develops a tall, straight, clean bole that has been valued and logged for its hard, attractive timber. Typically Proteaceae, the juvenile foliage may develop 2–5 deep, irregular lobes, while the mature leaves have a simpler shape. They are a deep, glossy green above and fine, silvery hairy below, distinguished by their heavy venation. Young shoots are grey and hairy, while the glossy, new leaves emerge a flushed rosy pink to red. The common name describes the attractive, fragrant, frothy blooms that foam from the branch tips in summer. Held in slender, dense, erect, bottlebrush-like spikes, the crisply curling, tubular, white flowers are tipped with 4 arching lobes, each with a protruding, hooked style. In autumn and winter, small, dark brown, beaked follicle fruit ripen and split open to release flat, winged seeds. This species is commonly known as the Ivory Curl Tree or Buckinghamia and has become popular in Australia as an ornamental since the 1950s, being widely planted as a garden specimen, a street tree or in public open spaces. Although large in its natural habitat, like so many rainforest trees, in cultivation *B. celsissima* grows in a stocky, spreading manner, attaining only about one-third of its natural height. *B. celsissima* requires rich, acid soil, adequate moisture and a sheltered site, but also needs plenty of sunlight to bloom well. This species may begin to bloom when very young.

B. celsissima; with typical Proteaceae fls.

B. celsissima; has rough, flaky bark with a bluish cast to it.

B. celsissima; photographed at the superb Mt Coot-tha Botanic Gardens in Brisbane, Qld, Australia.

B. celsissima; has charming, ivory bottlebrush-like spikes. Although this sp. fls when very young, it is fast growing and eventually requires plenty of space.

Bulnesia arborea

VERAWOOD

(Jacq.) Engl.   9 spp.

ZYGOPHYLLACEAE

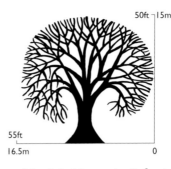

50ft ⌐15m
55ft
16.5m   0

ORIGIN	Colombia and Venezuela
HEIGHT	up to 15 m+ (50 ft+)
TYPE	evergreen flowering tree
STATUS	not threatened
HABITAT	coastal regions and dry foothills
GROWTH	slow
FLOWG	spring to autumn
DRY TOL.	high
SALT TOL.	moderate to high
LIGHT	full sun
SOIL	fertile, well-drained
NUTRIT.	balanced fertilizer annually; organic mulch
HAZARDS	none
PROBLEMS	weak-wooded
ENVIRON.	insect nectar
PROPAG.	seeds; cuttings; layers
LEAVES	pinnate; bright, olive-green; leaflets in 7–14 pairs; glossy, slightly folded
FLOWERS	showy; golden yellow; to 5 cm (2 in.); with cupped petals; held in terminal panicles
FRUIT	a samara, to 5 cm (2 in.); circular, 5-parted, papery, winged
USE	large flowering tree; street tree; specimen; public open space; bonsai subject; xerophytic
ZONE	10–12

THE *BULNESIA* CLAN is very close kin of *Guaiacum* (Lignum Vitae). In Venezuela, **Bulnesia arborea** is known as Maracaibo Lignum-vitae because of the density of its wood, although it is not considered quite an equal to *Guaiacum* in the commercial trade. **B. arborea** is a common tree of the dry shorelines and foothills of Colombia and Venezuela. When crowded in a forest, these slow-growing species may be relatively slender, with a tall, straight trunk that makes it desirable for timber. Planted in the open, however, **B. arborea** develops a more spreading crown, with its soaring branches dividing and sweeping downwards to form a cascade of supple stems that bear fine, glossy foliage that swirls around its axis. **B. arborea** could easily be mistaken for a legume. Both the deep green, very finely cut, feathery leaves and the brilliant yellow, 5-clawed flowers, held in panicles above the foliage, are strongly suggestive of the Caesalpiniaceae clan. However, its segmented, winged fruit, with 1 seed at the base of each of the 5 divisions, belies the kinship, nor does it evoke the fleshy, berry-like fruit of the related *Guaiacum*. It does not bloom as profusely as *Cassia*, for example, but it is, nevertheless, an attractive sight when in full bloom. The timber of **B. arborea** is renowned for its durability. Posts made from Verawood are recorded as having lasted for 300 years without rotting.

*** **B. sarmientoi**; (Lor. & Griseb), Trop. S America, to 18 m (60 ft). Known as PARAGUAY LIGNUM-VITAE and PAO-SANTO, this deciduous tree has an airy, arching and spreading crown. The leaves are small, rounded and leathery, with paired leaflets. The flowers are white and in axillary clusters. *B. sarmientoi* is much valued for an oil, known as Guaiac oil, which is distilled from the wood and used in making soap. (10–12)

NOTE: *B. arborea* is listed as weak-wooded and undesirable in Florida, USA.

B. arborea; the yellow fls greatly resemble Malpighia sp. In its native region, Verawood is valued for its dense, heavy wood, which is compared to Lignum Vitae, of the same family.

B. arborea; the 5 keeled wings of the fr. belie any relationship with the Legume clan.

B. arborea; shown at Fairchild Gardens, Miami, Florida.

B. arborea; timber of this sp. is renowned for its durability.

ORIGIN	C. and S America
HEIGHT	up to 10 m (33 ft)
TYPE	evergreen (or deciduous) flowering and fruiting tree
STATUS	not threatened
HABITAT	dry and moist limestone forests near coasts; dry, rocky, open lowland
GROWTH	moderate
FLOWG	mostly spring to autumn
DRY TOL.	high
SALT TOL.	moderate
LIGHT	full sun
SOIL	widely tolerant
NUTRIT.	balanced fertilizer annually; organic mulch
HAZARDS	none
PROBLEMS	none
ENVIRON.	bee nectar; wild fruit for birds
PROPAG.	seeds; greenwood cuttings
LEAVES	simple; rich green; to 10 cm (4 in.); elliptic, with wavy margins; base tapered
FLOWERS	showy; yellow; held in panicles; petals clawed; calyx with 10 glands at base
FRUIT	a drupe, to 2.3 cm (1 in.); dark yellow to red; ovoid; with sticky, dense, sweet pulp
USE	backyard tree; specimen; large planter; screening; small street tree; conservatory
ZONE	9–12

50ft — 15m

50ft
15m   0

Bunchosia argentea

PEANUT BUTTER TREE

(Jacq.) DC   55 spp

MALPIGHIACEAE

BUNCHOSIA SPECIES OF TROP. AMERICA are mostly small understorey trees of lowland humid and dry forests. *Bunchosia argentea* forms a dense, conical crown of short-stemmed, paired, wavy-edged leaves. Typical of this genus, the flowers, which are held in elongated racemes, have little, spreading, stalked (clawed), light yellow, wavy-edged petals that are set in a calyx bearing 8 prominent glands. The fruit is a broadly ovoid drupe tipped with a short, fused style. It has a very thin skin and a sticky, dense pulp that is sometimes compared to a cooked sweet potato. Apart from being a very attractive evergreen tree, *B. argentea* is equally desirable for its ornamental blooms and fruit that are borne freely for most of the year. This species is known as the Peanut Butter Tree, not because the fruit tastes of peanuts, but because the pulp has the consistency and texture of the product. The fruit are popular in their regions where they are eaten out-of-hand or made into milkshakes. They must be picked every day and stored in a refrigerator, however, as they spoil quickly. Both this species and *B. armeniaca* may tolerate light frosts.

*** *B. armeniaca*; ([Cav.] Rich.), S America, to 11 m (36 ft), CHICO MAMEY or CIRUELO is very similar to *B. argentea*. Leaves thicker and less wavy-edged, to 22.5 × 10 cm (9 × 4 in.). Flowers are held in compact, erect racemes and petals have fringed edges. The fruit is broad-ovoid, to 2.5 cm (1 in.), with dark red, thin skin covered with white down. Pulp is dark red, sweet, thin and rather dry, with 2 large seeds. (9–12) These are all honey plants.

*** *B. glandulosa*; ([Cav.] Rich.), Trop. America, to 9 m (30 ft), is known as STINKWOOD in the Lesser Antilles, in the W Indies. Leaves are light green, oblong, wavy-edged, to 9 cm (3.5 in.); they have 2 glands below. Flowers fewer per raceme; fruit egg-shaped, red or orange.

NOTE: These species may escape cultivation.

B. armeniaca; clawed, light yellow, wavy-edged petals; calyx bearing 8 glands.

B. argentea; these spp. of trop. America, are mostly small understorey trees of lowland humid and dry forests.

B. armeniaca; this fr. is not yet ripe enough to eat; it must deepen to red.

B. argentea; is equally desirable for its ornamental blooms and fr. that are borne freely for most of the year.

Bursera simaruba

GUMBO-LIMBO

(L.) Sarg.   (L.) Sarg.

Terebinthus simaruba; B. gummifera

BURSERACEAE

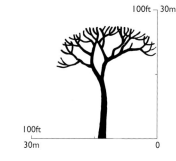

100ft — 30m

100ft
30m   0

ORIGIN	Trop. America
HEIGHT	up to 25 m (82 ft)
TYPE	deciduous foliage tree
STATUS	not threatened
HABITAT	dry, lowland thickets and woodlands
GROWTH	fast
FLOWG	intermittently, all year
DRY TOL.	high
SALT TOL.	high
LIGHT	full sun
SOIL	alkaline, well-drained
NUTRIT.	normally not necessary
HAZARDS	none
PROBLEMS	none
ENVIRON.	bee nectar; wild bird fruit
PROPAG.	seeds; very large cuttings
LEAVES	pinnate; bright green, lacquered
FLOWERS	fairly showy; creamy white; small, pollen rich; held in spidery, panicles
FRUIT	a drupe, to 1.3 cm (5 in.); dark red, fleshy; held in grape-like clusters
USE	seaside; street tree; massed as an accent; xerophytic
ZONE	10–12

BURSERA SIMARUBA is a singular, deeply tap-rooted native of Trop. America, with spongy, resinous wood and bulky, glabrous limbs covered with iridescent, rusty red skin that peels off in transparent sheets. When not in leaf, it resembles an overgrown herb rather than a tree, but with its buoyant, lustrous, new summer foliage it is suddenly transformed into a classic shade tree. It produces abundant, spidery panicles of creamy yellow, pollen-rich flowers that are adored by bees. These are followed by great bunches of succulent, red berries, to the delight of parrots and other fruit-eating birds. Traditionally, this species has been used for living fence posts, as very large limbs or large trees will root if planted. Horticulturally, *B. simaruba is* not usually highly regarded in its region but it makes a worthy subject for ornamental landscape use, especially if planted in groups, when the remarkably strong, fluid lines of the lustrous trunks may form abstract patterns. This tree is known in Florida as Gumbo-Limbo, but has earned some very descriptive nicknames: Red Belly Tree for its ruddy, smooth, swollen limbs, Tourist Tree for its thin, transparent, red and peeling skin and Turpentine Tree for the strong odour of its wood. *B. simaruba* produces a resin named American Elemi or Chibou that is used in making varnish and was employed by the Aztecs as an incense. A substitute for tea has been prepared from the leaves. These are important honey plants.

*** *B. frenningae*; (Correll), Bahama endemic, to 4.5 m (15 ft). An attractive dwarf *Bursera* named for Blanche Frenning of Goat Cay, Bahamas. A shrub or, rarely, a tree of dry scrublands; diffusely branched with reddish, flaky bark. (10–12)

*** *B. microphylla*; (A. Gray.), S USA to Mexico, to 3 m (10 ft). ELEPHANT WOOD is a shrub or tree with cherry-red limbs. The leaves are linear-oblong; the flowers are white. (8–11)

B. simaruba; succulent fr. is particularly adored by parrots.

B. simaruba; etiolated from growing in dense woodland, these specimens will fill out now they have been cleared from the choking tangle of the surrounding bush.

B. simaruba; known as the Tourist Tree for its red and peeling, skin-like bark.

B. frenningae; a charming, dwarf, endemic Bursera from the islands of the Bahamas.

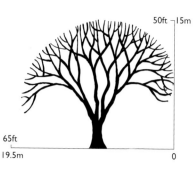

50ft ⌐15m

65ft
19.5m
0

Butea monosperma

FLAME-OF-THE-FOREST

(Lamb.) Taub.   2 spp.

Erythrina monosperma; B. frondosa

FABACEAE (Papilionoideae)

ORIGIN	India, Burma and Sri Lanka
HEIGHT	up to 15 m (50 ft)
TYPE	deciduous flowering tree
STATUS	not threatened
HABITAT	humid lowland forest
GROWTH	moderate
FLOWG	spring, before leaves
DRY TOL.	moderate
SALT TOL.	low
LIGHT	full sun
SOIL	fertile, well-drained
NUTRIT.	balanced fertilizer annually; deep, organic mulch
HAZARDS	none
PROBLEMS	sensitive to excess wet, dry or cold conditions
ENVIRON.	bird nectar
PROPAG.	seeds; cuttings; layers
LEAVES	3-pinnate; dullish green; with 3 leaflets to 30 cm (12 in.); rhombic, leathery
FLOWERS	showy; vivid vermilion; beaked, pea-like, to 5 cm (2 in.); held in dense racemes to 15 cm (6 in.)
FRUIT	a legume, to 10 cm (4 in.); silvery pubescent; initially bright tan, becoming beige with maturity
USE	spring-flowering tree; specimen; large planter; public open space
ZONE	10–12

THE *BUTEA* GENUS was named for the Earl of Bute (1713–1792), who maintained a botanic garden at Kew House in London. Without much structural beauty in the accepted sense, **Butea monosperma** acquires great character as it matures, often developing a gnarled, crooked trunk and rough, twisted, distorted limbs. With the onset of spring, before its new foliage, this unassuming tree of the wet coastal forests metamorphoses into opulent, vibrant bloom, strongly reminiscent of the *Erythrina* genus to which it was originally relegated. Each silvery-sheened, vermilion, beaked bloom is set in a velvety, blackish brown bud that opens to form its calyx. In its natural habitat, **B. monosperma** grows prolifically, creating a flaming jungle with its spring blossom, but when the seasons are too wet, dry or cold, this species may die back to its tuberous rootstock, to re-emerge when conditions become more favourable. The 3 long-petioled, silky, leathery leaflets resemble those of an overgrown haricot bean. **B. monosperma** is sacred to Brahmins. In India, its tough, card-like leaves were worn by Brahmin bachelors to indicate their dedication to their religious studies. They were also folded and used as a funnel to direct ghee onto the sacred fires during religious chanting. In its native regions, this species is a prodigious provider: an astringent, ruby red gum named Bengal Kino is extracted from its trunk and limbs and is popular for internal and external use; a seed-oil vermifuge, Muduga oil, is provided by the fruit, while the flowers give a brilliant, but fleeting, yellow or orange-red dye known as Tisso. Bark fibres are used for rough cordage and to make simple sails for boats called dhows, and are also processed for paper pulp. **B. monosperma** is very salt-resistant and xerophytic and is used to recover arid, salt lands. It is also a host tree for lac cultivation.

B. monosperma; with typically rangy growth, this sp. is nevertheless showy.

B. monosperma; this old specimen at Jardin Botanico de Cienfuegos is still blooming even after weathering severe hurricanes.

B. monosperma; has large, thin, pubescent pods.

B. monosperma; Flame-of-the-Forest or Parrot Tree puts on a spectacular display in spring – perhaps compensating for the otherwise scruffy framework of the tree.

73

Byrsonima crassifolia

NANCE

(L.) H.B.K.   130 spp.

B. coriacea

MALPIGHIACEAE

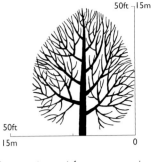

ORIGIN	C and S America; W Indies
HEIGHT	up to 10 m (33 ft)
TYPE	evergreen flowering and fruiting tree
STATUS	vulnerable in some areas
HABITAT	lowland moist or dry thickets and woodland
GROWTH	slow
FLOWG	spring to autumn
DRY TOL.	high
SALT TOL.	high
LIGHT	full sun
SOIL	fertile, well-drained
NUTRIT.	balanced fertilizer annually
HAZARDS	none
PROBLEMS	none
ENVIRON.	bee nectar; wild fruit for birds
PROPAG.	seeds (slow)
LEAVES	simple; rich green; shiny, paler below; with rusty red veins and petioles
FLOWERS	showy; yellow; held in dense, narrow, rusty-stemmed racemes
FRUIT	a drupe, to 5 cm (2 in.); rounded, yellow; pulp sour to sweet and aromatic
USE	small flowering tree; backyard tree; accent; large planter; small street tree; xerophytic
ZONE	9–11

BYRSONIMA CRASSIFOLIA is an exceedingly variable species with an extensive distribution in Trop. America – so much so, that there has been much taxonomic confusion. Plants in some parts of C and S America vary so much from those in the W Indies that they were considered by some as 2 separate species. Apart from its widely popular, berry-like fruit, *B. crassifolia* is a very ornamental small tree that grows slowly, becoming either round-topped and spreading or narrow and compact. In the wild, however, especially in arid areas, it is often distinctly distorted. Typically Malpighiaceae, the rich yellow, crumpled, clawed flowers have stamens with large, hairy, greyish anthers that form a prominent parasol at their centres. Held in crowded, erect, hairy racemes, the flowers deepen to dull orange with age, creating a vibrant, glowing canopy that is further emphasized by the velvety, rusty red of the young growth. The strongly pungent, rich yellow fruit has a thin skin and white, juicy, oily pulp, said to vary in flavour from insipid to sweet or acid. Nevertheless, *B. crassifolia* fruit is widely popular and is eaten fresh or cooked or is prepared as juice. Besides culinary value, it has several domestic uses: the rind gives a light brown dye and is employed in Guatemala for dyeing textiles; ink is sometimes made from the bitter, green fruit and the bark is used for tanning, while in Panama the fruit is fermented to make Chica, a popular drink. The hardwood is dull red or pinkish brown. These are honey plants.

*** *B. lucida*; (D.C.), (syn. *B. cuneata*), S Florida and W Indies, to 10 m (33 ft). GUANA- or LOCUST-BERRY is an attractive, small evergreen species with narrow, shiny, blue-green, spathulate leaves clustered towards the twig tips. Little, white, wheel-like blooms deepen to pink, red or yellow with age, creating a variegated effect. The fleshy, round, brownish fruit are sweet, edible and said to taste of cranberry. An excellent container subject. (9–11)

B. crassifolia; litter of old lvs and ripe fr.

B. crassifolia; with upright racemes of yellow fls, that deepen to a rich orange as they mature. This tree was photographed at the Fruit and Spice Park, Florida.

B. crassifolia; the whole tree is infused with a golden glow when it is in full bloom.

B. lucida; has charming, erect racemes of white fls that deepen to reddish pink with age, creating a variegated effect.

ORIGIN	W Indies; C America
HEIGHT	up to 12 m (40 ft)
TYPE	evergreen, small, flowering spiny tree
STATUS	endangered in the wild
HABITAT	arid limestone thickets
GROWTH	moderate
FLOWG	autumn to winter
DRY TOL.	high
SALT TOL.	fairly high
LIGHT	full sun
SOIL	alkaline, well-drained
NUTRIT.	balanced fertilizer in summer; organic mulch
HAZARDS	spiny
PROBLEMS	none
ENVIRON.	bee nectar
PROPAG.	seeds; softwood cuttings
LEAVES	2-pinnate; rich green, 5–10 cm (2–4 in.); leaflets oblique, leathery; strongly aromatic
FLOWERS	showy; bright yellow with orange or red standard; held in simple or compound, terminal, erect racemes
FRUIT	a legume, to 9 × 2 cm (3.5 × 0.8 in.); an oblong samaroid, highly burnished
USE	seaside; small flowering tree; accent; screening; barrier; large planter; xerophytic
ZONE	10–12

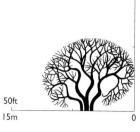

50ft ┐15m
50ft
15m 0

Caesalpinia echinata

INDIAN SAVIN TREE

L.   150 spp.

C. vesicaria

FABACEAE (Caesalpinioideae)

CAESALPINIA ECHINATA is a tough xerophytic, seaworthy species native to arid limestone thickets near the sea in drier parts of Mexico, C America and the eastern W Indies. This species is, nevertheless, an exuberant small tree, with its stout trunk and twigs mostly scattered with thick, corky spines. *C. echinata* is much branched and forms a dense, billowing mass, with lustrous, rich green, strongly aromatic foliage composed of leathery, 2-pinnate leaves, with large, oblique, blunt-tipped, oblong leaflets that are partially folded inwards along their margins. As may be seen below, this species may be sprawling and shrub-like, but also grows to form a sturdily trunked tree. The rich colour of the foliage sets off the striking, erect, slender panicles of its bright yellow, pea-like flowers, each with a red-splashed posterior petal. Beginning in winter, the blooms last well into spring, lightening an otherwise drab, winter landscape. With the last of the flowers, masses of swollen pea-pods are formed. As they mature, they become a burnished sienna-red, adding to the ornamental nature of this lovely member of the *Caesalpinia* genus. While lacking the seductive colours of its blooms, *C. echinata* is possibly more useful and handsome than its flamboyant but sometimes undisciplined relative, *C. pulcherrima*. Although surprisingly little known, Indian Savin has much potential for use as a landscape plant, lending itself especially for planting as a barrier or for screening in arid or coastal areas, where it may be kept short and dense. In its native regions, it has been found that an infusion of pods mixed with iron sulphate gives a permanent, black dye. Villagers of the Yucatan province of Mexico make a preparation of the powdered bark charcoal from *C. echinata* wood and use it as a domestic remedy for diarrhoea in children. Fine-grained heartwood is very tough and used to fashion musical instruments. *Caesalpinia* are important honey plants.

NOTE: This genus is currently under revision.

C. echinata; abundant, long-lived, erect, fresh yellow fls.

C. echinata; a small tree, with its stout trunks and twigs usually scattered with thick, corky spines.

C. echinata; a wealth of polished sienna-red, leathery sd pods are borne for several months.

C. echinata; has leathery, glossy, bright green foliage and clear yellow, long-lived blooms, and is a most desirable xerophytic sp.
Photographed at Fairchild Tropical Gardens, Miami, Florida.

75

Caesalpinia

Caesalpinia cassioides; (Willd.), (syn. *C. bicolor*), Peru, Ecuador and Columbia; to 7 m (23 ft). Cassia-leafed *Caesalpinia* is a rare ornamental sp. that is sparsely thorny may grow as a large shrub or a small tree. Light green and thin-textured, the pinnate lvs, with ovate notched lflts, are pale greyish below. The long-stemmed, scarlet, tubular-campanulate blooms are veined in darker red and have 10 perky, slightly exserted stamens. Fr. pod is to 4 cm (1.6 in). (9–11)

Caesalpinia ferrea; (Mart. ex Tul.), E Brazil, endemic; to 15 m (50 ft). BRAZILIAN IRONWOOD is a large, unarmed shrub or large tree with coarse, pinnate lvs. The little yellow fls are followed in great abundance by thick, oblong sd pods. It is also known as LEOPARD TREE because of its dramatic, light and dark, bluish grey and creamy, spotted bark. The heavy, hard wood is highly valued in its region. Popularly used in the subtropics as a street tree. (9–12)

Caesalpinia granidillo; (Pittier), (syn. *Libidibia punctata*); Venezuela; endemic, to 8 m (26 ft). Known commonly as BRIDAL VEIL, it is known as EBANO or GRANADILLO in Venezuela. The heartwood of this small sp. is hard, dense and heavy; it is considered equal to Ebony in its region, where it is known as Coffee-wood or Brown Ebony in the timber trade. Like *C. ferrea*, this sp. has mosaiced, ceramic-like bark. (10–12). **Note: this sp. is considered to be C. punctata (Willd.) by some authors.**

Caesalpinia sappan; (L.), Indomalaysia, up to 7 m (23 ft) ; SAPPANWOOD, BAKAM or PATTANGI is a small, prickly, straggling tree that is highly regarded in its region, where the heartwood is exported for the red and black dyes it yields. (In SE Asia, it is used to dye wool and calico.) *C. sappan* also has several medicinal properties, as well as producing tannin and hard, durable timber. It blooms in summer and autumn. (10–12)

Caesalpinia violacea; ([Mill.] Standl.), (syn. *C. brasiliensis*), Cuba; C America, to 18 m (59 ft). Yarua, Brasiletto, Chacte or Brazil wood, is unarmed. This sp. bears small, fragrant, yellow fls (1 petal, red-spotted) in erect spikes, to 25 cm (10 in.). Pinnate lvs with 4–10 pinnate, 12–16 lflts. This sp. is often confused with the Brazilian sp., *C. echinata*. (10–12) **Note:** when this genus is revised, this sp. will be placed in *Coulteria*.

Caesalpinia yucatanensis; (Greenman.), Mexico and Guatemala, to 6m (20ft). Immensely popular as a garden ornamental; the 2-pinnate foliage has 4 pairs of oval lflts and erect racemes of light yellow fls with a pale orange standard petal. Although its main flowg period is spring, it has flushes of bloom most of the year. **NOTE: this sp. has long been confused with *C. mexicana* and is regularly sold in the Florida trade under this name.** (10-12)

Caesalpinia coriaria; ([Jacq.] Willd.), (syn. *Libidibia coriaria*), from the Antilles and S Mexico to northern S America, to 9 m (30 ft). This small, thornless, decid. sp., Divi-divi, is renowned in the leather industry for the rich tannin secreted in its bitter, coiled pods. These legumes are said to contain from 30–40% tannin and a mature tree is considered capable of producing around 36 kg (79 lb) of pods each year. Bark is high in tannin, also. *C. coriaria* is a sp. of seasonal and coast. forests. The heartwood, which is dark brown or blackish and often streaked, is heavy, very hard, strong and durable; although it polishes well it is difficult to work. Wood yields a reddish dye and black dye has been prepared from fr. pods. This is an important bee plant. (10–12)

Calliandra surinamensis

PINK TASSEL-FLOWER

Benth   200 spp.

FABACEAE (Mimosoideae)

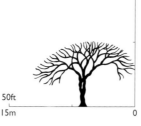

50ft ⌐15m

50ft
15m   0

FROM A SHORT, STURDY TRUNK the willowy limbs of the ***Calliandra surinamensis*** stretch and arch to form a wide spreading vase shape. For long periods, the uppermost surface of the branches, which carry small clusters of finely ferny foliage, is sprinkled with little, erect, stalkless, fragrant, powder-puff flowers, their dense tufts of white stamens seemingly dipped to half their length in bright pink dye. In early morning, the new blooms glisten freshly but, during the heat of the day, they slowly subside to preserve their pollen, expanding in the evening to receive their pollinators, the night-flying moths. *Calliandra* is Greek for 'beautiful stamens', while its specific name was chosen for Dutch Guiana (now Surinam), where it was first discovered. The filaments of the fragile pompoms are held in bundles. They spring from delicate, silky, narrow, white, frilly trumpets, which may be so formed as a guide for the pollinator's proboscis and to protect the base of the stamens. The little pinnate leaves, having photosynthesised during the day, close at night to conserve their fluids. Because of its arching habit, and the fact that its blooms are carried on the upper surface of its limbs, *C. surinamensis* is best viewed from above, making it a perfect choice for a sloping garden or planted to form a small allée.

*** ***C. haematocephala***; (Hassk.), (syn. *C. inaequilatera*), S America, to 6 m (20 ft). RED POWDER PUFF or LEHUA-HAOLE is usually shorter in cultivation and has coarser, darker, less glossy foliage than *C. surinamensis*. The large, deep rose-pink (rarely white) flowers of ***C. haematocephala*** are photoperiod sensitive, blooming mostly in the months when the days are short in length. There are several excellent, compact cultivars. (10–12)

ORIGIN	Northern S America
HEIGHT	up to 6 m (20 ft)
TYPE	evergreen, small flowering tree
STATUS	not threatened
HABITAT	dry woodland and brushland
GROWTH	moderate
FLOWG	year-round
DRY TOL.	high
SALT TOL.	low
LIGHT	full sun
SOIL	widely tolerant, well-drained
NUTRIT.	balanced fertilizer annually; organic mulch
HAZARDS	none
PROBLEMS	mealy bugs; scale
ENVIRON.	butterfly, moth, and hummingbird nectar
PROPAG.	seeds; cuttings
LEAVES	pinnate; rich green; 1–3 pairs of pinnae; leaflets to 17 mm, (6.7 in.), in 7–12 pairs
FLOWERS	showy; white and pink; dense bundles of fragile filaments held in slender, trumpet flowers; fragrant
FRUIT	a legume, up to 4 cm (1.5 in.); curved, brown, dehiscent
USE	small avenues and allées; specimen; flower border; large planter; median strip; xerophytic
ZONE	9–12

C. surinamensis; its rosy pink stamens are held in bundles.

C. surinamensis; its strong vase-shape lends itself to planting in small allées. Here it is seen framing a walkway at Andromeda Botanic Gardens, Barbados, in the West Indies.

C. surinamensis; slender limbs are garnished with pink fls, which open early morning and close at midday.

C. surinamensis; the woody, leguminous pods split open and curve back to expel the hard, shiny sds with great force.

ORIGIN	Australia, endemic
HEIGHT	up to 8 m (26 ft)
TYPE	evergreen, small flowering tree
STATUS	not threatened
HABITAT	moist woodland; river banks
GROWTH	moderate
FLOWG	intermittently, after rain
DRY TOL.	moderate
SALT TOL.	moderate
LIGHT	full sun
SOIL	fertile, water-retentive
NUTRIT.	balanced fertilizer annually; deep, organic mulch
HAZARDS	none
PROBLEMS	sooty mould; nematodes
ENVIRON.	nectar for birds
PROPAG.	seeds; semi-ripe cuttings
LEAVES	simple; dull green; to 6.5 cm (2.5 in.); linear, leathery, densely whorled; spicily aromatic
FLOWERS	showy; bright red; in densely spiralled, many-stamened bottlebrush spikes, to 20 cm (8 in.)
FRUIT	a capsule; urn-shaped; woody, light brown; crowded along stems
USE	small flowering tree; accent; courtyard; large planter; bonsai subject
ZONE	9–12

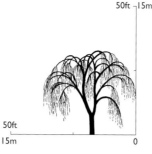

50ft ¬15m

50ft
15m   0

Callistemon viminalis

WEEPING BOTTLEBRUSH

(Sol. ex Gaertner) G. Don. ex Loud.   30 spp.

MYRTACEAE

THIS IS A ROBUST BUT GRACEFUL MEMBER of the vast tribe of Australian myrtles, which includes *Eucalyptus, Leptospermum, Melaleuca* and *Syzygium*. **Callistemon viminalis**, one of the most tropical of this genus, is widespread and common along banks of rivers and creeks in eucalyptus woodlands from the Cape York Peninsula in northern Qld, to Clarence River in the south. In the wild, **C. viminalis** is very varied in size and form and may become straggly, although in cultivation it usually forms a billowing, willowy specimen. It is easily distinguished from other species of this ornamental genus by its long, flexuous, weeping limbs, which are particularly splendid in spring, with their glowing flush of new, coppery, silky pubescent growth. The leaves are short, linear and whorled along their wiry stems. As they age, they stiffen and develop oil glands, which emit a pungent, spicily lemonish myrtle scent when crushed. Dangling from the tips of slender stems are bright red brushes of long-lasting, many-stamened flowers, rich in nectar. These blooms are distinguished by the base of their stamens being joined in a ring and all shed together as a unit. They are replaced by little, wooden, cup-shaped seed capsules that are clustered along the length of the stem. As the fruit ripens, it is by-passed by new leaf growth and, eventually, fresh blooms, which form on the new growth above. The canopy of this species provides good cover for small birds, especially native Scarlet Honeyeaters, which are about the same size and colour as the blooms. *Callistemon* species hybridize freely, resulting in a plethora of cultivars, many of which are similar in appearance and are dwarf or temperate in nature. Because of the great variation found in this species, it is mostly propagated from cuttings.

✱✱✱ *C. salignus*; ([Smith] Sweet), Qld, NSW, and SA, Australia, to 10 m (33 ft). WILLOW BOTTLEBRUSH, native to river flats and creek beds, has willowy foliage, slightly pendulous branches and a compact form. New growth is reddish; flowers are cream or pink. (8–10)

C. rigidus; fr. forms after the fls are pollinated and normal growth continues.

C. salignus; this widespread sp., with its willowy foliage and compact form, has attractive reddish new growth.

C. viminalis; a well established specimen at the Arboretum of Los Angeles, in California.

C. viminalis; a trop. sp. of Qld, northern Australia. This very varied sp. has been widely hybridized and may have pink, mauve or whitish fls, as well as its usual bright red or crimson.

79

Callitris macleayana

STRINGYBARK CYPRESS PINE

(F. Muell.) F. Muell   19spp (approx)

CUPRESSACEAE

100ft — 30m

75ft
22.5m   0

MOST SPECIES OF THE HANDSOME CYPRESS PINES occur in drier, open forests throughout much of Australia, with 2 species found in New Caledonia, in the S Pacific. *C. macleayana* has a scattered distribution in the wet uplands of both NE Qld and SE Qld. In these forests, the crown is often sparse and open, but in cultivation it has a dense, broadly conical crown, like most other *Callitris*. The related northern hemisphere *Cupressus* has opposite pairs of scale-like leaves, while leaves of *Callitris* are 3-ranked; juvenile *C. macleayana* have prickly, needle-like scales in whorls of 4. This species has thick, brown bark that splits into long 'tapes', hence the common name, and soft, easily worked, pale timber that contains aromatic resins which, in several other species, provide excellent protection against white ant attack, fungus or shipworm, but increase flammability. The resin exuded from the cut wood of many *Callitris* species is used for pharmaceuticals and varnishes, while the tannin-rich bark is used in tanning. *Callitris* timber has been used for flooring, framing and cabinetwork; the many knots stay tight, and add to its appeal when polished. *C. macleayana*s, like most of its genus, is adaptable in cultivation, tolerating frost in southern Australia and often turning a coppery red. Several species have been used successfully for hedges but, like most conifers, it will not tolerate hard pruning into bare stems.

*** *C. columellaris*; (F. Muell.), NE NSW and SE Qld, Australia, to 30 m (100 ft). BRIBIE ISLAND PINE once encompassed other species widespread through the dry inland, but is now narrowly limited to coastal areas, where it prefers well-drained, sandy soils over a water table. Forest trees have gnarled limbs and a billowing crown of dense, dark green foliage. (9–11)

*** *C. intratropica*; (R. T. Baker & H. G. Smith), north Australia endemic, to 25 m (82 ft). NORTHERN CYPRESS PINE occurs widely through the monsoon tropics. It is a handsome species, forming a cone-shaped crown and rough, dark, deeply furrowed bark. (9–12)

ORIGIN	Australia, endemic
HEIGHT	up to 45 m (148 ft)
TYPE	evergreen foliage tree
STATUS	not threatened
HABITAT	wet forests and rainforest margins
GROWTH	fast to moderate
FLOWG	intermittently
DRY TOL.	moderate to low
SALT TOL.	low
LIGHT	full sun to part shade
SOIL	porous; water-retentive
NUTRIT.	high-nitrogen fertilizer; organic mulch
HAZARDS	none
PROBLEMS	susceptible to fire
ENVIRON.	seeds for cockatoos
PROPAG.	seed
LEAVES	scales; rich green; whorled on soft, olive-green twigs; juvenile scales needle-like, to 3 mm (0.1 in.)
FLOWERS	male cones to 5 mm (0.2 in.) long; thick-walled, woody; dehiscent when ripe; with winged seeds
FRUIT	a cone, to 1.8 cm (0.7 in.); 6-valved, pointed, woody, dark brown shiny; dehiscent; held in sessile clusters; with winged seeds
USE	accent; specimen; hedges; street tree; public open space; windbreak; large planter; bonsai subject
ZONE	9–12

C. macleayana; these spherical cones will split open to release their winged sds.

C. macleayana; a handsome species with open growth, although, in cultivation it has a dense, broadly conical crown, like most other *Callitris*.

C. intratropica; this sp. is slow to germinate and establish, but makes an excellent street tree and windbreak.

C. intratropica; fine, scaly, grey-green foliage is held erect, in a brush-like manner. Lvs are burned to repel mosquitoes.

ORIGIN	Kenya to S Africa
HEIGHT	up to 15 m (50 ft)
TYPE	semi-deciduous flowering tree
STATUS	fairly rare in the wild
HABITAT	elevated coastal forests; high plateaux forest
GROWTH	slow
FLOWG	winter and summer
DRY TOL.	requires humidity
SALT TOL.	moderate
LIGHT	bright shade to full sun
SOIL	slightly acid, well-drained
NUTRIT.	high-potassium fertilizer; deep, organic mulch
HAZARDS	none
PROBLEMS	none
ENVIRON.	butterfly nectar; seeds for animals and birds
PROPAG.	(ripe) seeds; cuttings; grafting
LEAVES	simple; deep green; aromatic; margins may be wavy
FLOWERS	showy; white to pale pink; stamens pink with purplish, spotted glands; fragrant
FRUIT	a woody capsule, to 4 cm, (1.5 in.); 5-lobed; covered with warty protuberances
USE	seaside (sheltered); specimen; public open space; street tree; civic centre; large planter
ZONE	9–11

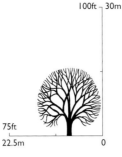

100ft – 30m

75ft
22.5m — 0

Calodendrum capense

CAPE CHESTNUT

(L. f.) Thunb.   2 spp.

RUTACEAE

THIS STUNNING, RARE TREE, one of the most beautiful of subtropical species, is native to highland forests from Kenya to Zimbabwe and the humid coastal forests of S Africa. *Calodendron capense,* which belongs to the citrus clan, forms a rounded, dense canopy over a stocky trunk. It is briefly deciduous but may remain evergreen in moist, forest conditions or under irrigation. The short-petioled, rich green leaves are aromatic and slightly folded, with sinuous margins. Its curious flowers are held in sumptuous, terminal panicles and are composed of 5 strap-like petals that are whitish, shading to pink, and stained a deep rose with maroon near their base. There are 10 stamens, 5 that are fertile and 5 that form flat staminodes resembling petals that are whitish touched with pink and spotted with maroon-purple glands. Equally unusual are the woody, 5-parted fruit that look like clusters of warty, bluntly spiny chestnuts. They enclose large, angular, shiny black seeds, containing an oil that is sometimes used in making soap. *C. capense* prefers soil that is free draining and deeply, but infrequently, watered. It has proved to thrive in inland coastal areas that are tempered by the proximity of the sea but sheltered from strong winds. The common name, Cape Chestnut, is somewhat of a misnomer as this tree is neither a chestnut nor solely native of the Cape of S Africa. It is very popular as a street tree or garden specimen in frost-free areas of California and Australia, as well as upland Hawaii, but does not do well in Florida, probably due to the high alkalinity of the soil. It is very slow growing and seedling trees may take 14 years to bloom. *C. capense* timber is pale yellow-brown, straight-grained, tough, easy to work and is used to make furniture. Monkeys, pigeons and parrots feed on the seeds and native swallowtail butterflies breed on it.

C. capense; fls with curious, flattened, petal-like stamens.

C. capense; timber is pale, yellow-brown, straight-grained, tough, easy to work and used to make furniture.

C. capense; the knobbly, chestnut-like fr. contain oily, black sds. Photographed in Mosman, Sydney, Australia.

C. capense; with shaggy, 5-petalled, sumptuous fls of glorious pink. Although fairly rare in the wild, this sp. is one of the most beautiful, subtrop. trees.

Calophyllum inophyllum

ALEXANDRIAN LAUREL

L. 187 spp.

GUTTIFERAE

ORIGIN	Trop. Asia to the Pacific
HEIGHT	up to 35 m (115 ft)
TYPE	evergreen, large foliage (flowering) tree
STATUS	not threatened
HABITAT	moist coastal woodland
GROWTH	fast at first, then slower
FLOWG	late spring and summer
DRY TOL.	moderate
SALT TOL.	very high
LIGHT	full sun to part shade
SOIL	humid, well-drained
NUTRIT.	balanced fertilizer annually; deep, organic mulch
HAZARDS	none
PROBLEMS	possibly invasive
ENVIRON.	insect nectar; seeds for bats
PROPAG.	seeds
LEAVES	simple; dark green; to 20 cm (8 in.); glossy, broadly elliptic; finely veined
FLOWERS	showy; creamy white; to 2 cm (0.8 in); with yellow stamens and red pistil; fragrant
FRUIT	a drupe, to 3.5 cm (1.4 in.); yellow to light brown when ripe; ball-like
USE	seaside; large shade tree; street tree; public open space; coastal windbreak; pollarded
ZONE	10–12

THE WORD *CALOPHYLLUM* is derived from Greek and means 'beautiful leaf'. *Calophyllum inophyllum*, one of many species native to its region, is a common, slow-growing tree of the coastal forests and scrubland of Trop. Asia, Australia and the Pacific. These species are distinguished by their yellow or whitish transparent latex and leathery, oblong-elliptic, deep green leaves that resemble *Garcinia*, and have many regular, closely set, parallel veins. For a brief period in spring and again in late summer, *C. inophyllum* bears masses of sweetly fragrant, ivory white blooms held in erect racemes. Each waxy bloom cradles a crown of golden stamens around a pinkish red pistil. The flowers, which are pollinated by insects, begin to open between 3–4 a.m., are wide open at sunrise and withering the next day. Following the flowers come trusses of golf-ball-sized, green fruit that are held for a long period until mature and brown. Their large, oily seeds are eaten by bats and are distributed by them. These seeds, known commercially as Punnai nuts, yield dark green, strongly aromatic, but somewhat toxic, Dilo- or Pinnay-oil, which, nevertheless, is used regionally for cooking and as a lighting fuel, as well as for many medicinal applications. The oil is also used in massage and is scented with Ylang-Ylang or other fragrant flowers for skin and hair oil. Crushed leaves are used traditionally in Polynesia to treat eye ailments. Apart from being a most desirable tree for streets, parks, urban landscapes, coastal and home gardens, *C. inophyllum* is also important commercially for its excellent timber, which is known as Borneo mahogany and is esteemed for its fine grain and is used for furniture and boatbuilding.

*** *C. sil*; (Lauterb.), Malesia to New Guinea and Australia, to 20 m (66 ft). ALLIGATOR BARK with fissured bark and superb, deep red, new growth; fruit is blue-green. (10–12)

NOTE: these species have escaped cultivation in some regions.

C. inophyllum; with golf ball-sized, young fr., which are waterproof and float well.

C. inophyllum; has splendid, sweetly fragrant, waxy fls with a pompom of golden stamens studded with a perky, red style at their centre.

C. inophyllum; this salt-resistant sp. has become widely popular for its handsome foliage and splendid blooms.

C. sil; Alligator Bark has stunning, dark red new growth, fragrant white fls and blue-green fr.

(1) ***Calophyllum brasiliensis***; (Combess.), (syn. *C. antillianum*; *C. calaba*), W Indies; C and S America, to 25 m (82 ft). BEAUTY LEAF or SANTE MARIA has a luxuriant, everg. canopy for shade, a salt-tol. par excellence and renowned timber resembling Mahogany. The trunk normally forms a straight axis and has light grey, fissured bark; lvs, which are smaller than *C. inophyllum*, are stiff, elliptic, to 7 cm (3 in). (2) The polygamous fls are much smaller than *C. inophyllum*, but deliciously scented and held in denser panicles, borne along the terminal twigs; male fls have about 40–50 stamens in a prominent orange cluster.

(3) *C. brasiliensis* also bears oily nuts, which are valued for their oil and medicinal qualities. The embryo is contained in a thick, waterproof shell, adapted to allow the fr. to float long distances and thus be distributed; they are also sought after by bats. Latex or resin from the trunk, called Balsamo de Maria has been employed medicinally. BELOW: In Cuba *C. brasiliensis* is used as agricultural windbreaks and is widely planted as a street tree. This photograph was taken at the Jardin Botanico Nationale of Cuba, where there is an extensive experiment and research into economic crops. (10–12)

Calotropis gigantea

GIANT MILK-WEED

(L.), Aiton   3 spp.

ASCLEPIADACEAE

CALOTROPIS GIGANTEA is one of the few ornamental flowering trees to thrive on some Micronesian atolls of the western Pacific. It is known as Crown Flower there and, although not native, proliferates along the sheltered shores of lagoons. Soft-woody, with straggling, languid growth, *C. gigantea* may grow as a shrub or develop a trunk of up to 25 cm (10 in.) in diameter; it has copious, rubbery, milky sap in all it parts and paired white, woolly, grey-green, stalkless leaves. Typical of the Milk-Weed family, the sturdy, little, crown-shaped flowers are held on long, pale green stalks in terminal, flat-topped cymes; they are succulent, furry and pale lilac-blue, with purple reflexed tips. Flowers are replaced by bizarre, ballooning, bladder-like fruit that are stuffed with seeds, each attached to a 'parachute' of silky hairs, which are used like kapok. Unpalatable to animals, *C. gigantea* quickly establishes itself on pastureland. It is particularly renowned for its fibrous bark (known as Madar in India and Yercum in W Africa), which is stripped to make textiles, fishing nets and bowstrings. This species is of religious, medicinal and economic significance in India, where it is sacred to the Hindu gods Siva and Karma. Its milky sap, Mudarine, coagulates when warm and is said to have a similar effect to digitalis. It is also used to treat dysentery, leprosy, elephantiasis, epilepsy, asthma and also many, minor, complaints. Charcoal is derived from the wood ash and has been used in the production of gunpowder. In Java, the flowers are candied, while in Africa the roots are used as chew sticks. *C. gigantea* is a splendid species for seaside or dry gardens but will require pruning for a compact crown.

*** *C. procera*; ([L.], Aiton), India, to 5 m (16 ft), FRENCH COTTON differs in its smaller leaves and flowers with erect corolla lobes, usually with a spot at the base. (10–12)

NOTE: these species may escape cultivation in sandy soils.

ORIGIN	Africa and India
HEIGHT	up to 6 m (20 ft)
TYPE	evergreen, small flowering and foliage tree
STATUS	not threatened
HABITAT	dry coastal and strand; over-grazed pasture land
GROWTH	fast
FLOWG	year-round
DRY TOL.	high
SALT TOL.	high
LIGHT	full sun
SOIL	tolerant, very well-drained
NUTRIT.	normally not necessary
HAZARDS	none
PROBLEMS	aphids
ENVIRON.	nectar for butterflies
PROPAG.	seeds; cuttings; layers
LEAVES	simple; silvery green; to 18 cm (8 in.); silky hairy
FLOWERS	showy; white, pinkish- or purple-tinged succulent; in umbels; petals reflexed
FRUIT	a follicle, to 12 cm (4.7 in.); balloon-like, filled with many seeds attached to fine, silky fibres
USE	seaside; specimen; large planter; coastal screening; xerophytic
ZONE	10–12

C. gigantea; has bladder-like fr. with many sds attached to long, silky threads.

C. procera; with powdery, crown-like blooms. The growth may be quite straggly, so to grow a full, bushy specimen this sp. must be regularly pruned.

C. gigantea; this sp. is happy to grow in sand, right on the shore line, and thrives in the shelter habitat of lagoons.

C. gigantea; showing its soft, deeply grooved bark and copious, milky latex. The bark fibres are known as Yercum in W Africa.

ORIGIN	Trop. America
HEIGHT	up to 10 m (33 ft)
TYPE	deciduous flowering tree
STATUS	uncommon in the wild
HABITAT	dry, semi-deciduous forest
GROWTH	moderate
FLOWG	winter
DRY TOL.	high
SALT TOL.	moderate
LIGHT	full sun
SOIL	rich, deep, well-drained
NUTRIT.	balanced fertilizer annually
HAZARDS	none
PROBLEMS	none
ENVIRON.	bee nectar
PROPAG.	seeds; cuttings; layers
LEAVES	simple; rich green; to 5–7 cm (2–2.7 in.); elliptic, shiny
FLOWERS	showy; ivory-white; with 1 enlarged, white sepal; flowers tiny; slightly fragrant
FRUIT	a capsule, to 1 cm (0.4 in.); cylindrical; 2-valved
USE	winter-flowering tree; specimen; public open space; xerophytic
ZONE	10–12

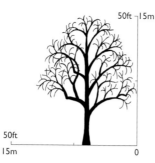

50ft ⌐15m

50ft
15m   0

Calycophyllum candidissimum

DEGAME

(Vahl.) DC.   6 spp.

Macrocnemum candidissimum

RUBIACEAE

EVEN WHEN LEAFLESS, *Calycophyllum candidissimum* is strikingly lovely. It has a tall, lean, upward-stretching silhouette of sinewy, layered limbs that are luminous with rusty red, flaking bark, and its new foliage, which is transparent and sealing wax red, makes it incandescent against the spring sunshine. In Cuba, it has been given the colourful, descriptive names of Prawn's Broomstick and Gourd Stick, which reflect its florid, bony structure. The opposite, petioled, thin-textured, elliptic leaves are pointed at each end, shiny green above and paler below. During the dry winter months, *C. candidissimum* puts on a display of unique blooms that closely resemble those of its close relative, *Pogonopus speciosus*, also of the Rubiaceae clan. With the maturity of the small, white, 4-lobed, slightly fragrant flowers, which are held in crowded, branched corymbs at the ends of the twigs, several flowers in each cluster produce an enlarged, white, leaf-like calyx lobe. Over its long flowering period, *C. candidissimum* is punctuated with these little, eye-catching, fluttering, snowy white banners. The sapwood is pale yellow, while the heartwood is greyish, strong, resilient and fine-textured and takes a good polish; it has been popular for construction, cabinetwork and agricultural implements. Although rare in cultivation, this splendid tree qualifies as an excellent choice for landscape use. In its native regions, *C. candidissimum* is considered to be an important honey plant.

✳✳✳ *C. spruceanum*; (Hook.), Peru, Bolivia and Brazil, to 25 m (82 ft). MULATTO or MULATEIRO-DE-VARZEA is native to Brazil, where it grows near rivers and is occasionally inundated. This lanky, sparsely branched tree blooms in late winter and bears ample panicles of small, simple, fragrant, starry, pure white flowers without enlarged calyx lobes. Its bark, like *C. candidissimum*, is smooth and reddish. (10–12)

C. candidissimum; the tiny fls have large, white, long-stemmed sepals.

C. candidissimum; a young specimen is shown glowing in the early-morning sunlight at the Jardin Botanico Nationale, Cuba.

C. candidissimum; with glowing red bark, which resembles that of some spp. of the Myrtle family.

C. candidissimum; a few, shaggy, red-barked limbs support the sparse foliage of this charming sp.

Camellia sinensis

TEA

(L.) Kuntz.   200 spp.

Thea sinensis

THEACEAE

50ft ⌐15m

50ft
15m   0

TEA OF COMMERCE consists of the cured young leaves and tender tips of the small tree *Camellia sinensis*, which originated near the source of the Irrawaddy River, on the border of N Burma and SW China. It is a straggling tree or small shrub, with dark green, smooth, shiny, finely toothed leaves. The white or pale yellow flowers are like miniature, cultivated *Camellia*, with a typical boss of bright yellow stamens at their centres. The leaves of *C. sinensis* contain alkaloids such as caffeine, theobromine and a volatile oil, all of which give tea its stimulating effects and unique flavour. Tea was originally used medicinally, but gradually became the chief beverage of China in the 5th century AD, although it did not reach Europe until the 17th century. Finally, it was the 'wild tea', *C. sinensis* var. *assamica* ([Masters] Kitam.), a larger leafed SE Asian variety known as Assam hybrid, which was found to be more suited to cultivation in the humid British colonies of Ceylon (now Sri Lanka) and Assam, in India, that became more widely cultivated for modern industry. Tea trees are pruned to waist height to accommodate the pickers, who nip off the young tips of the shoots; for finer teas, only the very young leaves are taken. These leaves are withered, rolled, fermented, dried and sorted into grades to make English-type black tea (such as Pekoe, Orange Pekoe and Souchong). Alternatively, China or green tea (Gunpowder or Hyson) is produced by steaming the rolled leaves without withering or fermenting them. Although green tea is a little bitter compared with black tea, connoisseurs consider it more stimulating and better for the health. Chinese teas are often scented by adding fragrant flower petals of such species as *Jasminum sambac*, *Michelia* spp. and *Murraya paniculata* to the leaves when they are drying. Brick tea is a cheap, coarse tea that is mixed with a glutinous substance and moulded into 'bricks' in China; it is popular in Tibet, Siberia and Mongolia.

ORIGIN	Assam, India
HEIGHT	5–15 m (16–50 ft)
TYPE	evergreen foliage tree
STATUS	limited distribution
HABITAT	cool, humid tropical highlands
GROWTH	slow
FLOWG	winter
DRY TOL.	low
SALT TOL.	low
LIGHT	partial shade to full sun
SOIL	humid, slightly acid
NUTRIT.	magnesium-rich fertilizer; deep, organic mulch
HAZARDS	none
PROBLEMS	camellia die-back; fungus
ENVIRON.	insect nectar
PROPAG.	seeds; cuttings; layers
LEAVES	simple; dark green, glossy leathery; serrated, with black-tipped teeth
FLOWERS	showy; white, to 2 cm (0.8 in.); 7–8 waxy petals; many bright yellow stamens; lightly fragrant
FRUIT	a capsule, to 1 cm (0.4 in.); 3-celled, hard-shelled, containing 3 seeds
USE	small tree for cooler sites; specimen; hedging; botanic collection; bonsai subject; container; conservatory
ZONE	8–10

C. sinensis; white, or pale yellow fls like miniature, cultivated *Camellia*.

C. sinensis; kept low to accommodate the tea pickers in a tea garden in Alexandra Bay in N Qld, Australia. The trees on the right are not cut to the same extent.

C. sinensis; showing the 3-celled, green fr. of this slow-growing sp.

C. sinensis; a compact tree with handsome, dark green, glossy foliage. Only small, new lvs are picked.

An impressive tea garden that is situated in the Boh Tea Plantation in the Cameron Highlands, Peninsular Malaysia.

Cananga odorata

YLANG-YLANG

(Lam.) Hook. f. & Thoms.   2 spp.

Canangium odoratum

ANNONACEAE

50ft ─ 15m

50ft

15m   0

THE RENOWNED *Cananga odorata* is a very fast-growing tree that is particular about its habitat – if crowded, it will bolt upwards to become fastigiate and abort its lower limbs. In its infancy, this tree appears somewhat herbaceous, having green bark and whorls of softly woody, over-sized branches divided into very long, willowy stems. The simple, thin, bright green, juvenile leaves, which are evenly spaced along the entire length of these long stems, appear to be pinnate, but as the tree matures it develops a woody habit and a lax, full, wide crown. *C. odorata* is renowned for its remarkable flowers that have 6 narrow, waxy, dull yellow petals that are dangled like tiny banana skins from a stout stalk. They are powerfully fragrant and their beautiful scent will carry far across a garden. Traditionally, in India, *C. odorata* was mixed with coconut oil to prepare Macassar oil, used as a gentleman's hair dressing, hence antimacassars that protected chair backs, so fashionable and necessary in the 19th century. Known in the trade as Ylang-Ylang, this species is cultivated for its essential oil, which is extracted from the flowers and used in the making of perfume. There are productive plantations in Madagascar and other islands off the E African coast, where it is an important crop; tons of the flowers are harvested and dried yearly, particularly for a French perfume house. In Polynesia, flowers are used in leis or steeped in coconut oil and used as a hair, body or massage oil. *C. odorata* is vigorous and easily cultivated and is often grown on tea plantations in Sri Lanka for its lightweight, odourless timber, which is cut for plywood and used to make tea chests. It is also used in Qld, Australia, for rainforest regeneration because of its rapid growth and its bird- and bat-attracting fruit.

NOTE: *C. odorata* has become naturalized in some regions.

ORIGIN	India, SE Asia to Australia
HEIGHT	up to 20 m (66 ft)
TYPE	evergreen, small flowering tree
STATUS	not threatened
HABITAT	evergreen woodland
GROWTH	fast
FLOWG	year-round
DRY TOL.	moderate
SALT TOL.	moderate
LIGHT	full sun
SOIL	rich, well-drained
NUTRIT.	balanced fertilizer yearly; deep, organic mulch
HAZARDS	none
PROBLEMS	weak, brittle wood
ENVIRON.	insect nectar; wild fruit for birds and bats
PROPAG.	seeds; cuttings
LEAVES	simple; bright green; to 20 cm (8 in.); oblong-ovate, in 2 ranks
FLOWERS	showy; citron-yellow; with 6 long, waxy petals held in 2 ranks; intensely fragrant
FRUIT	a syncarp, to 2.5 cm (1 in.); fleshy, oblong, black when ripe
USE	small shade tree; specimen; courtyard; large planter; public open space; civic centre; large conservatory
ZONE	10–12

C. odorata; cultivated in trop. regions where their strongly fragrant blooms are harvested to extract an essential oil used in perfumes.

C. odorata; the fr., which will ripen black, is eaten by birds and bats.

C. odorata; long, willowy stems with opposite lvs that give the appearance of being pinnate.

C. odorata var. *fruticosa*; a sterile, dwarf form that grows up to 2 m (6.6 ft) high, with extra petals and smaller lvs.

Canarium ovatum

PILI NUT

Engler   77 spp.

BURSERACEAE

ORIGIN	E Asia to Philippines
HEIGHT	up to 20 m (66 ft)
TYPE	evergreen, dioecious, fruiting tree
STATUS	vulnerable
HABITAT	humid tropical forests
GROWTH	moderate
FLOWG	year-round
DRY TOL.	low
SALT TOL.	low
LIGHT	full sun
SOIL	humid, rich, deep
NUTRIT.	high-potassium fertilizer; deep, organic mulch
HAZARDS	none
PROBLEMS	none
ENVIRON.	insect nectar
PROPAG.	seeds
LEAVES	pinnate; deep green; leaflets in 3–7 pairs, plus terminal leaflet
FLOWERS	inconspicuous; yellowish white; very small, 3-parted, on sturdy, branched inflorescence
FRUIT	a drupe, to 7 cm (2.75 in.); triangular, 3-valved; blue-black skinned; kernel (or nut) white, oily, edible
USE	shade tree; street tree; nut tree; public open space
ZONE	10–12

100ft – 30m
75ft
22.5m   0

CANARIUM SPECIES occur mainly in the Indo-Malaysian–NW Pacific region, with 2 species in Africa. Native of lowland rainforests, these trees form lush canopies of large, rich green leaves and plank-like buttresses – even small aerial roots. Although dioecious, some male trees are able to produce perfect flowers with functional pistils; they produce smaller fruit but are also capable of fertilizing female flowers. *Canarium* are prolific once established and are valued for their bluish black, pulpy fruit that are dangled on sturdy cords and filled with white, oily pulp, with hard-shelled, spindle-shaped, almond-flavoured nuts that are eaten fresh or roasted or otherwise processed for their oil. They are not perishable and keep very well in storage. **Canarium ovatum** is the Pili nut of the Philippines, where it is popular as a sweet or salted confectionery and was for many years harvested almost entirely from wild trees. The oil is used industrially to make sun-tan lotions and cosmetics, and for cooking. Some *Canarium* spp. exude a fragrant, sticky, pale yellow resin that is processed to make varnishes or incense for religious ceremonies. In Indonesia, traditionally the bark is used to alleviate malaria and the leaves for vertigo. Its hard, reddish timber is considered mahogany-like.

*** **C. australianum**; (F. Meull.), N Australia and New Guinea, to 25 m (82 ft). SCRUB TURPENTINE is a coastal species. The fruit is small, bluish purple; its oily seeds are eaten. Wood is useful and has a turpentine odour. A medicinally useful species. (10–12)

*** **C. vulgare**; (Leenhouts), (syn. *C. commune*), Malaysia, to 25 m (82 ft). KENARI-NUT or JAVA ALMOND has nutritious nuts containing 11% protein and a high oil content, known as Solomon Nut oil (SLN). In the Solomon Is, where the fruit is harvested from wild trees, the islanders swing from the treetops using handmade ropes, which leads to many fatal accidents. *Canarium* trees take about 6–8 years to bear fruits from seeds. (10–12)

C. ovatum; has small, long-stalked, 3-parted, female fls.

C. ovatum; has delicious, protein-rich nuts known regionally as Pili Nuts, Pak Lam or Chinese Olives.

C. vulgare; Java Almond is valued for these blue-black, pulpy fr, which are dangled on sturdy cords.

Canarium australianum; this hardy, often coast. sp. forms a bouyant canopy of large, glossy, pinnate lvs. The wood has a turpentine smell when cut.

89

Canella winterana

PEPPER CINNAMON

(L.) Gaertn.   1–2 spp.

Winterana canella; Canella alba

CANELLACEAE

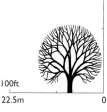

100ft ⌐ 30m

100ft

22.5m   0

THIS FAIRLY RARE, SMALL TREE is native to thickets on dry, coastal limestone throughout the W Indies and parts of S Florida. With a deep green, dense crown of obovate or spoon-shaped, leathery, aromatic leaves, **Canella winterana** is a superb xerophytic species. Fragrant flowers, which are borne terminally in tight clusters, are clasped first in little, round, frosted, blue-green sepals. As these buds open, they reveal rich red stamens surrounded by 5 little, fleshy, dark red petals that are purplish on their outer surface. Flowers are replaced by equally ornamental, crimson, strongly aromatic berries. **C. winterana** is a source of Canella Bark, which has an aroma of cinnamon and cloves and was used by early settlers as a condiment, medicinally as a tonic and stimulant or to flavour and enhance tobacco. Canella Bark was exported, to a limited extent, from the Bahamas earlier last century, chiefly for medicinal purposes. Like cinnamon, the orange-coloured, inner bark was cut into quills, which yielded about 1% of essential oil. It was discovered that if Canella flowers were dried and then rehydrated in warm water, they smelled of musk and could be used as such. When gathered and dried, the berries are reported to be hot like black pepper. Despite its great usefulness, the leaves and stems of this species proved toxic to poultry in feeding trials in St Croix, in the Virgin Islands, while in Puerto Rico, crushed leaves and twigs were said to be thrown into rivers to stupefy fish before catching them. Although prodigiously slow growing and drought-resistant, *C. winterana* is a superb, classic evergreen and is well worth planting for its aromatic foliage and its ornamental flowers and fruit. The sapwood is olive-brown and the heartwood is blackish in colour. The wood is hard and very heavy, but seldom used because of its small size. It is an important honey plant.

ORIGIN	Florida, USA; W Indies
HEIGHT	up to 15 m (50 ft)
TYPE	evergreen flowering and fruiting tree
STATUS	vulnerable
HABITAT	dry coastal woodland on limestone
GROWTH	slow
FLOWG	intermittently, all year
DRY TOL.	high
SALT TOL.	moderate to high
LIGHT	part shade to full sun
SOIL	alkaline, fertile
NUTRIT.	balanced fertilizer yearly
HAZARDS	possibly toxic parts
PROBLEMS	aphids; sooty mould
ENVIRON.	bee nectar; wild fruit for birds
PROPAG.	seeds
LEAVES	simple; dark green, to 10 cm (4 in.); glossy, aromatic
FLOWERS	showy; purple, violet or red; held in compact cymes; fragrant
FRUIT	a berry, to 1 cm (0.4 in.); bright crimson-red, ripening purplish; held in compact clusters
USE	shade tree; specimen; small fruit tree; accent; xerophytic; bonsai subject; conservatory
ZONE	9–12

C. winterana; with pungent, berry-like, rich crimson fr.

C. winterana; tight, posies of waxy, blue-bloomed buds slowly open to reveal the cheerful, little crimson fls that have bright golden 'eyes' at their centres.

C. winterana; a young tree in the dry, rocky, native woodland in George Town, Grand Cayman, W Indies.

C. winterana; orange-coloured inner bark was traditionally cut into 'quills' that yielded an essential oil.

90

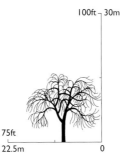

100ft - 30m

75ft
22.5m   0

Casimiroa edulis

WHITE SAPOTE

Le Llave & Lex.   5 spp.

RUTACEAE

ORIGIN	Mexico; S America
HEIGHT	up to 18 m (60 ft)
TYPE	evergreen fruiting tree
STATUS	not threatened
HABITAT	dryish highland forests at 600–1,000 m (2,000–3,000 ft)
GROWTH	moderate
FLOWG	winter (poss. also autumn)
DRY TOL.	moderate
SALT TOL.	moderate
LIGHT	full sun
SOIL	fertile, well-drained
NUTRIT.	citrus-type fertilizer; deep, organic mulch
HAZARDS	seeds toxic
PROBLEMS	fruit flies; black scale
ENVIRON.	bee nectar; wild bird fruit
PROPAG.	seeds; grafts; layers
LEAVES	3–7 foliate; deep green; leaflets to 12.5 cm (5 in.); petiole to 10 cm (4 in.)
FLOWERS	inconspicuous; greenish yellow; in short, terminal or axillary clusters
FRUIT	a drupe, to 10 cm (4 in.); yellow-green; pulp cream, somewhat peach-flavoured; seeds large, white
USE	small shade tree; small fruit tree; agricultural shade; screening; backyard tree
ZONE	8–10

CASIMIROA EDULIS is a vigorous, subtropical species of the citrus clan, native of high elevations of C America. This is a much-branched tree, with light grey, thick, warty bark, and often long, drooping branches. Its foliage is palmately compound and mostly evergreen but may shed leaves in light frosts. Small, odourless, greenish white, winter flowers are followed by apple-shaped, pale yellow, thin-skinned fruit containing soft, buttery, creamy white or yellow flesh that is sweet but sometimes bitter-resinous. *C. edulis* fruit has a remarkably high food value, almost as rich in protein, carbohydrate and vitamins as banana. It is sometimes described as being peach-flavoured, and in Mexico it is popular for use in milkshakes and ice creams, although in some areas it is considered unhealthy if eaten in quantity. The bark, leaves and seeds contain a glucoside named Casimirosine that has proved to have an hypnotic and sedative affect. Regionally, it is used medicinally to induce sleep, and a decoction of the leaves is also used to treat diabetes, while in China it is popularly used to lower blood pressure. There has been medical research into these various properties but with little commercial success to date. Although literature often reports that *C. edulis* does not flourish below a 900 m (1,500 ft) elevation, the tree is grown successfully at sea level in Florida, Hawaii and Puerto Rico. It will endure droughts, but requires adequate moisture to fruit well. Fruiting from seed takes 7–8 years but only 4–5 years from grafted stock. These are honey plants.
*** *C. sapota*; (Oerst.), S Mexico to Nicaragua, to 12 m (39 ft). Woolly-leafed White Sapote usually has larger, thicker leaflets that are velvety white on their undersides. Flowers are 4-parted. Fruit is up to 11.25 cm (4.4 in.) wide, ovoid, irregular and knobbly, with rough, pitted skin and somewhat bitter flesh. (10–12)

C. edulis; has many medical applications (used for hypertension in China).

C. edulis; its bark contains a glucoside called Casimirosine that has proved to have an hypnotic and sedative affect.

C. edulis; has thin-skinned fr. with soft, buttery, resinous flesh that is said to be mildly soporific if eaten in quantity.

C. edulis; this fecund, multi-trunked Citrus relative grows at the Fruit and Spice Park in Homestead, Florida.

Cassia fistula

SHOWER OF GOLD

L.   30 spp.

C. excelsia

FABACEAE (Caesalpinioideae)

CASSIA FISTULA is a short-trunked tree with wide-spreading, smoothly barked, heavy limbs and soft leaves that are bright green and slightly silvery downy when young; as they age, they darken and thicken. Although deciduous, this species is seldom leafless in equatorial regions and may change leaves a small number at a time. Few trees are more lovely in bloom; draped in cascades of fragrant, yellow flowers, the Shower of Gold greatly resembles the temperate region's Laburnum and is known in Asia as Indian Laburnum. In full bloom, *C. fistula* lights up a garden on a dull day by casting a golden glow on everything surrounding it. Although it flowers over a relatively long period, from early to late spring, it can sometimes be triggered into bloom later by light pruning. *C. fistula* is fairly slow growing but is easy to propagate, although in drier regions it may become leggy and benefit from early shaping to promote a good canopy structure. Like many species in this large family, the huge, cylindrical fruit take approximately a year to mature. The pods have their ceramic-like, orange seeds tightly packed in a sweet, sticky pulp that has great appeal to monkeys, birds and other animals, thus aiding their dispersal. In India and the Middle East, the sweet, honey-like pulp is used as a laxative. Indeed, in the days before refrigeration, in Egypt the pods were harvested, set out for several days and sprinkled with water to encourage fermentation, so as to be able to preserve the pulp for this purpose. In India, the pulp is used to enhance tobacco, while in Sri Lanka, the blossoms are used for votive temple offerings. In Indonesia, the flowers and leaves are used as purgatives and the roots to treat scabies and skin ulcers. The reddish heartwood is very hard, heavy and durable and is suitable for construction, as well as for cabinet and inlay work.

ORIGIN	India
HEIGHT	up to 20 m (66 ft)
TYPE	semi-deciduous flowering tree
STATUS	not threatened
HABITAT	dry deciduous forest
GROWTH	fairly slow
FLOW G	early to late spring
DRY TOL.	moderate to high
SALT TOL.	moderate
LIGHT	full sun
SOIL	fertile, well-drained
NUTRIT.	general fertilizer yearly; organic mulch
HAZARDS	none
PROBLEMS	susceptible to scale
ENVIRON.	seeds and pulp eaten by birds and monkeys
PROPAG.	seeds (soaked first)
LEAVES	pinnate, bright green; 16 pairs leaflets, thin-textured
FLOWERS	showy; clear yellow; in long racemes, 15–75 cm (6–30 in.); slightly fragrant
FRUIT	a legume, to 60 cm (24 in.); blackish brown, tubular; seeds in sweet, sticky pulp
USE	flowering tree; avenue or street; specimen; public open space; civic centre
ZONE	10–12

C. fistula; ceramic-like sds are tightly packed in a sweet, sticky pulp.

C. fistula; after a prodigiously dry spring, this Golden Shower photographed in Cairns, N Qld, Australia, has responded to heavy rain and is overloaded with bloom.

C. fistula; a pale yellow cultivar (probably *fistula × javanica*) grows at Fairchild Tropical Gardens in Miami, Florida.

C. fistula; with pale, skin-like bark. The reddish heartwood is very hard, heavy and durable.

Cassia afrofistula; (Brenan.), (syn. *C. sieberiana*), E Africa, to 10 m (33 ft). AFRICAN LABURNUM, MBARAKA or KIANGI is a small, decid. tree of the dry African savannahs or forest edge along river valleys. Tough, leathery, dull green lvs with oblong, lflts are adapted to withstand long, arid seasons. Buds, stalks and young pods are pubescent. Blackish sd pods are cylindrical and somewhat compressed to 60 cm (24 in.). Tree photographed at the Kampong, in Miami, Florida. (9–11)

Cassia bakeriana; (Craib.), Myanmar, to 12 m (39 ft). PINK CASSIA is a fairly rare *Cassia*, native to semi-open, lowland to medium elevation forests. It forms a superb, widespread canopy, with lvs in flattened clusters. Young lvs are dense, velvety, silky hairy. Spring fls are held in upright, unbranched, dark, red-purple, stalked clusters. Deep pink fls are clasped in hairy, dark red-purple calyxes; blooms fade to almost white with age. Fr. is brown or grey, narrowly tubular and finely hairy. (10–12)

Cassia brewsteri; ([F. Meull.[Benth.), Qld, Australia, shrub or tree, to 12 m (39 ft). LEICHHARDT BEAN is native to dry rainforest and open woodland. Young growth is thinly downy. It is distinguished by its generous panicles of yellow blooms that deepen to orange and rusty red. Fr. is a long, dark brown, cylindrical pod containing many sds set in spongy tissue. Aborigines eat young, roasted sds. This is an autumn-flowg sp. (10–12)

Cassia marksiana; ([Bailey] Domin.) (syn. *Cassia brewsteri* var. *marksiana*), to 25 m (82 ft). This fragrant sp. is still relatively rare and largely unknown in its native Australia, where it is found in humid lowland rainforest. In cultivation, this fast-growing sp., which prefers a sunny position, is fairly frost-hardy. Spring flowg. (9–12) NOTE: **some authors consider this sp. to be a variety of** *C. brewsteri.*

93

Cassia grandis; (L. f.), C and S America, to 30 m (66 ft). Horse Cassia is also known as Coral Shower or Canafistula. This is one of the first *Cassia* to bloom in the spring; it virtually explodes into bloom after the first rains, although the fls are relatively short-lived. The large, swollen, black pods are thought to resemble a horse's male organ - hence its common name. This is an important bee plant. A spring-flowg sp. (10–12)

Cassia javanica; (L.), (syn. *C. nodosa*), SE Asia, from 25–40 m (82–131 ft). Known as Apple-Blossom Cassia or Javanese Cassia, this sp. has a spiny trunk. In spring, it bears masses of bubbly, fragrant, rose-pink blooms that gradually fade to palest pink, giving them a variegated appearance. The heartwood is beautifully marked and is used for house building in Java. Here it is shown in N Qld, Australia. A spring-flowg sp. (10–12)

Cassia javanica × grandis; (Gainepain), (syn. *C. renigera*), Commonly known as Red Cassia, this Burmese, spontaneous hybrid has softly hairy twigs and young foliage. Lvs with 13–21 prs of lflts that are oblong and blunt-tipped, as in *C. grandis*. The fls are deep, rose-pink and slightly smaller than *C. fistula × indochinensis*, in shorter, more compact clusters. Cylindrical fr. is very long and narrow. Blooming in early summer. (10–12)

Cassia moschata; (HBK.), from Cuba to C and S America, to 20 m (66 ft). Bronze Shower or Canafistula Sabanera blooms in early spring. With a wide-spreading habit, the twiggy canopy tumbles around its slender superstructure. New, softly pubescent, loosely packed blooms are clear yellow but deepen to orange or brick-red with age. This superb tree was photographed in spring at the Jardin Botanico de Cienfuegos, Cuba. (10–12)

Cassia × nealii; (Irwin and Barneby), Hawaii, to 10 m (33 ft). This var., which is widely known as Rainbow Shower, was first produced in Hawaii by applying pollen from *C. fistula* to *C. javanica*. It was named in honour of Marie C. Neal, who wrote the classic *In Gardens of Hawaii*. This tree has fragrant fls that emerge creamy yellow and gradually fade to deep rose-pink with age. The timber of this sp. is excellent. Spring flowg. (**10–12**)

Cassia sp. (undescribed), Paluma Range, Qld, Australia, to 8 m (26 ft). This unnamed sp. occurs in the margins of upland rainforest and adjacent *Eucalyptus* forest. It is a small tree with a compact crown of glossy, dark green foliage and chains of rich, gold-yellow fls. The underside of the new growth is often purplish. It is very similar to the native *C. tomentella*, of Qld, (Velvet Cassia), for the soft-hairiness of its young shoots. (**10–12**)

Cassia queenslandica; (C. White), Qld, Australia, to 15 m (50 ft). There are several yellow-flowered spp. of Cassia native to eastern Australia and they tend to be rather similar. *C. queenslandica* is distinguished by its lvs, which have 10–16 ovate, leathery lflts and its pendulous infl., to 35 cm (14 in) long. The slender fr. pod is finely ribbed, to 50 cm (20 in.), with the sds held transversely. Spring flowg. (**10–12**)

Cassia roxburghii; (DC.), (syn. *C. marginata*), S India and Sri Lanka, to 10 m (33 ft). Commonly called Red Laburnum, Ceylon Senna or Roxburgh's Cassia, this is a stunning, most original *Cassia*, with neat, tumbling, layered foliage. Pinkish red and white fls are held in little racemes along upper axils of the lvs and persist for many weeks. Fairly slow growing, this sp. blooms in late summer or early autumn. (**10–12**)

Castanospermum australe

MORETON BAY CHESTNUT

A. Cunn. ex Mudie   12 spp.

FABACEAE (Papilionoideae)

MORETON BAY CHESTNUT, or Black-Bean Tree, is a slow-growing tree of the silty, coastal rainforests and riverbanks of NE Australia and the large island of New Caledonia in the SW Pacific. This species is not, in fact, a chestnut, or even related to that family, but is one of the most distinguished members of the Fabaceae (legume) family, with an open, rounded, evergreen crown of lustrous pinnate leaves that have slender, slightly curved leaflets. However, even without its singular flowers *Castanospermum australe* would still be a most desirable tree. The flowers are ramiflorous, that is, blooming on the old wood, trunk and major branches, and this means that they are hidden amongst the leaves. They are held in copious racemes, but if it were not for the fact that they are so brilliantly coloured, they probably would not be seen or admired, although they are no secret to the native Lorikeets that feed on their sweet nectar. Contained in an inflated, orange calyx, each little bouffant, greenish yellow pea-flower gradually deepens in colour to orange, then turns deep red as it matures, giving the impression of great variegation. Curving, whiskery stamens add to the vibrant drama of the inflorescence, giving it a plume-like air. The flowers are succeeded by obese, woody, cylindrical pods that contain large, globose, chestnut-like, dark brown seeds. These are poisonous but recently have been studied as a possible HIV vaccine. Researchers have found Castanospermine in all parts of the tree, but mainly in the seeds. It alters the surface of a virus, making it non-infectious. Despite being toxic, traditionally these seeds were eaten by the Aborigines in Australia, who usually roasted them for a long time before consuming them. Timber of *C. australe* is hard and heavy. It is used to make furniture of a teak-like quality. The cut bark smells of cucumber.

100ft — 30m	
110ft	
33m	0

ORIGIN	Australia and N Caledonia
HEIGHT	up to 40 m (130 ft)
TYPE	deciduous, large flowering tree
STATUS	not threatened
HABITAT	coastal forests; lowland rainforests
GROWTH	slow
FLOWG	spring
DRY TOL.	low
SALT TOL.	low
LIGHT	full sun
SOIL	rich, slightly acid loam
NUTRIT.	high-potassium fertilizer; deep, organic mulch
HAZARDS	seeds poisonous
PROBLEMS	none
ENVIRON.	nectar for birds
PROPAG.	seeds
LEAVES	pinnate; rich green; to 15 cm (6 in.); leaflets 11–15, leathery
FLOWERS	showy; yellow to orange, then red; to 4 cm (1.5 in.); ramniflorous, in racemes
FRUIT	a legume, to 30 cm (12 in.); oblong, curved; seeds 5, black or dark brown, very large and chestnut-like
USE	flowering tree; public open space; street tree; specimen
ZONE	9–12

C. australe; the very thick, woody fr. contain large, poisonous, chestnut-like sds.

C. australe; the little pea blooms are held directly on the limbs in copious racemes. They change from yellow to deep red before they abort.

C. australe; in Yungaburra, N Qld, the red carpet below tells of the abundant spring bloom within its canopy.

C. australe; timber is hard, heavy and has a Teak-like quality. It is used to make high quality furniture.

ORIGIN	Honduras; Nicaragua
HEIGHT	up to 45 m (148 ft)
TYPE	deciduous, monoecious or dioecious, large foliage tree
STATUS	not threatened
HABITAT	openings in moist lowland forest
GROWTH	fast
FLOWG	year-round
DRY TOL.	low
SALT TOL.	low
LIGHT	full sun
SOIL	rich, well-drained
NUTRIT.	balanced fertilizer yearly
HAZARDS	none
PROBLEMS	none
ENVIRON.	nectar for insects; wild fruit for birds
PROPAG.	seeds, shortly viable
LEAVES	simple; bright green; to 40 × 20 cm (16 × 5 in.); oblong, cordate; rusty hairy petioles and veins
FLOWERS	inconspicuous; yellow or orange; held in crowded, head-like, scaly clusters, in leaf axils
FRUIT	fig-like, multiple, to 10 cm (4 in.); green to yellow to orange, then red; mollusc-like, in dense clusters; seeds white, papery
USE	specimen; source of rubber; botanic collection; public open space
ZONE	10–12

100ft ⌐ 30m
75ft
22.5m ⌐ 0

Castilla elastica

PANAMA RUBBER TREE

Sessé   3 spp.

C. lactiflora; C. panamensis

MORACEAE

A ROBUST, HEAVILY TRUNKED TREE, becoming buttressed in age, *Castilla elastica* has spreading limbs divided into long, drooping, stout, hairy twigs that hold two rows of large, coarse, densely brown-hairy leaves. This species, which is a monoecious species, has greenish yellow male and female flowers held in crowded clusters at leaf axils. Female flowers are followed by mollusc-like, succulent, reddish fruit with juicy pulp that is sweetish and edible and contains one pendulous, white, papery seed. *C. elastica* has copious rubbery latex and in the 20th century was an important source of rubber. When the 15th-century explorer Christopher Columbus came upon this species in the Americas, he was fascinated to find both the Olmecs and Aztecs using its latex in various ways, particularly as bouncing balls called Pelota to play games known as Tlachtl. Traditionally, the trees have been tapped locally and the rubbery latex, which dries to become tough but resilient, fashioned into useful artifacts. When *C. elastica* trees are 8–10 years old, they may yield up to 25 kg (55 lb) of latex apiece, albeit of poor quality. In fact, until 1920, most of the world's rubber supply came from *C. elastica* and *Hevea brasiliensis* trees tapped in Amazonia. *C. elastica* was extensively cultivated in C America for this purpose but it was found difficult to tap the trees for their latex and *Hevea brasiliensis* finally superseded this species in the Panama rubber industry. Currently, the latex of *Castilla elastica* is often tinted with natural dyes and used to fashion local handcrafts. Excellent raincoats are also made by coating heavy cotton cloth with crude rubber. The pale grey bark, which strips off easily, is used as cord. Locally, mats are made by beating out the bark and these are used as blankets and for clothing.

NOTE: *C. elastica* has proved to be an invasive species.

C. elastica; has coarse, oval lvs that are also heavily veined.

C. elastica; with distinctive, pale grey bark, which strips off easily and is used as cord.

C. elastica; a sturdy old specimen at Cienfuegos, Cuba.

C. elastica; photographed in spring with its curious, mollusc-like fr. (below) and fls (above), in the superb arboretum of the Jardin Botanico de Cienfuegos, Cuba.

97

Casuarina equisetifolia

SHE-OAK

L.   17 spp.

CASUARINACEAE

100ft ┌ 30m

75ft
22.5m   0

ORIGIN	Asia to Australia and the Pacific
HEIGHT	up to 35 m (115 ft)
TYPE	evergreen, large, dioecious foliage tree
STATUS	not threatened
HABITAT	sandy coastal strand
GROWTH	fast
FLOWG	summer
DRY TOL.	high
SALT TOL.	high
LIGHT	full sun
SOIL	well-drained
NUTRIT.	normally not necessary
HAZARDS	none
PROBLEMS	shallow-rooted; invasive
ENVIRON.	none (wind-pollinated)
PROPAG.	seeds
LEAVES	scales; grey-green; minute, held in nodal whorls around needle-like stems
FLOWERS	inconspicuous; females, in cones; males, in cylindrical catkins
FRUIT	a cone, to 2 cm (0.8 in.); globose, woody; with tiny, winged seeds
USE	seaside; windbreak; coastal screening; hedges; topiary; xerophytic
ZONE	9–12

BEEFWOOD, HORSETAIL, Sea Willow, Australian- or Whistling-Pine are just a few of the common names given to this ubiquitous pioneer tree of tropical strands, with its remarkable ability to grow with its roots in the surf. Like *Gymnostoma*, *Casuarina* species are not conifers because, although very reduced and modified, they have actual flowers with stamens and cone-like fruit with an embryo. The apparent needle-like leaves are actually modified twigs that affect photosynthesis; the true leaves are reduced to minuscule, tooth-like scales and held at the joints of the twigs. *Casuarina equisetifolia* grows rapidly to form a tall, slender, sparsely limbed tree with a thin crown of wiry, drooping, green, needle-like twigs. The bark is a light, greyish brown and becomes rough, furrowed and shaggy with age. The twigs, which function as leaves, remain green and are shed systematically. Minute, staminate flowers, crowded in rings in the leaf scales, are held in narrow, cylindrical, terminal clusters, while minute, pistillate flowers that lack petals form ball-like clusters of dark red styles. The fine-textured, reddish brown heartwood (known in its native Australia as She-Oak, Ironwood or Beefwood) is very hard and heavy, but susceptible to termites. It burns with great heat and is used for domestic fuel. This is an important species in Polynesia where it is known as Toa. Traditionally, its wood has been used to fashion spears and clubs. When young, *C. equisetifolia* may be shaped into many forms and is popular for hedges and topiary. *** *C. cunninghamiana*; (Miq.), E Australia, to 20 m (65 ft). RIVER SHE-OAK is a fast-growing species of riverbanks and brackish lagoons. It has a dense, ballooning canopy and a tendency to sucker. Its timber is hard and durable and is used to make shingles and axe handles and for ornamental joinery. It is an excellent wood for fuel. (8–12)

NOTE: *C. equisetifolia* is a very invasive species.

C. equisetifolia; tiny cones hold winged sds.

C. equisetifolia; in the islands of Hawaii where, as throughout the tropic. coasts, it helps to bind the sands and collect salty deposits from the sea winds.

C. equisetifolia; typical reddish, flaking bark conceals the hard, fine-textured, reddish brown heartwood.

C. cunninghamiana; this dark-foliaged sp. is easily recognized in its natural habitat in N Qld, Australia.

Catalpa longissima

SPANISH OAK

(Jacq.) Dum. Cours.   11 spp.

Macrocatalpa longissima

BIGNONIACEAE

ORIGIN	Cuba and the Bahamas
HEIGHT	up to 25 m (82 ft)
TYPE	semi-deciduous flowering tree
STATUS	uncommon to rare in some habitats
HABITAT	dry lowland woodland
GROWTH	fairly slow
FLOW'G	spring, or intermittently
DRY TOL.	high
SALT TOL.	moderate
LIGHT	full sun
SOIL	fertile, well-drained
NUTRIT.	balanced fertilizer yearly
HAZARDS	none
PROBLEMS	somewhat brittle wood
ENVIRON.	bee nectar
PROPAG.	very fresh seeds
LEAVES	simple; bright green; to 11 × 4 cm (4.3 × 1.5 in.); elliptic, shiny, leathery
FLOWERS	showy; whitish pink trumpets; frilly petals, with purple-striped, yellow throats
FRUIT	a capsule, to 67 cm (26.3 in.); string-like; seeds winged; shortly viable
USE	large flowering tree; public open space; large planter; specimen; xerophytic
ZONE	9–12

CATALPA LONGISSIMA tends to be anonymous most of the year. A relative of the grander *C. bignonioides*, or Common Catalpa, of N America, the Spanish Oak bears little family resemblance. This is a large, evergreen species that usually forms a tall, straight bole that is furrowed and ridged, becoming buttressed with age and supporting a buoyant, fairly slender crown of narrow, wavy, lightish green leaves held on arching, drooping, limbs. *C. longissima* begins flowering when it is still small, triggered into bloom after rain breaks a long, dry period. Then only the height of a tall shrub, it foams in effervescent bundles of pale pink blossoms. The little, inflated, crimped trumpets are typically Bignoniaceae and specially detailed, white, blushed pink, with purple bee lines and a yellow-splashed, inflated throat. In each bundle, a few flowers open at one time; they are short-lived and soon abort. Only one fruit develops from a flower cluster. It is exceedingly long, thin and wire-like and is dangled from the tree for months before it matures and splits longitudinally into 2 curving parts. If they are to be harvested for their minute, winged, shortly viable seeds, these fruit must be observed very carefully. The light, pinkish brown timber is finely marked with dark lines resembling oak and is highly valued for making fine furniture, for flooring, boat building and general construction. *C. longissima* was widely cut in the early days of development but large trees are now rare in many regions. These species are honey trees.

*** *C. punctata*; (Griseb.), Cuba and the Bahamas, to 10 m (33 ft). ROBLE DE OLOR; native of dry woodland. Oblong, leathery leaves are scurfy scaly below, punctured with tiny translucent glands, called *punctata*. This species differs from *C. longissima* in having flowers that are light yellow with orange and brown bands. (10–12)

C. longissima; at Fairchild Gardens, Florida, showing its gauzy, new spring foliage.

C. longissima; fls are typically Bignoniaceae and are held in lavish bundles after a dry period is broken by heavy rain.

C. punctata; lvs are rounded, thicker and spathulate. Its small fls are yellow with an orange and brown, banded throat.

C. longissima; the light, pinkish brown timber is finely marked with dark lines resembling oak .

99

Cavanillesia platanifolia

QUIPO

(Bonpl.) HBK   3 spp.

MALVACEAE (formerly Bombacaceae)

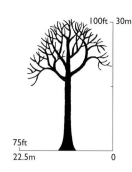

100ft ⌐ 30m

75ft
22.5m   0

THE QUIPO, OR PANAMA CANOE TREE, is a monumental pachycaul, which often dominates the moist and dry forests from Panama to Peru. It closely resembles the Baobab, with its obese, smooth, soaring trunk and sparse crown of angular, stretching limbs carrying 5–7 lobed, long-petioled leaves. In spring, before the new foliage, come small, red, waxy flowers filled with many stamens and cupped in heavily tomentose calyxes. In winter, when its gaunt skeleton is leafless, *Cavanillesia platanifolia* is enlivened by bundles of large, iridescent, rusty red, 5-winged samaras that hold the spindle-shaped, indehiscent, lightweight fruit that have evolved to be blown along the ground by the wind and thus dispersed. Like Balsawood (*Ochroma pyramidalis*), *C. platanifolia* grows so very rapidly that its wood is extremely lightweight. Traditionally, the soft, pithy wood has been used locally to make dugout canoes and rafts for the great rivers of this equatorial region. These rafts are designed to float heavier timber down the rivers. Logs, which have escaped the coastal logging operations and floated away, have been found washed up on the shores of the islands of the Azores, towards the coast of Spain, having drifted across the Caribbean Sea and Atlantic Ocean, creating a hazard for yachts and small ships.

*** *C. arborea*; (K. Schum.), (syn. *Pourretia tuberculata*), Brazil, to 30 m (100 ft). IMBARÉ or BARRIGUDA-BRANCA develops a hugely swollen, bottle-shaped trunk that could be taken for that of a Baobab. Leaves are rounded, deep green, deeply veined, with long petioles. Small, white flowers are held rigidly erect on stout, tomentose stems and cupped firmly in thick, rusty pubescent calyxes; the blooms have an abundant, dishevelled bundle of white stamens. Fruit to 25 cm (10 in.), similar to *C. platanifolia*. (10–12)

ORIGIN	Panama to Peru
HEIGHT	up to 65 m (213 ft)
TYPE	deciduous, large, pachycaul timber tree
STATUS	not threatened
HABITAT	lowland, moist and dry forest
GROWTH	fast
FLOWG.	spring, before leaves
DRY TOL.	high
SALT TOL.	low
LIGHT	full sun
SOIL	well-drained, humid
NUTRIT.	balanced fertilizer annually
HAZARDS	none
PROBLEMS	none
ENVIRON.	insect nectar
PROPAG.	fresh seeds
LEAVES	simple; rich green; large, shallowly 5–7 lobed; smooth, long-petioled
FLOWERS	fairly showy; 5 red petals; to 5 cm (2 in.); stamens in 5 clusters; set in tomentose calyxes
FRUIT	a samara, to 10 cm (4 in.); spindle-shaped, with 5 longitudinal, reddish wings; containing 1 seed
USE	specimen; public open space; botanic collection
ZONE	10–12

C. platanifolia; a vigorous, pachycaul tree with a straight, solitary trunk, which is traditionally used to make canoes in its native Panama. Photographed at Jardin Botanico, Cienfuegos, Cuba.

C. arborea; cupped blooms are held rigidly erect on tomentose stems.

C. platanifolia; iridescent, rusty red, 5-winged samaras hold spindle-shaped, indehiscent, lightweight fr.

C. platanifolia; an old tree showing its tendency to become bottle-shaped in age.

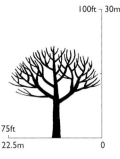

100ft ⌐ 30m

75ft
22.5m ———————————————— 0

ORIGIN	Trop. America
HEIGHT	up to 20 m (66 ft)
TYPE	evergreen, dioecious foliage tree
STATUS	not threatened
HABITAT	moist limestone; cleared land
GROWTH	fast
FLOWG	intermittently, all year
DRY TOL.	moderate
SALT TOL.	low
LIGHT	bright shade to full sun
SOIL	rich, water-retentive
NUTRIT.	balanced fertilizer annually; deep, organic mulch
HAZARDS	none
PROBLEMS	possibly invasive
ENVIRON.	fruit for bats, birds and animals
PROPAG.	seeds (slow); cuttings
LEAVES	palmate; dull green; to 60 cm (24 in.); pubescent, silvery white below
FLOWERS	showy; pale yellow; gelatinous, sweet, edible, in fingered clusters on long stems
FRUIT	a nutlet; minute, multiple; to 12 cm (4.7 in.); sweet, jelly-like, finger-shaped; eaten by bats
USE	small shade tree; large planter; specimen; accent; humid shade garden; courtyard; large conservatory
ZONE	9–12

Cecropia peltata

TRUMPET TREE

L.   75 spp.

C. asperima

CECROPIACEAE

CECROPIA PELTATA tends to be more of a fast-growing, short-lived, mammoth herb than a tree. It has a slender trunk, often with stilt roots supporting a sparsely branched canopy of soft stems that hold spirals of massive, rounded, palmate, 7–9 lobed leaves. These are dull, dark green above, silvery white below. The succulent, woody trunk is solid, but the limbs are hollow, as are the long leaf petioles, which are cut and used as blow tubes or trumpets, hence the common name. These voids are often inhabited by Azteca ants, which feed on food substances (glycogens) secreted at the petiole bases. Hollow internodes are burrowed into by pregnant female ants, which raise their broods there and attack other predators, such as leaf-cutting ants (*Attadiscigera* species), which have very powerful jaws. Flowers are dioecious and are held in paired, finger-like clusters. When ripe, these greyish, hollow, long-fingered 'hands' of female flowers are edible, being sweet, slightly gelatinous and filled with minute seed. These pioneer trees stand out on the wooded slopes of their rich, humid habitat, signalling their presence by the silvery flashes of their foliage as it is stirred by the slightest breeze. Discarded brown and bright silver leaves curl up into fantastic contortions as they dry and are much prized by florists. Known as Yagrumo in Puerto Rico, the soft, brittle wood is combined with cement and made into an insulation board. In Trop. America, the wood is named Imbauba and is used for making boxes, crates, paper pulp and also matches. (It ignites easily and is used for lighting fires by means of friction.) In Cuba, the dried leaves of *C. peltata* are smoked to alleviate asthma, while the caustic sap has been used to make a crude type of rubber.

*** *C. palmata*; (Willd.), W Indies to Brazil, to 15 m (50 ft). SNAKEWOOD TREE differs in having long, blunt-tipped leaves with 7–11 lobes. (10–12)

C. peltata; with sweet, edible, long fingered fr.

C. peltata; pale grey bark and soft, weak, lightweight, brittle timber is subject to attack by termites.

C. peltata; as green and white lvs fall and dry, they contort to create splendid shapes, much sought after by florists.

C. peltata; is a fast-growing sp., which makes an attractive ornamental because of its dramatic foliage, as well as its intriguing, edible, jelly-like, fingered fr.

Cedrela odorata

WEST INDIAN CEDAR

L.   8 spp.

C. sintenisii

MELIACEAE

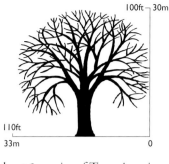

THIS CLOSE RELATIVE of *Swietenia* and *Toona* is one of about 8 species of Trop. American *Cedrela*, which are valued for their fine timber. **Cedrela odorata** grows very quickly and under suitable conditions eventually attains great height. The sinuous, stout trunk has smooth, grey bark at first, later becoming rough, furrowed and slightly buttressed with age. With its upward-sweeping, heavy limbs, **C. odorata** forms a billowing crown of long, graceful, pinnate leaves that are pinkish red on emergence. This tree is easily recognized by its languidly drooping pinnae that lend the tree an exhausted air. Diminutive, greenish cream flowers are held erect in slender, terminal clusters and are eventually replaced by small, oval, woody capsules that imitate those of mahogany, splitting open when ripe into 5 valves, each of which contains many long, winged seeds. It is the flowers and fruit that differentiate *Cedrela* from the very closely related, *Toona*. *Cedrela* flowers have their ovaries raised on cylindrical discs and the seeds of its larger fruit are winged only on the lower part. The heartwood of **C. odorata** is lightweight and reddish brown, with prominent growth rings, and, although reminiscent of mahogany in colour, it is softer, tougher, more lightweight and easily worked. This wood contains a strongly aromatic oil, causing the timber to smell of garlic when freshly cut (as do the leaves and twigs), which results in the timber being repellent to insects. Apart from use in general construction, furniture and cabinetry, cedar wood is highly valued as a lining for cigar boxes and the interiors of wardrobes because of its pleasant aroma. Curiously, at some stage **C. odorata** was planted on the island of Stromboli, off the coast of southern Italy, and is now naturalized there. This is an important honey tree.

ORIGIN	Trop. America
HEIGHT	up to 30 m (100 ft)
TYPE	deciduous, large foliage (timber) tree
STATUS	rare in some habitats
HABITAT	dry lowland woodland
GROWTH	very fast
FLOWG.	summer
DRY TOL.	high
SALT TOL.	moderate
LIGHT	full sun
SOIL	deep, fertile
NUTRIT.	balanced fertilizer annually
HAZARDS	none
PROBLEMS	borers
ENVIRON.	moth and bee nectar
PROPAG.	seeds (fresh)
LEAVES	pinnate; deep green; leaflets 10–22, oblique, ovate
FLOWERS	fairly showy; greenish white, held in erect panicles
FRUIT	a capsule, to 4 cm (1.5 in.), woody, dehiscent, held in branched panicles; seeds winged
USE	large shade tree; public open space; street tree; xerophytic
ZONE	10–12

C. odorata; in Cuba, this sp. is important for use in making cigar boxes. Closely related to Mahogany, it is also considered one of the most desirable of all timbers in Trop. America.

C. odorata; with widely branched panicles of small, white fls.

C. odorata; fr. capsules become woody before they open to form star-like shapes and to expel their sds.

C. odorata; wood is used for lining cigar boxes and the interiors of closets as it imparts a pleasant aroma.

A view of rich farmland in the magnificent valley of Vigñales, near Pinar del Rio in western Cuba. *Cedrela odorata* is an important, indigenous timber in Cuba, where it is used to line the boxes for their renowned cigars.

Ceiba pentandra

KAPOK

(L.) Gaertn.   11+ spp.

Bombax pentandrum; Eriodendron anfractuosum

MALVACEAE (Formerly bombacaceae)

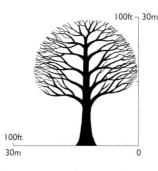

100ft – 30m

100ft
30m   0

CEIBA PENTANDRA is possibly the noblest tropical tree. It has immense, buttressed roots anchoring the colossal, lofty, thorny mast and supporting a massive spiral of horizontal limbs that hold billowing, palmately lobed foliage in level planes of bright green. A towering pachycaul, its prodigious superstructure has adapted to grow in all corners of the tropics. As it matures, it sheds its lower limbs, becoming pole-like. In winter, clustered at the stem ends, small, green, acorn-shaped calyxes open to reveal the cupped, compact, pale yellow or whitish, heavily waxy flowers with sturdy, curling, golden stamens. Nocturnal and bat-pollinated, they have a milky odour. After pollination, they are replaced by large, boat-shaped, felty pods filled with milky hairs. When they split open, the tree looks like it is covered in giant cotton balls. Eventually, the little seeds, which are attached to long, silky hairs, are launched to float far and wide. It is this silk that provides the famed kapok that is used to fill pillows, cushions and mattresses. Kapok was used in Europe during World War 11 for padding lifesaving jackets. *C. pentandra* is the tallest species in Africa, where it is planted for its cotton crop; it often signals the location of a village from far away and is revered in some customs as a habitat for spirits. The wood is very soft and exceedingly lightweight, rather like Balsawood. The young fruits and seeds are eaten or made into food-cake for cattle; the leaves and roots are medicinal. An important honey plant.

*** *C. aesculifolia*; ([HBK] Britt. & Bak. f.), to 25 m (82 ft), C America. With a spiny trunk and branches. Flowers are yellow or white, with purple stamens. (10–12)

NOTE: *C. pentandra* may be invasive.

C. pentandra; with clusters of waxy yellow nocturnal fls with milky odour.

C. pentandra; a volunteer sapling in a car park in Grand Cayman, W Indies, demonstrates its remarkable structure.

C. pentandra; after pollination, fls are replaced by large, boat-shaped, felty pods stuffed with silky hairs.

C. pentandra; a fairly young specimen growing in the brackish, coral sand of the Cayman Is in the W Indies.

(1) ***Ceiba acuminata***; (Rose) Mexico, to 10 m (33 ft). This charming, small, slow-growing tree with a dense, rounded crown of digitate lvs was photographed in the arboretum of the Jardin Botanico de Cienfuegos, Cuba.

(2) The little blooms with their curling strap-like petals and sprightly, deep pink stamens measure about 10 cm (4 in.) across. (10–12)

The massive, buttressed trunk of this venerable ***C. pentandra*** was photographed several times at the Singapore Botanic Gardens, but it was not until this gentleman was asked to stand beside it that the gargantuan scale was obvious.

Ceratonia siliqua

CAROB

L.   2 spp.

FABACEAE (Caesalpinioideae)

50ft 15m
50ft
15m   0

ORIGIN	Arabia
HEIGHT	up to 10 m (33 ft)
TYPE	evergreen, dioecious, small fruiting tree
STATUS	threatened in the wild
HABITAT	fertile, slightly humid coastal plains or valleys
GROWTH	slow
FLOWG.	spring
DRY TOL.	high
SALT TOL.	moderate
LIGHT	full sun
SOIL	fertile, well-drained
NUTRIT.	balanced fertilizer annually
HAZARDS	none
PROBLEMS	none
ENVIRON.	bee nectar; fruit for bats
PROPAG.	seeds (soaked in water); cuttings; layers
LEAVES	pinnate; bright green above, dull green below; leaflets oval, leathery
FLOWERS	inconspicuous; yellow-green, tinted red, petal-less, dioecious; males are pungently scented
FRUIT	a legume, to 30 cm (12 in.); black-brown, ridged, swollen; seeds set in sweet mucilage
USE	seaside; shade tree; small street tree; specimen; fodder plant; xerophytic
ZONE	8–10

CERATONIA SILIQUA has hefty, twisting limbs supporting a wide, coarse canopy that gains great character as it matures. It is dioecious, with just the female trees bearing fruit, but 5% of male trees are normally needed for pollination in plantations. In spring, minute, petal-less flowers are held along old branches. The males are catkin-like, with a pungent smell, and the females are solitary. Their embryos form into little, green, sturdy beans that become black-brown as they ripen and may be eaten by bats, which disperse the seeds. Depending upon the amount of humidity, fleshy fruit grow up to 30 cm (12 in.) long, with large seeds embedded in a sweet, mucilaginous pulp that is about 50% sugar, as well as a gum, tragasol, a substitute for gum tragacanth. *C. siliqua*, a very slow-growing, drought-resistant and long-lived species, has found many uses and has long been valued in the subtropics as a source of fodder. Both its leaves and fruit are used. The *Bible* tells of John the Baptist's 'husks that the swine did eat', a supposed reference to the Carob beans recorded as having sustained St John when he wandered in the wilderness. (*C. siliqua* is often called St John's Bread.) It has also earned its place in history as it was the foliage and the ripe, juicy fruit swollen with sweet mucilage that nourished Wellington's cavalry when they wintered along the north Spanish coast during the Peninsular War between 1808–14. Perhaps its greatest fame, however, is the claim that its large seeds were the original carat weight used by jewellers and apothecaries. The fruit is fermented to make alcohol and the seeds have been used as a coffee and chocolate substitute, as a colouring for bouillon cubes or as a diabetic flour suitable for use as a baby food. A type of confectionery is derived from the pulp. The heavy, red timber is used for furniture. The seeds must be soaked for 24 hours before sowing. This is an important honey plant.

C. siliqua; minute, petal-less, staminous male fls are semen-scented.

C. siliqua; in Altea, on the central coast of Spain, where it is one of the commonest trees. It is grown as a cash crop and is known there as Algarroba.

C. siliqua; curious, petal-less female fls are held erect on a sturdy, red stem.

C. siliqua; heavy, leathery and indehiscent, Carob beans have sweet, juicy mucilage around their sds.

50ft — 15m

50ft
15m — 0

Ceratopetalum gummiferum

CHRISTMAS BUSH

Sm.   5 spp.

CUNONIACEAE

ORIGIN	Australia, endemic
HEIGHT	up to 10 m (33 ft)
TYPE	evergreen, small flowering tree
STATUS	protected species
HABITAT	open forests; rainforest gullies; coastal scrub
GROWTH	moderate
FLOWG	spring
DRY TOL.	moderate
SALT TOL.	moderate
LIGHT	full sun
SOIL	well-drained, acid loam
NUTRIT.	high-potassium fertilizer; deep, organic mulch
HAZARDS	none
PROBLEMS	difficult to propagate
ENVIRON.	insect nectar
PROPAG.	seeds; cuttings
LEAVES	3-pinnate; dark green above, paler below; with serrated margins
FLOWERS	showy; white, to 6 mm (0.2 in.); 5-parted calyx enlarges to 2.5 cm (1 in.) and turns deep red
FRUIT	a capsule, to 5 mm (0.2 in.) diam.; woody; with a single seed and persistent, red calyx lobes
USE	specimen; accent; summer-flowering small tree; large container; civic centre; bright conservatory
ZONE	9–11

CERATOPETALUM GUMMIFERUM is considered by many to be Australia's most beautiful flowering tree. Native of NSW and Qld, *C. gummiferum* is usually found as a tall shrub but may, under ideal conditions, reach 10 m (33 ft), with a slender trunk and a dense, fine-textured, low-branching crown. If Australians are asked why they so love this species, they will say for its stunning, red Christmas blooms, but they may be surprised to learn that it begins flowering in spring, when the flowers are minuscule and white, not red. At this time they are surrounded by 5 little, creamy white sepals, that, over the next month or two, as the petals fall, gradually enlarge to 4 times their original size, and blush first pink and then red. This evolved to protect the little fruit capsules and to provide the wings with which they can float away from the tree. By midsummer – Christmas-time in the southern hemisphere – the flowers have given way to tiny, ripe fruit, the sepals have deepened to a beautiful cherry red and the dry bushland is illuminated by the spectacle of its billowing, flaming filigree, which is perfect for use as Christmas decorations. *C. gummiferum* tolerates light frost. Modern Australian cultivars include forms with pure white bracts or specific shades of red.

*** *C. apetalum*; (D. Don); NSW and Qld, Australia, to 33 m (108 ft). COACHWOOD or SCENTED SATINWOOD is one of the most important timber trees of SE Australia. It is found in the coastal brush forests and has a clear, robust trunk that may become buttressed with age. The long, narrow leaves are simple, with serrated margins, and are an unusual pale blue or purple as they emerge. The sepals of the starry, little flower are white but turn red as they mature. The heartwood, which is fragrant and smells of caramel, is pale pink and contains red sap. This renowned timber was popular in the past for coach-building; latterly it has been used to make marine ply. (9–11)

C. gummiferum; little white, starry fls are followed by red calyxes.

C. apetalum; starry cream 'fls' redden as they mature into sd capsules.

C. gummiferum; a sturdy specimen in the cool uplands of N Qld, Australia.

C. gummiferum; many Australians consider this small tree their favourite native sp. for its stunning, red Christmas blooms.

Cerbera manghas

PONG-PONG

L.

3–4 spp.

APOCYNACEAE

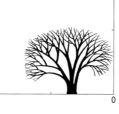

50ft – 15m

50ft
15m 0

CERBERA MANGHAS, a coastal dweller of Polynesia westwards to SE Asia and the eastern shores of Africa, is adapted to endure littoral life. Although generally found as a small tree, it may reach to 20 m (66 ft). Its copious, acrid latex and leathery, lacquered leaves, its woody, polished, plum-like fruit, its heavily waxy blooms and densely branched, supple superstructure have all evolved to withstand tough conditions. Clustered on sturdy, erect panicles are held abundant posies of large, funnel-shaped, pale ivory, pink-eyed flowers set in sturdy, pale green calyxes. The sweet fragrance of the blooms compensates for the poisonous nature of the large, ruby-red, lacquered fruit, the oily seeds of which are reported to contain the heart poison, cerebin. In the Philippines, it is used for stupefying and catching fish, and elsewhere as a ritual ordeal poison. In spite of this, in some places the bark, leaves and milky latex are taken internally as an emetic and purgative. The name *Cerbera* alludes to the toxic nature of the plant and derives from Cerberus, the name of the three-headed dog from Greek mythology that guarded the entrance to Hades, the underworld. The fruit is covered in thick, fibrous webbing and, waterproof and lightweight, it floats in the sea or in rivers to be distributed by the currents. *C. manghas* is in bloom almost continuously. To thrive, it demands very little, just well-drained soil.

*** *C. odollam*; (Gaertn.), from India to the Pacific, to 10 m (38 ft). YELLOW-EYED CERBERA, SEA-MANGO, BUTA BUTA or REVA is a species of the littoral forests. It is a bushy, narrowly crowned tree with greyish white, pustular bark. Its leaves are narrowly elliptic, dark, glossy green and they wither to orange-brown. Its flowers are distinguished by having yellow, rather than red, 'eyes' and spherical fruit. (10–12)

NOTE: these two species are often treated as one by some authors.

ORIGIN	Seychelles to Pacific
HEIGHT	up to 20 m (66 ft)
TYPE	evergreen, small flowering and foliage tree
STATUS	not threatened
HABITAT	rocky, sandy coastal woodland
GROWTH	moderate
FLOWG	year-round
DRY TOL.	high
SALT TOL.	high
LIGHT	full sun
SOIL	very well-drained
NUTRIT.	balanced fertilizer annually; organic mulch
HAZARDS	seeds and latex very toxic
PROBLEMS	none
ENVIRON.	insect nectar
PROPAG.	seeds
LEAVES	simple; dark green, to 30 cm (12 in.); spathulate, glossy, spiralled
FLOWERS	showy; white, with pink or yellow throat; held in large, lax clusters; fragrant
FRUIT	a drupe, to 10 cm (4 in.); ovoid; paired or not; fleshy, fibrous, dark pink to black
USE	seaside; small street tree; small flowering tree; accent; courtyard; large planter; conservatory; xerophytic
ZONE	10–12

C. manghas; showing their kinship to *Plumeria* and *Nerium oleander*, these delightful, fragrant blooms belie their toxic qualities.

C. manghas; with waterproof, lightweight, toxic fr. that is designed to float.

C. manghas; growing in the coast. town of Cairns, N Qld, where it is popular as a small, street tree.

C. manghas; narrow-elliptical lvs, while in *C. odollam* they are narrow-obovate.

ORIGIN	Trop. America
HEIGHT	up to 10 m (33 ft)
TYPE	evergreen, small flowering shrub or tree
STATUS	not threatened
HABITAT	thickets and woodland margins; wasteground
GROWTH	fast
FLOW'G	intermittently, all year
DRY TOL.	moderate to high
SALT TOL.	moderate
LIGHT	bright shade to full sun
SOIL	fertile, water-retentive
NUTRIT.	balanced fertilizer annually; organic mulch
HAZARDS	parts toxic to livestock
PROBLEMS	nematodes; scale; thrips
ENVIRON.	moth and butterfly nectar; wild fruit for birds
PROPAG.	seeds; greenwood cuttings
LEAVES	simple; rich green above, paler below; shiny; oblong, thin-textured
FLOWERS	showy; chalky white; tubular, 5-lobed, to 2 cm (0.8 in.); fragrant
FRUIT	a berry, to 1.7 cm (0.7 in.); elliptic, purplish black; containing several seeds
USE	hedging; screening; specimen; flower border; container; accent; conservatory
ZONE	9–12

50ft ⌐ 15m

50ft
15m ——————— 0

Cestrum diurnum

DAY JESSAMINE

L.   175 spp.

C. fastigiatum; C. diurnum var. fastigiatum

SOLANACEAE

WHILE NOT AS CELEBRATED as *Cestrum nocturnum* (known as Night-Blooming Jessamine), **Cestrum diurnum** shares many of its ornamental characteristics. Day Jessamine is so called, not because it blooms during the day (as does *C. nocturnum*), but because it is diurnally (daytime) fragrant, whereas the other is nocturnally (nightime) fragrant. Another distinguishing feature is the fruit; **C. diurnum** has inky purple berries, while those of *C. nocturnum* are white. **C. diurnum** grows to be a sizeable tree in some habitats, but its sibling is more shrub-like. While not as showy or as strongly perfumed, the flowers of **C. diurnum** are, nevertheless, quite splendid. After a rainy break during a dry period, they transform this commonplace, shrubby tree with their pearly white clusters. Unfortunately, the blooming period is relatively short and the flowers are fairly rapidly transformed into masses of succulent, pale green, then blackish purple berries that are known as Ink Berries in Hawaii and the W Indies. Both species attract fruit-eating birds with their succulent fruit, which explains why they are both so widely naturalized, even becoming a pest in some regions. Strangely, the fruit and leaves are considered toxic for livestock, although in Mexico both parts of the plant have been recorded as being used as a treatment for epilepsy and certain other disorders. They also play a role in religious rituals. The wood is whitish and hard. This easily propagated and fast-growing genus responds well to hard pruning, which produces a compact growth and abundant blooms; it is excellent for use as hedging or screening.

*** **C. nocturnum**; (L.), W Indies, up to 5 m (16 ft). NIGHT-BLOOMING JESSAMINE, semi-scandent species. Slim, tubular flowers spread their petals open at night. (9–12)

NOTE: these species are listed as invasive in Florida, USA.

C. diurnum; inky, purplish black fr. is sought after by birds.

C. nocturnum; nocturnally fragrant, these slender tubes reflex their petals in the evening.

C. diurnum; is triggered into bloom by rain after a dry period.

C. diurnum; with slender, pearly white trumpets with strongly reflexed petals. This sp. is fragrant during the day, attracting diurnal pollinators.

Chorisia speciosa

SILK FLOSS TREE

Kunth. 114 spp.

MALVACEAE (Formerly Bombacaceae)

100ft – 30m

75ft
22.5m   0

ORIGIN	Brazil, Argentina
HEIGHT	up to 20 m (66 ft)
TYPE	deciduous flowering tree
STATUS	not threatened
HABITAT	dry deciduous forests
GROWTH	fast
FLOWG	autumn
DRY TOL.	high
SALT TOL.	moderate
LIGHT	full sun
SOIL	rich, well-drained
NUTRIT.	balanced fertilizer annually
HAZARDS	spiny trunk
PROBLEMS	none
ENVIRON.	insect and bird nectar
PROPAG.	seeds; layers; grafting
LEAVES	palmate; deep green; leaflets to 12.5 cm (5 in.); lanceolate, long-petioled
FLOWERS	showy; pink, lavender, white or yellow, with whitish throat, to 12.5 cm (5 in.)
FRUIT	a capsule, to 20 cm (8 in.); woody, oblong; dehiscent; with seeds embedded in fine, silky fibre
USE	autumn-flowering tree; public open space; large planter; specimen; large conservatory; xerophytic
ZONE	8–10

LIKE *BOMBAX CEIBA*, the bright green, bottle-shaped trunk of the renowned **Chorisia** *speciosa* is covered in stout spines when it is young. As the heavy, wide-spreading limbs develop their whorled and layered structure, they become supported by massive buttresses. The leaves are large, digitate and glabrous, with long petioles. Autumn or early winter is marked by the emergence of the blooms from large, purplish buds that punctuate the thick, greyish stems. As the emerging buds swell, they burst open to reveal their luxuriant contents and suddenly the drab tree pulsates with colour, creating the impression of a swarm of silken butterflies. Plump and Hibiscus-like, the blooms have 5 flaring petals, shading from pink, lavender or yellow to milky white at the throat, and a stout staminal column. (It is said that no two *C. speciosa* have flowers exactly the same colour.) After the flowers are finished, large, 5-valved, greenish brown, velvety, dehiscent seed pods develop that are packed with diaphanous silky threads, or floss. These are used to fill pillows in some areas. *Chorisia*, and even more so *Montezuma*, clearly illustrate the confusion of earlier botanists in assigning plants to either the Bombax or the Hibiscus families, resolved by their recent amalgamation. Much research has been done on this species at the Kampong, of the National Tropical Botanic Gardens in Miami, Florida, where several superb, new hybrids have been created, as well as successful grafting. *C. speciosa* thrives in subtropical and frost-free regions.

*** *C. insignis*; (Kunth), Peru, Argentina, to 15 m (50 ft). The trunk is green and swollen, but has very small spines. This species has oblong-obovate leaflets, to 12.5 cm (5 in.), with serrated margins, and abundant, showy, white or yellow blooms. (10–11)

NOTE: the genus *Chorisia* has recently been included in the genus *Ceiba*.

C. speciosa; a large specimen at the Royal Botanic Gardens in Sydney, Australia.

C. speciosus; delicate, Hibiscus-like blooms may be lavender, deep pink or yellow, with golden, freckled throats; at a distance they resemble silken butterflies.

C. insignis; the white form of this illustrious, S American genus.

C. speciosa; when young, the green-skinned trunk is visciously armed with stout spines.

ORIGIN	Trop. America to Trop. Africa
HEIGHT	up to 6 m (20 ft)
TYPE	evergreen, shrubby, small fruiting and foliage tree
STATUS	vulnerable
HABITAT	coastal shoreline and sandy thickets
GROWTH	slow
FLOWG	year-round
DRY TOL.	high
SALT TOL.	high
LIGHT	bright shade to full sun
SOIL	very well-drained
NUTRIT.	balanced fertilizer annually; organic mulch
HAZARDS	none
PROBLEMS	none
ENVIRON.	bee nectar; wild fruit for birds and agoutis
PROPAG.	seeds; cuttings; layers
LEAVES	simple; rich green; almost round; shiny, leathery
FLOWERS	inconspicuous; greenish white; in erect clusters at leaf axils
FRUIT	a drupe, to 4 cm (1.5 in.); pink, crimson, whitish or purple; fleshy, edible; seed oily
USE	seaside; backyard tree; screening; hedging; dune stabilization; planter; topiary; xerophytic
ZONE	10—12

50ft — 100ft

50ft

15m — 0

Chrysobalanus icaco

COCOPLUM

L. 2 spp.

CHRYSOBALANACEAE

CHRYSOBALANUS ICACO is easily distinguished by its long, flexible, whip-like limbs clad in evenly spaced, stiffly erect, rounded, leathery leaves. It is slow growing and may form a scrambling shrub or, eventually, attain tree-like stature. In its sandy, coastal habitats, *C. icaco* often forms large, rambling, impenetrable thickets. For this reason, it has been planted in some regions to stabilize sand dunes. Greenish white, little flowers are held in erect clusters in the leaf axils and develop into spongy, white- or purple-skinned fruit. The purple-, or red-, skinned form is considered sweeter and to have more flavour than the white. The fruit contain a large nut-like, 5-ridged, edible seed that yields an oil, said to have been used domestically by the Carib Indians, who also strung seeds on twigs for use as candles. This is a fruit that many older inhabitants of the W Indies will remember eating on their way to school. Cocoplum was never planted, it just grew along the beaches and among the sandy thickets of the dry coastal areas and, like so many wild species, provided much more than food. Being rich in tannins, the astringent bark, fruit and leaves have been employed as a cure for dyspepsia and diarrhoea, as well as for skin complaints. Honeybees love the little, greenish white flowers and agoutis adore the large, plum-like, thin-skinned fruit that has astringent, fairly sweet, white, spongy flesh. In W Africa, stinging ants inhabit the plant, making nests in the leaves and keeping off intruders whilst they feed on the secretions of the fruit. *C. icaco* has become popular in the Americas for use as a seaside hedge plant, a popular form being *C. icaco* var. 'Red Tip', compact in form, with coppery red new growth. In Mexico, the leaves and fruit are processed for a black dye. This is a honey plant.

NOTE: *C. icaco* has become naturalized in E Africa, Vietnam and Fiji.

C. icaco; tiny fls are held stiffly erect at leaf bases and are charged with nectar.

C. icaco; a fine specimen at the Queen Elizabeth II Botanical Park.

C. icaco; white-skinned form of the fr. with soft, sweetish, spongy flesh.

C. icaco; a purplish variety along the sandy coast of Grand Cayman, where it is considered sweeter than the white form.

Chrysophyllum cainito

STAR APPLE

L.   43 spp.

Achras canaito

SAPOTACEAE

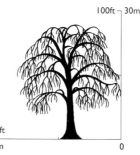

ORIGIN	Trop. America
HEIGHT	up to 30 m (100 ft)
TYPE	semi-deciduous, large fruiting (foliage) tree
STATUS	not threatened
HABITAT	low to medium elevation, humid woodlands
GROWTH	moderate
FLOWG	spring to summer
DRY TOL.	high
SALT TOL.	moderate
LIGHT	full sun
SOIL	fertile, well-drained
NUTRIT.	balanced fertilizer annually; organic mulch
HAZARDS	none
PROBLEMS	none
ENVIRON.	wild fruit for birds and bats
PROPAG.	seeds; cuttings
LEAVES	simple; dark green, coppery tomentose below; to 12 cm (4.7 in.); oblong to ovate
FLOWERS	inconspicuous; white or greenish; rusty pubescent, clustered at leaf bases
FRUIT	a berry, to 7.5 cm (3 in.); greenish or purplish; plum-like; flesh is sweet, jelly-like, with milky latex
USE	large shade tree; street tree; backyard tree; screening; specimen; large planter; conservatory
ZONE	10–12

ALTHOUGH **CHRYSOPHYLLUM CAINITO** is indigenous to most parts of Trop. America, it thrives in subtropical regions and is widely cultivated from Africa to SE Asia and Australia. *C. cainito* has milky sap characteristic of the Sapotaceae, which includes *Pouteria*, *Manilkara* and *Mimusops*, and is a splendid, decorative tree, most worthy as a garden ornamental. Growing to a medium height, it has a spreading, drooping, airy crown with dark, lacquered, leathery leaves that flash their superb, fiery, coppery suede linings when they are stirred by the breeze. Tiny, whitish purple, bisexual flowers are held in axillary clusters along the upper surface of the bearing twigs. Following the flowers, plump, apple-sized fruit are borne in great abundance. It has a thick, glossy rind filled with a gummy latex, while the edible, sweet flesh is white or purple and jelly-like, with several flattened, brown seeds. The common name, Star Apple, arose from the stellate arrangement of the fruit's cells and seeds. These number about 8 and in cross section form a star. Unfortunately, as with many common names, it may be confused with *Averrhoa carambola*, which is known as Star Fruit. Depending on humidity, *C. cainito* may retain its foliage in dry months or become completely deciduous. In Jamaica, because *C. cainito* never drops its fruit, the harvesters have to climb the trees to get it and it is known there as the Mean Tree. An unkind person may be referred to as being as 'mean as a Star Apple'. The wood is hard, heavy, strong and durable and used in construction and carpentry.

*** *C. splendens*; (Sprengl.), (syn. *Villocupsis splendens*), Brazil, up to 18 m (59 ft). COW'S TONGUE or LINGUA DE VACA is a superb, pyramidal-crowned species with dark green, leathery foliage, bronze velvety below. The fruit differs from *C. cainito* in being long, narrow, pale rusty plush, with 4 sharp angles; the pulp is reddish. (10–12)

C. cainito; with its rusty fls held at lf axils.

C. cainito; cultivated for its dark green, coppery-suede lined lvs. This sp. earned its common name Star Apple because of the star-shaped arrangement of the fr.

C. cainito; naked, but 'fully loaded' in the dry season, at the Fruit and Spice Park in Homestead, Florida.

C. cainito; is a splendidly, decorative tree, most worthy as a garden ornamental.

(1) *Chrysophyllum imperiale*; ([Linden ex Koch. and Fintelmann] Bentham and Hooker), (syn. *Chloroluma imperialis*; *Planchonella imperialis*), Brazil, to 15 m (50 ft). This tree was photographed at the Royal Botanic Gardens in Sydney, where it was planted by Prince Alfred, Duke of Edinburgh, in 1868. (2) At first glance, the enormous, heavily veined whorled lvs, with spinous-serrate margins and large, nippled fr. may suggest a species of the *Terminalia* clan. Native of lowland forests of Brazil's Atlantic coast, which has suffered degradation from urban development, this magnificent endemic is on the Red List of endangered species. (9–11)

(3) *Chrysophyllum oliviforme*; (L.), (syn. *C. monopyrenum*), USA and W Indies, to 10 m (33 ft). Satin Leaf, Damson Plum or Caimitillo, this is an elegant sp. with small, lustrous, leathery, dark green lvs, which, like *C. cainito*, are velvety, rusty pubescent below. (4) The olive-like fr. is dark purple, with a single sd and filled with dryish pulp. It is edible – but just. *C. oliviforme* is fairly slow growing and an excellent tree for smaller gardens, as well as for street planting. Unfortunately, some gardeners find the abundant fr. messy. (10–12) **NOTE: in some environments *C. oliviforme* has proved invasive, because the fr. may be widely dispersed by birds.**

Cinnamomum verum

CINNAMON BARK TREE

(Bl.) J. Presl.

C. zeylanicum

LAURACEAE

350 spp.

ORIGIN	S India; Sri Lanka
HEIGHT	8–17 m (26–56 ft)
TYPE	evergreen foliage tree
STATUS	not threatened
HABITAT	moist, well-drained soils, from sea level up to 700 m (2,300 ft)
GROWTH	slow
FLOWG	late spring to autumn
DRY TOL.	low
SALT TOL.	low
LIGHT	bright shade or full sun
SOIL	rich, humid, sandy; acid
NUTRIT.	high-potassium fertilizer; deep, organic mulch
HAZARDS	none
PROBLEMS	scale insects
ENVIRON.	bee nectar; wild bird fruit
PROPAG.	fresh seeds; cuttings; layers
LEAVES	simple; deep green; 3–5 longitudinal veins; lacquered; aromatic
FLOWERS	inconspicuous; yellowish white; in open panicles
FRUIT	a berry, to 1.4 cm (0.5 in.); purplish black; with a cup-like, persistent calyx
USE	small shade tree; humid shade tree; large planter; botanic collection; conservatory
ZONE	10–12

CINNAMON IS ONE OF THE EARLIEST RECORDED SPICES; it was used in China around 3,000 BC and is mentioned several times in the *Bible*. Aromatic bark and oil of this species were the first exported commodities of Ceylon (now Sri Lanka), even then commanding fabulous prices. ***Cinnamomum verum*** was previously known as *C. zeylanicum*, meaning from Ceylon. Like many of its huge clan, this species is a most handsome tree, with a widely spreading, dense crown and sturdy, erect trunk that has smooth, papery, spicily pungent bark. Aromatic, leathery and highly lacquered, the dark green leaves have the distinctive 3–5 longitudinal veins of the genus; they are brilliant red on emerging but soon deepen to rich, dark green. Expanded panicles of tiny, yellowish white flowers attract bees and are followed by little, black berries, which are widely distributed by the birds. In traditional cultivation, ***C.* verum** was grown as a bush, with seeds sown directly in a circle of about 1.3 m (4 ft) in diameter. As the saplings developed (up to 2 years), they were cut close to the ground after the rainy season, when the young bark was easily detached from stems. Saplings then resprouted and cultivation continued. Currently, trees are planted in plantations and coppiced every 2 years. After 10 years, rootstocks are removed, split up and replanted. The spicy, inner bark is detached from the outer skin and cut into short lengths. It dries a rich brown and contracts into quills. Other commercial bi-products include oleoresins and eugenol, essential oils extracted by steam distillation from bark, twigs or leaves. These oils are used as flavourings and for perfumes, soaps, incense and pharmaceuticals. However, they should be avoided during pregnancy as they may cause miscarriage. The unripe fruit, known as Cassia Buds, are also dried for seasoning. All species are honey plants

NOTE: many *Cinnamomum* spp. have proved invasive in some regions.

C. verum; fls held in light, airy panicles.

C. verum; the spicy inner bark is removed from the outer skin and cut into short lengths; it dries a rich brown and contracts into 'quills', which are sold as Cinnamon sticks.

C. verum; leathery, highly lacquered lvs have distinctive, 3–5 longitudinal veins. New growth is brilliant red.

C. verum; showing stripped bark. Commercial bark 'quills' are stripped from young saplings in the spring.

Cinnamomum aromaticum; (Nees.), (syn. *C. cassia*), Burma; endemic, to 13 m (43 ft). CASSIA BARK, C. LIGNEA, CHINESE- or BASTARD-CINNAMON is one of the oldest recorded spices (referred to in the *Bible* as the 'spice from India'). Bark is coarser than *C. verum*, but nevertheless made into quills and used to flavour food, toothpaste, incense and medicines. Lvs are distilled for oil for flavouring. Sds are sought after and spread by birds, bats and squirrels. Both *C. aromaticum* and *C. camphora* have less oil content than *C. verum* but are more pungent. **NOTE: an invasive sp.** (10–12)

Cinnamomum iners; (Reinw. ex Blume), Indomal., to 20 m (66 ft). WILD CINNAMON or KAYU MANIS is one of the commonest trees of thickets and waste spaces in Malaysia. This sp. is very closely allied with true Cinnamon, *C. verum*. New flushes of lvs occur several times a year when rain follows a dry spell; at first they are reddish pink fading to cream and then fresh green. The rancid smell of the fls attracts insects and beetles. Bark is used as a food flavouring and a tonic drink, as well as for making joss-sticks. Photographs taken at Singapore Botanic Gardens. (10–12)

Cinnamomum camphora; ([L.] J. Presl.), China, Japan and Taiwan, to 13 m (43 ft). CAMPHOR, CAMPHOR LAUREL or HO WOOD grows best at higher elevations or in the subtropics. Distillation of clippings, roots or wood chips provide solid, white camphor crystals and a volatile oil. Crystals were an ancient incense, perfume, embalming aid and the original mothball. Camphor oil is analgesic, as well as antiseptic. Chests lined with Camphor wood are used to preserve fine linen. Shown above are wild *C. camphora* trees in the Gold Coast of southern Qld, Australia, **where it is considered a noxious weed.** (8–11)

Citrus sinensis

SWEET ORANGE

(L.) Osbeck.   16 spp.

RUTACEAE

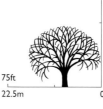

100ft ⌐ 30m

75ft

22.5m   0

SWEET ORANGE WAS INTRODUCED INTO EUROPE from China and Indo-China before 400 AD and brought to the New World by Christopher Columbus and other Spanish explorers. *Citrus sinensis* is not, in fact, considered a pure species but possibly a hybrid of *C. maxima* and *C. reticulata*; there are, in fact, only 16 true species of *Citrus*, but many long-established, natural hybrids. *C. sinensis* is a splendid small tree with a glossy, globular crown and fragrant, waxy blooms. It will grow both in the tropics and subtropics but is happier in the latter, which is demonstrated by the fact that the best fruit is grown in California and Florida, in the USA, in Australia and in the Mediterranean region. In the lowland tropics, some varieties of oranges may grow and fruit well, developing good flavour, but their skin remains yellowish green even when fully ripe, lacking the glowing, orange tones that appeal to consumers. *Citrus* must be propagated vegetatively to maintain their cultivar integrity and, due to their susceptibility to root nematodes and fungi, require grafting onto vigorous, resistant rootstock. Seedlings of Rough Orange, *C. aurantium*, or Rough Lemon, *C. jambhiri* and also related species such as *Clausena lansium*, *Swinglea glutinosa* or *Triphasia trifolia*, all of which adapt this species to different growing conditions, are used for this purpose. Being so popular and high in vitamin C, 66% of the fruit crop is processed into a fresh, pasteurized, concentrated or powdered form of orange juice. The peel yields an aromatic oil for use in making toilet soap, while an extract from the leaves, twigs and young fruit is known commercially as Petitgrain oil and is used in aromatherapy. *Citrus* species require full sun, preferring a well-drained, fertile sandy loam and a sheltered position protected from strong, drying winds. *Citrus* species are important honey plants.

ORIGIN	S China; Vietnam
HEIGHT	8–13 m (26–43 ft)
TYPE	evergreen, small fruiting tree
STATUS	not threatened
HABITAT	humid lowland plains
GROWTH	moderate
FLOWG	late spring and summer
DRY TOL.	moderate
SALT TOL.	low
LIGHT	full sun
SOIL	well-drained, fertile loam
NUTRIT.	complete, slow-release fertilizer, autumn and spring
HAZARDS	spiny
PROBLEMS	sooty mould; root nematodes
ENVIRON.	bee nectar
PROPAG.	grafted onto rootstock
LEAVES	simple; rich green; to 15 cm (6 in.); oblong to elliptic; winged petioles
FLOWERS	showy; creamy white; to 3.7 cm (1.5 in.); waxy; fragrant
FRUIT	a berry (hesperidium); to 9 cm (3.5 in.); oval to flattened; thin peel, sweet flesh
USE	backyard tree; large planter; accent; conservatory; bonsai subject
ZONE	9–10

C. sinensis; with heavily fragrant, waxy blooms.

C. sinensis; an orange grove in the Costa Blanca in Spain, near Valencia, where some of the world's finest oranges are grown in its perfect, frost-free environ.

C. sinensis; this photograph was taken near Valencia, N Spain, a region famous for its orange groves.

C. sinensis; local oranges in Cayman Is are not brightly orange-skinned but are just as sweet and juicy inside.

Citrus aurantifolia; (Swingle), Trop. Asia, to 5 m (16 ft). Mostly known as KEY LIME or WEST INDIAN LIME, grows in a dense, irregular manner, with its thorny twigs and branches criss-crossing in all directions. Being a pure sp., ***C. aurantifolia*** may be grown from sd (unlike most Citrus) that are grafted onto rootstock. They are usually picked when they are green, just before they turn yellow, when they are more aromatic. (10–12)

Citrus aurantium; (L.), (syn. *C. bigardia*), SE Asia, to 9 m (30 ft). Called SOUR-, or SEVILLE-, ORANGE or BIGARADE, this sp. is thought to be a natural cross between *C. maxima* and *C. reticulata* and was, for many centuries, the only *Citrus* of the Mediterranean. The roots are resistant to phytophthora rot and young plants are used as rootstock for sp. types of *Citrus*. ***C. aurantium*** is particularly renowned for making marmalade. (9–11)

Citrus limon; (Tan.), (syn. *C. limonum*), origin unknown, to 7 m (23 ft). The LEMON was first recorded in China around 1,000 AD; it spread in popularity across Asia to the Mediterranean around 1,150 AD and has been widely cultivated in that area ever since. It is thought to be a hybrid of *C. medica* and *C. aurantiifolia*. Essential lemon oil is extracted from the peel. This is strictly a warm temperate or subtrop. sp. (8–10)

Citrus margarita, ([Swing.] Lour), (*Fortunella margarita*) S China, to 5 m (16 ft), KUMQUAT or COMQUAT is subtrop. Bushy, and compact, it is both decorative and edible, and widely used as a container plant. Unlike other *Citrus*, the entire fr. may be eaten – pulp, rind and skin. Fls are fragrant but lvs are not aromatic; skin is oily aromatic and slightly spicy; whitish pith is sweet and inner pulp sour and lemonish. Requires grafting. Fruitg in summer. (9–11)

Citrus maxima; (Merrill), (syn. *C. grandis*), SE Asia to Philippines, to 15 m (50 ft). PUMMELO, SHADDOCK or BALI LEMON is a trop. sp. demonstrated here at Fruit and Spice Park, Homestead, Florida. This is a true sp. and the largest of all the *Citrus*. The fr. is enormous, to 8 kg (18 lbs). The flesh may be pink or white, sweet and very juicy, while the very thick skin is popular for making candied peel. (10–12)

Citrus medica; (L.), Indian endemic, to 7 m. (23 ft) CITRON, CIDRAN or ETROG has curious, elongated fr. and is said to have been brought from northern India to the Mediterranean by Alexander the Great. The 'fingered' form shown here, var. *sarcodactylis* ([Noot] Swingle), which is known as Buddha's Hand, is split into finger-like sections that have little flesh but are very aromatic. The peel is a major source of candied peel. (9–11)

Citrus reticulata; (Blanco.), (syn. *C. deliciosa*; *C. nobilis*), SE Asia, to 7 m. (23 ft) This is the popular MANDARIN or TANGERINE ORANGE. Apart from being delicious, *C. reticulata* is a very ornamental and abundant var. Many forms have been developed ('Clementine', 'Cleopatra', 'Dancy', 'Kinnow', etc.) and they all have peel that detaches easily from the sweet flesh. This sp. is better in the subtropics. (9–11)

Citrus × paradisi; (Macfad.), (hybrid from *C. maxima* × *C. sinensis*), GRAPEFRUIT, POMELO or PAMPLEMOUSSE. It forms a fairly small, sparse, spreading canopy with regular, spiny branching. All parts are large – lvs, spines, fls and fr.; the lvs have winged petioles. This trop. sp. is very alkaline- and drought-tolerant and easy to grow in the tropics. Cvs include red-fleshed vars like 'Red Blush' and 'Star Ruby'. (10–12)

ORIGIN	S China
HEIGHT	up to 12 m (39 ft)
TYPE	evergreen fruiting tree
STATUS	limited natural distribution
HABITAT	humid lowland woodland
GROWTH	fast, given suitable habitat
FLOWG	summer
DRY TOL.	moderate
SALT TOL.	low
LIGHT	full sun
SOIL	fertile, well-drained
NUTRIT.	fertilizer as for citrus; deep, organic mulch
HAZARDS	none
PROBLEMS	none
ENVIRON.	bee nectar; wild fruit for birds
PROPAG.	seeds; cuttings; grafting
LEAVES	pinnate; bright green; 5–9 foliate; leaflets ovate to lanceolate
FLOWERS	showy; ivory-white; held in cymose panicles; fragrant
FRUIT	a berry, to 2.5 cm (1 in.); globose, 5-celled; tawny yellow, resembling tiny limes; held in abundant clusters
USE	shade tree; specimen; backyard tree
ZONE	10–12

50ft ⌐ 15m

50ft
15m   0

Clausena lansium

WAMPI

(Lour.) Skeels.   23 spp.

Cookia punctata; Cookia wampi

RUTACEAE

CLAUSENA LANSIUM, a native of S China, is, like *Casimiroa edulis*, a distant relative of *Citrus*. *C. lansium* is equally valuable as a fruit tree or an ornamental. It has an upward-stretching habit and flexible limbs clad with spirally arranged, dark green, glossy, pinnate leaves that are slightly wavy but with coarsely toothed margins. Like most of the Rutaceae, they are aromatic; in this case they smell of anise when crushed. Held in spreading panicles, its tiny, white, fragrant flowers transform into small, globose or oval fruit resembling diminutive lemons arranged in branched, grape-like clusters. These fruit have a tough, thin, pliable, yellowish, minutely hairy rind that is oily and resinous and detaches easily from the yellowish white, mucilaginous flesh. Vaguely divided into 5 sections, the flesh is very juicy, with a taste of grapes or gooseberries, depending upon the variety, that is, either sweet or pleasantly sour. In Thailand, this is one of the most popular of fruit and they are eaten raw or made into marmalade or drinks. In Sri Lanka, they are popular for flavouring meat curries. *C. lansium* is native to humid habitats and requires watering in areas with a long, dry season, but given good conditions, it is relatively fast growing. Although it will tolerate limestone soils, *C. lansium* thrives best on rich, well-drained loam. The wood is white and close-grained, resembling boxwood.

*** *C. excavata*; (Burm. f.), India to SE Asia and New Guinea, up to 13 m (43 ft). PINK LIMEBERRY is a very widely distributed species, with lax, spreading growth and limbs ending in tassels of long, slender leaves. The twigs and leaf stalks are finely hairy, with a unattractive smell of resin, lime and ivy when crushed. The fruit is rounded, to 10 cm (4 in.), pulpy, translucent pink and gland-dotted, with a sour smell of resinous oranges. (10–12) Like *Citrus*, these species are important honey plants.

C. lansium; with wide panicles of tiny white fragrant fls.

C. lansium; anchored by a sturdy trunk. Wood is white and close-grained, resembling Boxwood.

C. lansium; in the arboretum of fruit trees at the Kampong of the National Botanic Garden in Miami, Florida.

C. lansium; long, abundant clusters of little fr., which resemble tiny lemons and are considered to taste of grapes or gooseberries. Crushed lvs are anise-pungent.

Clerodendrum minahassae

TUBE FLOWER

Teijsm. & Binn.   400 spp.

LAMIACEAE

ORIGIN	Celebes
HEIGHT	up to 7 m (23 ft)
TYPE	deciduous, small flowering (fruiting) tree
STATUS	limited distribution
HABITAT	humid lowland woodland
GROWTH	fast
FLOWG	late spring to late summer
DRY TOL.	moderate
SALT TOL.	low
LIGHT	bright shade or full sun
SOIL	fertile, well-drained
NUTRIT.	general fertilizer yearly; deep, organic mulch
HAZARDS	none
PROBLEMS	none
ENVIRON.	butterfly nectar
PROPAG.	seeds; cuttings; layers
LEAVES	simple; bright green; smooth, to 18 cm (7 in.); deeply veined
FLOWERS	showy; light yellow to white; held in terminal cymes; calyx fleshy, bright red, persistent
FRUIT	a drupe, to 1 cm (0.4 in.); blue or blue-black; fleshy, juicy, set in persistent calyx
USE	specimen; flower border; large planter; screening; conservatory
ZONE	10–12

THIS HUGE VERBENA GENUS is more renowned for its climbers, shrubs and the large Verbena clan than for its trees. Species are characterized by the prominent stamens and the frequently slender tube of the corolla, specifically adapted for moth or butterfly pollination. *Clerodendrum minahassae*, a soft-wooded, fast-growing and short-lived species, is more often a large shrub, although it is rated as a small tree. The large, deeply quilted, bright green leaves are held at an almost vertical angle on stout, grooved petioles. Evolving in spectacular flushes several times during the season, large, terminal cymes of white or light yellow flowers first emerge as eye-catching, pleated, pink-tinged buds set in stout, fleshy, deep green calyxes. With the expansion of its very long-tubed blooms, from each of which springs several crimson stamens, *C. minahassae* becomes a fountain of colour. As the flowers abort, the calyxes remain. They thicken and become a rich red, with little, juicy, blue or blue-black, berry-like fruit at their centres, and so the tree continues to decorate the landscape even without its blooms.

*** *C. quadriloculare*; ([Blanco]Merr.), Philippines, up to 8 m (26 ft), STAR BURST is similar to *C. minahassae* but has deeper green leaves that are rich violet below. Even without its sumptuous blooms, this species is a superb, foliage plant. With its winter display of massive, very long, pink-tubed, white blooms – often likened to fireworks – it is one of the most spectacular, winter-blooming tropical trees. (10–12)

*** *C. tomentosum*; ([Vent.] R. Br.), Australia, up to 15 m (50 ft). Known as LOLLY BUSH or HAIRY CLERODENDRUM, this is a spreading, woody species of rainforests and coastal, wet, sclerophyll forests. The tubular flowers are creamy white with long, whiskery stamens. The black, berry-like, glossy fruit is set in persistent, fleshy, red calyxes. (10–12)

NOTE: *C. quadriloculare*, along with some other spp., can sucker aggressively.

C. minahassae; with ornamental, bright red calyxes and blue fr.

C. minahassae; has a large, lax form with drooping, heavily veined lvs, pleated, rosy fl. buds and sprightly, long-tubed, white blooms with perky, red stamens.

C. minahassae; a heavy, coarse canopy of deeply quilted, bright green lvs.

C. quadriloculare; handsome dark foliage and exquisite winter blooms of the Star Burst Clerodendrum.

ORIGIN	W Indies
HEIGHT	up to 20 m (66 ft)
TYPE	evergreen, dioecious foliage tree
STATUS	vulnerable
HABITAT	dry, coastal limestone woodlands
GROWTH	slow
FLOWG	intermittently, all year
DRY TOL.	high
SALT TOL.	high
LIGHT	deep shade to full sun
SOIL	well-drained, fertile
NUTRIT.	balanced fertilizer annually; organic mulch
HAZARDS	poisonous fruit
PROBLEMS	scale insects
ENVIRON.	nectar for insects; fruit for bats
PROPAG.	seeds; cuttings; layers
LEAVES	simple; deep green; to 18 × 10 cm (7 × 4 in.); very thick, rigid, obovate
FLOWERS	showy; white, tinged pink; heavy, waxy petals
FRUIT	a capsule, to 8 cm (3 in.); very pale green, ripening brown; yellow seeds set in orange-red pulp, with latex
USE	seaside; small shade tree; indoor plant; large planter; screening; espaliered; conservatory; xerophytic
ZONE	10–12

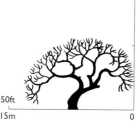

50ft ─15m
50ft
15m
0

PITCH APPLE

Jacq.   145 spp.

C. retusa; C. major

GUTIFFERAE

LIKE MOST MEMBERS of this genus, **Clusia rosea** may begin life as an epiphyte quite capable of destroying its host by strangulation or suffocation. This is a rugged tree, able to withstand drought, salt-spray, hurricanes, full sun or deep shade. The thick, rubbery leaves are almost indestructible; they remain on the limbs for a long time and they are often used as an autograph book, with the names being engraved on the pliable, waxy surface. There is a record that early Spanish Conquistadors used the leaves as playing cards, using a pin to mark out the figures in spots. The *Clusia* genus carries both male and female flowers on different plants. The male flower has a dense pad of stamens, all curving in a ring towards the centre, where there is a mass of reduced, depressed stamens covered with viscid, shiny resin to attract pollinators. The fruit is a tough, rubbery ball full of latex. It is yellow-green, ripening brown, and splitting into 7–9 parts that contain many yellow seeds set in orange-red pulp. Although considered poisonous, they are eaten by bats. In early times in the W Indies, the fruit was boiled in water and the viscous, waterproof, pitch-like latex skimmed off and used as caulking for the seams of wooden boats. The yellow, resinous latex of the bark, fruit and other parts of the tree hardens upon exposure and has been used as plaster and in local medicine. The heartwood is reddish brown, hard and heavy, but difficult to saw and susceptible to termites. Because of its slow growth and its endurance of low light, it is possible that *C. rosea* would do extremely well indoors, perhaps playing the 21st-century role of a 19th-century Aspidistra (Cast Iron Plant) in withstanding demanding conditions.
❋❋❋ *C. flava*; (Jacq.) W Indies, C America, up to 10 m (33 ft). CARD GUM or TAR POT has smaller parts and yellow flowers. Possibly scrambling; forming thickets. (10–12)

C. rosea; male fl. with staminal pad with shiny, viscid resin.

C. rosea; an established Pitch Apple Tree provides shade at the airport in Grand Cayman. The persistent lvs are thick, rubbery and very long-lived.

C. rosea; the fr. is divided into 7–9 parts that form a star shape when mature.

C. rosea; dehiscent fr. is a tough, rubbery ball full of orange-red pulp with latex; it is yellow-green, ripening brown.

Coccoloba uvifera

SEA GRAPE

(L.) L.   120 spp.

POLYGONACEAE

THIS STURDY, WORTHY TREE of the Trop. American coasts has a habit of stretching itself along the sand and pushing its heavy limbs through the undergrowth. ***Coccoloba uvifera*** is as ubiquitous along the coastlines of Trop. America as the coconut and has a unique beauty; its trunk has smooth, pale grey bark that flakes in large patches to reveal the creams and salmons of the inner flesh. The leaves are stiff, leathery platters with prominent, waxy, bright red veins; as they age, they turn orange and red. Small, white or greenish white, nectar-rich flowers are held in erect, narrow spikes and are popular with honeybees. As the flowers fade and the fruit begins to form, its weight draws the spike downwards. The fruit is the most astonishing feature of this species: mellow, sweet, succulent, reddish purple 'grapes' that are delicious and popular as a fresh fruit. They are also made into drinks or jellies and in some regions are used for a wine-like beverage. *C. uvifera* is truly a garden designer's tree, not only because of its dynamic physique, but also for its versatility. Totally salt- and wind-resistant and adaptable for many uses, Sea Grape may be left to grow into its characteristic, natural form, lightly pruned in its youth so as to form a wind screen or hedge or shaped into a small shade tree. In Miami, USA, it is often drastically pruned to provide ground cover. To have a fruiting tree, a female form must be planted; it is therefore best to propagate it from cuttings. W. Indian kino, a red and astringent substance, was extracted from the bark and used in tanning and dyeing. The heartwood is reddish brown, hard and heavy, but very susceptible to attack by dry-wood termites and, as *C. uvifera* often harbours these insects, care should be taken if the trees are planted near buildings. It is popular regionally as a fuel wood. This is an important honey plant.

ORIGIN	Trop America
HEIGHT	up to 15 m (49 ft)
TYPE	evergreen, dioecious foliage tree
STATUS	vulnerable coastal habitats
HABITAT	coastal strand and limestone thickets
GROWTH	slow to moderate
FLOWG	spring and autumn
DRY TOL.	high
SALT TOL.	high
LIGHT	full sun
SOIL	very well-drained
NUTRIT.	balanced fertilizer annually
HAZARDS	none
PROBLEMS	messy leaf drop; may harbour termites
ENVIRON.	bee nectar; wild fruit for birds and bats
PROPAG.	seeds; cuttings; layers
LEAVES	simple; dull green; to 20 cm (8 in.) diam.; orbicular, thick, stiff, red-veined
FLOWERS	inconspicuous; whitish green; held in slender, arching spikes
FRUIT	an achene, to 2 cm (0.8 in.); green, then red to purple; in grape-like clusters
USE	seaside; small shade tree, screening; hedges; large planter; conservatory; xerophytic
ZONE	10–12

100ft ⌐ 30m

75ft

22.5m   0

C. uvifera; has spikes of greenish white fls.

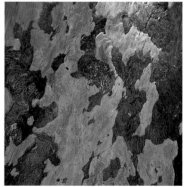

C. uvifera; a young cluster of juicy, edible Sea Grapes, much adored by doves and pigeons, as well as the indigenous population.

C. uvifera; with its unmistakable, heavy, lazy growth patterns. The wood is bright red when cut and very heavy.

C. uvifera; with an exquisite patchwork of flaking, pale grey bark that reveals the creams and salmons of the inner bark.

(1) *Coccoloba diversifolia*; (Jacq.), (syn. *C. floridana; C. laurifolia*), S Florida; W Indies, to 10 m (33 ft). PIGEON PLUM or UVA DE PALOMA is a compact, oval-crowned, small tree, often with several trunks, (2) that has the same ornamental, multi-coloured bark as *C. uvifera*. The lvs are very diversely shaped, which presents problems in selecting trees for grouping in the landscape. Like the Cocoplum, Pigeon Plum provides a larder for fruit-eating birds, particularly local pigeons and ground doves. *C. diversifolia* is popularly planted as a specimen or accent, being somewhat fastigiate and slow growing. Photographed at the Jardin Botanico Nationale, in Cuba. (10–12)

(3) *Coccoloba pubescens*; (L.), (syn. *C. grandifolia*), W Indies, to 13 m (43 ft), PLATTER-LEAF or MOUNTAIN GRAPE. The orbicular lvs are pubescent below and clasped basally by large, hairy, sheathing ochrea. Sapling lvs may reach 50 × 80 cm (20 × 31 in.) and in the 19th century were gilded as a curiosity. Canopy lvs on mature trees are much smaller, often only 7.5 × 10 cm, (3 × 4 in.) or more. Terminal inflorescent spikes, to 18 cm (7 in.), bear greenish white fls. Fr. is globose to ovoid, to 6 mm (0.2 in.), greenish, tinged pink, and eaten locally, where it is often known as 'raisin'. (4) a young specimen at Ernesto's Good Earth Nursery in Miami, Florida. (10–12)

Cochlospermum vitifolium

BRAZILIAN ROSE

(Willd.) Spreng.   12 spp.

C. hibiscoides

BIXACEAE

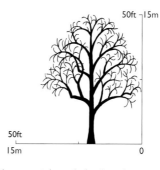

50ft ⌐15m

50ft
15m   0

ORIGIN	Mexico; C and S America
HEIGHT	up to 12 m (39 ft)
TYPE	deciduous, smallish flowering tree
STATUS	not threatened
HABITAT	arid, stony scrubland; savannahs
GROWTH	fast
FLOWG	late winter to spring
DRY TOL.	high
SALT TOL.	moderate
LIGHT	full sun
SOIL	fertile, very well-drained
NUTRIT.	apply fertilizer very sparingly
HAZARDS	none
PROBLEMS	root rot in poorly drained conditions
ENVIRON.	bee nectar
PROPAG.	seeds; large cuttings
LEAVES	palmately lobed; tawny green, pale grey below; to 22 cm (8.6 in.); margins toothed
FLOWERS	showy; bright yellow; to 12 cm (4.7 in.); many curling, orange stamens; rose-like
FRUIT	a capsule, to 7.5 cm (3 in.); velvety-pubescent; with many seeds in fine, silky down
USE	small flowering tree; specimen; screening; large planter; xerophytic
ZONE	10–12

COCHLOSPERMUM VITIFOLIUM is an austere, frugal tree with polished, pale grey, stubby branches that remain skeletal and naked for long periods. The sudden emergence of its great, silken, rose-like blooms, their golden bowls filled with orange, curling stamens, makes it difficult to believe that they have not been attached for decoration. As the flowers fade, new, deep green foliage emerges to provide summer shade. The leaves, which have long, red petioles, are deeply, palmately lobed, with toothed margins. With the new foliage, the flowers are transformed into dark brown, oval, thin-skinned, 5-lobed pods that contain several kidney-shaped seeds embedded in masses of soft, silky wool that is traditionally used for filling pillows and said to induce sleep. A superb, double-flowered form, var. *plenum* (shown below), lacks a functional pistil and does not produce fruit. *C. vitifolium* is a stalwart, xeromorphic native of the harshest habitats: arid, stony hillsides and savannahs. In its region, the fibrous bark of this species provides cordage and juice for Chica, a beer-like beverage. *Cochlospermum* wood is whitish to light brown; the heartwood is soft, spongy, very lightweight and perishable. The inner bark is streaked brown, fibrous, slightly bitter and yields a gum. Because it grows easily from large cuttings, *C. vitifolium* is often used as a living fence. *Cochlospermum* species require a dry, well-drained, sunny position. These are honey plants.
*** *C. gillivraei*; (Benth.) NE Australia and New Guinea, to 12 m (39 ft). Cotton Tree or Gillivray's Kapok Bush is widespread in coastal woodlands. The flowers are bright yellow with red stamens. The fruit is a fragile capsule, with brownish black skin. (10–12)
*** *C. religiosum*; (L.), Burma and India. Katira is a source of the insoluble gum, Karaya, used as a substitute for gum tragacanth, which is used in the food, textile and pharmaceutical industries. The tree is held sacred and is planted near temples. (10–12)

C. vitifolium; simple fls with many stamens quickly transform into large fr.

C. vitifolium var. *plenum*; with double blooms like full-blown roses, does not make fr. and is possibly the ultimate sp. for a dry garden.

C. vitifolium; an austere, frugal sp., with pale grey, stubby branches, which remain skeletal for long periods.

C. gillivraei; fragile fr. has 2 layers of delicate skin, which separate and dehisce to release silken sds.

ORIGIN	NE Trop. Africa
HEIGHT	up to 7 m (23 ft)
TYPE	evergreen, fruiting small tree or tall shrub
STATUS	vulnerable in the wild
HABITAT	understorey of high-elevation humid forests
GROWTH	moderate
FLOWG	spring
DRY TOL.	low
SALT TOL.	low
LIGHT	light shade to full sun
SOIL	humid, rich, acid
NUTRIT.	high-potassium fertilizer; deep, organic mulch
HAZARDS	none
PROBLEMS	coffee leaf disease; scale insects
ENVIRON.	bee nectar
PROPAG.	seeds; semi-ripe cuttings
LEAVES	simple; dark green, paler below; to 10 × 8 cm (4 × 3 in.); glossy, heavily veined
FLOWERS	showy; snowy white; in axillary clusters along stem tops; fragrant
FRUIT	a berry, to 15 mm (0.6 in.); ripening red, yellow or purple; seeds ellipsoid, olive green
USE	small flowering tree or shrub; backyard tree; accent; humid shade; large container; conservatory
ZONE	10–12

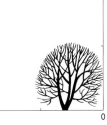

50ft – 15m

50ft
15m — 0

ARABIAN COFFEE

L.   90 spp.

RUBIACEAE

COFFEA ARABICA is an attractive, flowering species belonging to the same family as *Ixora* and *Gardenia* and is popularly grown as an ornamental (and has escaped cultivation in many regions). Distinguished by its large, deeply veined, elliptic leaves, this species forms a dense, dark green crown. Its small, white, jasmine-like blooms are very fragrant, providing nectar for bees that produce a white honey with a characteristic coffee taste. The berry fruit have a red, pulpy skin and it is the large, fermented seeds of these berries that produce coffee. The flesh is removed before the seeds are processed. After washing and drying, the remaining thin, greyish, parchment-like skin is also removed and the 'beans' are ready for roasting. The flavour and quality of coffee is greatly influenced by the soil, fertilizers, altitude and climate of the growing region. Because it is an understorey plant of high-elevation forests, *C. arabica* requires light shade to thrive and is commonly overplanted with suitable, fast-growing, thin-canopied trees (mostly leguminous), with roots capable of fixing nitrogen in the soil. In his gardener's bible, *Tropical Planting and Gardening*, H. F. Macmillan says, 'The use of coffee as a beverage was first known in Abyssinia about the beginning of the 15th century. It was introduced to England in 1662....' In fact, the first coffee shop recorded is the *Angel* in High St, Oxford, England, in 1650. Macmillan was referring to Arabian coffee, the species most planted commercially. Irrigation channels dating from 1350 AD still remain at high altitudes in Yemen.

*** *C. canephora*; (Pierre ex Frohner), ROBUSTA COFFEE, of the lowland, humid tropics in the Congo Basin. The beans are considered of a lower quality than *C. arabica*. It is often used in the manufacture of instant coffees. (10–12)

NOTE: species of *Coffea* have become naturalized in N Qld's rainforests.

C. arabica; with masses of starry, short-stalked, white, fragrant blooms.

C. arabica; thin, fleshy, red skin covers the 'beans'. This is removed before the beans are processed.

C. arabica; masses of small, lustrous, red berries replace the the fls. They contain large sds known as 'beans'.

C. arabica; Coffee is a very ornamental sp., with glossy foliage, starry, white, fragrant fls and masses of brilliant red berries.

Cola acuminata

COLA NUT

(Pal.) Schott. & Endl.   125 spp.

C. vera

MALVACEAE (formerly Sterculiaceae)

COLA ACUMINATA is a sought-after native of the rapidly shrinking forests of Trop. W Africa. Traditionally a trade item along caravan routes in the Sahara, **C. acuminata** was domesticated in W Africa, where it retains an important place in the regional culture as a symbol of hospitality. It grows to form a fairly tall, dense crown, with its young growth densely rusty tomentose; its tough, stout leaf stalks remain attached to stems after the long-pointed, strongly veined leaves have fallen. In spring, even on young trees compact umbels of small, ornamental, long-stemmed flowers emerge from the axils of the leaves. They have no petals, only showy, pale cream or yellowish, star-shaped calyxes with 5 oblong, spreading, waxy, long-pointed lobes that are striped reddish or purple at their base. The fruit is very curious, being an enormous syncarp composed of 4 or 5 large, stout, warty, leathery, green follicles that are stalkless but joined to the carpel at their base. Each follicle 'pod' contains large, irregular, bitter nuts that are creamy pink at first but change to rosy red as they ripen. (A rare, white form is more highly valued.) It is mainly for these nuts, which contain 2% caffeine and also theobromine and kolanin, that this tree is cultivated. Domestically, they act as a masticatory and stimulant, as well as being considered a tonic for the digestive system. They are also taken for headaches, depression and nervous conditions. Earlier in the 20th century, they ranked next to the African Oil Palm (*Elaeis oleifera*) in importance to the Trop. W Africa export trade and were shipped to Europe for use in various preparations, such as Kola wine, chocolate and various medicinal concoctions. Now, of course, they are also widely exported as an ingredient for the carbonated soft drinks industry.

NOTE: C. acuminata has become naturalized in parts of the W Indies.

ORIGIN	Trop. W Africa
HEIGHT	up to 20 m (66 ft)
TYPE	evergreen flowering and fruiting tree
STATUS	scarce in native habitats
HABITAT	humid lowland forests
GROWTH	moderate
FLOWG	spring
DRY TOL.	moderate
SALT TOL.	low
LIGHT	full sun
SOIL	deep, rich, well-drained
NUTRIT.	balanced fertilizer annually; deep, organic mulch
HAZARDS	none
PROBLEMS	none
ENVIRON.	insect nectar
PROPAG.	seeds; ripe-wood cuttings
LEAVES	simple; bright green; to 20 cm (8 in.); elliptic, leathery
FLOWERS	showy; pale yellow, with a purplish or reddish, striped throat; no petals, star-shaped calyxes; in panicles
FRUIT	a follicle, to 8 × 20 cm (3 × 8 in.); leathery, woody; seeds large, 5–6 per pod
USE	shade tree; flowering tree; street tree; botanic collection; large container; conservatory
ZONE	10–12

C. acuminata; with highly ornamental, petal-less blooms.

C. acuminata; the large, pulpy sds, which contain caffein, theobromin and kolanin, are used in making Cola, carbonated drinks.

C. acuminata; a sturdy specimen thriving at Cienfuegos Botanic Gardens in south-eastern Cuba.

C. acuminata; with smooth, pale grey bark.

ORIGIN	Madagascar, endemic
HEIGHT	up to 15 m (49 ft)
TYPE	deciduous flowering tree
STATUS	endangered
HABITAT	moist coastal woodland
GROWTH	moderate
FLOWG	autumn into winter
DRY TOL.	moderate
SALT TOL.	low
LIGHT	full sun
SOIL	rich, well-drained
NUTRIT.	balanced fertilizer annually; deep, organic mulch
HAZARDS	none
PROBLEMS	none
ENVIRON.	nectar for birds and insects
PROPAG.	seeds
LEAVES	2-pinnate; rich green; leaflets held in 15–25 pairs; feathery
FLOWERS	showy; vivid scarlet; held in dense, horizontal, conical clusters
FRUIT	a legume, to 30 cm (12 in.); oblong, flattened; with several lozenge-shaped seeds
USE	autumn-flowering tree; specimen; street tree; public open space; courtyard
ZONE	10–12

100ft — 30m

75ft
22.5m — 0

Colvillea racemosa

COLVILLE'S GLORY

Bojer. ex Hook.   1 sp.

FABACEAE (Caesalpinioideae)

THE HUGE ISLAND OF MADAGASCAR, off the SE coast of Africa, is the birthplace of many of the most spectacular tropical plants. *Colvillea racemosa*, like its close relative, *Delonix regia* (Poinciana), is endemic there. These 2 trees share many characteristics, *C. racemosa* strongly resembling the Poinciana, but without its flowers, although its pinkish, coppery-coloured trunk is usually taller and stouter. They have the same layered, fine, ferny foliage but *C. racemosa* does not develop such a widely spreading parasol crown. In early spring and summer, this species remains quite anonymous, but in the drab days of late summer and early autumn, it begins to display its blooms, which are held in huge, erect, long-stemmed clusters and spring from the extreme tips of its flexible limbs. These magnificent inflorescences are composed of erect, silky, crowded cones of small, bubbly, deep scarlet sepals and pale orange petals filled with golden stamens; it is estimated that 1 flower cone may bear as many as 200 silky buds. As each terminal flower cone matures, the basal blooms open first and during a period of about 6 weeks the cones of buds slowly put on their spectacular show. The gilded blooms attract iridescent, darting, nectar-imbibing birds, and the flowers are held out on sturdy stalks and at a convenient angle to accommodate them. As they fade, the spent blooms carpet the ground below. The flowers are followed by large, flat, oblong pods filled with lozenge-shaped seeds layed horizontally in grooves. This splendid tree was discovered in 1824 by the botanist Wenceslas Bojer (1797–1856), who was responsible for identifying so much of the flora of Madagascar. He discovered a single specimen growing in hills near Majunga on the island's north-west coast and named it after Sir Charles Colville, who was then the governor of Mauritius.

C. racemosa; large, ripe fr. pods with its sds held horizontally.

C. racemosa; its pinkish, coppery-coloured trunk is usually taller and stouter than *Delonix regia*.

C. racemosa; does not develop a spreading, parasol crown nor the wealth of bloom of *Delonix regia*.

C. racemosa; magnificent infls. are composed of erect, silky, crowded cones of small, bubbly, deep scarlet sepals and paler, orange petals filled with perky, golden stamens.

127

Conocarpus erectus

GREEN BUTTONWOOD

L.   2 spp.

C. procumbens

COMBRETACEAE

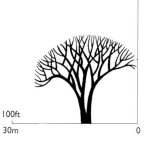

100ft – 30m

100ft
30m   0

THIS IS AN UNDISCIPLINED NATIVE of coastal regions of Trop. America. **Conocarpus** *erectus* belongs to the edges of mangrove and brackish swamps where it forms extensive, impenetrable thickets by sprawling and rooting as its limbs touch the ground. It continues to grow by looping and weaving its heavy, rough-barked limbs in all directions. The ovate, crisply succulent leaves have slightly winged petioles. Long-stalked, minute, greenish, fragrant flowers transform into curious fruit, which look like tiny, compressed, pinkish pine cones. The fruit comprises dry, 2-winged, overlapping drupes that separate at maturity. These little fruit are composed of a tissue that adapts them to flotation and dispersal by water. In some areas, the form *C. erectus* var. *sericeus*, known as Silver Buttonwood, is found. Shown below is a photograph of a thicket of both the green and silver forms that have spontaneously evolved at the edge of a brackish swamp. Both forms are popular garden subjects used as small, salt-resistant or xerophytic shade trees, screening or hedging. Although **C. erectus** is native to brackish swamps, it will grow equally in dry sites, marl-filled land with a high, brackish water table and poor, sandy soils. *Conocarpus* is popular for planting in the United Arab Emirates, in the Middle East, where great advances have been made in the reclaiming and the greening of the desert with the development of desalinated irrigation. Because this species may be propagated from large cuttings, it has been planted as a living fence in some water-retentive areas. **C. erectus** heartwood is yellow-brown, very heavy and hard, with a fine texture that takes a good polish. However, it is susceptible to dry-wood termites. It burns slowly and makes an excellent charcoal. Bark and leaves contain tannins. Research has not yet determined why this species is known as Buttonwood.

ORIGIN	Trop. America; W Africa
HEIGHT	up to 20 m (66 ft)
TYPE	evergreen foliage tree
STATUS	not threatened
HABITAT	brackish coastal swamp
GROWTH	moderate
FLOWG	year-round
DRY TOL.	high
SALT TOL.	high
LIGHT	full sun
SOIL	tolerant, water-retentive
NUTRIT.	normally not necessary
HAZARDS	none
PROBLEMS	none
ENVIRON.	insect nectar
PROPAG.	seeds; cuttings; layers
LEAVES	simple; bright green or silver-tomentose; to 10 cm (4 in.); succulent-crisp
FLOWERS	inconspicuous; purplish white; held in tiny, fuzzy balls; fragrant
FRUIT	a drupe, to 4.5 mm (0.2 in.); cone-like; purplish brown, persistent
USE	seaside; small shade tree; screening; specimen; hedging; source of charcoal; xerophytic
ZONE	10–11

C. erectus var. *sericeus*; a silver form with young fr.

C. erectus; habitat in a brackish inland wetland at Queen Elizabeth II Botanic Park in the Cayman Is, W Indies.

C. erectus; both the green and silver forms have evolved spontaneously at the edge of this brackish swamp.

C. erectus var. *sericeus*; known as Silver Buttonwood, is a popular, salt-resistant, ornamental.

An inland brackish, Buttonwood wetland on Little Cayman in the Cayman Is, W Indies, which is a breeding ground for the endangered Whistling Duck (*Dendrocygna* sp.).

Cordia dodecandra

ZIRICOTE

DC.   320 spp.

BORAGINACEAE

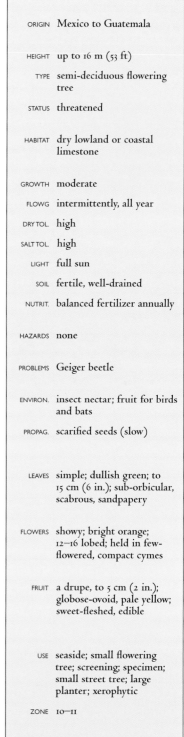

ORIGIN	Mexico to Guatemala
HEIGHT	up to 16 m (53 ft)
TYPE	semi-deciduous flowering tree
STATUS	threatened
HABITAT	dry lowland or coastal limestone
GROWTH	moderate
FLOWG	intermittently, all year
DRY TOL.	high
SALT TOL.	high
LIGHT	full sun
SOIL	fertile, well-drained
NUTRIT.	balanced fertilizer annually
HAZARDS	none
PROBLEMS	Geiger beetle
ENVIRON.	insect nectar; fruit for birds and bats
PROPAG.	scarified seeds (slow)
LEAVES	simple; dullish green; to 15 cm (6 in.); sub-orbicular, scabrous, sandpapery
FLOWERS	showy; bright orange; 12–16 lobed; held in few-flowered, compact cymes
FRUIT	a drupe, to 5 cm (2 in.); globose-ovoid, pale yellow; sweet-fleshed, edible
USE	seaside; small flowering tree; screening; specimen; small street tree; large planter; xerophytic
ZONE	10–11

CORDIA IS A WIDESPREAD GENUS of splendidly ornamental flowering and timber trees, making it difficult to choose the most significant species. Chiefly native to Trop. America, they are also found in India, Trop. Africa and the Middle East. **Cordia dodecandra**, of dry, lowland regions of Mexico and Guatemala, was selected not only for its form and attractive blooms, but also for its remarkable timber. **C. dodecandra**, like many Cordias, is a fairly slow-growing species, which tends to form a bulky framework with an open canopy of tough, grey green, scabrous leaves. (These are sometimes used as a type of sandpaper.) Large, and intensely orange, the flowers are very unusual, with their 12–16 petals giving the impression of being pleated and deeply crimped along their edges. **C. dodecandra** is cultivated locally for its fruit, which is slightly pear-shaped and pale yellow when ripe. Its flesh is sweetish and considered a delicacy regionally, although other reports suggest it to be rather unappetizing. However, **C. dodecandra** is most renowned for its timber, known widely as Ziricote, Ciricote or Chackpote. It has a dense, hard, dark heartwood that has the extraordinary property of being self-lubricating. This timber has several uses, notably as a component of ships' stuffing boxes – where the propeller shaft exits the hull and a perfect seal must be maintained. It is said that when Far-Eastern shipbuilders discovered this phenomenon, they toured Yucatan in Mexico and bought up all the trees they could find, rendering **C. dodecandra** virtually extinct in the region. Since then, there has been some reafforestation. The bark, flowers and fruit are used to make a cough syrup.

*** **C. rickseckeri**; (Millsp.), (syn. *C. sebestena* var. *brachycalyx*), Puerto Rico and Virgin Is, to 8 m (26 ft). Dog Almond is a rare but worthy species for its sturdy growth, brilliant, orange-scarlet flowers and egg-shaped, calyx-enveloped fruit. (10–12)

C. dodecandra; Jardin Botanico de Cienfuegos in Cuba; this specimen provides a framework for epiphytes, as well as a larder for birds.

C. dodecandra; with large, pleated, fiery orange fls.

C. dodecandra; fr. turns pale yellow when ripe. It has sweetish flesh and is considered delicious by some.

C. dodecandra; has dense, hard, dark-coloured heartwood, which is self-lubricating.

Cordia alliodora; ([Ruiz. & Pavon.] Cham.), (syn. *Cerdana alliodora*), Trop. America, to 30 m (100 ft). Cypre, Onion Cordia or Laurel Blanco is one of the most important timber trees of its region, known commercially as Cypre or Ecuador Laurel. It forms a huge, mast-like trunk with limbs developing high up in a layered, whorled fashion. Crushed lvs smell of garlic. An important bee plant. (10–12)

Cordia boissieri; (A. DC.), SW USA to Mexico, to 8 m (26 ft). Texas Olive or Ancahuita, is slow growing, forming a mop-head of tough, slightly hairy, silvery green foliage. Clusters of chalky white, funnel form fls with luminous yellow throats lend this sp. a freshly laundered appeal. Built to withstand drought and seaside environs, this is an excellent subject for small gardens. The hard sds need scarifying before sowing. (8–10)

Cordia dentata; (Poir.), (syn. *Cordia alba*), Trop. America, to 10 m (33 ft). White Manjack or Flor de Angel loses its lvs in prolonged drought but will remain everg. under irrigation. The exquisite, frilly, pale yellow or white fls are sweetly fragrant and, along with the fleshy white fr., which are filled with sweet sticky pulp, provide a luscious larder for birds and bees. This is an excellent plant for screening or as background filler. (10–12)

Cordia dichotoma; (Forster f.), N Qld, and NT Australia, to 23 m (75 ft). This *Cordia* has many names in its wide region that vividly describe the sticky, mucus-like flesh of its fleshy, pink or yellowish fr. In Australia, it is called Glue Berry or Snot Berry. *C. dichotoma* is conical to cylindric when young, becoming rounded with arching growth in maturity. It has small, white or yellowish fls that are held in loose cymes. (10–12)

Cordia gerascanthus; (L.), W Indies to C America, to 20 m (66 ft). Spanish Elm or Princewood is mostly anonymous in its dry woodland habitats but, with a shower of rain, it is triggered into frothy, fragrant, white bloom, illuminating the canopy. Quickly, the fls transform into dry, papery fr. that persists for many weeks. *C. gerascanthus* does not have berries, but has small, dry fr. with calyx attached, serving as a 'parachute'. (10–12)

Cordia goeldeiana; (Huber.), S America, from 10–20 m (33–66 ft). Known as Freijo or Cordia-preto in Brazil. The small, semi-decid. tree blooms in spring. It has small umbels of tiny, 5-petalled, orange blooms set in narrow, cylindrical calyxes, which persist after the fls have aborted. This calyx protects the young sd. The fr. are a decorative salmon colour and brighten up this rather dull tree. (10–12)

Cordia laevigata; (L.), (syn *C. nitida*), W Indies and C America, to 15 m (50 ft). Red Manjack or W. Indian Cherry is native of dry to moist lowlands. It begins with a strictly tiered, whorled formation but eventually develops a neatly rounded canopy. Young parts rusty, brown hairy; fls creamy white. The bright red, lacquered berries, full of juicy pulp, are adored by wild birds, especially doves and pigeons and are often fed to chickens. (10–12)

Cordia lutea; (Lam.), Ecuador, Galapagos, Peru, to 8 m (26 ft). Peruvian Cordia is found wild on arid slopes and mesas near water courses. It forms a stout trunk with grey, exfoliating bark. The rounded, bright green lvs are glabrous above, pale green pubescent below. Most of the year, it carries its cheerful, bright, light yellow blooms over its widely arching, exuberant canopy and is very popular for use as a specimen or for screening. (9–11)

Cordia myxa; (L.), India to Australia, to 12 m (39 ft). Sudan Teak, Sebesten or Assyrian Plum is a small, shrubby sp. It has naturalized in Africa and is also widely planted in the Mediterranean. Dioec., the tiny male and female, white to cream fls are held in loose terminal panicles. The fr. is either yellow or orange-pink to black with sweet, sticky, mucilaginous flesh. Blooming and fruitg year-round. (10–12)

Cordia subcordata; (Lam.), E Africa to Trop. Asia, Pacific and Australia, to 15 m (50 ft). Known as Marer in Kenya, and Sea Trumpet in Malaysia, this sp. grows along coast. strands, often just above the high tide mark. Because of its enormous distribution, the fls of this sp. vary from white, yellow-orange to red. The obovoid fr. is eaten in some parts of its range. Here it is shown as a street tree in Cairns, N Qld, Australia. (10–12)

Cordia sebestena; (L.), W Indies to Venezuela, to 10 m (33 ft), is mostly widely known as the Geiger Tree, but is also called Scarlet Cordia, Lolu or Kou-Haole. Tough, slow growing, very salt-resistant and xerophytic, this sp. is possibly the most popular *Cordia* for ornamental planting. *C. sebestena* may be decid. or everg., depending on humidity, but in cultivation it is often ever-blooming. Its fls, which are often likened to Geraniums, vary between deep red or orange and light orange, while the large fr., which is creamy white, fleshy, to 2.5 cm (1 in), has found local medical use and is considered edible by some. Heartwood is dark brown, hard, heavy and fine-textured; it has been used in some regions for carpentry. Propagated, like most *Cordia* spp., by sds (scarified, very slow) or cuttings. (10–12)

133

Couroupita guianensis

CANNONBALL TREE

Aublet.   4 spp.

C. antilliana

LECYTHIDACEAE

COUROUPITA GUIANENSIS is one of the most remarkable and renowned tropical trees. Commonly known as Cannonball Tree, this is a robust species with a stout, straight trunk and a lax, sparse crown, with large, glossy leaves clustered in spirals towards the ends of its flexuous branches. The narrowly elliptic leaves are borne singly or alternately on yellow green petioles. Curious, cauliflorous flowers are held on long, swirling stems that emerge from the trunk in tumbling, ropy tangles. This arrangement has evolved in this way specifically to facilitate the pollination of the flowers by bats or *Xylocarpa* bees. The singular flowers are short-lived and have 6 petals, which are yellowish red on the outside and rosy red within. Typically Lecythidaceae, they comprise 220 stamens, many of which are infertile, arranged across a disc at the lower part of the flower and folded upwards to connect with the fringed ovary. They are pungently fragrant at night to attract their swift-flying pollinators. The petals and stamens soon fall, leaving the pistil and calyx to be shed later. As if this were not novelty enough, the fruit, which resemble cannonballs or spherical gourds, are attached directly to the trunk or the flowering 'ropes'. Usually, a single fruit develops on a branch, taking about a year to mature. It does not split open but falls and decays with a cheesy smelling, greenish pulp that is filled with seeds, which turns purplish or bluish on contact with the air. In the jungle, the fruit sway and clash, creating loud reports like artillery fire, and when they litter the ground, it looks like an artillery company has bivouacked underneath. The light brown wood is soft and lightweight and although not durable, it is used in some regions for boxes and interior work. It is reported that a depilatory is made from the pulp of the fruit. In dry areas, trees may shed their leaves twice a year and prove messy.

ORIGIN	Trop. America
HEIGHT	up to 35 m (115 ft)
TYPE	deciduous or evergreen flowering tree
STATUS	not threatened
HABITAT	humid rainforest
GROWTH	fast
FLOWG	year-round
DRY TOL.	moderate
SALT TOL.	low
LIGHT	full sun
SOIL	rich, deep, humid
NUTRIT.	balanced fertilizer annually; deep, organic mulch
HAZARDS	none
PROBLEMS	none
ENVIRON.	bat and bee nectar
PROPAG.	fresh seeds
LEAVES	simple; bright green; to 31 × 10 cm (12 × 4 in.); whorled, glossy
FLOWERS	showy; dull, rosy red; to 6 cm (2.4 in.) held on long, dangling, woody stems; nocturnally fragrant
FRUIT	a capsule, to 24 cm (9.4 in.); round, woody, like cannonballs; containing up to 300 seeds in greenish pulp
USE	large flowering tree; public open space; specimen; botanic collection
ZONE	10—12

C. guianensis; with curious, cauliflorous fls.

C. guianensis; a magnificent specimen at the Jardin Botanico de Cienfuegos, Cuba, showing its tangled, swirling skirt of long, fl. stalks around its base.

C. guianensis; tumbling, ropy tangles are adapted specifically to facilitate the pollinators, bats and wild bees.

C. guianensis; 'cannon-ball' fr. are held on stout cords and sway and crash around in the wind.

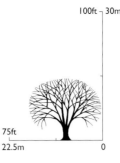

ORIGIN	SE Asia to N Australia
HEIGHT	up to 15 m (50 ft)
TYPE	briefly deciduous, small flowering tree
STATUS	rare in Australia
HABITAT	humid river valleys; open monsoon forest
GROWTH	slow
FLOW'G	spring, with new leaves
DRY TOL.	moderate
SALT TOL.	low
LIGHT	full sun or bright shade
SOIL	rich, slightly acid
NUTRIT.	high-potassium fertilizer; deep, organic mulch
HAZARDS	poisonous fruit
PROBLEMS	none
ENVIRON.	insect nectar
PROPAG.	fresh seeds; suckers; stem or root cuttings
LEAVES	3-foliate; rich green, white below; leaflets lanceolate, to 7 cm (2.7 in.)
FLOWERS	showy; white, fading to golden yellow; to 5 cm (2 in.); stamens long, purple
FRUIT	a berry, to 5 cm (2 in.); speckled white; seeds black, set in pinkish yellow pulp
USE	small flowering tree; humid shade garden; large planter; specimen; fodder plant; conservatory
ZONE	10–12

Crateva religiosa

SACRED GARLIC PEAR

Forster f. non auct.   6 spp.

CAPPARIDACEAE

NATIVE TO RIVER BANKS, the gravelly alluvium of stream beds or the dry, deep, boulder formations of sub-Himalayan tracts is *Crateva religiosa*, a slow-growing, small tree with a much-branched crown of glossy foliage. Its bark is conspicuously spotted white and the branches are pale to yellow-green with 3-foliate, long-petioled, rich green leaves that are much paler below, with a finely tapered apex and clustered towards the ends of twigs. In early spring, *C. religiosa* drops its leaves, but with the onset of warmer weather, the new foliage ushers in large, handsome blooms, which, so typical of the Capparidaceae family, are 4-petalled with long, whiskery, purple stamens. Although reminiscent of *Bauhinia* blooms, their rich cream petals deepen in colour, almost to orange, as they age and are curiously garlic scented. The pale, tawny fruit, which is ovoid to nearly spherical, is dangled on a long, sturdy stalk; it is about the size of a tennis ball, with smooth, leathery, speckled skin. Embedded within its inedible, poisonous, fleshy, garlicky, pinkish pulp are many largish, horseshoe-shaped seeds. In India, the pulp was mixed with mortar to make cement, or employed as a mordant in dyeing, while the foliage is used as fodder. The wood is smooth and close-grained; it works easily and is used in local villages for drums and artifacts. *C. religiosa* is held sacred in India and has traditionally been planted around tombs and temples, where the blossoms are plucked to be used as religious offerings; it is also often grown in graveyards.

*** *C. adansonii*; (DC.), Kenya; Burma to S China, to 20 m (66 ft). NAGARIDA (Kenya) is a very drought-tolerant, savannah tree with a widely spreading crown and a stout, often twisted trunk. Leaves are 3-foliate, with blunt-tipped leaflets, to 5–10 cm (2–4 in.). Abundant, lop-sided flowers are slightly smaller than *C. religiosa*; petals, cream, deepening to ochre; stamens, white. Subsp. *trifolia* ([Roxb.] Jacobs); flowers, with deep red stamens. (10–12)

C. religiosa; with long-stemmed, speckled, tennis ball-sized fr.

C. adansonii; a superbly floriferous sp. photographed in Darwin, N Australia.

C. religiosa; a slow-growing small tree with a much-branched crown of glossy foliage.

C. religiosa; white, fls deepen to a rich yellow and are distinguished by slender, whiskery, purple, stamens. They smell faintly of garlic.

Crescentia cujete

CALABASH

L.   6 spp

C. acuminata; C. arborea

BIGNONIACEAE

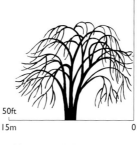

50ft ⌐15m

50ft
15m   0

CRESCENTIA CUJETE is a cauliflorous, stiffly branched, small tree with long, wand-like branches criss-crossing its centre in a haphazard way. Year round, little, yellow or tan flowers cling to the old stems. In the evening, their pungent, musky, cabbage scent attracts their nocturnal pollinators. Following the flowers, huge, curious fruit form into colossal, green globes that mature to a light tan and are filled with a white, floury pulp embedded with many seeds. These gourds bear nectaries thought to attract stinging ants, which ward off predatory herbivores such as goats. The large fruit may be shaped by tying a cord carefully around the girth of a developing gourd to distort it as it grows. Calabash shells have served as kitchen receptacles since ancient times, and their precious seeds have been dispersed around the tropical world by sailors from island to continent. The hard, smooth shell polishes well and is finely carved for ritual use in some regions of Africa. In the wild, *C. cujete* is often host to many epiphytes, especially bromeliads and orchids, and may be seen, almost leafless, burdened with its decorative guests. Blocks of *Crescentia* wood on which to mount epiphytic plants are sold commercially. In some regions, the young fruit is pickled. In Nicaragua, the seeds are cooked and used to make a beverage, while in Hawaii, the dried gourds filled with their seeds are used as hula rattles. Although moderately hard, heavy and flexible, the light brown heartwood is mostly only used domestically, for tool handles or fuel.

*** *C. alata*; (HBK), Mexico to Costa Rica, up to 8 m (26 ft). Known as TECOMATE or JICARA, this species has a more erect habit, with slender limbs. *Crescentia alata* has smaller fruit than *C. cujete* and its 3–5-parted leaves have winged petioles. The flowers are tan brown, with yellow throats. (9–12)

ORIGIN	C America
HEIGHT	up to 10 m (33 ft)
TYPE	semi-deciduous, small foliage tree
STATUS	vulnerable
HABITAT	coastal scrub; dry lowland, in clearings
GROWTH	slow
FLOW G	year-round
DRY TOL.	high
SALT TOL.	moderate
LIGHT	full sun
SOIL	fertile, well-drained
NUTRIT.	balanced fertilizer annually
HAZARDS	poisonous seeds
PROBLEMS	none
ENVIRON.	bat nectar
PROPAG.	seeds; misted cuttings
LEAVES	simple; dark green; to 27 cm (10.6 in.); oblanceolate, in whorls at nodes
FLOWERS	inconspicuous; yellow or whitish; bell-shaped, sessile, cauliflorous; with musky scent
FRUIT	a calabash, to 30 × 20 cm (12 × 8 in.); woody, smooth, indehiscent; many seeds, in pulp
USE	specimen; curiosity; useful fruit; support for epiphytes; botanic collection; large conservatory; xerophytic
ZONE	10–12

C. cujete; whitish, cauliflorous blooms are musky-pungent to attract bats.

C. cujete; showing its wildly disorganized, whip-like growth patterns. These trees carry many epiphytes on their rough-barked limbs and trunks.

C. alata; the pungent, musky, cabbage-scented, nocturnal fls attract bats. They abort at dawn.

C. alata; a young calabash. The fr. of this sp. is smaller and narrower than those of *C. cujete.*

ORIGIN	Australia; Pacific Is
HEIGHT	up to 12 m (39 ft)
TYPE	evergreen foliage tree
STATUS	not threatened
HABITAT	coastal and inland scrub; rocky outcrops
GROWTH	moderate
FLOWG	early spring
DRY TOL.	high
SALT TOL.	high
LIGHT	full sun
SOIL	fertile, well-drained
NUTRIT.	balanced fertilizer annually; organic mulch
HAZARDS	none
PROBLEMS	none
ENVIRON.	wild fruit for birds
PROPAG.	seeds; layers
LEAVES	pinnate; dull green; leaflets rounded, leathery with wavy margins
FLOWERS	inconspicuous; dull white; in tiny, erect, axillary panicles
FRUIT	a capsule, to 1.25 cm (0.5 in.); 3-valved, yellow; seeds with bright, orange-red arils
USE	seaside; shade tree; street tree; public open space; screening; xerophytic
ZONE	9–11

50ft ⌐15m

50ft
15m   0

Cupaniopsis anacardioides

TUCKEROO

(A. Rich.) Radlk.   60 spp.

SAPINDACEAE

CUPANIOPSIS ANACARDIOIDES is an Australian tree native to its east coast from the frost-free zone north of Sydney to Cape York Peninsula and the Northern Territory. It is found in sandy, coastal scrublands and is therefore a useful species for seaside planting, enduring a certain amount of exposure to salt-laden winds. *C. anacardioides* is very similar to *Blighia sapida*, to which it is closely related, with its smooth, pale grey trunk and limbs and relaxed habit of growth. Like the *Blighia*, Tuckeroo has a widespread, dense, shady, evergreen crown that is mostly wider than it is tall and is easily contained below overhead wires. The leaves are pinnate with 2–12 blunt, leathery leaflets. *C. anacardioides* also recalls the Cashew (*Anacardium*), for which it is named, but is not related. It is versatile as regards to soil and will withstand strong winds. Small panicles of greyish white flowers are borne in spring. Being a polygamous genus, unisexual and bisexual flowers are held on the same tree or on separate trees. Because of this, not all trees bear the highly decorative fruit that follow the flowers in summer and it should therefore be propagated vegetatively from a fruiting tree. These deep yellow, then brown, leathery, 3-valved capsules burst open when they are ripe to reveal 3 dark brown, glossy seeds embedded in a bright scarlet-red, pulpy aril. In Australia and California, this species has been found to be an excellent choice for street planting. The wood of *C. anacardioides* is pinkish and relatively tough and is used for building in some parts of its range. Because of its reddish colour, it is often known as Carrotwood.
*** *C. flagelliformis* var. *flagelliformis*; (Bailey), N Qld, to 6 m (20 ft). BROWN TUCKEROO, a superb tree of humid sites with deep red, velvety fruit and red new growth. (10–12)

NOTE: *C. anacardioides* has proved invasive and undesirable in S Florida.

C. anacardioides; little, drab white, uni, or bisexual fls.

C. anacardioides; a somewhat battered specimen growing in its natural habitat in N Qld, Australia.

C. anacardioides; lvs are pinnate with 2–12 blunt, leathery lflts.

C. anacardioides; typical of the Sapindaceae, the 3-celled fr. of this sp. contain large, ornamental sds with red arils (to attract birds).

Cussonia spicata

COMMON CABBAGE TREE

Thunb.   25 spp.

ARALIACEAE

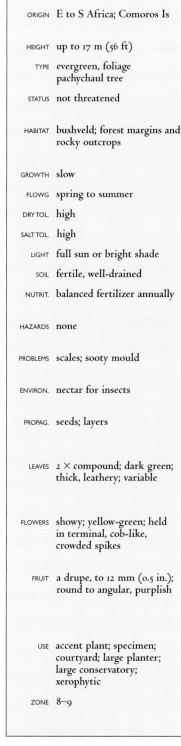

IT IS EASY TO SEE THE KINSHIP of this African tree to the Australian Umbrella Tree, *Schefflera actinophylla*. Both their grand many-lobed leaves and remarkable, octopus-shaped flower panicles tell of shared genes. This is a genus that grows in varied environments: a few species are truly tropical, some are subtropical and others are warm-temperate. Many have long been popular as greenhouse specimens in temperate regions. ***Cussonia spicata***, the Common Cabbage Tree, could be said to be marginally tropical and, while it may grow in much cooler areas, it is badly burned by frost. *C. spicata* begins life with few to no branches but, as it slowly matures, it divides 2 or 3 times, or even more in very old trees, to form a wide canopy. Thick, leathery, 5–12 foliate leaves are clustered at the ends of limbs; they are very often palmately compound in young plants, but eventually become digitately compound. An enormous, densely packed panicle of radiating inflorescences is arranged in bundles of 8–12 spikes. The little, stemless flower buds are crowded onto ends of their stout spikes to resemble a corn cob. As the flowers open, they reveal their tiny, yellowish green petals and sprightly stamens. The wood of *Cussonia* species is usually soft, light and strong and has found some local use.

*** ***C. paniculata***; (Ecklon. & Zeyh), S Africa, to 4.5 m (15 ft), is known as the HIGHVELD CABBAGE TREE or HOEVELDSE KEIPERSOL, which describes its habitat. The greyish, blue-green leaves are composed of 7–11 radiating leaflets, which are not subdivided. The flowers are yellow-green and the fruit is purple when ripe. (9–11)

*** ***C. sphaerocephala***; (Thunb.), Natal, S Africa, to 10 m (33 ft). NATAL FOREST CABBAGE TREE is a tall, sparsely-branched, evergreen tree. The leaves are in compact, rounded heads at trunk tips. The flowers are greenish yellow, the fruit purple. (9–11)

ORIGIN	E to S Africa; Comoros Is
HEIGHT	up to 17 m (56 ft)
TYPE	evergreen, foliage pachychaul tree
STATUS	not threatened
HABITAT	bushveld; forest margins and rocky outcrops
GROWTH	slow
FLOWG	spring to summer
DRY TOL.	high
SALT TOL.	high
LIGHT	full sun or bright shade
SOIL	fertile, well-drained
NUTRIT.	balanced fertilizer annually
HAZARDS	none
PROBLEMS	scales; sooty mould
ENVIRON.	nectar for insects
PROPAG.	seeds; layers
LEAVES	2 × compound; dark green; thick, leathery; variable
FLOWERS	showy; yellow-green; held in terminal, cob-like, crowded spikes
FRUIT	a drupe, to 12 mm (0.5 in.); round to angular, purplish
USE	accent plant; specimen; courtyard; large planter; large conservatory; xerophytic
ZONE	8–9

C. spicata; a double umbel of corncob-like fl. spikes.

C. paniculata; has large, compound, blue-green lvs clustered at the ends of its branches and dominates a planting of succulents at Huntingdon Gardens in Los Angeles.

C. spicata; lvs are mostly palmately compound in young plants but eventually become digitately compound.

C. sphaerocephala; at Kirstenbosch Botanic Gardens in Cape Town, S Africa. This is a sparsely-limbed sp.

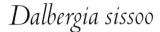

Dalbergia sissoo

INDIAN ROSEWOOD

Roxb. ex DC.   100 spp.

FABACEAE (Papilionoideae)

ORIGIN	India, endemic
HEIGHT	up to 20 m (66 ft)
TYPE	semi-deciduous, foliage timber tree
STATUS	limited distribution
HABITAT	coastal woodlands
GROWTH	fast
FLOWG	spring to summer
DRY TOL.	high
SALT TOL.	moderate to high
LIGHT	bright shade or full sun
SOIL	alkaline, well-drained
NUTRIT.	high-nitrogen fertilizer; organic mulch
HAZARDS	none
PROBLEMS	vigorous suckering
ENVIRON.	bee nectar
PROPAG.	seeds; cuttings; suckers; root cuttings
LEAVES	pinnate; bright green, to 18 cm (7 in.); leaflets diamond-shaped
FLOWERS	inconspicuous; yellowish white, abundant; fragrant
FRUIT	a legume, to 10 cm (4 in.), flat, thin, indehiscent; with 1–4 seeds
USE	shade tree; screening; street tree; specimen; windbreaks; civic centre; xerophytic
ZONE	10–12

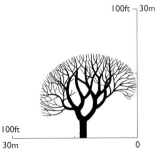

100ft – 30m

100ft
30m   0

DALBERGIA SISSOO is native of the coastal sandy soils or limestone woodlands of India, where it is an important timber tree. This is a very fast-growing species, which is astonishing considering the quality of its timber and the infertility of its native habitats. *D. sissoo* develops a relaxed, graceful framework of upward-thrusting, smoothly slender limbs supported by a sturdy, rough, pale grey trunk, with its bark peeling off in longitudinal strips. The airy, bright green crown is composed of large pinnate leaves with 3–5 oval, alternate, short-petioled leaflets. Although tiny, the masses of yellowish white, pea-like spring flowers, held in short-stemmed panicles at leaf axils and twig tips, are sweetly scented and popular with honeybees. They are quickly followed by bundles of smooth, thin, light brown pods containing 1–4 flat seeds. Because of its light canopy, this species is suitable for planting on lawns, allowing the passage of sufficient filtered sunlight for grass to thrive below. The tree will take severe pruning and shaping but care should be taken to avoid damaging roots as suckers may develop. *D. sissoo* has been widely cultivated for reafforestation, as well as for windbreaks to secure dry ridges and filled land, especially on poor, alkaline soils. This is 1 of 2 species known as Indian Rosewood (the other is *D. latifolia*) because the attractively grained wood has a rose-like fragrance. It is elastic and easy to work, making it ideal for construction and shipbuilding. In its native India, the wood of *D. sissoo* is considered unrivalled for fine, sculptural carving.

*** *D. melanoxylon*; (Guill. & Perro.), Trop. Africa, up to 35 m (115 ft). AFRICAN BLACKWOOD, MPINGA or AFRICAN EBONY, a deciduous, savannah tree, has spines that are actually the hardened tips of short branches. The heartwood is ebony-like but even harder; it has been made famous by the Mkonde carvers of Tanzania. (10–12)

D. sissoo; long-petioled, light green, thin textured lvs.

D. melanoxylon; the black, ebony-like heartwood is extremely hard and dense, making it a challenge to carve.

D. sissoo; the flat, indehiscent fr. is typical of the *Dalbergia* genus.

D. sissoo; forms an airy crown of luminous foliage, leaving the sun to penetrate to the ground below and making it an excellent specimen for planting on a lawn.

Delonix regia

POINCIANA

(Bojer.) Raf.   12 spp.

FABACEAE (Caesalpinioideae)

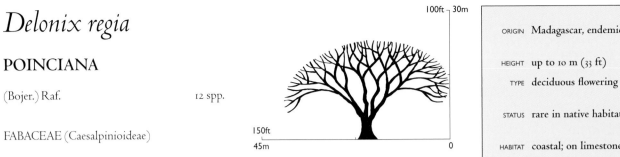

THE WORLD-RENOWNED *Delonix regia* from Madagascar, with its low-spreading parasol of radiating limbs and twigs, stands gauntly naked for the dry months of the year, save for its long, dark brown, sabre-like seed pods. These, like the fruit of *Cassia* species, are held for a full year before they mature and fall. With the first heavy, early summer rains, just before the emergence of tender, green, ferny foliage, the tree explodes into flamboyant, vivid scarlet bloom that pulsates against the sapphire of the tropical sky. The light green, delicately ferny, bipinnate leaves may have up to 1,000 leaflets. **D. regia** grows quickly but takes about 5 years to mature and bloom fully. *Delonix* flowers are usually brilliant scarlet, with the larger, standard petal splashed white and crimson; flowers may also be darker or much paler, even pure yellow. Although it did not take long for early plant collectors and ships' crews to carry the seeds and distribute them to all parts of the tropics, this species has become very rare in the wild. **D. regia** is light-sensitive; trees that grow beside street lamps remain evergreen and do not bloom, or may produce flowers on the side away from the light. The somewhat weak wood and aggressive roots of this species may cause a problem near masonry; it should not be planted near paths and pools. The heartwood is heavy, coarse-grained, brittle and very susceptible to termites.

*** **D. elata**; ([L.] Gamble), to 15 m (50 ft), Kenya. MWANGI or SUKELA is a timber tree of dry, thorn bush savannahs, with a spreading, rounded, arching habit and soft, grey-downy, semi-evergreen, young foliage. The flowers are held in wide corymbs, opening one at a time. They resemble whiskered pansies, with white petals fading to deep yellow, large pale green calyxes and long, purple-red stamens. Flowers, to 20 cm (8 in.). (10–12)

ORIGIN	Madagascar, endemic
HEIGHT	up to 10 m (33 ft)
TYPE	deciduous flowering tree
STATUS	rare in native habitat
HABITAT	coastal; on limestone hills
GROWTH	moderate
FLOWG	summer, before leaves
DRY TOL.	high
SALT TOL.	high
LIGHT	full sun
SOIL	well-drained, fertile
NUTRIT.	balanced fertilizer annually
HAZARDS	none
PROBLEMS	invasive roots
ENVIRON.	insect nectar
PROPAG.	seeds; large cuttings
LEAVES	2-pinnate; bright green, to 30 cm (12 in.); with up to 1,000 leaflets
FLOWERS	showy; scarlet, orange or yellow, to 8 cm (3 in.); petals clawed, standard petal splashed white and crimson
FRUIT	a legume, to 60 × 5.6 cm (24 × 2.2 in.); strap-like, woody, dark brown
USE	seaside; summer-flowering tree; street tree; specimen; bonsai subject; xerophytic
ZONE	10–11

D. regia; in early summer, masses of luminous, scarlet blooms pulsate against the sapphire-blue of the trop. summer sky.

D. regia; showing the enormous sd. pods, which have their sds set horizontally.

D. regia; the aggressive, surface roots of this tree may cause a problem near masonry.

D. elata; this sp. was photographed in the garden of an exotic tree collector at Mt Molloy near Cairns, N Qld, Australia.

(**1**) *Delonix regia*, or Royal Poinciana or Flamboyant, is without doubt the monarch of all the trop. flowg trees. This sturdy, drought- and salt-resistant endemic of Madagascar is now considered virtually extinct in its original habitat. As ubiquitous as the Coconut palm, this tree, with its joyous summer colour, is a universal floral symbol of the trop. and subtrop. world.

(**2** and **3**) *Delonix regia* var. *flava*; (Stehlé.) has golden yellow fls, with their posterior petal splashed scarlet and white. This form is relatively rare and much in demand. Because it does not necessarily come true from sd, var. *flava* is sometimes successfully grafted on to seedlings of the regular form.

In early summer, the wide, parasol crown of *Delonix regia* pulsates with colour.

Deplanchea tetraphylla

GOLDEN BOUQUET TREE

(R. Br.) Meull.   5 spp.

D. hirsuta

BIGNONIACEAE

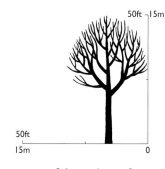

DESPITE ITS GENERAL IMPRESSION of being a native of humid rainforests, **Deplanchea tetraphylla** is a species of the rainforest margins, open forest and poor, sandy scrubland. This is a handsome, fast-growing, angular, evergreen species with an upward-stretching, sparsely branched crown, with its bright green foliage clustered towards the ends of the branches. Its large, heavily veined leaves, with golden hairy undersides, have their wavy edges neatly inrolled like the hems of fine linen, while the new growth is purple-tinged. *D. tetraphylla* begins to bloom when very young. During the dry season, in late winter or early spring, little, long-stalked, golden yellow, elongated trumpet flowers held erect in opulent, circular bouquets are massed in very large, flat thyrses that are nestled in the terminal whorls of leaves. (In tropical regions, this species may bloom intermittently, year-round.) It may be difficult to believe that *D. tetraphylla* is a member of the Bignoniaceae tribe – kin to *Tabebuia* and *Spathodea*, with their flamboyant trumpet flowers. Even the curious, velvety, pancake-like fruit gives few clues until, when mature, these elongated capsules become dry and packed with typical Bignoniaceae papery, winged seeds. In cultivation, this species prefers a warm, well-irrigated, sunny spot away from the tangle of its native scrubland. It likes to be protected from strong winds and gives shelter to flocks of Lorikeets and Flying Foxes (fruit bats) that are attracted to its nectar-rich blooms.

*** **D. bancana**; (Van Steenis), (syn. *Dipthanthera bañcaña*) Malaysia to Borneo; to 30 m (100 ft). YELLOW PAGODA FLOWER is a lofty tree with fluted buttresses and a rather open crown. The large leaves are cordate, wavy-edged and golden hairy below. The tree blooms when it is very young and carries clear yellow, long-stalked flowers that are held in magnificent, dense, pyramidal (or pagoda-shaped) clusters. (10–12)

ORIGIN	New Guinea and NE Australia
HEIGHT	5–20 m (16–66 ft)
TYPE	evergreen, small flowering tree
STATUS	not threatened
HABITAT	sandy, coastal scrub; monsoon forest margins
GROWTH	fast
FLOWG	spring, or year-round
DRY TOL.	moderate
SALT TOL.	moderate to high
LIGHT	exposed in full sun
SOIL	widely tolerant, well-drained
NUTRIT.	balanced fertilizer annually; deep, organic mulch
HAZARDS	none
PROBLEMS	rather brittle limbs; seeds susceptible to damping off
ENVIRON.	nectar for birds and bats
PROPAG.	fresh seeds
LEAVES	simple; rich green above, paler below; leathery; with wavy margins
FLOWERS	showy; dull yellow; long-stalked, in crowded, terminal thyrses
FRUIT	a follicle, to 15 cm (6 in.); oval-shaped, flat, woody; with papery, winged seeds
USE	seaside; accent; specimen; street tree; civic centre; large planter; large conservatory
ZONE	10–11

D. tetraphylla; with grandly dramatic, wavy lvs with golden hairy undersides.

D. tetraphylla; large heads of long-stalked, yellow blooms, with long, whiskery stamens do not resemble the normal, large trumpets of the Bignonia family.

D. tetraphylla; these large, woody fr. pods are stuffed with winged sds, which will disperse on the wind.

D. tetraphylla; a sp. with excellent statistics: simplicity of shape, dramatic lvs and unique bouquets of fls.

ORIGIN	Trop. W Africa
HEIGHT	up to 20 m (66 ft)
TYPE	evergreen fruiting tree
STATUS	not threatened
HABITAT	lowland, evergreen humid or semi-dry forests
GROWTH	moderate
FLOWG	spring
DRY TOL.	moderate
SALT TOL.	moderate
LIGHT	full sun
SOIL	fertile; humid; deep
NUTRIT.	general fertilizer annually; deep, organic mulch
HAZARDS	none
PROBLEMS	none
ENVIRON.	insect nectar
PROPAG.	seeds
LEAVES	pinnate; bright green; with 3–7 leaflets, to 13 cm (5 in.) long
FLOWERS	fairly showy; yellowish white; held in branched, erect, rusty hairy panicles; fragrant
FRUIT	a legume, to 2 × 2.5 cm (0.8 × 1 in.); flat, obovoid; velvety black, with thin, brittle shells and red, edible pulp
USE	shade tree; street tree; fruiting tree; public open space
ZONE	10–12

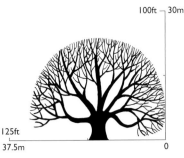

100ft — 30m
125ft
37.5m   0

Dialium guineense

VELVET TAMARIND

Willd.   40 spp.

FABACEAE (Caesalpinioideae)

ALTHOUGH SOMETIMES FOUND IN SAVANNAH VEGETATION as a shrub, ***Dialium guineense*** is also native of lowland, evergreen humid forest where it forms a wide-spreading canopy over a short, stocky, slightly buttressed trunk. The large, rounded, congested crown of slightly wavy-edged, bright green leaflets are held loosely and lend vibrant buoyancy to the spreading canopy. All parts of this *Dialium* are rusty pubescent: the young growth, stems and leaf petioles, as well as the flattened, branched flower panicles. The little, yellowish white or pinkish blooms, which are clasped in rusty velvety calyxes, characterize this genus by having only 2 stamens, while most leguminous plants have 10 or more. The most remarkable feature of *D. guineense* is, however, its singular fruit, which is held well above the foliage on wide-spreading, branched panicles. These indehiscent pods are flat discs of jet black velvet with thin, brittle shells enclosing 2 seeds surrounded by an orange-red, sweetly acid, farinaceous, edible pulp. They are known as Velvet Tamarinds and are used locally in the preparation of chutneys and preserves. The sapwood is whitish but the handsome, evenly grained heartwood is reddish brown with pink streaks.

*** ***D. indum***; (L), (*D. cochinensis*), Malaysia, to 20 m, (65 ft). KERANJI, of lowland forest, has 2–5 pairs of glabrous leaflets. Black, velvety fruit, to 5 cm (2 in.), has sweet, edible pulp and is sold in markets. The timber is important locally. (10–12)

*** ***D. orientale***; (Bak. f.), Kenya, to 18 m (60 ft), MPEPETA or SHISHOBLE of coastal, dry, evergreen forests is found either as a tree or a many-stemmed shrub. Leaves have elliptic-lanceolate leaflets in 1–4 pairs. Petal-less, whitish flowers are held on much-branched, wide panicles. The fruit is red, edible, round, to 2 cm (0.8 in.). The sapwood is white, the heartwood is red-brown, with pink streaks and a fine, even texture. (10–12)

D. guineense; with airy panicles of tiny fls.

D. guineense; rounded, slightly wavy-edged, bright green lflts loosely held, form a buoyant canopy.

D. guineense; thin-shelled fr. contains a sweetly acid, edible pulp. These fr. are rather old and the pulp is dryish.

D. guineense; an established specimen in the arboretum of the Jardin Botanico du Cienfuegos, in Cuba, and part of their extensive economic collection of trop. trees.

Dillenia indica

ELEPHANT APPLE

L.   60 spp.

D. speciosa

DILLENIACEAE

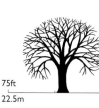

THIS DISTINGUISHED ASIAN BEAUTY thrives in humid forests of river valleys. Under ideal conditions, **Dillenia indica** attains a stout, straight trunk with wide-spreading branches that grow to form a broad, rounded, shady crown. Every aspect of this SE Asian species has a special merit, including the bark, which is luminous, rusty red and flakes in small, delicate scales. The lush canopy is composed of handsome, oblong leaves with a finely pointed apex, sharply toothed margins and strikingly prominent, parallel veins, which give them an elegant, deeply ribbed surface. The foliage is a perfect foil for the huge, nodding, milky white, waxy, Magnolia-like flowers that cup a coronet of curling, golden stamens. From this rises a sturdy, nectar-charged style, its apex radiating to form a striking, white 'daisy'. Unlike the other *Dillenia* described here, the petals of **D. indica** do not open completely and the flowers tend to hang downwards. They are lightly fragrant and attract bees and other insects as pollinators. To complete the superb design, the fruit of **D. indica** develops within the fleshy, membranous sepals of the flowers, which enlarge to enclose the large, fleshy fruit, forming a green 'cabbage' head containing many kidney-shaped, light brown seeds embedded in transparent, gelatinous sap. This fruit is especially designed to float and be dispersed by river currents. While not overly delicious, this pleasantly acid fruit is considered to taste of unripe apple and in many parts of its region is used as a vegetable in curries or is made into drinks or jellies. The pulp also serves locally as a hair wash. Dried, the leaves are used to polish ivory, while their juice is applied to the scalp to prevent baldness. The bark is used medicinally to treat the mouth infection, thrush. The wood ash is added to clay bricks to increase their fire resistance.

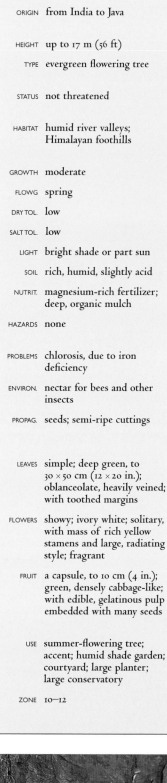

ORIGIN	from India to Java
HEIGHT	up to 17 m (56 ft)
TYPE	evergreen flowering tree
STATUS	not threatened
HABITAT	humid river valleys; Himalayan foothills
GROWTH	moderate
FLOWG	spring
DRY TOL.	low
SALT TOL.	low
LIGHT	bright shade or part sun
SOIL	rich, humid, slightly acid
NUTRIT.	magnesium-rich fertilizer; deep, organic mulch
HAZARDS	none
PROBLEMS	chlorosis, due to iron deficiency
ENVIRON.	nectar for bees and other insects
PROPAG.	seeds; semi-ripe cuttings
LEAVES	simple; deep green, to 30 × 50 cm (12 × 20 in.); oblanceolate, heavily veined; with toothed margins
FLOWERS	showy; ivory white; solitary, with mass of rich yellow stamens and large, radiating style; fragrant
FRUIT	a capsule, to 10 cm (4 in.); green, densely cabbage-like; with edible, gelatinous pulp embedded with many seeds
USE	summer-flowering tree; accent; humid shade garden; courtyard; large planter; large conservatory
ZONE	10–12

D. indica; with spectular, white, nodding blooms.

D. indica; finely and deeply veined foliage held in giant whorls; magnificent, pendent, white blooms and huge, succulent fr. add to the glamour of this sp.

D. indica; Elephant Apple is edible and, although not particularly delicious, is eaten in various ways in some regions.

D. indica; known as Red Beech for the luminous, rusty red bark which flakes in small, delicate scales.

(1) **D. alata**; ([R. Br. ex D.C.] Martelli), Australia, to 8 m (26 ft). Known as RED BEECH for its bright red, flaky bark. It is found in coast., rainforest swamps and blooms year-round, but requires a humid position. Its roots may prove invasive. Fr. is red and dehisces into a star-shape, like *D. suffruticosa*, but with white, rather than red, arils. (10–12) (2) **D. excelsa**; (Gilg.), Malaysia, to 35 m (115 ft). SIMPOH UNGU or PURPLE SIMPOH is a superb sp. with large, fragrant, ephemeral fls distinguished by their mass of purple stamens and reddish purple sepals. Fls emit a very penetrating, vapourous odour, which attracts honeybees. Fr. is reddish in bud. (10–12)

(3) **D. suffruticosa**, ([Griff.] Martelli), (syn. *Wormia burbidgei*), Malaysia, to 10 m (33 ft). SIMPOH AIR, WORMIA or SHRUBBY DILLENIA is a semi-scandent sp. of swamp forest and wasteland. This sp. has ever-growing shoots and is seldom out of bloom; fls, to 10 cm (4 in), are yellow with white stamens and fade after a single day. (4) Showing fr. of *D. suffruticosa* with a star-shaped arrangement of segments containing sds with red arils. The large, toothed, cabbage-like lvs are often used as wrapping for market food. (10–12)

(**Above**) **D. philippinensis**; (Rolfe.), Philippines, to 12 m (39 ft). A densely shrubby, small tree of lowland, Dipterocarp forests, which is broadly pyramidal and easily confused with a small *D. indica*. It is distinguished by its large fls, to 18 cm (7 in.) diam., that open up fully; petals are thin-textured and stamens purplish. Fleshy sepals of the fr. are eaten and also used to make cough syrup and, like *D. indica*, a hair shampoo. Bark yields a red dye. (10–12)

Dimocarpus longan

LONGAN

Lour   5 spp.

Euphoria longan; Nephelium longana

SAPINDACEAE

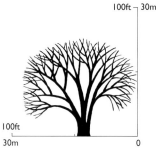

DIMOCARPUS LONGAN is auspiciously named Longyan in China, due to its shiny, dark seed, resembling a dragon's eye. It comes from highland Burma and S China and hence tolerates more cold than Lychee, even surviving some frost. **D. longan** appears to bloom and crop more heavily with cooler winters. In many, more tropical Asian villages, it is often grown for shade rather than its irregular harvest. This species grows rapidly on a range of soils, if provided with abundant water during the growing season and some protection from the strongest sun. *D. longan* has wavy-edged, pinnate leaves that emerge deep, wine-red, turning glossy, rich green and minutely grey velvety below. The young twigs are brownish grey woolly, as are the masses of little, yellowish white blooms that are held in large, terminal cymes. The ripe fruit, which weighs down its branched panicle, resembles the Lychee, but its crusty skin is almost smooth, with a fine honeycomb pattern. The mucilaginous, musky-sweet flesh is usually eaten raw, although it is also canned in syrup or dried. In some areas, the fruit is believed to improve brain function. In SE Asia, various parts of the tree are prepared therapeutically: dried fruits for insomnia, amnesia and mental health and seeds as a shampoo, as well as being ground into powder to treat skin diseases. The high-quality timber is used for furniture and carving. Named cultivars with superior fruit are propagated by layering or grafting. 'Kohala', which is favoured commercially, has large fruit and sweet, spicy flesh. Vietnamese cultivars show better promise than those of the more equatorial tropics. Var. *malesiana* of Borneo, to 15m (50ft). Isau has sweet, juicy, musky, melon-flavoured flesh, while var. *kakus*, also of Borneo, known as Kakus, is similar, but with less juicy fruit and smaller leaves. These are honey plants

ORIGIN	India and Burma to S China and Malesia
HEIGHT	10–40 m (33–131 ft)
TYPE	evergreen fruiting or foliage tree
STATUS	not threatened
HABITAT	humid, mountain woodlands
GROWTH	fast
FLOWG	spring
DRY TOL.	low
SALT TOL.	low
LIGHT	sheltered, full sun
SOIL	fertile, water-retentive
NUTRIT.	rich, organic fertilizer and deep, organic mulch
HAZARDS	none
PROBLEMS	nutritional deficiencies
ENVIRON.	butterfly nectar; wild fruit for birds
PROPAG.	fresh seeds; layers
LEAVES	pinnate; deep green, glossy; with 2–4 pairs leaflets; new growth, deep red
FLOWERS	showy; yellowish white; in erect cymes, to 40 cm (16 in.), held in upper leaf axils; fragrant
FRUIT	a drupe, to 2.5 cm (1 in.); globose, almost smooth, yellow-brown; with mucilaginous, musky, sweet flesh
USE	small shade tree; backyard tree; small flowering tree; specimen
ZONE	8–10

D. longan; the ripe fr. is similar to the Lychee but its crusty skin is almost smooth, marked with a fine honeycomb pattern. In China, this sp. is known as li-chi-nu, 'slave of Lychee'.

D. longan; nectar-rich blooms attract flocks of little, orange butterflies.

D. longan; a popular fr. in SE Asia, where it is eaten fresh, canned or dried.

D. longan; forms a billowing canopy showing its close links with Lychee. This sp. prefers a cool winter.

Flecker Botanic Gardens, lies 4 km from Cairns City centre in trop., N Qld, Australia, on the coast of the Great Barrier Reef. It is part of a complex of 3 areas of botanical and environmental importance, administered by Cairns City Council. Flecker Gardens is situated on the site of a nursery established in 1888 by Eugene Fitzalan, a botanical collector who opened his collection to the public. In 1971, the gardens were named in honour of Dr. Hugo Flecker, the founder of the Northern Qld Naturalist Club and Flecker Herbarium. These superb gardens are dedicated to conservation of rare and threatened plants of both native and exotic origins. Of particular interest is their extensive collection of ginger and related spp.

Diospyros ebenum

EBONY

Koenig.   475 spp.

EBENACEAE

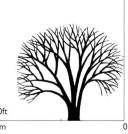

DIOSPYROS IS A WIDELY DISTRIBUTED GENUS, with most of its species sharing 2 characteristics: their dense, gloomy, evergreen crowns of dull, dark green leaves and their grey or black bark. This huge genus is acclaimed not only for the delicious, edible fruit of many of the species, but also for the extraordinarily fine timbers of others. Most celebrated is **Diospyros ebenum**, a slow-growing tree with hard, dense, heavy, black heartwood that is the ebony of commerce. **D. ebenum**, native to humid coastal and lowland forests of India and Sri Lanka, forms a densely foliaged, rounded crown when young, becoming more open and heavy-limbed in age. This is a monoecious species, with separate male and female flowers held on the same tree, but mainly hidden amongst the foliage; male flowers are in axillary clusters while the females, cupped in thick, heavy sepals, are solitary. The tannic ebony fruit is very ornamental, being round and golf ball sized, with a glowing, rusty brown, velvety skin. Like all the *Diospyros* clan, **D. ebenum** carries prominent, persistent sepals attached at its base. Reflecting the measured formation of its dense heartwood, the finely crusty, very dark grey or blackish bark is often matted in green mosses and lichens. Ebony wood has been renowned throughout history for its solid, almost metallic, qualities. It has been used to make small objects such as jewellery or chess pieces, or luxury domestic items like piano keys or inlay for fine furniture. Because of its slow growth, **D. ebenum** is becoming increasingly rare.

*** Other important, ebony-like timbers of the *Diospyros* genus include: *D. celebica*; (Bahk.), Sulawesi, MACASSAR EBONY. *D. haplostylis*; (Bolvin), Madagascar, MADAGASCAR EBONY. *D. mespiliformis*; (Hochst. ex A. DC.), Africa, AFRICAN EBONY and *D. montana*; (Roxb.), Indo-Malesia, BOMBAY EBONY.

ORIGIN	India to Sri Lanka
HEIGHT	up to 20 m (66 ft)
TYPE	evergreen monoecious tree
STATUS	threatened
HABITAT	humid coastal and lowland forests
GROWTH	slow
FLOWG	spring
DRY TOL.	low
SALT TOL.	low
LIGHT	full sun
SOIL	rich, water-retentive
NUTRIT.	balanced fertilizer annually; deep, organic mulch
HAZARDS	none
PROBLEMS	none
ENVIRON.	insect nectar; wild fruit
PROPAG.	seeds; grafting
LEAVES	simple; rich green; oblong-elliptic, glabrous
FLOWERS	inconspicuous; white, waxy axillary; fragrant
FRUIT	a berry, to 4 cm (1.5 in.); globose; brown velvety
USE	shade tree; specimen; collection; large planter; bonsai subject; conservatory
ZONE	10—12

D. ebenum; with golf ball sized, rusty velvety fr.

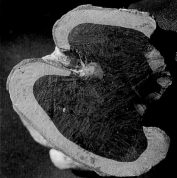

D. ebenum; this proverbially slow-growing sp. at the Jardin Botanico du Cienfuegos in Cuba, where it forms a part of their trop., economic crop collection.

D. ebenum; the finely crusty, very dark grey or blackish bark is often matted in green mosses and lichens.

D. ebenum; the dense, heavy, incredibly fine-grained heartwood of this sp. makes it very desirable.

Diospyros blancoi; (A. DC.), (syn. *D. discolor*), Philippines; to 33 m (98 ft). Known regionally as Velvet Apple, Butterfruit or Mabolo, this sp. is grown for its natural elegance, as well as its most attractive plush fr. Held in pairs, the fr. has a sturdy calyx and velvety, pinkish brown to reddish purple skin and a mellow taste of a moist, not very sweet, over ripe apple. The furry skin is unpalatable and fr. must be peeled before eating. (10–12)

Diospyros dignya; (Jacq.), (syn. *D. ebenaster*), Mexico to C America, to 20 m (66 ft). Black Sapote, Zapote Negro (Spanish), or Caca Poule (French E Africa), slow growing, with a wide, corpulent canopy over gouty, blackish framework. Fr. is smooth and globose, to 10 cm (4 in) with green skin and very soft, sweet, jelly-like, blackish pulp. Mostly blended with milk, fr. juice or alcohol. A liqueur is distilled from the ripe pulp in C America. (10–12)

Diospyros kaki (Rosb.), Not known in the wild; to 14 m (46 ft). Kaki, Persimmon or Japanese Persimmon is deciduous with grey, peeling to furrowed bark. Dark green, ovate to obovate glossy lvs, to 20 cm (8 in). Fr. is globose to depressed, with large, persistent calyxes. The fr. ripens in late autumn to early winter after lvs. have turned a glorious red or orange. Sometimes used for bonsai. Strictly warm-temperate to subtrop. (8–10)

Diospyros malabarica; ([Desr.] Kostel), (syn. *D. embryopteris*), Trop Asia, Gaub or Timbiri has heavily sticky fr., which is used for caulking boats; Tunka Oil is extracted from sds. This tree, at the Royal Botanic Garden in Trinidad, was photographed where it was found, demonstrating the extraordinary phenomonen of its spring flush of new growth. It is known there as Butter-Fruit (like *D. blancoi*) for its yellow, soft, buttery texture. (10–12)

Dipterocarpus grandiflorus

APITONG

Blanco   69 spp.

DIPTEROCARPACEAE

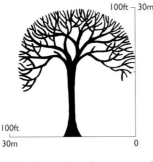

100ft – 30m

100ft
30m   0

THE VAST, LOWLAND TROPICAL FORESTS of Indo-Malaysia are largely composed of 16 genera and 680 species of the Dipterocarpaceae family that fall into 2 ecologically distinct groups – semi-evergreen, massive species of less disturbed, moist lowland forest and deciduous species that form the basis of dry Dipterocarp forests. Most important of this related group are *Dipterocarpus*, *Dryobalanops*, *Hopea* and *Shorea*. The fruit of *Dipterocarpus* and *Hopea* are 2-winged, *Shorea* has 3 wings and *Dryobalanops* 5. (*Dipterocarpus* means 'two-winged fruit'.) *Dipterocarpus grandiflorus*, an evergreen of humid forests, is known in the Philippines as Apitong; it has a straight bole to 30 m (100 ft) before the crown and is usually buttressed. Typical of its genus, the large, ovate leaves have straight, parallel side veins, bending just before the margin and strongly raised below. Buds are narrowly conical, protected by large stipules that soon fall, leaving scars. Typically, the flowering – often gregarious – and fruiting are seasonal and in response to a dry spell. *D. grandiflorus* flowers are very large and held in short, axillary, unbranched clusters. Each bloom has 5 petals, twisted together into an open-mouthed funnel and fused at the base, while the fruit is a 1-seeded nut with 2 large shuttlecock-like wings that are elongated calyx lobes, enabling fruit to be dispersed by wind. *Dipterocarpus* species provide tough, lightweight timbers that are widely used in heavy construction and for wharf pilings and power poles. These trees have flaky, pale grey or brownish bark, studded with small, corky pustules (breathing pores or lenticels) and yield a natural, reddish resin known as Dammar that is more or less fluid and exudes from the trunk, gradually hardening into 'tears'. It is collected commercially and used for making varnishes and for caulking boats. An oil, Balaw, is also obtained from the trunk.

ORIGIN	Andaman Is to Philippines
HEIGHT	up to 50 m (164 ft)
TYPE	evergreen foliage tree
STATUS	not threatened
HABITAT	in lowland rainforests
GROWTH	slow
FLOWG	after dry spell
DRY TOL.	moderate
SALT TOL.	low
LIGHT	bright shade
SOIL	humid, fertile, deep
NUTRIT.	balanced fertilizer annually; deep, organic mulch
HAZARDS	none
PROBLEMS	none
ENVIRON.	insect nectar
PROPAG.	fresh seeds
LEAVES	simple; deep green, obovate, variable, to 30 × 18 cm (12 × 7 in.); smooth, leathery
FLOWERS	showy; white or cream, rose-tinged within; to 8 cm (3 in.) diam.; petals pin-wheeled; slightly fragrant
FRUIT	a nut, to 15 cm (6 in.); with a 2-winged, persistent calyx containing a single seed
USE	botanical collection; timber tree; public open space
ZONE	10–12

D. grandiflorus; with attractive, large, star-like, pinwheel blooms.

D. grandiflorus; in Dipterocarp forests, the canopy is so lofty that one must study the forest floor to identify the spp. by their litter below.

Dipterocarp forest in Indomalaysia is largely composed of 16 genera and 680 spp. of the Dipterocarpaceae.

D. grandiflorus; has a straight bole to 30 m (100 ft), before the crown, and is usually buttressed.

Dipterocarp forest on rocky cliffs in Klany Gate, in the state of Selangor, Malaysia,
with the steely, blue-grey foliage of *Shorea curtsii* in the foreground.

Dodonaea viscosa

HOP BUSH

(L.) Jacq,   68 spp.

D. angustifolia

SAPINDACEAE

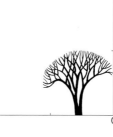

50ft — 15m

50ft / 15m   0

BECAUSE OF THE REMARKABLY EXTENSIVE DISTRIBUTION of **Dodonaea** *viscosa*, it naturally displays great variation in leaf shape and stature. Of the 68 species of *Dodonaea*, all but 2 occur in Australia, including **D**. *viscosa*, which is distributed through most warm parts of the world. Often called Varnish Leaf, this pioneer species grows as a multi-stemmed bush or small tree with grey-brown, narrowly, but deeply ridged and fissured bark and angular twigs. The light green leaves are lanceolate-elliptic and short-petioled, with their margins tightly inrolled and wavy. They are particularly distinguished by their viscid, lustrous upper surface, caused by a resinous excretion. In tropical habitats, tiny, petal-less, white flowers are borne irregularly throughout the year, in erect, short-stalked, viscid, axillary racemes. They are replaced by inflated, 3-winged, ornamental, pale green fruit that usually becomes tinged reddish, or pale, salmon pink before drying to a papery, pale buff pink and splitting open to disclose 1–2 round, black seeds in each segment. In Australia, **D**. *viscosa* is known as Hop Bush because its dried fruit are said to have been used as hops by the early Australian settlers. The stems of the dried fruit are highly regarded by florists for dried floral arrangements. The fresh fruit has been used in some parts of its range to stun and catch fish and the leaves and roots have been used medicinally. Cv. 'Purpurea' is an excellent and popular form, with rich, red-purple foliage.

*** **D**. *platyptera*; (F. Muell.), Australian endemic, to 7 m (23 ft). Small, dioecious shrub or multi-stemmed small tree of coastal vine thickets or fringes of lowland freshwater streams. With slightly fissured, pale grey bark and smooth, narrow-oval, light green leaves, greenish cream flowers and abundant clusters of 3-4 segmented fruit. (9–11)

NOTE: *D. viscosa* may escape cultivation in some regions.

ORIGIN	Pan-tropical to warm temperate regions
HEIGHT	up to 8 m (26 ft)
TYPE	evergreen foliage and fruiting shrub or small tree
STATUS	not threatened
HABITAT	dry coastal limestone, scrubland; in wooded grassland
GROWTH	slow
FLOWG	year round in the tropics
DRY TOL.	high
SALT TOL.	high
LIGHT	full sun
SOIL	fertile, well-drained
NUTRIT.	balanced fertilizer annually
HAZARDS	none
PROBLEMS	none
ENVIRON.	wind-pollinated
PROPAG.	seeds; cuttings
LEAVES	simple; yellowish green; possibly willow-like, viscid sticky; lustrous
FLOWERS	inconspicuous; white or greenish yellow; in short, axillary racemes
FRUIT	a capsule, to 2 cm (0.8 in.); rounded, 3-winged; base cordate
USE	seaside; coastal hedging or screening; accent; planter; coastal median strip; to stabilize sand; xerophytic
ZONE	9–11

D. viscosa; has racemes of tiny white fls and lvs with inrolled margins.

D. viscosa; inflated, 3-winged, ornamental, pale green fruit usually become tinged reddish, or pale, salmon-pink before drying to a papery, pale buff.

D. viscosa; in a sand dune habitat in Little Cayman, W Indies.

D. viscosa; with grey-brown, narrowly but deeply-ridged, fissured bark and angular twigs.

ORIGIN	from Trop Asia to the Pacific Is
HEIGHT	up to 20 m (66 ft)
TYPE	evergreen flowering or foliage tree
STATUS	not threatened
HABITAT	swampy coastal lowland
GROWTH	fast
FLOWG.	summer to year-round
DRY TOL.	moderate
SALT TOL.	high
LIGHT	part shade to full sun
SOIL	widely tolerant
NUTRIT.	balanced fertilizer annually; deep, organic mulch
HAZARDS	none
PROBLEMS	none
ENVIRON.	bat and moth nectar
PROPAG.	fresh seeds
LEAVES	pinnate; rich green, to 35 cm (13.8 in.); leaflets broadly elliptic, glossy
FLOWERS	showy; creamy white, long-tubed trumpets; to 18 cm (7 in.); nocturnally fragrant
FRUIT	a capsule, to 70 × 3 cm (27.5 × 1.2 in.); cylindrical, ribbed; seeds corky, winged
USE	seaside; flowering tree; shade tree; public open space; street tree; courtyard
ZONE	10–12

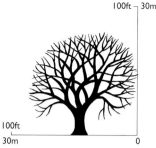

100ft – 30m
100ft
30m
0

Dolichandrone spathacea

MANGROVE TRUMPET TREE

(L. f.) K. Schum.   10 spp.

D. rheedii; Bignonia spathacea

BIGNONIACEAE

DOLICHANDRONE SPATHACEA is a relatively lofty tree with a slender, cone-shaped outline, somewhat resembling Tabebuia and sharing the typical trumpet flowers of the Bignoniaceae family. **D. spathacea** is native to swampy, coastal mangrove, although it will adapt to drier sites. Its trunk has pale, yellow-grey bark, which flakes off in small, irregular shards, and its base is often fluted into small buttresses. This is a vigorous, voluptuous species with lustrous, rich green, coarsely pinnate foliage tumbling over its loose-limbed crown. Typical of its genus, **D. spathacea** has nocturnal blooms. Buds are arranged in short, squat clusters at the branch tips and at dusk a single, large bloom unfolds and falls off at sunrise. The corolla is held in a leathery, long-beaked calyx that spills out its pipe-like, crumpled, obliquely curving, white trumpet to present its sweet nectar to their pollinators, the moths, which are lured by the blooms' ghostly hue and intense fragrance. Corky, winged seeds, held in strap-like, ribbed, dehiscent capsules, are adapted to the watery environment and designed for flotation. The young flowers and fruit are eaten as a vegetable in Burma and the leaves are employed medicinally for the mouth infection, thrush. The pale, lightweight wood is useful for fishnet floats and wooden shoes.

*** **D. atrovirens**, (Sprague), (syn. *Bignonia crispa*; *D. crispa*), India. TEMPLE FLOWER blooms from spring to summer with pearly white blooms on huge, drooping boughs of glossy foliage. The young flowers and fruit are eaten as a vegetable, particularly by the Brahmins in India. The useful wood is yellowish brown. (10–12)

*** **D. serrulata**; ([D.C. Seem.), Burma to Thailand, to 25 m (82 ft). Deciduous, with a narrow crown. Flowers, white, to 21 cm (8 in.), held in short clusters; eaten locally. Fruit, to 85 cm (33 in.), spirally twisted; seeds, with transparent wings. (10–12)

D. spathacea; these pipe-like, white trumpets are held in a leathery, beak-like calyx.

D. spathacea; on the banks of one of the many wetlands habitats at Fairchild Tropical Gardens in Miami, Florida.

D. atrovirens; fr. is a curved, tomentose capsule packed with winged sds.

D. atrovirens; the Temple Flower from India is used in the evenings – when it opens – to adorn the idols of Vishnu in Hindu temples.

153

Dombeya rotundifolia

WILD PEAR

(Hochst.) Planch   225 spp.

D. reticulata; D. spectabilis

MALVACEAE (formerly Sterculiaceae)

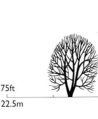

100ft — 30m

75ft
22.5m   0

IN LATE WINTER, when the savannahs of S to E Africa are parched and bleached from the long, dry season, this robust, shapely tree clads its naked, charcoal-grey limbs in spectacular, snowy white or pale pink blossoms and takes centre stage as harbinger of spring. In effervescent bundles, little, fragrant flowers cover every inch of every twig, attracting bees and butterflies. (This species is the larval plant for the butterfly *Caprona pillaana*.) In Zambia and Kenya, **Dombeya rotundifolia** is known as Wild Pear because it recalls the spring blossom of the European Pear (*Prunus communis*). As furry leaf buds burst forth on the rusty red, velvety new growth, and sharply scalloped, rounded leaves fill out and deepen to rich green, the little floral bouquets gradually fade to pinkish brown and finally, to a papery buff. They persist, as is the unfortunate manner of most of the *Dombeya* clan, long into summer, before rotting and floating away, carrying small, ripe, silky-hairy fruit capsules to begin life elsewhere. Although these trees are known to withstand savannah fires, they are popular for use as firewood, as the wood has the advantage of burning very slowly. The trees are widely cut for this use. Sadly, this is the fate of so many trees in regions without the convenience of gas or electricity, often leading to the gradual disappearance of some species. Otherwise, the wood is used to make bows and tool handles. **D. rotundifolia** is known for its medicinal qualities and both the Zulu and Shangaan people of southern Africa drink concoctions made from the bark to alleviate intestinal ulcers. The women also drink a concoction to hasten the onset of labour when it is delayed. The young bark of most species strips away easily from the trunk and large limbs. It is used as cordage and fibre by the local people, but this eventually causes mortal damage to the tree.

ORIGIN	E to S Africa and Madagascar
HEIGHT	up to 15 m (50 ft)
TYPE	deciduous, small flowering tree
STATUS	threatened
HABITAT	high, dry savannahs
GROWTH	moderate
FLOWG	spring to early summer
DRY TOL.	high
SALT TOL.	low
LIGHT	full sun
SOIL	fertile, well-drained
NUTRIT.	balanced fertilizer annually
HAZARDS	none
PROBLEMS	none
ENVIRON.	nectar for butterflies
PROPAG.	seeds; softwood cuttings
LEAVES	simple; red pubescent, rounded to lobed, margins toothed, to 18 × 13 cm (7 × 5.1 in.)
FLOWERS	showy; white to pale pink, in abundant panicles; drying to pale tan; persistent; fragrant
FRUIT	a capsule, to 7 cm (2.7 in.); 3–5 valved; dehiscent
USE	small flowering tree; accent; specimen; large planter; xerophytic
ZONE	9–10

D. rotundifolia; photographed at the Arboretum of Los Angeles. Typical of its genus, the white or pale pink blooms become pinkish tan with age.

D. rotundifolia; the white form with aging panicles of spring fls.

D. rotundifolia; all parts are velvety hairy. Pink-flowered forms are more reddish hairy than the white form.

D. rotundifolia; is widely cut for firewood as the wood has the advantage of burning very slowly.

(1) ***Dombeya cacuminum***; (Hochr.), Madagascar endemic, to 10 m (33 ft). The tall, multi-trunked STRAWBERRY SNOW-BALL TREE dangles its bounty of rose-pink blooms. (2) Typical of the *Dombeya* clan, they will persist on the tree and turn papery brown. Many of these spp. are an important source of fibre for villagers. Photographed at the Arboretum of Los Angeles. (10–12) (3) ***Dombeya burgessiae***; Gerard ex Harv.), to 6 m (20 ft), E Africa and Madagascar. PINK WILD PEAR is a small tree that occurs along forest margins and in rocky places in high rainfall regions. Lvs are ovate, to 18 × 18 cm (7 × 7 in.), bluntly 3–5 lobed; hairy below. The fls are held in many-bloomed, axillary heads. This is a very variable sp. (10–12)

(4 and 5) *Dombeya* hybrid species: ***D. × cayeuxii***; (André), (syn. *D. burgessiae*), S and E Africa, hybridized with ***D. × wallichii***; ([Lindley] BD Jackson), Madagascar, to 7 m (23 ft). The stems are bristly hairy and the lvs are dark green, large, cordate and toothed. The fls are pink and finely veined, held in axillary, pendent, umbellate cymes. This popular hybrid, garden ornamental is variable, with many forms. The blooms of this mature specimen, which can be as large as *Hydrangea*, were just fading when they were photographed at Huntingdon Gardens in Pasadena, California, USA. All of the 225 spp. of *Dombeya* are native to Africa, with 187 of them found only in Madagascar. (10–12)

Dovyalis hebecarpa

CEYLON GOOSEBERRY

Warb.   15 spp.

Aberia gardneri

FLACOURTIACEAE

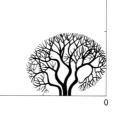

ORIGIN	India and Sri Lanka
HEIGHT	up to 7 m (23 ft)
TYPE	evergreen, dioecious, small fruiting tree
STATUS	not threatened
HABITAT	lowland, humid woodland thickets
GROWTH	moderate
FLOWG	late spring to autumn
DRY TOL.	moderate
SALT TOL.	low
LIGHT	full sun
SOIL	widely tolerant, well-drained
NUTRIT.	balanced fertilizer annually; deep, organic mulch
HAZARDS	spiny stems
PROBLEMS	Caribbean fruit fly
ENVIRON.	insect nectar; wild fruit for birds
PROPAG.	seeds; cuttings
LEAVES	simple; pale green, to 10 cm (4 in.); lanceolate to ovate, margins wavy-edged
FLOWERS	inconspicuous; greenish, with males and females on different plants
FRUIT	a berry, to 2.8 cm (1 in.); maroon-purple, with sour, purple pulp
USE	screening; small backyard tree; living barrier; large planter
ZONE	9–10

DOVYALIS (OR *DORYALIS*) *HEBECARPA* is a dioecious, evergreen, shrubby species with grey, slightly scaly bark and slender, greenish grey twigs armed with sharp, grey spines. The long-pointed leaves are often wavy-toothed on their margins and are held alternately zigzagged in 2 rows along the twigs. They are shiny green above, softly hairy and yellow-green below. Their little, round, velvety hairy berries become purplish in maturity and have a persistent style at their apex. Their ripe, purple pulp is sweet-and-sour, with a taste reminiscent of gooseberries, hence their common name. *D. hebecarpa* is eaten fresh, with sugar, or is cooked, juiced or made into preserves and is an excellent source of vitamin C. In Hawaii, it is mixed with papaya or guava to make jam, while in Israel it is a source of jelly for export. H.R. Macmillan, in his *Tropical Gardening and Planting*, suggests that this species is a good choice for encouraging birds into the garden because, '...it has been estimated that one bird will eat at least 50–100 caterpillars per day,' providing excellent, organic pest control.

*** **D. abyssinica**; ([A. Rich.]Warb.), (syn. *D. engleri*), NE Africa, to 10 m (33 ft), ABYSSINIAN GOOSEBERRY is a common species in Kenyan highland forest over 1,800 m (6,000 ft). It is deciduous and is with or without spines. The flowers are green, the males clustered and the females solitary, and the globose-ovoid fruit has the colour and flavour similar to that of rather astringent apricots. (8–11)

*** **D. caffra**; (Hook. f.), S and E Africa, to 9 m (30 ft). KEI APPLE is a subtropical species that copes equally well with seaside and xerophytic conditions. This species has straight, prominent spines and aromatic, little, bright yellow 'apples', with minutely downy skin and mealy, juicy, highly acid flesh. Widely used as hedging. (9–11)

NOTE: some *Dovyalis* spp. have escaped cultivation in some regions.

D. hebecarpa; small, staminous male fls.

D. hebecarpa; the Ceylon Gooseberry, photographed at the Fruit and Spice Park in Florida. This small tree is armed with very sharp, short, grey spines.

D. abyssinica; this globose-ovoid fr. has the colour and flavour of rather astringent apricots.

D. caffra; of subtrop. regions of S and E Africa, where it is known as Kei Apple. This little fr. is highly acidic.

ORIGIN	sub-Himalayas to Burma
HEIGHT	up to 25 m (82 ft)
TYPE	evergreen, large foliage (flowering) tree
STATUS	not threatened
HABITAT	in moist habitats and along the banks of streams
GROWTH	fast
FLOWG	year-round
DRY TOL.	moderate
SALT TOL.	low
LIGHT	high
SOIL	water-retentive, fertile
NUTRIT.	balanced fertilizer annually; deep, organic mulch
HAZARDS	none
PROBLEMS	brittle wood
ENVIRON.	bat nectar; wild fruit for birds
PROPAG.	seeds; large cuttings
LEAVES	simple; deep green; very long, narrow, to 33 × 10 cm (13 × 4 in.); held distichously
FLOWERS	showy; white; held in large heads; nocturnal; bat-pollinated; with a smell of sour milk
FRUIT	capsule, to 3 cm (1.2 in.); with persistent calyx and style; splits into 6 parts
USE	specimen; humid garden tree; public open space; large planter; conservatory
ZONE	10–12

100ft – 30m

75ft
22.5m   0

Duabanga grandiflora

DUABANGA

([Roxb. ex DC] Walp.)   2 spp.

D. sonneratioides; Lagerstroemia grandiflora

SONNERATIACEAE

OF THE RARE SONNERATIACEAE FAMILY, *Duabanga grandiflora* is closely allied to the *Sonneratia* species native to mangrove forests and tidal swamps of the Indian and Pacific Oceans, although at one time it was thought to be a *Lagerstroemia*. This species is commonly found on stream banks of warm, moist climate, from the sub-Himalayan tract in India through to the Malay Peninsula. It very quickly becomes a tall, evergreen tree with a smooth, greyish brown trunk prominently marked by hoop-shaped ridges, shield-shaped leaf scars and a bark that peels off in flakes. *D. grandiflora* is easy to spot in the jungle by its athletic, upward growth and whorls of long, horizontal branches that become massive and steeply drooping with age. These slender limbs are draped in superbly glossy, deep green, narrow-oval leaves, which emerge rosy pink and are held distichously along their length. They are brought into the same plane by the twigs twisting, rather than by the leaf stalks. The large, white flowers are held in sumptuous heads at the tips of the drooping limbs. They are nocturnal, opening at night, when they emit a strong smell of sour milk – evidently to attract their pollinators, the bats. Around 5 p.m., the large, crumpled, 4–8 lobed blooms emerge from their thick, leathery, green calyxes, unfolding to release their whirling mass of powdery, white anthers. The petals curl back to reveal large drops of sweet, clear nectar around the base of the ovary; by daybreak, the petals and stamens litter the ground. *D. grandiflora* blooms while still very young. The fruit capsule is seated in the persistent calyx and surmounted by a sturdy style. It splits longitudinally into 6 cells as it matures, to release its minute seeds. Known as Lampati in the timber trade, the soft wood is used for making plywood for tea chests and for the manufacture of matches.

D. grandiflora; fr. held in heavy, star-shaped, persistent calyxes.

D. grandiflora; smooth, greyish brown trunk prominently marked by shield-shaped lf scars and peeling in flakes.

D. grandiflora; Duabanga is easily recognized by its bold foliage and long, slender, tumbling limbs.

D. grandifolia; fls, with their thick calyxes, show their kinship to the Sonneratiaceae family (common mangrove spp. of the Indian and Pacific Oceans).

157

Duranta erecta

PIGEONBERRY

L.   17 spp.

D. repens; D. plumieri

VERBENACEAE

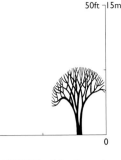

50ft ⌐15m

50ft
15m   0

POPULAR THROUGHOUT THE TROPICS AND SUBTROPICS, this American species is usually grown as a shrub, although it may attain the status of a small tree in the wild. **Duranta erecta** is extremely variable (polymorphic) in its form, being erect, trailing or even scrambling at times and either spiny or unarmed. It has a naturally disorganized, messy growth pattern, with its stiff, often awkward, slender limbs criss-crossing in all directions. The flowers are typical of the Verbenaceae family. They vary greatly in colour, ranging from blue or lavender to deep purple or even white (**D. erecta f. alba**); sometimes, the tiny, tubular flowers have a white 'eye'. Blooms are held terminally in narrow, curving racemes on arching stems, giving the tree an airy grace. With great speed, the sturdy, grooved calyxes thicken and the flowers abort, turning golden yellow as the embryos develop within; their calyxes remain as an outer skin, forming a 'beak' at the apex of the fruit. The combination of blue blooms and golden fruit is superb and widely popular because of the rarity of blue-flowering, tropical trees. Although pigeons and other birds are fond of these bitter, fleshy 'berries', they are considered poisonous to humans. In parts of Mexico, the berries are steeped in liquid that is then considered lethal to gnats and mosquitoes. Pigeonberry wood is light brown and hard, while the inner bark is light grey and bitter, and in some regions is said to have medicinal applications, as do the leaves. *D. erecta* is particularly popular as a hedge plant because of its dense, complicated growth and slender spines but, of course, if it is clipped, it will have fewer flowers. A superb, new cultivar introduced from Japan and known as 'Geisha Girl' has deep purple petals outlined in pale mauve, as well as several cream and green variegated forms that are popular in SE Asia.

NOTE: this species has escaped cultivation in subtropical regions of Australia.

ORIGIN	from southern USA to Brazil
HEIGHT	up to 8 m (26 ft)
TYPE	semi-deciduous, small flowering tree
STATUS	not threatened
HABITAT	dry scrub; pinelands; rocky outcrops
GROWTH	fast
FLOWG	year-round, in the tropics
DRY TOL.	high
SALT TOL.	moderate
LIGHT	full sun
SOIL	fertile, well-drained
NUTRIT.	organic fertilizer twice a year; organic mulch
HAZARDS	spiny; toxic fruit
PROBLEMS	none
ENVIRON.	insect nectar; wild fruit for birds
PROPAG.	seeds; cuttings
LEAVES	simple; bright green; ovate-elliptic; with serrated margins
FLOWERS	showy; blue, lilac, lavender or purple; rarely white; in long panicles; sweetly fragrant
FRUIT	a drupe, to 11 mm (0.4 in.); globular, beaked; deep yellow; enclosed in ripe calyx
USE	hedges; screening; specimen; accent; large planter; civic centre; xerophytic
ZONE	9–12

D. erecta; the little, Verbena-like blooms vary greatly in colour, ranging from blue or lavender to deep purple or even white, and sometimes have a white 'eye'.

D. erecta; these charming, golden berries are toxic to humans but not to birds.

D. erecta f. alba; is a superb form that has chalky white fls.

D. erecta; forming a tall, impenetrable barrier in Cairns, N Qld, Australia.

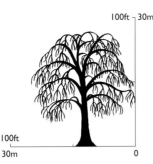

100ft ⌐ 30m

100ft
30m

0

ORIGIN	Malaysia and Borneo to Indonesia
HEIGHT	20–45 m (66–148 ft)
TYPE	evergreen, large fruiting tree
STATUS	not threatened
HABITAT	lowland humid forests
GROWTH	moderate
FLOWG	summer and winter
DRY TOL.	low to moderate
SALT TOL.	low
LIGHT	full sun
SOIL	fertile, well-drained
NUTRIT.	high-potassium fertilizer; deep, organic mulch
HAZARDS	none
PROBLEMS	root fungus and canker
ENVIRON.	nectar and wild fruit for bats
PROPAG.	very fresh seeds; cuttings; grafts
LEAVES	simple; glossy green, silver-bronze below, to 18 cm (7 in.); held in 2 ranks, elliptic to oblong
FLOWERS	showy; pink to yellow or greenish white; cauliflorous; nocturnal; with a smell of milk
FRUIT	a capsule, to 35 cm (13. 8 in.); densely spiny, ellipsoid to globose, olive-green; with creamy, pungently aromatic flesh
USE	large fruit tree; public open space; humid shade garden; botanic collection; conservatory
ZONE	10–12

Durio zibethinus

DURIAN

Murray   27 spp.

MALVACEAE (formerly Bombacaceae)

THE RENOWNED OR INFAMOUS *Durio zibethinus* is a huge rainforest tree with a massive straight trunk with bulky buttresses and topped with a whorl of almost horizontal limbs, typical of the Bombacaceae tribe. The large, simple leaves are glossy green with silver-bronze undersides. Flowers (with a smell of milk) and fruit (high in food value, being 2.5% protein) are held directly on the old wood of the trunk and branches. The greenish or creamy white blooms open in the afternoon, between 2.00–3.00 p.m. They are typically 5-petalled and are usually borne twice a year, in winter and summer. At night, they are visited by fruit bats that feed on the nectar, although some of them also eat the flowers. The fruit takes about 3 months to mature and is not fully ripe until it drops from the tree, but within a few days it splits into 5 sections. The pulp quickly becomes rancid and is considered spoilt and inedible. The taste, or stench, of this celebrated Asian fruit seems hard to define but has been described as reminiscent of banana custard mixed with rotten onions and strained through old socks, making the fruit an acquired taste. The smell draws animals as well as man: elephants, tigers, deer, pig, rhinoceros, tapir and monkey all find their way to the feast, obviously making the harvesting of the wild fruit dangerous in remote regions. *D. zibethinus* is an imposing fruit resembling a small jakfruit (jackfruit); the main difference between the two, apart from the smell, is that jakfruit has white latex and Durian has none. Dangled on a stout stalk, Durian is covered with coarse, stubby, sharp-pointed spines and is divided into 4–5 segments that are filled with large seeds, each embedded in its creamy or yellow, glutinous, custardy aril. Locally, *D. zibethinus* is most popularly eaten fresh, but is often used as a vegetable, preserved as a jam, sun-dried or made into a paste. The protein-rich seeds are also an important food and are roasted or boiled.

D. zibethinus; the nectar-rich fls are pollinated by bats and also eaten by them.

D. zibethinus; forms a tall, straight trunk and lush, conical crown of horizontal limbs and large, handsome lvs.

D. zibethinus; with creamy, pungent flesh, embedded with large sds. Photographed in Irian Jaya, Indonesia.

D. zibethinus; easily confused with jakfruit (jackfruit); Durio is of the Bombax tribe, but jakfruit is a gigantic fig. The spines on Durian are much sharper and longer.

159

Elaeocarpus angustifolius

BLUE QUANDONG

Blume.   60 spp.

E. grandis

ELAEOCARPACEAE

ELAEOCARPUS IS A GENUS celebrated for its unusual, deeply fringed flowers, its excellent timber and, particularly, for its extraordinary, bright blue fruit. Held high above its lofty, buttressed, light grey trunk, *Elaeocarpus angustifolius* has a superb, horizontally layered crown of deep green, finely toothed leaves that turn red as they age, resulting at times in the tree bearing single limbs of bright red foliage. In summer, arising from twigs at the scars of fallen leaves, curious inflorescences develop that are spirally arranged in narrow, unbranched racemes. They hold fragrant, white blooms that are turned to hang downwards, reminiscent of lily-of-the-valley. Each little, bell-shaped bloom is clasped in narrow, finely pointed sepals, with its petals deeply incised to give the appearance of a shaggy fringe. The marble-sized, cobalt-blue fruit that follows has thin, edible, somewhat acid pulp enclosing a deeply wrinkled, brown, 4-seeded stone that has found many uses in its region. Australians use them for craftwork and necklaces; in Hawaii they are used for leis. The light, pale, soft wood has been popular for general indoor work, leading to over-cutting in some parts. Easily grown, *E. angustifolius* has been widely used in Australia for forest regeneration.

*** *E. dentatus*; ([Forst. & Forst. f.] Vahl.), New Zealand, to 18 m (60 ft). Although a large tree in nature, this species is more often a shrub in cultivation. Leaves oblong to ovate, with serrated margins. The flowers are white, abundant; the fruit is small, purple grey. (9–11)

*** *E. ferruginiflorus*; (CT White) NE Qld, to 10 m, (33 ft). MOUNTAIN QUANDONG is a rare, slow-growing highland tree; rusty, felty foliage and blue-green fruit. (9–11)

*** *E. sphaericus*; ([Gaertn.] Schum.) India, Malaysia, to 15 m (50 m). INDIAN BEAD TREE has large, elliptic, serrulate leaves and racemes of pendulous, fragrant, white flowers. The fruit is globose and purple. (10–12)

E. angustifolius; curious, little, fringed fls held in narrow, 1-sided racemes at the tips of the branches. They attract many moths and butterflies – their pollinators.

E. angustifolius; with amazing, marble-sized, cobalt-blue fruit.

E. angustifolius; a group of young trees in Julatten, N Qld, demonstrating the formation of their lofty, pale grey trunks.

E. ferruginifolius; found up to 1,550 m (5086 m) in forests in the Wet Tropics World Heritage Area of NE Qld.

(1) *Elaeocarpus arnhemicus*; (F. Muell.), N Qld, (Cape York Pen.), northern NT, Australia and N Guinea, to 15 m (50 ft). BONY QUANDONG is an everg. native of coast. monsoon vine thickets or monsoon forests; it is a tough, small tree with very leathery, oval, tapering lvs, with serrated margins. Its lightly scented, fringed fls are very small and held in crowded, slender racemes in autumn to winter. (2) The small, thin-fleshed, long-lived, edible fr. measures to 1.5 cm (0.6 in.), with a hard, deeply pitted stone containing the sd. The fr. is particularly distinct, being an almost iridescent cobalt-blue and held in abundant clusters; it is particularly attractive to birds, especially pigeons. Germination from sd may prove erratic and difficult, but this sp. may be propagated from cuttings. *E. arnhemicus* is a very dry- and salt-tol. sp. (10–12) *Elaeocarpus bancroftii* (Meull. and Bailey), Australia, to 15 m (50 ft). JOHNSTONE RIVER ALMOND is one of many rainforest sp. of this exceptional genus in NE Qld. The lvs are distinguished by having 5–8 pairs of lateral veins; the margins have shallow, irregular teeth. (3) Creamy fringed fls are held in dense clusters. (4) The abundant, bluish, edible fr. measures to 4 cm (1.6 in.) diam., and has edible kernels. (10–12)

2

1

3

4

(1) *Elaeocarpus foveolatus*; (F. Muell.), N Qld, Australia endemic, to 30 m (100 ft). WHITE QUANDONG is a fairly rare sp. of this genus, found in both high- and lowland habitats. It has a buttressed trunk and compact crown of rich green, lacquered foliage that is bright, coppery pink on emergence. The small, white fls give way to blue fr. with a hard, inner stone. *E. foveolatus* is sparingly cultivated but worthy, being much smaller in cultivation and vigorous growth; its hard sds, which germinate erratically, must be scarified before planting. (10–12) (3) *Elaeocarpus serratus*; (L.), India and Malaysia, to 20 m (66 ft). CEYLON OLIVE (VERALU in Sri Lanka), a native of wet lowlands, has a rounded, compact crown with light, yellowish white trunk and slow to moderate growth. It has smaller lvs with serrated margins; as they age they turn rich orange or red. (2) The olive-like fr. is not blue, like most of these spp., but dull, greenish yellow, containing large, knobbly sds; the pulp is acidic, and is popular locally for pickling or for adding to curries. *E. serratus* is used locally as a backyard shade tree or for street planting. (10–12) (4) *Elaeocarpus* sp. This undescribed sp. was photographed on a farm near Maalan, N Qld, Australia, *E. arnhemicus* (F. Muell.). It is a large tree to 30 m (100 ft) of lowland monsoon forest. The abundant spikes of creamy white, lightly scented fls and small, deep blue fr. make this a most ornamental sp. (10–12)

ORIGIN	Trop. America
HEIGHT	up to 30 m (100 ft)
TYPE	deciduous; large foliage tree
STATUS	not threatened
HABITAT	dry, lowland forest and savannahs
GROWTH	fast
FLOWG	spring, with new leaves
DRY TOL.	high
SALT TOL.	moderate
LIGHT	full sun
SOIL	fertile, well-drained
NUTRIT.	not normally necessary
HAZARDS	none
PROBLEMS	fungus; invasive roots
ENVIRON.	insect nectar
PROPAG.	seeds
LEAVES	2-pinnate; deep green; pinnae, to 24 pairs; leaflets, to 50
FLOWERS	inconspicuous; greenish white, in dense heads, to 1.5 cm (0.5 in.) diam.
FRUIT	a legume, to 10 cm (4 in.) diam.; coiled, flat; with several seeds
USE	public open space; botanic collection; possible fodder plant; xerophytic
ZONE	10–12

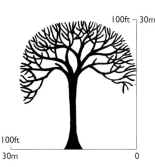

100ft – 30m
100ft
30m
0

Enterolobium cyclocarpum

EARPOD TREE

(Jacq.) Griseb.   5 spp.

Mimosa cyclocarpa

FABACEAE (Mimosoideae)

THIS VOLUPTUOUS GIANT requires its immense, stocky trunk and widely radiating surface roots in order to support its huge, spare, heavy-limbed, horizontal canopy that is layered with coarse, ferny foliage. In late spring, the verdant parasol is profusely sprinkled with tiny, white, fluffy, star-like flowers, which are followed by its distinctive seed pods. The fruit has earned **Enterolobium cyclocarpum** its common names Devil's-, Elephant's- or Monkey's-Ear, as the large, green legume is spiralled into a crinkled doughnut shape with a hole in the centre. On maturation the fruit thicken and become blackish brown and woody; local craftspeople often polish them for tourist artifacts. Most native trees of the countryside have their domestic, agricultural and economic uses and *E. cyclocarpum* is no exception. Young fruit and leaves are used as animal fodder (thus the seeds are dispersed). However, it is reported in Brazil that this has caused lesions in livestock. Both fruit and bark contain tannin and are also employed as a soap substitute, while the bark yields a medicine for colds and a gum that can be substituted for gum arabic. In some regions, the seeds are toasted and eaten. Rich brown, hard and durable, the heartwood has a reddish tinge. It is resistant to dry-wood termites and is widely used as a substitute for walnut or cedar for panelling, furniture and veneers. In Puerto Rico, the fast-growing *E. cyclocarpum* was once popularly planted as a shade tree but was attacked by a fungal disease, which caused it to collapse suddenly and rot. *** *E. contortisiliquum*; ([Vell.] Morong.), Argentina to Brazil, to 35 m (115 ft). Known as TIMBURI or ORELHA-DE-MACAO, it has dark brown fruit, which contains saponin, but it differs in being rounded and heart-shaped. The timber is strong and resistant. (9–11)

NOTE: these species may prove invasive in some areas.

E. cyclocarpum; known as Devil's Ear.

E. contortisiliquum; old woody fr. The fr. of this sp. is somewhat less spiralled and has an ear-like shape.

E. cyclocarpum; the parasol is profusely sprinkled with tiny, white fls, followed by masses of its distinctive sd pods.

E. contortisiliquum; at Fairchild Tropical Gardens, Miami, Florida. Both spp. of *Enterolobium* have wide-spreading, heavy limbs and fairly sparse foliage.

Eperua falcata

BOOTLACE TREE

Aublet.   14 spp.

FABACEAE (Caesalpinioideae)

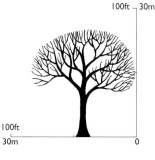

DESPITE ITS SINGULAR BLOOMS, **Eperua falcata** remains largely unknown outside its immediate region. Native of humid, lowland forests of Guyana, northern S America, this giant, robust forest tree forms a wide-spreading, sparsely limbed, evergreen canopy of asymmetric, leathery, pale green leaflets that dry black. Like *Kigelia pinnata*, the African Sausage tree, *E. falcata* has flagellate inflorescences – clusters of flowers are dangled on long, pendant, sturdy stems, which form a fringe at the base of the canopy. With 4 thick, concave sepals clasping a solitary, roundish, fringed petal and 10 long, crimson stamens, the luminous pink or dull red, trumpet-shaped flowers are nocturnally, pungently fragrant and specifically evolved to appeal to their designated pollinators, the bats. From each inflorescence, a single luminous, deep, mauve-pink woody fruit is formed that is, perhaps, even more spectacular than the blooms and recalls the large, flat pods of *Saraca cauliflora*, except for being shorter, a little wider and hooked like a scimitar. They explode on opening, flinging their seed up to 30 m (100 ft). *E. falcata* is one of several handsome species of the *Eperua* genus in this region, and early in its development its hard, reddish brown streaked timber, known as Wallaba, became renowned for its resistance to decay in water. Logs were shipped along coasts to be used for telegraph poles, construction and as roof shingles, particularly in Trinidad where Wallaba-roofed houses still stand. Infusions made from Eperua are believed to promote the growth of thick hair.

*** **E. purpurea**; (Benth.), Venezuela and Colombia, to 30 m (100 ft). Native of rainforests and river valleys, this species has abundant, intensely rosy purple blooms in autumn. This tree was considered the most beautiful of all flowering legumes by the renowned Brazilian botanist, Dr. Adolpho Ducke. (10–12)

ORIGIN	Guyana, endemic
HEIGHT	up to 35 m (115 ft)
TYPE	evergreen, large flowering tree
STATUS	threatened
HABITAT	humid lowland forests and swamps, often on humus-rich sand
GROWTH	moderate
FLOWG	spring
DRY TOL.	moderate
SALT TOL.	low
LIGHT	bright shade to full sun
SOIL	rich, deep, humid
NUTRIT.	balanced fertilizer annually; deep, organic mulch
HAZARDS	none
PROBLEMS	none
ENVIRON.	bat nectar
PROPAG.	seeds
LEAVES	pinnate; light green; leaflets oblong, with slightly undulate margins
FLOWERS	showy; red or pink; with 4 sepals and 1 large, fringed petal; held on long 'cords'; nocturnally pungent
FRUIT	a legume, to 30 cm (12 in.); scimitar-shaped; luminous, pinkish red; explodes on opening
USE	shade tree; specimen; street tree; public open space; civic centre; botanic collection; timber tree
ZONE	10–12

E. falcata; Bootlace Tree with heavy, rosy pink calyxes cupping a solitary, roundish, fringed petal that is nocturnally pungent. Photographed at the Royal Botanic Gardens in Trinidad.

E. falcata; the scimitar-shaped pod echoes that of the leguminous, *Saraca cauliflora*.

E. falcata; following the bat-pollinated fls come ornamental pods, dangled ready to split open and spill their beans.

E. falcata; fls hang down on long cords forming a fringe around the canopy.

ORIGIN	China and Japan
HEIGHT	up to 9 m (30 ft)
TYPE	evergreen, small foliage tree
STATUS	not threatened
HABITAT	evergreen lowland woodland
GROWTH	moderate
FLOWG	autumn to winter
DRY TOL.	high
SALT TOL.	moderate
LIGHT	bright shade to full sun
SOIL	rich, humid, well-drained
NUTRIT.	high-potassium fertilizer in spring; deep, organic mulch
HAZARDS	seeds slightly poisonous
PROBLEMS	fire blight; root fungus; mealy bugs
ENVIRON.	bee nectar
PROPAG.	seeds; layering; grafting
LEAVES	simple; rich green, rusty below; heavily veined; sharply toothed
FLOWERS	showy; dingy white; held in erect, rusty tomentose panicles; intensely fragrant
FRUIT	a pome, to 4 cm (1.5 in.); orange-yellow; edible; does not set fruit in the tropics
USE	small shade tree; small fruiting tree; accent; specimen; large planter; conservatory; xerophytic
ZONE	8–10

50ft ⌐15m

50ft
15m 0

Eriobotrya japonica

LOQUAT

(Thunb.) Lindley   26 spp.

Photinia japonica

ROSACEAE

ERIOBOTRYA JAPONICA is native to Japan and S China and is famous for its delicious fruit. Although this subtropical species will grow tolerably well in the shorter daylight hours of the tropics, it will bloom but rarely sets fruit. It is, however, often grown in the tropics for its compact stature and superb, large, quilted, deeply veined and toothed leaves. In cooler climates, as the sturdy, erect panicles of dingy white, strongly fragrant, rose-like winter flowers fade, small, fleshy, edible, apricot-flavoured fruit are formed. *E. japonica* is a member of the great rose family – which leads to a consideration of temperate fruit. Plants such as strawberry, raspberry and blackberries and trees including peach, almond, nectarine, pear, plum, apple and cherry, as well as apricot, quince and loquat, are all of the Rosaceae or Rose family. Fruit like grape, fig, persimmon, blueberry and cranberry are from other clans. Tropical fruit species, on the other hand, are infinitely more diversified. Members of the amorphous Rose clan share many of the same genes and, therefore, are prone to many of the same pests and diseases. (*E. japonica*, for example, inherits the Rose family's weakness to fireblight.) In the Mediterranean, however, Loquat is grown commercially (under protective cloth to keep out flies), to be used as a base for jams and jellies. Loquats are also eaten raw, are stewed or made into pickles. There are over 200 cultivars in Japan. These are important honey plants.

*** *E. deflexa*; ([Hemsl.], Nak.), Taiwan, to 10 m (33 ft). A similar, robust species but with smaller fruit. It has very ornamental, deep reddish, new growth and larger, pure white, showier flowers thato. are set in rusty brown stalks and calyxes. Cv. 'Bronze Improved': leaves, vivid bronze when young, later, rich green. (9–11)

NOTE: *E. japonica* is listed undesirably invasive in **NSW, Australia.**

E. japonica; erect panicles of rusty tomentose, rose-like fls.

E. deflexa; at Thuret Jardin des Plants in Cap d'Antibes, S France, where it thrives in the frost-free environment.

E. japonica; in the Mediterranean, it is grown extensively commercially, the fr. being used as a base for jams and jellies.

E. japonica; a member of the rose family, Loquat inherits the family's weakness to the devastating fireblight. In Japan, there are over 200 vars. of this popular, aromatic, native fr.

Erythrina variegata

MOUNTAIN EBONY

L.   112 spp.

E. indica; E. orientalis

FABACEAE (Papilionoideae)

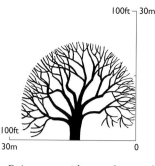

ERYTHRINA BLOOMS ARE DESIGNED for bird pollination. Being very widespread around the tropics, these species are pollinated by different types of nectar-loving birds. Those of S America have narrowly rolled petals to accommodate long-billed hummingbirds, while other species have their flowers twisted back for passerines and others have long peduncles as perches for non-hovering sunbirds. ***Erythrina variegata*** occurs naturally from E Africa to the Indian Ocean islands, west to Polynesia, and is the commonest *Erythrina* species. It is a spherically crowned, much-branched tree with grey-green, furrowed bark exfoliating in papery strips and scattered with conical thorns in its early years. Its 3-foliate leaves have large, triangular leaflets held on long petioles. Packed in tapering spikes, its luminous, scarlet, cockscomb flowers are illuminated by their electric violet stamens; they are held on stout stalks at a near horizontal angle, giving an impression of fiery darts. Following the flowers are fat, beaked, woody pods, which are brown, curved and packed with ornamental, enamelled, dark red seeds, which are popular for leis in Hawaii. *Erythrina* species contain powerful, narcotic alkaloids. Fast growing, ***E. variegata***, which may be easily grown from very large cuttings, is planted for coffee shade, windbreaks and as a support for black-pepper vines. In Polynesia, the soft wood is sometimes used in boatbuilding and light construction.

*** var. 'Alba' has pure white flowers.

*** var. *variegata*; a decorative form with the veins and midribs of its leaves boldly marked creamy yellow. In areas of high rainfall, this variety is hardly deciduous.

*** cv. 'Tropical Coral' is a relatively recent innovation, popular in Hawaii, with the compact, fastigiate form of Lombardy Poplar. Its stems are very spiny.

NOTE: *E. variegata* has escaped cultivation in some Pacific Is.

ORIGIN	from India to the Philippines and Pacific
HEIGHT	up to 20 m (66 ft)
TYPE	deciduous flowering tree
STATUS	not threatened
HABITAT	dry lowland woodland
GROWTH	fast
FLOWG	winter to early spring
DRY TOL.	high
SALT TOL.	high
LIGHT	full sun
SOIL	fertile, very well-drained
NUTRIT.	balanced fertilizer annually
HAZARDS	spiny, toxic, with alkaloids
PROBLEMS	tip borers
ENVIRON.	bird nectar
PROPAG.	seeds; large cuttings
LEAVES	3-foliate; green or variegated; leaflets to 21 cm (8.2 in.)
FLOWERS	showy; scarlet or crimson; held in dense spikes; to 20 cm (8 in.)
FRUIT	legume, to 40 × 3 cm (16 × 1.2 in.); linear, cylindric; woody
USE	seaside; summer shade tree; winter-flowering tree; street tree; civic centre; agri-cultural shade; xerophytic
ZONE	10—12

E. variegata; a luminous cockscomb spike of blooms.

E. variegata; sadly, this fine old specimen with its spring blooms at Fairchild Tropical Gardens in Miami, Florida, has been removed to make way for a new Visitors' Centre.

E. variegata; var. *variegata*; with vividly variegated lvs. In areas of high rainfall, this variety often retains its lvs.

E. variegata var. 'Alba' is a charming, pure white form.

Erythrina abyssinica; (Lam. ex DC.), (syn. *E. tomentosa*), from Trop. Africa to Himalayas, to 14 m (46 ft). RED HOT POKER TREE, deciduous, spiny, slow-growing tree of savannahs and scrub. Young lvs are densely woolly; woody fr. pods velvety and shortly constricted. Sds are vermilion and black. Lightweight, whitish wood is used for drums, fishnet floats and brake blocks. Red sds are made into necklaces. Shown above in Havana, Cuba, in the spring. (10–12)

Erythrina burttii; (E.G. Baker f.), Kenya and Tanzania, to 25 m (82 ft). MBOOSI is a fairly rare sp. of lowland coast. plains, usually forming a flat-topped, open canopy. Young bark is green. Fls have velvety pubescent calyxes and are flame-coloured in lax racemes appearing before lvs. Fr. pods are somewhat papery; sds are few, orange, and oblong. Here is shown an old, hurricane-ravaged specimen at the Jardin Botanico de Cienfuegos in Cuba. (10–12)

Erythrina caffra; (Thunb.), (syn. *E. insignis*), eastern S Africa, to 18 m (59 ft), LUCKY BEAN TREE is semi-everg.; limbs often prickly. Fls are orange-scarlet (rarely cream); standard petal is relatively short, broad and curved. Fr. is slender and slightly constricted between sds. *E. caffra* is considered to have magical properties in S Africa. Lf poultices are used locally to treat venereal sores and an infusion of lvs is used for earache. KZN, S Africa. (9–11)

Erythrina coralloides; (A. DC.), E Mexico to Arizona, USA, to 7 m (23 ft). Known as the NAKED CORAL TREE, this sp. grows as a tall shrub or small tree. Trunk and limbs are slightly prickly and densely rusty hairy. Lflts are deltoid to suborbicular. Fls are brilliant red, in wide, short, dense racemes. This old specimen at Huntingdon Gardens in Pasedena, California, shows the disorganized, weeping habit of this distinctive sp. (9–11)

Erythrina crista-galli; (L.), (syn. *E. pulcherrima*; *E. laurifolia*), S America, to 9 m (30 ft). Cockspur Coral is a subtrop. sp. of cooler regions east of the Andes. Blooming summer to autumn, *E. crista-galli* is popularly planted in cooler gardens or treated as a perennial in some temperate areas, where it is cut back by frost in winter. It requires a dry position. Photographed at the Royal Botanic Garden in Sydney, Australia. (8–10)

Erythrina decora; (Harms.), Namibia, S Africa, to 7 m (23 ft), Namib Coral Tree is a shrubby, medium-sized tree found in warm, arid (often rocky), bushveld. Twigs are greyish white with woolly hairs and some prickles. Fls on sturdy, woolly stems; calyxes are cream-tomentose. Fr. is a cylindrical pod, deeply constricted between sds, which are red with a black spot and slightly hairy. Sds are used to decorate Namibian herdsmen's horn trumpets. (9–11)

Erythrina dominguezii; (Hassler), Argentina, Brazil, Bolivia, Paraguay. This coral-coloured beauty was photographed in the spring at Jardin Botanico de Cienfuegos in Cuba, where there is an important collection of this genus. This venerable specimen has been affected by a hurricane or two. *E. dominguezii*, with its abundant bloom, is surely one of the most outstanding sp. of this superb genus. (9–11)

Erythrina fusca; (Loureiro), (syn. *E. glauca*), SE Asia to New Guinea to Fiji and Trop. America, to 26 m (85 ft). Swamp Immortelle is a very widespread sp., armed with blunt spines on its trunk. Lvs are dull green, silvery below. Fls vary greatly from region to region, from dull, purple-red to light orange or bright orange-red. The velvety sd pods contain dark brown or black sds. Depicted, is a tree at Waimea Arboretum, Hawaii. (10–12)

Erythrina lysistemon; (Hutch.), S Africa endemic, to 10 m (33 ft), COMMON CORAL TREE, or KAFFIRBOOM, very common locally, is a semi-decid. sp. occurring in bushveld and coast. bush. Lvs have a thorny midrib, rachis and petiole. Fls are bright red (rarely pink). Fr. are slender, deep brown pods, deeply constricted between sds. Fls attract many insect and bird spp. Lvs and bark are browsed by game. Limbs planted as live fence posts. (9–11)

Erythrina speciosa; (Andr.), Brazil endemic, to 5 m (16 ft). Known in Brazil as MULUNGU-DO-LITTORAL or ERITRINA-CANDELABRO, this is a spiny, fast-growing native of the Atlantic coast. rainforest. It has pink or bright red fls distinguished by extra long, rolled petals for hummingbirds. Fr. are slim, long and not constricted between sds. Blooming from winter to autumn. Photographed at the Arboretum of Los Angeles, Pasadena, USA. (9–11)

Erythrina × *sykesii*; (Barneby and Krukoff), Hort. This hybrid sp. has been known as *E. indica* in the horticultural trade of Australia. It was photographed at the renowned Huntingdon Gardens in Pasadena, California. Two trees of this sp. frame the main entrance to the display gardens. Their broad crowns of ascending, prickly limbs held masses of flaming orange, spring blooms. (9–11)

Erythrina verspitilio: (Benth.), Australia, 10–30 m (33–100 ft). BAT'S-WING CORAL TREE is widespread in subtrop. and trop. open forest. Stout, mottled trunk is corky and armed with large, conical spines. Mature lvs are trifoliate and lflts are much wider than long, resembling a bat's wings. Fls are salmon-pink to scarlet (in NT), open and pea-shaped, with prominent stamens. They are borne in long, pendent racemes. (9–12)

Eucalyptus deglupta

RAINBOW GUM

Blume. 600+ spp.

E. multiflora; E. naudiniana

MYRTACEAE (Telocalyptus)

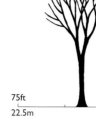

100ft – 30m

75ft
22.5m – 0

EUCALYPTUS IS A LARGELY AUSTRALIAN GENUS, although some species are found in Malesia and the Philippines. Within this extraordinary genus, which is adapted to a huge diversity of habitats found within its natural range, species are cultivated for their timber and wood fibre. They are renowned for their nectar-rich blooms, which produce a wide range of honeys, while their essential oils are used in perfumery and medicines. Many species are highly valued as ornamentals. They range in habit from exceptionally tall, fast-growing species to shrubby mallees. *Eucalypts* are heterophyllous (having more than one type of leaf), with a marked difference between juvenile and adult leaves. **Eucalyptus deglupta** originates in the tropical regions from New Guinea to the island of Mindanao in the Celebes Sea and is found in primary forests, along stream banks from sea level to 600 m (2,000 ft) altitude. Known as Rainbow Gum, **E. deglupta** has a lofty, mast-like trunk, simple, lanceolate leaves that are aromatic when crushed and splendid, abundant umbels of fragrant, nectar-rich, creamy white blooms. The bark peels off layer by layer in narrow, cardboard ribbons to reveal the inner bright green surface that, as it is exposed to the air, gradually changes to blue, then purple and finally brick-red. Combined with the pink-grey outer skin, it creates a superbly decorative effect. In the Philippines, pulverized bark is used in traditional medicine to reduce fatigue. Like many *Eucalyptus*, **E. deglupta** is shallow-rooted, brittle-limbed and easily toppled in a hurricane. These are important honey plants.

*** **E. salmonophloia**; (F. Muell.), W Australia, to 24 m. SALMON GUM has deep salmon new bark turning grey as it ages. The leaves are bright green; the flowers in umbels, white. (9–11)

NOTE: many *Eucalyptus* species have proved invasive in some regions.

ORIGIN	Sulawesi to Philippines and New Guinea
HEIGHT	up to 70 m (229 ft)
TYPE	evergreen, large foliage tree
STATUS	not threatened
HABITAT	lowland humid forests
GROWTH	very fast
FLOWG	several times a year
DRY TOL.	moderate
SALT TOL.	moderate to high
LIGHT	full sun
SOIL	deep, humid, well-drained
NUTRIT.	normally not necessary
HAZARDS	brittle, falling limbs; shallow roots
PROBLEMS	phytophthora root rot; blue-gum tip sucker
ENVIRON.	bee nectar
PROPAG.	seeds (have long viability)
LEAVES	simple; pale green; to 15 × 7.5 cm (6 × 3 in.); ovate; very aromatic
FLOWERS	showy; creamy white, small, in profuse, terminal umbels; fragrant
FRUIT	a capsule, to 3 mm (0.1 in.); 4-valved; held in abundant umbels
USE	public open space; street tree; specimen
ZONE	10–12

E. deglupta; at the Arboretum of Los Angeles, California. Like most of its amorphous family, the Rainbow Gum tends to have brittle limbs and shallow roots.

E. deglupta; with fragrant, nectar-filled fls. Fls. several times a year.

E. deglupta; with small fr. capsules held in abundance.

E. deglupta; peeling off in narrow, cardboard-like ribbons, creating an exquisite jigsaw of rainbow-hued bark.

(1) *Eucalyptus confertiflora*; (F. Muell.), from northern Australia to New Guinea, to 12 m (39 ft). This 'half-barked' Gum is widespread in open and savannah woodland where, very often, the soil is poorly drained and even seasonally waterlogged. This sp. usually carries its large, fluffy clusters of cream, nectar-rich fls (2) before its new lvs, which are bright purple or claret-coloured on emergence. The lvs are large, dull, grey-green in colour and are mostly finely hairy. Mainly spring blooming; the infls are held in compound, dense clusters, often on bare branchlets before the new lvs. This sp. is a source of firewood, as well as providing nectar for native bees. The timber is both tough and very durable. (10–12)

(3) *Eucalyptus miniata*; (Cunn. ex Schauer.), Australia (W Aust, NT, Qld.), to 30 m (100 ft). WOOLLYBUTT or DARWIN WOOLLYBUTT, an ornamental sp., widely distributed in open forests and woodlands in tablelands and sandstone country in trop. northern areas of Australia. It is another half-barked sp., with rough, flaking bark at the base of its smooth, whitish trunk. It is distinguished by (4) deep, prune-red young stems, grey-green, slightly sickle-shaped lvs and large, orange or scarlet blooms. Fr. is cylindrical to ovoid, and usually a ribbed, woody capsule with 3 deeply enclosed valves. *E. miniata* provides copious nectar for native bees. Inner bark is used for an infusion to treat diarrhoea. Limbs are used by Aborigines to make didjeridoos. Shown here growing as a street tree in Cairns, N Qld. (10–11)

(1) *Eucalyptus platyphylla*; (F. Meull.), from N Qld, Australia to New Guinea, to 20 m (66 ft). POPLAR GUM is closely related to *E. alba* (included with it by some authors). This sp. grows on moist flats and ridges of N Qld from near the tip of Cape York Peninsula, south to Rockhampton, within 100 km (62 miles) of the coast. This sp. may become decid. in the dry season. It has white, grey or tan bark that is also decid. and often powdery. Juvenile lvs are alternate, broadly lanceolate to ovate, short-petioled; adult lvs are alternate, orbicular, cordate or rhomboid, rarely lanceolate, rounded, thin-textured, grey-green. (2) Infl. is axillary, simple, umbels 3–7-flowered; buds are ovoid. Fr. is hemispherical to turbinate; several-ribbed. With its striking, pale bark, large, thick, leathery lvs and fluffy white fls, Poplar Gum is very ornamental and worthy of cultivation. (10–12)

(3) *Eucalyptus ptychocarpa*; (F. Meull.), W Aust.; NT; Qld, Australia, endemic, to 12 m (39 ft). This is the widely popular SWAMP-, OR SPRING-BLOODWOOD, which is widely planted as a street tree throughout Qld. Native of the banks of freshwater springs and streams in lowland or sandstone regions or coast. monsoon forest, this sp. is fast growing from sd, and forms a dense, spreading crown of drooping branches. The brown-grey bark is rough and fibrous. Juvenile lvs are opposite, lanceolate to broadly lanceolate, stalked, occasionally peltate. Adult lvs mostly alternate, narrowly ovate or lanceolate, thick, green or grey-green. Infl. is terminal, 3–7-flowered, corymbose panicles. (4 and 5) The colour of the fls, which are a good source of nectar, varies from deep to pale pink to white, with the ovoid or clavate buds dusted with glaucous tomen. (10–12) NOTE: this sp. is now *Corymbia ptychocarpa*.

(1) ***Eucalyptus phoenicia***; (F. Muell.), North Australia endemic, to 10 m (33 ft). SCARLET GUM is a slender, multi-trunked tree with a spreading, open crown. The lower trunk has fibrous, flaky, yellowish brown bark, while the branches are smooth and yellowish. The lvs are greyish green, narrow, to 15 cm (6 in.). (2) Held in large, dense, globular umbels, the nectar-rich winter blooms are typically fiery orange. Fr. are urn-shaped, woody, with a narrow neck, to 3.3 cm (1.3 in.) ***E. phoenicia*** is a worthy ornamental with showy fls and bark. It prefers a sunny, well-drained site. (3) ***Eucalyptus pruinosa***; (Schauer), N Australia endemic, to 8 m (26 ft). This small, decorative sp. is slow growing and develops a somewhat crooked, stumpy framework. It is found in monsoon savannah woodland, often in poorly drained, black, cracking soils. ***E. pruinosa*** may remain a shrubby mallée. The sp. name derives from the broad, stem-clasping, pruinose, bluish silver young lvs that age to grey-green. Fls are held in glaucous buds with a conical calyx that opens to form a small, dense, creamy, fluffy head. Fr. is an elongated, cup-shaped, woody capsule, to 1.2 cm (0.5 in.). Aborigines wind strips of the inner bark round the body and limbs to help soothe pains and rheumatism. (10–12)

Eugenia uniflora

SURINAM CHERRY

L.

550 spp.

E. michellii

MYRTACEAE

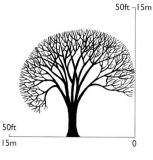

50ft ⌐15m

50ft
15m   0

ORIGIN	S America
HEIGHT	up to 10 m (33 ft)
TYPE	evergreen, small fruiting tree
STATUS	not threatened
HABITAT	lowland, in limestone thickets
GROWTH	slow
FLOW'G	spring, or sporadically
DRY TOL.	high
SALT TOL.	moderate
LIGHT	full sun
SOIL	fertile, well-drained
NUTRIT.	balanced fertilizer in spring; organic mulch
HAZARDS	none
PROBLEMS	may be invasive
ENVIRON.	bee nectar; wild bird fruit
PROPAG.	seeds
LEAVES	simple; rich green; to 6 x 3.5 cm (2.5 × 1.3 in.); ovate-lanceolate, glabrous; with red, new growth
FLOWERS	showy; creamy white, tinged pink; held on long, slender stalks; fragrant
FRUIT	a berry, to 3 cm (1.2 in.); 8-ribbed, bright red; juicy, sweet
USE	backyard tree; hedging and screening; accent; topiary; large planter; bonsai subject; median strip; xerophytic
ZONE	10–12

APART FROM 2 SPECIES, the genus *Eugenia* (550 species) is found in the New World, while the closely related *Syzygium* genus (1,000 species) are found exclusively in the Old World. Until recently, most *Syzygium* were included in the *Eugenia* genus. ***Eugenia uniflora***, which is native to light, sandy stream banks of Brazil, grows with a much-branched, shrubby habit, with neat, dense foliage and coppery new growth. Typical of its genus, the attractive, little fragrant flowers are creamy white with many stamens, and held on long, slender stalks. Pectin-rich, slightly resinous-flavoured fruit form rapidly as the blooms fade. They are cherry-like, depressed-globose, 8-ribbed and resemble diminutive, waxy, red pumpkins. There are 2 distinct varieties of *E. uniflora*, the more common, bright red form and a rarer, dark crimson to nearly black type, which tends to be sweeter and less resinous. Their popularity is mixed; there are many who find them too peppery, sour or resinous, while others find them utterly delicious – sweet, extremely juicy and slightly spicy – provided they are very ripe. In their region, these fruit are eaten out-of-hand or have general, culinary use, stewed or made into jellies and refreshing juice. In SE Asia, the green fruit are pickled in vinegar and salt. Crushed leaves are steeped in boiling water to make a home remedy to soothe irritated skin or for use as an insect repellent. Because of its measured growth and fine foliage, *E. uniflora* is widely planted as a slow- growing, fine-textured hedge or for tall screening in gardens of Trop. America.
*** Cultivars include: 'Black': large fruit, nectarine flavour. 'Chamba': large, juicy, sweet. 'Lolita': small fruit; 2 crops a year. 'Nacha': very large fruit, rather acid; 2 crops a year. 'Vermilion': large fruit, nectarine flavour. 'Westree 369': medium fruit; bears all year. *Eugenia* species are important honey plants

NOTE: *E. uniflora* is considered invasive in some regions.

E. uniflora; with little pumpkin-like fr. They need to be very ripe before their spicy, sweet flesh may be appreciated.

E. uniflora; with typical little nectar-rich, fragrant fls.

E. uniflora; with dense, fine foliage, popular as a tall hedge or screen, thus providing a living larder for man and birds.

E. uniflora; typical of the Myrtaceae, this sp. has hard, heavy, sinuous wood and bark that peels off in strips.

Eugenia luschnathiana; ([O. Berg.] B. D. Jackson), (syn. *Phyllocalyx luschnathiana*), Brazil endemic, to 9 m. (30 ft). Pɪᴛᴏᴍʙᴀ or Uᴠᴀʟʜᴀ ᴅᴇ Cᴀᴍᴘᴀ, is popular, aromatic fr. These are larger than those of Grumichama and are described as being soft and sweet like an apricot. This sp. is intolerant of alkaline soils, requiring deep, humid, acid soil. *E. luschnathiana* is often grafted onto *E. uniflora* stock, which is alkaline-tolerant. (10–12)

Eugenia reinwardtiana; ([Blume] D. C.), N Qld, Australia, to 3m. (10ft). Bᴇᴀᴄʜ Cʜᴇʀʀʏ is native to dry to moist vine thickets. Slow growing, it is the sole Australian member of this genus (the rest have been redesignated as *Acmena*, *Acmenosperma*, *Syzygium* and *Waterhousia*). Happy in shade or full sun, this sp. is grown for its neat, dense habit and its delicous, little glossy red fr. Typically, the small, leathery lvs emerge bright red. (10–12)

Trop. American pastureland, the typical habitat for the slow growing, xerophytic *Myrtaceae* tribe.

Euphorbia punicea

JAMAICAN POINSETTIA

Sw.

2,000 spp.

E. tryana

EUPHORBIACEAE (Euphorbioideae)

50ft ⌐15m

50ft
15m 0

LIKE ANY LARGE, ISOLATED TROPICAL ISLAND, Jamaica is home to many remarkable endemic plants. One of the most ornamental is the Jamaican Poinsettia, *Euphorbia punicea*, a much-branched, thornless shrub or small tree. This handsome species is common in the central and western parishes on rocky limestone in open woodlands and thickets, from sea level to 1,000 m (3,300 ft). *E. punicea* has thickish, glabrous limbs that contain copious, milky latex. (It is the presence of sap that distinguishes euphorbias from cactus.) The narrowly-oblong, thinly succulent leaves are clustered in whorls at the ends of the twigs. Nestled in their apex are clusters of large, vivid, butterfly blooms that recall the Crown of Thorns, *Euphorbia millii*. In reality, they comprise small, branched clusters with each, tiny, yellow flower (cyathium) embellished by a pair of brilliant scarlet, crimson or pinkish orange, leaf-like bracts (involucres) at its base. On closer inspection, the cyathia, which are either male or female, have curious raised, oval, window-like glands and bizarre sexual parts. This very slow-growing species detests having wet roots and must be planted in very well-drained soil. Although it will tolerate seaside conditions, if it is to perform well it should be sheltered from the full force of the wind.

*** *E. gymnota*; (Urb.), Bahamas endemic, to 6 m (20 ft), a large shrub or small tree. This glabrous species is very similar to *E. punicea*. It has fleshy, somewhat rubbery, dichotomous branching, with its linear-oblanceolate, greyish green leaves densely, spirally arranged at the tips of the many twigs. Flowers (or cyathia) are held terminally in dense clusters on stout pedicles; they are reddish. This species is a promising ornamental (10–12)

NOTE: *Euphorbia* sap is not water soluble, so must be rinsed out with alcohol.

ORIGIN	Jamaica, endemic
HEIGHT	3–10 m (10–33 ft)
TYPE	evergreen, small flowering tree
STATUS	very rare and vulnerable
HABITAT	on limestone, in open thickets and dry scrubland
GROWTH	slow
FLOWG	year-round
DRY TOL.	high
SALT TOL.	high
LIGHT	full sun
SOIL	rich. very well-drained
NUTRIT.	balanced fertilizer annually
HAZARDS	irritating toxic sap
PROBLEMS	none
ENVIRON.	insect nectar
PROPAG.	seeds; layers
LEAVES	simple; dark green, paler below; narrow-oblong; thin, smooth
FLOWERS	showy; brilliant scarlet, crimson or pinkish orange bracts; held in cymes
FRUIT	a capsule, to 1 cm (0.4 in.); dry, 3-celled dehiscent
USE	seaside; small flowering tree; accent; large planter; bonsai subject; civic centre; xerophytic
ZONE	10–12

E. punicea; little dry, 3-celled, dehiscent fr. capsules.

E. punicea; fls resemble small Poinsettia fls and decorate the tree all year. Although it is possible to layer this sp., it is probably better propagated by sd, despite being very slow growing.

E. punicea; all parts have milky latex. This sp. requires very well-drained soil to do well.

E. gymnota; this slow-growing Bahamas endemic is not often used in Florida horticulture, but it has great potential.

(1) ***Euphorbia tirucalli***; (L.), Africa, to 10 m (33 ft), PENCIL-, MILK-, FINGER -, or BONE-TREE, RUBBER EUPHORBIA or, in Australia, NAKED LADY, is a very poisonous sp., full of caustic, irritating sap that is said to cause blindness in contact with the eyes. This sap is used regionally as fish poison. *E. tirucalli* slowly forms a fleshy trunk and succulent branches. Thin, pencil-like stems usually carry a few, narrow, green lvs that abort early but are usually absent. This xerophytic sp. can be grown very easily from large limbs, which should be left for several days to 'bleed' their sap and 'heel' over. In many parts of the tropics, *E. tirucalli* is planted as barriers or boundary fences and, in Africa, frequently marks graveyards. (2) Tiny petal-less, creamy white stamened fls held at shoot tips. (3) A brilliantly flame-coloured, new var. known as 'Sticks of Fire'. (9–12)

(4) ***Euphorbia candelabrum***; (Kotschy), S Africa to NE Africa, to 20 m (66 ft). TREE CACTUS or GIANT EUPHORBE, photographed on the seaside esplanade in Altea, Costa Blanca, in S Spain. Fairly fast growing, it is popular as an ornamental in dry regions of the Mediterranean. Like all *Euphorbia*, *E. candelabrum* contains a poisonous and irritating milky latex that is used regionally to stun and catch fish. (9–11)

(5) ***Euphorbia ingens***; (E. Mey.), Africa, to 12 m (39 ft). CANDELABRA TREE is a true xerophyte with no lvs to manufacture chlorophyll. Fleshy stems perform like lvs, with 4–5 flanges to increase surface area, thus reducing the loss of water by transpiration. Each flange has strong, sharp spines. Stems are brittle and, when broken, exude milky, toxic sap. Blooms early spring. Latex is used as 'lime' to snare birds. Regionally, this sp. has several medicinal uses. Photographed in the wild in KZN, S Africa. (9–12) Both spp. will grow from large cuttings.

Fagraea fragrans

TEMBUSU

Roxb.   35 spp.

GENTIANACEAE (formerly Loganiaceae)

FRAGRAEA FRAGRANS is a slow-growing, single-trunked species that originally forms a narrow crown of perpendicular branches that droop downwards at their tips. In maturity, the trunk becomes deeply fissured and horizontal growth begins, with the tree developing middle-age spread and losing its youthful silhouette. The tumbling, flexible limbs have dense, terminal clusters of elliptic, thin-textured and short-petioled leaves. *F. fragrans* blooms twice during the year, once in summer and again in autumn. After a brief dry spell, the tree bears masses of tightly clustered, pearly white and intensely nocturnally fragrant flowers that deepen in colour to deep ivory over a period of several days. Although charming, the flowers, which tend to be hidden in the foliage, develop a sour smell and, as they age, they begin to abort. Slowly, after about 3 months, orange-red berries are formed, which, although very bitter, are a choice delicacy for the flying foxes (fruit bats) that fly in from far away to raid the trees for their sweet harvest. In the moonlight, the stately Tembusu is a tall, gauzy halo of tumbling, willowy limbs surrounded by an eerie swirling of screeching flying foxes and the pungently acrid odour of small, bruised, red berries. By this means, the seeds are dispersed far and wide. Medicinally, concoctions of bark are used against fever and leaves are used to alleviate severe diarrhoea. The timber is a heavy, durable hardwood that is often used locally in construction and furniture. *F. fragrans* tolerates low fertility and the poor aeration of heavy, clay soils and, in some regions, is planted to check soil erosion.

*** *F. ceilanica*; (Thunb.), India to Malesia, to 12 m (40 ft). Evergreen climber, shrub or small tree, often with aerial roots. The leaves are fleshy, narrowly-elliptic or obovate. The flowers are white or pale yellow, fragrant. The fruit is purple-black. (10–12)

ORIGIN	N India to Malesia
HEIGHT	up to 30 m (100 ft)
TYPE	evergreen, large flowering tree
STATUS	not threatened
HABITAT	open and swampy, lowland forest
GROWTH	slow
FLOWG	late spring and autumn
DRY TOL.	moderate
SALT TOL.	low
LIGHT	high
SOIL	tolerates heavy, poor soils
NUTRIT.	balanced fertilizer annually; deep, organic mulch
HAZARDS	none
PROBLEMS	none
ENVIRON.	moth nectar; bird and bat fruit
PROPAG.	seeds (slow)
LEAVES	simple; deep green; to 15 cm (6 in.); elliptic; tipped, thin-textured
FLOWERS	showy; pearly white, later yellow; held in stalked clusters; intensely fragrant, nocturnal
FRUIT	a berry to 1 cm, (0.4 in.); globose, on thick stalks; orange then scarlet; seeds roughly angled
USE	street tree; public open space; specimen in large garden; bonsai subject
ZONE	10–12

F. fragrans; pearly white, nocturnally fragrant fls.

F. fragrans; a mature specimen at the Singapore Botanic Gardens where it thrives in the heavy island clay. This tree is just beginning to develop a more horizontal growth.

F. fragrans; bitter, acrid-sweet berries, but delicious lollipops for flying foxes.

F. ceilanica; this sp. may be an everg. climber, shrub or small tree, often with aerial roots (epiphytic), like a fig.

Fagraea berteriana; (Gray ex Benth.), Pacific and Trop. Australia, to 15 m (50 ft). Pua-Kenikeni or Ten Cent Flower is popular in Hawaii where its highly fragrant, long-tubed white fls are used for leis or soaked in coconut oil to make a perfumed body and hair oil. Fls deepen to orange with age. Fr., to 2.5 cm (1 in.), fleshy, with many sds, are loved by birds. Blooming summer and autumn. This sp. requires rich, humid soil. Sometimes epiphytic. (10–12)

Fagraea cambagei; (A. Gray), (syn. *F. gracilipes* ; *F. elata*), from NE Qld, Australia to New Guinea, Aru Is and Pacific, to 10 m (33 ft), Mulgrave Plum, Pink Jitta or Porcelain Fruit is a slow-growing, shade-tolerant sp. of coast. bushland or swamps above mangrove. Lvs are thick, leathery, shiny; fls are white and fragrant, in terminal clusters. In NE Qld, fr. varies from hot pink in the south to pure white in the north. (10–12)

Fagraea crenulata; (Maingay ex C.B. Clark), Indochina, Malay Peninsula, Sumatra and Borneo, to 15 m (50 ft). Cabbage Tree, or Malabera is a fast-growing sp. of swampy land. This sp. has wide-spreading, sympoidal growth, a thorny trunk and extremely large, leathery lvs, and crowded, terminal panicles of small, white fls. It hates to be crowded and requires shelter from strong wind to prevent lvs from tearing. (10–12)

Fagraea racemosa; (Jack ex Wall.), Indo-China to Solomons and N Australia, to 13 m (43 ft). False Coffee is a slender, narrow tree with pendulous limbs, native to low-lying, swampy land. Lvs are opposite, large, smooth and leathery, to 20 cm (8 in.). Scented, pure white fls are held on pendulous terminal racemes all year. Much used in Malaysian native medicine. Photographed in autumn on Pulau Ubin, a small island off Singapore. (10–12)

179

This historic, native *F. fragrans* was growing on the site of the Singapore Botanic Gardens before the land was cleared for the installation of the gardens in 1859. It is featured on the Singapore $5 note. This specimen demonstrates how, having begun life as a slender young thing, it has widened its girth in old age. Seated at the base of the tree, an elderly woman performs a private, religious ritual, drawing spiritual inspiration from the sacred tree.

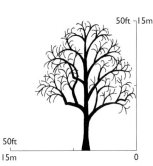

50ft – 15m

50ft
15m   0

Fernandoa magnifica

SNAKE TREE

Seem.   14 spp.

Kigelia lanceolata

BIGNONIACEAE

ORIGIN	E Africa
HEIGHT	9–18 m (30–59 ft)
TYPE	deciduous, small flowering tree
STATUS	rare in the wild
HABITAT	dry or humid evergreen or deciduous woodland
GROWTH	moderate to fast
FLOW'G	spring
DRY TOL.	moderate to high
SALT TOL.	low
LIGHT	full sun
SOIL	fertile, well-drained
NUTRIT.	balanced fertilizer annually; deep, organic mulch
HAZARDS	none
PROBLEMS	none
ENVIRON.	insect nectar
PROPAG.	seeds (fresh)
LEAVES	pinnate; deep green; to 30 cm (12 in.); leaflets to 9.5 cm (3.7 in.)
FLOWERS	showy; red trumpet, bright yellow throat; held in up to 10 flowered cymes
FRUIT	a capsule, to 100 × 2.5 cm (39.4 × 1 in.); cylindrical, twisted; seeds winged
USE	specimen; small flowering tree; accent; large planter; civic centre; xerophytic
ZONE	10–12

KNOWN AS MLANGA-LANGA in Kenya, Snake Tree is one of a closely related group of outstanding E African natives of the illustrious Bignoniaceae family that includes *Kigelia*, *Markhamia*, *Spathodea* and *Stereospermum*. All have extraordinarily beautiful, showy trumpet flowers. *Fernandoa magnifica*, which is no exception, is a vigorous species with an angular framework of slender limbs, which are an iridescent rusty red. In spring, before the new foliage, flower buds emerge, swelling and splitting to release gorgeous, crumpled, fiery scarlet or rich orange trumpets, their yawning mouths revealing brilliant golden throats. Fernandoa blooms are precocious and are aborted soon after pollination. Typical of the Bignoniaceae genus, the flowers are followed by cylindrical seed pods packed with winged seeds. In this case, the pods are spirally twisted, slender, woody and very long – up to 1 m (3.3 ft) in length. When dry, they spin, forming amazing optical gymnastics as they writhe in the breeze and so earning it the nickname Snake Tree. The heartwood, which is tough, orange-yellowish and dark streaked, is moderately hard and valued for making fine furniture and cabinetry. The Wagiriama tribe obtain a medicine for chest complaints from the tree roots.

*** *F. adenophylla*; ([Wall. ex Don] Steenis), (syn. *Heterophragma adenophyllum*), Indo-China to Malesia, to 15 m (50 ft). PETTHAN is native to open forests and secondary growth. While not as spectacular as *F. magnifica*, it is nevertheless popular as a garden ornamental. The trunk has smooth, shallowly fissured, pale brown bark and all young parts are rusty hairy. Leaves, with 2–4 pairs of leaflets that are rusty hairy below. Large thyrses of broadly funnel-shaped, cream or yellow-tan, spring flowers have inflated, densely hairy, bell-shaped calyxes. Fruit pods are ribbed and spirally twisted. Flowers are eaten fresh or in stir-fries in Thailand. Heartwood timber is tough, moderately hard and pale cream or yellow in colour, streaked orange. (**10–12**)

F. magnifica; the blooms are short-lived but are quickly replaced.

F. adenophylla; an enormous fr. pod, which spirals snake-like in the wind, on display at Waimea Arboretum, Hawaii.

F. adenophylla; large funnel-shaped, cream or yellow-tan fls. with inflated, densely hairy, bell-shaped calyxes.

F. magnifica; a vigorous sp., it has an angular framework of slender limbs, which are an iridescent rusty red. Photographed in Zimbabwe.

Ficus benjamina

WEEPING FIG

L.   750 spp.

MORACEAE

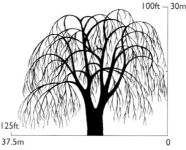

ORIGIN	SE Asia to Australia
HEIGHT	up to 80 m (262 ft)
TYPE	evergreen, very large foliage tree
STATUS	not threatened
HABITAT	humid tropical forests
GROWTH	fast
FLOWG	spring
DRY TOL.	high
SALT TOL.	moderate
LIGHT	bright shade or full sun
SOIL	humid, fertile, deep
NUTRIT.	possibly a high-nitrogen fertilizer
HAZARDS	none
PROBLEMS	invasive roots; toxic sap
ENVIRON.	wild fruit for birds
PROPAG.	seeds; cuttings; layers
LEAVES	simple; bright green; to 13 × 6.5 cm (5.21 × 2.5 in.); ovate, glossy; with elongated drip tip
FLOWERS	inconspicuous; minute, unisexual; enclosed within the fruit
FRUIT	a fig, to 1 × 0.8 cm (0.4 × 0.3 in.); berry-like; orange, pink or red
USE	large shade tree; public open space; hedges and screening; large planter; topiary; bonsai subject
ZONE	10—12

FICUS IS ONE OF THE GREAT TROPICAL PLANT GENERA, with species varying from evergreen to deciduous, monoecious to dioecious, from giant trees to shrubs, climbers, creepers and ground covers. Many are epiphytic or 'stranglers', but they all share two factors: milky sap and bizarre flowers. *Ficus benjamina*, a forest giant, is deservedly popular as it is adaptable and fast growing, as well as being exceedingly elegant. Left alone, with adequate space, the Weeping Fig will develop a voluptuous, verdant crown with finely layered foliage billowing and cascading over its massive superstructure. Typical of its genus, many minute flowers are wholly enclosed inside a fleshy receptacle (the fig). They are pollinated by tiny wasps that enter through a special hole at the base of the fruit to lay eggs in the special 'gall flowers' within; eventually, the pupae feed on the ovaries. The staminate *Ficus* flowers are timed to open just as the male and female wasps emerge from their pupae. The wasps mate, and emerge from the fruit covered in pollen. *F. benjamina* may begin life as an epiphyte but, in fact, the lack of its wasp pollinators in many regions leaves the fruit infertile — fortunately for environmentalists. This species does not develop aerial roots like the Banyan Fig, only fine, wire-like, rusty red strings (usually easy enough to remove) from its lower limbs. Its subterranean roots, however, are extensive, both above and below the ground, and very invasive as they seek out water sources, causing problems with plumbing pipes and swimming pools and causing heave to driveways and the foundations of buildings. There are many superb cultivars including: 'Exotica', a refined form with a strongly weeping habit, leaves long-pointed with twisting tips; 'Golden King', habit pyramidal, tall, narrow; 'Rysenhout', branches spreading upwards; 'Variegata', rich, green leaves splashed white

NOTE: many species of *Ficus* have proved invasive in some regions.

F. benjamina; small, berry-like figs, much sought after by birds.

F. benjamina; a wide-spreading, tumbling crown of compact foliage, provides a voluminous refuge for visitors to the Royal Botanic Gardens in Sydney, Australia.

F. benjamina; popular subject for hedging and topiary, even though it requires constant grooming.

F. benjamina cv. 'Variegata'; one of several vars. of variegated forms.

Ficus aspera; (Forst. f.), (syn. *F. parcellii*), Vanuatu (W Pacific), endemic, to 20 m (66 ft). This is the CLOWN FIG, either a decid. or everg. sp., depending on its culture. This is a fast-growing, ornamental sp. with much of its foliage spotted and splashed in variegation. With small, velvety, reddish fr. It has no aggressive roots, making it an excellent garden subject. *F. aspera* cvs. 'Cannonii' or 'Parcellii' are more strongly variegated. (10–12)

Ficus aurea; (Nutt.), Florida, USA; W Indies, to 20 m (66 ft). Known as the STRANGLER FIG, this is a robust, fast-growing and aggressive sp. common in dry coast. areas. *F. aurea* is a master strangler, lodging its sd in a crotch or crevice, where it sprouts and grows, eventually enveloping its victim. The large, leathery lvs have yellow veins and petioles. The fr. is red and berry-like and is an important food for native pigeons. (10–12)

Ficus auriculata; (Lour.), (syn. *F. roxburghii*), Himalayas to Indo-China and S China, to 12 m (39 ft). ROXBURGH'S FIG has a low, spreading form with a superb, billowing crown of large, glossy lvs that emerge deep red. Edible (but not really delicious) figs are borne in amazing abundance on lower limbs and, fungus-like, on surface roots (inset), forming soft mounds on the ground below the tree. Young lvs are eaten in Thailand. (10–12)

Ficus binnendijkii; (Miq.), (syn. *F. longifolia*), Malaya, Java and Borneo, to 30 m (100 ft). This is a delightful sp. that has recently made its debut as a house plant in garden centres. Its leathery, narrow, weeping lvs form a dense canopy in showering masses. In our photograph, it is shown planted as a lush, billowing screen. Sold variously as 'Allii', 'Amstell Queen', 'Mr. Longfellow' or 'Turban' in horticulture. (10–12)

Ficus celebica; (Blume, Bijdr.), (*F. lancifolia; F. acuminatissima*), Malaysia, Philippines, New Guinea, to 12 m (39 ft). WILLOW-LEAFED FIG is a sp. of lowland to medium elevations in thickets and forests. Its delicate, airy crown of wiry, willow-like foliage veils its slenderly branched framework, making this a most desirable sp. This tree was photographed at the Singapore Botanic Gardens. (10–12)

Ficus cyathistipula; (Warb.), Trop. Africa, to 15 m (50 ft). Known as KACHERE, this *Ficus* is outstanding for its dense foliage composed of thick, narrow, polished lvs, which are clasped at the base of their petioles by prominent, rusty papery stipules. Round, warty, yellow-green fr. follow tiny greenish fls. This ornamental sp. is without aggressive roots, and most suitable for planting as a specimen or for screening. (10–12)

Ficus dammaropsis; (Diels.), New Guinea endemic, to 13 m (43 ft). The DINNER PLATE FIG is a straggly branched sp. with no buttresses or aerial roots. It is grown particularly for its superb, large lvs that are deeply veined and wavy-margined; they are dull green and glabrous above, paler below, often with red veins. The fr. is large, purple and scaly. Given fertile, humid, slightly acid soil, this sp. is an outstanding ornamental. (10–12)

Ficus drupacea var. ***pubescens***; ([Roth.] Comer.), (syn. *F. payapa ; F. mysorensis*), SE Asia, to 20 m (66 ft). MYSORE or BROWN WOOLLY FIG is a large, spreading, everg. sp. that forms a thick, trunk-like mass from its main limbs, and massive, horizontal roots along the surface below. This is a very hairy sp., with buds and young twigs covered in a rusty fuzz. Ripe fr. is velvety red; abundant, in the lf axils. (10–12)

Ficus elastica; (Roth. ex. Hom.), (syn. *F. belgica; F. rubra*), Himalayas to Malaysia and Java, to 60 m (197 ft). The INDIAN RUBBER PLANT is probably best known as an indoor plant but sadly, it is extinct in the wild. It has copious, gummy latex. This was the original source of rubber (hence its name), but it was superseded by *Hevea brasiliensis*. There are many ornamental cvs. with silver, red and variegated lvs. Inset: var. 'Rubra'. (9–12)

Ficus lyrata; (Warb. ex De Wilde. and Durand), (syn. *F. pandurata*), Trop. W and C Africa, to 12 m (39 ft). FIDDLE-LEAF or BANJO FIG, a popular indoor plant, is named for its large, undulate, lyrate or fiddle-shaped lvs. As a garden specimen, it forms a handsome, rounded, very coarse-textured crown and has no aggressive roots, although the fleshy fr. may prove a nuisance. This sp. is xerophytic and reasonably slow growing. (10–12)

Ficus macrophylla; (Desf. ex Pers.), (syn. *F. macrocarpa*). NSW and Qld, Australia, to 55 m (180 ft). MORETON BAY FIG is a very large *Ficus* that forms a heavy crown over a relatively short, stout trunk. If given shelter it may grow to elevations up to 2,000 m (6,562 ft). Fr. is a favourite of Australia's fruit-eating bats, which infest the trees and scatter the fr. to rot (and smell) during the fruitg season. Photographed in Brisbane, Qld. (9–12)

Ficus natalensis; (Hoscht.), (syn. *F. triangularis*), to 30 m (100 ft), Trop. and S Africa. NATAL FIG is an epiphytic or terrestrial shrub or tree and may sometimes become a strangler. Popularly grown for its thick, leathery, triangular-shaped lvs, held in whorls resembling 4-leafed clovers. They have no visible veins on the upper surface but are paler below with pinkish midribs. Ornamental, berry-like fr. ripens rusty brown and is eaten by birds. (9–12)

Ficus platypoda; (A. Cunn. ex Miq.), (syns. *F. microphylla*, *F. rubiginosa*), NSW to N Australia, to 30 m (100 ft). Rusty or Port Jackson Fig. Widespread in dry hills and coast. forests. Lvs are leathery, elliptic-oblong and rusty pubescent below. Fr. is yellow, turning to red, dotted with warts. Popular ornamental for its low-branching, fine-textured canopy and unaggressive root system. **NOTE: a pest in some parts of Australia and New Zealand.** (9–11)

Ficus pleurocarpa; (F. Meull.) NE Qld., Australia, to 35 m (115 ft), known as the Banana Fig, is a rainforest sp. of humid, volcanic soils; it could be mistaken for a young *F. macrophylla* with its compact, dome-like canopy. The long, ribbed, orange-yellow, fleshy fr. distinguishes it and earns it its common name. These fr. are not palatable to humans but are eaten by birds and mammals. This tree was photographed in Cairns, N Qld. (10–12)

Ficus pseudopalma; (Blanco) a Philippine endemic, to 6 m (20 ft). The Dracaena- or Palm-leaf-Fig is a most distinctive sp. Small, erect and pachycaul, glabrous throughout and sparsely- or un-branched. Enormous lvs (to 1 m (3.3 ft) are held terminally, whorled, in palm-like fashion. The oblong-ovoid, ridged fr. is greenish purple, spotted white. Photographed at Fruit and Spice Park in Homestead, S Florida,. (10–12)

Ficus racemosa; (L.), (syn *F. glomerata*; *F. vesca*), Sri Lanka, S China, S and SE Asia to Australia, to 20 m (66 ft). This is a summer and winter-decid. rami- and cauliflorus tree with spreading crown with no strangling or aerial roots, and is never epiphytic. Figs are borne in clusters on much-divided, leafless tubercle-branches; stalked, sub-globose, initially green, with white flecks, later scarlet, densely puberulent, to 4 cm (1.6 in.), edible. (10–12)

Ficus religiosa; (L.), from India to Indo-China, to 35 m (115 ft). The famous SACRED FIG is a noble tree with long-petioled, poplar-like foliage and few, if any, aerial roots. Many trees have religious significance on the Indian subcontinent and Buddhists believe that Buddha attained enlightenment beneath one of these trees. They worship it and are forbidden to fell or harm any part of it. The bark is used to treat gonorrhea, and the fr. to treat asthma. (10–12)

Ficus sycamorus; (L.), widespread in Africa, to 25 m (82 ft), SYCAMORE FIG or EGYPTIAN SYCAMORE is a thick-branched, possibly buttressed, briefly decid. sp., with powdery bark, which varies greatly in colour – greenish, pinkish or cream. Native to humid habitats. The large, leathery lvs are edible and cooked locally as relish. Figs are reddish orange and eaten fresh or dried and sought by birds and animals. Bark and latex are used medicinally in the region. (9–12)

Ficus benghalensis; (L.), (syn. *F. indica*), India and Pakistan, to 30 m (100 ft). BANYAN TREE, the most renowned Ficus, is sacred to Hindus and famous for its monstrous, trunk-like, aerial roots, which descend to become accessory trunks (pillar roots) to support the heavy limbs on an ever-widening canopy. This established, but small specimen, at Fairchild Tropical Gardens in Miami, Florida, demonstrates perfectly the habit of this sp. of stretching its heavy limbs and growing vertical pillar roots to prop them up. In India, one ancient tree is said to house an entire village. A 200-year-old tree in the Botanic Gardens in Calcutta, India, has a canopy covering 1.6 hectares (4 acres) with 1,000 subsidiary trunks formed from aerial roots. (10–12)

Filicium decipiens

FERN TREE

(Wight. & Arn.) Hook. f   3 spp.

SAPINDACEAE

100ft ⌐ 30m

75ft
22.5m   0

ORIGIN	E Africa, India and Sri Lanka
HEIGHT	5–20 m (16–66 ft)
TYPE	evergreen, small foliage tree
STATUS	not threatened
HABITAT	river gorges and valleys
GROWTH	slow
FLOWG	spring
DRY TOL.	moderate
SALT TOL.	moderate
LIGHT	partial shade to full sun
SOIL	fertile, water-retentive
NUTRIT.	high-nitrogen fertilizer; deep, organic mulch
HAZARDS	none
PROBLEMS	none
ENVIRON.	nectar for insects; wild fruit for birds
PROPAG.	fresh seeds; layers
LEAVES	pinnate; dark green; to 25 cm (10 in.); glossy, leathery; winged petiole
FLOWERS	inconspicuous; whitish; held in small panicles; to 15 cm (6 in.)
FRUIT	a drupe, to 0.5 cm (0.2 in.); red to purplish black; held in large panicles
USE	small shade tree; accent; screening; large planter; shade garden; public open space; civic centre
ZONE	10–12

FILICIUM DECIPIENS is native to river gorges and valleys of the lower elevations, thriving in the fertile, humid soils. This species is an exceedingly distinguished smallish tree with a formal, rounded crown of deep green foliage, with its trunk and limbs conspicuously leaf scarred. It is characterized by its leaves, which are curiously fern-like; they are fairly large and mimic the shape of a polypod fern, with slightly wavy, crimped, stemless leaflets and a distinctly winged rachis. In spring, inconspicuous, tiny, white flowers are held terminally in erect panicles, but tend to be hidden within the foliage. They are followed by small, widely branched clusters of ornamental, ovoid, red fruit that ripens purplish black and is shortly viable; for propagation, they should be harvested and sown as soon as they ripen. *F. decipiens* was only introduced into Trop. America in the late 1970s and was named the Japanese Fern Tree. It did not take long for this species to be considered ornamentally desirable. However, it did not seem to set fertile seed in Florida, probably because of an absence of pollinators, unlike in Hawaii, where it fruits abundantly. Consequently, in Florida, this very ornamental, slow- growing species was found to be difficult to propagate by cuttings or layers and it remained fairly rare in the horticultural trade, adding, of course, to its demand and value. Because of its small stature, compact shape and low-branching habit, *F. decipiens* lends itself to shaping for formal plantings, small gardens and courtyards. It is also superb for use as a background screen for colourful, floral plantings. *F. decipiens* has long been popular in its native E Africa and in India for its hard, tough, reddish timber, known as Pehimbiya, which was traditionally used in the making of cartwheels and barrels.

NOTE: this species may escape cultivation.

F. decipiens; with compact, distinctive, fern-like foliage. Slow-growing and xerophytic, this spectacular sp. has many uses for a small garden.

F. decipiens; small, whitish, spring fls.

F. decipiens; small, ovoid, purplish fr., which is shortly viable and should be harvested and sown as soon as it ripens.

F. decipiens; the distinctive, dark green, lvs have striking, winged petioles and mimic the 'Polypod' ferns.

100ft – 30m

75ft

22.5m — 0

Firmiana colorata

INDIAN PARASOL TREE

(Roxb.) R. Br.   12 spp.

Sterculia colorata

MALVACEAE (formerly Sterculiaceae)

ORIGIN	India to Java
HEIGHT	up to 25 m (82 ft)
TYPE	deciduous flowering tree
STATUS	not threatened
HABITAT	in open areas, along margins of dry forest
GROWTH	fast
FLOWG	early spring, before leaves
DRY TOL.	high
SALT TOL.	low
LIGHT	full sun
SOIL	fertile, well-drained
NUTRIT.	high-potassium fertilizer
HAZARDS	none
PROBLEMS	brittle wood
ENVIRON.	insect nectar
PROPAG.	fresh seeds
LEAVES	palmately lobed; rich green; to 30 cm (12 in.); ovate or maple-like, glossy
FLOWERS	showy; coral-orange; a slender, bell-shaped calyx with no petals
FRUIT	follicle, to 8 cm (3 in.); red, waxy, papery; dehiscent; seeds black
USE	large flowering tree; public open space; specimen; fodder plant; xerophytic
ZONE	9–11

THE VEDDAHS OF SRI LANKA chanted odes of worship to their Malaiparutti (or Parasol) Trees, believing them to be possessed of spirits. This tree of the dry Asian woodlands transforms itself from a naked skeleton to a gaudy living coral in early spring, clothing the tips of its branches with a great profusion of vivid, velvety, coral-orange, tubular, petal-less flowers, held in stiff, erect clusters, recalling the closely related *Brachychiton*. For further drama, its brilliant, pinkish red fruit follicles are suspended on long stalks in groups of 4–5. As they mature, each papery follicle spreads open to reveal its yellowish interior, thus forming a perfect parasol, with the little ovoid seeds dangling around the edges. As the fruit disperses, the tree's covering changes into a summer cloak of shallowly lobed leaves. Despite the display, *Firmiana colorata* has several humble domestic uses. The broadly fissured, wrinkled, greenish grey bark is resinous, with a disagreeable odour. It peels off like paper to be converted into rope and, sometimes, bark cloth by the local people, who also use the fresh twigs and leaves for cattle fodder. The whitish wood is very soft and light, with no distinction between sap- and heartwood, but it has been popular in Gold Coast, W Africa, for use as shingles; it expands when moist owing to the resin content, thus making a roof more watertight. In SE Asia, it is used for making concrete moulds.

*** *F. simplex*; (R. Br.), (*F. platanifolia*; *Sterculia platanifolia*), E Asia, to 20 m (66 ft). PARASOL TREE, or JAPANESE VARNISH TREE, is deciduous with palmately lobed leaves. Little, cream flowers are followed by huge bundles of reddish, papery, leaf-like follicles. It is subtropical and very popular as a street tree in Japan. In China, the Parasol Tree was commonly planted in the gardens of poets and scholars, who made it their emblem. Propagate from fresh seed as soon as it ripens. (9–11)

F. colorata; waxy, tubular, petal-less fls recall those of *Brachychiton acerifolius*.

F. colorata; the same specimen (as shown on the right) blooming in early spring before the new lvs.

F. colorata; brilliant, pinkish red follicles; as they mature, each papery fr. will spread open to form a perfect parasol.

F. colorata; photographed in autumn, before it loses its lvs at the Jardin Botanico de Cienfuegos in Cuba.

Flacourtia indica

GOVERNOR'S PLUM

(Burm. f.) Merr.   15 spp.

F. ramontchi; F. separia

FLACOURTIACEAE

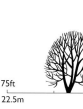

100ft ¬ 30m

75ft
22.5m   0

FLACOURTIA, WHICH ARE EASILY CONFUSED with the closely related *Dovyalis*, are mostly grown as bushy shrubs but may attain tree status. ***Flacourtia indica***, a small, vigorous species from Trop. Africa to S and E Asia, is native from humid limestone coasts and lowland valleys to high, dry savannahs and hillsides, ensuring its tolerance of a wide variety of soils and conditions. Bright green, long-tipped, obovate leaves are coral-red as they emerge. Flowers are small, greenish, without petals and the little globose, 6-celled, dark red fruit are tipped by 5-6 short, radiating styles and have juicy, astringent, yellow pulp. Although dioecious, *F. indica* has the ability to set fruit without male pollen. This species has long been grown throughout the tropics as a backyard specimen or, because it is often but not always, spiny, as a boundary screen. Fruits and young shoots are edible; a preparation of fruit and wood is used against roundworms, while leaves are used as an antidote to snake bite. The bark is said to be effective against rheumatism, gout and skin disease and the roots are used to treat skin allergies. Fruit of *F. indica* matures in 60 days from pollination and is eaten fresh, stewed, juiced or made into jams, jellies or pickles. Fresh foliage is used as fodder and the crooked wood for fuel.
*** *F. inermis*; (Roxb.), origin unknown, to 10 m (33 ft). Lovi-Lovi or Tomi-Tomi is thornless (*inermis* means thornless). This species has a compact, rounded crown and new growth is flushed deep coral-red. Abundant reddish pink 'cherries' have a simple nipple at their tip; they are exceedingly sour. The leaves wither red. (9–11)
*** *F. jangomas*, ([Lour.] Rausch.), India, to 10 m (33 ft). Rukam or Paniala is a densely spiny species with large leaves and spectacular, new, pinkish growth. Fruit is reddish brown with yellow-green pulp; it has a ring of persistent styles at tip. (10–12)

NOTE: some of these species have proved invasive in some regions.

ORIGIN	from E Africa to S Asia
HEIGHT	up to 15 m (50 ft)
TYPE	deciduous. dioecious, small fruiting tree
STATUS	not threatened
HABITAT	coastal to higher elevations; savannah or forest
GROWTH	moderate
FLOWG	year-round
DRY TOL.	moderate to high
SALT TOL.	low
LIGHT	full sun
SOIL	fertile. widely tolerant
NUTRIT.	balanced fertilizer annually; organic mulch
HAZARDS	spiny
PROBLEMS	fruit fly; possibly invasive
ENVIRON.	bee nectar; wild fruit for birds
PROPAG.	seeds; cuttings; grafting
LEAVES	simple; deep green; to 9 × 6 cm (7.5 × 2.5 in.); elliptic, leathery; with toothed margins
FLOWERS	inconspicuous; pale green sepals (without petals); many stamens
FRUIT	a berry, to 2.5 cm (1 in.); red black; translucent, astringent flesh; with up to 10 seeds
USE	small backyard tree; hedges; living barriers; large planter; median strip; fodder plant
ZONE	10–12

F. indica; Governor's Plum with small lvs and red fr. with astringent, yellow pulp.

F. indica; although this sp. may grow as a relatively large tree, it is more commonly found as a bushy shrub like this one at the Fruit and Spice Park in Homestead, Florida.

F. inermis; Lovi-Lovi has masses of small, ornamental, reddish pink 'cherries' that are exceedingly sour.

F. jangomas; is a most decorative, but spiny sp., with large lvs and spectacular, pinkish flushes of new growth.

50ft – 15m

50ft
15m — 0

Flindersia brayleyana

QLD MAPLE

F. Meull.   16 spp.

RUTACEAE

ORIGIN	N Qld, Australia, endemic
HEIGHT	up to 12 m (39 ft)
TYPE	semi-deciduous, flowering timber tree
STATUS	scarce in natural habitat
HABITAT	wet, to very wet, lowland and highland rainforest
GROWTH	fast
FLOWG	late spring to summer
DRY TOL.	moderate
SALT TOL.	low
LIGHT	full sun
SOIL	fertile, humid, acid
NUTRIT.	magnesium-rich fertilizer; deep, organic mulch
HAZARDS	none
PROBLEMS	becomes root bound; trees blow over in cyclones
ENVIRON.	nectar for beetles
PROPAG.	fresh seeds (fast)
LEAVES	pinnate; dark green; with large, drooping leaflets; leaves crowded terminally
FLOWERS	showy; white; held very small in large panicles; scented
FRUIT	a capsule, to 10 cm (4 in.); woody, thick, with warty surface; containing papery seeds
USE	small street tree; specimen; accent; civic centre; large planter; screening; bonsai subject
ZONE	10–11

FLINDERSIA IS A GENUS of the citrus family and famous for its timber. Of the 16 species, 11 are endemic to Australia and found mostly on volcanic soils in coastal and highland rainforests. Fast growing from seed, *Flindersia brayleyana* develops a dense canopy of large, glossy, leathery, parapinnate leaves over a sturdy trunk that is brightened in late spring or early summer by huge, terminal, foaming panicles of tiny, white, honey-scented flowers. They are followed by large, woody, warty capsules that resemble the fruit of *Toona* or *Cedrela*, being composed of 4–6 valves that split open to release papery seeds. *F. brayleyana* is one of the most desirable species, both as an ornamental and for its superb, pink-toned, maple-like timber that looks like ruffled fabric. It has been so extensively logged for cabinetry work that it is scarce in its natural habitat, but has become popular as an ornamental and is widely planted, even as far south as Sydney, where it has proved to be surprisingly cold-hardy. *F. brayleyana* grows poorly if its root system is stunted in any way and is best planted when fairly small. Dried seed pods are popular with floral arrangers.

*** *F. australis*; (R. Br.), Qld to NSW, to 40 m (131 ft). CROW'S ASH or AUSTRALIAN TEAK has a flanged trunk and a dense, oval crown. The flowers are white and the robust, bluntly spiky fruit, to 10 cm (4 in), persists on the tree intact for some months after opening. The durable, yellow-brown timber has a high oil content and is highly flammable; it has, however, long been in demand for building and flooring. (10–11)

*** *F. schottiana*; (F. Meull.), from NSW, Australia, to New Guinea, to 50 m (165 ft). CUDGERIE is a fast-growing, sparsely branched, pioneer tree, planted for timber and forest regeneration. The leaves have been described as being 'held in a singular manner, resembling the splayed, primary feathers of a bird's wing'. It bears masses of honey-scented, white flowers in summer and is hardy except in heavy frosts. (10–12)

F. brayleana; ornamental woody, warty fr. pods are sought after by florists.

F. schottiana; a compact, handsome sp. of wet and dry rainforests that is renowned for its excellent timber.

F. brayleyana; fast growing from sd, the Qld Maple develops a dense, relaxed canopy.

F. brayleyana; enormous, foaming panicles of tiny fls in late spring or early summer. They are sweetly scented to attract beetles, which are their pollinators.

(1) ***Flindersia bourjotiana***; (F. Muell.), NE Qld, Australia, to 30 m (100 ft). QLD SILVER ASH is found from sea level to 900 m (2,953 ft), on wet, heavy soils. With a striking, erect, columnar form, this sp. has bright green, pinnate lvs and very small, white fls. The pale yellow timber is used extensively for flooring and cabinetmaking. (10–12) (2) ***Flindersia ifflaiana***; (F. Meull.), Qld, Australia; to 10 m (33 ft). CAIRNS HICKORY ASH forms a neat, rounded crown. Distinguished by 6–12, drooping leaflets and the margins of its lf stem being angular or possibly winged. Spring fls are white, in expanded panicles. (10–12) (3) Fr., with blunt, warty spines, persist several months. (10–12) (4) ***Flindersia oppositifolia***; (F. Muell.), north east Qld, Australia, to 6 m (20 ft), MOUNTAIN SILKWOOD is a small, rare, montane rainforest sp. that forms a bushy canopy. The deep red fls are unusual, resembling *F pimenteliana* (F. Muell.) of N Qld, N Guinea and Solomon Is. The lvs of *F. oppositifolia* are unifoliate, with 1 lflt, but with an appendage. Young lvs are reddish. (10–12)

'White Christmas' on the trop. Atherton tablelands just inland from Cairns, N Qld, a festive finale to a record drought, with mass flowg of every *Flindersia brayleyana* throughout the remnant patches of once continuous rainforest, now rich dairy pasture.

ORIGIN	SE Asia
HEIGHT	up to 12 m (40 ft)
TYPE	evergreen, briefly deciduous flowering tree
STATUS	not threatened
HABITAT	humid or dry evergreen forests
GROWTH	moderate
FLOWG	spring
DRY TOL.	moderate
SALT TOL.	moderate
LIGHT	full sun
SOIL	deep, friable, humid
NUTRIT.	balanced fertilizer annually; deep, organic mulch
HAZARDS	brittle, weak limbs
PROBLEMS	canker; powdery mildew
ENVIRON.	bee nectar
PROPAG.	seeds; grafts
LEAVES	pinnate; light green, silvery below; leaflets elliptic-oblong
FLOWERS	showy; white; held in large, erect, branched panicles; fragrant
FRUIT	a samara, to 3.5 cm (1.3 in.); winged at one end; held in branched bundles; with 1 seed
USE	small street tree; specimen; accent; large planter; civic centre; screening
ZONE	8–11

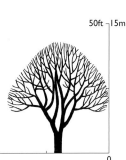

50ft ⌐ 15m

50ft
15m   0

Fraxinus griffithii

GRIFFITH'S ASH

Clarke.   65 spp

F. formosana

OLEACEAE

FRAXINUS IS A LARGE GENUS of mostly deciduous trees of the Olive family that are largely native to the temperate regions of the northern hemisphere. Many are valued for their strong, elastic timbers used for cricket bats, tennis racquets and other sporting equipment. *Fraxinus* species differ from other members of the Oleaceae in having pinnate leaves and winged fruit. One group of species is known as the 'Flowering Ashes' and *Fraxinus griffithii*, one of the few tropical species of this genus, belongs to this group. The distinctive bark of its trunk and main limbs is mottled grey and cream. It forms a billowing, rounded canopy of superb foliage comprised of elliptic-oblong leaflets that are pale green above and silvery below. In spring, tiny, white, 4-petalled flowers are held in very large, showy, branched, terminal panicles. By autumn, these blooms have transformed into bundles of delicate, winged fruit that are even more decorative than the flowers for, as they ripen, they become blushed a glowing, russet-pink. *F. griffithii* will tolerate light frosts.

*** *F. floribunda*; (Wall.) S, to 25 m (81 ft). HIMALAYAN MANNA ASH is related to *F. ornus* of S Europe and Asia Minor. It is found in deciduous forests up to 1,200 m (4,000 ft). This briefly deciduous tree is particularly distinguished by its dark brown, deeply fissured bark, young shoots which are mauve and finely pubescent, and its black buds during the winter months. Leaflets are narrowly ovate, tapering and finely toothed. In spring, flowers, which are white with 4 petals, are fragrant and held in abundant, branched clusters at the end of twigs, appearing with the emerging leaves. *F. floribunda* is dioecious, so only the female trees carry the very desirable, densely clustered, winged fruit, which is held on pendent, slender stalks. (8–10) These are honey trees.

F. griffithii; grand panicles of tiny, white, 4-petalled fls followed by decorative fr.

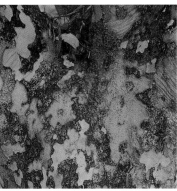

F. griffithii; the smooth, distinctive bark of its trunk and main limbs is mottled grey and cream.

F. griffithii; is widely grown in warm climates as a street tree and ornamental specimen for a small garden.

F. griffithii; in autumn, the blooms have transformed into bundles of delicate, winged fr., which are even more decorative than the fls.

Garcinia mangostana

MANGOSTEEN

L.   200 spp.

GUTTIFERAE

GARCINIA MANGOSTANA is a tree that bears its fruit in an unusual way; only female plants are known, but luckily they do not require a male for fertilization. This phenomenon is known as parthenogenesis. **G. mangostana** is a smallish, handsome, conical tree with yellow sap and large, leathery leaves. The flowers have 4 thick, persistent sepals (2 outer yellowish ones, 2 inner red ones) and 4 small, red petals surrounding a prominent, 5–8-celled, mushroom-shaped ovary with a sessile, star-shaped stigma attached at the tip (it remains imprinted on the base of the fruit) and short, impotent stamens arranged around the base of the ovary. Blooms do not open until midday, with petals falling before sunset. The globular fruit, which are held on twiggy limbs, have smooth, dense, reddish purple, bitter rind that may be almost woody, thus preserving the contents for a long time. This rind is valued for its tannin and as a dye. Within are 5–8 fleshy, snowy white, succulent segments (or arils), often corresponding to the number of lobes at the tip of the stigma. The flesh is sweetly, meltingly delicious and considered by some to resemble a mixture of grape and strawberry. The famous American tropical plant explorer, David Fairchild, declared Mangosteen to be the Queen of Fruits and eagerly set about trying to grow it in Florida, USA, but found his wonder tree reluctant to flourish anywhere but in deep, rich, acid soils in equatorial regions of high humidity, with no dry season. Because of its deep taproot, this species can be very difficult to transplant. **G. mangostana** is propagated almost exclusively by seed which, since they are apomictic, with no sexual embryo, breed true to type. Much research has been done into propagation vegetatively, but with poor results. It may take up to 15 years to bear fruit from seed but, once it begins, it bears heavily for many years.

ORIGIN	SE Asia
HEIGHT	up to 10 m (33 ft)
TYPE	evergreen, small fruiting tree
STATUS	rare in the wild
HABITAT	humid, equatorial regions, with no dry season
GROWTH	slow
FLOWG	spring and autumn
DRY TOL.	low
SALT TOL.	low
LIGHT	sheltered sun or part shade
SOIL	fertile, humid, acid
NUTRIT.	organic fertilizer; deep, organic mulch
HAZARDS	none
PROBLEMS	thread fungus; canker
ENVIRON.	insect nectar
PROPAG.	sow fresh seeds in pots (resents root disturbance, even as seedlings)
LEAVES	simple; rich green, paler below; to 25 × 10 cm (9.8 × 4 in.); elliptic, leathery
FLOWERS	showy; rose-pink or yellow; to 4 cm (1.5 in.) diam.; 4 thick, rounded sepals and 4 petals
FRUIT	a berry, to 7.5 cm (3 in.); purple-black; pericarp thick; seeds 1–2, set in juicy, white aril
USE	botanic collection; small fruit tree; humid shade garden; bonsai subject
ZONE	11–12

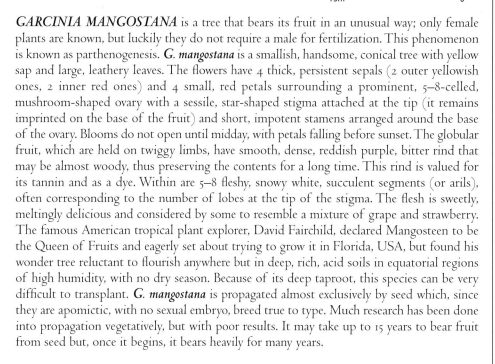

G. mangostana; a mushroom-shaped ovary with a sessile, star-shaped stigma.

G. mangostana; has distinctive, large sepals that persist at the base of the fr., while the stigma lobes persist to form a star-like pattern at the tip.

G. mangostana; the smooth, dense, reddish purple, bitter rind of the fr. may be almost woody, thus preserving it.

G. mangostana; slow growing, forming a dense canopy of large, leathery lvs. At the Botanical Ark, N Qld, Australia.

Garcinia aristata; ([Griseb.] Borh.), (syn. *Rheedia aristata*), Cuban endemic, up to 10 m (33 ft). Known as MANAJAU or ESPUELA DE CABALLERA, is found in semi-decid. forests on alkaline soils in Cuba, where it is used for treating asthma and skin problems. Slow growing, it forms a very narrow, fastigiate crown. The lvs are elliptical and glossy, to 7.5 cm (3 in). Fls are clustered on side shoots. (**10–12**)

Garcinia dulcis; ([Roxb.] Kurz.), (syn. *Xanthochymus tinctoria*), from S India to Malaya, up to 7 m (23 ft). Named GOURKA, or MUNDU, this is an ornamental, conical tree with a straight trunk and drooping limbs. Bright yellow, thin-skinned fr. has edible, juicy, sour pulp enclosing 1–4 sds. Unripe fr. yields a resin from which (an inferior) gamboge colour is extracted and used to make yellow artist's paint. (**10–12**)

Garcinia livingstonei; (T. Anderson), Trop. Africa, up to 20 m (66 ft). In Kenya this sp. is called MTOTOZI and is found from the coast. forests to the banks of the Thika River (of *Flame Trees of Thika* fame), to the north of Nairobi. The damson-like fr. are held on mature wood and are edible. Photographed at the Fruit and Spice Park, Homestead, Florida. (**10–12**)

Garcinia spicata; (Hook. f.), India and Sri Lanka, up to 10 m (33 ft). With a wide-spreading form and luxuriant, deep green foliage. The large, polished lvs are broadly elliptic, to 20 cm (8 in.), while emergent lvs are bright, coppery pink. Abundant white, waxy, stemless fls encrust the stems of twigs and are followed by smooth, globose, dark green fr., to 2.5 cm (1 in.). (**10–12**)

Garcinia xanthochymus, (Hook. f. ex Anderson), from N India to W Himalayas, to 13 m (43 ft). GAMBOGE is a wide-spreading sp. with enormous, drooping lvs and globose, apple-sized, golden yellow fr. It is renowned, however for its sap, which, when tapped, yields a yellow pigment known as 'gamboge' that is used in making watercolour paint and for dyeing Buddhist priests' robes. (This sp. is not the only *Garcinia* to provide this important pigment.) (10–12)

Garcinia cymosum f. *pendula*, ([K. Schum.] IM Turner and PF Stevens), (syn. *Tripetalum cymosum*), New Guinea endemic. Photographed at Foster Gardens in Honolulu, Hawaii. This rare, slow-growing, fastigiate sp. forms a compact, almost untapered pillar of foliage with tightly weeping, pendulous branches. It has bright red, edible fr. and is traditionally grown in New Guinea villages. Inset shows a small specimen at Flecker Gardens in Cairns, N Qld, Australia. (10–12)

The *Garcinia* clan are known for their compact crowns and distinctive shapes; many are slim and fastigiate, like *G. aristata* and *G. cymosum*, but this photograph of *Garcinia xanthochymus* taken in the Royal Botanic Gardens in Trinidad, shows the extraordinary pyramidal shaped canopy developed by this sp. *G. xanthochymus* has hard, heavy, coarse-grained wood with many knots. In India, young lvs are considered edible and eaten raw, cooked as spinach or added to a curry. Fr. is edible but sour. Young twigs and lvs are prepared to be used as disinfectant.

ORIGIN	from India to Malaysia
HEIGHT	up to 12 m (40 ft)
TYPE	evergreen flowering tree
STATUS	vulnerable
HABITAT	high elevation, humid evergreen forests
GROWTH	moderate
FLOWG	spring
DRY TOL.	low
SALT TOL.	low
LIGHT	bright, shifting shade
SOIL	rich, humid, acid
NUTRIT.	magnesium-rich fertilizer; deep, organic mulch
HAZARDS	none
PROBLEMS	chlorosis; sooty mould
ENVIRON.	moth nectar
PROPAG.	seeds; cuttings; layers
LEAVES	simple; deep green, to 45 cm (18 in.); lustrous, leathery
FLOWERS	showy; ivory white, fading to deep cream then buttery yellow; intensely fragrant
FRUIT	a berry, to 4×3 cm (1.5 × 1.2 in.); tawny yellow; ovoid, ribbed, tipped with persistent calyx
USE	small flowering tree; accent; large planter; courtyard; conservatory
ZONE	10–12

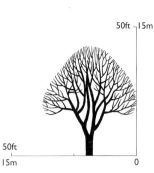

50ft 15m
50ft
15m   0

Gardenia carinata

RANDA

Wallich.   60 spp.

RUBIACEAE

KNOWN AS RANDA OR CHEMPAKA UTAN in Malaysia, this lovely, vigorous, little Asian, evergreen forest tree forms an upwardly stretching and spreading, sturdy framework of smooth, grey branches. *Gardenia carinata* has large, glossy, rich green, tapered leaves that are whorled along the ends of the supple limbs to compose a luxuriant, rounded or oval crown. About 4 years after planting, young saplings begin to bloom. Early in the evening, the large, solitary, intensely fragrant, 6–9-petalled, solitary flowers open a pale cream, turning a deep cream by the following afternoon and a rich, buttery yellow on the third day, before they finally abort. *G. carinata* fruit is a broadly oblong, indehiscent, yellow berry with 6–7 ridges and is tipped by the persistent calyx tube of the old flower. Preparations are made from the fruit for use in herbal medicine and it is particularly prescribed for influenza and colds. *Gardenia* species require rich, well-drained, neutral to acid soil and prefer light, shifting shade. This species is easily grown from seed.

*** *G. imperialis*; (K. Schum.), Trop. Africa, to 20 m (66 ft), SHINING GARDENIA is a large tree native to swamps and riversides with stout limbs, sympodial growth and large, obovate, sessile, polished leaves 20–50 cm (8–20 in.), with small pouches at their base; young parts are viscid. Huge, white, 5-lobed flowers have a corolla tube to 23 cm (9 in.) in length. Fruits ellipsoid, to 5 cm (2 in.). (10–12)

*** *G. tubifera*; (Wall.), Malaysia to Borneo, to 18 m (60 ft), WATER GARDENIA or CHEMPAKA UTAN is fairly common on riversides, especially on tidal beaches and in lowland forests. The trunk of *G. tubifera* is pale grey, with smooth or finely cracked bark, and has a sympodial habit of branching. Buds and twigs are glabrous and varnished with a pale yellow resin. Obovate leaves are very variable in size, up to 4 cm (10 in.). Fragrant flowers, to 9 cm (3.5 in.) diam. are white, turning orange. (10–12)

G. carinata; as they age, the fls become rich, buttery yellow and less fragrant.

G. carinata; this everg. tree has an upwardly stretching framework of smooth, grey branches.

G. carinata; an indehiscent, (yellow) berry with 6–7 ridges and tipped by the persistent calyx tube of the fl.

G. carinata; early in the evening, the large, solitary, intensely fragrant, 6–9 petalled fls open pale cream, deepening in colour by the following afternoon.

Gardenia cornuta; (Helms.), S Africa, to 5 m (16.4 ft). NATAL GARDENIA is a shrub or small tree in bushveld and thickets; it is densely branched with smooth, grey limbs, the lustrous, obovate lvs, with slightly undulate margins, are clustered in whorls of 3. White, long-tubed, fragrant fls fade to deep cream. Fr. is ovoid, yellow to orange with a persistent calyx (and eaten by monkeys). Fr. and roots are used medicinally. This sp., like most Gardenias, needs acid soil. (9–12)

Gardenia posquerioides; (S. Moore), E Africa, to 7 m (23 ft). MUKUMUTI is found as an understorey small tree of the forest and has an erect, compact habit of growth and leathery, narrowly oblong lvs whorled around the tips of short, stubby, whitish twigs. Large, solitary, 8-petalled fls with inrolled petals open white but gradually deepen to yellow with age. Calyx tube with 8 lobes to 2.5 cm (1 in.), remains persistent on spindle-shaped fr. (10–12)

Gardenia taitensis; (DC), Polynesia, to 6 m (20 ft). TIARE is famous in the Pacific for its powerfully fragrant fls, which are popular for use in leis and fresh head garlands. As with many of their strongly-perfumed fls, the Polynesians use them to scent their coconut body oil. This sp., with its large, lacquered, water-resistant lvs, is native of coast. woodlands and thickets and is relatively salt-tol. (10–12)

Gardenia thunbergia; (L. f.), S Africa endemic, to 5 m (16 ft). WHITE GARDENIA is a small tree or shrub with short, rigid branches with large, glossy, dark green lvs clustered at their tips. Solitary and intensely fragrant, the white, pinwheel blooms have many slender, overlapping petals; they fade to cream as they age. Each large bloom measures to 10 cm (4 in.) diam. Blooming from winter to spring. (9–11)

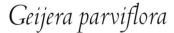

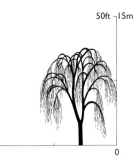

50ft ⌐15m

50ft
15m   0

ORIGIN	E Australia, endemic
HEIGHT	up to 9 m (30 ft)
TYPE	evergreen, small flowering and foliage tree
STATUS	not common in the wild
HABITAT	semi-arid plains; on red or sandy soils
GROWTH	slow
FLOWG	winter and spring
DRY TOL.	high
SALT TOL.	moderate
LIGHT	full sun
SOIL	fertile, water-retentive
NUTRIT.	balanced fertilizer annually; organic mulch
HAZARDS	none
PROBLEMS	none
ENVIRON.	nectar for insects
PROPAG.	seeds
LEAVES	simple; grey-green; linear, leathery, with oil glands; pleasantly aromatic
FLOWERS	showy; silvery white; bell-shaped; with 5 triangular lobes; held in loose panicles
FRUIT	a carpel, to 6 mm (0.2 in.); globular, warty; containing many black seeds
USE	specimen; street tree; public open space; large planter; civic centre ; fodder plant; xerophytic
ZONE	9–11

Geijera parviflora

WILGA

Lindley   8 spp.

RUTACEAE

THIS CITRUS-RELATIVE is found in the semi-arid regions from northern S Australia to Qld, in Australia, and will tolerate temperate as well as tropical conditions. *Geijera* are a small genus of 8 species, distributed from New Guinea and eastern Australia to New Caledonia, in the South Pacific. ***Geijera parviflora*** is a small, slow-growing tree that develops a deep root system and a dense, low-branching, rounded crown, with its supple, long twigs tumbling downwards from the main limbs. As with many of the Rutaceae family, the long, narrow, grey-green leaves have many tiny oil glands and give off a pleasant, aromatic smell when crushed. In late winter or early spring, along with many of the first Wattles, *G. parviflora* produces masses of tiny, creamy white blooms that have 5 little, triangular lobes and 5 short stamens arranged around a bright yellow, sticky 'pad' containing ovaries and pistils. Small, warty, citrus-like fruit become brownish and contain a single, black, shiny seed. Known most commonly as Wilga in its native land, these are often the only trees to be seen on an arid plain and are quite striking, resembling a Weeping Willow. Being very deep-rooted and having scabrid, oily leaves, this species is well-equipped to withstand long droughts. *G. parviflora* is adored by livestock that frequently nibble the lower twigs and foliage, thus shearing it off in a horizontal plain (it is sometimes called Sheep Bush). Unfortunately, animals often eat the young saplings before they have a chance to mature, causing this species to become rare in some areas.

*** *G. salicifolia*; (Schott.), NSW to Qld; to 25 m (82 ft). Known as Scrub Wilga, found in the rain- and brush-forests. The leaves are lance-shaped, usually broad, but a narrow-leafed form also exists. Timber is useful. Another species: var. *salicifolia*, Narrow-Leafed Brush Wilga of Hunter River, has aromatic leaves. (9–11)

G. parviflora; curious little 5-parted fls have a 'sticky pad' at their centres.

G. parviflora; fr. are small, green, warty and citrus-like; they dry brownish and contain a single, black, shiny sd.

G. parviflora; with masses of creamy white blooms in late winter or early spring, along with the Wattles.

G. parviflora; in the extensive Australian collection at the Arboretum of Los Angeles. This is a slow-growing, deep-rooted, weeping sp., well adapted to arid conditions.

Genipa americana

MARMALADE BOX

L.   7 spp.

G. caruto; G. americana var. caruto

RUBIACEAE

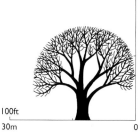

GENIPA AMERICANA is often grown for its beauty and summer shade, as well as for its fruit. This is a medium-sized, robust tree with a spreading crown of extremely handsome, dark green, deeply veined, leathery leaves on stout twigs with the same distinctively smooth, grey bark as the trunk. *Genipa americana*, not to be confused with Genip (*Blighia sapida*), is very closely related to *Gardenia*, as may be seen from the fruit. Native to regions of moderate to high rainfall, **G. americana** is also tolerant of a dry season but loses its leaves. Following the fragrant, pale yellow flowers, large, aromatic fruit as big as an orange develop, and are held singly erect on stout stalks. The leathery skin is yellowish brown to greyish, with a purplish, sour pulp within. As they ripen, they become soft and emit a strong, rather pungent odour, somewhat reminiscent of overripe apples. To avoid ravaging bats, the fruit is harvested before it is completely mature and then stored in the dark until it is ripe. **G. americana** may be eaten fresh, pulverized to make a cooling drink or made into marmalade or preserves. Fermented fruit is used by Amerindians to make an alcoholic beverage known as Genipapo. The unripe fruit exudes a juice that turns blue-black on contact with the skin and has provided an indelible blue dye (Genipin) that is used by the Amerindians for tattooing and body paint. The tonic, diuretic fruit has been used regionally to treat anaemia and liver problems and is being tested for its antibiotic and antiseptic properties. Apart from its virtue as a fruit tree, **G. americana** has valuable timber, which is yellowish brown, with sometimes a pinkish or purplish blue caste. The heartwood is hard, heavy, strong and flexible and has been employed in many ways, from tool handles, furniture and cabinetwork to shipbuilding. Of easy culture, **G. americana** is often planted regionally along farm boundaries using freshly cut, stout limbs.

ORIGIN	Trop. America
HEIGHT	up to 20 m (66 ft)
TYPE	deciduous or evergreen foliage or fruiting tree
STATUS	not threatened
HABITAT	moist, coastal limestone woodlands
GROWTH	moderate
FLOWG	spring to autumn
DRY TOL.	moderate
SALT TOL.	moderate
LIGHT	full sun to partial shade
SOIL	rich, humid, well-drained
NUTRIT.	balanced fertilizer annually; deep, organic mulch
HAZARDS	none
PROBLEMS	none
ENVIRON.	bee nectar; fruit for bats
PROPAG.	seeds; large cuttings; grafting
LEAVES	simple; deep green; to 30 × 10 cm (12 × 4 in.); paler below, elliptic-obovate; deeply veined
FLOWERS	showy; pale yellow; to 4 cm (1.5 in.); held in terminal cymes; slightly fragrant
FRUIT	a berry, to 12 cm (4.7 in.); elliptic, yellow-brown; leathery; with sour, pungent, edible pulp
USE	summer shade tree; fruiting and flowering tree; specimen; large planter; screening
ZONE	10—12

G. americana; large, showy, pale yellow fls have reddish brown centres.

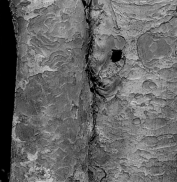

G. americana; This fruitg tree was photographed at the Wild Fowl Trust in Trinidad, where it is an important native. Fr. is not yet ripe and will become yellowish.

G. americana; is known locally as Marmalade Box for its fr., which is fermented as an alcoholic beverage.

G. americana; distinctively smooth, grey bark on its trunk and heavy limbs.

200

ORIGIN	Trop. America
HEIGHT	up to 10 m (33 ft)
TYPE	deciduous, small flowering tree
STATUS	not threatened
HABITAT	dry lowland woodland and wasteland
GROWTH	fast
FLOWG	early spring, when leafless
DRY TOL.	high
SALT TOL.	moderate
LIGHT	full sun
SOIL	well-drained
NUTRIT.	normally not necessary
HAZARDS	poisonous roots and bark
PROBLEMS	weak-wooded and invasive
ENVIRON.	bee nectar
PROPAG.	seeds; large cuttings
LEAVES	pinnate; dull green; to 30 cm (12 in.); softly pubescent
FLOWERS	showy; pale pink, lilac or white; held in short-stalked soft racemes, to 15 cm (6 in.)
FRUIT	a legume, to 15 × 2 cm (6 × 0.8 in.); dark brown, linear; explosive on ripening
USE	small flowering tree; specimen; living fence posts; agricultural shade; land stabilization; xerophytic
ZONE	10—12

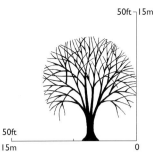

50ft ⌐ 15m

50ft
15m   0

Gliricidia sepium

QUICK STICK

(Jacq.) Kunth. ex Walp..   4 spp.

G. maculata

FABACEAE (Papilionoideae)

GLIRICIDIA SEPIUM is a demure, leggy-limbed tree for much of the year, unassuming until early spring when, as if impersonating an apple or cherry blossom, it is suddenly swathed in frothy, nectar-rich, pinkish mauve blossom. Plush leaf buds gradually unfurl as the delicate flowers fade and transform into velvety, green pods, leaving the tree to slip into obscurity once more. In Jamaica, **G. sepium** leaves are used to combat colds and fever; they are either placed fresh under a bed sheet to draw out the fever or are boiled in water and drunk as a cure. The foliage is also considered medicinal for livestock and is planted as living corral posts so the animals can eat the leaves. In many regions, the nitrogen-rich, fresh foliage is used as green manure. Rapid in growth and of easy culture, *G. sepium* has a somewhat untidy and lanky growth and benefits from correctional pruning. Nevertheless, it has been widely used as coffee shade in some areas and is generally known as Madre de Cacao in Spanish regions. Because of its explosive fruit pods, which may eject seeds up to 40 m (131 ft), this species can prove invasive. The roots and bark are toxic and employed to stun and catch fish in the countryside, where fishermen throw ground-up bark into a stream and wait for the dazed fish to rise to the surface. In Mexico, the same preparations are mixed with ground maize and used to poison rats and mice. The sapwood is light brown and the heartwood dark brown, turning reddish on exposure. It is hard, heavy, strong and termite-proof. The handsome timber is sometimes used for railway ties and general construction. Quick Stick won its curious name from its ability to root and grow from large, limb cuttings and is therefore very popular for fence posts. This is an important honey plant

NOTE: G. sepium is considered invasive in some regions.

G. sepium; with heavy clusters of charming, pink, nectar-rich, pea-like fls.

G. sepium; popularly planted as a living fence in Cuba and many islands of the W Indies.

G. sepium; smooth, pock-marked bark. Roots and bark are toxic and employed as fish poison.

G. sepium; is known as Quick Stick in the W Indies because of the ability of large limbs to be used as cuttings. Foaming, pink blossoms herald the early spring.

Gmelina arborea

SNAPDRAGON TREE

Roxb.   35 spp.

P. tomentosa

LAMIACEAE

100ft ⌐ 30m
75ft
22.5m   0

GMELINA ARBOREA grows in an erect, spreading, much-branched manner to form a large, shady crown. It has pale grey, corky bark, which exfoliates in broad, scurfy flakes, while its branchlets and young growth are clothed in a fine, pale, brownish or yellow, hairy pubescence. The large, limp, heart-shaped leaves are rough, leathery and tawny-tomentose below; they fall at the onset of the dry months. Small, velvety, exquisitely scented flowers, which are arranged in long, narrow, branched thyrses at the ends of the naked twigs, appear with the first signs of spring. Each tawny brown and bright yellow bloom resembles those of the snouty snapdragon and is held in a cup-shaped, densely brown hairy calyx. The zygomorphic corolla is funnel-shaped, with a wide mouth and 5 very unequal lobes; the upper 2 are fused together and curved slightly backwards, while the lower 3 are fused together and curved forwards, with the middle lobe much larger. Unfortunately, like so many large, deciduous, flowering species, *G. arborea* holds these delicate blossoms high up in the vibrant tropical sky and this detracts from their ornamental impact. The fruit is an oblong drupe with a leathery rind. It is yellow when ripe and is full of an aromatic, edible pulp which, when mixed with the pounded root, has medicinal use. The hard, very strong, light-coloured timber neither warps nor splits and is durable under water, making it excellent for use as pilings. Cured timber is also employed for making canoes and house posts, as well as for carving images, ornaments and musical instruments. Wood ash and flowers are employed for dyeing and the roots have great medicinal value as a blood purifier and antidote to poisons. In India, it is prepared to treat gonorrhea and bladder problems. Strangely, although they do not contain saponin, the bruised leaves give a strong, frothing liquid.

ORIGIN	from Pakistan to the Malay Peninsula
HEIGHT	up to 25 m (82 ft)
TYPE	deciduous, large flowering tree
STATUS	not threatened
HABITAT	coastal or lowland deciduous forest
GROWTH	fast
FLOWG	early to late spring
DRY TOL.	high
SALT TOL.	moderate
LIGHT	full sun
SOIL	deep, well-drained
NUTRIT.	balanced fertilizer annually
HAZARDS	none
PROBLEMS	none
ENVIRON.	moth nectar
PROPAG.	seeds; cuttings
LEAVES	simple; dull green; to 25 × 15 cm (10 × 2 in.); ovate, slightly papery
FLOWERS	showy; yellow; zygomorphic; possibly tinged brown; held in long, narrow thyrses; strongly fragrant
FRUIT	a drupe, to 2 cm (0.8 in.); smooth, yellow; with aromatic, edible pulp
USE	large flowering tree; public open space; specimen; xerophytic
ZONE	10—12

G. arborea; small, golden yellow, plum-like fr. with aromatic, edible flesh.

G. arborea; delicate Snapdragon-like, exquisitely scented blooms are held high on the bare bones of a leafless canopy and are difficult to appreciate against a vibrant blue, trop. sky.

G. arborea; a towering old specimen at Fairchild Tropical Gardens with its summer foliage.

G. arborea; has pale grey, corky bark, which exfoliates in broad, scurfy flakes.

(1) *Gmelina dalrympleana*; ([F. Meull.] H.J Lam), from New Guinea to N Qld., Australia, to 20 m (66 ft). DALRYMPLE'S WHITE BEECH or GREY TEAK grows as a tall shrub or a medium-sized tree, is native of moist lowland, monsoon forests or coast. thickets, and has smooth, grey-brown bark. Distinguished by its dark green foliage. (2) Little pink or lilac fls with a yellow-splashed, lower lip and a dark blue, maroon or purple calyx. Berry-like fr. is pink or magenta. Blooming in spring. Tolerates light shade, but requires ample humidity. Timber of mature trees is used by Aborigines for dugout canoes. (10–12) (3 and 4) *Gmelina fasciculiflora*; (Benth.), NE Qld, Australia, to 15 m (50 ft). NORTHERN WHITE BEECH is endemic to wet rainforest from near sea level to 800 m (2,625 ft). Fls are zygomorphic and variable, but typically white with a purple 'bib' and held in upright panicles. Fr. is blue-purple, to 2 cm (0.8 in.); it has an unpleasant odour and stains fingers when crushed; cut for timber. (9–12) Also *Gmelina leichhardtii*, ([F. Meull.] Benth.), Australia, to 40 m (131 ft). WHITE- or QLD-BEECH or GREY TEAK is a hardy, fairly fast growing, sp., grown from sd (may be slow to germinate). This sp. of warm, coast. or riverine rainforests blooms most profusely once every few years. Little white fls are marked purple, followed by berry-like, purplish blue drupes, to 2.5 cm (1 in.). Celebrated for its timber, it is considered equal to Red Cedar (*Toona ciliata*). (10–12)

Gnetum gnemon

MENINJAU

L.   28 spp.

GNETACEAE

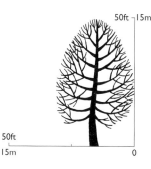

50ft ⌐15m

50ft
15m   0

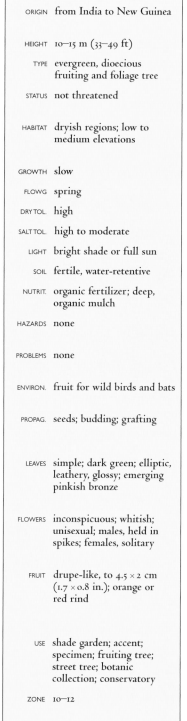

GNETUM GNEMON, with its curious name, is a primitive plant, which, like *Podocarpus*, is on the cusp between gymnosperms and angiosperms. Like *Podocarpus* (a gymnosperm), its seeds are not enclosed in an ovary but, as in angiosperms, *G. gnemon* has water-transporting vessels in its wood, flower-like structures and an embryo with 2 cotelydons. It is further distinguished by its monopoidal growth, forming a narrow, pyramidal crown over a distinctive, grey-barked trunk that has ring-like thickenings at the nodes of young stems resembling those of a coconut palm. *G. gnemon* has a canopy of thick, glossy, leathery, elliptic leaves, held in pairs along slender, drooping, flexible dark stems; they emerge a pinkish bronze colour, deepening to a dark green as they mature. In some regions, young, tender leaves are eaten as a spinach. Little, inconspicuous, male flowers are held in small, stiff, crowded spikes in the leaf axils, while the minute female blooms are solitary, erect ovules surrounded by 3 'envelopes'. *G. gnemon* bears male and female 'cones', with the 'fruit' being, in fact, its actual seed; the ovoid, pale, yellowish green fruit may ripen orange or red. This popular, slow-growing species has long been cultivated for its leaves and fruit in the drier regions of China, Malaysia and Java. Known as Meninjau in Malaysia, the edible, pulpy, somewhat tasteless rind of the fruit is eaten boiled or roasted. Excellent crackers, known as Emping Belinjau, are made from the slightly bitter kernels. After the brittle seed coats are removed, they are sliced very thinly and pounded flat into discs, then set to dry in the sun until they are crisp and kept for months. They are reminiscent of the cassava bread of the W Indies and are served salted or coated with caramel. Many species of this genus (including *G. gnemon*) are valued for the fibre yielded from their bark, which is used to make cord or woven into sacks, particularly in New Guinea.

G. gnemon; fr. in 2 stages of development.

G. gnemon; these small, oval, red-fleshed sds have developed from the narrow spikes of female fls of this curious, primitive plant.

G, gnemon; smooth, leathery elliptic lvs are held in pairs along slender, drooping, flexible dark stems.

G. gnemon; in Singapore, delicious Emping Belinjau crackers are made from fr. kernels.

ORIGIN	E Australia, endemic
HEIGHT	17 m–40 m, (56–131 ft)
TYPE	evergreen, very large flowering and foliage tree
STATUS	rare in the wild
HABITAT	gullies, forests and rainforests
GROWTH	fast
FLOWG	spring
DRY TOL.	moderate
SALT TOL.	moderate
LIGHT	full sun
SOIL	rich, acid, well-drained
NUTRIT.	high-potassium fertilizer; deep, organic mulch
HAZARDS	irritant hairs on fruit
PROBLEMS	scale; sooty mould
ENVIRON.	bee and bird nectar
PROPAG.	fresh seeds; cuttings
LEAVES	simple; silvery green, silver below; deeply, pinnately lobed, fern-like
FLOWERS	showy; golden orange; narrow, bell shaped; with stout, curving stamens; held in dense, 1-sided 'brush'
FRUIT	a follicle, to 2.5 cm (1 in.); pod-like, leathery
USE	small or large shade tree; street tree; public open space; large planter
ZONE	8–11

100ft — 30m
75ft
22.5m — 0

SILKY OAK

A.M. Cunn. ex R. Br.   261 spp.

PROTEACEAE

GREVILLEA ROBUSTA is a fast-growing, somewhat conical tree of irregularly spaced, spreading limbs around a robust, cylindrical trunk. The foliage is composed of ferny, doubly pinnately-lobed leaves, which are dark green above and silky, silvery white below; young shoots are densely, silvery hairy. In spring or early summer, **G. robusta** is garlanded with dazzling, spidery flowers. Typically Proteaceae, these remarkable, bright yellow or burnished yellow, fringed blooms are composed of upturned, 1-sided, densely packed, tubular flowers with stout, curving stamens. Like all Grevillea blooms, they are adored by bees and nectar-loving birds. The fruit are dark brown, woody, boat-shaped follicles. Sadly, **G. robusta** flowers poorly in the lowland tropics, but it is still worth planting, however, for its handsome, silvery foliage, although it has brittle wood and may be attacked by scale insects and disfigured by sooty mould. In 1938, the Hawaiian government planted 100,000 trees for afforestation and erosion control in forest reserves, but it was found that this species did not take well to monoculture. The name Silky Oak derives from the silky, oak-like grain of its wood, which is prized for cabinetry. *Grevillea* species are classed as important honey plants.

*** **G. banksii**; (R. Br.), Qld, Australia, to 7 m (23 ft), RED FLOWERED SILKY OAK, a very variable coastal species found in some areas in an almost prostrate form, has profuse cream, pink or red flowers in spring. It has poisonous hairs on its ovaries, causing a skin rash in some people; horses have died from eating them. (9–11)

*** **G. hilliana**; (F. Meull.), from NSW to N Qld, Australia, to 30 m (100 ft). WHITE YIEL YIEL, a rainforest species, has a dense crown of dark green leaves covered with silky, silvery hairs. This evergreen is quite fast growing from fresh seed and has beautifully figured, hard, heavy wood. (9–11) NOTE: all *Grevillea* require acid soil.

NOTE:*Grevillea robusta* is listed as invasive in California, USA.

G. robusta; with spidery, nectar-rich blooms.

G. hilliana; this rainforest sp. has a dense crown of dark green lvs covered with silky, silvery hairs.

G. robusta; ferny, doubly, pinnately-lobed lvs that are dark green above and silky, silvery white below.

G. robusta; somewhat conical, fast-growing Australian tree has irregularly spaced, spreading limbs around a robust, cylindrical trunk.

(1 and 2) *Grevillea baileyana*; (McGill.); Qld, Australia and New Guinea, to 25 m (82 ft) (in cultivation, usually to 10 m [33 ft]). WHITE OAK is a fast-growing, suckering sp. of wet rainforests. Like many Proteaceae, the juvenile lvs are simple whereas mature lvs become deeply lobed; they are rich, glossy green above and rusty plush below, making this sp. desirable as a specimen or garden accent, while dried lvs are very popular with florists. In spring, the dense, conical canopy foams with a profusion of fragrant white fls held in bottlebrush spikes. Although short-lived, their profuse nectar attracts nectar-loving birds as well as insects. Easily propagated from fresh sds (10–12) (3 and 4), *Grevillea glauca*; (Knight), N Qld, Australia and New Guinea, to 12 m (39 ft). This silvery foliaged sp., photographed in Cairns, N Qld, is distinguished by its ash-grey trunk and limbs that contrast with the foliage. It is known (with typical Australian humour), as BUSHMAN'S CLOTHESPEG for its woody, egg-shaped, strongly hinged fr. that splits open very slightly and may be manipulated like a pincer. (10–12)

ORIGIN	S Africa
HEIGHT	up to 7 m (23 ft)
TYPE	evergreen tall shrub or small flowering tree
STATUS	limited distribution
HABITAT	humid mountain slopes and bushland
GROWTH	moderate
FLOWG	spring
DRY TOL.	high
SALT TOL.	low
LIGHT	full sun, bright shade
SOIL	rich, well-drained
NUTRIT.	organic fertilizer; deep, organic mulch
HAZARDS	none
PROBLEMS	none
ENVIRON.	nectar for birds
PROPAG.	seeds; cuttings; layering; root suckers
LEAVES	simple; bright green, rounded, somewhat lobed; margins coarsely toothed
FLOWERS	showy; scarlet, in dense, cylindrical mass; campanulate; with many stamens
FRUIT	a capsule, to 2 cm (0.8 in.); 4–5 celled, dehiscent; with many seeds
USE	specimen; large planter; accent; flowering border; bright conservatory
ZONE	9–10

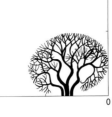

50ft ⌐15m
50ft
15m ⌐   0

Greyia sutherlandii

NATAL BOTTLEBRUSH

Hook. & Harv.   3 spp.

GREYIACEAE

THE GENUS *GREYIA* was named in honour of Sir George Grey (1812–1898), Governor of the Cape Colony in S Africa at the time when the first species were discovered growing on the rocky slopes of the Drakensberg Mountains of Natal. It remains a small family of a single genus of three species of shrubs and small, soft-wooded trees, all of them endemic to S Africa. *Greyia sutherlandii* is quite slow growing, forming a coarse parasol of stubby, angular, plump twigs as it matures. It is distinguished by its simple, alternate leaves that are held by stout petioles that sheath at their base but are without stipules. The fleshy, bright green, geranium-like leaves are rounded, irregularly coarsely toothed, somewhat lobed and grouped towards the ends of the stout, reddish limbs. In spring, the tips of the drab twigs sprout lavish, tightly packed cones of bright scarlet flowers, to 12 cm (4.7 in.), each one a little, waxy bell filled with copious nectar and spouting many pollen-tipped, whiskery, red stamens. Like *Schotia* of the same regions, these blooms are much sought after by nectar-loving sunbirds. The flowers are followed in the autumn by conical fruit capsules that are 2 cm (0.8 in.) long and which split open at one end to release many little seeds. The wood is lightweight, soft and supple and is used for carvings and household tools. *G. sutherlandii* is the most celebrated of its genus and very popular in Mediterranean gardens, where the mild, frost-free climate is ideal. These are not tropical species, but will grow in the cooler subtropics.
*** *G. radlkoferi*; (Szyszyl.), S Africa, to 8 m (26 ft). TRANSVAAL BOTTLEBRUSH occurs in montane (often rocky) grassland. It closely resembles *G. sutherlandii*, but is larger in all its parts. The leaves are tomentose below when young. The third species of this rare genus is *G. flanaganii*,which is restricted to the eastern Cape. It has smaller leaves and drooping, red flowers. (9–11)

G. sutherlandii; fls begin to open from the base upwards.

G. sutherlandii; scarlet cones of bell-shaped blooms are adapted specifically for nectar-loving birds. Fls open from the base of the spike and secrete copious amounts of nectar.

G. sutherlandii; stubby, soft growth is most disorganized and unattractive during the dry season without lvs.

G. sutherlandii; fleshy, bright green lvs are rounded, coarsely toothed and lobed.

Guaiacum officinale

LIGNUM VITAE

L.   65 spp.

ZYGOPHYLLACEAE

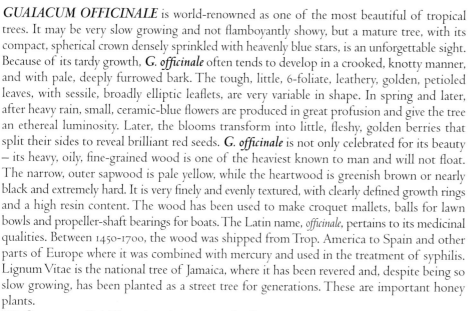

50ft ⌐15m

50ft
15m   0

GUAIACUM OFFICINALE is world-renowned as one of the most beautiful of tropical trees. It may be very slow growing and not flamboyantly showy, but a mature tree, with its compact, spherical crown densely sprinkled with heavenly blue stars, is an unforgettable sight. Because of its tardy growth, **G. officinale** often tends to develop in a crooked, knotty manner, and with pale, deeply furrowed bark. The tough, little, 6-foliate, leathery, golden, petioled leaves, with sessile, broadly elliptic leaflets, are very variable in shape. In spring and later, after heavy rain, small, ceramic-blue flowers are produced in great profusion and give the tree an ethereal luminosity. Later, the blooms transform into little, fleshy, golden berries that split their sides to reveal brilliant red seeds. **G. officinale** is not only celebrated for its beauty – its heavy, oily, fine-grained wood is one of the heaviest known to man and will not float. The narrow, outer sapwood is pale yellow, while the heartwood is greenish brown or nearly black and extremely hard. It is very finely and evenly textured, with clearly defined growth rings and a high resin content. The wood has been used to make croquet mallets, balls for lawn bowls and propeller-shaft bearings for boats. The Latin name, *officinale*, pertains to its medicinal qualities. Between 1450-1700, the wood was shipped from Trop. America to Spain and other parts of Europe where it was combined with mercury and used in the treatment of syphilis. Lignum Vitae is the national tree of Jamaica, where it has been revered and, despite being so slow growing, has been planted as a street tree for generations. These are important honey plants.

*** **G. sanctum**; (L.), Trop. America, to 10 m (33 ft). BASTARD LIGNUM VITAE or GUAYACAN is very similar to *G. officinale*, but less compact. Leaves are larger; flowers are larger, but not as abundant; wood is less heavy, dense and hard. (10–12)

ORIGIN	Trop. America
HEIGHT	up to 10 m (33 ft)
TYPE	evergreen, small flowering tree
STATUS	endangered
HABITAT	dry and humid coastal woodland
GROWTH	slow
FLOWG	intermittently, after rain
DRY TOL.	moderate to high
SALT TOL.	high
LIGHT	full sun
SOIL	fertile, water-retentive
NUTRIT.	high-potassium fertilizer; organic mulch
HAZARDS	none
PROBLEMS	none
ENVIRON.	bee nectar; wild bird seed
PROPAG.	seeds
LEAVES	6-foliate; yellowish green; to 9 cm (3.5 in.); leathery, glabrous, with yellow petioles
FLOWERS	showy; deep to light blue; held in clusters
FRUIT	a capsule, to 2 cm (0.8 in.); golden yellow; seeds with red aril
USE	seaside; small flowering tree; large planter; accent; courtyard; civic centre; bonsai subject; xerophytic
ZONE	10–12

G. officinale; with small, enchanting, ceramic-blue blooms.

G. officinale; old established tree in Bodden Town, Grand Cayman, W Indies, is drenched in starry blooms after a heavy shower. Little blooms infuse the tree with an azure aura.

G. officinale; fleshy, little, golden berries split their sides to reveal their brilliant red sds.

G. sanctum growing in native, arid, coast. habitat in the Turks and Caicos Is in the W Indies.

ORIGIN	Old World Tropics
HEIGHT	up to 10 m (33 ft)
TYPE	evergreen, small coastal tree
STATUS	not threatened
HABITAT	coastal strand; rocky or sandy coastal habitats
GROWTH	moderate
FLOWG	all year, mainly summer
DRY TOL.	moderate
SALT TOL.	high
LIGHT	full sun or bright shade
SOIL	well-drained
NUTRIT.	balanced fertilizer annually; deep, organic mulch
HAZARDS	none
PROBLEMS	none
ENVIRON.	nectar for moths
PROPAG.	seeds; cuttings; layers
LEAVES	simple; bright green; to 25 cm (9.8 in.); obovate, sparsely hairy below
FLOWERS	showy; white; to 4 cm (10 in.) long; tubular; held in long-stemmed clusters; nocturnally fragrant
FRUIT	a drupe, to 3 cm (1.2 in.) diam.; whitish to brownish; faintly ridged; marked with calyx scar at tip
USE	seaside; screening; large planter; courtyard; accent; specimen; coastal median strip
ZONE	10–12

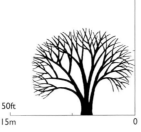

50ft
15m

50ft
15m   0

Guettarda speciosa

SEA RANDIA

L.   80 spp.

RUBIACEAE

ALTHOUGH A MEMBER of the *Ixora* and *Gardenia* family, *Guettarda* species are mostly much less flamboyant than their cousins, often with dull foliage and smaller, insignificant flowers. However, **Guettarda speciosa**, which superficially resembles the beautiful *Gardenia taitensis*, native of the Pacific Is, is an exception. *G. speciosa* also has large, glossy, handsome foliage, white, fragrant blooms and built-in salt-resistance, being a strand species that grows naturally above the high water mark. The deeply veined leaves are tough and leathery, with an impermeable, polished surface and tautly inrolled margins; in many regions, the stems and veins are bright yellow. The flowers are moth-pollinated and have long tubes to accommodate the moths' probosces, and bright, white petals to make them visible at night. They open about one hour after sunset and the spent corollas abort next morning, leaving the pistil attached. Long-stemmed fruit distinguishes this species; it is rounded, faintly ribbed and slightly flattened on the top, from where the persistent calyx is finally aborted. These fruit are commonly found in beach litter, appearing as pale, brownish, small woody 'stones', with 4-6 grooves, and surrounded by numerous fibres that are left from the mesocarp. In some parts of India, *G. speciosa* is known as Funeral Flower because perfume from the blooms is extracted from dew wrung from funeral muslin that has been draped over the tree at night. This small, spreading, generously foliaged species has many landscape uses, particularly in coastal gardens. *** **G. scabra**; ([L.] Lam.), Trop. America, to 10 m (33 ft). ROUGH VELVETSEED, VELVET-BERRY or GREENHEART is a species of coastal thickets and moist, limestone brushland. It has small, ovate, scabrous leaves and narrow, rusty-hairy, pinkish, long-tubed flowers and new growth. The fruit is berry-like, red and velvety. (10–12)

G. speciosa; long-stalked, sea-worthy fr.

G. speciosa; these bright white, long-tubed, fragrant fls open at night and abort in the morning, leaving behind their slender pistils.

G. scabra; has small ovate, scabrous lvs and narrow, rusty hairy, pinkish, long-tubed fls and new growth.

G. speciosa; is a small, everg., generously foliaged sp. that has evolved to have perfect sea-worthiness.

Gustavia superba

MEMBRILLO

(Kunth.) Berg.

to 41 spp.

LECYTHIDACEAE

ORIGIN	from Costa Rica to Colombia
HEIGHT	up to 15 m (49 ft)
TYPE	evergreen flowering tree
STATUS	limited distribution
HABITAT	humid woodlands and rainforest
GROWTH	moderate
FLOWG	year-round
DRY TOL.	moderate
SALT TOL.	low
LIGHT	bright shade or sheltered sun
SOIL	moist, fertile, slightly acid
NUTRIT.	magnesium-rich fertilizer; deep, organic mulch
HAZARDS	none
PROBLEMS	iron deficiencies
ENVIRON.	nectar for wild bees; wild fruit for birds
PROPAG.	seeds; layers
LEAVES	simple; deep green; to 128 cm (50 in.); oblanceolate; leathery, deeply veined
FLOWERS	showy; creamy white to pale pink; to 15 cm (6 in.) diam.; very fragrant
FRUIT	berry-like, to 10 cm (4 in.); orange; with a persistent calyx; seeds buried in edible pulp
USE	small flowering tree; humid shade garden; accent; large planter; courtyard; conservatory
ZONE	11–12

THIS DISTINCTIVE, DENSELY CROWNED TREE of the rainforests and swampy woodland regions of C and northern S America was named for King Gustave III of Sweden. *Gustavia superba* is a sumptuously exotic species, with huge, rich green, leathery, lanceolate, deeply veined, stemless leaves that taper towards their base and are clustered at the ends of branches. Superb, fragrant, large, waxy blooms are held cauliflorously along the main stems and limbs, peeking from the luxuriant, green foliage. They have between 7–9 wavy petals that are white within, reddish pink without, and rich yellow at their base, with a coronet of creamy yellow, waxy stamens blushed deep rose cupped at their tips. Like those of *Lecythis* and *Bertholletia* species, these blooms are adapted for pollination by Trigonid bees. The curious fruit comprises old flower calyxes, which form the mesocarp (flesh) of the large berry, but is 'sliced off' at its top surface to expose the pericarp (ovary) where, when the fruit is ripe, seeds ooze out in the deliquescence (juices) within. The orange pulp of the fruit is said to be high in vitamin A and considered a delicacy in Colombia, where it is known as Chupa. Unfortunately for this exquisite, tropical beauty, *G. superba* harbours a repulsive odour; locally, it is given names like Flower of Death and Corpse Tree for the overpoweringly foetid odour not of its blooms, but of its cut wood.

*** *G. hexapetala*; ([Aubl.] Sm.), (syn. *G. pterocarpa*), Amazonia, Guianas and N Venezuela, to 20 m (66 ft). This species differs from others in having reddish brown bark. Its leaves are smaller, to 24 cm (9.5 in.), with petioles that are 15 cm (6 in.) long. The flowers are white, with white stamens that have yellow bases; the lobed calyx is rusty-pubescent. The fruit matures yellow-orange, with a persistent calyx. (10–12)

G. superba; fr. formed from the calyxes and capped with a thin 'lid'.

G. superba; despite being called Stinkwood, this small sp. conceals singularly exotic, pale pink blooms cupping a neat mass of inwardly curving, purple-pink stamens.

G. superba; large, deeply veined, new lvs are produced in grand flushes of reddish pink.

G. superba; a multi-stemmed specimen. Its large lvs are clustered at the ends of branches.

(1) **Gustavia augusta**; (L.), (syn. *G. insignis*), Guianas and Amazonian rainforest, to 22 m (72 ft). This much-branched sp. often remains shrubby in cultivation. It has large, slender lvs to 48 × 13 cm (19 × 5 in.) that may have serrated margins towards the upper half of the blade. (2) Fleshy fls are held in racemes of 1–8 and are usually held above the lvs. They are white, often tinged with pink, with a fringe-like corona of pink to violet stamens and have a light scent, comparable to that of water-lilies. Typical of this genus, the fleshy, globose fr., with no persistant calyx, are held on sturdy stalks. *G. augusta* is known as STINKWOOD (or JENIPARANA in Brazil) for its foul-smelling lvs, trunk and roots. Ash of the foetid bark is used by the natives to coat pellets of an hallucinogenic snuff paste made from the bark of local *Virola* tree spp. (10–12) (3) **Gustavia gracillima**; (Miers.), W Colombia, is a small, slender tree with narrow, elliptic or lanceolate lvs to 46 × 3.5 cm (18 × 1.4 in.). (4) The fls, although somewhat hidden in the lf axils or on the stems, are a very lovely, deep lavender or cerise-pink colour, with a deeper corona of stamens. (10–12)

Gymnostoma rumphianum

WEEPING RU

(Miq.) L.A.S. Johnson   18 spp.

Casuarina rumphiana

CASUARINACEAE

50ft ⌐15m

50ft
15m   0

ORIGIN	E Malesia
HEIGHT	up to 15 m (50 ft)
TYPE	evergreen foliage tree
STATUS	not threatened
HABITAT	humid mountain forests; heath forests and serpentine soils
GROWTH	slow
FLOWG	spring
DRY TOL.	moderate
SALT TOL.	moderate
LIGHT	full sun
SOIL	acid, well-drained
NUTRIT.	balanced fertilizer annually; deep, organic mulch
HAZARDS	none
PROBLEMS	none
ENVIRON.	none
PROPAG.	seeds; cuttings; layers (the latter preferable for female forms)
LEAVES	needles; deep green; hanging in tassels at ends of drooping twigs
FLOWERS	inconspicuous; grey-brown; held in cylindrical catkins
FRUIT	a 'cone,' to 2 cm (0.8 in.); globose, woody; filled with winged samaras; 1-seeded
USE	specimen; large planter; accent; screening; street tree
ZONE	10–12

GYMNOSTOMA IS A GENUS OF 18 SPECIES found from Malaysia to the W Pacific that very closely resemble *Casuarina* and used to go by that name, but now taxonomists have reclassified them. *Gymnostoma* differ from *Casuarina* in the morphology of their stems and fruiting cones. Although trees of the Casuarinaceae family look like conifers, they are not, because, although very reduced and modified, they have actual flowers with stamens and fruit which, although cone-like, has an embryo. The apparent needle-like leaves are actually modified twigs (cladodes), which effect photosynthesis, and are reduced to minuscule, tooth-like scales. *Gymnostoma rumphianum* is a slow-growing native of the mountain forests of the Philippines, Celebes and Moluccas Is. It forms a slender, upward-thrusting, vase-shaped framework tipped with drooping twigs, with needle-like leaves hanging in vertical, airy, unbranched, green tassels. *G. rumphianum* was named after G. E. Rumpf (1628–1702), the Dutch botanist who did much work in Amboina (or Ambon), an island in the Central Moluccas, in Indonesia.
*** *G. australianum*; (L.A.S. Johnson), N. Qld, Australia, to 10 m (33 ft), DAINTREE PINE, a rare species of rainforest margins, grows to a formal, conical shape in full sun. (9–11)
*** *G. nobile*; ([Whitmore] L.A.S. Johnson), (syn. *Casuarina nobilis*), Borneo to the Philippines, to 15 m (50 ft). Known as BORNEO RU or RHU RONANG. This is a very beautiful, slow-growing species, with the needle twigs crowded near the branch tips so that the whole plant has a dense, plume-like, rounded shape when young. As it matures, the crown becomes more open but still remains attractive. (10–12)
*** *G. papuanum*; ([S. Moore] L.A.S. Johnson), (syn. *Casuarina papuana*), New Guinea endemic. NEW GUINEA RU has soft, 'fluffy' foliage; strongly weeping limbs. (10–12)

G. papuanum; New Guinea Ru has soft, 'fluffy' foliage and strongly weeping limbs.

G. rumphianum; Weeping Ru of Malaysia, a close relative of the She Oak, is a slow-growing sp. found in mountains from northern Philippines to the Moluccas.

G. australianum; a rare sp. that forms a superb, symmetrical crown and is popular in its region as a tub specimen.

G. australianum; in their natural, riverside habitat in Noah, NW Qld, Australia.

212

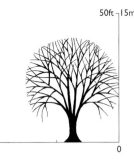

50ft — 15m

50ft
15m — 0

Haematoxylum campechianum

LOGWOOD

L.   3 spp.

FABACEAE (Caesalpinioideae)

ORIGIN	Trop. America
HEIGHT	up to 10 m (33 ft)
TYPE	semi-deciduous flowering tree
STATUS	not threatened
HABITAT	dry, coastal limestone woodland, in humid sink holes
GROWTH	slow
FLOWG	winter to early summer
DRY TOL.	high
SALT TOL.	high
LIGHT	full sun
SOIL	tolerant, water-retentive
NUTRIT.	normally not necessary
HAZARDS	very spiny
PROBLEMS	none
ENVIRON.	bee nectar
PROPAG.	seeds
LEAVES	pinnate; dull to bright green; leaflets in 2–4 pairs; 10 cm (4 in.); wedge-shaped, notched at tips
FLOWERS	showy; pale yellow; in spikes, to 10 cm (4 in.); fragrant
FRUIT	a legume, to 5 cm (2 in.); papery pods held in abundant bundles
USE	seaside; flowering tree; living barrier; xerophytic
ZONE	9–10

From the Greek, *haima* (blood), and *xylon* (wood), comes *Haematoxylum*; the specific name, *campechianum* refers to Campeche, a Mexican state where this species is native and has long been one of the most important species. ***Haematoxylum campechianum*** is a bulky, heavy-limbed tree, with ridged or fluted trunks, pale grey, exfoliating bark and long, vicious spines. But this drab tree is transformed after heavy rain when it billows with the little, creamy yellow, fuzzy catkins of its heavily fragrant, nectar-rich flowers that drone with bees. Soon, it is laden with thin, papery, pointed, flat pods, which are held in messy bundles and remain attached for many months. Dye and ink (haematoxylin) is obtained from the heartwood of this tree by shredding and boiling it with iron salts. The colour changes from scarlet to yellowish and finally black as it cools. For centuries, *H. campechianum* was an important export in its region and it led to the establishment of the British colony of Belize, on the Caribbean coast of C America. Privateers first obtained their supplies by capturing Spanish vessels sailing from Campeche for Spain. Later, in the 17th century, settlements were set up to cut wood on Belize's shores. The heartwood was sawn into logs and rasped into shavings, often by prisoners or slaves. In some parts of the W Indies, Logwood was introduced by the settlers as a cash crop and has subsequently invaded some of those islands. In the early days, its fresh, red dye was mixed with wax to polish wooden floors but, as synthetic dyes replaced organic ones, the tree was no longer used and, because of its invasive and brutally thorny nature, it became a scourge in many areas. The heavy, dense, Campechy-wood timber was also used to make floors and furniture. In some regions, an essential oil is extracted from the flowers and used to make a perfume. This is an important honey plant.

NOTE: *H. campechianum* has proved invasive in some lowland regions.

H. campechianum; bundles of fecund, papery pods follow the fls.

H. campechianum; with a thorny, bony superstructure, plays host to dry-forest bromeliads and orchids.

H. campechianum; are loaded with blooms several times a year. Many people are allergic to the pollen.

H. campechianum; this drab tree is transformed as it billows with creamy yellow, fuzzy little catkins of its heavily fragrant, nectar-rich fls droning with drunken bees.

213

Hamelia patens

FIREBUSH

Jacq.   16 spp.

H. erecta

RUBIACEAE

50ft ┐ 15m

50ft

15m   0

THIS EXUBERANT SPECIES of moist, limestone thickets has become legendary for its enthusiastic growth, generous bloom and adaptable nature. **Hamelia patens** is a shrubby, small tree that grows in partly shady, dryish corners where little else will thrive. A cousin of the *Ixora* and *Gardenia*, this species is easily recognized by its hotly flushed, softly downy foliage, petioles, twigs and widely forking flower cymes. With flexible, purplish-tinged, angled and minutely hairy limbs, **H. patens** forms a soft, billowing, globular crown of dull green, reddish-veined leaves, harmonizing with the slender, curving, branched, reddish cymes of slim, tubular, scarlet flowers that have extrafloral nectaries perfectly adapted for regional hummingbirds. They continue to secrete for many days after they fall. The Spanish common name for this species, Coralillo, refers to the resemblance of the cluster of flowers to a coral necklace. The small, sour, dark red to black-purple berries that follow are adored by fruit-eating birds and are said to be edible as well as medicinal. They are sometimes fermented to make an alcoholic drink. The smooth, greyish bark is easily stripped and has been used as tanbark or cordage in parts of its range. The leaves and stems have also been employed for tanning. The small calliper wood is light brown and hard. **H. patens** responds well to hard, annual pruning.

✳✳✳ **H. cuprea**; (Griseb.), Jamaica to Hispaniola, to 10 m (33 ft). FIRE BELLS is a larger, more compact and tree-like species found in coastal thickets and limestone hillsides. It is glabrous throughout, with yellowish green, crisp foliage and bell-shaped flowers, which vary from pure, bright yellow to infused bright orange; they are larger and less constricted than *H. patens*. This species blooms in flushes most of the year, after rain breaks a dry period. It is xerophytic and quite salt-resistant. (**10–12**)

ORIGIN	Trop. America
HEIGHT	up to 7 m (23 ft)
TYPE	evergreen tall shrub or small flowering tree
STATUS	not threatened
HABITAT	wasteland; thickets; roadsides
GROWTH	fast
FLOWG	year-round
DRY TOL.	high
SALT TOL.	moderate
LIGHT	full sun to bright shade
SOIL	well-drained
NUTRIT.	balanced fertilizer after pruning; organic mulch
HAZARDS	none
PROBLEMS	none
ENVIRON.	hummingbird nectar; wild fruit for birds
PROPAG.	seeds; cuttings; layers
LEAVES	simple; dull green; to 5 × 10 cm (2 × 4 in.); obovate, pubescent; flushed reddish in cold periods; red petioles
FLOWERS	showy; orange-scarlet or crimson; to 2 cm (0.8 in.); downy, tubular
FRUIT	a berry, to 8 mm (0.2 in.); red to purple and finally black; fleshy
USE	small flowering tree; shade garden; screening; planter; xerophytic; civic centre; conservatory
ZONE	10–12

H. patens; fr. scarlet, then black when ripe.

H. patens; with darting, tubular blooms, reminiscent of *Cuphea ignea*, the Cigar Flower, of the Lythraceae family. These fiery-coloured tubes attract hummingbirds.

H. patens; tolerates fairly low light and humidity, making this a very useful plant for dry, difficult corners.

H. cuprea; with bright yellow or orange-yellow bell-shaped fls, which are larger and less constricted than *H. patens*.

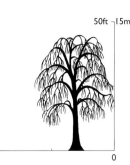
ORIGIN	E Australia, endemic
HEIGHT	up to 12 m (39 ft)
TYPE	evergreen, foliage timber tree
STATUS	rare in the wild
HABITAT	lowland rainforest; coastal scrub
GROWTH	fast
FLOWG	intermittently, all year
DRY TOL.	moderate to high
SALT TOL.	high
LIGHT	full sun or bright shade
SOIL	fertile, humid, well-drained
NUTRIT.	balanced fertilizer annually; deep, organic mulch
HAZARDS	none
PROBLEMS	caterpillars
ENVIRON.	insect nectar; wild fruit for birds
PROPAG.	seeds (soak first)
LEAVES	pinnate; dark green; glossy; leaflets 8–10, oblong-lanceolate, to 15 cm (6 in.)
FLOWERS	showy; greenish or yellowish white; with spirally twisted style; held in long, drooping panicles
FRUIT	a capsule, to 3 cm (1.2 in.); orange or yellow; inflated, 2-lobed; with shiny, black seeds
USE	small shade tree; small street tree; public open space; large planter; civic centre; specimen
ZONE	9–10

Harpullia pendula

TULIPWOOD

Planch. ex F Meull..   37 spp.

SAPINDACEAE

KNOWN AS TULIPWOOD, this fairly slow-growing Australian endemic of lowland rainforests and coastal scrubs is often found in sandy soils near the sea. *Harpullia pendula* is an exuberant, evergreen tree, with flexuous limbs tumbling around its narrow, soaring crown, composed of polished, pinnate leaves. Following the brief spring blooming, when it is quietly draped with drooping panicles of greenish or yellowish white flowers, *H. pendula* puts on a lavish display of pendulous, bright yellow or orange fruit that, sumptuous and fiery, illuminate the tree and cause it to appear to glow from within. During the summer months, each flaming, inflated, 2-lobed capsule opens to reveal a luminous tangerine interior. Dangling by a long, slim thread from these are jet black seeds, which seem reluctant to disperse. This species is renowned for its deep yellow timber, which is marked in black and thought to resemble tulips. *H. pendula* was once a common tree in the drier rainforests in NSW to N Qld, but is now quite rare in the wild. Nevertheless, it is popular as a street tree because of its superb, evergreen canopy and its benign root system.

*** *H. arborea*, ([Blanco] Radilk.), (syn. *H. imbricata*; *H. tomentosa*), India to N Australia, to 15 m (50 ft). HARPUL (trade name) or COOKTOWN TULIPWOOD (Australia), is a fast-growing rainforest tree that requires a sheltered, humid position. *H. arborea* is sparsely branched to begin with, but eventually develops a shapely form, with a dense crown of glossy foliage. Little greenish yellow, faintly fragrant flowers are held in pendulous panicles in spring and are followed by masses of inflated, bright red, or orange, fruit. *H. arborea* is valued as one of the great tropical timbers for its superbly marked, hard, fine-grained wood, used traditionally to make fine cabinetry. It was found suitable for planting as a host tree for the lac insect prior to the development of plastics. (10–12)

H. arborea; with long, drooping panicles of little greenish yellow fls.

H. arborea; a well-established specimen at Fairchild Tropical Gardens in Miami, Florida.

H. arborea; masses of inflated, bright red or orange fr. that splits open to show its fiery lining.

H. pendula; glowing, inflated fr. illuminates the tree during an abundant harvest. Gradually each little ballooned capsule splits open to release its shiny, black sds.

215

Harpullia

(1) ***Harpullia ramiflora*;** (Radlk.), Malesia and E Australia, to 9 m (30 ft). CAPE YORK TULIPWOOD or CLAUDIE TULIPWOOD is a reasonably fast-growing, multi-trunked sp., of lowland, riverine or gallery rainforests, that is of easy culture and makes an excellent, everg. street tree. The luxuriant foliage of *Harpullia ramniflora* distinguishes this sp.; the compound lvs are composed of 8–12 large, heavily veined lflts held in a drooping manner. The specific Latin name, *ramiflora*, describes the fls and fr., which are borne in clusters attached directly onto major stems and trunks.

(2) Fragrant white fls that are cupped in sturdy, hairy, bell-shaped calyxes are not very conspicuous but the fr. most certainly are. (3) Typical of this genus, the black sds are encased in golden yellow arils and are revealed as the orange-red fr. split open. Great bundles of fr. cascade from the limbs to decorate the sombre, coarse canopy of enormous, pinnate lvs. *H. ramiflora* is easily grown from fresh sd and, although it is native to humid habitats, it can tolerate a certain amount of dryness. (10–12)

ORIGIN	Old World Tropics
HEIGHT	up to 10 m (33 ft)
TYPE	evergreen small foliage tree
STATUS	not threatened
HABITAT	humid coastal regions; mangrove swamps
GROWTH	slow
FLOWG	year-round
DRY TOL.	moderate
SALT TOL.	high
LIGHT	bright shade to full sun
SOIL	fertile, water-retentive
NUTRIT.	balanced fertilizer annually; deep, organic mulch
HAZARDS	none
PROBLEMS	none
ENVIRON.	insect nectar
PROPAG.	seeds; ripe-wood cuttings
LEAVES	simple; deep green, bright silver below; to 36 × 12 cm (14 × 5 in.); ovate-lanceolate
FLOWERS	inconspicuous; yellow-green, with no petals; calyx, bell-shaped, toothed
FRUIT	a follicle, to 7.5 cm (3 in.); ellipsoid, woody, beaked, keeled for flotation
USE	seaside; small shade tree; screening; humid shade garden
ZONE	10–12

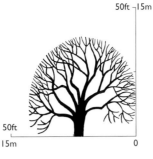

50ft ⌐15m
50ft
15m   0

Heritiera littoralis

LOOKING GLASS TREE

Dryand.   30 spp.

MALVACEAE (formerly Sterculiaceae)

HERITIERA LITTORALIS is found in crowded colonies at river mouths or in mangrove swamps where the river water mingles with the sea. Highly adapted to life on the seashore, this species even tolerates salt water from the highest tides, if flushed by fresh water. The Sunarbans, the world's largest mangrove forest lining the Ganges Delta, derives its name from this species, known as Sundri. Slow-growing, *H. littoralis* develops wide-spreading, shallow roots, often forming sinuous, ribbon-like, smooth-barked plank buttresses in old age. It has a luxuriant crown of large, glossy leaves, their undersurface covered with flat, scurfy, silver scales that may flash and glitter in the breeze like little mirrors. Tiny, petal-less flowers comprise dull purple, toothed, bell-shaped calyxes that hang in yellowish green tassels from leaf axils. Seeds are contained in an oblong, walnut-like, woody beaked fruit that is keeled to aid its flotation (which may last for several weeks) and hence its wider distribution. The seeds and bark contain tannin. In Malaya, the seeds are used medicinally and are sometimes eaten with fish. *H. littoralis* is valued in its native region for its dark brown, exceedingly tough wood – possibly the toughest of Malaysian timbers – and is used for building boats and for making masts for dhows, poles and wheel hubs.
*** *H. macrophylla*; (Wall. ex Vogel), India and Burma, to 30 m (100 ft). Leaves to 35 cm (13.8 in.), bright green, opaque silvery below. Flowers small, pinkish yellow, in open panicles; tough fruit is beaked. Much valued for its timber. (10–12)
*** *H. trifoliata*; ([Sprague] Sprague), (syn. *Tarrietia utalis*), W Africa, to 28 m (90 ft). Niangon is a large forest tree with a straight bole, to about 18 m (60 ft), and flying buttresses. Leaves are coriaceous, simple on seedlings but digitate on mature wood. Small flowers held in axillary panicles. Fruit are unilaterally winged. (10–12)

H. littoralis; with beaked, woody fr. with keels for flotation.

H. littoralis; with wide-spreading, shallow roots that form sinuous ribbon-like, plank buttresses in old age.

H. littoralis; this is a sp. adapted to living in inundated sites. It is valued in its region for its exceedingly tough timber.

H. littoralis; designed for coast. life, this salt-resistant sp. is known as the Looking Glass Tree for its leathery lvs, which have flashy, silvery linings.

217

Hernandia nymphaeifolia

SEA HEARSE

([C. Presl.] Kubitzki)   22 spp.

H. ovigera; H. peltata.

HERNANDIACEAE

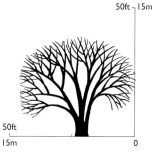

AT FIRST GLANCE, this species could be mistaken for *Thespesia populneus* but, on close inspection, it will be seen that the leaves of **Hernandia nymphaeifolia** are peltate, with the stalk attached near the centre. (The specific name, *nymphaeifolia*, refers to the similarity to those of the water lily, *Nymphaea*.) The 4-parted flowers, which are held in large panicles, are composed of 1 female and 2 males. They are petal-less, with the females having 4 large, cup-shaped, fleshy sepals that ultimately envelop the fruit. The swollen fruit case is greenish yellow, fleshy and hollow, resembling a little polished apple, and actually has the same pleasant, mellow fragrance. It encloses a hard, blackish, oily drupe that is longitudinally ridged and 1-seeded. At its base is a large hole through which, when ripe, the large seed oozes out. In Polynesia, *H. nymphaeifolia* is cultivated for its unusual flowers and black, grooved seeds, which are often strung into necklaces. These oily seeds are also burned for candles, but produce a great deal of smoke. Being fast growing, of easy culture and of a smallish, compact stature, Sea Hearse is popular for street planting in coastal areas. The lightweight, soft, greyish wood is sometimes used in the same manner as Balsawood or as tinder.

*** *H. sonora*; (L.), W Indies, to 20 m (66 ft). JACK-IN-A-BOX has its peltate, oval leaves held vertically on stiff, pale green petioles. The flowers are yellowish white in stout, erect panicles. The fruit is a pumpkin-like, ridged, greenish or reddish capsule, with a hole at its base. In India, where it has been introduced, the bark, seeds and leaves are used medicinally as a purge and the juice as a painless depilatory. A preparation of the roots is also popular there as an antidote to fish poisoning. Like *H. nymphaeifolia*, the seeds are burnt for candles. The soft sapwood and the heartwood are barely distinguishable. (10–12)

ORIGIN	Old World Tropics
HEIGHT	up to 10 m (33 ft)
TYPE	evergreen, small flowering tree
STATUS	not threatened
HABITAT	moist coastal woodland; rocky and sandy coasts
GROWTH	fast
FLOWG	intermittently, all year
DRY TOL.	moderate
SALT TOL.	high
LIGHT	full sun
SOIL	rich, humid, water-retentive
NUTRIT.	not normally necessary
HAZARDS	none
PROBLEMS	none
ENVIRON.	insect nectar
PROPAG.	seeds
LEAVES	simple; rich green; to 10 cm (4 in.); broadly ovate; long-petioled
FLOWERS	showy; greenish yellow; monoecious; held in silvery panicles
FRUIT	a capsule, to 5 cm (2 in.); greenish white, globular; with apical hole
USE	seaside; shade tree; coastal street tree; specimen; seaside screening; large planter
ZONE	10–12

H. sonora; 4-part flowers held in large panicles.

H. nymphaeifolia; a lushly foliaged strand tree found along sheltered beaches with high rainfall. This sp. deserves to be more widely planted in trop. coast. gardens.

H. sonora; fr. is a pumpkin-like, ridged, greenish or reddish capsule with a hole at its base.

H. sonora; lightweight, soft, greyish wood is sometimes used in the same manner as Balsawood or as domestic tinder.

ORIGIN	Amazon Basin
HEIGHT	up to 20 m (66 ft)
TYPE	deciduous foliage tree
STATUS	not threatened
HABITAT	rainforest; along river banks
GROWTH	fast
FLOW G	summer
DRY TOL.	moderate
SALT TOL.	low
LIGHT	bright shade
SOIL	fertile, water-retentive
NUTRIT.	high-nitrogen fertilizer; deep, organic mulch
HAZARDS	seeds poisonous
PROBLEMS	fungus (S American leaf blight)
ENVIRON.	pollination effected by wind
PROPAG.	very fresh seeds; bud grafting onto seedlings
LEAVES	3-foliate; dark green; 30–60 cm (12–24 in.); spirally arranged
FLOWERS	showy; pale yellow; in large panicles; fragrant
FRUIT	a capsule, large, 3-lobed; held in stalked clusters; exploding on opening; seeds speckled, to 2.5 cm (1 in.)
USE	humid shade garden; specimen; botanic collection
ZONE	11–12

100ft – 30m
75ft
22.5m
0

Hevea brasiliensis

PARA RUBBER TREE

(A. Juss.) Meull.   12 spp.

Siphona brasiliensis

EUPHORBIACEAE (Crotonoideae)

IN THE 18TH AND 19TH CENTURIES, the Omagua, a once powerful tribe of the Upper Amazon, fashioned a variety of rubber products for domestic use and trade, including water bottles, balls, boots and elastic bands. Such items attracted the attention of visitors to Amazonia and the British took raw latex back home, where they found that it could rub out pencil marks, hence the name, rubber. *Hevea brasiliensis* has smooth, greyish bark and stout branches supporting a lustrous, rounded crown of long-stalked, 3-fingered leaves. Sweetly scented, petal-less, minuscule, whitish flowers are held in airy, terminal panicles, with the male and female flowers grouped together, and pollination is effected by the wind. The seeds of *H. brasiliensis* look very like those of *Ricinus communis* (Castor Oil) and are explicitly designed for its riverside habitat. The fruit explodes noisily, ejecting the tough-shelled, brown-speckled, egg-like seeds up to 20 m (66 ft), often sending them into the river currents where they may float for up to 2 months. In Brazil, it is said that most of the seeds are destroyed by Piranha fish, but despite this, the seeds are notoriously shortly viable and must be sown when absolutely fresh. Although the seeds contain cyanic poisons, they are a staple food of the local people, who soak them for prolonged periods or boil them to remove the toxins. Out of more than 1,000 species of tropical trees that contain rubbery latex, *H. basiliensis* is the only one found to have latex of any real commercial importance. Strangely enough, although it is a Brazilian native, this species has been grown more extensively in Sri Lanka and the Malay Archipelago than in its native land. Rubber trees are ready to be tapped for their latex at about 7 years old. The cutting lines follow the spiralled latex vessels of the bark and great care is taken not to cut or damage the cambium layer.

H. brasiliensis; with 4-lobed capsules held in drooping, branched clusters.

H. brasiliensis; tapping lines follow spiralled latex vessels of the bark. Care must be taken not to cut the cambium layer.

H. brasiliensis; fr. explode with a loud retort when ripe, causing the large, speckled sds to fly far from the tree.

H. brasiliensis; a small, abandoned rubber plantation on the small island of Pulau Ubin off the coast of Singapore.

219

Hibiscus tiliaceus

SEA HIBISCUS

Arruda.   300 spp.

H. abutiloides

MALVACEAE

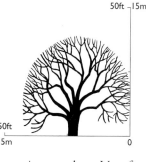

ORIGIN	Pan Tropical
HEIGHT	up to 10 m (33 ft)
TYPE	evergreen, small flowering tree
STATUS	not threatened
HABITAT	coastal swamps; edges of mangrove swamps
GROWTH	fast
FLOWG	year-round
DRY TOL.	high
SALT TOL.	high
LIGHT	full sun
SOIL	well-drained
NUTRIT.	normally not necessary
HAZARDS	none
PROBLEMS	straggling, pliable growth; messy leaf drop
ENVIRON.	insect nectar
PROPAG.	seeds; large cuttings
LEAVES	simple; rich green, paler below; to 16 cm (6 in.); cordate, long-petioled
FLOWERS	showy; yellow, fading to deep-orange, with dark maroon 'eye'; petals overlapped
FRUIT	a capsule, to 4 cm (1.5 in.); 5-celled, dehiscent; with reddish seeds
USE	seaside; coastal screening; fast-growing shade tree; coastal street tree; sand stabilization; xerophytic
ZONE	10–12

LIKE MANY TREES OF SALINE SWAMPS, ***Hibiscus tiliaceus*** is a wanderer. Very fast growing, this species has gangling, softly pubescent, heavy limbs, which are almost scandent and may, like the *Conocarpus*, root if they touch the ground, sending up a fresh crown of stems. In soft mud, it may form impenetrable thickets. Unfortunately, *H. tiliaceus* is also shallow-rooted and requires constant hard pruning in order to form a stable, solitary specimen. Superficially, this species may be confused with Sea-Grape, but its large, broad, heart-shaped leaves are thin-textured. Flowers, held in terminal clusters, are attractive and hibiscus-like, but open one at a time, emerging light yellow with a dark, maroon 'eye', and gradually changing to deep orange before falling in the evening. *H. tiliaceus* is very important to the Polynesians, who use the lightweight wood for the outriggers of their canoes. Flowers are used for medicine, having laxative properties, and green bark, which peels off easily in wide strips, is employed in the making of fine fibre for dance skirts worn in religious festivals, as strainers for a ceremonial drink and is beaten out to make traditional, tapa bark cloth. In other parts of the Pacific, it is woven into rope and fishing nets. Young leaves and green bark has been eaten in times of famine. Sapwood is whitish and the heartwood a dark, greenish brown; it is moderately soft, heavy and porous and used chiefly for fuel and as net floats or corks. Large limbs may be planted as living posts and are often cropped as a source of green bark. *H. tiliaceus* is an excellent choice for dense, sea-worthy screening and hedging; it may be planted in situ by criss-crossing stakes of semi-mature wood and regularly pruning the new shoots until a dense growth is achieved. *H. tiliaceus* has been widely planted to contain beach erosion and for coastal rehabilitation. This is a honey plant.

NOTE: *H. tiliaceus* has proved invasive in some lowland regions.

H. tiliaceus; Mahoe is a shallow-rooted sp. and requires constant, hard pruning in order to form a solitary, stable specimen.

H. tiliaceus; the blooms slowly age to deep orange before falling in the evening.

H. tiliaceus; with 5-celled, dehiscent, dried fr. full of reddish sds.

H. tiliaceus; light yellow fls deepen to rich yellow at noon.

(1) *Hibiscus elatus*; (Sw.), Cuba and Jamaica, to 25 m (82 ft). BLUE MAHOE or CUBAN BAST is native of dry woodlands. Very similar to *H. tiliaceus*, *H. elatus* has orange fls that fade dark red; they have narrow, widely separated petals. *H. elatus* is highly regarded for its excellent hardwood, which is used for furniture and construction. Much sturdier and slower growing than Sea Hibiscus, this sp. resists hurricanes. Photographed in their native Cuba, where they are popular as street trees. (10–12) (2) *Hibiscus tiliaceus* var. *populneus*; a popular form with elongated, undulate lvs. This form is found in various colour combinations, including deep, brownish purple or (as above) pale green and cream variegations. (3) *Hibiscus tiliaceus* cv. 'Royal Flush'

has superb, deep purple new growth. Young lvs have a white bloom below. As the foliage matures, it becomes deep green, flushed slightly with purple. A similar form has lvs splotched pink, purple and cream. (4) *Hibiscus kokio*; (Hillebr.) Hawaiian endemic, to 7 m (23 ft). Known as KOKI'O or KOKI'O ULA'ULA, this is a very variable shrub or small tree that may have red, orange or yellow fls. (5) *Hibiscus waimea*; (A. Heller), Hawaiian endemic, to 10 m (33 ft). KOKI'O KEA is its common name. It has densely stellate branches and petioles. The white fls last only a day and deepen to pinkish in the evening; they are strongly fragrant. These 2 Hawaiian endemics are threatened with extinction. (10–12)

Hura crepitans

SAND-BOX TREE

L.   2 spp.

H. senegalensis

EUPHORBIACEAE (Euphorbioideae)

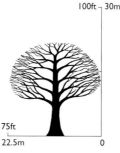

100ft — 30m

75ft
22.5m   0

HURA CREPITANS is a fast-growing Trop. American tree of the Euphorbiaceae family, with a heavy trunk and limbs that are covered with spines. It also has the typical, acrid latex of its tribe, which is extremely toxic and may cause temporary blindness. This species has distinctive characteristics that clearly explain one of Nature's singular sexual mechanisms. The monoecious nature of *H. crepitans* is typical of the Euphorbias, which means that instead of having male stamens and female pistils and ovaries on the same flower head, it has the two sexes on the same inflorescence. In this case, they are very easily distinguished, being rather large and showy. The males are deep red and clustered in a 'corn cob', to 3 cm (1.2 in.) long, while the female, poised above the male, resembles a stout-stemmed, red parasol with an ovary at its base. The seeds that follow are contained in a flattened, pumpkin-like schizocarp made up of many seed carpels, or sections, that become hard and woody as they ripen. The fruit splits open explosively with a loud report, scattering the carpels, which expel their seeds up to 14 m (46 ft) away, sometimes causing problems by frightening livestock. At one time, the young seed pods were very fashionable as an accessory for a writing desk. They were held together by wire or by pouring melted lead into the centre. The pod was then decorated, polished and used as a paperweight, or filled with fine sand that was used for blotting letters. The toxic sap has been used to treat leprosy. It is also used as a fish poison, and is said to kill even anaconda snakes. *Hura* timber is useful and known as Assacu; the heartwood is pale, yellowish brown to dark brown, moderately soft and lightweight, but very susceptible to termites. Traditionally, it has been used to fashion dugout canoes. Currently, the timber more often serves as fuel or to make crates and boxes.

ORIGIN	Trop. America
HEIGHT	up to 20 m (66 ft)
TYPE	semi-deciduous foliage tree
STATUS	not threatened
HABITAT	moist coastal forests
GROWTH	fast
FLOWG	winter to summer
DRY TOL.	high
SALT TOL.	moderate
LIGHT	full sun
SOIL	fertile, well-drained
NUTRIT.	balanced fertilizer annually
HAZARDS	spiny trunk; toxic sap
PROBLEMS	weak-wooded
ENVIRON.	insect nectar
PROPAG.	seeds; large cuttings
LEAVES	simple; deep green; to 15 × 12 cm (6 × 4.7 in.); long-petioled, elongated cordate
FLOWERS	inconspicuous; dark red; monoecious; held in pairs, terminally
FRUIT	a schizocarp, to 8 × 4 cm (3.15 × 1.5 in.); tangerine-like; with about 20 sections
USE	large shade tree; public open space; botanic collection; xerophytic
ZONE	10—12

H. crepitans; dried fr. is composed of many segments, like an orange.

H. crepitans; Sand-Box demonstrates the monoecious arrangements of sexual parts. Above, is the withered, female organ with its (already) swelling embryo, while dangled below is the male.

H. crepitans; a young specimen showing the characteristic, stocky growth habit.

H. crepitans; trunk and limbs, which are covered with spines, have acrid, very poisonous latex.

ORIGIN	Trop. America
HEIGHT	up to 33 m (108 ft)
TYPE	evergreen, large foliage tree
STATUS	vulnerable
HABITAT	lowland dry forests
GROWTH	slow
FLOWG	spring to autumn
DRY TOL.	high
SALT TOL.	moderate
LIGHT	full sun
SOIL	deep, fertile
NUTRIT.	balanced fertilizer annually; organic mulch
HAZARDS	none
PROBLEMS	sheds large branches
ENVIRON.	bee nectar
PROPAG.	seeds
LEAVES	2-lobed; bright green, to 4 cm (1.5 in.); leaflets asymmetric, thick, with yellow petioles and veins
FLOWERS	inconspicuous; milky white; narrow-petalled; held in erect clusters
FRUIT	a legume, to 10 cm (4 in.); thickly woody; with thick, pale yellow pulp; dark red seeds
USE	large shade tree; public open space; xerophytic
ZONE	10—12

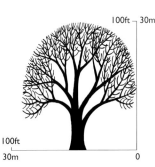

100ft – 30m

100ft
30m   0

Hymenaea courbaril

WEST INDIAN LOCUST

L.   16 spp.

FABACEAE (Caesalpinioideae)

HYMENAEA COURBARIL is one of the noble trees of Trop. America and has been planted in parks all over the tropical world. **H. courbaril** has a heavy, smooth-barked trunk that grows straight and tall in the open but tends to become distorted in deep shade. It forms a voluminous, wide-spreading canopy that it supports with robust buttresses in old age. This species is usually evergreen, except during prolonged drought, when it may lose some of its foliage. Although this is a member of the vast legume family, it has few of the obvious family characteristics. The twinned, oblique, leathery leaves, the knobby, hairy, floral panicles and buds of the narrow-petalled, white flowers and the distorted, rocky seed pods, with their flattened, dark red seeds set in edible, smelly, mealy pulp, do not really add up to a recognizable Caesalpinioideae species. Nor do they meet the usual specifications for a distinguished tree. However, it is difficult not to be impressed by the grandeur of a worthy, old Locust Tree or Stinking Toe. Its heartwood is dark, red-brown, often streaked blackish, very hard, heavy, strong and extremely resistant to termites. Known as Courbaril in the trade, this is considered one of the most valuable of American timbers, sometimes being compared to mahogany. **H. courbaril** has also been valued for its high-grade Copal resin, obtained from bark incisions, or exuded from the base of the tree and known as Gumamini or Brazil Copal. It is used in making varnish, patent leather and church incense. South American Indians stitched lightweight canoes from the bark.
*** **H. verrucosa**; (Gaertner), (syn. *Trachylobium verucosa*), E Africa and Seychelles, to 33 m (108 ft), GUM COPAL TREE with a tall, clear bole to 15 m (50 ft). This species is the source of Madagascar Copal and timber. Both species are important bee plants. (10—12)

H. courbaril; with heavy, rocky, indehiscent fr.

H. courbaril; a copal resin obtained from bark incisions, or exuded from the base of the tree, is known as 'Brazil Copal'.

H. courbaril; all parts of this sp. are thick and heavy; the leathery, yellow-petioled lvs are 2-parted in a cloven manner.

H. courbaril; old Stinking Toe in a pasture in Grand Cayman, where it must have been planted by a farmer-sailor who collected sd in S America, as it is not native to these islands.

223

Hymenosporum flavum

NATIVE FRANGIPANI

(Hook.) F. Meull.   I spp.

PITTOSPORACEAE

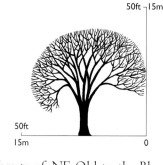

50ft ⌐15m

50ft
15m   0

THIS MONOTYPIC GENUS, native of upland rainforests of NE Qld to the Blue Mountains in E Australia, and also to New Guinea, is closely related to the *Pittosporum*. Fast growing and undemanding, the trunk is grey and roughish, with sparse branching. In its natural habitat it may reach 20 m (66 ft), but in cultivation it is usually much shorter. *Hymenosporum flavum* has a slender, erect framework holding radiating whorls of twiggy limbs and forming a superb, evergreen crown of large, glossy, deep green, leathery, slightly folded leaves, which are velvety below. In late spring, the canopy is lavishly garnished with creamy white, salverform flowers that are intensely honey fragrant, reminiscent of frangipani (hence its common name). They are held in lax, terminal panicles to 20 cm (8 in.) diameter. As they mature over several days, they turn deep, golden yellow. Small, flattish capsules follow, filled with small, winged seeds. The scientific name of this species comes from the Greek, *hymen*, a membrane, and *sporos*, a seed, referring to the membranously winged seeds that set this species apart from *Pittosporum*. **H. flavum** grows quickly, given plenty of moisture and well-drained, humus-rich soil, when it will shoot up to form a loose, columnar shape. Surprisingly, however, this species may perform best in slightly unfavourable situations, where it is forced to stay small and bushy, often blooming more profusely. Because of its tendency to become leggy at first, it may be advisable to prune back new growth from a young age, to ensure a well formed, compact shape. **H. flavum** is an adaptable species, with a wide climate tolerance; it is widely planted in Australia from Sydney to north Qld. It will withstand full sun and some frost, but requires humidity and shelter from strong winds. Propagation is easily done by fresh seeds or from cuttings.

ORIGIN	E Australia and New Guinea
HEIGHT	up to 12 m (39 ft)
TYPE	evergreen, small flowering tree
STATUS	not threatened
HABITAT	coastal and lowland rainforest
GROWTH	fast
FLOWG	late spring to summer
DRY TOL.	moderate to low
SALT TOL.	high
LIGHT	full, sheltered sun
SOIL	humus-rich, well-drained
NUTRIT.	high-potassium fertilizer; deep, organic mulch
HAZARDS	none
PROBLEMS	none
ENVIRON.	bee and butterfly nectar
PROPAG.	seeds; cuttings; layers
LEAVES	simple; dark green; to 15 cm (6 in.); leathery, glossy; velvety below
FLOWERS	showy; creamy white, deepening to ochre yellow; long salverform; very fragrant
FRUIT	a capsule, to 2.5 cm (1 in.); seeds flat, with a membranous wing
USE	seaside; small flowering tree; courtyard; large planter; specimen; civic centre; conservatory
ZONE	9–11

H. flavum; luxuriant, dark green foliage and white fls, which deepen to gold.

H. flavum; abundant, honey-pungent blooms are perfectly set off against polished leathery, dark green foliage. This Qld variety has dark, reddish brown centres to its blooms.

H. flavum; dehiscent capsules contain flat sds with a membranous wings.

H. flavum; in late spring at the Los Angeles Arboretum, short-lived blooms carpet the ground below the tree.

224

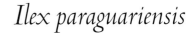
ORIGIN	S America
HEIGHT	up to 15 m (50 ft)
TYPE	evergreen foliage tree
STATUS	vulnerable
HABITAT	cool, humid tropical highlands
GROWTH	slow
FLOWG	year-round
DRY TOL.	low
SALT TOL.	low
LIGHT	bright shade
SOIL	rich, slightly acid
NUTRIT.	rich compost and deep, organic mulch
HAZARDS	none
PROBLEMS	scales; nematodes
ENVIRON.	wild fruit for birds
PROPAG.	seeds (very slow); misted cuttings; grafts
LEAVES	simple; dull to mid green; to 11 × 5.5 cm (4.3 × 2.2 in.); obovate
FLOWERS	inconspicuous; greenish white; dioecious; 4-petalled; axillary
FRUIT	a berry, to 5.5 mm (0.2 in.); globose, red; with 4 seeds
USE	small tree for higher elevations; botanic collection; bonsai subject; conservatory
ZONE	9–11

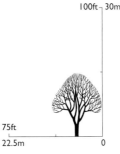

100ft 30m
75ft
22.5m 0

Ilex paraguariensis

MATÉ

A. St. Hil.　　　400 spp.

AQUIFOLIACEAE

THROUGH THE MILLENNIA, herbal beverages have been brewed from the dried leaves of specific plants known to either mildly stimulate or calm the nerves, to elevate the mind and spirit or to help bodily functions. From Brazil and Argentina to Paraguay and Uraguay, the most popular brewed beverage is Yerba Maté, derived from the leaves of a holly, *Ilex paraguariensis*, a slender, dioecious, evergreen native to high, cool, humid elevations near streams and river valleys, where it is found in stands known as manchas. The leaves are dull green, leathery, obovate-oblong and caffeine-rich, with serrated margins, and the flowers are small and greenish white, with the female flowers giving way to red, globose, holly-like fruit. The young leaves are harvested in much the same way as tea (*Camellia sinensis*). After they are dried, they are finely ground and packaged. Although it is infused in the same manner as tea, the sweet, aromatic Yerba Maté is imbibed directly from the spout of a teapot, from a gourd (a Maté) or from a glass, using a tube known as a Bombilla, which has a strainer at its end. Mineral rich, *I. paraguariensis* is recognized as a stimulant, diuretic and anti-rheumatic, as well as having the power to increase intellectual lucidity and vigour. Currently, it is being studied for its antioxidant properties.

*** *I. cassine*; (L.), Florida, USA and W Indies, to 8 m (26 ft). DAHOON HOLLY is a small, slow-growing, dioecious tree of coastal swamps and moist, coastal forests. It has simple, oblanceolate, leathery leaves, with shallow teeth. The little, greenish white flowers are held in small, hairy clusters at terminal leaf bases. It flowers in spring, with fruit ripe in winter. *Ilex cassine* may be propagated by seeds, but these are sexually unreliable so, if a fruiting tree is required, it should be done vegetatively by cuttings or layering from a female tree. *Ilex* species dislike being transplanted, even as seedlings, and are often sensitive to pruning. (8–11)

I. cassine; with compact, branched heads of tiny, greenish white fls.

I. paraguariensis; lvs are dull green, leathery, obovate-oblong with serrated margins.

I. cassine; typical of this dioec. genus, the luscious crimson berries are held on female trees only.

I. paraguariensis; in S America, lvs are used to make Yerba Maté, a mildly stimulating tea. Photographed at Tropical Fruit World in Qld, Australia.

Inga jinicuil

ICE CREAM BEAN

Harms.   350 spp.

LEGUMINOSAE (Mimosoideae

100ft — 30m

110ft
33m   0

ORIGIN	from Mexico to Costa Rica
HEIGHT	up to 20 m (66 ft)
TYPE	evergreen fruiting tree
STATUS	not threatened
HABITAT	moist, lowland slopes
GROWTH	fast
FLOWG	year-round
DRY TOL.	moderate
SALT TOL.	moderate
LIGHT	full sun
SOIL	fertile, well-drained
NUTRIT.	normally not necessary; deep, organic mulch
HAZARDS	none
PROBLEMS	brittle wood; caterpillars
ENVIRON.	bee and bat nectar
PROPAG.	seeds; misted cuttings
LEAVES	pinnate; rich green, leaflets in 3–4 pairs, with winged midrib
FLOWERS	showy; creamy white; held in clusters; with fragile, thread-like stamens; fragrant
FRUIT	a legume, to 20 × 5 cm (8 × 2 in.); plump, ridged longitudinally; seeds set in sweet, white pulp
USE	large shade tree; street tree; public open space; xerophytic
ZONE	10–12

INGA JINICUIL, A VERY FAST-GROWING SPECIES from C America, has been widely introduced to parts of the W Indies as coffee shade. This vigorous, ebullient legume forms a dense, wide-spreading umbrella crown with handsome, bright green, glossy, coarsely pinnate foliage that is distinguished by its prominently winged rachis, or leaf stalk. Irregularly throughout the year, the verdant parasol of *I. jinicuil* is sprinkled with creamy white, starry pompoms of its large, mimosa-like flowers, which tend to be easily damaged and scorched brown by high winds and heavy rain. Huge, heavy, swollen, multi-ridged, bean-like pods replace the flowers. They are light green and have well-defined, raised, moulded rims. As they mature, they darken in colour but do not split open on ripening. This robust packaging protects a cache of slightly sweet, white, creamy, high-protein pulp, the taste of which is likened to vanilla ice cream and which is considered a delicacy by some, particularly children. Embedded in this pulp are several oblong seeds. *Inga* species are important honey plants.

*** *I. laurina*, ([Sw.] Willd. ex L.), W Indies and C America, to 9 m (20 ft). SPANISH OAK, SWEET PEA or POIS DOUX is a widely distributed species of moist, lowland limestone areas. It has been commonly planted for shade in coffee or cocoa plantations. The flower of *I. laurina* differs from *I. jinicuil* in that it takes the form of a short bottlebrush of white, thread-like stamens. (10–12)

*** *I. vera*; (Willd.), (syn. *I. inga*), W Indies, to 20 m (66 ft). Known in Spanish-speaking islands as GUABA or GUAMA, or in French as POIS DOUX, this fast-growing, evergreen species is the commonest coffee shade tree and has become naturalized throughout many regions. The sweetish, white pulp of its fruit is also edible. (10–12)

NOTE: these species have the potential to be invasive.

I jinicuil; fragile, like thistle down, these fls deepen to ochre during the day.

I. jinicuil, a pod pulled open to show the interior, with sds buried in sweet cottony pulp. Although not equal to ice cream, children usually enjoy it.

I. jinicuil; the pinnate lvs are distinguished by their winged rachis.

I. jinicuil; this vigorous, ebullient legume forms a dense, wide-spreading, umbrella crown.

ORIGIN	from Mascarenes to Australia and Fiji
HEIGHT	up to 20 m (66 ft)
TYPE	evergreen flowering tree
STATUS	not threatened
HABITAT	sea coasts; mangrove swamps; river banks
GROWTH	moderate
FLOWG	summer
DRY TOL.	moderate
SALT TOL.	high
LIGHT	full sun
SOIL	very well-drained
NUTRIT.	balanced fertilizer annually; organic mulch
HAZARDS	none
PROBLEMS	none
ENVIRON.	nectar for insects
PROPAG.	seeds; cuttings
LEAVES	simple pinnate; rich green; 1–2 pairs of blunt leaflets; thick, leathery
FLOWERS	showy; white or pink; with 1 large petal; downy, 4-parted; persistent calyx; 3 red stamens; very fragrant
FRUIT	a legume, to 20 cm (8 in.); thick, leathery; with 3–6 flattened, globose seeds
USE	seaside; coastal street tree; specimen; timber tree; shade tree
ZONE	11–12

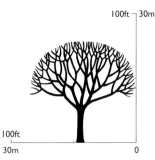

100ft – 30m

100ft
30m 0

Intsia bijuga

IPIL

(Colebr.) Kuntze   3 spp.

FABACEAE (Caesalpinioideae)

ALTHOUGH THIS EVERGREEN TREE is widely distributed, it is particularly prolific along the sandy coastlines of the Fijian and Tongan islands, in the South Pacific, where it is used for making canoes. *Intsia bijuga* is known in this region as Kwila, and as Ipil in other parts of the Pacific. It is a vigorous species, with smooth, grey, erect limbs and large, leathery, pinnate foliage, but it is particularly distinguished by its very fragrant blooms. Closely related to the *Afzelia* genus of Africa, these genera are distinguished by their curious flowers, comprising a large, solitary petal. *I. bijuga* has either a white or pink petal that is set in a heavy, furry, strongly cupped, 4-parted calyx. Each bloom has 3 long, bright crimson stamens that add gaiety to the large, crowded clusters. The fruit is a large, thick, leathery pod containing 3–6 round seeds. The wood is moderately heavy and hard. It is used for interior work, although it needs to be thoroughly seasoned or it develops dark stains. *I. bijuga* is an excellent tree for seaside or street planting. It is the national tree of the island of Guam.

✽✽✽ *I. palembanica*; (Miq.), (syn. *Afzelia palembanica*), to 40 m (131 ft), Indo-China to Malesia. Known variously as MERBAU, BORNEO- or MALACCA-TEAK, this very large, deciduous, strongly buttressed tree of lowland or coastal forest and mangrove forests has a tall, clear bole with pinkish grey bark, shallowly pocked with small, roundish scaling pieces. Leaflets of this species are held in 3–4 pairs and the fruit pods, which are larger than *I. bijuga* (to 30 cm [12 in.]), have flat seeds. *I. palembanica*, famous regionally as a timber tree, with timber known as Merbau, greatly resembles another legume, *Koompassia excelsa*, which grows in the same environment and, at 80 m (262 ft), is one of the tallest trees in the forest. (10–12)

I. bijuga; little pale yellow, furry calyxed fls with a single petal.

I. bijuga; planted as a street tree in Cairns, N Qld, on the Great Barrier Reef.

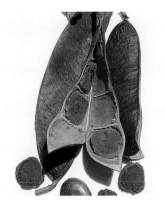

I. bijuga; with large, thick, leathery sd pods and flattened, globose sds.

I. bijuga; with opulent clusters of curious, 1-petalled fls cupped in concave, greenish sepals. The bright crimson stamens lend a little colour.

Ixora pavetta

TORCHWOOD

Andrews   300 spp.

I. parviflora

RUBIACEAE

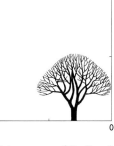

50ft ⌐15m

50ft
15m   0

THIS *IXORA*, A COMMON EVERGREEN SPECIES from drier parts of India, does not reach the high standards set by the stunning colour of the blooms of most of its family. *Ixora pavetta* is densely branched, with large, glossy leaves, and forms a lush, compact canopy. Although not as colourful as many of the popularly cultivated Ixora, the compact, spiky heads of cream flowers are held in erect, reddish-stalked clusters at the ends of the branchlets, making a strong visual impact with their regular, rather powerful, design, and with the added compensation of their sweet fragrance. This shrubby, little tree is perfectly designed for screening and does well in bright shade. The ripe fruit is eaten by local people. The leaves are given as fodder to buffaloes, whilst the green branches burn brightly. Traditionally, they were bound together and used as torches, hence the common name, Torchwood. Before the advent of telephones in India, these torches were used by runners, who carried letters by night when it was cooler and the offices were closed. The wood of *I. pavetta* is quite small in diameter, but is very hard and close-grained and is used for furniture, turning and building. *** *I. thwaitesii*; (Hook. f.), Sri Lanka, endemic, to 6 m (20 ft). BOLA DE NIEVE, CORONA DE REINA and RICE FLOWER were some of the names given to this small tree by early settlers in the W Indies. It has large, glabrous, oblanceolate to elliptic leaves, which are often undulate along their margins, and compact heads of starry, pure white flowers, which persist on the plant, becoming brown with age. Known also as White Ceylon Ixora, this species is popular for its fresh fragrance. It blooms all year but seldom, if ever, sets seeds in many regions of Trop. America, possibly because of the lack of pollinators. (10–12)

NOTE: *I. thwaitesii* is a freely suckering species.

ORIGIN	Trop. Asia
HEIGHT	up to 7 m (23 ft)
TYPE	evergreen, small flowering tree
STATUS	not threatened
HABITAT	dry woodland
GROWTH	slow
FLOWG	spring
DRY TOL.	high
SALT TOL.	low
LIGHT	bright shade to full sun
SOIL	fertile, slightly acid
NUTRIT.	magnesium-rich fertilizer; deep, organic mulch
HAZARDS	none
PROBLEMS	none
ENVIRON.	butterfly nectar
PROPAG.	seeds; greenwood cuttings
LEAVES	simple; dark green; to 13 cm (5 in.); oblong-elliptic, sub-sessile, leathery
FLOWERS	showy; dingy white, possibly tinged pink; held in compact heads; fragrant
FRUIT	a berry, to 0.5 cm (0.2 in.); shiny, black, 2-lobed
USE	screening; shade garden; large planter; accent; specimen; conservatory; xerophytic
ZONE	10–12

I. pavetta; the green wood of this sturdy, little Indian, everg. tree burns readily.

I. pavetta; spiky heads of cream fls with reflexed petals and long, exserted pistils are held in erect, reddish-stemmed clusters at ends of branchlets.

I thwaitesii; compact heads of starry pure white flowers persist on the plant and become brown with age.

I pavetta; the timber is hard and close-grained, used for furniture, turning and building.

Jacaranda mimosifolia

JACARANDA

100ft – 30m

100ft

30m — 0

D. Don.   34 spp.

J. ovalifolia; J. acutifolia;

BIGNONIACEAE

ORIGIN	Argentina and Brazil
HEIGHT	up to 16 m (53 ft)
TYPE	deciduous flowering tree
STATUS	not threatened
HABITAT	on dry, rocky hillsides
GROWTH	fast
FLOWG	mid to late spring
DRY TOL.	high
SALT TOL.	low
LIGHT	full sun
SOIL	fertile, well-drained
NUTRIT.	high-potassium fertilizer; organic mulch
HAZARDS	none
PROBLEMS	attack by termites
ENVIRON.	bee nectar
PROPAG.	seeds; cuttings; layers
LEAVES	2-pinnate; light green; to 30 cm (12 in.); very fine and feathery
FLOWERS	showy; blue-purple; bell-shaped, in large, terminal panicles
FRUIT	a capsule, to 6 cm (2.4 in.); rounded, disc-like; green, then woody; with winged seeds
USE	specimen; small flowering tree; small street tree; public open space; xerophytic
ZONE	9–11

THIS SOUTH AMERICAN BEAUTY is celebrated throughout the subtropics and warm-temperate regions for its enchanting, blue-purple flowers. *Jacaranda mimosifolia* is native to southern Brasil and northern Argentina. Although this genus appears to be of the Fabaceae, it is, in fact, Bignoniaceae, and related to the *Tabebuia*, as seen on close inspection of the little, inflated trumpet flowers. This is a graceful tree, even without its blooms, with a light green, round-headed crown of delicate, filmy foliage layered over its slender branch tips. In mid to late spring, it forms large, loose, airy panicles of flowers and is shrouded in misty clouds of silken, bluish purple blossom that constantly falls to, and carpets, the ground. Eventually, one or two fruit capsules develop from a flower cluster. When ripe, they split open along the edges to reveal very dark brown, winged seeds. Although *J. mimosifolia* does not prosper or bloom at sea level in the true tropics and requires a cool, dry winter, there are many other superb species of *Jacaranda* – all from the Americas – which, although none so lavishly floriferous as *J. mimosifolia*, are, nevertheless, worthy of, and suitable for, planting as flowering ornamentals. Despite being deciduous, this species is a great favourite (like *Delonix regia*) as an avenue tree. There are some lovely cultivars available such as: 'Rosea', with pale, mauvish pink flowers, 'Violet Candles', with congested, erect, deep purple spikes, and 'White Christmas (or 'Alba'), an Australian cultivar with pure white trumpets that flowers during late spring or early summer, which is Christmas-time in Australia. These are honey plants.

*** *J. copaia*; ([Aublett.] D. Don.), NE S America, to 30 m (100 ft). PARAPARA, or FUTUI has pale to dark blue flowers in narrowly erect inflorescences; leaves are larger and coarser. Fruit is long, narrow. Timber (Palisander) is much valued for its pulp. (10–12)

J. mimosifolia; little bluish purple, bell-like trumpets held in large panicles.

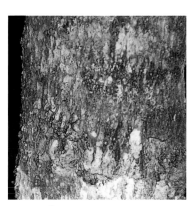

J. mimosifolia; thin, rough, grey bark. Timber is light brown and soft.

J. mimosifolia; fr. are flattened, green, fleshy discs that become dark brown and woody as they ripen.

J. mimosifolia; Jacaranda is one of the most popular flowering trees of the subtropics. Here it is showing off its sping bloom in Ravenshoe, N Qld, Australia.

Jacaranda

(1) ***Jacaranda caerulea***, ([L.] Griseb.), W Indies, to 12 m (39 ft). In the Bahamas this sp. is known as CANCER TREE, while in Cuba it is ABBEY MACHO. This is a superb *Jacaranda* with bright green, buoyant, glossy foliage and delicate, sky-blue, purple or white blooms that are held in erect, widely branched panicles at the tips of the twigs. It is very drought hardy and blooms for a fairly long period in the spring. (10–12) (2) ***Jacaranda cuspidifolia***; (Mart. ex DC.) of S America, to 12 m (39 ft). Lvs to 50 cm (19.5 in.) and infl. to 20 cm (8 in.). Thus, although this sp. is very similar to *J. mimosifolia*, the lvs are larger (and coarser); the fl. spikes are shorter. Fr. are rounded, thin, tan-brown and wavy-edged. This sp. blooms when very young and continues sporadically all year with large panicles of delicate, lavender-blue, Delphinium-like fls with white throats (there is a pure white form). (9–11) (3) ***Jacaranda jasminoides***; ([Thunb.] Sandw.), (syn. *J. pubescens*), from Mexico to Brazil, to 7 m (23 ft). CAROBA-BRAVA is one of the names given to this small, sparsely branched sp. by the Brazilians. Although the velvety, rich purple fls are not as numerous as other spp., they make up for it by being much larger. *J. jasminoides* blooms when quite young. (9–11)

An avenue of *Jacaranda mimosifolia* forms a lavender tunnel down this street in Mosman, Sydney, in late spring. The problem is, that the petals may stain the cars.

ORIGIN	W Indies and N S America
HEIGHT	up to 6 m (20 ft)
TYPE	evergreen, small flowering and fruiting tree
STATUS	habitats vulnerable
HABITAT	dry and moist coastal scrubland and beaches
GROWTH	very slow
FLOWG	winter to summer
DRY TOL.	high
SALT TOL.	high
LIGHT	full sun or bright shade
SOIL	fertile, well-drained
NUTRIT.	balanced fertilizer twice a year; organic mulch
HAZARDS	poisonous fruit
PROBLEMS	none
ENVIRON.	nectar for insects; wild fruit for birds
PROPAG.	seeds; layers
LEAVES	simple; grey-green; spathulate; thick, leathery; whorled towards ends of twigs
FLOWERS	fairly showy; creamy white; in crowded, erect racemes; fragrant
FRUIT	a berry, to 10 mm (0.4 in.); orbicular, thin-shelled; with bitter, toxic, orange pulp
USE	seaside; specimen; accent; large planter; screening; bonsai subject; conservatory; xerophytic
ZONE	10–12

50ft — 15m

50ft
15m — 0

Jacquinia arborea

BARBASCO

Vahl.   35 spp.

J. armillaris var. arborea; J. barbasco

THEOPHRASTACEAE

JACQUINIA ARBOREA is a common, small evergreen tree along the coasts of many of the islands of the W Indies, where it thrives in sandy soils and withstands strong, salt-laden sea breezes. Like many xerophytic plants, this is a proverbially slow-growing species, which takes many years to attain its full height. It is recognized by its compact, much-branched, rounded crown of stiff, spoon-shaped, grey-green leaves. The bark is smooth or finely fissured and dark brown; the light brown or yellowish inner bark is bitter. Typically, the spoon-shaped rigid leaves are held on much-forked, stout, whitish grey scaly twigs and are arranged in a spiralled manner, mostly in clusters of 3 or more near the apex. They are distinguished by their short, yellowish petioles and strongly inrolled margins. Issuing from the twig tips are erect, stout spikes (or racemes) of little, creamy white, bell-shaped, fragrant flowers that are set in thick, overlapping, green calyxes. Later, as little berry fruit develop, the old flower stalks are bent down by their weight, until the entire crown is decorated with tumbling chains of bright scarlet, thin-shelled berries that are filled with an orange-red, bitter pulp that is considered poisonous to humans. The crushed fruit of this and related species have been used to poison and stupefy fish prior to catching them.

✳✳✳ *J. aurantiaca*; (Aiton. f.), Mexico endemic, to 8 m (26 ft). Known as CHICA. During the colonial period in Colombia, miners separated gold from sediment rich in iron oxide by employing the glutinous sap of several plants, including crushed leaves of Piper and Weinmannia species and *J. aurantiaca*. When mixed with water, the foamy sap captured the iron oxide flakes, allowing the gold particles to settle at the bottom of the pan. This is an extremely ornamental species with bright green foliage that contrasts pleasingly with bright orange flowers. (9–11)

J. arborea; with terminal spikes of little, fragrant white fls.

J. arborea; crown is adorned with tumbling chains of bright scarlet, thin-shelled berries filled with orange-red pulp and small hard, brown sds.

J. aurantiaca; an ornamental sp. with bright green foliage contrasting pleasingly with bright orange fls.

J. arborea; a robust old specimen that has taken many years to form its stout trunk.

231

Jatropha curcas

PHYSIC NUT

L.   175 spp.

Curcas indica

EUPHORBIACEAE (Crotonoideae)

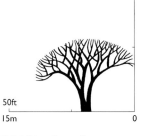

50ft ⌐15m

50ft
15m   0

ORIGIN	Trop. America
HEIGHT	up to 8 m (26 ft)
TYPE	deciduous foliage and fruiting tree
STATUS	not threatened
HABITAT	wasteground; dry lowland thickets
GROWTH	fast
FLOWG	irregularly, all year
DRY TOL.	high
SALT TOL.	moderate
LIGHT	full sun
SOIL	well-drained
NUTRIT.	generally not necessary
HAZARDS	toxic parts
PROBLEMS	none
ENVIRON.	insect and bee nectar
PROPAG.	seeds; large cuttings
LEAVES	simple; dull green; long-petioled; ovate or cordate; 3–5-lobed
FLOWERS	inconspicuous; yellow-green; in branched clusters
FRUIT	a capsule, to 4 cm (1.5 in.); 3-parted; dehiscent; oily seeds that are very poisonous
USE	small foliage tree; living barrier; reclaiming deserts; binding sand dunes; xerophytic
ZONE	10–12

WITH NO REAL INTRINSIC ORNAMENTAL VALUE, *Jatropha curcas*, a Euphorbiaceae species, has played an enormously important role in the everyday lives of the peoples of its wide region. Gaunt, and somewhat gouty, with a sparse, thin, deciduous crown of a few, spreading, soft, spongy limbs, *J. curcas* has small, insignificant, yellow-green flowers and toxic, oily seeds. Early explorers found this species growing as a living hedge around the Indian village compounds of the W Indies and Mexico. This was not only because the foliage was unpalatable to animals and so kept them away from the living areas, but because almost all parts of the plant had been found to be useful. Since then, *J. curcas* has been widely cultivated throughout the tropical world, and the seeds, leaves and sap have been employed in home remedies. The pleasantly flavoured, oily seeds were traditionally roasted and eaten, despite being dangerously toxic unless prepared correctly. Used mainly as a drastic purgative, they are known medically as Semen-, Ricini-, Marjora- or Barbados-Nuts, or Pignons d'Inde. In Nigeria, Physic Nut stems are used as a foaming chew stick, and in other regions the clear, pressed seed oil has been used for making soap and candles and as a lighting oil. In Sri Lanka, it was even tried as a high-octane fuel. Medicinally, *J. curcas* is being studied for anti-tumour properties. In Mexico, a lac, or varnish, was obtained from scale insects propagated on the bark and in Guatemala, an infusion of the leaves was used to set dyes on cotton.

*** *J. integerrima*; (Jacq.), Cuba and Hispaniola, to 6 m (20 ft), known as PEREGRINA, grows as a large, open shrub. Its glossy, green leaves are mostly unlobed. It has ornamental, small, crimson flowers in clusters all year round, although it is most spectacular in the cooler months. Cv. 'Compacta' is shorter and bushier. (10–12)

NOTE: *J. curcas* has proved invasive in some regions.

J. curcas; with large, toxic, oily sds.

J. curcas; this sp. is cropped in drier regions of W Africa and Sri Lanka, where sd oil is used as a source of alternative fuel for motor engines.

J. curcas; gaunt and somewhat gouty, with a sparse, thin, decid. crown of a few spreading, soft, spongy limbs.

J. integerrima; endemic of Cuba and Hispaniola, Peregrina is a popular ornamental that blooms year-round.

ORIGIN	from Barbados to Cuba, Bahamas and Jamaica
HEIGHT	up to 20 m (66 ft)
TYPE	evergreen foliage tree
STATUS	endangered
HABITAT	woodland, on dry, rocky slopes
GROWTH	slow
FLOWG	spring to summer
DRY TOL.	high
SALT TOL.	moderate
LIGHT	full sun
SOIL	fertile; well-drained
NUTRIT.	high-nitrogen fertilizer; deep, organic mulch
HAZARDS	none
PROBLEMS	none
ENVIRON.	seeds for birds
PROPAG.	seeds; cuttings
LEAVES	needle-like; light green or glaucous; 4-ranked
FLOWERS	cones; subglobose or reniform; maturing in 8 months
FRUIT	a cone, to 6.5 cm (2.5 in.); bluish, scaly; male cones, yellow; females, berry-like, bluish
USE	conservation; accent; screening; windbreak; xerophytic
ZONE	10—12

100ft — 30m

75ft

22.5m — 0

THIS W INDIAN JUNIPER is threatened with extinction and is rigorously protected in its natural habitat. ***Juniperus barbadensis*** is a distinguished member of this illustrious clan. The trunk of this Juniper has thin bark that separates in strips and growth is lax and graceful, with the upper, slender limbs ascending and the lower ones drooping, causing the tree to form a soft, cone-shaped crown over the years. Small, pungent, ovate leaves are 1 mm (0.04 in.), with the apex incurved, with a narrow oil gland. Male, pollen-bearing, berry-like 'cones' are yellow, while the decorative, bluish green, rounded females remain on the tree for 8 months before they are mature; they contain 1 or, rarely, 2 seeds. Correll & Correll wrote in the *Flora of Bahamas*, 'Some authors would include our plant in *J. bermudiana* L. (of Bermuda). That species, however, is usually a much larger, more robust plant. Our plant (*J. barbadensis*) is actually more closely allied to *J. silicicola (Small), Bailey, [of sandy soils]* and further study may prove them to be cospecific.'

*** *J. bermudiana*; (L.), Bermuda endemic. Known as BERMUDA CEDAR, this W Indian Juniper is very closely related to *J. barbadensis*. It is also an endangered and protected species, which is usually much larger and more vigorous. Its stout, 4-sided twigs are about 1.5 mm (0.06 in.) in diameter and its mature leaves more than 1.5 mm (0.06 in.) long. Once prolific in Bermuda, this species is now almost extinct. (9—12)

*** *J. chinensis*; (L.), China, Mongolia and Japan; tree or shrub to 20 m (66 ft). CHINESE JUNIPER is widely popular in both warm-temperate to subtropical or tropical regions. It forms a typically compact, conical crown and has been much hybridized. Cvs 'Parsonii', low growing, grey-green foliage. 'Torulosa', taller variety, with twisted branches. ''Blue Vase', broadly spreading with blue-green foliage. (4—12)

J. barbadensis; with little, bluish female cones.

J. chinensis; with a compact, conical crown, this is popular for formal planting in SE Asia as an accent.

J. barbadensis; growth is lax and graceful, with the upper, slender limbs ascending and the lower ones drooping.

J. chinensis var.'Torulosa'; is a popular, fairly slow-growing form of *J. chinensis* and excellent as an accent plant.

233

Khaya anthotheca

AFRICAN MAHOGANY

(Stapf. ex Bak. f.)   7 spp.

K. nyasica

MELIACEAE

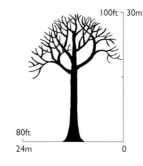

ORIGIN	C and SE Africa
HEIGHT	up to 50 m (164 ft)
TYPE	semi-deciduous, large, foliage timber tree
STATUS	not threatened
HABITAT	evergreen forests, medium to higher elevations
GROWTH	fast
FLOWG	spring
DRY TOL.	moderate
SALT TOL.	moderate
LIGHT	full sun
SOIL	deep, fertile, humid
NUTRIT.	balanced fertilizer annually; deep, organic mulch
HAZARDS	none
PROBLEMS	may be invasive
ENVIRON.	bee nectar
PROPAG.	seeds
LEAVES	pinnate; bright green; 15 x 30 cm (6 × 12 in.); with 4–10 pairs of leathery leaflets
FLOWERS	inconspicuous; white; in large, abundant, erect panicles; fragrant
FRUIT	a capsule, to 8 cm (3 in.); woody, erect, 4–5 parted, dehiscent; with winged seeds
USE	shade tree; avenue tree; public open space
ZONE	9–12

KHAYA ANTHOTHECA, a magnificent tree with a massive, pole-like trunk anchored by remarkable buttresses, is native of evergreen forests, especially along rivers and streams. Very similar to *Swietenia*, **K. anthotheca** has larger leaves, abundant panicles of fragrant, white flowers and erect, 4–5-valved, thick, woody fruit echoing those of *Swietenia mahogani*. It is only under exceptional circumstances that this species grows to its full potential, being commonly found at about 20 m (66 ft), but it can develop into a giant, like a famous specimen recorded at Mt Selinda in Zimbabwe, known as the Big Tree, which was 65 m (213 ft) high, with a trunk girth of up to 5 m (16 ft). Although **K. anthotheca** is known to have destructive surface roots and is reputedly unstable in shallow, clay soils, there was a row of venerable trees that dominated the small town of Zomba, Malawi, E Africa, where it has long been the most popular of local timbers for furniture and cabinetmaking. **K. anthotheca** has, until recently, been known as *K. nyasica*, Nyasaland being the former name for Malawi. It is the most popular timber tree in many parts of C and E Africa, where mature specimens are widely cut for milling. Although not universally considered as fine as Trop. American mahoganies, *Khaya* is similarly reddish in colour, easy to work, takes a fine finish and polishes with little trouble. The bark is thick, bitter and astringent. An infusion is prepared from it and drunk by locals to relieve colds, while the winged seeds are crushed and boiled to extract oil, which is then rubbed into the scalp to kill vermin. These are honey plants.

*** **K. senegalensis**; (Juss. A.), W Africa, SENEGALESE MAHOGANY or BISSELON is very similar to *K. anthotheca*; a distinguishing feature is the persistent encrustation of dark bark on the lower portion of the otherwise smooth trunks. (10–12)

K. anthotheca; at Montgomery Botanical Centre in Miami, Florida. This specimen demonstrates the typically pole-like form of its trunk.

K. senegalensis; lower trunk is distinguished by persistent encrustation of bark.

K. anthotheca; at Kirstenbosch Botanic Gardens, in Cape Town, S Africa, where it is native.

K. senegalensis; emergent lvs are reddish.

ORIGIN	Trop. Africa
HEIGHT	up to 16 m (53 ft)
TYPE	semi-deciduous flowering tree
STATUS	not threatened
HABITAT	dry savannahs and woodlands
GROWTH	fast, then moderate
FLOWG	intermittently, all year
DRY TOL.	high
SALT TOL.	moderate
LIGHT	full sun
SOIL	fertile, water-retentive
NUTRIT.	balanced fertilizer annually; organic mulch
HAZARDS	poisonous fruit
PROBLEMS	none
ENVIRON.	bat and bird nectar
PROPAG.	seeds
LEAVES	pinnate; dull green; to 50 cm (20 in.); coarse, leathery; leaflets to 20 × 6 cm (8 × 2.4 in.); margins wavy
FLOWERS	showy; yellow-ochre, lined maroon; held on long, stout, dangling cords; nocturnally pungent
FRUIT	a berry, to 1 m x 18 cm (40 × 7 in.); pendulous, sausage-like; with many seeds in dense pulp
USE	specimen; public open space; curiosity; botanic collection; xerophytic
ZONE	9–12

100ft — 30m
100ft
30m   0

THIS CURIOUS AFRICAN NATIVE has an ungainly, wide-spreading crown of coarse foliage. Stout, drooping branches are naked to a great length but end in a profusion of large, leathery, sallow green, pinnate leaves. *Kigelia africana* has a flagellate inflorescence that is pendulous and composed of a sumptuous cascade of crinkled, finely pleated trumpets, yellow-ochre externally and lined dark red within. Specifically evolved for bat pollination, these fleshy blooms, which are hung on cords 3 m (10 ft) long, have a strong, pungent, nocturnal odour to attract these animals. Because of their convenient structure and succulent nature, the flowers are eaten by cattle and antelope. Following the flowers, obese, heavy, tawny, sausage-like fruit are formed and dangled on long, stout cords. These fruit may weigh up to 6.8 kg (15 lb) and can be dangerous to those below when they fall. Unripe, these gourd-like fruit are very poisonous, but locally the pulp has been found to have medicinal value in the treatment of syphilis and rheumatism and is also used as a purgative. In some regions, they are also powdered and used as dressings for sores and ulcers. Ripe fruit, while not edible, are baked and added to native beer to aid fermentation. In Malawi, the fruit has also been considered to have protective qualities. In his book, *Trees of Central Africa*, Keith Coates Palgrave describes how the local people, being deeply fearful of whirlwinds, would hang a fruit in a corner of their house as a powerful charm to ward off any damage. Palgrave also talks of an historic *K. africana* growing on the border of Zimbabwe and Zambia where the explorer, Dr. David Livingstone, is said to have pitched his tent just before he saw Victoria Falls. He is said to have carved his initials on its trunk. *Kigelia* wood is fairly strong and tough and is used to make dugout canoes and mortars for pounding maize.

K. africana; with fleshy, 2-toned, pleated and crumpled, nocturnal blooms.

K. africana; obese, heavy, tawny, 'sausage-like' fr. form, dangling on long, stout cords.

K. africana; the fls are held on long, thick, pendent stems, making it easier for the bats to locate them.

K. africana; photographed on a dry veldt in northern KZN, S Africa. It was late winter and still too early for new lvs and fls. This tree appears to have been browsed by animals.

235

Kleinhovia hospita

GUEST TREE

L.   1 sp.

MALVACEAE (formerly Sterculiaceae)

THIS VOLUPTUOUS, TROPICAL ASIAN TREE holds its crown of large, long-petioled, oval or heart-shaped, pointed leaves over a stout, deeply ribbed trunk. At a distance, with its large, fresh green, rounded leaves and the billowing froth of little pale or deep pink summer blooms, *Kleinhovia hospita* may well recall a gargantuan Begonia. However, without its blooms, it could be mistaken for a Sea Hibiscus (*Hibiscus tiliaceus*). On closer inspection, however, it is seen that the 5 deep-rose sepals of the flowers fall off early, leaving little transparent, unequal, pale pink petals, the uppermost of which has a claw- or hook-shaped apex. These diminutive blooms are nectar-rich, making this tree an important bee plant. The 5-celled ovaries, which evolve into small, inflated, 3-celled, pinkish green seed capsules and persist on the red-stalked panicles like tiny limpets on finely branched coral, contain 1 or 2 globose, warty, whitish seeds in each valve. Linnaeus gave this tree (which is monospecific, or the only species of its genus) the specific name *hospita* because of its many resident 'guests' – epiphytic herbs, mosses, lizards and snakes. They make the tree their home largely because of its accommodating bark and damp, lush habitat. In India, where *K. hospita* is widely planted as an avenue tree, the trunk is sometimes deeply knotted and this twisted wood, which is hard and attractively black streaked, has long been valued for knife and kris (dagger) handles. It is called Pelet Wood and the search for Pelet trees was a serious occupation; sometimes, deliberate damage was done to the trees by slashing them to create the desirable abnormalities. The bark and leaves smell of bitter almonds (prussic acid) and are poisonous. In Malaya, they are used as an insecticide, popularly employed to eradicate head lice. The leaves, steeped in hot water, have been used for eyewash. *K. hospita* requires very well-drained soil. This is a honey plant.

ORIGIN	from Trop. Asia to Australia and the Pacific
HEIGHT	up to 20 m (66 ft)
TYPE	evergreen flowering tree
STATUS	not threatened
HABITAT	humid coastal forests and lowlands
GROWTH	moderate
FLOWG	late spring to autumn
DRY TOL.	moderate
SALT TOL.	moderate
LIGHT	full sun
SOIL	humid, well-drained
NUTRIT.	balanced fertilizer annually; deep, organic mulch
HAZARDS	bark and leaves toxic
PROBLEMS	none
ENVIRON.	nectar for bees
PROPAG.	seeds; layers; suckers
LEAVES	simple; rich green; to 25 × 24 cm (10 × 9.5 in.); cordate, long-petioled
FLOWERS	showy; pale pink; calyxes deep rose; held in widely branched panicles
FRUIT	a capsule, to 2.5 cm (1 in.); pyriform, inflated, 3-parted; with 1 or 2 warty, whitish seeds; held on reddish panicles
USE	large flowering tree; shade tree; public open space; street tree; specimen; civic centre
ZONE	10–12

K. hospita; with inflated, 3-parted, fleshy fr.

K. hospita; with its large fresh green, rounded lvs and billowing froth of little pink, blooms, it may well recall a gargantuan Begonia.

K. hospita; photographed at the Jardin Botanico, Cienfuegos, Cuba, in full spring bloom.

K. hospita; wood is sometimes deeply knotted, twisted and attractively black-streaked and is much sought after.

Koelreuteria elegans

GOLDEN RAIN TREE

(Seem.) AC Sm.   3 spp.

K. formosana

SAPINDACEAE

ORIGIN	Taiwan and Fiji
HEIGHT	up to 18 m (59 ft)
TYPE	deciduous flowering tree
STATUS	not threatened
HABITAT	dry or moist lowland woodland
GROWTH	moderate
FLOW'G	summer
DRY TOL.	high
SALT TOL.	low
LIGHT	full sun
SOIL	fairly rich, well-drained
NUTRIT.	balanced fertilizer + magnesium; organic mulch
HAZARDS	none
PROBLEMS	scales; mushroom rot
ENVIRON.	insect nectar
PROPAG.	seeds
LEAVES	2-pinnate; yellowish green; to 45 cm (17.7 in.); pinnae, 9–15 leaflets, toothed
FLOWERS	showy; yellow; tiny, 4-petalled, lop-sided; held in loose, many-flowered erect racemes
FRUIT	a capsule, to 3 cm (1.2 in.); reddish, bladder-like, inflated; 3 seeds, black
USE	small flowering tree; street tree; courtyard; specimen; civic centre; large planter; xerophytic
ZONE	9–11

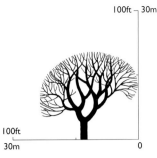

THIS KOELREUTERIA, from Taiwan and the Fiji Is, is a species with much to offer as an ornamental: a desirable size and shape, brilliant blooms, decorative fruit and autumnal colour. *Koelreuteria elegans* is a subtropical species and in equatorial regions may remain considerably smaller than its optimum height, possibly with fairly sparse growth. However, in its natural environment it reaches noble dimensions. The charm of **K. elegans** is that it is colourful from spring to autumn. The reddish, new spring leaves are quite elegant, being 2-pinnate and coarsely fern-like, with leaflets that are strongly toothed along their margins, with a tendency to droop and tremble from their axis, giving the tree a delicate yet sprightly air. In midsummer, great branched pyramids of tiny, lopsided, vivid yellow blooms enliven the tree's canopy. As they fade, they float down from their candelabra in a gentle, golden rain, hence their common name. As the last flowers fall, seed pods begin to swell to form inflated, 3-valved capsules that redden with age, becoming a flushed, iridescent salmon-red and wreathing the crown in bright, flame pink, reminiscent at a distance of Bougainvillea blooms. As the weather cools, the leaves begin to take on their rich yellow autumn hue and the fruit fade; soon the show is over until next summer. **K. elegans** may send up suckers on damaged roots.

*** **K. paniculata**; (Laxm.), N India, China and Korea, to 15 m (50 ft). GOLDEN RAIN TREE, VARNISH TREE or PRIDE OF INDIA is very similar but more cold-tolerant than **K. elegans**. The flowers are used medicinally and are a source of yellow dye in China. The young fruit varies from bright pink to blood red. (4–10)

NOTE: *Koelreuteria* **spp. may sucker and seed freely, becoming invasive in some areas.**

K. elegans; tiny bright yellow fls are held in erect panicles and fall like 'summer rain'.

K. elegans; following the fls, persistent, dried, pinkish-red fr. capsules that resemble Bougainvillea decorate the tree.

K. elegans; with its pale bark flaking in small palettes.

K. elegans; on the Gold Coast, Qld, Australia, where this sp. flourishes and has proved invasive in some areas.

Kopsia arborea

PENANG SLOE

(Bl.) Blume   25 spp.

K. flavida

APOCYNACEAE

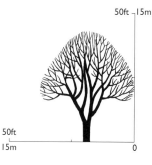

50ft ⌐15m

50ft
15m   0

ORIGIN	from Java to New Guinea, and Australia
HEIGHT	up to 12 m (40 ft)
TYPE	evergreen, small flowering tree
STATUS	not threatened
HABITAT	lowland rainforest
GROWTH	slow to moderate
FLOWG	late spring to summer
DRY TOL.	moderate
SALT TOL.	high
LIGHT	full sun to bright shade
SOIL	fertile, well-drained
NUTRIT.	balanced fertilizer twice a year; deep, organic mulch
HAZARDS	possibly poisonous parts
PROBLEMS	none
ENVIRON.	nectar; fruit for wild birds
PROPAG.	seeds; cuttings; layers
LEAVES	simple; vivid green; narrow-lanceolate; thin-textured; glabrous
FLOWERS	showy; white; narrow petals, salverform; slender tube to 2.5 cm (1 in.); held in crowded, terminal clusters
FRUIT	a drupe, to 2.5 cm (1 in.); fleshy, plum-like; dark, purplish blue covered in blue-grey bloom
USE	seaside; small shade tree; accent; screening; large planter; courtyard; coastal civic centre
ZONE	10—12

KOPSIA GENUS is one of the Apocynaceae trinity, *Kopsia*, *Ochrosia* and *Cerbera*, which closely resemble each other and mostly perform the same functions horticulturally. *Kopsia* species are easily distinguished from the other 2 genera by their paired leaves, which are thin-textured and sometimes slightly wavy-edged. **Kopsia arborea** is a fairly slow growing species, with smooth bark and limbs that are readily distinguished by being a pale buff colour. Multi-stemmed, this species forms a luxuriant, conical, bushy form. with its lower limbs drooping, often to the ground, making it an ideal species for screening. As in all *Kopsia*, **K. arborea** has copious, milky sap in all its green parts. Even without its abundant blooms, this is a handsome, vigorous, compact, small tree with the deepest blue-green, polished foliage that tends to hang vertically. Held in terminal panicles, the pristine, starry flowers are pure white with no colouring except for the little, golden stamens at their throat. These slender-tubed, salverform flowers have 5 narrow, flaring petals. The fruit are little, deep, violet-black wild plums covered with an attractive, powdery, blue-grey bloom, and look very much like sloes. Perhaps the most appealing element of this superb species, however, are the brilliant scarlet, aging leaves that punctuate the crown. Slender, twinned, terminal leaves are held erect on their long petioles and from a distance they resemble brightly coloured blooms. In Florida, *Ochrosia elliptica* is often mistakenly offered in the horticultural trade under **Kopsia arborea**.
*** **K. fruticosa**; ([Ker-Gaw] A. D.C.), Malaysia, to 6 m (20 ft). Known as SHRUB VINCA because of the similarity of the flowers to those of *Vinca*. This small *Kopsia* is widely popular as a garden subject. Oval leaves are thin-textured, yellow-green, very glossy above; flowers are pink, with a red eye. This species prefers rich, slightly acid soil. (**10—12**)

K. arborea; toxic purplish blue 'plums' are dangerous – especially for children.

K. arborea; a salt-tol. sp. from Java, Indonesia, photographed at Forest Gardens in N Qld, Australia, where it is also native.

K. arborea; paired lvs become rich red as they age.

K. fruticosa; this little beauty is known as Shrub Vinca for the similarity of the fls to those of *Vinca*.

(1 and 2) ***Kopsia pruniformis***; (Bakh. f.) Java endemic, to 10 m (33 ft). Known as JAVA PRUNE for its large, blue-black, plum-like fr., this is a handsome, vigorous, small tree with deepest, blue-green, polished foliage. In terminal panicles, the pristine white, starry fls have only the palest of yellow stamens marking their narrow, raised throats. Like *K. arborea*, old lvs wither to blood red, punctuating the sombre crown with their brilliant colour. This densely branched, drought-tol. everg. makes an excellent accent or screen. (10–12) (3 and 4) ***Kopsia singapurensis***; (Ridl.), Malaysia to Singapore, to 8 m (26 ft). SINGAPORE KOPSIA or WHITE KOPSIA is a small everg. tree or large shrub of lax, open growth. Twice a year in the wild, in late winter and again in autumn, it becomes enveloped in fresh white blossom. In cultivation, it may bloom more frequently. Like *K. fruticosa*, this sp. has a red- or pink-stained 'eye'. The small, glossy fr. is held in abundant clusters. These spp. are of easy culture from fresh sd, greenwood cuttings or layers. There has been some very successful cross-pollination of some of these spp. A pollen cross of *K. singapurensis* × *K. fruticosa* has produced a spectacular, free-blooming, large shrub at the Singapore Botanic Gardens. (10–12)

Lagerstroemia speciosa

QUEEN OF FLOWERS

L.   53 spp.

L. flos-reginae
LYTHRACEAE

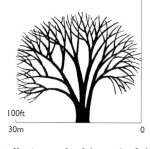

100ft — 30m
100ft
30m   0

THE CELEBRATED QUEEN OF FLOWERS is the most alluring and celebrated of this fairly large, renowned genus of flowering Asian-Pacific trees. *Lagerstroemia speciosa* grows to be an erect, bulky tree with rigidly twiggy, broom-like branches and a dense, sinewy trunk with pale bark that flakes off in large patches. The oblong-lanceolate, rich green leaves are pale below and deeply veined; typically they turn coppery red before they are shed in late autumn. In early summer, with the waxy, reddish, new growth, young, pale grey or rusty-pubescent flower panicles form in sumptuous cones of rich purple or pink. Their glorious, crinkled, 6-petalled blooms fade greatly as they age and give the impression of being variegated. These blooms are considered to be rose-like in Asia and are known in many parts as Rose of India. Although *L. speciosa* will grow and flower in poor soil, this species does not thrive or put on its best show in such conditions. It will only realize its full, fabulous potential in deep, rich, slightly acid loam. These species are also fussy about being transplanted, requiring careful root pruning well in advance. To encourage a full-bodied canopy, some limb pruning should be done as soon as the flowers fade. Apart from their ornamental value, most of *Lagerstroemia* species are highly valued for their timber in Trop. Asia, where they are grown and milled for their wood. This is considered equal to teak in quality, although the surface turns a dirty mauve colour on exposure to the air. Reddish, very dense and resistant to salt air and sea water, it is known as Banglang in the trade and is employed for boatbuilding and constructing wharves or for marine planking and railway sleepers. Seasoned timber takes a superb polish and is used, like mahogany, for panelling. In SE Asia, preparations of *L. speciosa* are used as remedies for diabetes and urinary tract problems. The bark yields a yellow dye. ❋❋❋ Var. *rosea* has pink flowers.

ORIGIN	Trop. Asia
HEIGHT	up to 25 m (82 ft)
TYPE	deciduous, large flowering tree
STATUS	not threatened
HABITAT	moist forest; swampy valleys
GROWTH	moderate
FLOWG	summer
DRY TOL.	moderate
SALT TOL.	low
LIGHT	full sun
SOIL	rich, humid, slightly acid
NUTRIT.	low-nitrogen fertilizer; deep, organic mulch
HAZARDS	none
PROBLEMS	scales; aphids; caterpillars
ENVIRON.	insect nectar
PROPAG.	seeds; softwood cuttings
LEAVES	simple; rich green; to 19 × 8.5 cm (7.5 × 3.4 in.); 2-ranked, oblong
FLOWERS	showy; purple, pink or whitish; held in downy panicles to 40 cm (15.7 in.)
FRUIT	a capsule, to 2.5 cm (1 in.); woody, glabrous; with winged seeds, persistent for a long period
USE	small flowering tree; specimen; street tree; public open space; courtyard; large planter
ZONE	10–12

L. speciosa; with abundant, persistent, woody capsules in autumn.

L. speciosa; in their native regions, these spp. are as valued as much for their hard, tough timber as for their ravishing fls.

L. speciosa; the rich green lvs typically turn coppery red before they are shed in late autumn.

L. archeriana; a small sp. of Indonesia, N Guinea and Australia, with fls set in red calyxes.

(1) ***Lagerstroemia floribunda***; (Jack.), Malaya, Thailand and Burma, to 20 m (66 ft). Known as Bungor, Kedah, or Late Crepe Myrtle, this sp., as the name suggests, is a late (autumn) bloomer. This sp. forms a dense, bushy, conical or broadly cylindrical crown; the trunk becomes fluted in age. As usual, the bark is pale, creamy brown, flaking in large, thin, angular patches. Large, foamy blooms are held in generous, pale, velvety panicles of lavender or pink that fade to white, giving it a variegated appearance. This is an abundant sp. in open country and limestone hills of its regions. (10–12) (2) ***Lagerstroemia loudonii***; (Teysm. and Binn.), Burma and Thailand, to 13 m (43 ft). Loudon's Crepe Myrtle is a tough sp. that may withstand considerable cold and high winds. The large, fringed blooms are dark to light lilac, fading to bluish white and tend to be more showy, being held on naked limbs before the new lvs. (10–12) (**previous page**) ***Lagerstroemia archeriana***; (Bailey) N Qld and W Australia, Timor and New Guinea, to 4 m (13 ft). Native Crepe Myrtle is a tall shrub which, although a trop. sp., will adapt to warm-temperate conditions. Its purple fls fade to pale lavender. These delicate, frilly blooms (page 240) are set in distinctive, ruby-red, waxy calyxes, which add to the general colour. This sp. must have adequate sun and space for its roots. (10–12)

A glorious thicket of *Lagerstroemia speciosa*, the Queen of Flowers, in full, summer bloom at the Jardin Botanico Nationale, Cuba.

Lagunaria patersonii

COW ITCH

(Andrews) G. Don f.   1 sp

MALVACEAE

50ft ⌐15m

50ft
15m   0

THIS MEMBER OF THE *HIBISCUS* FAMILY, a solitary species of its genus *Lagunaria*, is native to coastal Queensland, as well as Norfolk Island (the home of the celebrated Norfolk Island Pine, *Araucaria heterophylla*) and Lord Howe Island. *Lagunaria patersonii* has long been popular for seaside planting in NSW, Qld, NT and other regions of Australia. It usually grows in an elegant, erect, narrow, pyramidal fashion, with a dense, low-branching crown. The trunk has dark grey, shallowly fissured bark, while the dense foliage comprises dull green, rough-textured, oval leaves that are scurfy-white on their undersurface. As new leaves emerge, they are a delicate, velvety green, softening the outline and providing a pleasing contrast to the sombre pyramid. Held on stout, furry stalks, the small, pointed flower buds are also pale green and velvety; they open to release rose-pink to magenta, spreading, silken, recurved petals arranged around a sturdy staminal column of golden anthers topped with pale green stigmas. *L. patersonii* blooms over a long period, from spring until early autumn. These blooms resemble those of hibiscus, as do the the 5-celled, egg-shaped, conical fruit. Their form echoes the flower buds in being velvety and pale green. As it matures, the fruit dries a dark brown and becomes woody, eventually splitting open to reveal its contents. The 5 valves are covered with very fine hairs that have an irritating effect on the skin when handled. They are known as 'cow itch', an unfortunate name to be associated with such an attractive tree. Set in each of the valves are 5 reddish tan seeds, which germinate readily, although the young plants need plenty of moisture and protection from the wind and cold. *L. patersonii* can withstand low temperatures, as well as sea winds, if protected and may grow on solid limestone, provided the soil is humid.

ORIGIN	Norfolk Is and Australia
HEIGHT	up to 15 m (50 ft)
TYPE	evergreen flowering tree
STATUS	not threatened
HABITAT	moist coastal forests; seasonal stream banks in dry hinterland
GROWTH	fast
FLOWG	spring to early autumn
DRY TOL.	moderate
SALT TOL.	high
LIGHT	full sun
SOIL	fertile, well-drained
NUTRIT.	balanced fertilizer annually; deep, organic mulch
HAZARDS	irritating hairs on fruit
PROBLEMS	none
ENVIRON.	insect nectar
PROPAG.	seeds – handle with care
LEAVES	simple; dull green, white scurfy below; new leaves very pale green
FLOWERS	showy; rose-pink to mauve; hibiscus-like, with velvety petals that are recurved
FRUIT	capsule, to 4 cm (1.5 in.); hard, egg-shaped, 5-valved, dehiscent; with irritating hairs; packed with reddish seeds
USE	seaside; specimen; coastal street tree; large planter; civic centre
ZONE	9–12

L. patersonii; dehiscent fr. are typical of the *Hibiscus* clan.

L. patersonii; Hibiscus-like, with spreading, silken, recurved petals arranged around a sturdy staminal column of golden anthers.

L. patersonii; a fine specimen at Sydney Botanic Garden, Australia, showing its elegant habit of growth.

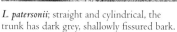

L. patersonii; straight and cylindrical, the trunk has dark grey, shallowly fissured bark.

ORIGIN	Malay Peninsula, endemic
HEIGHT	up to 17 m (56 ft)
TYPE	evergreen, small fruiting tree
STATUS	rare in the wild
HABITAT	rainforest and humid river valleys
GROWTH	slow
FLOWG	spring and autumn
DRY TOL.	low
SALT TOL.	low
LIGHT	sheltered sun or part shade
SOIL	rich, slightly acid; humid
NUTRIT.	organic compost and deep, organic mulch
HAZARDS	none
PROBLEMS	scale; sugar cane borer
ENVIRON.	nectar for insects
PROPAG.	seeds; grafting; layers
LEAVES	pinnate; dull green; leaflets 5–9, oval, leathery, to 26 × 10 cm (8.5 × 4 in.)
FLOWERS	showy; yellow; held on long, solitary or clustered spikes; cauliflorous
FRUIT	a berry, to 3.7 cm (1.4 in.); tawny yellow; with milky rind and translucent, sweet, juicy flesh
USE	small shade tree; street tree in high rainfall areas; backyard tree; specimen
ZONE	11–12

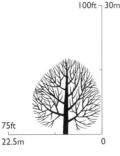

100ft – 30m
75ft
22.5m — 0

Lansium domesticum

LANGSAT

Correa. Serr.   3 spp.

MELIACEAE

LANSIUM DOMESTICUM, a native of Malaysia, was distributed throughout Malesia in prehistoric times and has long been established as one of the most popular fruits of this equatorial region. *L. domesticum* forms a slender, fairly tall tree with a deeply fluted, straight trunk and erect, open crown of coarse, pinnate, dull green foliage. This is a cauliflorous species, with flowers and fruit held directly on the limbs or trunk. Yellow flowers are held in hairy, solitary or clustered spikes on the limbs or trunk and fruit is produced abundantly. There are 2 distinct forms of *L. domesticum*. *Langsat* is a meagre tree that has oblong fruit with pale, greyish buff rind containing much disagreeable latex. It is native to the north of the Malay Peninsula. *Duku*, the more popular variety, is found in the south and is a robust tree with larger, rounder fruit that have a thick, brownish buff rind. It is easily split into 5 parts and has no latex. Characteristic of *Duku* fruit is their easily peeled, thin, crusty rind, and at least 1 of the 5 translucent, sweet, fleshy segments, or arils, encloses a very large, bitter seed. Those without seeds are the sweetest, but they are smaller than fruit containing seeds. Unlike most native fruit of SE Asia, there has been little hybridization of this species, except 1 sterile, infraspecific hybrid of *Duku* × *Langsat*, known as Longkon and developed in Thailand. *L. domesticum* superficially resembles *Clausena lansium* and *Dimocarpus longan*, although all 3 are of different families. *L. domesticum* demands an equatorial climate with no dry season and usually bears twice a year, in summer and winter. It is very slow growing, taking up to 15 years to bear fruit from seed, but this is faster than from grafting or layering. (Seeds must be sown fresh.) Locally, the fruit is eaten fresh, dried and preserved, or made into jams or juice. In Java, the peel is dried and used for incense. In the Philippines, it is burned to produce smoke to deter mosquitoes. This is strictly an equatorial species.

L. domesticum; this thin-skinned fr. peels easily.

L. domesticum; a very slow-growing sp., taking up to 15 years to bear fr. from sd.

L. domesticum; one of the most popular fr. of Malaysia.

L. domesticum; being held directly on the limbs or trunk makes harvesting much easier. Photographed at The Botanical Ark in N Qld, Australia.

Lawsonia inermis

HENNA

L.   1 sp.

L. alba

LYTHRACEAE

50ft — 15m

50ft
15m   0

ORIGIN	Old World Tropics
HEIGHT	up to 7 m (23 ft)
TYPE	semi-deciduous, small flowering tree
STATUS	not threatened
HABITAT	dry, coastal secondary scrub wasteland
GROWTH	fast
FLOWG	year-round
DRY TOL.	high
SALT TOL.	moderate
LIGHT	full sun
SOIL	fertile, well-drained
NUTRIT.	balanced fertilizer annually; organic mulch
HAZARDS	sometimes spiny
PROBLEMS	sooty mould
ENVIRON.	bee nectar
PROPAG.	seeds; cuttings; layers
LEAVES	simple; rich green, ovate, succulent, crisp
FLOWERS	showy; creamy white or light red; held in terminal panicles; very fragrant
FRUIT	a capsule, to 2.5 cm (1 in.); dry, persistent; indehiscent
USE	small flowering tree; hedging and screening; specimen; planter; courtyard; civic centre; xerophytic
ZONE	10—12

LAWSONIA INERMIS IS A MONOTYPIC SPECIES that grows as a small, much-branched, multi-trunked tree or shrub. It is glabrous throughout but occasionally the slender twigs may end in a spine. It is easy to see the genetic affinity between *Lagerstroemia* and *Lawsonia*: the sinewy limbs and flaking bark, the oval leaves and, most of all, the frilly, little flowers. *L. inermis* has 2 forms: one with creamy white blooms, the other with light red; both are heavily fragrant, although the cream form is more intensely so. These flowers, which are distilled for their perfume, are produced in quick succession all year round and are followed by dry, indehiscent capsules, which are produced abundantly and remain for long periods. They inhibit flowering and should be removed regularly. Ancient Egyptians, who used *L. inermis* to dye their bodies and for the swathing cloths of their mummies, dried the small, oval leaves, which were then powdered and made into a paste. For centuries, this paste, which gives a dull, orange-yellow to red or blackish dye and is known as henna, has been used traditionally in Islamic culture for staining the hair, beards, nails and skin. In India, Henna-dyeing is an art form known as Mendhi, and plays an important part in marriage ceremonies. Intricate patterns are applied to the feet and hands of the bride and her female guests and the colouring may last for several weeks. Henna is also used as a hair conditioner and colouring and is often mixed with the flower heads of chamomile (*Chamaemelum nobile*) for use on the hair. Because *L. inermis* grows in a dense manner and tolerates close pruning, it is particularly lends itself for use as hedging. It is sometimes known as Egyptian Privet because of its wide use in the Middle East for this purpose. The roots, bark, leaves and flowers have all been used in home remedies and have many medical applications.

L. inermis; a mature specimen of Henna, demonstrating its tree-like stature at Waimea Arboretum, Hawaii.

L. inermis; the heavily fragrant fls resemble miniature Crepe Myrtles.

L. inermis var. *rubra*; is a little less fragrant, and perhaps has a smaller habit.

L. inermis; dry, indehiscent capsules, which are produced abundantly and may remain for long periods.

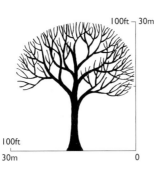

Lecythis zabucajo

MONKEY POT

(Lam.) de Wit.   22 spp.

L. glauca

LECYTHIDACEAE

ORIGIN	Brazil and Guiana
HEIGHT	up to 35 m (115 ft)
TYPE	deciduous, large fruiting (nut) tree
STATUS	threatened
HABITAT	humid fertile lowlands and river valleys
GROWTH	moderate
FLOWG	spring
DRY TOL.	moderate to low
SALT TOL.	low
LIGHT	full sun
SOIL	deep, rich, humid
NUTRIT.	organic compost and deep mulch
HAZARDS	possibly toxic seeds
PROBLEMS	none
ENVIRON.	insect nectar; fruit for monkeys
PROPAG.	seeds; semi-ripe cuttings
LEAVES	simple; deep green, to 12 × 6 cm (4.7 × 2.4 in.); elliptic, glabrous, papery; with scalloped margins
FLOWERS	showy; yellow or white, with purple margins; androphore, rose pink
FRUIT	a capsule, to 20 × 26 cm (8 × 10 in.); globose, with convex 'lid'; seeds spindle-shaped and deeply ridged
USE	large flowering and fruiting tree; public open space; botanic collection; humid, shade garden
ZONE	11–12

LECYTHIS ZABUCAJO, one of several excellent species of its genus, is a forest giant that forms a great, clear bole in the rainforest but is much smaller in cultivation. A member of the Lecythidaceae clan, with its intriguing reproductive mechanics, **L. zabucajo** has large, unequal, 6-petalled flowers, with its stamens borne on the interior of a hinged flap (androphore) that is arched over to connect with the pistils held in the centre. These ephemeral blooms are most attractive, being a pale, lavender-pink with purplish throats and are heavily fragrant, particularly at midday when they attract not only bees, but also scrambling insects to effect their pollination. Typically, this extraordinary floral arrangement is succeeded by an equally curious fruit, in this case a pod, which resembles that of the closely related Brazil Nut (*Bertholletia exselsa*). It looks and feels like a thick, rustic, brown clay pot (and is often used as such) and has a round disc-like lid plugging a hole at its base. The fruit takes 18 months to mature, at which time the lid drops down to release long, wrinkled, oily seeds. This is different from the Brazil Nut, which requires the fruit to be broken open, but, in fact, presents a problem to the harvesters, as bats are able to help themselves to the luscious contents. The seeds are known generally as Sapucaia nuts and are delicious; indeed, connoisseurs consider them superior to Brazil nuts. They are eaten fresh or roasted and are used to make fine confectionery in their native region. In Brazil, oil from the nuts is used to make soap. Large pods are used domestically as kitchen vessels and plant pots. Dried fruit are also used to trap monkeys by baiting the insides with sugar. When the monkey grabs the bait, it is unable to retract its clenched fist, hence another common name, Monkey Pot. Lecythis seeds have been found to accumulate toxic levels of selenium from the soil. The wood of many *Lecythis* species is hard, durable and much desired and this popularity threatens these superb trees.

L. zabucajo; with attractive, delicate, waxy pink fls.

L. zabucajo; Sapucaia Nuts are most delicious; indeed connoisseurs consider them superior to Brazil Nuts.

L. zabucajo; the heavy, wooden fr. capsules, with hinged lids, normally contain delicious Sapucaia Nuts.

L. zabucajo; at the Jardin Botanico de Cienfuegos, Cuba. This sp. is closely related to the Cannonball Tree and the Brazil Nut.

Leptospermum madidum

WEEPING TEA TREE

A. Bean   79 SPP

MYRTACEAE

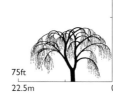

ORIGIN	Northern Territory, Australia, endemic
HEIGHT	up to 10 m (33 ft)
TYPE	evergreen, small flowering and foliage tree
STATUS	restricted habitat
HABITAT	along banks of lowland freshwater streams
GROWTH	slow
FLOWG	spring
DRY TOL.	high
SALT TOL.	moderate
LIGHT	full sun
SOIL	slightly acid, sandy loam
NUTRIT.	high-nitrogen fertilizer; organic compost and mulch
HAZARDS	none
PROBLEMS	none
ENVIRON.	nectar for bees and beetles
PROPAG.	seeds; cuttings of semi-ripe wood
LEAVES	simple; dull green; narrow, aromatic, with oil glands
FLOWERS	fairly showy; white; small, solitary or in small groups; held in leaf axils
FRUIT	a capsule, to 0.4 cm (0.2 in.) diam.; brown when ripe; with many very fine seeds
USE	seaside; specimen; public open space; courtyard; large planter; small street tree
ZONE	10–12

LEPTOSPERMUM are members of the great Myrtaceae clan and very closely related to *Melaleuca* and *Callistemon*. Of the 79 species of *Leptospermum*, all but 3 are endemic to Australia, where they are esteemed for their glossy, usually aromatic foliage and for their small but abundant blooms. Most species of *Leptospermum* are found in warm-temperate regions but there are several worthy subtropical and tropical species. **Leptospermum madidum** is popular for small gardens in Queensland and other parts of Australia's tropical north. There are 2 main subspecies in cultivation: subsp. *sativum* (A. Bean) is, perhaps, premier, with fine, willowy, light green foliage, strongly weeping limbs, contorted trunks and peeling white bark; subsp. *madidum* (A. Bean), Cape York Pen., Qld, has deeper green, coarser foliage and a less strongly pendulous habit. Both subspecies are native to creek banks. They serve as superior tropical substitutes for Weeping Willow.

*** **L. petersonii**; (Bail.), (syn. *L. citratrum*), Qld to NSW , to 5 m (16 ft). A small tree or shrub found on sandy creekbanks and rocky slopes with flaky bark, elliptic, strongly lemon-scented leaves and white flowers with pale red bracts. This sp. is commonly grown in Guatemala and Kenya for its popular, lemon-scented Tea Tree oil. (9–11)

*** **L. scoparium**; (Forst. & Forst.), New Zealand and Australia, to 4 m (13 ft). MANUKA or TEA TREE is probably the best known species, being very popular as a florist's flower. It has small, narrow leaves and masses of little, white, pink or red flowers. Captain Cook and his crew are said to have used these little, aromatic leaves to brew a tea, thus giving the common name, Tea Tree, to this genus. *L. scoparium* is warm-temperate or marginally subtropical but is grown successfully at higher elevations in Hawaii and other parts of the highland tropics. There are many cultivars of this species. (8–10)

L. madidum subsp. *sativum*; in spring bud.

L. madidum subsp. *sativum*; this strongly weeping form is very popular in Qld, Australia. It was photographed in Cairns, on the Great Barrier Reef.

L. madidum subsp. *madidum*; a popular, slow-growing sp. with wide-spreading, airy but less weeping growth.

L. madidum subsp. *madidum*; with strongly weeping limbs, contorted trunks and attractive, peeling, white bark.

246

50ft — 15m

50ft
15m — 0

Leucadendron argenteum

SILVER TREE

Meissn.   79 spp

PROTEACEAE

ORIGIN	Cape Town, S Africa, endemic
HEIGHT	up to 9 m (29 ft)
TYPE	dioecious, small foliage tree
STATUS	endangered
HABITAT	forest margins, on acid sandy soils
GROWTH	fast
FLOWG	winter and early spring
DRY TOL.	high
SALT TOL.	low
LIGHT	full sun
SOIL	slightly acid, well-drained
NUTRIT.	allergic to phosphates; organic compost and mulch
HAZARDS	none
PROBLEMS	magnesium deficiencies
ENVIRON.	insect and bird nectar
PROPAG.	seeds (fresh)
LEAVES	simple; grey, covered in pale, silvery hairs; whorled around twig tips
FLOWERS	insignificant; silver scaly; dioecious; surrounded by a dense whorl of silvery bracts
FRUIT	a winged nutlet, produced in female, cone-like heads
USE	botanic collection; large planter; specimen; xerophytic
ZONE	9–11

LEUCADENDRON ARGENTEUM, which is almost extinct and found only on some slopes of Table Mountain, in Cape Town, South Africa, must surely top the list of desirable silver-leafed plants. Its thick, leathery leaves are densely covered in silky velvety, bright silver hairs. They glint and sparkle in the sunlight and are designed to withstand long periods of drought. Although the flowers tend to be insignificant, they are surrounded by conspicuous, silvery bracts, highly valued by flower arrangers, as are the fruit, which are formed in large cones and are covered in spirals of bright, silvery bracts that persist for several years. Being dioecious, fruit will be sterile without male pollen nearby. *L. argenteum* belongs to the ancient Proteaceae family, with curious but beautiful blooms, and is mostly confined to Gondwanaland, the name used for a hypothetical land mass of the southern hemisphere, separated at the end of the Paleozoic period. Proteaceae are distinguished by the congested heads of their blooms, as in the tubular or bottlebrush compositions of the Australian *Grevillea*, *Buckinghamia* or *Alloxylon*, or the massive, leafy, cone-like or fringed ones of S African *Protea*, *Leucospermum* or *Leucodendron*. The *Leucadendron* genus is particularly celebrated by *L. argenteum,* for whom the genus was named: *leucos* from the Greek, meaning 'white', and *dendron*, meaning 'tree', thus *Leucadendron argenteum* means Silver Tree. Like all members of the Proteaceae, these plants are extremely sensitive to nitrates and phosphates, which may be toxic to it even at moderate levels. However, they may suffer magnesium deficiencies. (A dilute solution of magnesium sulphate can be applied spring and autumn.) *L. argenteum* is not a tropical species but will grow in acid soils in warm subtropical and Mediterranean climates. It is intolerant of any root disturbance and is not frost-hardy. Dried leaves are sold to tourists as bookmarks.

L. argenteum; a young female fl. surrounded by silvery bracts.

L. argenteum; with distinctive, pale, closely ringed bark.

L. argenteum; with persistent old fr., which may remain on the tree for years.

L. argenteum; a small group of trees growing at the Kirstenbosch Botanic Gardens, Cape Town, S Africa, on the slopes of Table Mountain.

Leucaena leucocephala

WILD TAMARIND

(Lam.) de Wit.   22 spp.

FABACEAE (Mimosoideae)

50ft — 15m

50ft
15m   0

ORIGIN	Trop. America and Old World Tropics
HEIGHT	up to 10 m (33 ft)
TYPE	deciduous foliage tree
STATUS	not threatened
HABITAT	dry, coastal regions; wasteground
GROWTH	fast
FLOWG	year-round
DRY TOL.	high
SALT TOL.	high
LIGHT	full sun
SOIL	well-drained
NUTRIT.	normally not necessary
HAZARDS	toxic leaves and fruit pods
PROBLEMS	extremely invasive
ENVIRON.	bee nectar
PROPAG.	seeds; cuttings
LEAVES	2-pinnate; greyish green; pinnae 3–10 pairs, very feathery
FLOWERS	showy; creamy white; in terminal clusters; with long-stalked pompoms of white stamens
FRUIT	a legume, to 15 cm (6 in.); dehiscent, papery; with many seeds
USE	xerophytic; agricultural shade; land reclamation; fodder for cattle, goats and sheep; firewood
ZONE	10–12

LEUCAENA LEUCOCEPHALA, with its exuberant growth and prodigious production of papery pods that disperse their seeds with shameless promiscuity, is undisputedly one of the most invasive of tropical trees. *L. leucaena* is a small, deciduous, spreading tree with a brittle, muscular, smooth, greyish brown trunk and wand-like, stretching limbs supporting an airy crown of softly feathery, pinnate leaves. Terminal clusters of long-stalked flowers with pompoms of thread-like stamens are quickly followed by bundles of dark brown, flat, thin pods, which, as they split open and shed their seeds, rapidly establish dense thickets along roadsides, in abandoned pastures and on cleared land. When crushed, all parts of this tree have a slight smell of onions. Despite its invasive ways, *L. leucaeana* has found usefulness in some of the most infertile and difficult corners of the tropical regions and in arid areas has long been used to provide agricultural shade or screening, for charcoal or firewood, to rebuild soil through the nitrogen-fixing bacteria of its root nodules or as a forage crop. However, the leaves and pods contain mimosine and are poisonous to many domestic animals, such as horses, donkeys, mules, pigs and rabbits, which all lose their hair after grazing on this leguminous tree. Curiously, cattle, goats and sheep show little ill effects from eating it. Studies have found that the consequence of the poison can be counteracted considerably by adding soluble iron salts to animal feed. In Hawaii, all parts of the tree are used by dairymen as cattle fodder because it has a high protein content. In the Philippines, the green pods have been cooked as a vegetable and the seeds have been used as a coffee substitute. For the xerophytic gardener, *L. leucaena* could be the solution for the greening of a difficult, private desert. An important honey plant.

NOTE: this species is usually regarded as a noxious weed.

L. leucocephala; white, staminous balls.

L. leucocephala; this shamelessly profligate sp. regularly beguiles as it becomes decked out in soft, new, ferny foliage and starry white blooms.

L. leucocephala; bundles of papery pods stuffed with sds that have been used as a coffee substitute in the Philippines.

L. leucocephala; used for charcoal or firewood and to rebuild soil through nitrogen-fixing bacteria of roots.

248

ORIGIN	China, Korea and Japan
HEIGHT	up to 10 m (33 ft)
TYPE	evergreen, small flowering tree
STATUS	not threatened
HABITAT	humid lowland woodland
GROWTH	fast
FLOWG	late summer
DRY TOL.	moderate
SALT TOL.	low
LIGHT	full sun
SOIL	fertile, water-retentive
NUTRIT.	balanced fertilizer annually; deep, organic mulch
HAZARDS	toxic fruit
PROBLEMS	aphids; scale insects
ENVIRON.	bee nectar; wild fruit for birds
PROPAG.	seeds; cuttings; layers
LEAVES	simple; dark green; smooth, shiny, to 10 cm (4 in.); long-pointed
FLOWERS	showy; white; held in crowded panicles; 10 x 20 cm (4 × 5 in.); very fragrant
FRUIT	a drupe, to 1 cm (0.4 in.); blue-black; fleshy, berry-like; held in large clusters
USE	specimen; screening and hedging; courtyard; large planter; civic centre; topiary
ZONE	7–11

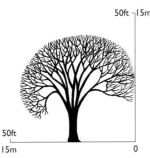

50ft ⌐15m

50ft

15m   0

Ligustrum lucidum

GLOSSY PRIVET

Ait. f.   40 spp.

L. magnoliifolium

OLEACEAE

LIGUSTRUM LUCIDUM is the most tree-like of common privets and while none of this genus is truly tropical in origin, is often grown there as a small, evergreen tree. This species is distinguished by its large, polished (= *lucidum*), dark green leaves, which are narrowly ovate and long-pointed, with sunken veins. Because of its shiny foliage, this is also known as Wax Privet or White Wax Tree. Late summer ushers in the plume-like spires of heavily fragrant, creamy white, nectar-rich flowers, which attract many bees; the resulting honey is considered very desirable. Flowers are followed by ample, but poisonous, grape-like clusters of purple-black, fleshy berries, which persist for most of the winter. **L. lucidum** is popular as a specimen tree not only for its foliage, but also for the rhythmic curves of its trunk and limbs. It is closely related, and similar, to *L. japonicum* (Thunb.), Japanese Privet, which differs in having smaller obovate leaves, with more prominent veins below and flowers held in denser, longer panicles. The Chinese value *Ligustrum* greatly. The fruit is said to aid kidney function, strengthen muscles, relieve rheumatism and prevent hair loss. It is also said to prevent bone-marrow loss in chemotherapy patients, as well as have potential as a treatment for HIV. The Chinese also use an oil infusion from the flowers to treat sunburn. Leaves, young shoots and bark yield a strong, yellow dye. Cvs include 'Aureo-variegatum' and 'Excelsum Superbum'. *** **L. sinensis**; (Lour.), Central China endemic, to 6 m (20 ft). CHINESE PRIVET is semi-deciduous or evergreen and densely downy in most of its parts. Leaves are olive-green above, pale below, with a downy midrib. The off white flowers, in large, erect clusters, are fragrant and borne in midsummer. Fruit is claret, or black-purple in colour. (7–11)

NOTE: *L. lucidum* is considered a noxious weed in parts of Australia.

L. lucidum; bunches of grape-like, purple-black, fleshy berries persist for months.

L. lucidum; a close relative of the Jasmines, the Glossy Privet has characteristic thick, glossy, waxy lvs and honey-fragrant panicles of white fls.

L. japonicum; very similar, but with smaller lvs and denser heads of fls.

L. lucidum; is the most tree-like of this genus. Because of its shiny foliage, it is called Glossy Privet.

249

Litchi chinensis

LYCHEE

Sonn.   1 sp.

Nephelium litchi

SAPINDACEAE

THE SOAPBERRY FAMILY, Sapindaceae, is renowned for its edible fruits – longan, Spanish lime, ackee, rambutan and lychee. *Litchi chinensis* has been so long in cultivation that wild forms, apart from naturalized escapees, are practically unknown. Cultivars of Litchi were discussed in one of the earliest treatises on fruit cultivation, written by a Chinese scholar, Tsai Hsiang, in 1079 AD. *L. chinensis* is slow growing and long-lived, forming a billowing, globular crown with coppery red, new growth. The attractive, erect panicles of greenish white, spring blooms are followed in early summer by the most decorative of fruit. Held in long-stemmed, drooping clusters, the rosy red, thin-skinned, warty fruit is filled with sweet, juicy, translucent flesh that has a high vitamin C content. This is not strictly a tropical species, its natural habitat having hot, humid summers and cool, misty, frost-free and dry winters. The optimum climate for *L. chinensis* is described as intermediate between that of the sweet orange and avocado. Although tolerant of a wide range of soils, this species, which is tap-rooted, does best on deep, moist, well-drained, fertile soils requiring plenty of moisture during the drier, fruiting months. *L. chinensis* seeds are shortly viable and must be sown when not more than 4–5 days old. Lychee fruit are mostly eaten fresh, although they are commonly canned or dried, when they resemble very large, luscious raisins. A grafted tree will fruit from between 2–5 years. However, it may not be in prime condition until it is 20–40 years old and may continue to produce for 100 years or more. In China, the seeds are used as an analgesic for neuralgia and the fruit peel to treat diarrhoea. The fruit retains its quality for only 3–5 days without refrigeration. Excellent cvs include 'Brewster', 'Royal Chen', 'Tai So', 'Haak Yip' and 'Bengal'. This is a honey plant.

ORIGIN	from S China to W Malaysia
HEIGHT	up to 20 m (66 ft)
TYPE	evergreen fruiting tree
STATUS	extinct in the wild
HABITAT	high rainfall in subtropical regions
GROWTH	slow
FLOWG	spring
DRY TOL.	moderate
SALT TOL.	low
LIGHT	full sun
SOIL	deep, fertile, water-retentive
NUTRIT.	organic fertilizer (mulch encourages root fungus)
HAZARDS	none
PROBLEMS	mushroom root rot; leaf fungus
ENVIRON.	bee nectar; bat fruit
PROPAG.	fresh seed; layers
LEAVES	pinnate; dark green, paler below; elliptic, sharply pointed
FLOWERS	inconspicuous; whitish green or yellowish; held in terminal panicles
FRUIT	a drupe, to 4 cm + (1.5 in.); bright red to purple when ripe; seeds with sweet, transluscent arils
USE	shade tree; street tree; backyard tree; screening; specimen; bonsai subject; large, bright conservatory
ZONE	10–11

L. chinensis; rosy-red, thin-skinned, warty fruit contain sweet, juicy translucent, fleshy arils that have a high vitamin C content.

L. chinensis; with erect, airy panicles of tiny fls in spring.

L. chinensis; skin peels away to reveal succulent, sweet white, pungently fragrant arils surrounding a large, black sd.

L. chinensis; slow growing and long-lived, this sp. forms a superb, globular crown with coppery red, new growth.

A small, simple, Buddhist shrine in a public park in Bangkok is decorated daily with fresh fls and fr. and demonstrates a celebration of nature.

Lonchocarpus violaceus

WEST INDIAN LILAC

(Jacq.) D.C.   130 spp.

L. caribaeus

FABACEAE (Papilionoideae)

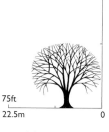

100ft ─ 30m

75ft
22.5m ──────────────── 0

LONCHOCARPUS, a large genus of white- to pink- or violet-bloomed leguminous trees native of tropical and subtropical mangrove swamps, limestone hillsides, dry plains or river banks, are mostly found in the Americas, with a few species in Africa and Madagascar. They are very closely related to *Dalbergia* and *Robinia*. **Lonchocarpus violaceus** is a small, fast- growing, evergreen species, which forms a spreading canopy of a few, long, wand-like limbs over a fairly short trunk. It carries its bluntly tipped, large, pinnate leaves along the length of its arching limbs. When the early spring rains break the long winter drought, upright spikes of glorious, rose-violet, fragrant blooms appear along the slender wands of the branch tips. From the uppermost leaf axils little pea-like flowers, which are splotched yellow and white, are held erect in slender racemes. They are short-lived and are soon followed by bundles of flat, oblong, green pods that gradually turn a pale, straw colour and persist for a long time without dehiscing. As the flowers are confined to the tops of the uppermost limbs, *L. violaceus* is often best viewed from above, making it a perfect candidate for a downward-sloping garden. This is a tree of dry, limestone hills and is an excellent choice for a xerophytic garden. Like many species in this genus, it has fibrous bark that strips off easily and this has been utilized to make ropes and cords. The leaves are used in the preparation of home remedies. *Lonchocarpus* are very closely related to *Gliricidia* and they share the same toxic properties, which have long been exploited in their native lands, often as a poison to stun and catch fish. Several species have been developed commercially as sources for rotenone insecticides. Some *Lonchocarpus* are quite cold-tolerant and may support temperatures down to -4C (25F), with short-lived frosts. These species are renowned as honey trees.

ORIGIN	W Indies and Colombia
HEIGHT	up to 15 m (50 ft)
TYPE	evergreen flowering tree
STATUS	not threatened
HABITAT	dry limestone hills
GROWTH	moderate
FLOWG	spring
DRY TOL.	high
SALT TOL.	moderate
LIGHT	full sun
SOIL	fertile, friable
NUTRIT.	balanced fertilizer annually
HAZARDS	poison parts
PROBLEMS	none
ENVIRON.	bee nectar
PROPAG.	seeds; cuttings
LEAVES	pinnate; rich green; leaflets in 3–4 pairs, to 10 cm (4 in.); long, blunt-tipped
FLOWERS	showy; white or rose violet; held in upright racemes to 20 cm (8 in.); fragrant
FRUIT	a legume, to 8 × 4 cm (3 × 1.5 in.); oblong, flattened; with 1–3 seeds
USE	small flowering tree; small shade tree; large planter; accent; civic centre; xerophytic
ZONE	10—12

L. violaceus; an arching cat-walk of violet blooms.

L. violaceus; a happy young specimen showing off its arching, plumey growth and spring blooms.

L. violaceus; abundant bundles of persistent sd pods, which gradually turn brown and papery.

L. violaceus; like many sp. in this genus, the fibrous bark strips off easily and is used for ropes and cords.

(1) **Lonchocarpus domingensis**, ([Pers.] DC.), (syn. *L. sericeus*), Trop. America, to 15 m (50 ft). Known as GUAMA in Cuba, where this old specimen was photographed in the Jardin Botanico de Cienfuegos. In other parts of its range, it is called GENO-GENO and RIVIERE SAVONETTE. This is a decid. sp. of dry coast. woodlands that blooms mostly in spring. Pinnate lvs with 1–3 pairs of suborbicular to oblong-elliptic lflts, broadly rounded at the base and covered below in fine, soft, silky hairs. (2) Fls are pea-like, bright rose-purple, and standard white at the base. Like others of its genus, *L. domingensis* is a honey plant. (10–12) (3) **Lonchocarpus longistylus**; (Pitt.), endemic of Mexico, to 18 m (59 ft). Known as MAYAN LILAC, this tree was

photographed at the Jardin Botanico Nationale, Cuba, in full, late spring bloom. In its native Mexico, the ancient Mayans fermented the bark in honey and water to make an intoxicating drink called Balcha (these days, named Pitarilla); it was imbibed at religious ceremonies and offered to the gods. (10–12) (4) **Lonchocarpus pentaphyllus**; ([Poiret.] DC), (syn. *L. latifolius*), Trop. America, to 10 m (33 ft). Known as FORTVENTURA, SWAMP DOGWOOD, WATER-WOOD or SAVONETTE, this is a widely distributed sp. native of wet forests and banks of streams. Lvs are alternate-pinnate with elliptic lflts to 15 cm (6 in.) long. Fls are pea-shaped, purple, in erect racemes. The heartwood is reddish, hard, heavy and strong, and is used for pilings. (10–12)

Lophanthera lactescens

GOLDEN CHAIN TREE

Ducke 4 spp.

MALPIGHIACEAE

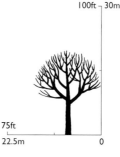

100ft – 30m

75ft
22.5m — 0

ORIGIN	Brazil, endemic
HEIGHT	up to 20 m (66 ft)
TYPE	semi-deciduous flowering tree
STATUS	threatened
HABITAT	Amazon rainforests and river valleys
GROWTH	moderate to fast
FLOWG	late summer
DRY TOL.	moderate
SALT TOL.	low
LIGHT	full sun to bright shade
SOIL	rich, humid, slightly acid
NUTRIT.	organic fertilizer; deep, organic mulch
HAZARDS	none
PROBLEMS	none
ENVIRON.	bee nectar
PROPAG.	seeds; cuttings; layers
LEAVES	simple; mid green; to 22 × 11 cm (8.6 × 4.3 in.); obovate, apex rounded or obtuse
FLOWERS	showy; golden yellow; held in pendulous terminal thyrse of up to 300 small flowers
FRUIT	a schizocarp, to 5 cm (2 in.); dry, pale grey, pea-like; with a single black seed within
USE	specimen; humid garden; courtyard; street tree; large planter; civic centre; large, bright conservatory
ZONE	11–12

THE VAST COUNTRY OF BRAZIL stretches 3,600 km (2,240 miles) at its widest point, encompassing dry plains as well as the rich rainforests of the Amazon Basin, and is thus home to a vast cornucopia of flora. One of the loveliest of Brazilian flowering trees, and indeed of the tropical world, is **Lophanthera lactescens**, a member of the largely Trop. American *Malpighiaceae* family. The specific name, *lactescens*, refers to its bitter, milky sap. This species is very closely related to *Byrsonima*, as may be seen by the structure of the (inverted) inflorescence. *L. lactescens* is a semi-deciduous species of the rainforests and riverbanks of Amazonia. As it grows, it often develops 2 or 3 trunks, which support its lean, compact, erect form, with its huge whorls of large, handsome, mid green leaves. In late summer, pendulous chains of minute, long-tubed, yellow flowers hang from the tips of the twigs, creating an elegant, candelabrum effect. There are up to 300 tiny, upwardly curving, long, slender-tubed flowers in each chain. The blooms open from the apex of the raceme, taking several weeks to mature before the ones at the bottom are faded. Following the flowers, little, pale grey, pea-sized fruit are formed and dangled on soft, slender 'strings', with each fruit containing a single, shiny, brown-black seed. A great many fruit are produced in early spring; they should be collected and sown immediately they are ripe to ensure viability. *L. lactescens* is very sensitive to transplanting, therefore it is advisable to sow the seeds in peat pots and to plant them where they are to grow as soon as possible. This is one of the reasons *L. lactescens* remains relatively rare in ornamental horticulture, although it has proved very successful in the tropical north of Australia. The heartwood is yellowish and moderately heavy, compact, durable and resistant to attack by insects. This is a honey plant.

L. lactescens; with masses of young, green (later grey), pea-like fr.

L. lactescens; each pendulous raceme of this rare, Brazilian endemic holds up to 500 tiny fls charged with copious nectar to attract bees.

L. lactescens; surprisingly tol. and easy to grow (with fresh sds), and popular as a street tree in Cairns, N Qld, Australia.

L. lactescens; thin, pale grey, warty bark has bitter, milky sap.

100ft 30m

75ft
22.5m   0

Lophostemon confertus

BRUSH BOX

(R. Br.) P.G. Wilson & Waterhouse   4 spp.

Tristania conferta

MYRTACEAE

ORIGIN	E and NE Australia
HEIGHT	up to 54 m (177 ft)
TYPE	evergreen, very large foliage and timber tree
STATUS	not threatened
HABITAT	mixed or transitional rainforest, on wet schlerophyll
GROWTH	moderate
FLOWG	spring and summer
DRY TOL.	moderate
SALT TOL.	low
LIGHT	full sun or part shade
SOIL	acid, fertile, water-retentive
NUTRIT.	magnesium-rich fertilizer; deep, organic mulch
HAZARDS	none
PROBLEMS	none
ENVIRON.	nectar for insects
PROPAG.	seeds; layers
LEAVES	simple; dark green (or variegated); leathery; grouped in pseudo whorls
FLOWERS	showy; white; widely spreading lobes with crested stamens, in bundles
FRUIT	a capsule, to 13 mm (0.5 in.) long; goblet-shaped, containing many narrow seeds
USE	shade tree; street tree; specimen; public open space; large planter; conservatory
ZONE	9–11

LOPHOSTEMON is named from the Greek words *lophis*, meaning crest, and *stemon*, meaning stamen, referring to its fringed, or crested stamens. This is a regionally widespread genus found from NSW to Qld, on the margins of coastal rainforests, in Eucalypt woodlands and on river flats, on moist, acid soils. **Lophostemon confertus** is a forest mammoth, which soars to 54 m (177 ft) through the rainforest canopy, with a clean, straight trunk, anchored by massive, narrow buttresses. Its young trunk has grey, scaly bark which, like many half-barked *Eucalyptus*, persists at its base, but sloughs off higher up to reveal a smooth, luminous, rusty pink or orange, inner bark. The young shoots exude a milky sap that smells of vinegar when they are cut, hence one of its common names, Vinegar Tree. To begin with, **L. confertus** has densely conical growth but it develops a more spreading habit with age. From spring to summer, it carries little, white flowers with widely spreading lobes and numerous, protruding stamens in 5 feathery bundles. Later, come small, goblet-shaped, woody fruit capsules (closely resembling those of *Eucalyptus*) filled with narrow, wedge-shaped seeds. Curiously, this giant myrtle is very popular for street planting in Australia. Of course, it does not attain such giddy heights in cultivation, when it is frequently found at about 10–15 m (33–50 ft). Its ornamental timber is highly regarded, being strong and dense. In its native Australia, it has been used for shipbuilding, for constructing bridges and wharves and for hardwood floors, while the bark is employed in tanning. **L. confertus** has been planted for afforestation in Hawaii.

*** var. 'Variegatus' is a highly ornamental form that is much smaller and thus popular for domestic planting in Australia and New Zealand. There is a new, dwarf cultivar known as 'Billy Bunter' that forms a rounded shrub.

L. confertus; delightful and original blooms with feathery, white stamens.

L. confertus var. 'Variegatus'; at Auckland Botanic Gardens, New Zealand, demonstrating its half-barked trunk.

L. confertus var. 'Variegatus'; showing the small, vase-like fr., which has a kinship to the *Eucalyptus*.

L. confertus; photographed at Lake Morris in N Qld, this Australian endemic is closely related to *Eucalyptus* and has been an important timber tree for many years.

Lysiloma sabicu

SABICU

Benth.   9 spp.

FABACAEAE (mimosoideae)

THIS SPLENDID LITTLE LEGUME may superficially resemble *Albizia lebbek* or *Leucaena leucocephala* (Wild Tamarind — a pet name given to many finely pinnate, parasol-crowned legumes). Spineless, with gracefully arching limbs, the **Lysiloma sabicu** carries a mantle of fresh green, feathery foliage that is a mellow, russet-pink when it first emerges. The smooth, young, lustrous, brown bark stretched over its muscular stems resembles the sinewy skin of animal limbs and the tree is descriptively named Horse Flesh in the Bahamas. As it ages, the bark splits and peels longitudinally, often in a spiral fashion, lending the trunk a deeply shaggy appearance. In spring, little, creamy yellow flowers sit like dandelion down on the spreading twigs but they soon turn into broad, thin, papery pods. Despite its quiet grace, filmy crown and delicate framework, this is a rugged, thrifty little tree with built-in salt and drought-tolerance, prepared for any challenge; *L. sabicu* is as much at home by the sea as on arid, rocky slopes. This species performs excellently as a lawn specimen because its light, airy crown allows plenty of sunlight to penetrate to the grass below. It also has unaggressive roots. The hard, strong, durable reddish heartwood is likened to mahogany and has been used in boatbuilding. These are excellent honey plants.

*** **L. latisiliquum**; ([L.] Benth.), W Indies to C America, to 16 m (52 ft). Known as TAMARINDILLO, this xerophytic species forms a light, feathery, pyramidal crown, with its limbs curving downwards. It is a larger tree than *L. sabicu*. The leaves are much finer, with 10–33 pairs of leaflets. The mimosa-like, pure white, cottony flowers are set in deep red calyxes. As they are pollinated, the blooms turn rose-pink and then collapse. The fruit are smaller, to 12 cm (4.7 in.) and are pointed at their apex. The dark brown timber is particularly highly regarded in Cuba. (**10–12**)

ORIGIN	Cuba and Bahamas
HEIGHT	up to 8 m (26 ft)
TYPE	evergreen, small foliage tree
STATUS	restricted distribution
HABITAT	dry, coastal thickets and woodland
GROWTH	moderate
FLOWG	spring to summer
DRY TOL.	high
SALT TOL.	high
LIGHT	full sun
SOIL	fertile, well-drained
NUTRIT.	balanced fertilizer annually
HAZARDS	none
PROBLEMS	none
ENVIRON.	bee nectar
PROPAG.	seeds
LEAVES	pinnate; bright green, paler below; leaflets, to 7 pairs; new growth reddish
FLOWERS	inconspicuous; creamy yellow; held in mimosa-like heads, to 2.5 cm (1 in.)
FRUIT	a legume, to 15 cm (6 in.); flat, leathery, mahogany red; with several seeds
USE	seaside; small shade tree; coastal street tree; specimen; large planter; civic centre; xerophytic
ZONE	10–11

L. sabicu; creamy yellow fls are more substantial than *L. latisliquum*.

L. sabicu; known as Horse Flesh in the Bahamas, this hardy, little tree performs very well by the sea or in arid areas.

L. sabicu; flat, papery and pearly pinkish, the fr., which, like those of *Albizia lebbek*, persist on the tree for a long time.

L. latisiliquum; fls are pure white and fluffy and sit like dandelion's down on the spreading twigs.

Macadamia integrifolia

MACADAMIA NUT

Maiden & Betch   12 spp.

PROTEACEAE (Grevilleoideae – Macadamieae)

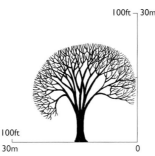

100ft – 30m

100ft
30m   0

ORIGIN	Qld, Australia, endemic
HEIGHT	up to 20 m (66 ft)
TYPE	evergreen; flowering nut tree
STATUS	vulnerable
HABITAT	humid mountain slopes; coastal rainforest
GROWTH	slow
FLOWG	spring, or year-round
DRY TOL.	moderate
SALT TOL.	low
LIGHT	full sun
SOIL	water-retentive, sandy loam
NUTRIT.	organic fertilizer; deep, organic mulch
HAZARDS	allergic to phosphates
PROBLEMS	phytophthera root rot; anthracnose
ENVIRON.	bee nectar
PROPAG.	fresh seeds; grafting
LEAVES	simple; dark green, to 14 cm (5.5 in.); glossy, oblong to obovate; in whorls of 3
FLOWERS	showy; white; held in pendent, bottlebrush-like spikes, to 30 cm (12 in.)
FRUIT	a drupe, to 35 cm (14 in.) diam.; globular, dehiscent; seeds, hard, brown
USE	flowering tree; shade tree; specimen; screening; backyard tree; large planter; conservatory
ZONE	9–12

MACADAMIA INTEGRIFOLIA is a long-lived, evergreen native of tropical and subtropical coastal rainforests of Qld and NSW that forms a dense, compact, rounded canopy over a sturdy trunk. The narrow, leathery, wavy-margined leaves are whorled at the branch tips and the inflorescences – typically Proteaceae – are pendulous, crowded spikes of little, creamy white, curling, tubular flowers arising from lower leaf axils. The fruit, which has a hard, smooth-skinned, polished, tan shell, contains a sweet, crisp, oily white kernel that resembles hazelnut in flavour and is marketed like almonds, cracked, shelled, roasted, sugared or salted. It is widely accepted as the most delicious of all nuts and the most expensive, and is the only international commercial food crop that originates in Australia. Oil is extracted commercially and used in cosmetics. Of the 12 species of *Macadamia*, 10 are endemic to Australia. Of these, only *M. integrifolia* (Smooth-shelled) and *Macadamia tetraphylla* (Rough-shelled) have been found to be non-toxic, other species having poisonous (cyanide) fruit. Some **M. integrifolia** varieties produce nuts all year round, whereas *M. tetraphylla* is more seasonal. Very slow growing, most trees bear fruit 6–15 years after planting from seed; grafted plants are generally faster. *M. integrifolia* tolerates a pH from 4.5–8, but does particularly well on deep, well-drained loams and sandy loams. Although young trees are sensitive to frost, mature trees can withstand moderate freezes.

*** **M. whelanii**; ([FM Bailey] FM Bailey), Qld, Australia, to 30 m (100 ft). WHELAN'S SILKY OAK is native to very wet, lowland rainforest. It is an attractive species with masses of white flowers held on stiff, erect branches in late spring. New leaves emerge bright red. Although the fruit contains cyanogenetic toxins, the Aborigines are known to have eaten them. This species grows best in humus-rich soil. (10–12) These are important honey plants.

M. integrifolia; thick outer shells eventually fall away to leave the hard, oily nut.

M. whelanii; a native of very wet sites, this large sp. has spectacular fls but toxic fr.

M. integrifolia; a Macadamia plantation at Tinaroo, N Qld, Australia.

M. integrifolia; typical of the Proteaceae clan, these creamy white, fls are adapted for insect pollination with their stout 'bottlebrush' of nectar-filled fls.

Macaranga tanarius

HAIRY MAHANG

Meull. – Arg.   280 spp.

Ricinus tanarius

EUPHORBIACEAE (Acalyphpoideae)

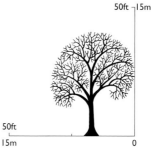

AT FIRST GLANCE, this species could be mistaken for a Portia Tree, *Thespesia populneus*. *Macaranga* species belong to the great Euphorbia family. They are dioecious, their minuscule, male flowers held in congested, much-branched, coral-like panicles, while the females are bell-shaped and solitary, in slender clusters. This genus is also distinguished by its peltate leaves that have long, hollow petioles attached at their centres. ***Macaranga tanarius*** is one of many Malaysian *Macarangas* and the most widespread and common, extending southwards to E Australia, where it is a pioneer species in clearings in coastal rainforests. *M. tanarius* is very fast growing, said to grow to 2 m (6.5 ft) per year under favourable conditions, and is highly regarded for its ability to regenerate naturally on degraded, rainforest land. Male and female flowers are greenish white, the fruit smooth, 2-valved, tipped with soft, green spines. *** *M. grandifolia*; ([Blanco.] Merr.), Philippines endemic, to 7 m (23 ft). CORAL TREE is a popular garden ornamental in many parts of the tropics for its extraordinarily grandiose leaves, which are rounded-ovate in form, with prominent, reddish veins and the stem attached towards the centre of the leaf blade. In appearance, this tree could be thought a relative of the Castor Oil plant, *Ricinus communis*. The long, tubular, hollow petiole has a large, leaf-like stipule clasping its base and, as in *Cecropia*, it may be inhabited by ants. There is often a sticky substance adhering to the hairy undersides of the leaves. The flowers are pinkish red and the males are held in coral-like, congested inflorescences. (10–12)
*** *M. peltata*; ([Roxb.] Meull.), India and Sri Lanka. Known as KENDA, the soft timber provides plywood for chests in Sri Lanka, while the leaves are used for steaming Jaggery, a coarse, dark sugar made from palm tree sap. (10–12)

NOTE: these species may prove invasive.

ORIGIN	from Malaysia to Australia
HEIGHT	up to 10 m (33 ft)
TYPE	evergreen, dioecious foliage tree
STATUS	not threatened
HABITAT	pioneer tree; widespread in disturbed or coastal areas
GROWTH	fast
FLOWG	year-round
DRY TOL.	moderate
SALT TOL.	high
LIGHT	full sun or bright shade
SOIL	humid, fertile
NUTRIT.	normally not necessary
HAZARDS	poisonous; spiny seeds
PROBLEMS	messy leaves; greedy roots
ENVIRON.	nectar for insects
PROPAG.	seeds; large cuttings
LEAVES	simple; bright green, to 23 cm (9.1 cm.); cordate, peltate; with long, hollow petioles
FLOWERS	showy; rosy red; male staminate catkins, axillary; females, solitary
FRUIT	a capsule, to 0.5 cm (0.2 in.); 2-valved, with soft spines
USE	seaside; large planter; accent; screening; courtyard; specimen
ZONE	10–12

M. tanarius; tiny, bell-shaped, female fls.

M. tanarius; photographed at Flecker Botanic Gardens, Cairns, Qld, Australia. This fast-growing, pioneer tree is popular for its ability to regenerate degraded forest land.

M. grandifolia; is easily confused with the Castor Oil tree. It has grandiose, long-petioled, peltate lvs.

M. grandifolia; coral-like male fls are held at the base of the lvs.

ORIGIN	SE USA, endemic
HEIGHT	up to 25 m (82 ft)
TYPE	evergreen, large flowering tree
STATUS	becoming rare in the wild
HABITAT	humid valleys and river banks
GROWTH	slow
FLOWG	summer to autumn
DRY TOL.	moderate
SALT TOL.	low
LIGHT	full sun or bright shade
SOIL	rich, water-retentive
NUTRIT.	organic fertilizer; deep, organic mulch
HAZARDS	none
PROBLEMS	none
ENVIRON.	nectar for beetles
PROPAG.	seeds; cuttings; layers
LEAVES	simple; rich green; with thick, inrolled margins, to 20 cm (8 in.); polished above, rusty felty below
FLOWERS	showy; ivory white; large, fleshy, cupped; intensely fragrant
FRUIT	a cone, to 10 cm (4 in.); aggregation of follicles; seeds ceramic-like, glossy red
USE	large flowering tree; street tree; specimen; public open space; very large planter; large conservatory
ZONE	7–10

100ft ⌐ 30m
75ft
22.5m   0

Magnolia grandiflora

MAGNOLIA

L.   100 spp.

MAGNOLIACEAE

MAGNOLIA ranks among the most ancient of the angiosperm genera. They are distinguished by their pungent odour and large, spathe-like, terminal, deciduous stipule (ochrea), which is attached to the stem, leaving a circular scar as it detaches. Flower buds also have an ochrea, and the petals are thick, with a powerful fragrance. Stamens and pistils are held in a cone-like column with up to 200 stamens that are massed around its base and shed as the flower is pollinated, while upwardly flaring pistils remain attached to the thick, columnar centre (torus). Their embryos develop into a compact cone of dry, furry follicles, which eventually contain large, hard, scarlet seeds, held by long threads. *Magnolia grandiflora*, the most renowned of its genus, is endemic to southern USA and is a warm-temperate species, but may grow in higher elevations of the tropics and subtropics. Many *Magnolia* are native to the mountains of Burma, China and SE Asia, as well as high elevations of Trop. America. *Magnolia* bark contains an essential oil used to treat peptic ulcers, vomiting and asthma, as well as typhoid, malaria and salmonella. Very slow growing, it is usually grafted to speed up its flowering cycle; it takes up to 20 years to bloom from seed. There are many cultivars, including a dwarf, 'Little Gem', which shows promising heat-tolerance.

*** ***M. liliifera***, ([L.] Baill.), (syn. *Talauma hodgsonii*), Himalayas to Borneo, to 15 m (50 ft). TALAUMA is native to humid, undisturbed forest. New growth is rose-purple. Flowers to 15 cm (6 in.), the petals are pale, rose-beige and smell of guava. (8–10)

*** ***M. splendens***, (Urban), (syn. *Talauma splendens*), Puerto Rico, to 25 m (82 ft). LAUREL SABINO, with very fragrant, creamy flowers, to 7.5 cm (3 in.), blooming year-round. It is threatened with extinction as it has been cut extensively for its hard, olive-green, spicily aromatic wood that is used locally to make furniture. (10–12)

M. grandiflora; fl. bud with large, woolly, brownish ochrea.

M. grandiflora; a large specimen growing in Atherton, N Qld, Australia,

M. grandiflora; young follicle fr. forming from a composite of female embryos. Ceramic-like sds are bright scarlet.

M. grandiflora; showing the magnificent pink torus with its flame-like pistils. The 'matchstick' stamens have already aborted. Petals are thick, with a powerful, citrus fragrance.

259

Majidea zanguebarica

BLACK PEARL TREE

Kirk. ex Oliv.   5 spp.

Harpullia zanguebarica

SAPINDACEAE

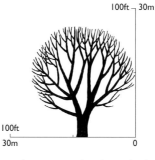

100ft — 30m

100ft
30m   0

MAJIDEA ZANGUEBARICA is a slow-growing species that, when young, has long, lank, sparsely clad limbs, with its tomentose, pinnate foliage clustered towards their ends. With age, the growth gradually fills out to compose a conical crown of soft, feathery leaves over a rough-barked trunk. Small, pale, yellowish, pink or greenish flowers have deep orange styles and are held in densely branched, velvety, terminal panicles with large, pale green, leafy bracts. Although not very showy, they are quite attractive, especially as the flowers fade and inflated seed pods begin to develop, looking from a distance like small flame-red butterflies amongst the velvety, pale green bracts. It is these fruit pods which, like those of the *Harpullia*, are the most dramatic, visual detail of this elegant tree. As they mature, they balloon out, changing from soft green to pale, yellowish tan, eventually dehiscing widely to reveal their startlingly luminous, scarlet lining and several opalescent, blue-black seeds that are covered with a pale grey bloom, making them resemble little, black pearls. In the Witu forests of the Kenyan coast, near the mouth of the Tana River, ***M. zanguebarica*** species grow to a greater size and are cut for their fine timber. This tree is closely related to the famous *Harpullia* genus and was until recently classified as such. Timber of *Harpullia* and *Majidea* is world-renowned for its hard, fine-grained wood that has been used traditionally to make fine cabinetry.

*** ***M. fosteri***; ([Sprague] Radlk.) (syn. *Harpullia fosteri*), to 30 m (100 ft), from W Africa to Sudan. This forest giant, variously known as Berekum, Mampong or Tombel, is distinguished by its angled, velvety hairy branchlets. The flowers are held in dense, terminal panicles. They have a yellowish calyx, red disk and pink anthers. The inflated fruit is brownish and pink within, while the seeds are blue. (10–12)

ORIGIN	Kenya, endemic
HEIGHT	up to 25 m (82 ft)
TYPE	semi-deciduous, large foliage tree
STATUS	vulnerable
HABITAT	lowland or coastal humid forests
GROWTH	slow
FLOW'G	winter
DRY TOL.	high
SALT TOL.	moderate
LIGHT	full sun
SOIL	rich, well-drained
NUTRIT.	balanced fertilizer annually
HAZARDS	none
PROBLEMS	none
ENVIRON.	insect nectar
PROPAG.	seeds
LEAVES	pinnate; dullish green; to 20 cm (8 in.); to 10 pairs of leaflets, oblique, elliptic, undulate, tomentose
FLOWERS	inconspicuous; whitish or yellowish green; 5 sepals and 4 petals, with short claw; in dense, terminal panicle
FRUIT	capsule, to 6 cm (2.4 in.); much inflated, 3-parted, lined with rich red; seeds black, pearl-like
USE	small shade tree; street tree; public open space; specimen; large planter; xerophytic
ZONE	10–12

M. zanguebarica; with curious, deep orange, expanded, disc-like styles.

M. zanguebarica; drab yellow-beige fr. are suddenly transformed when they open to reveal their scarlet linings and dangle their remarkable 'black pearl' sds.

M. zanguebarica; pale, yellowish, pink or reddish fls are held in densely branched, velvety, terminal panicles.

M. zanguebarica; slow-growing, the Black Pearl tree forms a conical crown of dull green, soft, feathery lvs.

ORIGIN	Trop. America
HEIGHT	up to 6 m (20 ft)
TYPE	evergreen, small fruiting tree
STATUS	not threatened
HABITAT	rocky limestone, from sea level to 1,000 m (3,280 ft)
GROWTH	moderate
FLOWG	intermittently, all year
DRY TOL.	high
SALT TOL.	moderate to high
LIGHT	full sun
SOIL	rich, well-drained
NUTRIT.	organic fertilizer; organic mulch
HAZARDS	none
PROBLEMS	nematodes; sooty mould
ENVIRON.	bee nectar; fruit for birds
PROPAG.	seeds; cuttings; layers
LEAVES	simple; rich green; to 10 cm (4 in.); ovate-lanceolate, glabrous
FLOWERS	showy; red to rose pink; to 1.5 cm (0.6 in.); with 5 clawed petals; held in small umbels
FRUIT	a drupe, to 2 cm (0.8 in.); bright red to crimson; glossy; pulp, orange, sour to sweet
USE	small flowering tree; backyard tree; courtyard; accent; large planter; bonsai subject; xerophytic
ZONE	10–12

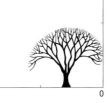

50ft — 15m
50ft
15m — 0

L.   40 spp.
M. punicifolia
MALPIGHIACEAE

APART FROM BEING A REGIONALLY IMPORTANT FRUIT TREE, *Malpighia glabra* serves many purposes in the garden, not least as a decorative specimen for a small space. It is much branched, developing a graceful vase shape, with arching limbs, deep, glossy green foliage and smoothish, grey bark. The little, wheel-like, rosy red, pale, lilac-pink or whitish blooms, centred with bright yellow stamens, are typical of the *Malpighia* clan. Several times a year, they smother the tree with their bright stars, attracting clouds of bees. The round, slightly flattened, crimson, cherry-like fruit is well known to have a very high vitamin C content. Although they greatly resemble the temperate Cherry (*Prunus cerasus*), the flavour varies considerably from quite sour to fairly sweet. Marie C. Neale, in *Gardens of Hawaii*, says that years ago many acres of **M.** *glabra* were planted in the islands and great quantities of the fruit were shipped to N America, until it lost out in competition with synthetic vitamin firms. The cherries mature in 30 days and are eaten fresh or are juiced and used as a beverage or processed into purée. Selected plants may be propagated from cuttings or grafted onto seedling stock – it has even been successfully espaliered by some growers – but cross-pollination is required for good fruit production. It is not clear why this species is known as Barbados Cherry. **M.** *glabra* is often confused with *M. emarginata*, a very similar species. These are a honey trees.

*** **M. emarginata**; (Sessé & Moc, ex DC), (syn. *M. punicifolia*), W Indies; Mexico to Venezuela and Peru, to 6 m (20 ft). WEST INDIAN CHERRY, CEREZA or ACEROLA grows as a much-branched shrub or small tree with stiff branchlets. It is much smaller in all its parts than *M. glabra*. The flowers are pink or purple; the fruit are red, to 1.75 cm (0.69 in.) diameter, edible and rather sour, but very high in vitamin C. (10–12)

M. glabra; with little pinwheel, pink fls.

M. glabra; with tough, fairly smooth bark and many arching limbs, it develops a graceful vase shape.

M. glabra; forms a twiggy shrub or small tree. The little red fr. are quite sour but very high in vitamin C.

M. glabra; the juicy, round, slightly flattened, crimson, cherry-like fr. are eaten fresh, juiced and used as a beverage or processed into purée.

Mammea americana

MAMMEY APPLE

L.   50 spp.

GUTTIFERAE

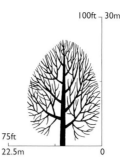

MAMMEA AMERICANA is a noble, long-lived species with a splendid, glossy, dark green, voluminous crown supported by a stoutly erect trunk, which may be grey brown and smooth or slightly fissured. Short-petioled, dark green leaves are leathery and distinguished by their many, closely arranged, parallel, lateral veins. Large, white, waxy, fragrant flowers are borne on thick stalks and are mostly hidden in the leaves. They are monecious; male blooms are camellia-like, composed of 6 heavily waxy, ivory-white petals with a coronet of golden stamens at the centre, while the females have a sturdy pistil. In the French W Indies, an aromatic liqueur, Eau de Creole, or Creme de Creole, is distilled from these flowers. The fruit of *M. americana* is very like Sapodilla or Mamey Sapote of the Sapotaceae genus. It has rough, leathery, russet skin and soft, sweet, apricot-flavoured flesh, which is deep yellow, orange or reddish, with milky latex. It is delicious and usually eaten raw or made into marmalade, chutney or preserves. Embedded in the pulp are 2–4 large, oblong, red-brown seeds with a rough surface. The flesh immediately surrounding the seeds is bitter, while the seeds themselves are poisonous, especially to certain types of insects and to chickens; in some regions they are also used as a toxic bait to stun fish. *M. americana* is fairly slow growing and begins to bear fruit after 6–8 years from seed, or from 4–5 years from grafts. The sapwood is light brown and the heartwood reddish brown, with a surface often flecked with small, oily exudations. It is hard, heavy and strong, but susceptible to termites. The bark contains a gummy, pale yellow latex, which, along with powdered seeds, has been used as an insecticide to extract chiggers and insects from the skin, as well as to kill ticks and parasites that live on dogs and other animals.

ORIGIN	W Indies
HEIGHT	up to 20 m (66 ft)
TYPE	evergreen, monoecious fruiting tree
STATUS	threatened
HABITAT	moist coastal forests, up to 1,250 m (4,100 ft)
GROWTH	moderate
FLOWG	spring to summer
DRY TOL.	moderate
SALT TOL.	moderate
LIGHT	full sun or bright shade
SOIL	humid, rich, water-retentive
NUTRIT.	balanced fertilizer annually; deep, organic fertilizer
HAZARDS	seeds poisonous
PROBLEMS	borer; spider mites
ENVIRON.	insect nectar; bat and bird fruit
PROPAG.	seeds; grafts
LEAVES	simple; dark green; to 17 × 9 cm (7 × 3.5 in.); elliptic, thick, with many parallel veins
FLOWERS	showy; ivory white; to 5 cm (2 in.); 6 waxy petals; monoecious; fragrant
FRUIT	a drupe, to 15 cm (6 in.); thick skin and yellow or reddish flesh; with whitish latex sap
USE	large shade tree; large fruiting tree; street tree; public open space
ZONE	10–12

M. americana; this moderately young specimen at Andromeda Botanic Gardens, Bathsheba, Barbados, demonstrates its powerful growth habit.

M. americana; male fl. with golden stamens.

M. americana; with large, thick-skinned, deep yellow or russet, sweet-fleshed fr. containing white latex.

M. americana; the crown is supported by a stout trunk that may be grey-brown and smooth or slightly fissured

ORIGIN	from N India to Malayasia
HEIGHT	up to 30 m (100 ft)
TYPE	evergreen, large fruiting tree
STATUS	not threatened
HABITAT	humid tropical forests
GROWTH	moderate
FLOWG.	spring
DRY TOL.	moderate
SALT TOL.	moderate
LIGHT	full sun
SOIL	rich, well-drained
NUTRIT.	high phosphate and potassium; organic mulch
HAZARDS	possibly irritates skin
PROBLEMS	anthracnose; scale
ENVIRON.	bee nectar; wild fruit for birds and bats
PROPAG.	seeds; budding and grafting
LEAVES	simple; rich green; to 30 × 7 cm (12 × 3 in.); oblong-elliptic to lance-shaped; with red new growth
FLOWERS	showy; pinkish white or yellowish; held in red or pink clusters on red-stemmed panicles; fragrant
FRUIT	a drupe, to 25 × 10 cm (9 .8 × 4 in.); ovoid-oblong; yellow, green or red; with sweet, aromatic flesh
USE	backyard tree; large shade tree; street tree; large flowering tree; public open space; specimen
ZONE	10–12

Mangifera indica

MANGO

L.   40–60 spp.

ANACARDIACEAE

MANGIFERA INDICA is thought to have been in cultivation for so long that its natural distribution has been obscured. Grown in the open, it forms a very dense, round crown of large, leathery, lance-shaped, drooping leaves over a stout trunk. In late winter and early spring, a flush of new, bright red leaves are borne, followed by tiny, yellow-green to pink, fragrant flowers held in erect, red-stemmed, showy panicles. The legendary, aromatic, heavy fruit is truly a masterpiece. Almost heart-shaped, dangling on its long, stout stalk, the luminous, ripe fruit is mostly blushed pink, red or purple, with a delicate, iridescent, powdery bloom. During the early weeks of summer, when mangoes are plentiful and cheap, the local population seems to become crazed by a social phenomenon sometimes called Mango Madness. Proprietors have been known to stand guard over their trees with a gun or to protect them with a ferocious dog tied under the tree. *M. indica* has been recorded and cultivated in India for over 4,000 years and is revered by Buddhists and Hindus, who use its leaves as decoration at weddings in the hope that the couple will give birth to a son. In Hindu tradition, this species is regarded as the tree of destiny or fate, and it figures prominently in rituals and ceremonies. Almost every part of *M. indica* has been employed medicinally. The astringent bark is used to check haemorrhaging and diarrhoea and leaves are used to alleviate coughs, chest ailments, skin irritations and dental problems. The flowers are considered an aphrodisiac and are also used to repel mosquitoes. The bark and leaves yield a yellow dye and the seeds are ground up to treat scorpion stings. Mango needs a dry season to promote flowering and pollination. There are many superb, regional varieties and cultivars. An important honey plant.

NOTE: considered invasive in tropical Australia, where it is widely dispersed by fruit bats.

M. indica; fragrant, red-stalked spring fls.

M. indica; '...Mango tree, oh so pretty...' and so it is when flushed with its new, spring growth.

M. indica; in spring, the tree becomes flushed brilliant crimson with its new red lvs.

M. indica; dangling luminous globes, which illuminate the trees in early summer. Apart from banana, the mango is the most widely regarded of trop. fr. in all its regions.

263

Manilkara zapota

SAPODILLA

(L.) Van Royen.   65 spp.

Achras zapota

SAPOTACEAE

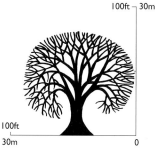

100ft – 30m

100ft

30m   **0**

MANILKARA ZAPOTA is one of the few fruit trees to thrive in the poor, wind-swept, low-lying, coral islands of the W Indies. *M. zapota* is a very slow-growing but undemanding tree that takes time to form its dense, widespread, shiny, dark, evergreen canopy over a bulky, deeply furrowed trunk and limbs that contain copious, white, milky latex. Throughout the year, light, yellowish green, bell-shaped flowers are held singly on brown, hairy stalks, slowly transforming to tawny, rough-skinned, round or oval fruit that is smaller but very similar in appearance and taste to Mammey Zapote, *Pouteria sapota*. Sapodilla fruit are thin-skinned, with sweet, brownish, slightly grainy flesh with milky sap. They taste of mellow pea, with over-tones of caramel. Because it is a favourite food of bats, the fruit is often picked greenish, before the bats are attracted to it, and ripened in the dark. It is mostly eaten raw but may be made into preserves and syrup. There are several excellent, large, sweet varieties that may be successfully grafted onto wild rootstock. *M. zapota* is, however, more widely renowned for its milky latex known as Chicle, which is the main source of chewing gum. The tree is cultivated commercially in C America, particularly in the Yucatan region of Mexico, Guatemala and Honduras, where it is grown in plantations and tapped every 2–3 years during the rainy season, in the same manner as rubber. The milky sap is condensed by heating and the resulting gum is kneaded with a stick and fashioned into small cakes for export. *M. zapota* wood is dark red, very hard and heavy, strong, tough and durable and is a popular timber, where available, for general and heavy construction, cabinetwork and furniture. Being evergreen, alkaline-tolerant and totally salt-resistant, this species is an excellent tree for seaside planting; it even thrives in 'dirty' sand.

ORIGIN	from S Mexico to C America
HEIGHT	up to 30 m (100 ft)
TYPE	evergreen, large fruiting tree
STATUS	not threatened
HABITAT	lowland and coastal forests
GROWTH	slow
FLOWG	all year (mostly summer)
DRY TOL.	high
SALT TOL.	high
LIGHT	full sun
SOIL	fertile, well-drained
NUTRIT.	balanced fertilizer annually
HAZARDS	none
PROBLEMS	none
ENVIRON.	nectar for moths; fruit for bats, monkeys and birds
PROPAG.	seeds; grafting
LEAVES	simple; deep green; ovate; whorled towards ends of smaller limbs
FLOWERS	inconspicuous; yellowish green; small, bell-shaped, in brownish hairy, lateral clusters; fragrant
FRUIT	a berry, to 10 cm (4 in.); globose to oval; seeds black, set in sweet, edible pulp
USE	seaside; backyard tree; shade tree; coastal street tree; public open space; xerophytic
ZONE	10–12

M. zapota; with little, tomentose, bell-shaped, fragrant fls.

M. zapota; often picked green and ripened in a dark cupboard to ensure that bats do not find them first. The slightly grainy flesh is reminiscent of an over ripe pear with caramel overtones.

M. zapota; with a wide-spreading, everg. canopy, this slow-growing sp. has 'chicle' latex, used to make chewing-gum.

M. zapota; a freshly cut trunk at Fairchild Tropical Gardens, Miami, Florida, haemorrhaging its copious, milky latex.

(1) **Manilkara jaimiqui**; (Wright), (syn. *Mimusops emarginata*; *Manilkara bahamensis*), Florida, Cuba, Bahamas and Hispaniola, to 10 m (33 ft). Known as WILD DILLY or KANAPALEI, this sp. has typical milky latex and tough, leathery lvs. Nodding, sturdily stemmed, light yellow, bell-shaped fls give way to long-stemmed fr., to 3.5 cm (1.4 in), which are rounded and slightly flattened. This is a wonderfully compact tree with neat, erect, bluish green foliage. (10–12) (2) **Manilkara kauki**; ([L.] Dubard), (syn. *Mimusops kauki*), Coast. areas of Trop. Asia to the Pacific region and NE Qld, Australia, to 20 m (66 ft). SAWAH OR SAWAI (Malay) or WONGAI (Australia) is native to rocky headlands and lowland coast. forest. It is renowned for its durable wood, which is known in the Asian trade as *Mimusops*. It has dense, upswept growth and dense, rich green foliage; the leathery lvs are rusty or silvery below. (3) The orange-red, egg-shaped fr. has a dryish, pale cream, sweet flesh, which is edible but rather flavourless. This is a slow-growing, sun-loving, salt-resistant sp. (10–12) (4) **Manilkara roxburghiana**; ([Wight.] RM Parker), (syn. *Mimusops roxburghiana*), India endemic, to 25 m (82 ft), is known as MIMUSOPS in Florida, USA, where it is extremely popular for seaside planting. Superb, large, leathery, very dark green, polished lvs are neatly whorled around the smaller limbs and twigs, to create a lush, rounded canopy. It is a large, everg., slow-growing sp., valued for its strong, reddish brown timber. Shown here at the Jardin Botanico de Cienfuegos, Cuba, covered in lichen and epiphytes. (10–12)

265

Maniltoa browneoides

HANDKERCHIEF TREE

Harms. 20—25 spp.

M. gemmipara

FABACEAE (Caesalpinioidea)

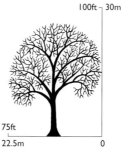

MANILTOA BROWNEOIDES is a very handsome, rare tree from the rainforests of New Guinea with a short trunk and an oval crown of large, parapinnate, leathery, shiny leaves. *M. browneoides*, which has flushes of flowers and new foliage at frequent intervals during the year, belongs to the same group of leguminous trees as *Amherstia, Brownea* and *Saraca. Maniltoa* has its flowers and new leaves encased in large, cone-shaped, papery, brown scales. The white, many-stamened flowers resemble those of *Brownea*. When they first open, they are very attractive but turn brown fairly quickly as the petals become damaged and pollinators deplete the pollen. However, *M. browneoides* is actually admired more for its young, new leaves than for its blooms. Curiously, its embryonic leaves are contained in large, rusty tomentose buds that eventually split open to dangle them in limp bundles from the tips of twigs, until the leaves have manufactured their chlorophyll and strengthened into normal foliage. *Amherstia* and *Saraca* have pinkish, new leaves, while *Brownea*'s are also blotched or spotted. Those of *M. browneoides* are even more spectacular, however, being creamy white. As they emerge, the tree appears to be hung with hundreds of large, limp, white handkerchiefs. Within a few days, the new leaves have deepened to green. Fruit forms into fat, beaked, leathery pods, each with a single seed.

*** *Maniltoa lenticellata*; (C. White), N Qld, Australia, to New Guinea, to 22 m (72 ft). Known as Cascading Maniltoa, its 'handkerchiefs' do not form a solid mass but cascade down from their large, cone-shaped buds, covering the tree. Initially pinkish, they become cream and then turn light green. Superb, short-lived, white or pink, large-stamened flowers emerge at the same time. This species is easily differentiated from *M. browneoides* by its strongly weeping growth. (10—12)

ORIGIN	New Guinea, endemic
HEIGHT	up to 25 m (82 ft)
TYPE	evergreen, large flowering tree
STATUS	fairly rare in the wild
HABITAT	tropical, lowland humid forest
GROWTH	moderate to slow
FLOWG	at intervals, year-round
DRY TOL.	low
SALT TOL.	low
LIGHT	full sun or bright shade
SOIL	slightly acid, humid
NUTRIT.	organic fertilizer; deep, organic mulch
HAZARDS	none
PROBLEMS	none
ENVIRON.	nectar for insects
PROPAG.	seeds; cuttings under mist
LEAVES	pinnate; rich green; leaflets oblong-lanceolate, leathery, shiny; new leaves, white
FLOWERS	showy; white, with long stamens; clustered in a ball, open for a short time
FRUIT	a legume, to 3 cm (1.2 in.); many fat, beaked pods form in a cluster; 1-seeded
USE	street tree; specimen; public open space; shade tree; specimen; large, bright conservatory
ZONE	11—12

M. browneoides; fresh, white, delicate blooms that resemble *Brownea*.

M. browneoides; limp, white 'handkerchiefs' of new lvs distinguish this New Guinea endemic and signal their presence from a great distance, as they dangle from the tips of the twigs.

M. browneoides; this *Maniltoa*, at the Singapore Botanic Gardens, hangs out its new lvs like damp, white napkins.

M. lenticellata; 'handkerchiefs' do not form a solid mass, but cascade, with the fls from their large, cone-shaped buds.

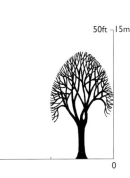

50ft ⌐15m

50ft
15m   0

ORIGIN	Trop. E Africa
HEIGHT	up to 13 m (43 ft)
TYPE	deciduous, small flowering tree
STATUS	not threatened
HABITAT	edges of forests and river banks
GROWTH	fairly fast
FLOWG	year-round
DRY TOL.	moderate
SALT TOL.	low
LIGHT	full sun
SOIL	rich, humid, friable
NUTRIT.	organic fertilizer; deep, organic mulch
HAZARDS	none
PROBLEMS	none
ENVIRON.	bee and insect nectar
PROPAG.	seeds
LEAVES	pinnate; bright green; leaflets 7– 11, oblong, to 20 cm (8 in.); deeply veined
FLOWERS	showy; yellow, throats striped red; small, funnelform trumpets, to 5 cm (2 in.)
FRUIT	capsule, to 130 × 2 cm (51 × 0.8 in.); scaly, ribbed, ribbon-like; with winged seeds
USE	small flowering tree; accent; humid shade garden; large planter; large, bright conservatory
ZONE	10–12

Markhamia lutea

SIALA

(Benth.) K. Schum.   10 spp.

M. hildebrandtii; M. platycalyx

BIGNONIACEAE

MARKHAMIA LUTEA is a superb E African native that develops graceful, often curving, slender trunks and a distinctive, slender, oblong or pyramidal crown. The bark is greyish or reddish brown, flaking in irregular strips and patches. Held in lavish, erect, densely brown-tomentose, terminal panicles, the funnelform, yellow trumpet flowers have their throats spotted and streaked scarlet, resembling *Tabebuia*, to which it is closely related. Typical of the Bignoniaceae family, **M. lutea** has its seeds in long, ribbon-like seed pods, which can be messy, especially as they are produced year-round. Like Tabebuia, the winged seeds are only briefly viable and must be sown fresh. **M. lutea** is perhaps the most widely valued indigenous tree in the high plateaux of the Lake Victoria region in Kenya where, amongst many other uses, it is cut for durable poles used in the process of curing tobacco. It is often left standing on agricultural land because its slender bole and narrow crown do not throw too much shade over the crops and its large leaves are used for mulching. Despite its domestic usefulness, **M. lutea** is widely sought after as an attractive ornamental. Fresh Siala wood is yellow-white, drying to pale, yellow-brown; it is hard, tough, fairly flexible and close-grained.

*** **M. acuminata**; (Schum. ex Engl.), (syn. *M. zanguebarica*), E. Africa, to 10 m (33 ft). Mtawanda is a much-branched tree. Leaves to 30 cm (12 in.); the wood is useful. (10–12)

*** **M. stipulata**; ([Wallich.] Seem.), (syn. *Dolichandrone stipulata*), SE Asia, to 15 m (50 ft). This is a deciduous (rarely evergreen) species; leaflets, to 30 cm (12 in.) long. The inflorescence comprises narrow, unbranched clusters of cream or brownish yellow flowers that have a disagreeable odour and are cupped in brown, velvety calyxes that are split on one side. Var. *pierrii* has yellow flowers, or flowers that are tinged red. (10–12)

M. lutea; this fast-growing sp. quickly develops a slender crown.

M. stipulata var. *pierrii*; this is a red form photographed at Jardin Botanico de Cienfuegos, Cuba.

M. acuminata; an E African native, known there as Mtawanda. It is valued locally for its heartwood.

M. lutea; photographed at Millaa Millaa in N Qld, Australia. This specimen was showing off its sumptuous yellow, funnel-shaped trumpets. They are set in rusty tomentose calyxes.

Melaleuca leucadendra

WEEPING PAPERBARK

(L.) L.   220 spp.

MYRTACEAE

FOUND ALONG BANKS of freshwater streams, lowland wetlands, around lagoons billabongs or seasonally flooded swampy areas, *Melaleuca leucadendra* tolerates a wide variety of soils. This large, wide-spreading tree forms a dense crown of pendulous branches and foliage. From late autumn and through the winter months, this species bears abundant, cylindrical spikes of greenish or creamy white flowers. The genus *Melaleuca*s is closely linked to *Callistemon*, as may be seen from studying the little, nectar-rich 'bottlebrush' blooms; unlike *Callistemon*, the stamens of **M. leucadendra** are in bundles. Its pollen-laden flowers are adored by bees, nectar-loving birds and bats. Like most of the species of this large genus, **M. leucadendra** is named Paperbark for its thick, pale, papery, flaking epidermis that peels, layer upon layer, like dry onion skin. The thick bark insulates the trunk to withstand fire and has been used traditionally by the Australian aborigines for making bedding, shelters, water containers, small canoes, fire tinder and for wrapping corpses. Bark has also been used for packing fruit and as insulation for roofs and boats. **M. leucadendra** is popular in its native Australia, where its shape and size makes it perfect for street planting. In Malaya, it is often clipped into narrow shapes; in Hawaii, it was planted for afforestation. An aromatic infusion is made from the pungent leaves and drunk, inhaled or applied externally for coughs, colds, headaches and general sickness. The timber is used for posts, poles and bush construction. *** **Melaleuca dealbata**; (S.T. Blake), Australia and New Guinea, to 20 m (66 ft). BLUE- or GREY-PAPERBARK, native to low-lying, humid, sandy, silty sites in open woodland and coastal sandstone hills, has blue-grey foliage and densely hairy branchlets and flowers in congested spikes. This species is renowned for its very strong wood that never rots. (10–12)

NOTE: M. leucadendra may escape cultivation in some regions.

ORIGIN	from Malesia and New Guinea to Australia
HEIGHT	up to 30 m (100 ft)
TYPE	evergreen, large flowering tree
STATUS	not threatened
HABITAT	stream banks and swamp margins; in lowland woodlands and heaths
GROWTH	moderately fast
FLOWG	winter (and intermittently)
DRY TOL.	low
SALT TOL.	moderat to high
LIGHT	full sun
SOIL	fertile, water-retentive
NUTRIT.	not normally necessary
HAZARDS	none
PROBLEMS	possibly invasive; brittle
ENVIRON.	nectar for bees, birds and bats
PROPAG.	seeds (minuscule)
LEAVES	simple; greyish green, to 18 × 5 cm (7 × 2 in.); narrow-ovate
FLOWERS	showy; creamy white or greenish; with many stamens crowded terminally into bottlebrush
FRUIT	a capsule, to 0.4 cm (0.2 in.); 3-celled, cup-shaped; seeds extremely small
USE	coastal garden; public open space; street tree; accent; topiary
ZONE	10–12

100ft – 30m
75ft
22.5m   0

M. quinquenervia; the fragile 'bottlebrush' fls are charged with nectar.

M. quinquinervia; photographed growing innocuously in its riverine habitat at Hartley's Creek, N Qld, Australia.

M. quinquenervia; with pale, papery, flaking bark and abundant, nectar-rich fls, it is popular as a street tree in Cairns, Qld.

Melaleuca dealbata; an attractive, large, spreading tree with blue-grey foliage and densely hairy branchlets.

Melaleuca argentea; (W. Fitzg.), Australia and New Guinea, to 20 m (66 ft). SILVER-LEAVED PAPERBARK is a tall, spreading tree, with slender, pendulous branches and silvery green foliage, native to riverbanks in deep, sandy loam. Bark is papery, creamy white to grey. Lvs are silvery and silky hairy when young. Fls are cream to greenish cream; strongly scented. Blooming in winter. Lvs are used by aborigines to flavour meat in cooking. (10–12)

Melaleuca bracteata; (F. Meull.) (syn. *M. genistiifolia*), BLACK TEA TREE is extremely fine-leafed. Two popular cvs are: *M. bracteata* cv. 'Revolution Gold' (above), tall, pyramidal or fastigiate to 5 m (16 ft). Young, golden growth often burns in hot conditions. Prefers subtropics or uplands tropics. Cv. 'Golden Gem' (inset) a smallish, spreading, golden-foliaged shrub, which may develop a serpentine trunk with age. (9–11)

Melaleuca cajeputi; (Powell), from Myanmar to Australia, to 30 m (98 ft). PAPERBARK is native of swampy sites, stream banks and coast. swamp and is a large tree with dense, erect foliage. New lvs are silvery, fls greenish or creamy white. Cajeput Oil, used medicinally like Eucalyptus Oil, is distilled from lvs. Bark is used by aborigines to make shelters, bedding and containers. Popular as a street tree and a specimen. (9–11).

Melaleuca linariifolia; (J.E. Smith), N and E Australia endemic, to 10 m (33 ft). FLAX-LEAFED- or NARROW-LEAFED-PAPERBARK or SNOW-IN-SUMMER is found along the estuaries and streams from NSW to Qld. Over rugged trunks and limbs, this tree forms a spreading canopy of fine, soft, bluish green foliage that, in late spring, is sprinkled with tiny bundles of fluffy white fls. *M. linariifolia* does not tolerate alkaline soil. (9–11)

Melaleuca minutifolia; (Sm.), N Australia endemic, to 10 m (33 ft). This is a fairly rare, multi-branched sp. of the far north of Australia, where it is found in open woodland or in stands on flats and in depressions in shallow, seasonally flooded, gravelly or sandy loams. It usually grows up to 7 m (23 ft), but here a fine old specimen is shown planted in a public open space in Cairns, Qld. *Minutifolia* describes the fine, loosely packed, scaly lvs. The prolific white fls that develop in late spring or summer, are also minute.(10–12)

Melaleuca viridiflora; (Sol. ex Gaertner), northern Australia endemic, to 15 m (50 ft). BROAD-LEAVED PAPERBARK is native of streambanks, swamps, lagoons and billabongs, often forming dense stands in open woodland. Blooms early spring; colour varies greatly from green to cream, white, pink or red (as in inset). Above, is var. 'Burgundy', with narrower, more weeping foliage. The whitish, layered, fibrous papery bark was used by aborigines for tinder, fish traps, cooking and bedding. The typically broad, thick lvs mimic the phyllodes of many trop. Australian acacias and were used to make infusions to treat coughs and colds. (10–12)

Melaleuca quinquenervia; ([Cav.] ST Blake), Malaysia to Australia and New Caledonia, to 30 m (100 ft), these Paperbark trees were photographed in the Everglades in S Florida, USA, where thousands of acres have been invaded by them. In fact, the local government originally 'seeded' the area to dry up the swamps. This species found paradise when its fine sds were further aerially sprayed over the fringes of the Everglades, but now *M. quinquinervia* tops the area's list of invasive plants. As the thick, layered bark insulates the trunk to withstand fire, it established itself after fires swept through native vegetation in New Caledonia, where it has established pure stands and has been proved difficult to eradicate. (10-12)

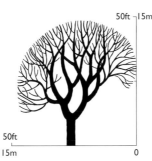

50ft ⌐15m

50ft
15m   0

Melia azedarach

PERSIAN LILAC

L.   3 spp.

M. dubia

MELIACEAE

ORIGIN	from Asia to Australia
HEIGHT	up to 15 m (50 ft)
TYPE	deciduous flowering (fruiting) tree
STATUS	not threatened
HABITAT	dry woodland; cleared land
GROWTH	very fast
FLOWG	intermittently, in tropics
DRY TOL.	high
SALT TOL.	high
LIGHT	full sun
SOIL	well-drained
NUTRIT.	general fertilizer annually
HAZARDS	poison; narcotic fruit; leaves toxic
PROBLEMS	weak-wooded
ENVIRON.	insect nectar; wild fruit for birds
PROPAG.	seeds
LEAVES	2-pinnate; light green, to 80 cm (20 in.); leaflets to 10 cm (4 in.), toothed, pungent
FLOWERS	showy; pale, purplish white; in erect, airy panicles; with purple staminal column; fragrant
FRUIT	a drupe, to 2.5 cm (1 in.); oval, yellow; poisonous to humans
USE	seaside; small flowering tree; specimen; small street tree; coastal civic centre; xerophytic
ZONE	7–12

MELIA AZEDARACH is extremely drought-tolerant, being a pachycaul species, and is grown widely in Arabia and around the Mediterranean. Fast growing, it forms a shapely, conical tree with crowded, abruptly spreading branches that form a rounded or flattened crown of delicate, fern-like foliage. Its 2-pinnate leaves have long-pointed, saw-toothed leaflets that are bitter and pungent when crushed. *M. azedarach* is deciduous and a spring bloomer. Its terminal, branched, long-stalked, flower panicles are attached laterally and bear little, showy, fragrant blooms that have pale purple, slightly coiled petals surrounding a narrow, stout, deep purple, staminal tube. Strangely, the abundant, round, berry-like, golden yellow fruit is extremely poisonous to humans, although it is sought after by birds, especially parrots. In the tropics, where *M. azedarach* seems to outgrow itself, it becomes ungainly and brittle, losing its symmetry and allure. Limbs snap off easily or tend to die back at their tips, especially if it is severely pruned. In the Mediterranean, where it flowers in late spring, it maintains a more compact structure and tolerates drastic pruning. It is appreciated there as much for its profuse, decorative berries, which persist for many months, as for its flowers. Known in its region as Ceylon Cedar or Mahogany, the heartwood, which is hard, durable and attractively marked, but susceptible to dry-wood termites, is used for construction. The bark and leaves have many medicinal and insecticidal applications, including for skin diseases and fever. They are also used to make a tonic. The leaves are used for fodder, the bark yields a red dye and fibre is stripped to make rope. In Australia, *M. azedarach* var. *australasica* (C. DC.), is one of the few deciduous trees and is known as White Cedar. It is often stripped in late summer by caterpillars.

NOTE: *M. azedarach* has proved invasive in many lowland regions.

M. azedarach; fr. is toxic to humans, but not to birds.

M. azedarach; in the Mediterranean, it maintains a more compact structure and even seems to tol. drastic pruning.

M. azedarach; this relatively short-lived small tree quickly forms a soft, billowing mass. It resents pruning of old wood.

M. azedarach; Persian Lilac has sweetly fragrant, pale lilac fls that have a deep violet staminal tube. A preparation of these blooms is used as an insecticide in some regions.

271

Melicoccus bijugatus

SPANISH LIME

Jacq.   2 spp.

SAPINDACEAE

ORIGIN	Trop. America
HEIGHT	up to 20 m (66 ft)
TYPE	evergreen fruiting tree
STATUS	not threatened
HABITAT	dry, coastal limestone woodland
GROWTH	slow
FLOW'G	spring
DRY TOL.	high
SALT TOL.	high
LIGHT	full sun
SOIL	fertile, well-drained
NUTRIT.	balanced fertilizer annually
HAZARDS	slippery fruit
PROBLEMS	citrus black fly; root rot
ENVIRON.	bee nectar; wild bird fruit
PROPAG.	seeds; layers; grafting
LEAVES	pinnate; dullish, light green; leaflets in 4 pairs; elliptic; with winged axis
FLOWERS	inconspicuous; greenish white; in crowded, long-stemmed clusters; fragrant
FRUIT	a drupe, to 3 cm (1.2 in.); with a globose, green, thin, shell-like skin; juicy, translucent, jelly-like pulp
USE	seaside; shade tree; street tree; specimen; xerophytic
ZONE	10–12

MELICOCCUS BIJUGATUS is a distinctive species, native to Colombia, Venezuela and the Guianas and is also very common in the W Indies, where it mostly known as Genip. This classic species has a robust, smooth, pale grey trunk with a skin-like bark, orange-brown, gritty, inner bark and a distinctive, dense, compact, evergreen globe of greyish green leaves, each with a slightly winged axis. At once drab and refined, *M. bijugatus* has the ability to weather the strongest seaside storms and to endure the direst of droughts. Curiously, this species may be either hermaphroditic (bisexual), having male and female flowers on the same inflorescence, or dioecious, with the sexes on separate trees. Swathed in bees, the abundant, small, whitish, honey-fragrant spring flowers are held in little, erect, spikey racemes. They are followed by green, leathery and crispy-skinned, small, round fruit, held in drooping, grape-like clusters. This has yellow to salmon-orange, gelatinous, sweet, edible flesh, containing 1–2 large seeds that are edible when roasted. A Spanish Lime fruit of good quality resembles a small lychee and tells of the close family relationship. There is a caution, however. Because the fruit are very jelly-like, slippery and about the size of a large marble, they are a choking hazard to small children. Regionally, a decoction is made from the bark and used to alieviate dysentery. The sapwood is light brown and the heartwood light brown or pale, yellow-grey, of medium weight and fairly hard, but reportedly not resistant to decay. It has, however, found some use for cabinetwork. *M. bijugatus* develops slowly, taking 7–10 years to produce fruit from seed or 4–5 years from vegetative reproduction. The fruit takes from 90–150 days to mature. These trees dislike hard pruning and if damaged by hurricanes, take a long time to recover. These are an important honey plants.

M. bijugatus; long-stemmed, greenish white fragrant fls.

M. bijugatus; are popularly eaten out-of-hand but the jelly-like flesh is very slippery, about the size of marbles, and may block the windpipe to choke a small child.

M. bijugatus; with a distinctively rounded mop of tough, drought- and salt-resistant, everg. foliage.

M. bijugatus; a robust smooth, skin-like, pale grey trunk with orange-brown, gritty, inner bark.

ORIGIN	from India to Malay Peninsula
HEIGHT	up to 18 m (60 ft)
TYPE	evergreen foliage tree
STATUS	vulnerable
HABITAT	evergreen humid forests
GROWTH	slow
FLOWG	spring and autumn
DRY TOL.	moderate
SALT TOL.	moderate
LIGHT	full sun or bright shade
SOIL	rich, slightly acid
NUTRIT.	magnesium-rich fertilizer; deep, organic mulch
HAZARDS	toxic resin
PROBLEMS	none
ENVIRON.	bee and insect nectar
PROPAG.	fresh seeds; misted cuttings
LEAVES	simple; deep green; to 15 cm (6 in.); lanceolate, leathery; new leaves are Venetian red
FLOWERS	showy; white; with 4 petals; many yellow stamens; sweetly fragrant
FRUIT	a drupe, to 5 cm (2 in.); spherical, with woody rind; persistent stigma at tip and calyxes at base
USE	small flowering tree; small street tree; specimen; large planter; civic centre; accent; bonsai subject
ZONE	10—12

100ft – 30m
75ft
22.5m   0

Mesua ferrea

POACHED EGG TREE

L.   40 spp.

GUTTIFERAE

IN ITS YOUTH, THIS SLOW-GROWING tropical Asian tree has a neat, densely conical shape, developing into a more oval or oblong form after many years. In autumn and again in spring, the leathery, long-pointed leaves are brilliant, waxy, Venetian red when they first emerge, igniting the tree with their vibrancy and giving the impression at a distance that the tree is in full, fiery bloom. As they mature, the leaves become bright green, with pearly white tomen on the undersides. The flowers of **Mesua ferrea** closely resemble those of *Mammea americana* (also Guttiferae) and are exceptionally attractive, being fairly large, with white, waxy petals, a profusion of golden, thread-like stamens in their centre and a sweet fragrance, reminiscent of face powder. In India, these blooms, which are considered to arouse sexual desire, are dried and put into cotton sachets for scenting clothes and for filling the pillows of bridal beds. They are also considered to have medical properties. The aromatic stamens are prepared for fever and the buds for dysentery. In Indonesia, extracts are prepared and given to help mental disturbance. The 1-celled fruit is the size of a golf ball and has a pointed tip, with its base enclosed in fleshy sepals. It has a woody rind and contains up to 4 seeds. Locally, Nahur oil is extracted from the oily, pulpy fruit and used as a lubricant, for domestic illumination and to alieviate skin diseases. Resin from the bark, which is slightly toxic, is used to make varnish. Medically, it has found use as a heart stimulant, for treating anaemia and for its anti-inflammatory and antibacterial properties. The timber is, like Lignum Vitae, renowned for its iron-like qualities: close-grained, very hard and reddish brown, **M. ferrea** wood has proved suitable in its region for railway sleepers and heavy machinery parts. This tree is considered sacred in India and is frequently planted near temples, where the fragrant blooms are picked for offerings. This is a honey plant.

M. *ferrea*; with a fragrance of face powder.

M. *ferrea*; the new lvs, Venetian-red when they first emerge, ignite the tree with their vibrancy.

M. *ferrea*; golf ball-sized, the 1-celled fr. has a pointed tip and its base is enclosed in fleshy sepals.

M. *ferrea*; at Fairchild Tropical Gardens, Miami, Florida, this tree appears to be in full bloom, with its extravagant display of new foliage. Sadly, it was removed to make way for a new visitors' centre.

273

Metrosideros polymorpha

OHI'A

Gaudich.

50 spp.

M. collina subsp. *polymorpha*

MYRTACEAE

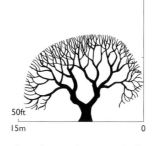

50ft ─ 15m

50ft

15m   0

ORIGIN	Hawaii, endemic
HEIGHT	up to 30 m (100 ft)
TYPE	evergreen, large (or small) flowering tree
STATUS	vulnerable
HABITAT	volcanic rainforests
GROWTH	fairly slow
FLOWG	summer
DRY TOL.	low
SALT TOL.	moderate to high
LIGHT	full sun
SOIL	fertile, acid loam
NUTRIT.	magnesium-rich fertilizer
HAZARDS	none
PROBLEMS	caterpillars
ENVIRON.	nectar for birds
PROPAG.	seeds; layers
LEAVES	simple; grey-green, silvery pubescent; leathery; obovate to orbicular, with yellow petioles and veins
FLOWERS	showy; rich red; with 5 petals and sepals; large brushes of red stamens; nectar-filled
FRUIT	a capsule, 3-celled, to 9 mm (0.3 in.); leathery; with minuscule seeds
USE	seaside; small flowering tree; specimen; collection; large planter; bonsai subject
ZONE	9–11

CLOSELY ALLIED WITH *Syzygiums*, the *Metrosideros* genus is found on volcanic soils from S Africa and E Malaysia to Australia and the Pacific. Fairly slow growing, the Hawaiian endemic **Metrosideros polymorpha** may attain great heights in rainforest areas amongst giant tree ferns or remain as a prostrate shrub. It develops a solid, rugged trunk with its limbs covered in dark, fissured or flaky bark and a relatively open canopy of greyish or yellow-green foliage. The leaves are leathery, rounded and variously silvery grey pubescent, especially the new growth. Billowing pompoms of rich red, staminous flowers decorate the silvery, new growth in the winter and midsummer months. They are laden with sweet nectar and are a critical food source for several Hawaiian honeycreepers, especially the 'I'iwa, with its colour-coordinated, scarlet plumage. **M. polymorpha** leaf is resistant to volcanic fumes as their stomata have the ability to close. They are also popular locally for use in making leis. **M. polymorpha** is one of the most spectacular, native trees of Hawaii and is its most abundant native species, especially on the Big Island and on Kauai, where it is found from the dry lowlands to sub-alpine and volcanic elevations. Ohi'a wood was once considered sacred and was used exclusively for carving temple images and war gods; using it for other purposes could result in execution. There are 8 varieties of this species recorded in the islands and a number of varieties of this species are recognized.

*** **M. excelsus**; (Sol. & Gaertn.), (syn. *M. tomentosus*), New Zealand endemic, to 20 m (66 ft). POHUTUKAWA or CHRISTMAS TREE is smothered in brilliant crimson blooms in summer, which is Christmas-time in New Zealand, and has been considered to be amongst the most spectacular of all woody flowering plants. It has densely white-tomentose branchlets and small, ovate, coriaceous leaves with recurved margins and is densely grey felty below. **M. excelsus** will survive coastal conditions provided the soil is not saline. (9–11)

M. polymorpha; with rounded, silvery grey, felty emergent lvs.

M. polymorpha; these red, pompom blooms are engorged with sweet juices to entice their pollinators – small, nectar-loving birds and butterflies will perform this function.

M. polymorpha; a well-established small, bushy form photographed at Foster Gardens in Honolulu, Hawaii.

M. polymorpha; with a rugged trunk and limbs covered in dark, sooty grey, fissured or flaky bark.

ORIGIN	Himalayas, India and China
HEIGHT	up to 35 m (115 ft)
TYPE	evergreen, large flowering tree
STATUS	becoming rare
HABITAT	humid evergreen forest
GROWTH	fast
FLOWG	spring to autumn
DRY TOL.	moderate
SALT TOL.	low
LIGHT	sheltered sun
SOIL	rich, slightly acid
NUTRIT.	organic fertilizer; deep, organic mulch
HAZARDS	none
PROBLEMS	scales; sooty mould
ENVIRON.	moth nectar
PROPAG.	seeds; misted cuttings
LEAVES	simple; deep green, to 28 × 11 cm (11 × 4.5 in.); long-ovate, glossy
FLOWERS	showy; creamy white to deep yellow; waxy, Magnolia-like; very fragrant
FRUIT	a capsule; oval, greyish brown; in pendent bundles on sturdy stalks; seeds black, with a bright red aril
USE	flowering tree; humid shade garden; accent; courtyard; large planter; conservatory
ZONE	10–12

100ft – 30m
100ft
30m
0

Michelia champaca

CHAMPAK

L.   30 spp.

MAGNOLIACEAE

MICHELIA CHAMPAKA is a member of the renowned *Magnolia* family. It is a splendid species with pale, smooth bark and a rounded crown of dark, glossy, deep-green foliage. *M. champaca* begins to bloom in mid spring, continuing until the onset of winter. The light orange or deep yellow, many-petalled flowers resemble little, shaggy *Magnolia* — to which they are closely related — and are intensely perfumed, especially at night, when they are redolent of fragrant incense. Greyish brown, warty-spotted fruit, held in large, pendent bundles on stout cords, split open when they are ripe to release their small, black seeds, which are enveloped in bright scarlet arils. *M. champaca* is held in special reverence by the Hindus and is considered sacred to the god, Vishnu. It is commonly planted around Hindu and Jain temples. In Combatore, in India, so great is the reputed sanctity of the tree that nobody wearing shoes is permitted to approach under its shadow. The flowers yield the celebrated Champac perfume. They are also prepared to treat kidney disease and to relieve inflamed eyes. The fine-grained heartwood is dark purple when freshly cut, turning brown as it dries. It is considered an excellent building timber and is also a popular material for making tea boxes and furniture and for sacred carvings. It is also used for domestic fuel. For these reasons, this species is becoming rare in the wild.

✳✳✳ *M.* var. *alba* (D.C.), Java endemic. Small tree with white flowers, called PAKLAN in China or PAKALANA in Hawaii. This attractive variety is of uncertain origin, possibly a hybrid between *M. champaca* and *M. montana*. It rarely sets seed. (10–12)

✳✳✳ *M. figo*; ([Lour.] Spreng.), China endemic, to 5 m (16 ft). BANANA SHRUB is an evergreen, tall, much-branched shrub. The flowers are banana scented. Fairly cold-tolerant. (9–11)

NOTE: this genus does not tolerate root disturbance.

M. champaca var. *alba*; has smaller, white fls and purple stamens.

M. figo; a cold-tol. small tree or shrub with miniature, Magnolia-like blooms with a strong banana scent.

M. champaca; bundles of warty, spotted grey fr. opening to reveal black sds enveloped in fleshy red arils.

M. champaca; is a densely foliaged small tree covered in intensely fragrant, golden blooms from spring to autumn. It is not difficult to see their affinity with Magnolias.

275

Millettia pinnata

PONGAM

(L.) Pierre   90 spp.

Millettia pinnata

FABACEAE (Papilionoideae)

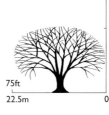

MILLETTIA PINNATA is a good-looking, well-groomed tree found naturally in mangrove forests and humid river flats. The spreading, bouffant crown is splendidly, symmetrically rounded, with its branches arched in a graceful manner. Deep, rich green leaves are widely ovate and polished, giving **M. pinnata** a healthy, vigorous appearance, while the racemes of little, pendent, pea-like, pinkish mauve flowers with purplish brown calyxes are gently scented. At their best, they may be quite lavish and have been described as wisteria-like. Despite their appeal, they are short-lived and soon followed by inflated, pointed, oval, woody seed capsules, which are undoubtedly a displeasing feature of this otherwise impeccable tree. The poisonous, triangular fruit tend to be messy and, being pebble-like, are a nuisance underfoot on paths or lawns. Their fecundity may also be unwelcome – they germinate rapidly wherever they fall. However, **M. pinnata** provides more than intrinsic beauty. In India, the seeds are pressed to yield a red oil, Pongam oil, which burns well and is used as a fuel for lamps, as well as an insecticide. The juice of the roots has antiseptic qualities and is applied to sores or is used for cleaning teeth and strengthening gums. The smooth, grey bark exudes a black gum. A preparation of the bark is used in the Orient to treat poisoned wounds and as an embrocation for skin problems. The seeds and roots are said to poison fish and are used to stun them, although they have not been reported as being fatal to man. Locally, the hard, yellowish wood is not considered durable, but is used regionally for domestic fuel. The leaves and young growth are fed to cattle and other animals, especially in times of drought. **M. pinnata** is a honey plant.

NOTE: *M. pinnata* was known as *Pongamia pinnata* – potentially invasive in Florida, USA.

ORIGIN	from Indo-Malaysia to Australia
HEIGHT	up to 15 m (50 ft)
TYPE	semi-deciduous foliage and flowering tree
STATUS	not threatened
HABITAT	humid coastal forests and river valleys
GROWTH	fast
FLOWG	spring to autumn
DRY TOL.	high
SALT TOL.	moderate to high
LIGHT	full sun
SOIL	widely tolerant
NUTRIT.	balanced fertilizer annually; organic mulch
HAZARDS	toxic fruit
PROBLEMS	messy fruit; caterpillars
ENVIRON.	bee nectar
PROPAG.	seeds
LEAVES	pinnate; rich green to 45 cm (18 in.); leaflets 5–9, glossy, ovate, slightly foetid
FLOWERS	showy; pinkish mauve or white; set in purplish brown calyxes; held in narrow racemes, to 12.5 cm (5 in.)
FRUIT	a legume, to 5 cm (2 in.); oblique, woody; indehiscent; held on stout stalks
USE	seaside; small shade tree; street tree; screening; civic centre; xerophytic
ZONE	10–12

M. pinnata; with tough, fecund, pebbly, messy fr.

M. pinnata; while not spectacular, the little pea-like, Pongam fls are lavish and short-lived, but pleasantly perfumed to attract honeybees. This sp. is grown mostly for its foliage.

M. pinnata; has a symmetrically rounded, spreading crown.

M. pinnata; a preparation of the bark is used in the Orient to treat poisoned wounds.

(1) **Millettia atropurpurea**; ([Wall.] Benth.), (syn. *Whitfordiodendron pubescens*), India to Sumatra, to 30m (100ft). PURPLE MILLETTIA is very closely related to *Andira inermis*, this widespread, Asian tree has been renamed several times in fairly quick succession, although it is still often found in botanic gardens around the tropics labelled with its old name, *M. atropurpurea*. Native of poor, stony, laterite soils, it is slow at first but grows quite rapidly once established. *M. atropurpurea* is easily recognized by its neat, densely cylindrical crown of pinnate lvs that is often low to the ground. (2) Blooms after a long dry period, the large, pea-like, dark purple blooms are held in tightly packed infl., mostly hidden within the canopy; spent blooms carpet the ground below the tree, testimony to its hidden beauty. (3) The fr. that follows is very large, to 19 x 6.5 cm (7.5 x 2.5 in.), dehiscent, leathery with 1 or 2 large sds per pod. (4) **Millettia dura**; (Don.), E Africa, to 13 m (43 ft). MWANGA (Kenya), a slow-growing sp., which grows as a shrub or small tree, is found in secondary scrub or at the forest edge. All parts are rusty velvety when young. Fls are held in drooping panicles. Wood is tough and used for hoe handles. (10–12)

NOTE: *Millettia atropurpurea* is now known as *Callerya atropurpurea*.

Millingtonia hortensis

CORK TREE

L. f   1 sp.

M. pinnata

BIGNONIACEAE

100ft ⌐ 30m

75ft

22.5m   0

BECAUSE OF ITS SPEEDY GROWTH and ease of culture, *Millingtonia hortensis* is extensively cultivated as a street tree and ornamental in most of India and countries bordering the Arabian Sea. This is a tall, lean, stately tree with a high, elongated crown of erect limbs, which rise vertically from the straight axis of the trunk. As they stretch upwards, their flexible tips droop downwards, giving the tree a slender, graceful outline. Because the foliage and inflorescence are lightly covered with a waxy, silvery white pubescence, the tree tends to have an ethereal quality, especially when it shimmers in the breeze. Cracked and furrowed with corky fissures, the yellowish bark peels away easily and in Asia an inferior cork is made from this. Although a member of Bignoniaceae, the foliage and slender-tubed flowers strongly resemble those of jasmine. In late spring and again in autumn, the tree is luminous with profuse sprays of starry white, delicately fragrant, nocturnal blooms. As they are visited by their pollinators, they deepen to yellow and abort but do not fall, as they are caught on the sturdy stigma and remain suspended for several days. Finally, they float down to form a starry carpet underneath the tall, misty giant. *M. hortensis*, while never quite leafless, loses some of its foliage during the dry period, usually in spring. Although easily transplanted, even when quite large this tree has shallow roots and brittle wood and is easily damaged in high winds. For this reason, it should be planted in a sheltered position. *M. hortensis* is mostly propagated from suckers, although the resulting shape may be less desirable than that produced by seed. However, in some regions, where the pollinating moth is absent, the tree does not form fruit. This species blooms when only about 3 m (10 ft). The dried leaves have been used as an inferior substitute for opium, and the fragrant flowers are sometimes added to the final rinsing water when washing hair.

ORIGIN	from SE Asia to Philippines
HEIGHT	up to 26 m (85 ft)
TYPE	evergreen flowering tree
STATUS	not threatened
HABITAT	humid lowland forests
GROWTH	fast
FLOWG	late spring and autumn
DRY TOL.	high
SALT TOL.	moderate
LIGHT	full, sheltered sun
SOIL	fertile, well-drained
NUTRIT.	balanced fertilizer annually
HAZARDS	none
PROBLEMS	shallow roots; brittle wood; suckering
ENVIRON.	bat and moth nectar
PROPAG.	seeds; large cuttings of limbs; suckers (root cuttings)
LEAVES	3-pinnate; rich green; to 1 m (3.3 ft); leaflets to 6 × 3 cm (2.5 × 1.2 in.), elliptic
FLOWERS	showy; white, pale yellow in age; tubular, to 5 cm (2 in.); nocturnally fragrant
FRUIT	a capsule, to 35 × 2 cm (14 × 0.8 in.); linear, flat; seeds winged
USE	street tree; public open space; specimen; xerophytic
ZONE	10—12

M. hortensis; large, slender, Jasmine-like blooms.

M. hortensis; a fast-growing Cork tree near the historic Holttum Hall at Singapore Botanic Gardens. This tree demonstrates the narrow, upward thrusting growth of this sp.

M. hortensis; even the ferny, 2-pinnate lvs are strongly reminiscent of Jasmine.

M. hortensis; bark is cracked and furrowed with corky fissures; yellowish bark peels away easily and is used as cork in Asia.

ORIGIN	from India to the Pacific
HEIGHT	up to 15 m (50 ft)
TYPE	evergreen foliage (fruiting) tree
STATUS	not threatened
HABITAT	humid lowland forests
GROWTH	moderate
FLOWG	year-round
DRY TOL.	moderate
SALT TOL.	moderate
LIGHT	full sun
SOIL	humid, fertile
NUTRIT.	high-nitrogen fertilizer; deep, organic mulch
HAZARDS	none
PROBLEMS	none
ENVIRON.	bee nectar
PROPAG.	seeds; misted cuttings
LEAVES	simple; deep green; to 16 × 7.5 cm (6.5 × 3 in.); oblong-elliptic; with wavy margins
FLOWERS	inconspicuous; whitish; to 1.5 cm (0.6 in.); petals are brown-papery in age; very fragrant
FRUIT	a berry, to 2.5 cm (1 in.); ovoid or globose; sweetish, floury, edible
USE	small shade tree; street tree; public open space; civic centre; screening
ZONE	10–12

100ft – 30m
75ft
22.5m — 0

Mimusops elengi

SPANISH CHERRY

L.   41 spp.

SAPOTACEAE

MIMUSOPS ELENGI, a vigorous, evergreen Asian species, is widely grown for its classically dense, fine-textured, dark green, spherical crown of oval leaves over a sturdy trunk. Small, nodding, drab white, papery flowers are hidden in the foliage, but they have a pungently sweet fragrance to attracts the attention of bees. Although a member of the large, bountiful Sapotaceae, renowned for its exotic fruit, **M. elengi** has little to offer in this regard, just a small, ovoid, orange-red berry with floury, yellow, edible but insipid pulp. **M. elengi** provides generously in other ways and has been widely distributed throughout the tropics and subtropics for its adaptability and usefulness. Its flowers are popular in India for making festive garlands and for filling pillows, as they retain their sweet scent long after they have been dried; perfume is sometimes distilled from them. In its native region, a bitter tonic is extracted from the bark and used to treat snakebite and in the distillation of an alcoholic beverage, Arrack. Oil is obtained from the seeds and is used to make paint, as well as for cooking and burning. A preparation of bark is prescribed to treat fevers, scabies and eczema. In W Africa, a brown dye is extracted from the bark. The Australian form of **M. elengi** differs in having flat leaf margins, smaller, spherical fruit and a more layered growth. This is a honey plant.
*** **M. caffra,** (E. Mey. ex DC.), S Africa endemic, to 10 m (33 ft), MILKWOOD is very wind-resistant, with small, diamond-shaped leaves, and is commonly planted as windbreaks. The flowers are whitish; the ovoid fruit is scarlet when ripe. (9–11)

NOTE: *Mimusops* was once included in *Manilkara*. The genus *Mimusops* extends from Africa, Madagascar and Asia to Australia and the Pacific. It differs from the genus *Manilkara* (pan-tropical) in having 4-parted flowers, while *Manilkara's* are 3-parted.

M. elengi; tiny blooms are popular for making festive garlands in India.

M. caffra; known as Milkwood, the little ovoid fr. of this sp. is golden yellow turning scarlet on ripening.

M. elengi; olive-like, with sweet, insipid, floury pulp.

M. elengi; at the wonderful Fruit and Spice Park in Homestead, S Florida. This specimen shows the classic, spherical form of this everg. sp. that makes it so popular for planting.

Monodora myristica

CALABASH NUTMEG

(Gaertn.) Dunal. 15 spp.

ANNONACEAE

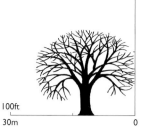

IN ITS RAIN FOREST AND RIVERBANK HABITATS, this exotic African cousin of the Custard Apple grows up to 30 m (100 ft), with a huge, lush crown supported by a grey-barked trunk that, with age, becomes vertically corrugated with distinctly rounded ridges. The huge, oblong leaves of *Monodora myristica* are particularly handsome. They emerge purple but turn deep, rich green, satiny glaucous above and pale, metallic green below, with prominent veins and a stout, purplish petiole. *M. myristica* deservedly ranks as one of the most renowned tropical species for its fragrant blooms that are unsurpassed in beauty and originality. Like festive decorations, these curious blooms dangle on long, sturdy cords, which are actually modified twigs. They abort if the flower is not fertilized, or thicken and become woody if it is. Typical of its clan, the flowers are heavily waxy and composed of 3 calyx lobes and 3 petals, set in 2 whorls. Somewhat reminiscent of an orchid, the arching, yellowish calyx lobes are crisply frilled, their margins edged and splotched with deep red, while the petals are paler with purplish red spots. Slightly cupped, they form a canopy over the crowded stamens and stout pistils, eventually uniting to create a 1-celled ovary, which evolves into a large, woody syncarp fruit that is filled with aromatic pulp. In their region, the large, pungent seeds embedded within are used like nutmeg to flavour food, or are roasted, ground and applied to heal wounds or to the forehead to relieve headaches. In cultivation, however, *M. myristica* mostly lacks its beetle pollinator, thus seldom setting fruit.

*** *M. crispata*; (Engl. & Diels), (syn. *M. angolensis*), Trop. W. Africa, to 9 m (30 ft). Shrub or tree; leaves ovate, to 8 cm (20 in.). The outer petals are purple-variegated, the inner petals are long clawed; the sepals are lanceolate, the margins are crispate, rose and white. (10–12)

ORIGIN	Trop. Africa
HEIGHT	10–30 m (33–100 ft)
TYPE	deciduous, large or small flowering and fruiting tree
STATUS	not threatened
HABITAT	humid, lowland river valleys
GROWTH	moderate
FLOWG	late spring to summer
DRY TOL.	moderate to high
SALT TOL.	low
LIGHT	sheltered sun or bright shade
SOIL	deep, fertile loam
NUTRIT.	organic fertilizer; deep, organic mulch
HAZARDS	none
PROBLEMS	possible suckers
ENVIRON.	insect and bat nectar
PROPAG.	seeds; root cuttings (suckers); layers
LEAVES	simple; deep green, glaucous below, to 35 × 18 cm (14 × 7 in.); obovate
FLOWERS	showy; yellowish, marked purple-red; petals frilled; fragrant
FRUIT	a syncarp, to 30 cm (12 in.) diam.; woody, black; seeds, many, in fragrant pulp
USE	small or large flowering tree; humid shade garden; specimen; large planter; large conservatory
ZONE	10–12

M. myristica; superb young lvs that are satin-finished.

M. myristica; with a lush, rounded, dark green canopy.

M. myristica; a grey-barked trunk, which with age, becomes vertically corrugated with distinctly rounded ridges.

M. myristica; with exotic, silky, orchid-like fls dangled on stout, cord-like stems for their bat pollinators. This tree blooms at Jardin Botanico de Cienfuegos, Cuba, but does not fr.

ORIGIN	Puerto Rico, endemic
HEIGHT	up to 16 m (53 ft)
TYPE	evergreen flowering tree
STATUS	endangered
HABITAT	moist limestone woodland and swampland
GROWTH	moderate
FLOWG	year-round
DRY TOL.	moderate
SALT TOL.	low
LIGHT	full sun
SOIL	fertile, well-drained
NUTRIT.	balanced fertilizer annually; deep, organic mulch
HAZARDS	none
PROBLEMS	bollworm beetle
ENVIRON.	moth and bee nectar
PROPAG.	seeds; cuttings
LEAVES	simple; rich green; to 20 cm (8 in.); cordate, long-petioled
FLOWERS	showy; crimson to pink, orange-tan externally, to 15 cm (6 in.); stamens spiralled in staminal column
FRUIT	a capsule, to 2 cm (0.8 in.); ovoid; succulent when young, dry when mature; indehiscent
USE	shade tree; small street tree; public open space; specimen
ZONE	10—11

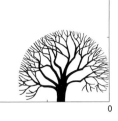

100ft — 30m

100ft
30m

0

Montezuma speciosissima

MAGA

Mocino & Sesse ex DC   1 sp.

Thespesia grandiflora

MALVACEAE (formerly Bombacaceae)

MONTEZUMA SPECIOSISSIMA, a luxuriant monospecific endemic of confused nomenclature, is the national tree of Puerto Rico. It is a vigorous, large-leafed tree, greatly resembling Seaside Mahoe (*Hibiscus tiliaceus*), with similar, heart-shaped leaves and soft, lax growth and rough, grey or brown and deeply furrowed bark on the trunks of larger trees. It is, however, the gorgeous, large, heavily petalled, rich, pinkish red, pink and white or, occasionally, pure white Hibiscus-like flowers that have made this tree so beloved and famous in Puerto Rico, where it is known as Maga. When *M. speciosissima* was first described by Spanish botanists, they had mixed up its herbarium specimens with their Mexican collections. In the ensuing confusion, they named the genus *Montezuma* in honour of the Aztec ruler in Mexico at the time of the Spanish Conquest. *M. speciosissima* was originally included in the Malvaceae – not surprising given its strong resemblance to the *Hibiscus*. Later, it was redesignated as being a monospecific member of the Bombacaceae, before these 2 families were finally united and this species was included once more in Malvaceae. This surely demonstrates the close association of these 2 great families. *M. speciosissima* has been widely planted in Puerto Rico as a street tree and in forest plantations. A few years ago, however, planting of this national treasure was ceased as it was found to host the bollworm beetle. The heartwood of *M. speciosissima* is a rich, chocolate-brown, heavy, fine-textured and very durable. Like *Hibiscus tiliaceus*, it has loose, fibrous bark on the young limbs and traditionally this has been stripped for use as cordage. The trees were found to sprout from stumps and, when coppiced, to produce long, vigorous shoots to provide quantities of fibre. This is a honey plant.

NOTE: recently, taxonomists have included the Bombacaceae family in Malvaceae.

M. speciosissima; differentiated by its cupped calyx and twisted staminal column.

M. speciosissima; rough bark is grey or brown and deeply furrowed on large trees.

M. speciosissima; one could be forgiven for confusing this Puerto Rican endemic with *Hibiscus tiliaceus* (Mahoe).

M. speciosissima; the thin-textured, heart-shaped lvs are long-petioled, as are the drooping, deep pink blooms, which are held terminally.

Morinda citrifolia

NONI

L.   80 spp.

M. quadrangularis
RUBIACEAE

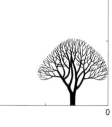

50ft ⌐15m

50ft
15m   0

MORINDA CITRIFOLIA is a dramatically foliaged, evergreen species of wastelands, pastures and sandy coasts. With its stout, 4-angled stems and shrubby habit of growth, this member of the *Gardenia* tribe is often so common in the lowland tropics as to go largely unnoticed or appreciated. In fact, **M. citrifolia** is a most desirable ornamental. It has great, rich green, deeply quilted leaves, tiny, white, waxy flowers held in slim, crowded panicles and bizarre, juicy, multiple fruit (syncarp), which is milky white, has a curious, cheese-like odour and resembles a scrubbed new potato. Although not very palatable, it is edible and is fed to pigs. Apart from its good looks, **M. citrifolia** has long been recognized for its healing properties and is used medicinally in all tropical regions. In the W Indies, where it was introduced long ago and it is known as Painkiller, the leaf is heated or wilted and pressed on painful swellings, a poultice of leaves is applied to wounds or to the head for headaches or crushed leaves are mixed in lard or camphor oil and are put on the face for the treatment of neuralgia or head colds. Recently, there has been a surge of interest in **M. citrifolia** as a homoeopathic cure-all, resulting in its being cultivated as a cash crop, particularly in Hawaii. In India, this species is cropped for its bark, which yields a permanent red dye known as Turkey Red, using *Symplocos racemosa*, which accumulates aluminium, as its mordant. It is used to print fabric.
*** var. *variegata*; green leaves boldly splashed with creamy white.
*** **M. reticulata**; (Benth.), N Qld, Australia, endemic, to 4 m (13 ft). MAPOON BUSH, a scrambling shrub of monsoon forests, is included to show the diversity of this genus. Like other Rubiaceae, it has enlarged bracts. The Aborigines used it as a dye plant and as a contraceptive. It is propagated from root cuttings, suckers and seeds. (10–12)

ORIGIN	from Trop. Asia to Australia
HEIGHT	up to 7 m (23 ft)
TYPE	evergreen, small fruiting tree
STATUS	not threatened
HABITAT	beach and lowland monsoon scrub on limestone wasteland; beach rainforest
GROWTH	moderate
FLOWG	year-round
DRY TOL.	high
SALT TOL.	high
LIGHT	full sun to part shade
SOIL	well-drained
NUTRIT.	a little organic fertilizer
HAZARDS	none
PROBLEMS	none
ENVIRON.	insect nectar
PROPAG.	seeds; cuttings
LEAVES	simple; deep green, paler below; to 2 5 × 12 cm (10 × 4.7 in.); oblong to elliptic
FLOWERS	inconspicuous; white; sessile, in dense, axillary panicles
FRUIT	a syncarp, to 13 cm (5.1 in.); whitish or greenish yellow; slightly translucent
USE	seaside; screening; accent; container; large planter; backyard tree; xerophytic; conservatory
ZONE	10–12

M. citrifolia; a dramatically foliaged sp. of wastelands, pastures and sandy coasts.

M. citrifolia; Noni has potato-like, medicinal fr., which has recently enjoyed great interest in the field of homoeopathy as a cure-all.

M. citrifolia var. *variegata*; a most desirable ornamental, which is much smaller than the regular sp.

M. reticulata; an endemic, scrambling shrub of Australian monsoon forests with showy, snowy bracts.

ORIGIN	Trop. Asia
HEIGHT	up to 10 m (33 ft)
TYPE	evergreen or deciduous flowering tree
STATUS	not threatened
HABITAT	dry coastal forests and cleared land
GROWTH	fast
FLOWG	year-round
DRY TOL.	very high
SALT TOL.	moderate
LIGHT	full sun
SOIL	very well-drained
NUTRIT.	low
HAZARDS	none
PROBLEMS	none
ENVIRON.	bird and bee nectar
PROPAG.	seeds; cuttings
LEAVES	2–3 pinnate; light green; to 45 cm (18 in.); feathery, thin-textured
FLOWERS	showy; creamy white; held in large, terminal racemes; fragrant
FRUIT	a capsule, to 50 × 1.5 cm (20 × 0.6 in.); 3-sided, dehiscent, light brown
USE	seaside; small flowering tree; coastal street tree; specimen; xerophytic
ZONE	10–12

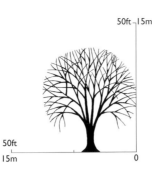

50ft–15m

50ft
15m
0

Moringa oleifera

HORSERADISH TREE

Lam.   12 spp.

M. pterygosperma

MORINGACEAE

MORINGA OLEIFERA is a fast-growing, long-lived, xerophytic pachycaul tree that may have an obese bole with age. Widely planted for ornament, it forms a spreading canopy of brittle limbs and delicate, light green, 3-pinnately compound, feathery foliage. Year round, it produces panicles of cream, fragrant blooms, quickly followed by large, 3-angled, bean-like pods. All parts of *M. oleifera* are edible and consumed, even the honey-scented flowers, which are added to stews. The tender, green, softly ferny leaves are eaten as spinach or salad, while the young, fat, ribbed fruit, known as Drumsticks, are filled with sweet, edible peas and the young pods are used raw or boiled as an ingredient of Madras Drumstick Curry. (When boiled, they are said to have the flavour of Asparagus.) *M. oleifera* is useful in many other ways: the scraped root is an excellent substitute for horseradish; the wood exudes a gum that is white at first, but later turns yellow then dark, red-brown and is used like gum tragacanth as a demulcent in confectionery and cough syrups. The oily, dried, winged seeds yield an important edible oil known as Ben oil. This used by watchmakers, as well as in perfumery and cosmetics, for salad oil, soap and machine oil. *M. oleifera* is easily grown and large limbs are planted for use as a living fence in many arid areas, especially Arabia, where little else grows. *** *M. ovalifolia*; (Dinter & Berger), Namibia, SW Africa, to 7 m (23 ft). AFRICAN MORINGO or PHANTOM TREE is a succulent, squat pachycaul with an obese, pale grey to coppery barked trunk that stores water. Leaves to 60 cm (24 in.), fruit to 40 cm (16 in.), flattened, pale green to grey pink. The leaves and fruit are browsed by elephant, giraffe and springbok. The root is edible but tastes sour. (9–11) These are important honey plants.

NOTE: *M. oleifera* has escaped cultivation in many parts of the world.

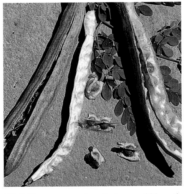

M. oleifera; young, winged sds are edible and taste a little like garden peas.

M. oleifera; soft, spongy wood is used as pulp for making cellophane and rayon, but otherwise has little value.

M. oleifera; the Horseradish Tree is a most undemanding and rewarding tree and is a prodigious provider.

M. oleifera; abundant panicles of this ever-blooming sp. are sweetly honey-fragrant and, like most parts of this amazing tree, edible, being added to curries and stews in some regions.

283

Morus alba

WHITE MULBERRY

L.   12 spp.

MORACEAE

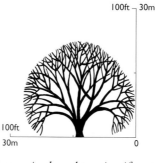

MORUS ALBA is native to warm-temperate regions but will grow in the subtropics, if not as well, to form an elegant shade tree with a pale grey trunk and low-sweeping, flexuous, zigzagged limbs clad in lush, rich green leaves that are paler below. Male and female flowers are mostly held on different trees (dioecious); they are short-stalked, in separate, drooping catkins. Pink or dark red, multiple fruit, or syncarp, is composed of the embryos from many female flowers. Although a member of the fig family, the fruit looks more like those of the *Rubus* or Blackberry genus. The leaves of **Morus alba** are important as the food of the silkworm, *Bombyx mori*. In Mexico and other regions, Mulberry trees (not to be confused with *Broussonetia papyrifera*, Paper Mulberry) are coppiced to produce long limbs from which bark is stripped and used for making bark cloth. Hallucinogens are present in uncooked shoots and unripe fruit. Extracts of leaves and root bark are used as a diuretic and to lower blood pressure. In Chinese medicine, preparations are concocted for coughs, colds and sore eyes. Other preparations have been found to decrease blood sugar levels and, in tests, to inhibit tumours. There are many excellent cultivars.

*** **M. australis**; (Poir.), Temp. E Asia, to 8 m (26 m), is very similar to *M. alba*. The leaves are variable, mostly 3–5 lobed with serrated margins; fruit is dark purple, very small, to 1.5 cm (0.6 in), but very sweet. (7–10)

*** **M. macroura**; (Miq.), India, Pakistan, Sri Lanka and S China, to 10 m (33 ft), SHAHTOOT or the KING WHITE (also KING RED) is a small, weeping, hardy species renowned for its very long, honey-sweet fruit, up to 20 cm (8 in.). (8–11)

*** **Morus nigra** (L.), SW Asia, to 15 m (50 ft). BLACK MULBERRY, is grown for its delicious, very dark red to blackish fruit that has a rather pleasant, sub-acid flavour. (5–9)

NOTE: these species have naturalized in many regions.

ORIGIN	C and E China, endemic
HEIGHT	to 16 m (53 ft)
TYPE	evergreen. dioecious fruiting tree
STATUS	vulnerable
HABITAT	deciduous dry woodland
GROWTH	fast
FLOW'G	spring
DRY TOL.	high
SALT TOL.	moderate
LIGHT	full sun
SOIL	deep, fertile loam
NUTRIT.	balanced fertilizer annually
HAZARDS	none
PROBLEMS	bacterial blight
ENVIRON.	(wind-pollinated) wild fruit for birds
PROPAG.	large cuttings; layers
LEAVES	simple; rich green; ovate to cordate; to 20 cm (8 in.); lobed or coarsely toothed
FLOWERS	inconspicuous; greenish yellow; in erect catkins, to 1 cm (0.4 in.); held at leaf axils
FRUIT	a syncarp, to 2.5 cm (1 in.); greenish white, ripening pink or red; sweet but poor flavour; edible
USE	shade tree; screening; backyard tree; fruiting tree; street tree; xerophytic
ZONE	4–11

M. alba; fast-growing but very long-lived (to 100 years or more).

M. nigra; here we see the little catkins held erect at lf axils. As they are pollinated, composite fr. forms; it becomes heavy and hangs down to ripen from red to black.

M. macroura; the famous Shahtoot, with elongated, honey-sweet fr.

M. alba; are coppiced to produce long limbs from which bark is stripped and used for making bark cloth.

ORIGIN	from W Indies to S America
HEIGHT	up to 8 m (26 ft)
TYPE	evergreen, small fruiting tree
STATUS	not threatened
HABITAT	lowland limestone thickets; wasteland
GROWTH	fast
FLOWG.	year-round
DRY TOL.	high
SALT TOL.	low
LIGHT	full sun
SOIL	well-drained
NUTRIT.	normally not necessary
HAZARDS	none
PROBLEMS	may be invasive; fruit fly
ENVIRON.	bee nectar; wild fruit for birds and bats
PROPAG.	seeds; cuttings
LEAVES	simple; green, silvery hairy below; lanceolate, base oblique; margins toothed
FLOWERS	showy; white; 5-petalled, with many yellow stamens
FRUIT	a berry, to 1.2 cm (0.5 in.); round, reddish or yellowish; pulp juicy, musky sweet
USE	small shade tree; backyard tree; large planter; specimen; xerophytic
ZONE	10–12

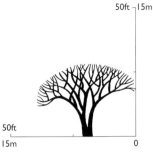

50ft ─15m

50ft
15m ─── 0

Muntingia calabura

CAPULIN

L.   1 sp.

TILIACEAE

FAST GROWING, **MUNTINGIA CALABURA** forms a distinctive, wide, arching parasol of horizontally layered, softly downy, oblique leaves that are 2-ranked and coarsely toothed. Because its little, drab white blooms are reminiscent of strawberry flowers, *M. calabura* is known as Strawberry Tree in some regions. These long-stalked flowers are borne continuously at leaf axils on the underside of twigs but last only a day, falling in the afternoons. They are specifically evolved for bee-pollination; their stalks elongate to present the bloom to the bees and then it is retracted below the leaves once pollination has taken place. Small, round, red or yellowish berry fruit are produced throughout the year. They are sweet, juicy and fig-like, with many minute seeds. *M. calabura* was briefly popular for planting in the new developments in some areas of the W Indies because of its ease of propagation, small scale and speed of growth, but it soon became obvious that this species could become invasive. In some areas, the fruit is considered a nuisance as it attracts bats and birds, which are their distributors. In Australia, it is the favourite of the Mistletoe Bird, which often fatally infests the tree with this parasitic plant. *M. calabura* is adapted to arid conditions, where it is often grown as a fuelwood. The sapwood is lighter coloured than the pale brown heartwood. This is lightweight, medium-textured or irregularly grained and very easily worked, but poorly resistant to decay. The bark yields a tough, silk-like fibre and is stripped for use as lashing, supports or rope. It is also used for basket-making. In Venezuela, an infusion of the young leaves is used as a tea and in Sri Lanka, where *M. calabura* is known as the Jam Tree, the fruit is used to make preserves. This is a honey plant.

NOTE: this species has proved very invasive in many regions.

M. calabura; with small, strawberry-like blooms.

M. calabura; Capulin is easily recognized for its stiff, wide-spreading canopy of soft, lance-shaped lvs. It is very fast growing and of easy culture.

M. calabura; wood is lightweight, medium-textured and very easily worked, but poorly resistant to decay.

M. calabura; little juicy, fig-like, red fr. that is sweet but undistinguished. It is adored (and spread) by birds and bats.

Murraya koenigii

CURRY LEAF

(L.) Spreng.   4 spp.

RUTACEAE

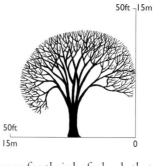

50ft ⌐15m

50ft
15m   0

MURRAYA KOENIGII, belongs to the Rutaceae family, famous for their leaf glands that secrete aromatic, ethereal oils – especially the Citrus clan. Known generally as Curry Leaf for its wonderfully sweet, curry-pungent foliage, *M. koenigii* is a most attractive, small tree, with a wide, neatly sumptuous, oval or rounded crown of soft, fine, greyish green foliage. This is composed of spirally arranged, pinnate leaves, with asymmetric, narrowly elliptic leaflets minutely notched along their margins. In spring, punctuating the tips of every slender, wand-like branch are the compact bouquets of fragrant, pearly white, nectar-rich flowers. They are followed by heavy clusters of juicy, flattened berries, which turn from dull red to bluish black as they ripen. They are sought after by birds and are freely distributed by them. *M. koenigii* is widely planted domestically in its native India and Sri Lanka and, indeed, anywhere in the tropical world where curry is an important dish. Indian Curry powder contains a subtle, complicated amalgam of pungent spices that vary slightly from dish to dish or region to region. Like the temperate Curry Plant, *Helichrysum italicum*, the leaves of *M. koenigii* are the prototype, but without the chilli. The leaves are used fresh or dried to flavour food and as a cure for dysentery. They are also processed to yield an oil that is used regionally in the soap industry. Although this is a splendid, small tree for ornament as well as evergreen shade, and is perfect for a patio or courtyard, it has the disadvantage of producing suckers, which may be a nuisance. It must be pointed out that, while the leaves of this species smell and taste of curry, they are in fact, used only as an addition to curry powder; they are not sufficiently pungent to replace it. This is a honey plant.

NOTE: *M. koenigii* suckers prolifically and may prove a problem in small gardens.

M. koenigii; with tight posies of little fragrant fls.

M. koenigii; Curry Leaf forms a multi-trunked, much-branched framework for it soft, fine, aromatic foliage. It is commonly planted as a backyard tree in curry-loving regions.

M. koenigii; small, juicy berries turn red and then black on ripening. They are a favourite of fruit-eating birds.

M. koenigii; with thick, cracked bark.

(1) ***Murraya paniculata***; ([L.] Jack.), (syn. *M. exotica*), SE Asia to Australia, to 7 m (23 ft). ORANGE JASMINE, MOCK ORANGE, BURMESE BOXWOOD (or ALAHE'HAOLE in Hawaii). Small tree found throughout SE Asia, particularly Burma, Thailand and N Malaysia, where it is known as Kemuning. (1) shows larger leafed cv. 'Lakeview'. Like *M. koenigii*, *M. paniculata* has small posies of white, waxy fls (2) which are intensely, orange-blossom fragrant. Fls are produced in great profusion after heavy rain breaks a dry period and are quickly followed by an abundance of small red berries. (3) In Java, the blooms are harvested for their essential oil, used in making perfume. In Burma and parts of Thailand, the wood and roots are ground up to produce the famous sweet-scented Thanaka Powder, which adorns the cheeks of many women of these regions. Yellow heartwood of larger specimens is valued commercially in Asia. This slow-growing sp. has a fine-textured, compact crown of leathery, glossy, pinnate foliage, which, unlike *M. koenigii*, has no pungency. *M. paniculata* lends itself to many formal uses in a small garden and is commonly planted in large containers or as a box-like hedge. This sp. does not tolerate root disturbance. Shrubby forms with smaller lvs are sold in Australia as *M. exotica*, while tree-like forms are labelled *M. paniculata*. (9 –12) **NOTE: *M. paniculata* is considered invasive in Florida, USA.**

A well-established *Murrayia paniculata* shading a pavilion at Foster Gardens, Honolulu, Hawaii. It is known there as Alahe'haole and the blooms are used in leis.

Myrciaria floribunda

GUAVABERRY

(West ex Wild.) Berg.

Eugenia floribunda

MYRTACEAE

40 spp.

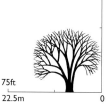

ORIGIN	Trop. America
HEIGHT	up to 15 m (50 ft)
TYPE	evergreen fruiting tree
STATUS	vulnerable
HABITAT	dry or humid coastal woodlands, to 300 m (1,000 ft)
GROWTH	very slow
FLOWG	winter to spring
DRY TOL.	high
SALT TOL.	moderate
LIGHT	full sun
SOIL	rich loam
NUTRIT.	organic fertilizer; organic mulch
HAZARDS	none
PROBLEMS	none
ENVIRON.	bee nectar; wild fruit for birds
PROPAG.	seeds
LEAVES	simple; deep green; to 9 cm (3.5 in.); lanceolate; long-pointed
FLOWERS	showy; white; almost stalkless; 4 fringed petals, with pompoms of golden stamens
FRUIT	a berry, to 10 mm (0.4 in.); globose, with rough, glandular spots; green, then red or deep yellow; up to 4 seeds
USE	small street tree; specimen; backyard tree; large planter; xerophytic; bonsai subject
ZONE	10–12

MYRCIARIA FLORIBUNDA is a native of dry or moist coastal woodlands in many parts of Trop. America and is especially handsome. It has a dense, rounded canopy over a slender framework of hard, muscular limbs, a mosaic of flaking bark and a delicate tracery of ever-dividing stems with neatly paired leaves. In old age, the bony bole is slightly flared into small buttresses at its base, with its pale tan or grey skin flaking off in circular discs to expose the glowing, golden brown, inner flesh. The elliptic to lanceolate, leathery leaves are covered with minute gland dots, which secrete an aromatic oil. Little, round, red or golden yellow berries follow the abundant, starry white blooms and mass of golden stamens, punctuating the bases of the narrow, twinned leaves along the length of the fine twigs. The fruit is stemless and clings to the leaf nodes. Its sweet, orange flesh is strongly, aromatically fragrant and makes a delicious, pungent-flavoured jam or juice. Christmas-time in most parts of the Lesser Antilles of the W Indies is Guavaberry Rum time. This delicious, aromatic, rum-based liqueur has been brewed for centuries and there are those with a special aptitude for making it. Very closely allied to *Eugenia*, the *Myrciaria* genus differs in having its hypanthium (fleshy calyx tube) prolonged beyond the ovary. *M. floribunda* is a slow-growing species and, although rarely cultivated in its region, is seldom destroyed, with wild trees left in pastures for their fruit. *M. floribunda* takes from 6–8 years to bear fruit from seed. A honey plant.

*** **M. dubia**, ([HBK] McVaugh), Amazon Basin, to 8 m (26 ft). CAMU CAMU is a slender, lowland tree that grows abundantly along the Xingu and Napo rivers. The round, sweet, juicy fruit has a particularly high vitamin C content, estimated to be 30 times that of citrus. It is eaten fresh or made into drinks and ice cream. (10–12)

M. floribunda; small pompom fls are held along the twigs at lf nodes.

M. floribunda; Guavaberry is prodigiously slow growing but very long-lived. This lovely specimen was photographed at the Jardin Botanico de Cienfuegos, Cuba.

M. floribunda; the Christmas crop means Guavaberry Rum time in the Virgin Is.

M. floribunda; with typical Myrtaceae hard, heavy wood, sinewy limbs, and peeling bark.

(Left) **Myrciaria cauliflora**; ([C, Martius.] C. Berg.), (syn. *Eugenia cauliflora*), S Brazil endemic, to 13 m (43 ft). Jaboticaba or Brazilian Grape Tree is one of the most important fruit trees in Brazil. Branching low on its trunk, the sinewy limbs form a vase-like structure. Excessively slow growing, this cauliflorous sp. bears at about 6 years from sd and 4 years from layers. It has, however, been found that, because of its compact, fibrous root system, this sp. transplants well. Jaboticaba fr. is often likened to the thick-skinned Muscadine grapes. This sp. is spectacular for courtyard and large planters. (10–12) (Right) **Myrciaria vexator**; (McVaugh), from Costa Rica and Panama to Venezuela, to 10 m (33 ft). Often found in pastures along roadsides, this ornamental, sp. has deep green, glossy, layered foliage and stunning, 2-toned, flaking bark. Dark purple and plum-sized, the thick-skinned fr. is delicious. This sp. is also slow-growing and even more ornamental than *M. cauliflora*. It is a relatively little known sp. and deserves to be more widely planted. (10–12)

A view taken at Fairchild Tropical Gardens in Miami, Florida, where much of the research for this book was done. Although most renowned for its superb palmatum, it also has an excellent, well-established arboretum, as well as areas featuring regional flora and fauna and endangered species.

Myrica cerifera

WAX MYRTLE

L.   55 spp.

MYRICACEAE

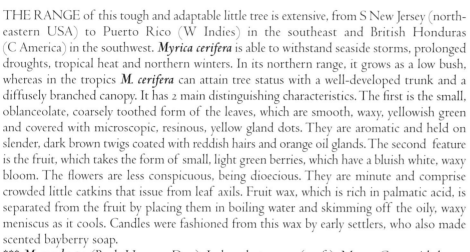

50ft — 15m

50ft
15m   0

ORIGIN	Trop. America
HEIGHT	up to 12 m (40 ft)
TYPE	evergreen, dioecious small tree or small shrub
STATUS	not threatened
HABITAT	moist coastal woodland, to 1,000 m (3,300 ft)
GROWTH	moderate
FLOWG	year-round
DRY TOL.	moderate
SALT TOL.	high
LIGHT	full sun or bright shade
SOIL	fertile, humid
NUTRIT.	balanced fertilizer annually; organic mulch
HAZARDS	none
PROBLEMS	invasive; leaves stain masonry
ENVIRON.	bee nectar; wild fruit for birds
PROPAG.	seeds; cuttings; suckers
LEAVES	simple; yellow-green, to 6.5 cm (2.5 in.); oblanceolate, gland dotted below; margins coarsely toothed
FLOWERS	inconspicuous; yellow-green; males in minute, axillary catkins
FRUIT	a drupe, to 3 mm (0.1 in.); bluish white; globose, waxy
USE	seaside; swampside; brackish sites; accent; coastal screening; topiary; large planter; xerophytic
ZONE	6–11

THE RANGE of this tough and adaptable little tree is extensive, from S New Jersey (northeastern USA) to Puerto Rico (W Indies) in the southeast and British Honduras (C America) in the southwest. *Myrica cerifera* is able to withstand seaside storms, prolonged droughts, tropical heat and northern winters. In its northern range, it grows as a low bush, whereas in the tropics *M. cerifera* can attain tree status with a well-developed trunk and a diffusely branched canopy. It has 2 main distinguishing characteristics. The first is the small, oblanceolate, coarsely toothed form of the leaves, which are smooth, waxy, yellowish green and covered with microscopic, resinous, yellow gland dots. They are aromatic and held on slender, dark brown twigs coated with reddish hairs and orange oil glands. The second feature is the fruit, which takes the form of small, light green berries, which have a bluish white, waxy bloom. The flowers are less conspicuous, being dioecious. They are minute and comprise crowded little catkins that issue from leaf axils. Fruit wax, which is rich in palmatic acid, is separated from the fruit by placing them in boiling water and skimming off the oily, waxy meniscus as it cools. Candles were fashioned from this wax by early settlers, who also made scented bayberry soap.

*** **M. esculenta**; (Buch-Ham. ex Don). Indomal., to 12 m (40 ft). MALAY GALE with leaves in rosettes. Fruit is bright, rose red to black, edible. The bark gives a yellow dye. (10–12)

*** **M. faya**, (Aiton), Azores and Canary Is, to 7 m (23 ft). The FIRE TREE is naturalized in Portugal. It was introduced into Hawaii for afforestation purposes in the 1880s but succeeded too well and in consequence has long been considered an invasive pest, as are many introduced species in Hawaii. Portuguese labourers there developed a method for making wine from the tiny, red, edible berries. (9–10)

M. cerifera; staminous male fls in crowded, catkin-like clusters.

M. cerifera; has narrow, thickened, serrated, waxy lvs and wax-covered fr., thus enabling this widespread sp. to endure cold, drought and seaside conditions.

M. cerifera; small, immature green fr. already has its oily, waxy 'bloom.'

M. cerifera; growing in brackish swampland along the causeway into Savannah, Georgia, USA.

ORIGIN	Molucca Is, endemic
HEIGHT	up to 23 m (75 ft)
TYPE	evergreen dioecious tree
STATUS	rare in the wild
HABITAT	humid volcanic lowlands, with even rainfall
GROWTH	slow
FLOWG	year-round
DRY TOL.	low
SALT TOL.	moderate
LIGHT	sheltered sun; part shade
SOIL	humid, fertile, acid
NUTRIT.	organic fertilizer; deep, organic mulch
HAZARDS	none
PROBLEMS	none
ENVIRON.	insect nectar
PROPAG.	seeds (very slow); cuttings; grafting
LEAVES	simple; dark green, silvery below; to 12 cm (4.7 in.); oblong, aromatic
FLOWERS	inconspicuous; yellow; to 1 cm (0.4 in.); no petals; sepals cup-shaped, 2–3 lobed; many stamens
FRUIT	a drupe, to 9 cm (3.5 in.); globose to ovoid; thick, yellowish skin; nut is dark brown, with red aril
USE	fruiting nut tree; shade tree; humid shade garden; specimen; botanic collection; large conservatory
ZONE	11–12

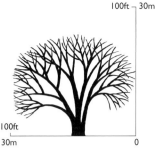

100ft – 30m
100ft
30m
0

Myristica fragrans

NUTMEG

(L.) Houtt.　　　72 spp.

MYRISTICACEAE

MYRISTICA FRAGRANS is endemic to the equatorial islands of the Moluccas but is now widespread throughout the tropics, being renowned for its extraordinary, 3-in-1 pale amber fruit that superficially resembles an apricot. Each component of this fruit has its culinary value. The nut, or seed, is the hard, brown, ovoid kernel known as nutmeg, which is enveloped in a curious, scarlet, pungently aromatic aril in the form of a succulent 'net' known as mace. Enclosing the kernel and aril is a thick, fleshy, juicy husk. In its native islands, the nuts are dispersed by Nutmeg Pigeons, *Ducula* spp., which feed on the mace but reject the nuts. When the fruit is harvested, mace and nutmegs are separated and dried, and the fleshy husks are processed as preserved fruit and jellies, while the mace is detached, flattened and dried. The pulp of dried nutmegs contains 25–40% of orange-coloured, aromatic oil. When processed, it is known as nutmeg butter and is used for scenting soaps, lotions and toothpaste and in cigarettes. Most nutmeg and mace are traded as ground spice for culinary use. In the W Indies, nutmeg is valued as a remedy for diarrhoea. Elsewhere, it is reputed to cure rheumatism, although an excess is toxic, hallucinatory and addictive. It also has a reputation for being an aphrodisiac. Although hermaphrodite (bisexual) trees exist, a female tree is usually needed to produce fruit as *M. fragrans* is dioecious. The seeds are slow to germinate, taking up to 30 months to sprout. Nutmeg requires well-drained, acid loam and a hot, maritime climate.
*** *M. insipida*; (R. Br.), N Qld, Australia, to 20 m (66 ft). This large, densely layered, spreading, dioecious, evergreen tree is dominant as a subcanopy rainforest tree, especially along the banks of streams. The seeds are distributed by migratory birds, which seek the thin aril. This species is very slow growing. (10–12)

M. fragrans; apricot-like fr. is dangled on sturdy stalks.

M. insipida; red aril covered sds are distributed by migratory birds, which seek the thin aril.

M. fragrans; extremely slow growing, this sp. forms a dense, everg. crown.

M. fragrans; 'nut' or kernel is the hard, brown, ovoid kernel, known as Nutmeg. It is enveloped in a scarlet, pungently aromatic aril in the form of a succulent 'net', known as Mace.

291

Myroxylon balsamum

BALSAM OF TOLU

(L.) Harms   2–3 spp.

M. toluiferum

FABACEAE (Papilionoideae)

100ft — 30m

115ft
34.5m   0

ORIGIN	from Venezuela to Peru
HEIGHT	up to 35 m (115 ft)
TYPE	evergreen or deciduous resinous tree
STATUS	not threatened
HABITAT	dry and humid forests
GROWTH	moderate
FLOWG	spring and late summer
DRY TOL.	high
SALT TOL.	moderate
LIGHT	full sun
SOIL	fertile, well-drained
NUTRIT.	balanced fertilizer annually
HAZARDS	none
PROBLEMS	none
ENVIRON.	nectar for bees
PROPAG.	seeds
LEAVES	pinnate; mid green; 3–13 leaflets ovate-oblong, to 9 cm (3.5 in.), glossy
FLOWERS	inconspicuous; white; held in pubescent racemes; sweetly fragrant
FRUIT	a legume, to 7.5 cm (3 in.); teardrop-shaped, winged pod with single seed
USE	specimen; public open space; botanic collection; street tree; xerophytic
ZONE	10–12

MYROXYLON ARE LEGUMINOUS, S AMERICAN SPECIES, with copious, citrus-flavoured resin. **Myroxylum balsamum** is a large, handsome tree, with a stiffly erect, spreading habit, carrying a layered canopy of large, pinnate leaves. It is popularly planted for shade or as street trees in S America. In spring and autumn, white fragrant flowers are held in small, erect spikes. These are followed in summer and winter by distinctive, lance-shaped, single-seeded winged fruit, used to flavour Aguardiente, a potent, clear rum commonly consumed throughout Latin America. There are 2 forms of this genus: **M. balsamum** var. **pereirae**, known as Balsam of Peru (native of C America), and **M. balsamum** var. **balsamus** (native of northern S America), also known as Balsam of Tolu (or Quiniquino). *Myroxylum* were cultivated by the Incas for medicinal use, to arrest bleeding and promote healing. In 1562, Pope Pius IV authorized Catholic clergy to use it as an anointing oil. Gradually, it became popular in Europe for use in perfumes and medicine. Traditionally, it was shipped from Peru's main port of Callao. Soon, the seeds were carried around the world and the tree became cultivated in many parts of the tropics. Currently, it is employed in the manufacture of ointments, as a flavouring for cough syrups and medicines and as a fragrance. The dark, treacly, oily, but sweetly pungent, resin of both varieties is mostly tapped like maple syrup. It has a cinnamon-vanilla scent and a sweet, citrus taste. It contains a high percentage of cinnamene, a volatile oil, with Tolu balsam having traces of other important constituents, including benzoic acid and vanillin. Apart from its resin, **M. balsamum** is valued for its strong timber, which is deep, rich red like mahogany, with a fine grain and a lasting, pleasant aroma. It is resistant to termites and is used for cabinetry and to make furniture. This is a honey plant.

M. balsamum var. *pereirae*; ([Royle] Harms.). Balsam of Peru, photographed at Jardin Botanico de Cienfuegos, Cuba. This is an economically important tree in its native C America.

M. balsamum; small, white, pea-like fls set in tomentose calyxes.

M. balsamum; distinctive, winged, lance-shaped fr. with a single sd. They are adapted for wind distribution.

M. balsamum; valued for its strong timber, which is deep, rich red like Mahogany, with a fine grain and lasting aroma.

ORIGIN	Nigeria and Guinea
HEIGHT	up to 7 m (23 ft)
TYPE	evergreen, small flowering tree
STATUS	rare in the wild
HABITAT	understorey in the rainforest
GROWTH	slow
FLOWG	spring
DRY TOL.	low
SALT TOL.	low
LIGHT	sheltered sun or light shade
SOIL	rich, humid, acid
NUTRIT.	organic fertilizer; deep, organic mulch
HAZARDS	possibly toxic parts
PROBLEMS	difficult to cultivate
ENVIRON.	nectar
PROPAG.	seeds
LEAVES	simple; rich green; to 22 × 9 cm (8 × 3.5 in.); elliptic; margins entire or undulate
FLOWERS	showy; purplish and yellow; 2 inner rows of petals; cauliflorous
FRUIT	a berry, to 4.5 cm (1.75 in.); dark orange to red-brown; with 1 kidney-shaped seed
USE	humid shade garden; botanic collection; large planter; curiosity; conservatory
ZONE	10–12

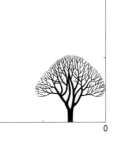

50ft 15m
50ft
15m 0

Napoleonaea imperialis

NAPOLEON'S HAT

Pal.   8 spp.

N. cuspidata

LECYTHIDACEAE

NAPOLEONAEA IMPERIALIS, of the equatorial rainforests of central W Africa, is not in the least flamboyant but nevertheless qualifies for its noble nomenclature. **N. imperialis** is a small, multi-trunked, loose-limbed tree or tall shrub. The curious, short-stemmed blooms are unique, albeit that they are mostly held out of sight, directly on the trunk and limbs or in the lower leaf axils. In 1808, when a French botanist, Ambroise Palisot Beauvois, first discovered the species on an expedition to W Africa, he declared that the bloom '...reproduces, with incredible accuracy, the royal crowns of France and Italy.' Beauvois naturally dedicated the genus to the Emperor Napoleon. The flower is almost stalkless, about 5 cm (2 in.) in diameter. It comprises 4 concentric circles, the outer 1 a dish-shaped circle of united purplish petals edged in yellow. This forms the flat 'brim' of the hat, or royal crown. Forming a fringed coronet in the centre, are 3 circles of stamens, 1 row sterile, 1 row joined and 1 row fertile. The colours are reddish, purplish and yellowish white. 'Red, white and blue...!' declared Beauvois, with much imagination and royal fervour. *Napoleonaea* genus belongs to the same clan as Barringtonia and Brazil Nut. Its edible fruit resembles a flattened guava in shape, having also a large, persistent calyx at its base. It is 5–6-celled, each cell containing a kidney-shaped, brown seed.

*** **N. heudelotii**, (Juss.), W Africa. Known as NAPOLEON'S BUTTON, the flowers of this small tree are to 8 cm (3 in.) diam., and are rich red. The fruit is globose, to 8 cm (3 in.), obscurely lobed, dark orange to red-brown. The fruit is eaten locally, and traditionally the rind of the fruit and bark are chewed to cure persistent coughs. (10–12)

*** **N. vogellii**; (Hook. & Planchon.), Nigeria, to 50 m (164 ft). WALLIA is found in riparian forest and along seashores. Used as a chewing stick in Nigeria. (10–12)

N. imperialis; a bloom fit for an emperor.

N. vogellii; Wallia, with paler colouring. Found in riparian forest and along sea-shores. Photographed at Kew Gardens.

N. imperialis; at the Royal Botanic Gardens, Trinidad, where it was planted early last century.

N. imperialis; the French botanist Ambroise Beauvois discovered this curious fl. in W Africa. He named it after the Emperor Napoleon.

Nauclea orientalis

LEICHHARDT PINE

(L.) L.   10 spp.

N. cordata

RUBIACEAE

A MEMBER OF THE IXORA CLAN and closely allied to *Sarcocephalus latifolius* (African Peach), the **Nauclea orientalis** has similar flowers and fruit. It is widely distributed from Trop. Asia to Australia and the Pacific and is found in rainforest, along streams and in swampy areas. The stout branches are whorled around a sturdy trunk with greyish brown, flaking bark. Typical of this group, *N. orientalis* has large, handsome leaves that are spoon-shaped, rich green, slightly wavy-edged and long-petioled, giving the tree a luxuriant canopy. Held on stout stalks, the remarkable, fragrant flowers contrast greatly with the foliage. They are set in globular heads of tiny, yellow calyxes, each of which holds a narrow, white tubular flower. This spiky, pincushion-like arrangement is rich in nectar to attract their butterfly pollinators. The lumpy potato-like, 2-celled, 2-seeded, tawny berry fruit that follows is also roughly globose and much smaller than *Sarcocephalus*. It has thin, crusty skin and thin, bitter pulp, which is juicy and edible, although not particularly palatable. The soft, pine-like timber of *N. orientalis* is greatly valued in the Indo-Malaysian area and is known in the trade as Kanluang. It is widely used to make packing cases. Although the tree may attain a stately height in humid habitats, it will probably develop as a much smaller tree under cultivation. It is advisable to plant *N. orientalis* in a sheltered position to provide protection for its large leaves. The bark yields a bright yellow dye. The leaves and bark are made into fish poisons, medicines and painkillers.

*** *N. diderrichii*, ([De Wildeman] Merrill), Trop. Africa, to 40 m (131 ft). A large tree, with furrowed, grey to brown bark and large, 40 cm (16 in.), elliptic leaves. The flowers in globose heads of white, yellow or green, to 3 cm (1 in). The fruit, to 4 cm (1.5 in.), globose, succulent, ribbed, white or grey to pale brown. (10–12)

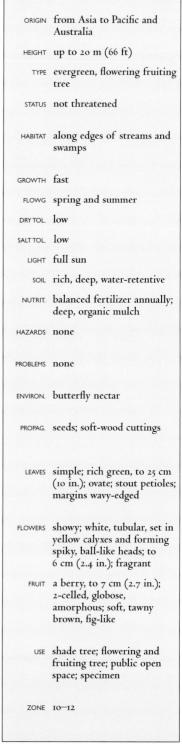

ORIGIN	from Asia to Pacific and Australia
HEIGHT	up to 20 m (66 ft)
TYPE	evergreen, flowering fruiting tree
STATUS	not threatened
HABITAT	along edges of streams and swamps
GROWTH	fast
FLOWG	spring and summer
DRY TOL.	low
SALT TOL.	low
LIGHT	full sun
SOIL	rich, deep, water-retentive
NUTRIT.	balanced fertilizer annually; deep, organic mulch
HAZARDS	none
PROBLEMS	none
ENVIRON.	butterfly nectar
PROPAG.	seeds; soft-wood cuttings
LEAVES	simple; rich green, to 25 cm (10 in.); ovate; stout petioles; margins wavy-edged
FLOWERS	showy; white, tubular, set in yellow calyxes and forming spiky, ball-like heads; to 6 cm (2.4 in.); fragrant
FRUIT	a berry, to 7 cm (2.7 in.); 2-celled, globose, amorphous; soft, tawny brown, fig-like
USE	shade tree; flowering and fruiting tree; public open space; specimen
ZONE	10–12

N. orientalis; a young, soft, fig-like fr.

N. orientalis; this widespread sp. of the rainforests and swamps has curious blooms. They are charged with sweet nectar and attract many butterflies, which pollinate them.

N. orientalis; growing wild at Toobanna in N Qld, Australia.

N. orientalis; stout branches are whorled around a sturdy trunk that has greyish brown, flaking bark.

ORIGIN	W Malaysia, endemic
HEIGHT	up to 25 m (82 ft)
TYPE	evergreen; dioecious fruiting tree
STATUS	vulnerable
HABITAT	lowland humid forests
GROWTH	fast
FLOWG	spring and summer
DRY TOL.	low
SALT TOL.	low
LIGHT	full sun
SOIL	humid, rich, acid
NUTRIT.	high-nitrogen and potassium fertilizer; organic mulch
HAZARDS	none
PROBLEMS	fruit fly; fungus
ENVIRON.	wild fruit for birds and bats
PROPAG.	seeds; layers; grafts
LEAVES	pinnate; bright green; with 1–2 pairs of elliptic leaflets, to 25 cm (1 in.)
FLOWERS	inconspicuous; whitish; small, in long-stemmed panicles
FRUIT	a drupe, to 6 cm (2.4 in.); red, with long, soft, curling spines; with a single, large seed with a translucent aril
USE	small shade tree; humid shade garden; backyard tree; large planter; conservatory
ZONE	10–12

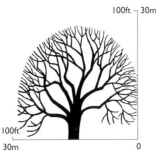

100ft — 30m
100ft
30m — 0

Nephelium lappaceum

RAMBUTAN

L.   22 spp.

Euphoria nephelium; Dimocarpus crinata

SAPINDACEAE

WITH THE MATURATION of its great harvest of softly spiny, glowing bundles of rich red fruit, *Nephelium lappaceum* is spectacularly ornamental. This is a somewhat bushy, wide-crowned tree, native to equatorial regions that have no pronounced dry season. This is a dioecious genus, although female trees have hermaphrodite flowers with a functioning pistil. It is, however, mostly propagated vegetatively by cuttings, grafts or layers as the seeds are so shortly viable and seedlings are variable. *N. lappaceum* has fruit typical of the large, fecund, Sapindaceae family and is endemic to Malaysia and closely related to *Litchi chinensis*. Extremely popular in SE Asia, this rich red, ovoid or rounded fruit is distinctive for its long, curling, soft spines. (The name Rambutan is derived from the Malay word *rambut*, meaning hair.) Like Lychee, Rambutan skin is almost shell-like and cracks away very easily to expose the deliciously creamy, translucent flesh of its aril, which surrounds the solitary seed. Superior strains have arils that detach freely from the seed, while in other less desirable forms they do not. In Malaysia, the former type is named Rambutan-lekang. The taste and quality of the fruit varies enormously, the best being juicy, with an appealing, mild, sub-acid flavour. The fruit is eaten fresh, stewed and canned or is made into jams and jellies. One of the problems encountered by farmers in the region is that bats adore this fruit and may devour great quantities. The fruit and leaves yield a red dye that is used to colour batik. The tough fruit skins are high in tannins and are used medicinally, as are the leaves and roots. Rambutan wood is handsome, reddish, dense and hard and suitable for many types of construction. *N. lappaceum* takes 5–6 years to bear from seed or 3–4 years grafted or layered. Summer is the main fruiting season, with possibly another, shorter, season during the winter months.

N. lappaceum; shell-like skin and soft spines.

N. lappaceum; a young tree photographed at Harvey Creek Exotic Gardens, Babinda, N Qld, Australia.

N. lappaceum; large, soft, pinnate lvs, which are bright green above and pale, white below.

N. lappaceum; is a softly spiny, red skinned fr., which is said to be the most popular of all SE Asian fr. Shown here is unripe fr., which will turn completely red as it matures.

Newbouldia laevis

BOUNDARY TREE

(Beauv.) Seem. ex Bur.   1 sp.

N. pentandra

BIGNONIACEAE

100ft ⌐ 30m

75ft
22.5m   0

THIS SUMPTUOUS, W AFRICAN member of the Bignoniaceae family is renowned in its region for its vigour. Because of its ability to grow from large limbs dug into the ground, *Newbouldia laevis* is popularly planted as a live fence in west tropical Africa to mark property boundaries or around sacred groves or shrines. Members of the Yoruba tribe hold this tree in superstitious regard and will not cut it with an axe or burn it, while the Ibo tribe consider it sacred and plant it outside a chief's house. ***N. laevis*** is a fast-growing species, forming a very erect, slender framework. In age, it may have a tall, bare trunk with bushy growth at its apex. Its polished, dark green, leathery, pinnate leaves are composed of 3–6 pairs of broadly-elliptic leaflets with serrated margins that are clustered and whorled towards their tips. *N. laevis* is not a graceful tree, but in summer it carries attractive blooms. Typical of the Bignoniaceae family, these flowers are narrowly campanulate trumpets and are held in crowded, spike-like panicles at the ends of lacquered, purplish-black shoots, which give extra drama to the terminal bouquets. The colour of the blooms varies greatly, from purplish pink, red-purple, deep purple, bluish or white; the yawning trumpets usually have striped throats. Each flower is clasped by an inflated calyx that splits down one side to allow the trumpets space to expand. Also typical of its family are the long, slender, purple-dotted fruit, which split down both sides of their length to reveal their neat packaging of layered seeds, which are winged at each end. As soon as they dry out, they float away on the wind. *N. laevis* has many medicinal uses and concoctions of the pounded roots are used for syphilis, intestinal problems or as a poultice for aching limbs. The leaves are sometimes used domestically to remove stains from fabric and hands. The heartwood is pale brown and moderately hard.

ORIGIN	Trop. W Africa
HEIGHT	up to 18 m (60 ft)
TYPE	evergreen flowering tree
STATUS	not threatened
HABITAT	dry secondary woodland and cleared land
GROWTH	fast
FLOWG	summer
DRY TOL.	high
SALT TOL.	moderate
LIGHT	full sun
SOIL	rich, well-drained
NUTRIT.	balanced ferttilizer annually; organic mulch
HAZARDS	none
PROBLEMS	none
ENVIRON.	insect nectar
PROPAG.	seeds; large cuttings
LEAVES	pinnate; rich green; to 60 cm (24 in.); leaflets glossy; with entire or toothed margins
FLOWERS	showy; white, pink or purple; to 5 cm (2 in.); wide-mouthed trumpets; fragrant
FRUIT	a capsule, to 30 cm (12 in.); cylindrical, slender, purple-dotted; seeds winged
USE	flowering tree; accent; specimen; large planter; median strip; civic centre; xerophytic; conservatory
ZONE	10–12

N. laevis; delicate, fragrant, purplish pink trumpets have golden throats and are held in glossy, purplish black, stalked infls, lending great drama to the grand, terminal fl. spikes.

N. laevis; a spent bloom showing its golden throat.

N. laevis; a neat packaging of layered sds, which are winged at each end and will soon float away on the wind.

N. laevis; fast-growing young Boundary Tree with columnar growth and large, polished, leathery foliage.

296

ORIGIN	Madagascar; Comores Is
HEIGHT	up to 10 m (33 ft)
TYPE	evergreen, small foliage tree
STATUS	limited habitat
HABITAT	dry coastal woodland
GROWTH	slow
FLOWG	spring to summer
DRY TOL.	high
SALT TOL.	high
LIGHT	full sun
SOIL	widely tolerant
NUTRIT.	balanced fertilizer annually
HAZARDS	none
PROBLEMS	none
ENVIRON.	insect nectar
PROPAG.	seeds; cuttings
LEAVES	simple; greyish green; obovate, tough, leathery; with tightly inrolled margins
FLOWERS	fairly showy; white; long-stalked, bell-shaped, 4-parted; in small panicles; fragrant
FRUIT	a drupe, to 2 m (0.8 in.); olive-like, green; ripening purplish
USE	seaside; specimen; coastal screening; street tree; median strip; large planter; pollarded; xerophytic
ZONE	10–12

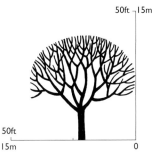

50ft ⌐15m

50ft
15m ⌐ 0

Noronhia emarginata

MADAGASCAR OLIVE

(Lam.) Thours. ex Hook.   40 spp.

Olea marginata; Noronhia chartacea

OLEACEAE

FOR A NEAT AND IMPERVIOUS seaside tree, **Noronhia emarginata** has no peer. From a very early age it displays superb characteristics: sturdy, supple, wind-resistant limbs and grey, leathery, oval leaves that are mostly held stiffly upright in an agreeable manner. These thickened leaves have a highly polished upper surface, with the edges rolled tightly under to give them even greater strength and to ensure that salty water does not adhere to them. Their petioles have the distinction of being so woody that they resemble small twigs. The little, long-stalked, milky-white or yellowish, thick, 4-petalled flowers are lightly fragrant. They are followed by green, olive-like drupes that mature purple. Surrounding a large, hard seed, the sweetish, cream-coloured flesh is considered edible in some parts of its region. These waxy drupes are waterproof and are dispersed to far-away shores by floating with the ocean currents. As *N. ermarginata* grows, it slowly develops a more open habit of muscular symmetry, with a loose, rhythmic, open growth, making it very desirable as a specimen for a seaside lawn, where it will allow sufficient light through for grass to thrive below. This splendid endemic of the coasts of Madagascar has always been considered to resemble the Mediterranean Olive and thus earned its common name, Madagascar Olive. Indeed, *N. emarginata* is a member of the olive family and was originally designated as *Olea marginata*. Being a very tolerant species, it will thrive in partial shade or full sun and is adaptable to a wide range of soils.

*** *N. louvelii*; (H. Perr.) Madagascar endemic, to 9 m (20 ft). Known locally as LETRAZO, this rare species is native to coastal forests from sea level to 900 m (3,000 ft). The leaves are leathery, brownish green above, yellowish below. The flowers are smaller, but similar to those of *N. emarginata*. (10–11)

N. emarginata; with little, waxy fls like lily of the valley.

N. emarginata; with tough, weatherproof bark.

N. emarginata; with little, long-stalked, oily 'olives', designed to float on the sea for distribution.

N. emarginata; is designed with inbuilt seaworthiness, making it an excellent choice for coast. planting. This specimen is on the waterfront in George Town, Cayman Is., W Indies.

Nuxia floribunda

FOREST ELDER

Benth.   15 spp.

Lachnopylis floribunda

LOGANIACEAE

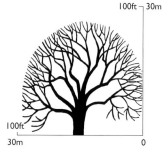

THE LATIN NAMES that are given to plants are usually usefully descriptive. *Floribunda* is an epithet that means many-flowered and graphically depicts the **Nuxia floribunda**. *Nuxia* is a relatively small genus confined to tropical E Africa and S Africa. It is in the same family as *Buddleja* and is popularly cultivated for its blooms. Like many species, the Forest Elder does not grow as tall in cultivation as it does in its natural habitat. With a sturdy trunk clad in finely corrugated, greyish bark, the arching limbs carry a densely buoyant crown of glossy foliage. The simple leaves are mostly held in whorls of 3; they are glabrous, slightly wavy and possibly toothed along their margins. The little, fragrant, creamy white flowers, which are somewhat reminiscent of *Buddleja saligna*, have 4 narrow petals and are held in branched, terminal and axillary, many-flowered sprays. Typical of this genus, the tiny, narrow calyx holding the flowers is viscid. The 2-valved fruit capsules contain minuscule seeds that are shortly viable. The heartwood is pale yellowish, hard, heavy and used in general carpentry. The leaves are browsed by game and the bark is used medicinally. This species is generally considered more ornamental than *N. congesta*.

*** ***N. congesta***; (R. Br. ex Fresen.), (syn. *Lachnopylis congesta*), from Kenya to S Africa, to 12 m (40 ft), COMMON WILD ELDER. In Kenya, this tree grows at the edges of dry, rocky forests and is known as Muranda by the Kikiyu tribe. As the epithet suggests, its summer flowers are held in crowded, congested heads of tiny, foamy, white flowers. They resemble those of the elderberry and are borne in great profusion, persisting on the tree long after they have faded. This species is distinguished also by its trunk, which has irregularly corrugated, rough, blackish bark that shreds in 'strings'. (9–11)

ORIGIN	Trop. and S Africa
HEIGHT	up to 25 m (82 ft)
TYPE	evergreen flowering tree
STATUS	not threatened
HABITAT	humid forest margins
GROWTH	moderate
FLOWG	late spring to summer
DRY TOL.	moderate
SALT TOL.	low
LIGHT	full sun
SOIL	deep, rich and friable
NUTRIT.	balanced fertilizer annually; deep, organic mulch
HAZARDS	none
PROBLEMS	none
ENVIRON.	bee and butterfly nectar
PROPAG.	fresh seed; semi-ripe cuttings
LEAVES	simple; rich green; oblong-elliptic; possibly toothed margins
FLOWERS	showy; creamy white; tiny, 4-parted; in airy panicles; very fragrant
FRUIT	a capsule, to 2 mm (0.08 in.); 2-valved, brown, glabrous
USE	flowering tree; specimen; small shade tree; small street tree; civic centre; large planter
ZONE	9–11

N. floribunda; closely related to Buddleja but it could be thought a Lilac. It is quite cold-tol. if given a sheltered, sunny spot. Photographed at the Arboretum of Los Angeles.

N. congesta; congested heads of tiny, persistent, very fragrant blooms.

N. floribunda; blooms abundantly in Los Angeles. It is found growing wild at the edges of humid forests.

N. congesta; resembles Elderberry and fls are borne in great profusion, persisting on the tree long after they have faded.

TREE-OF-SORROW

L.   2 spp.

OLEACEAE

ORIGIN	from India to Java
HEIGHT	up to 6 m (20 ft)
TYPE	evergreen, small flowering tree
STATUS	not threatened
HABITAT	Sub-Himalayan forest; high elevation forest
GROWTH	fast
FLOWG	all year, mainly winter
DRY TOL.	moderate
SALT TOL.	low
LIGHT	full sun
SOIL	fertile, friable
NUTRIT.	organic fertilizer annually; deep, organic mulch
HAZARDS	none
PROBLEMS	none
ENVIRON.	moth nectar
PROPAG.	seeds
LEAVES	simple; dull green; to 7 cm (2.7 in.); ovate-cordate, opposite, short-stalked
FLOWERS	showy; creamy white; 7-petalled; corolla tube orange; very fragrant
FRUIT	an achene, to 2 cm (0.8 in.); orbicular disc
USE	specimen; large planter; courtyard; topiary; hedging; conservatory
ZONE	10—12

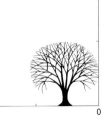

50ft ⌐15m

50ft
15m   0

NYCTANTHES ARBOR-TRISTIS is often found as a large, rambling, bony shrub in the wild, but may mature to attain tree status if left unchecked. The thin, rough, little leaves of this species are ovate, tapered to a point and mostly with serrated margins. *N. arbor-tristis* is quite undistinguished, except for its little, jasmine-like creamy white flowers that are clustered at the ends and along the twigs of its slender branchlets. These nocturnal blooms are powerfully fragrant. They have 7 slender petals, which are unequally lobed and somewhat rolled and twisted, surrounding a tiny, brilliant orange staminal tube. The fruit is quite large in comparison with the flowers, being a round, compressed disc containing 2 seeds. The names *arbor-tristis* and Tree-of-Sorrow refer to the night-flowering habit of this species. In India, there is a folktale about a certain king's daughter who fell in love with the Sun, who very soon deserted her. In despair, she killed herself and was cremated. From the spot where the princess's ashes fell, arose the Tree-of-Sorrow, which, unable to bear the sight of the sun, bloomed at night and dropped its flowers each morning. Because of this, for Hindus in India, *N. arbor-tristis* is a sacred tree and is planted around temples, where the fragrant flowers are used as votive offerings, especially to honour the God of Forests. The fallen corollas are swept up during the holy days and are preserved for future use. A rich orange dye is obtained from the tiny tubes and has been used as a cheap substitute for saffron and employed for colouring cotton cloth, especially Buddhist robes. *Nyctanthes* wood, although usually of small calliper, provides an excellent domestic fuel. Although it is sparsely branched in its natural form, *N. arbor-tristis* is often clipped into dense hedges or topiary.

N. arbor-tristis; tiny, fragrant fls that fall at dawn.

N. arbor-tristis; the tiny fls fall, leaving behind the little, tubular calyx and an embryo filled with minuscule sds.

N. arbor-tristis; with a distinctive, bright orange corolla tube.

N. arbor-tristis; forms a small, twiggy, airy canopy. It is a very sacred tree in India and planted around Hindu temples, where fallen blooms are used as votive offerings.

Ochroma pyramidale

BALSAWOOD

(Lam.) Urban.   1 sp.

O. lagopus

MALVACEAE (formerly BOMBACACEAE)

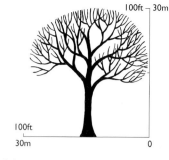

IN ITS HUMID JUNGLE HABITATS, **Ochroma pyramidale** is slightly buttressed, with its smooth, pinkish grey bole soaring up through the tangle to form an open crown of a few, coarse, spreading limbs. The large, leathery, heart-shaped, rusty red, velvety, petioled leaves are deep green above, pale yellowish below and heavily veined. The blooms are formed on stout stalks near the ends of the twigs. Each bloom is held stiffly erect, firmly cupped in heavy, rusty red, velvety calyxes holding huge, crumpled, succulent, creamy white, flaring petals, resembling a splendid chalice. They are bat-pollinated. The seeds are contained in massive, dehiscent, 10-angled, deeply spirally-ridged, plush, velvety pods, where they are embedded in brown, woolly fibre and require high temperatures to germinate. When the pods burst open, they spread their sections to imitate an enormous fluffy starfish. The woolly fibre from the seed pods has been used for filling pillows in India. Like *Cavanillesia platanifolia*, this monster Bombax grows so rapidly that it does not have time to develop heavy hardwood. It has, in fact, the lightest of all commercial timbers, being even lighter than cork. The sapwood is milled for its world-famous Balsawood, which played such an important role during World War ll, when it was used to make life rafts and belts and even British Mosquito bombers. Children's model aeroplanes were also made from this material, the parts neatly cut out in Balsawood, with the details stamped on in blue ink. Although perishable, Balsawood is used for insulation, fish-net floats and to make lightweight boxes that are used to ship cooler cargo on local boats. *O. pyramidale* is not suitable for normal planting but is most worthy of inclusion in an arboretum or a botanic collection, or even as a species for a large, public park.

ORIGIN	Trop. America
HEIGHT	up to 30 m (100 ft)
TYPE	evergreen, large flowering tree
STATUS	not threatened
HABITAT	moist, lowland limestone forest
GROWTH	fast
FLOWG	winter to summer
DRY TOL.	moderate
SALT TOL.	high
LIGHT	full sun
SOIL	fertile, water-retentive
NUTRIT.	generally not necessary; deep, organic mulch
HAZARDS	none
PROBLEMS	none
ENVIRON.	nectar for insects and bats
PROPAG.	seeds
LEAVES	simple; deep green, to 30 cm (12 in.) diam.; round, cordate, heavily veined; with long, stout petioles
FLOWERS	showy; white or yellow; to 15 cm (6 in.); solitary, tubular, erect, bell-shaped, with a heavy reddish calyx
FRUIT	a capsule, to 25 cm (10 in.); elongate, angular; seeds embedded in fibre
USE	public open space; botanic collection; curiosity
ZONE	10–12

O. pyramidale; huge, crumpled, cupped bell held in a heavy calyx.

O. pyramidale; every part of the phenomenally fast-growing, light-timbered Balsawood tree is exaggerated in size: the long-petioled lvs and lf blades, the fls and the fr.

O. pyramidale; the fr. dehisces to imitate a gargantuan, fluffy star-fish.

O. pyramidale; slightly buttressed, with a smooth, pinkish grey trunk and an open crown of a few, spreading limbs.

ORIGIN	Australia and New Caledonia
HEIGHT	up to 12 m (40 ft)
TYPE	evergreen, flowering tree
STATUS	not threatened
HABITAT	coastal woodland and dry thickets
GROWTH	moderate
FLOWG	summer
DRY TOL.	high
SALT TOL.	high
LIGHT	full sun or bright shade
SOIL	tolerates poor sandy soil
NUTRIT.	balanced fertilizer annually; organic mulch
HAZARDS	poisonous fruit
PROBLEMS	scale insects
ENVIRON.	nectar for insects
PROPAG.	seeds; layers
LEAVES	simple; rich green; held in whorls, to 15 cm (6 in.); elliptic, glabrous, leathery
FLOWERS	showy; ivory white; funnelform, in small, dense cymes; fragrant
FRUIT	a drupe, to 5 cm (2 in.); oval, angled, fleshy, bright, glossy red; with violet-scented pulp
USE	seaside; specimen; large planter; coastal screening; hedging; xerophytic
ZONE	10–12

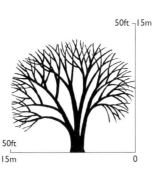

50ft ─ 15m
50ft
15m   0

Ochrosia elliptica

POKOSOLA

Labill.   30 spp.

APOCYNACEAE

ALTHOUGH THIS FAIRLY SLOW-GROWING SPECIES may attain a substantial height in the wild, as a garden ornamental it is usually found at about 5 m (16 ft). *Ochrosia elliptica* is a species that relishes a seaside environment but its thick, glossy, whorled, leathery foliage makes it a most worthy species for a multitude of horticultural uses. Small, fragrant, ivory cream, waxy stemless flowers develop in short clusters at, or near, the tips of the twigs. Although these little, simple blooms are attractive, the lacquered, brilliant, sealing-wax red fruit are infinitely more ornamental. Either paired or held in groups, the fleshy drupes have a mealy, violet-scented pulp that is extremely poisonous. They are held throughout the winter and spring and brighten up the sombre foliage. There are 3 members of the Apocynaceae genus that are very similar: *Cerbera*, *Kopsia* and *Ochrosia*. They all have deep green, leathery leaves, charming, white or pale yellow, funnelform flowers and fleshy, ornamental fruit. All 3 genera are remarkably salt-tolerant and have highly toxic sap. Both *Cerbera* and *Ochrosia* are xerophytic.
*** *O. mariannensis*; (A. DC. in DC.), S Pacific. FAGO has much larger and more elongated elliptic leaves that are lighter green and slightly folded and curved. This small tree forms a spreading, voluptuous canopy much decorated by its brilliant red, lacquered twinned fruit, which follow the posies of little starry white, waxy flowers. The wood is yellow and the roots yield a yellow dye. (10–12)
*** *O. oppositifolia*; ([Lam.] K. Schum.), W Polynesia to Mascarenes. FAO is a short to tall tree native to the coastal scrubs and woodlands. The flowers are small and white, in attractive crowded cymes; the paired fruit is yellow, ovoid, to 8 cm (3 in.). Although the fruit pulp is poisonous, the seed kernel is considered edible. (10–12)

O. elliptica; little, ivory, waxy, fragrant fls.

O. elliptica; very slow-growing, seaworthy and drought-resistant, it is undemanding and grown for its handsome foliage and fr.

O. mariannensis; with superb posies of little, long-tubed, starry white, waxy fls.

O. elliptica; Pokosola is the most widely planted of the *Ochrosia*. Its twinned, brilliantly lacquered fr., which smell strongly of violets (cyanide), are extremely poisonous.

301

Oncoba spinosa

FRIED EGG FLOWER

Forssk.   4 spp.

O. monacantha

FLACOURTIACEAE

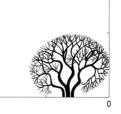

50ft ⌐15m

50ft

15m   0

ORIGIN	Arabia and Trop. Africa
HEIGHT	up to 7 m (23 ft)
TYPE	deciduous, flowering small tree
STATUS	not threatened
HABITAT	dry woodland or riparian forest
GROWTH	slow
FLOWG	spring
DRY TOL.	moderate to high
SALT TOL.	low
LIGHT	full sun
SOIL	rich, well-drained
NUTRIT.	balanced fertilizer annually; organic mulch
HAZARDS	spiny
PROBLEMS	none
ENVIRON.	bee nectar; wild bird fruit
PROPAG.	seeds
LEAVES	simple; deep green; reddish when young, to 9 × 5 cm (3.5 × 2 in.); elliptic; margins serrated
FLOWERS	showy; white; Camellia-like, with a boss of golden stamens and large style; fragrant
FRUIT	a berry, to 5 cm, (2 in.); yellowish brown; hard-shelled, shiny, pulpy within; many seeds
USE	small flowering tree; living barrier; courtyard; large planter; xerophytic
ZONE	9–11

ONCOBA SPINOSA, native of high elevation river valleys, and of bushveldt, is completely adapted to a rugged life. This small, densely woody, sparsely foliaged, shrubby species has leathery, long, elliptic, toothed leaves and is heavily armed with straight, axillary spines to 8 cm (3.1 in.) in length. In spring, the dull foliage is enlivened with wine-red, new leaves. At this time, and possibly at other intervals, this bony, spiny, unattractive, little tree is embellished with the most exquisite blooms. Delicate, waxy, milky white, with a golden-yellow 'yolk' of curling stamens at their centres, the lovely, fragrant *Camellia*-like blooms do look like fried eggs. Although they live for only 1 day, they are carried in succession over a long period. The flowers are followed by large, hard-shelled, rusty or golden brown berries that are filled with sweet pulp and many seeds. While not particularly delectable, this fruit is edible. The wood of *O. spinosa* is hard, pale brown and polishes well but, because of its small calliper, it is not in general use except for inlay and small cabinet work. In South Africa, this native is known as the Snuff-Box Tree and was, in fact, used to make such items. The fruit, too, was found a purpose, dried with its seeds inside, and used as a rattle.

*** *O. echinata*; (Oliv.), (syn. *Caloncoba echinata*), Upper Guinea, W Africa. The GORLI SHRUB has no thorns on its limbs but bears a densely spiny, yellow or orange, globose fruit filled with many seeds. The thin, leathery leaves (to 15 cm [6 in]) are oblong, short-pointed at the tip and wedge-shaped at the base. The short-stemmed flowers are white and much smaller than those of *O. spinosa*. Oil is extracted from the seeds, which consist of 46% hard, white, crystalline fat and is popular regionally as a hair dressing. The roots and leaves of both species are used medicinally. These are honey plants. (10–12)

O. spinosa; fr. is filled with sweet pulp that is edible but not very tasty.

O. spinosa; the Fried Egg Flower is so-called because its flat, white, fragrant blooms each have a 'yolk' of stamens at their centres.

O. spinosa; decked out in its summer foliage at the Fruit and Spice Park, Homestead, Florida, USA.

O. spinosa; a tough, spiny, xerophytic, decid., African sp.

ORIGIN	N Qld, Australia, endemic
HEIGHT	up to 25 m (82 ft)
TYPE	evergreen flowering and fruiting tree
STATUS	limited distribution
HABITAT	lowland wet rainforest, often along permanent streams and near swamps
GROWTH	moderately fast
FLOWG	early summer
DRY TOL.	moderate
SALT TOL.	low
LIGHT	full sun
SOIL	fertile, well-drained
NUTRIT.	balanced fertilizer annually; deep, organic mulch
HAZARDS	none
PROBLEMS	none
ENVIRON.	insect and bird nectar
PROPAG.	seeds (scarified); semi-ripe cuttings
LEAVES	pinnate; deep green; stoutly stalked, petiole finely, rusty hairy
FLOWERS	showy; pink, mauve or red; pea-like, set in bell-shaped, deeply toothed calyxes
FRUIT	a legume, to 10 cm (4 in.); brown, dehiscent; containing 2 or 3 flat, polished, hard red seeds
USE	street tree; specimen; shade tree; large flowering tree; public open space
ZONE	10–12

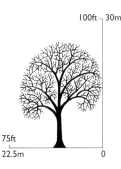

100ft — 30m

75ft
22.5m ⎯⎯⎯⎯ 0

Ormosia ormondii

YELLOW BEAN

(F. Muell.) Merr.   100 spp.

Podopetalum ormondii

FABACEAE (Papilionoideae)

LIKE MOST OF THIS LARGE CLAN, *Ormosia ormondii* is distinguished by the light tan, smoothish bark of its large trunk that becomes finely scaly on mature trees. This broad-crowned Australian endemic may become a mass of pink, red or mauve during a dry summer, when heavy rain breaks the drought in its lowland, monsoonal rainforest. At such times, it is considered one of the most spectacular species of this tropical region. *O. ormondii* forms a dense crown, with its foliage clustered towards the ends of the branches. Large, stout-stalked, pinnate leaves have rusty hairy petioles and deep green leaflets, with very short, reddish petioles. Pea-like flowers are held in crowded, branched panicles. They are clasped in elongated, bell-shaped calyxes with unequal, pointed teeth and comprise 5 pink petals with long stamens and slender, curved styles exserted. These panicles and all young shoots are finely rusty hairy. Blooms last for several weeks and provide nectar for many native birds and insects. Sharply beaked, brown, dry, dehiscent pods replace the flowers. They contain 1 or a few bright red, hard, flat, polished seeds that resemble those of *Adenanthera pavonina* and are similarly used for beadwork. Slow at first, *O. ormondii* grows steadily once established. Like many species of this large genus, the useful heartwood is salmon-coloured, with occasional darker streaks. It is coarse-textured and of medium weight.

*** *O. krugii*: (Urban), Puerto Rico and Lesser Antilles, to 18 m (60 ft). PERONÎA has abundant, dark violet flowers in summer. Fruit, to 10 cm (4 in.), is pointed at both ends, with 1–5 red seeds, with black spots. The heartwood is salmon-pink and useful. (10–12)

*** *O. nobilis*; (Tul.) Amazon Basin, to 7 m (23 ft), LADY BUG TREE is a small, drought-resistant tree of the savannahs. The seeds are red, with a black spot. *O. nobilis* has fine roots that grow under damaged bark and coalesce to repair it. (10–12)

O. ormondii; wood beans filled with hard, polished red sds.

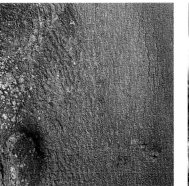

O. ormondii; with light tan, smoothish bark on its large trunk, which becomes finely scaly on mature trees.

O. ormondii; when rain breaks a drought, this sp. is considered one of the most spectacular flowg trees of its region.

O. ormondii; panicles and all young shoots are finely rusty hairy. Blooms last for several weeks and provide nectar for many native birds and insects.

Oroxylon indicum

MIDNIGHT HORROR

(L.) Kurtz.   1 sp.

BIGNONIACEAE

INFAMOUS FOR ITS NOCTURNAL SILHOUETTE AND SMELL, this somewhat invasive species of the wastelands and roadsides of Indo-Malaysia has become a collector's item. True to its Bignoniaceae heritage, its leaves are compound, its flowers are trumpet-shaped and its seed capsules generously filled with winged seeds. Unlike most of its kin, however, *Oroxylon indicum* is exaggerated in all its parts. Fast growing, lanky and sparsely limbed, this pachycaul tree blooms after attaining up to 10 m (33 ft), whereupon further upward growth ceases until, gradually, the lower buds break to give rise to further stiffly erect branches. Its enormous, long-petioled, coarsely pinnate leaves are held in giant parasols. They are divided 4 times, feather-fashion, and have wide branchlets holding relatively few pointed leaflets. Shooting up to 1.5 m (60 in.), the terminally erect, crowded inflorescence holds broadly lobed, funnel-shaped flowers that closely resemble those of *Markhamia* or *Kigelia*. Blushed reddish or purplish brown on the outside, they are yellowish or pinkish within, with copious nectar. They remain closed until about 10.00 p.m., when they open and give off a harsh odour that attracts bats to its nectar. After, the corolla is detached and shed. Each limb of *O. indicum* appears to bloom independently of the others. The flowers produce enormous, scimitar-shaped seed pods measuring up to 1.5 m (60 in.) in length. These are dangled from the tree like huge sabres. *O. indicum* is a provider to humans as well as to bats. Its young shoots are cooked as a vegetable and the bitter bark of its roots and stems are used medicinally. A dye is also made from it which, in Sarawak, is used to decorate rattan baskets. In Thailand, the flowers are harvested, chopped up and added to local dishes, usually with chillies.

ORIGIN	from India to Malaysia
HEIGHT	up to 20 m (66 ft)
TYPE	semi-deciduous flowering tree
STATUS	not threatened
HABITAT	clearings and roadsides; lowland woodlands
GROWTH	fast
FLOWG	summer
DRY TOL.	moderate
SALT TOL.	low
LIGHT	full sun to bright shade
SOIL	fertile, water-retentive
NUTRIT.	occasional dressings of balanced fertilizer
HAZARDS	none
PROBLEMS	may be invasive
ENVIRON.	nectar for bats
PROPAG.	seeds; cuttings
LEAVES	2–3 pinnate; rich green; to 2 m (7 ft) long; leaflets few, ovate, to 9 cm (3.5 in.); glossy
FLOWERS	showy; reddish, purple-brown, lined whitish yellow; with a harsh, pungent, nocturnal odour
FRUIT	a capsule, to 150 × 10 cm (60 × 4 in.); scimitar-shaped; seeds many, with papery wings
USE	flowering tree; curiosity; accent; botanic collection; public open space
ZONE	10–12

(tree height diagram: 100ft / 30m, 75ft, 22.5m, 0)

O. indicum; nocturnally malodorous fls are held erect in crowded infls.

O. indicum; enormous scimitar-shaped fr. are dangled like huge sabres. By the light of the moon, travellers may be charged with fear, especially as large bats swoop noiselessly around.

O. indicum; aborted after pollination by bats. They closely resemble those of *Markhamia* or *Kigelia*.

O. indicum; a sparse, fast-growing, Trop. Asian sp. known as Midnight Horror in some regions for its dagger-like fr.

ORIGIN	KwaZuluNatal, S Africa
HEIGHT	up to 10 m (33 ft)
TYPE	evergreen, flowering tall shrub or small tree
STATUS	a protected, endangered species
HABITAT	on coastal sand forest
GROWTH	slow
FLOWG	intermittently, all year
DRY TOL.	moderate
SALT TOL.	moderate
LIGHT	sheltered sun to part shade
SOIL	fertile, friable
NUTRIT.	organic fertilizer; deep, organic mulch
HAZARDS	none
PROBLEMS	none
ENVIRON.	nectar for moths
PROPAG.	seeds; cuttings; layers
LEAVES	simple, deep green; to 12 cm (4.7 in.); oblong-elliptic, glabrous, leathery, with asymmetric base
FLOWERS	showy; white, with long, slender tube; held in crowded corymbs; nocturnally fragrant
FRUIT	a berry, to 2.5 cm (1 in.); oval, fleshy, yellowish orange; held erect
USE	small flowering tree; patio; specimen; large planter; botanic collection; conservatory
ZONE	9–12

50ft ⌐15m

50ft
15m
0

Oxyanthus pyriformis

ZULU LOQUAT

40 spp

O. natalensis

RUBIACEAE

THESE SLOW-GROWING AFRICAN EDNDEMICS challenge their trop. American cousins in their beauty and innovation. **Oxyanthus pyriformis** is a native of the sand forest of KwaZuluNatal, in eastern S Africa. Like the rest of its genus, it mimics many of the characteristics of *Posoqueria latifolia*, the Needle Flower. Known regionally as Zulu Loquat (or Zoeloelikwart, in Afrikaans), **O. pyriformis** is found either as a multi-stemmed shrub or as a small, spreading tree. Dark green, glossy leaves are elliptic, large and leathery, with a lobed, strongly asymmetric base. Intermittently, after a heavy rain shower breaks a dry period, the tree is flushed with abundant blooms. It is a superb sight, with each flower cluster spouting its needle-like blooms and creating a shower of pearly white. The nocturnally fragrant, white flowers are held in tight, axillary clusters. Like those of *Posoqueria*, each bloom has a very long, slender tube up to 6 cm (2.4 in.) long and adapted to accommodate the proboscis of a local Hawk Moth. From each cluster of flowers, a single fruit is formed, an oval, fleshy, yellowish orange berry with a slender neck. **O. pyriformis** blooms when still relatively young.

*** **O. speciosus**; (D.C.), Trop. Africa, to 10 m (33 ft). Known as LISILURU in Kenya and WILD LOQUAT in S Africa (where the form is subsp. *gerradii*). This is a widespread, understorey, evergreen shrub or small forest tree, with smooth, reddish brown bark. The leaves are elliptic to narrowly ovate, very large, to 30 cm (12 in.), glossy dark green, with a rounded base. They have a tendancy to droop. The flowers are similar to *O. pyriformis* but with shorter tubes, to 3.5 cm (1.3 in.). (10–12)

*** **O. oxycarpus**; (S. Moore), Trop E. Africa, to 4 m (12 ft), is a small species with oblong-elliptic leaves, to 9 cm (3.5 in.). The flowers are white or cream in axillary clusters of 1–3, with a tube that is up to 13 cm (5 in.) long. (10–12)

O. pyriformis; rounded, fleshy with a slender neck.

O. pyriformis; young bark is smooth and reddish.

O. pyriformis; this specimen is growing at Queen Elizabeth II Botanic Park, Cayman Is, W Indies.

O. pyriformis; is a superb sight, with each fl. cluster spouting its cluster of needle-like blooms, creating a veritable shower of pearly white.

Pachira aquatica

GUIANA CHESTNUT

Aublet.   20 spp.

P. macrocarpa; Bombax aquaticum

MALVACEAE formerly BOMBACACEAE

PACHIRA AQUATICA forms heavy plank buttresses at the base of its stout trunk in order to support its corpulent, sumptuous, oval crown of glossy, palmate leaves. This fast-growing species is a native of the rich river estuaries along the coasts from Mexico to northern S America and Trinidad. Its dense, evergreen foliage is composed of large, long-petioled, digitate leaves with 3–9 entire, elliptic to obovate-oblong leaflets. *P. aquatica* is prized for its stunningly opulent, rusty plush, sometimes deeply ridged fruit that resemble cocoa pods. They may measure 30 cm (12 ins.) in length, weigh up to 3 kilos (6.6 lbs) and contain many large, starchy seeds embedded in whitish, fleshy, fibrous pulp. These seeds are roasted and eaten like chestnuts or ground into flour. (Staff at the Fruit and Spice Park in Florida report them to be less than delectable.) Equally significant, are the voluptuous flowers. In the evening, these extravagant, sweetly fragrant blooms unpeel their strap-like, yellowish white waxy petals and unfurl a massive brush of up to 700 purple- or crimson-tipped stamens for their nocturnal pollinators. The photograph (below left) of the freshly opened bloom was taken before it had been pollinated; in a few hours, it would have faded to a creamy tan in the sun, before collapsing and falling. The young leaves are prepared and eaten as a vegetable in some parts. In Guatemala, the skin of the green, immature fruit is used to treat hepatitis, while Choco Indians prepare the seeds as an anaesthetic. The bark provides a yellow dye used to tint sails and fishing nets. The large seeds are designed to withstand humidity and are capable of floating in water for months. It is not until they touch dry land that they begin to germinate. *P. insignis:* ([Sw.] Savigny), (syn. *P. loddigesii*), S America and W Indies, to 30m (100ft) Wild Chestnut or Wilid Cocoa, is superficially similar to *P. aquatica*. The pungent flowers, which may measure up to 30 cm (24in.) diam., have dark, rusty red calyxes, strap-like, crimson petals and red and white filaments. Fruit is rusty-velvety. (10–12) These are honey trees.

ORIGIN	Trop. C and S America
HEIGHT	up to 20 m (66 ft)
TYPE	evergreen flowering and fruiting tree
STATUS	not threatened
HABITAT	river estuaries; lowland rainforests
GROWTH	moderate
FLOW'G	year-round
DRY TOL.	low to moderate
SALT TOL.	low
LIGHT	full sun to bright shade
SOIL	rich, deep, humid
NUTRIT.	balanced fertilizer annually; deep, organic mulch
HAZARDS	none
PROBLEMS	none
ENVIRON.	nectar for bats
PROPAG.	seeds; cuttings; layers
LEAVES	palmate; rich green; with 5–9 leaflets, obovate to elliptic-lanceolate; long-petioled
FLOWERS	showy; yellowish white or pink to purple; petals long, narrow; nocturnally fragrant
FRUIT	a capsule, to 30 cm (12 in.); 5-valved, rusty-velvety, woody; seeds edible
USE	shade tree; flowering tree; humid shade tree; public open space; conservatory
ZONE	10–12

P. aquatica; a huge, velvety capsule with edible, chestnut-like sds.

P. aquatica; has stunning, nocturnal blooms that open in the early evening and fade by morning. Strongly fragrant, they are adapted for bat pollination.

P. aquatica; a fast-growing sp. is native of rich, river estuaries along the coasts from Mexico to north S America and Trinidad.

P. aquatica; with a stout, smooth-barked trunk, this sp. quickly stabilizes itself with large, plank buttresses.

1

2

3

4

Pachira glabra; ([A. Robyns] Pasq.), (syn. *Bombacopsis glabra*), from Mexico to the Guianas (including N. Brazil), to 17 m (56 ft). Known as SABA NUT or AMERICAN CHESTNUT, this small, vigorous sp. is native to alluvial plains and lowland rainforests. It is ornamental, distinguished by its glabrous, long-petioled, 5–7 foliate lvs and by its bright green trunk, limbs and fruit. (1) Nocturnal fls have light green, strap-like sepals and wiry, white, curving stamens. (2) Fr. is a capsule, to 12.5 cm (5 in.), containing many large, very fertile sds. It resembles a Cocoa pod. *P. glabra* is cultivated regionally for its sds, which are eaten fresh, boiled or roasted like chestnuts. (10–12)

Pachira quinata; (Seem.), (syn. *Bombacopsis quinatum*), from Nicaragua to Colombia, to 30 m (100 ft). POCHOTE is a S American sp. that has an unmistakable trunk that is studded with vicious, rusty red, stout spines. (3) It is also called CEDRO ESPINOSO or CEDRO MACHO for its fine, hardwood timber, which is prized regionally for making furniture, doors and windows. This relatively fast-growing, decid. giant has small, fragrant, white, nocturnal fls, (4) that are pollinated by moths. Fr. 5-valved, with sds enveloped in a fine woolly 'duvet' that aids in their dispersal. (10–12) These are honey trees.

Pangium edule

KEPAYANG

Reinw.   1 sp.

FLACOURTIACEAE

'*KEPAYANG IS ONE OF NATURE'S MONSTERS*, wrote E.J.H. Corner in *Wayside Trees of Malaya*. 'It is a poisonous tree with ungainly fruits suggesting a stomach crammed with big seeds.' Despite his misgivings, Corner acknowledges that this toxic monster has played a very important role in village life in SE Asia. *Pangium edule* is large, spreading and buttressed, with *Terminalia*-type branching. As a sapling, the leaves are lobed, but in maturity they become long-stalked and cordate. The flowers are small and whitish, while the fruit, known as Kelauk in Malaysia, is large, nippled and scurfy-skinned, weighing up to 3 kgs (6.6 lbs). It contains several large, angular seeds that have creamy white, oily kernels. On ripening, when the fruit becomes mushy, the seeds are removed and processed by washing, boiling and drying to remove the toxic enzyme. The seeds are pressed to extract their oil, known as Kepayang, and is sometimes used for cooking when coconut oil is scarce. By heating this oil, the toxins are destroyed but, because of a high olein content, it quickly becomes rancid. With the availability of cooking oils, the use of Kepayang has mostly died out. *P. edule* may now be quite rare in modern, built-up areas where more acceptable fruit is planted, but for generations it was included in the staple diet of many villagers in Malaysia and Borneo. A poison, glucoside (hydrocyanic acid), occurs in all parts of the tree, particularly the fruit kernel. This acid can be denatured, however, and rural people knew the art of doing so, devising ways to use the oily kernels and leaves. Glucoside, as a poison, can also serve as an antiseptic. Crushed, fresh seeds are commonly applied to sterilize wounds or are applied to boils. The leaves have been used externally to treat skin parasites. There is still much scientific study to be done on this chemically interesting species

ORIGIN	Malaysia
HEIGHT	up to 27 m (89 ft)
TYPE	deciduous fruiting tree
STATUS	rare in the wild
HABITAT	lowland humid forest
GROWTH	moderate
FLOWG	spring
DRY TOL.	moderate
SALT TOL.	moderate
LIGHT	full sun
SOIL	rich, humid, fertile
NUTRIT.	balanced fertilizer annually; deep, organic mulch
HAZARDS	all parts very toxic
PROBLEMS	none
ENVIRON.	nectar for insects
PROPAG.	seeds
LEAVES	simple; deep green, rusty scurfy below; oval or cordate, long-petioled
FLOWERS	inconspicuous; greenish white; to 5 cm (2 in.); with many stamens
FRUIT	a berry, to 30 cm (12 in.); with brown, scurfy skin and nipples at each end; many large, woody seeds
USE	botanic collection (not recommended for landscape planting)
ZONE	11–12

P. edule; with long, yellowish petioles and deeply veined, cordate lvs.

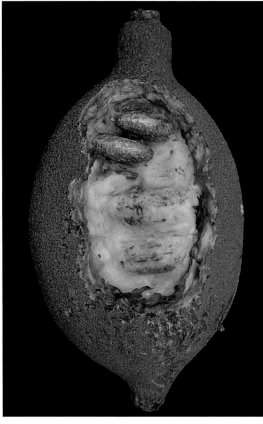

P. edule; the poison, glucoside, occurs in all parts of this tree, particularly the fr. kernel; however, this acid can be denatured by rural people who use the oily kernels and lvs.

P. edule; has an opulent canopy, concealing the poisonous fruit.

P. edule; distinctive, smooth, golden bark matches the fr.

ORIGIN	N Australia and New Guinea
HEIGHT	up to 10 m (33 ft)
TYPE	evergreen, small fruiting tree
STATUS	not threatened
HABITAT	monsoonal areas in open Eucalypt forest or dry scrub
GROWTH	slow
FLOWG	early spring
DRY TOL.	high
SALT TOL.	low
LIGHT	full sun
SOIL	deep, well-drained
NUTRIT.	balanced fertilizer annually
HAZARDS	none
PROBLEMS	none
ENVIRON.	wild bird and animal fruit
PROPAG.	fresh seeds; root suckers
LEAVES	simple; dull green, glabrous above, whitish hairy below
FLOWERS	inconspicuous; whitish cream; tubular; held in terminal or axillary panicles; scented
FRUIT	a drupe, to 4 cm (1.5 in.) long; skin orange scurfy; flesh yellow-orange, edible
USE	shade tree; fruit tree; specimen; xerophytic; bonsai subject
ZONE	10–12

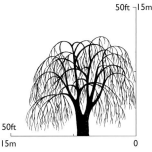

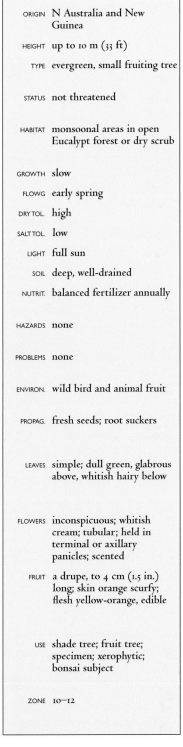

PARINARI IS THE UNLIKELY NAME of a fairly large genus widely distributed throughout the tropics. They are members of the Chrysobalanaceae family, closely related to the Rose clan, and are particularly valued for their fruit, which has been a important food for Australian Aboriginals. *Parinari nonda* has an singularly exotic-sounding name and is known commonly as Nonda Plum. It is native to the drier, monsoonal areas of N Australia, New Guinea and Solomon Is. A slow-growing, xerophytic species, *P. nonda* is distinguished by its contorted, twisted growth, corky bark and silver-lined leaves that are arranged regularly along strongly weeping, slender branchlets. Tiny, insignificant, whitish cream flowers are held in congested, axillary tomentose panicles. The fruit is ovoid with orange-brown skin and yellow-orange, firm, dry flesh that tastes of baked potato. They are held in great abundance and actually look like small, scurfy potatoes.

*** *P. curatellifolia* subsp. *mobola*; (Planchon ex Benth.), Trop Africa, to 15 m (50 ft). Known as MBOLA in Kenya, while further south it is GRYS APPEL (Afrikaans), SAND APPLE or HISSING TREE, because local people believe that the tree hisses when it is cut. Locally, this species is important for its very hard, pale brown to yellow-red timber that is used for poles, mortars and dugout canoes. Borer-proof, with a high silica content, this timber is not durable when exposed to the elements. It is recorded, however, that David Livingstone's grave originally had a headstone carved in a trunk of this species. The ovoid, russet-yellow, scurfy-skinned fruit, to 3.5 cm (1.3 in.), is described as having dry but delicious flesh. In Zambia, it is used to make a non-intoxicating drink, Luswazhi. (Fermented and distilled, it also provides an intoxicating beverage.) The fruit is used in many ways and the roots are highly valued for their medicinal properties. *P. curatellifolia* is strongly fire-resistant. (10–12)

P. nonda; tiny, whitish cream fls are held in congested, tomentose panicles.

P. nonda; distinguished by its contorted, twisted growth and fragmented, corky bark.

P. nonda; like small potatoes, the fr. has russet, scurfy skin and is described as having dry, but delicious flesh.

P. nonda; this tree in Cairns guards a memorial to commemorate the tragic death of a Japanese student. It is very appropriate for its strong, sturdy growth and weeping nature.

Parkia javanica

DRUMSTICK TREE

(Lam.) Merrill.　　　　　　　30 spp.

FABACEAE (Mimosoideae)

EDWIN A. MENNINGER, in his *Fantastic Trees*, says 'Like a woman holding some distasteful article at arm's length till she can get rid of it, a Parkia tree dangles its malodorous balls of flowers at the ends of long ropes that hang down under the trees...' These lofty, Asian natives of low-lying riversides and savannahs are an exceedingly handsome but curious genus. ***Parkia javanica*** has a tall, clear, smooth trunk and a crown of remarkably finely divided, ferny leaves over its flat-topped or parasol-shaped crown. In summer, ***P. javanica*** is decorated with a wonderful display of curious, fuzzy flowers that are held in tightly packed, globular knobs and dangled on the ends of long, sturdy stalks like drumsticks. Three types of flowers compose a single head: infertile ones near the stalk, males in the middle and bisexual ones at the apex. Nocturnally, their copious, watery nectar has a strong, sickly smell of sour milk. This extraordinarily original floral arrangement has been evolved specifically for bat-pollination. As they fade – after a single night – the embryos of the apical flowers develop into a large, dangling cluster of giant, spiralling, bean-like, pale green pods that contain fleshy seeds embedded in an orange-pink, bitter, mealy pulp. It is interesting that some species of *Parkia* have red (see below) rather than white flowers and are suspected of being pollinated by nectar-loving birds rather than bats.

*** ***P. speciosa***; (Hassk.), Malaysia endemic, to 45 m (148 ft), PARKIE or PETAI. Commonly grown in Asian gardens, this handsome, parasol-crowned shade tree is valued for its abundant harvest of 50 cm (20 in.) long, crisp, light green, bitter seed pods. These are dangled in bundles on long, stout, cord-like stems. They taste strongly of garlic, said to pervade the body of the eater, and contain edible seeds. These are eaten raw in salads or are pickled or cooked and eaten as a relish. They are known to have a diuretic effect and are eaten by local people to help control high blood pressure. (10–12)

ORIGIN	from India to Java
HEIGHT	up to 50 m (164 ft)
TYPE	semi-deciduous, large flowering and fruiting tree
STATUS	not threatened
HABITAT	humid lowland forests
GROWTH	slow
FLOWG	summer
DRY TOL.	moderate
SALT TOL.	low
LIGHT	full sun
SOIL	rich, deep, humid
NUTRIT.	balanced fertilizer annually; deep, organic mulch
HAZARDS	none
PROBLEMS	none
ENVIRON.	nectar for bats
PROPAG.	seeds (fast at first)
LEAVES	2-pinnate; rich green; leaflets in 15–30 pairs; pinnae to 13 mm (0.5 in.)
FLOWERS	showy; white, with yellow stamens; held on long, pendent stalks; with a smell of sour milk
FRUIT	a legume, to 15 cm (6 in.); many, forming from flower heads; containing edible, garlic-flavoured seeds
USE	large shade tree; large flowering tree; street tree; public open space
ZONE	10–11

P. javanica; pods are dangled on long, stout, cord-like stems.

P. speciosa; the bizarre fls, held on long, sturdy stalks, resemble drumsticks. They are composed of a collar of white, infertile fls with males around the middle and females below.

P. speciosa; embryos of the apical fls develop into a large, dangling cluster of giant, bean-like fr.

Parkia sumatrana; (Miq.) SE Asia. Some spp. have red fls and are possibly pollinated by nectar-loving birds (not bats).

ORIGIN	from Mexico to Honduras
HEIGHT	up to 7 m (23 ft)
TYPE	semi-deciduous, small flowering tree
STATUS	not threatened
HABITAT	dry lowland grasslands and coastal region
GROWTH	fast
FLOWG	spring to summer
DRY TOL.	high
SALT TOL.	high
LIGHT	full sun
SOIL	wide tolerance
NUTRIT.	occasional fertilizer
HAZARDS	very spiny
PROBLEMS	scales; root rot
ENVIRON.	insect nectar
PROPAG.	seeds
LEAVES	2-pinnate; bright green; saw-toothed; with terminal spines
FLOWERS	showy; bright yellow; with orange dot on lip; held in loose racemes; sweetly scented
FRUIT	a legume, to 10 cm (4 in.); flat, beaked; constricted between seeds
USE	seaside; small flowering tree; living barrier; accent; large coastal planter; xerophytic
ZONE	9–12

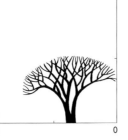

50ft 15m
50ft
15m
0

Parkinsonia aculeata

JERUSALEM THORN

L.   29 spp.

FABACEAE (Caesalpinioideae)

WHEN THE LEAVES of this common tropical tree are examined closely, the structure of its extraordinary leaf arrangement can be seen. The leaves are 2- or 3-pinnate, with the pinnae being composed of a wide, flat, winged midrib that holds tiny, rounded leaflets (pinules) along the length. At the base, where it joins the main stem, there is a very short, spine-tipped leaf-stalk (rachis) from which 2 or 3 pinnae arise. When this curious, leguminous tree is leafless, it continues to hold its leaf stalks and midribs – only the tiny leaflets are deciduous. Because of this arrangement, the *Parkinsonia aculeata* never appears truly leafless. Known as Jerusalem Thorn because of its popularity in Arabia, this graceful, little tree is remarkable for its slender, smooth, yellow-green or blue-green trunk and sparse, wiry branchlets and green saw-bladed leaves, which weave an attractively airy crown. *P. aculeata* is actually a tough, desert tree that is well equipped for its xerophytic life. The green skin of its trunk and the persistent leaf stalks are adapted to manufacture chlorophyll in the absence of normal leaves. Widely distributed early in the 19th century, *P. aculeata* has proved adaptable to desert conditions in Iran and other parts of the Middle East. Buoyant, spring blooms enrich this thrifty, elegant tree. In bloom, they are bright yellow, blotched orange, with the upper petal slightly larger and spotted red, but they turn red as they wither. Long, pointed pods, which are constricted between the oblong, dark brown seeds, follow the flowers. The sapwood is yellowish and the heartwood is light or reddish brown. The wood is moderately hard and heavy, but brittle and is most commonly used for fuel. The foliage and the seed pods are grazed by animals. An infusion of the leaves has be used in home remedies.

NOTE: *P. aculeata* has become seriously invasive in drier areas of Australia.

P. aculeata; with bundles of narrow, constricted pods.

P. aculeata; thin, grey bark over green skin that may manufacture chlorophyll when 'lvs' are shed.

P. aculeata; with a lean, muscled framework and sparse, misty foliage, this sp. is designed to cope with arid habitats.

P. aculeata; Jerusalem Thorn is transformed from its leggy, drab, green-grey anonymity by its joyous golden blooms.

311

A view of the entrance to the small, but exquisite, Andromeda Botanic Gardens, Bathsheba, Barbados, W Indies, where the legendary plantswoman, Iris Bannochie, spent many years amassing her collections and creating this beautiful national treasure. This is one of many botanic gardens visited in the search for worthy, trop. or subtrop. trees.

ORIGIN	Panama, endemic
HEIGHT	up to 7 m (23 ft)
TYPE	evergreen, small foliage tree
STATUS	not threatened
HABITAT	humid limestone woodlands
GROWTH	slow
FLOWG	spring and summer
DRY TOL.	moderate
SALT TOL.	low
LIGHT	full sun to bright shade
SOIL	fertile, humid
NUTRIT.	balanced fertilizer annually; deep, organic mulch
HAZARDS	none
PROBLEMS	none
ENVIRON.	bat and moth nectar
PROPAG.	seeds
LEAVES	3-foliate; light green; leaflets to 6.5 cm (2.5 in.); petioles winged
FLOWERS	showy; greenish white; to 5 cm (2 in.); bell-shaped, with frilly lips; cauliflorous
FRUIT	a capsule, to 54 cm (20 in.); dull, translucent yellow; pendent, pungent
USE	humid shade garden; specimen; curiosity; botanic collection; large conservatory
ZONE	10–12

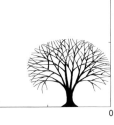

50ft—15m
50ft
15m
0

Parmentiera cerifera

CANDLE TREE

Seem.   9 spp

BIGNONIACEAE

LIKE ITS CLOSE RELATIVE the Calabash, **Parmentiera cerifera** branches from near the base of its trunk, its limbs spreading and arching in an untidy manner. This endemic Panamanian species, native to limestone formations, has a sparsely clad crown with thin, light green leaves with distinctive, winged petioles. Like the Calabash, the *P. cerifera* is cauliflorous. Split down one side, the curved, brownish calyx cups the frilly, greenish white flowers that are irregularly bell-shaped and folded upwards. Their throats are streaked a rosy pink to attract moths and bats. When the flowers have been pollinated, they abort and the tree then becomes covered with what may be the most bizarre of all fruit. Exuding a pungently aromatic fragrance reminiscent of overripe apples, the slim, waxy, yellow-ochre fruit look exactly like freshly dipped candles hanging out to dry. These fruit eventually fall and lie on the ground to ripen and rot, attracting cattle and other herbivores, which eat them and are responsible for the distribution of their seeds. (An interesting suggestion is that extinct megafauna, like dinosaurs, were their original gourmets.) Regionally, farmers use the fruit to fatten their livestock. In fields, where the Candle Tree provides shade, animals strip and eat the bark, as well as browse on the fruit. *P. cerifera* has been found to contain medicinal qualities and regionally the bark and roots have been employed therapeutically. The Candle Tree does not flower or fruit until it is relatively well established.

*** *P. aculeata*; (Kunth. & R.O. Williams), (syn *P. edulis*), C America, to 10 m (33 ft). Cow OKRA or GUAJILOTE has a spreading crown, with leaves whorled on short, spiny twigs. The waxy fruit is dull yellow, short, plump and ridged like okra or a gherkin. Australians call it Cucumber Tree. It is eaten locally or fed to farm animals. (10–12)

NOTE: these species have become invasive in N Australia.

P. cerifera; limbs spread and arch in a somewhat untidy manner.

P. aculeata; known as Cow Okra, these fr. are sometimes eaten, but more often fed to animals.

P. aculeata; curved, brownish calyx cups greenish white fls, which are irregularly bell-shaped and folded upwards.

P. cerifera; bears its slender, waxy fr. directly on its trunk and branches like candles hanging out to dry. When ripe, they have a sweetly pungent smell. They drop and rot below the tree.

Peltophorum pterocarpum

COPPER POD

(D.C.) Backer ex K. Heyne   8 spp.

Caesalpinea ferrugineum; P. roxburghii

FABACEAE (Caesalpinioideae)

THERE ARE 2 *PELTOPHORUMS* particularly popular in the tropics. They are very similar and difficult to differentiate, although 1 is a New World species and the other is native to the Old World. In spite of being hardier, the Trop. American species, *P. dubium* tends to be less popular. The Old World species, **Peltophorum pterocarpum**, is known as Copper Pod. After a somewhat untidy leaf drop at the end of the dry season, the tree rapidly reclads itself with luxuriant, dark, coppery red, softly tomentose, new growth, which gradually matures as finely pinnate, glossy, ferny foliage, to form a lavish canopy. Opulent, coppery red candelabra of velvety flower buds gradually open to present profuse, short-lived, golden yellow blooms, which are nocturnally fragrant and have a grape-like scent. There are 2 flushes of bloom each year. One of the charms of these great trees is the carpet of gold created below as they sprinkle their spent blooms, which will crackle underfoot. Huge, erect branches of fruit are held high on the canopy in autumn. As they ripen, the pods resemble smooth, burnished ox-blood leather and glow a fiery red at sunset. Many abort and spill their contents, while others turn blackish brown and remain on the tree, leading to its having an unruly look. Despite the rapid growth of *P. pterocarpum*, the timber is renowned in India and used for cabinetwork; the hard heartwood is blackish brown and the sapwood is whitish in colour. In Asia, this species is valued medicinally. It also provides a source of brown dye that is used to colour batik. In spite of its drawbacks, this is a worthy species, especially as it is so tolerant of drought and salt conditions. It should be pruned to reduce its bulk in dry months and never planted near buildings.

NOTE: *P. pterocarpum* has brittle wood, is shallow-rooted and vulnerable to termites.

100ft – 30m
100ft
30m   0

ORIGIN	from Trop. Asia to Australia
HEIGHT	up to 24 m (80 ft)
TYPE	evergreen, flowering tree
STATUS	not threatened
HABITAT	dry or moist coastal forest; deciduous woodland
GROWTH	fast
FLOWG	spring and summer
DRY TOL.	high
SALT TOL.	moderate to high
LIGHT	full sun
SOIL	widely tolerant
NUTRIT.	balanced fertilizer annually
HAZARDS	none
PROBLEMS	brittle; shallow roots
ENVIRON.	nectar
PROPAG.	seeds (hard and slow)
LEAVES	2-pinnate; rich, yellow-green; to 40 cm (16 in.); leaflets in 10–20 pairs
FLOWERS	showy; bright yellow; in erect racemes, to 20 cm (8 in.); with a grape-like scent
FRUIT	a legume, to 10 cm (4 in.); flat, indehiscent; bright, coppery red
USE	seaside; large flowering tree; street tree; specimen; xerophytic
ZONE	10–12

P. pterocarpum; burnished, dried fr. and new coppery growth glows in the setting sun.

P. pterocarpum; this sp. is more flamboyant than the other spp. because of the rusty copper of the tomen on the fl. buds and burnished ox-blood of their fr.

P. pterocarpum; blooming in the alkaline soils of Grand Bahama, where it is a popular street tree.

P. pterocarpum; despite Copper Pod's rapid growth, the timber is renowned in India and used for cabinetwork.

(1) ***Peltophorum africanum***; (Sond.), from Zambia to S Africa, to 10 m (33 ft). Black Wattle, Weeping Wattle or Huilboom is found in bushveld, often on sandy soils. It is densely crowned and smaller than the other 2 spp. but may reach 13 m (43 ft) (sometimes coppicing). Young shoots are densely covered with fine, rusty brown hairs. Lvs are feathery, with 4–9 prs. of pinnae; lflts usually 8–22prs. pinnae, densely hairy below. (2) Fls are held in erect, terminal, rusty brown, velvety racemes; petals aree yellow, crinkled, fragrant. (3) Fr. pods are flat, winged, with fine, velvety hairs. Wood is soft, with black heartwood, which is particularly popular for carving. Bark and roots are used for medicinal purposes. This is a breeding tree for several local butterflies. Flowg in spring and summer. In S Africa, the lvs of this tree are eaten by spittle bugs, which excrete frothing 'water' that drips from the crown, earning it the name, 'Weeping Wattle'. (9–12) (4) ***Peltophorum dubium***; ([Spreng.] Taub.), of S America, to 15 m (50 ft). Brasiletto, is less flamboyant than *P. pterocarpum* on the whole. (5) The spring and summer fls are light yellow with dark ochre tomen, but without the repeat blooming of *P. pterocarpum*. Fr. is smooth and a dull, grey-brown. (6) To compensate, lvs are glossy with 20–30 lflts per pinna, in a tidier, domed crown. This is the most cold hardy of these 3 spp., and, although it has brittle wood and shallow roots, appears to be more storm resistant. (9–11)

315

Persea americana

AVOCADO

Mill.   200 spp.

P. persea; P. gratissima

LAURACEAE

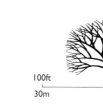

100ft — 30m

100ft

30m   0

PERSEA AMERICANA originated in C America and is recorded as having been grown for food since 8,000 BC. Early Spanish explorers discovered it in cultivation and took seeds to Spain in 1601. It is now grown in most warm regions. The fruit, widely known as Avocado, is considered one of the most nutritious in the world. There are 3 main forms of *P. americana*: Mexican (var. *drymifolia*), a subtropical, highland native with anise-scented leaves and small fruit; Guatemalan (var. *guatemalensis*), a semi-tropical, highland variety with large fruit to 2kg (4.4 lbs) that has a hard, brittle, warty skin; and W Indian (var. *americana*), from the tropical lowlands, a very large fruit, to 3kg (6.6 lbs), that is smooth, lacquered and bright green, with the lowest oil content. Fragrant, greenish white blooms are held in erect panicles. Each flower opens twice; the female (pistil) opens first, then, many hours later, it reopens with the male (stamens) phase. They have synchronous dichogamy, meaning that all trees in the area bloom at the same time and are either female or male positive at that point. Despite this, the trees may fruit only every second year. The fruit has oily, buttery pulp, rich in vitamins A, B and E, as well as potassium. In the Philippines, the ripe fruit is eaten mashed with milk and sugar or is even made into ice cream. Fresh pulp is massaged into the hair as a vitamin-rich hair tonic and restorer. An oil, the consistency of olive oil, is extracted from the pulp for domestic use, as well as being used for soaps and aromatherapy, and the oily seeds produce a reddish brown dye that has been used for marking clothing. The wood is soft and heavy but not durable. The leaves have proved toxic to goats and other animals, although most parts of the plant are used medicinally in some way. *P. americana* is fairly slow growing, taking 5–8 years to bear fruit from a seedling, or 3–4 years from grafted or budded stock. This is a honey plant.

ORIGIN	Trop. America
HEIGHT	up to 16 m (52 ft)
TYPE	semi-deciduous fruiting tree
STATUS	not threatened
HABITAT	coastal limestone; humid lowland
GROWTH	fast
FLOWG	summer to autumn
DRY TOL.	high
SALT TOL.	moderate
LIGHT	full sun
SOIL	rich, neutral to alkaline
NUTRIT.	balanced fertilizer twice a year; organic mulch
HAZARDS	none
PROBLEMS	root rot; scales
ENVIRON.	bee nectar; wild bird fruit
PROPAG.	seeds; tip cuttings; layers; grafts
LEAVES	simple; bright green; to 17 cm (6.7 in.); elliptic, glabrous; slightly aromatic
FLOWERS	fairly showy; greenish white; held in yellowish, branched clusters; fragrant
FRUIT	a drupe, to 20 cm (8 in.); ovoid, leathery-skinned; pulp whitish or yellowish, oily
USE	summer shade tree; backyard tree; xerophytic
ZONE	9–12

P. americana; with erect panicles of pale greenish, fragrant fls.

P. americana var. *americana*, the smooth, green-skinned, W Indian Avocado, which is the largest and least oily of the 3 types. Like all Avocados, it is rich in vitamins and potassium.

P. americana; the Avocado is a slow-growing sp. which takes 5–8 years to bear fr. from sd.

P. americana; the wood of this sp. is soft and heavy, but not durable.

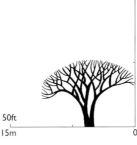

50ft ⌐15m

50ft
15m   0

Petrea arborea

TREE PETREA

H.B.K.   30 spp.

VERBENACEAE

ORIGIN	from northern S America to Trinidad
HEIGHT	up to 7 m (23 ft)
TYPE	semi-deciduous, small flowering tree
STATUS	rare in the wild
HABITAT	dry woodlands, on volcanic soils
GROWTH	slow
FLOWG	intermittently, year-round
DRY TOL.	high
SALT TOL.	moderate
LIGHT	full sun
SOIL	fertile, well-drained
NUTRIT.	magnesium-rich fertilizer
HAZARDS	none
PROBLEMS	none
ENVIRON.	insect nectar
PROPAG.	seeds; cuttings under mist; layers
LEAVES	simple; dullish green; to 16 × 8 cm (6 × 3 in.); elliptic, sandpapery
FLOWERS	showy; violet or blue; in abundant racemes; small flower aborts early; sepals paler than corolla
FRUIT	a drupe, to 7.5 cm (3 in.); obovoid; enclosed in calyx that acts as wings
USE	specimen; flowering border; large planter; accent; bonsai subject; bright conservatory
ZONE	10–12

A GRAND ALLÉE of *Petrea arborea* is planted as the centrepiece of the Royal Botanic Gardens of Trinidad, where they are native. Normally, this rather less spectacular and obscure species is overshadowed by its more famous sibling, *P. volubilis* (Purple Wreath or Sandpaper Vine), which is a scrambling vine from C America and the Lesser Antilles. Known locally as Tree Petrea or Lilac, *P. arborea* differs in having smaller leaves and flowers, with an upright, woody habit of growth of slender, grey, conspicuously lenticillate limbs. The thin-textured, greyish green foliage is typically rough and sandpapery on both surfaces. *P. arborea* blooms profusely about 3 times during the year, bearing nodding, densely pubescent sprays of violet or violet-blue flowers. Each flower is composed of a 5-lobed calyx (the narrow sepals resembling petals) that holds a small, velvety bloom in the centre. The sepal lobes are paler than the corolla, which soon drops away, while the sepals persist, fading and drying to a dull grey and finally serving as wings for the single seed embedded in the short, central tube. Although this species is often semi-deciduous in the wild, it tends to retain its leaves under irrigated cultivation.

*** *P. kohauttiana*; (Presl.), W Indies, known as FLEUR DE DIEU. This slow-growing species is either a straggling small tree or a liane, to 20 m (33 ft). The leaves are rigid and rough, to 7.5 cm (3 in.). The flowers are held in racemes, to 30 cm (12 in.); they are either pure violet or pure white in colour. The rigid, persistent calyx turns brown. Seedlings take about 2 years to bloom. (10–12)

*** *P. volubilis*;(L.), C America and Lesser Antilles, to 12 m (40 ft). PURPLE WREATH is more of a vine or scrambler but it may be coaxed into a tree form. It is so widely grown that it is included here. Cv. 'Albiflora' has stunning, white flowers. (9–12)

P. arborea; velvety, violet-blue fls abort early to leave the pale lilac sepals.

P. volubilis; the sublime white form, cv. 'Albiflora'.

P. kohauttiana; this is a lean, straggling sp. that either grows as a shrub or a tall liane. There is a white form as well.

P. arborea; an avenue of the Tree Petrea has long been the focal point of the historic Royal Botanic Gardens, Trinidad, where it is native.

Phyllanthus acidus

GOOSEBERRY TREE

(L.) Skeels.   600 spp.

Cicca acida; P. distichus

EUPHORBIACEAE

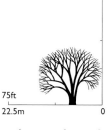

100ft ⌐ 30m

75ft
22.5m   0

PHYLLANTHUS ACIDUS IS A SMALL, DECIDUOUS TREE with greenish grey bark and a light, airy, spreading habit. The leaves appear pinnate but, characteristic of this singular genus of the great Euphorbiaceae family, they are actually phylloidal. The greenish or pinkish tinged midrib (or axis) that holds the drooping leaflets is actually a modified stem that is shed like leaves from stout twigs. Male and female flowers are held in unbranched racemes; males have a red calyx, females have a pale pink calyx. The ribbed, light yellow berries resemble diminutive squash but are sour like the gooseberry of the temperate zones. They are cauliflorous and densely clustered along the trunk and limbs, or held dangling from the younger twigs. In full harvest, the canopy of *P. acidus* appears illuminated within by its masses of translucent fruit. They may be eaten raw by those who appreciate their astringency, or made into preserves, confectionery, pickles or chutneys. *P. acidus* fruit are popular in SE Asia as a refreshing drink, for chutneys or as a substitute for tamarind in curries. The roots and seeds are used in local medicines. The heartwood is reddish brown, moderately hard, strong, fibrous and fine-grained. It is widely planted in tropical regions. Bees pollinate the flowers morning and evening.

*** *P. emblica*; (L.), (syn. *Emblica officinalis*), Trop. Asia, to 20 m (66 ft). EMBLICA, MYROBALAN or MALACCA TREE is a native of drier forests. This ornamental species has a wide, finely layered, deciduous, graceful canopy of pale green, feathery leaves. New growth is pinkish, and pale grey bark on the fluted trunk peels and flakes in scroll-like patches, revealing very smooth pale, pinkish buff, new bark that is green below the surface. The flowers are minute, pale, greenish white held at the leaf nodes. The fruit are round, plum-like, juicy, yellow, to 2 cm (0.8 in.), edible and high in vitamin C, but sour. (12–11) These are important honey plants.

NOTE: *P. acidus* has naturalized in lowland regions of many tropical countries.

ORIGIN	obscure – possibly Trop. Asia
HEIGHT	up to 10 m (33 ft)
TYPE	deciduous, small fruiting tree
STATUS	not threatened
HABITAT	coastal and dry limestone woodlands
GROWTH	moderate
FLOWG	late winter to spring
DRY TOL.	high
SALT TOL.	moderate
LIGHT	full sun
SOIL	fertile, well-drained
NUTRIT.	balanced fertilizer annually
HAZARDS	none
PROBLEMS	Phyllanthus caterpillar
ENVIRON.	bee nectar
PROPAG.	seeds; cuttings
LEAVES	simple; bright green; to 7 cm (2.7 in.); ovate; held in 2 rows along a 30 cm (12 in.) axis
FLOWERS	inconspicuous; reddish or pink; minute, in clusters along a slender axis
FRUIT	a berry, to 2 cm (0.8 in.); spherical, ridged; light yellow or greenish; with sour, juicy flesh
USE	backyard tree; accent; specimen; conservatory; large planter; xerophytic
ZONE	10–12

P. acidus; a regularly branched sp. with simple lvs set along a decid. rachis.

P. acidus; cauliflorous and densely clustered along the trunk and limbs or held dangling from the younger twigs, these little, 'gooseberry-like fr. are very sour.

P. emblica; fls are minute, pale, greenish white and held, with the new lvs, at the lf nodes.

P. emblica; this is a particularly alluring tree with a wide-spreading canopy of the finest, feathery foliage.

(1) **Phyllanthus angustifolius**; ([SW.] Sw.), (syn *P. linearis*), Jamaica and Cayman Is, to 6 m (20 ft), known in Cayman as DUPPY BUSH, this sp. appears to have its narrow, deep green, leathery lvs spiralled in clusters towards the ends of the branches. These apparent lvs are, however, flattened lf stalks, known as phylloclades, which have the appearance and function of a lf and vary greatly in size and width. (2) More curiously, fls and fr. are borne along the edges of these lf-like phylloclades. The tiny fls, which are held in small staminate or bisexual clusters at notches of the margins, may vary from pale buff to shades of red. Fr. is a capsule, to 4 mm (0.16 in.).

P. angustifolius may grow as a shrub or small tree and is native to dry, rocky thickets and woodlands. This sp. is very slow growing (by sd or cutting), but most ornamental and worthy of wider popularity as a stalwart xerophytic with a wide range of landscape uses. (10–12) (3) **Phyllanthus pectinata**; (Hook.) India endemic, to 30 m (100 ft). This curious, widely spreading tree has finely pinnate, yew-like foliage. (4) It clearly demonstrates phylloidal phenomenon with its fls and fr. dangled at the tips of its slender 'leaves.' (10–12) These are honey trees.

Phyllocarpus septentrionalis

CARDINAL TREE

J.D. Sm.   2 spp.

FABACEAE (Caesalpinioideae)

PHYLLOCARPUS SEPTENTRIONALIS is distinguished by its distinctive, wide-spreading, vase-shaped form and long, gangling, flexible limbs that arch vertically before curving abruptly downwards, with the vibrant green foliage forming a dense, tumbling cascade. The bark of its lean, low-branching trunk is dark grey and smoothish, except for numerous small, orange pustules. In late winter, the tree briefly loses its leaves and, soon after, celebrates the early spring with an extravaganza of lavish, lively, crimson blooms that thickly encrust its pale, naked limbs. The little flowers are sweetly fragrant and comprise 3 waxy, concave, scarlet sepals, which conceal the corolla within, and very long, sturdy, whiskery, red stamens. The large, flat, indehiscent, thin seed pods are winged along their upper sutures. This exceptional legume needs to be established in just the right habitat in order to flourish. In its natural habitat in the thinly wooded, dry, rocky hills up to 600 m (2,000 ft) of Guatemala and Honduras, where it is known as Flor de Mico or Monkey Flower Tree, *P. septentrionalis* is well adapted to the pulse of the seasons, as well as the type and chemical content of the soil. Edwin A. Menninger, in his *Flowering Trees of the World*, tells how seeds of this species were distributed widely in subtropical southern Florida early last century. They grew vigorously and remained evergreen but would not bloom. The trouble, it seems, is that in its naturally dry habitat *P. septentrionalis* is leafless and dormant in the winter and is awoken by the onset of heavy spring rains, but in Miami there is too much winter rain. Further south, in Cuba, this species has long been popular and is well established throughout the island, which seems to meet its exacting conditions. In areas of high rainfall, *P. septentrionalis* may develop weak crotches and split in storms; therefore, it should be carefully pruned to form a sturdy, balanced framework.

ORIGIN	Guatemala and Honduras
HEIGHT	up to 30 m (100 ft)
TYPE	semi-deciduous, large flowering tree
STATUS	vulnerable
HABITAT	dry rocky hills, to 300 m (1,000 ft), and ravines
GROWTH	fast
FLOWG	winter to early spring
DRY TOL.	high
SALT TOL.	moderate
LIGHT	full sun
SOIL	fertile, slightly acid
NUTRIT.	balanced fertilizer annually
HAZARDS	none
PROBLEMS	none
ENVIRON.	hummingbird nectar
PROPAG.	seeds
LEAVES	pinnate; rich green; leaflets in 4–8 pairs; to 8 × 4.5 cm (3 × 1.8 in.)
FLOWERS	showy; bright scarlet; held in crowded racemes; nectar-rich; fragrant
FRUIT	a legume, to 15 × 5 cm (6 × 2 in.); scale-like, flat, winged; seeds 1 or 2
USE	flowering tree; collection; specimen; public open space; xerophytic
ZONE	10–12

P. septentrionalis; with long wands of waxy red, fragrant fls.

P. septentrionalis; little fls are sweetly fragrant with very long, whiskery red stamens. There is nothing more stunning than to witness an iridescent hummingbird imbibing their nectar.

P. septentrionalis; in S Cuba with arching, tumbling limbs encrusted with little, cardinal-red blooms.

P. septentrionalis; bark of its trunk is dark grey and smoothish, except for numerous small, orange pustules.

320

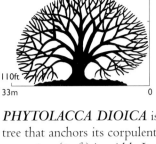

100ft — 30m
110ft
33m — 0

Phytolacca dioica

BELLA-SOMBRA

L.   25 spp.

P. arborea

PHYTOLACCACEAE

ORIGIN	Trop. S America
HEIGHT	up to 20 m (66 ft)
TYPE	evergreen, dioecious flowering tree
STATUS	not threatened
HABITAT	dry plains and woodlands
GROWTH	fast
FLOW'G	spring
DRY TOL.	high
SALT TOL.	moderate
LIGHT	full sun
SOIL	fertile, well-drained
NUTRIT.	balanced fertilizer annually
HAZARDS	possibly poisonous parts
PROBLEMS	none
ENVIRON.	wild fruit for birds
PROPAG.	seeds; large cuttings; root suckers
LEAVES	simple; green; to 10 cm (4 in.); petioles and midrib purplish pink; glabrous
FLOWERS	showy; white; held in slender, drooping racemes; to 10 cm (4 in.)
FRUIT	a berry, to 1.2 cm (0.5 in.); 7–10 celled; like a caterpillar; pale yellow, then black
USE	large shade tree; specimen; public open space; street tree; botanic collection; bosai subject; xerophytic
ZONE	9–11

PHYTOLACCA DIOICA is a fast-growing, soft, spongy trunked, elephantine pachycaul tree that anchors its corpulent superstructure by massive, widespread, swollen surface roots up to 18 m (60 ft) in width. It sometimes appears as if the bark has melted and spread around the base of the trunk. *P. dioica* grows rapidly to form a very dense, very widespreading crown to (20 m [66 ft]), with long, slender, pinkish petioled, drooping, glabrous leaves that are pale, silvery grey below. The canopy is usually wider than the height of the tree and is evergreen, except in colder climates where it may be semi-deciduous and may only develop as a large shrub. It is for its beautiful shade that this tree, a member of the Pokeweed family, is named Bella-Sombra. *P. dioica* is, perhaps, more of an overgrown herb than a serious, woody tree. Male and female blooms are carried on separate trees, the female trees being smaller and more gnarled than the males. The minute, white, many-stamened, wind-pollinated flowers are held in slender, nodding bottlebrush spikes at the tips of the twigs. They are extremely malodorous, even repelling insects and birds. As the compound ovary develops, it forms an elongated, jointed, multiple fruit that strongly resembles a mass of short, fat caterpillars. Each section contains a small, brownish seed. The massive ground structure that develops above the earth is part of the root system; it is often so elevated, bulky and bench-like that it may actually be used to sit on. From these obese anchors, arborescent suckers may develop. This curious device enables botanists to tell the age of the tree, since the spongy, fibrous pith of its trunk, which is 80% water, does not form age rings. *P. dioica* is, however, an extremely drought-resistant, long-lived species. In cooler climates it is semi-evergreen and may only develop as a large shrub.

P. dioica; white, staminous, male fls.

P. dioica; it sometimes appears as if the bark has melted and spread around the base of the trunk.

P. dioica; faded fls will form an elongated, jointed, multiple fr. that resembles little caterpillars.

P. dioica; seems to be more of a fast-growing, long-lived, gigantic herb than a woody tree. This curious specimen was photographed at Huntingdon Gardens, Pasadena, California.

321

Pimenta dioica

ALLSPICE

(L.) Merr.   2–5 spp.

Pimenta officinalis

MYRTACEAE

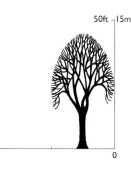

50ft ⌐15m

50ft
15m   0

PIMENTA DIOICA IS A DIGNIFIED SPECIES with majestic, sinewy, columnar growth. Typical of Myrtaceae, its pale bark exfoliates in strips, revealing the pinks and ochres of the inner flesh. Held erect, with their edges inrolled, the handsome, leathery, dark green leaves provide a dense, evergreen canopy. The mature leaves are deliciously aromatic and yield Pimento Leaf oil, an essential oil that is used for flavouring and perfumes. Little fragrant, staminous, nectar-rich, creamy white, 4-parted flowers are held in abundant panicles and are much loved by bees. It is the fruit that is the most important element of *P. dioica*. Small, globose, black and spicily pungent, it is said to combine the flavours of cinnamon, cloves and nutmeg, hence its common name, Allspice. Unripe fruit provides the famous culinary spice of commerce, and is used to make pickles, ketchups and sausages and in the curing of meat. Allspice is one of the most important exports of Jamaica and the main ingredient of their famous Jamaican Jerk seasoning. In Jamaica, where Allspice is known as Pimento, the liqueur, Pimento Dram, is distilled from the ripe berries and combined with rum, while Pimento Berry oil is derived from the dried spice. This is a slow-growing species and when reproduced from seeds, *P. dioica* takes 20 years to begin fruiting.

*** *P. racemosa*; ([Mill] Moore), (*P. acris*), Trop. America, to 13 m (43 ft). BAY RUM TREE is famous for its essential Myrcia or Bay Rum oil, which is distilled from the leaves and twigs. It is the main ingredient of Bay Rum, which is used in cosmetics and medicines. Bay Rum was originally prepared by using rum in the distillation. Compound Myrcia spirit (Bay Rum) is composed of bay oil, orange oil, pimenta oil, alcohol and water. (10–11) Pimenta species are important honey plants.

ORIGIN	Trop. America
HEIGHT	up to 13 m (43 ft)
TYPE	evergreen, small fruiting tree
STATUS	vulnerable
HABITAT	humid, lowland woodland and savannahs
GROWTH	slow
FLOWG	autumn
DRY TOL.	moderate
SALT TOL.	moderate
LIGHT	full sun or bright shade
SOIL	fertile, well-drained
NUTRIT.	balanced fertilizer annually
HAZARDS	none
PROBLEMS	rust; termites; borer
ENVIRON.	bee nectar; fruit for birds
PROPAG.	seeds; grafts
LEAVES	simple; dark green; oblong, glossy, leathery; strongly aromatic
FLOWERS	showy; creamy white; very small, 4-parted; nectar-rich, with many stamens; fragrant
FRUIT	a berry, to 6.5 cm (2.5 in.); globose, black; spicily pungent
USE	backyard tree; street tree; specimen; public open space; bonsai subject; conservatory
ZONE	10–12

P. racemosa; typical staminous, Myrtle fls are creamy white and nectar-rich.

P. dioica; is a lofty, noble tree with columnar growth. Aromatic Pimenta Leaf oil is distilled from the lvs. These trees are growing at the Royal Botanic Gardens, Trinidad.

P. racemosa; unripe fr. of the Bay Rum Tree. Jamaicans harvest these berries by stripping the trees.

P. dioica; typical of the Myrtaceae, the pale bark exfoliates in strips, revealing the pinks and ochres of the inner flesh.

Pinus caribaea

CARIBBEAN PITCH PINE

Morelet   93 spp.
Pinus hondurensis
PINACEAE

ORIGIN	Cuba, Bahamas and C America
HEIGHT	up to 30 m (100 ft)
TYPE	evergreen, large foliage tree
STATUS	threatened in some habitats
HABITAT	on sandy or clay soils; forming large stands
GROWTH	fast
FLOWG	spring
DRY TOL.	high
SALT TOL.	high
LIGHT	full sun
SOIL	clay or sandy soils
NUTRIT.	occasional fertilizer
HAZARDS	none
PROBLEMS	attack by termites
ENVIRON.	seeds for birds
PROPAG.	seeds
LEAVES	simple; dark green; to 30 cm (12 in.); scaly, needle-like; held in bundles of 2–3
FLOWERS	cones; moneocious; females few, with carpels; males many, catkin-like
FRUIT	a cone, to 7 cm (2.7 in.); reddish brown; narrowly conic, reflexed; with winged seeds
USE	seaside; coastal street tree; public open space; accent; timber tree; specimen; xerophytic
ZONE	9–11

TYPICAL OF THIS LARGE GENUS of northern hemisphere evergreens, **Pinus caribaea** is resinous, with a straight axis and an open, broad, round or irregular crown of whorled branches ending in clusters of needle-like foliage. This W Indian pine is easily recognized by the fact that the stiffly erect needles, to 25 cm (6 in.) are 3–4 per fascicle (bundle), crowded at their bases; they fall after 2 years. The conical cones are rusty brown when young. The bark is greyish, rough and thick, with long, scaly ridges and deep furrows that split to expose deep, reddish brown inner bark. The heartwood is reddish brown, soft, moderately lightweight and resinous. *P. caribaea* and other subtropical species (such as *P. radiata* and *P. ellotti*) are easily grown in commercial plantations, both for general construction timber and for paper pulp. *Pinus* species are very susceptible to termite attack.

*** var. *bahamensis*; (Griseb. Barret & Golfari), Cuba, Bahamas and Caicos Is, to 22 m. BAHAMAS PINE has 2 or 3 needles per fascicle. Cones are narrower, to 5 cm (2 in.).

*** var. *hondurensis*; (Barrett & Golfari), of C America, to 44 m (144 ft). Known as the HONDURANIAN PINE, it grows very quickly. Needles 3–4, possibly 5, per fascicle; cones, to 33 cm (13 in). In their native habitats, these Pines are widely logged and planted for the timber industry. Generally, the timber is reddish brown, soft and moderately lightweight and is considered superior to the other varieties.

*** *P. patula*; (Schldl. & Cham.), C and E Mexico, to 45 m (147 ft). PATULA PINE or MEXICAN WEEPING PINE, native of highland tropics and widely planted in the subtropics, with spreading crown of weeping, blue-green shoots. Cones, to 10 cm (4 in.), fascicles, grouped 2–5, stay closed for up to 20 years. Subsp. *tecunumanii* (Eguiluz & Perry), SE Mexico to Nicaragua, to 55 m. Needles held 3–4 per fasicle. Cones are long-stalked. (8–12)

P. caribaea; clusters of staminous fls.

P. caribaea; a young thicket growing in the Jardin Botanico de Cienfuegos, S Cuba.

P. patula; Mexican Weeping Pine is widely planted. This tree is growing in Sydney Botanic Garden, Australia

P. caribaea; cones collected at the Jardin Botanico Nationale, Cuba, where it is native.

323

Pisonia grandis var. alba

MOONLIGHT TREE

(R Br.) Span.   40 spp.

NYCTAGINACEAE

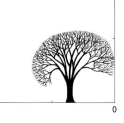

50ft ⌐15m

50ft
15m   0

ORIGIN	from Madagascar to the Pacific
HEIGHT	up to 5 m (16 ft)
TYPE	evergreen, small, dioecious foliage tree
STATUS	not threatened
HABITAT	atolls and islets with guano deposits
GROWTH	fast
FLOWG	year-round
DRY TOL.	moderate
SALT TOL.	high
LIGHT	full, or sheltered sun
SOIL	high in potassium
NUTRIT.	may require extra K; deep, organic mulch
HAZARDS	sticky fruit
PROBLEMS	none
ENVIRON.	insect nectar
PROPAG.	woody cuttings; layers
LEAVES	simple; bright green or yellowish; oblong-ovate; deeply veined
FLOWERS	inconspicuous; white; held in small, globular heads; dioecious
FRUIT	an achene, to 2 cm (0.8 in.); ridged or winged; very sticky when ripe
USE	seaside; accent; screening; courtyard; large planter; humid shade garden; conservatory
ZONE	10—12

PISONIA GRANDIS VAR. *ALBA* is popular in tropical gardens of SE Asia and the Pacific for its outstanding foliage. The parent, *P. grandis*, is a common native of the low elevation islands and atolls of the Pacific that have guano (deposits of sea bird excrement). *Pisonia* species are dioecious, with tiny, short-stalked whitish flowers held in crowded, globular heads. The warty, 5-ribbed fruit that follow are held in large, open clusters. They exude an incredibly sticky, mucilaginous discharge that is unaffected by water. Insects, and small birds attracted by the insects, become trapped by this 'glue', but the birds usually free themselves after losing feathers. On small coral cays along the Great Barrier Reef, Qld, Australia, 2 species of Noddys nest in *Pisonia* trees during the fruiting season and often become trapped by the fruit, leading to the death of many hundreds of birds. The light, soft wood of *P. grandis* (more substantial than var. *alba*) is known as Puka Wood and is used to make canoes in the Pacific. Var. *alba* is sterile, producing neither flowers nor the nuisance fruit. Its compact canopy of large, soft, succulent deeply veined leaves is naturally a luminous, pale, yellow-green and creates a stunning accent against a dark background. The best colour develops in full, sheltered sun or very bright shade. In the Pacific Is, its edible, succulent foliage is eaten as spinach, hence its other common names, Lettuce- or Cabbage-Tree.

*** *P. brunoniana*; (Endl.), (syn. *P. inermis* [non Jacq.]), from Hawaii to Norfolk and Lord Howe Is, to New Zealand and Australia, to 6 m (20 ft). PAPALA KEPAU, is a common understorey tree of humid forests. Multi-trunked, pale grey barked, it has elliptical, shiny leaves. The flowers are pale pink and held on stout stalks. Var. *variegata*; 'Para-para' is an attractive, variegated form popular in New Zealand. (9—11)

P. brunoniana; globular heads of tiny, pink fls.

P. grandis var. *alba*; the Moonlight or Lettuce Tree photographed in the spectacular Mandai Gardens, Singapore. These gardens are particularly famous for their orchid displays.

P. brunoniana; with incredibly sticky fr. capable of ensaring small birds.

P. brunoniana var. *variegata*; a superb form from New Zealand, which is very popular as an ornamental.

Pithecellobium arboreum

COJOBA

ORIGIN	W Indies and C America	
HEIGHT	up to 16 m (53 ft)	
TYPE	evergreen foliage tree	
STATUS	not threatened	
HABITAT	along streams, banks and cliff bases, in moist woodland	
GROWTH	fast	
FLOWG	spring to summer	
DRY TOL.	high	
SALT TOL.	moderate to high	
LIGHT	full sun	
SOIL	widely tolerant	
NUTRIT.	occasional fertilizer	
HAZARDS	spiny; irritant	
PROBLEMS	weak-wooded; may be invasive	
ENVIRON.	bee nectar; wild fruit for birds	
PROPAG.	seeds	
LEAVES	2-pinnate; bright green; axis minutely brown hairy; numerous small, narrow leaflets; finely feathery	
FLOWERS	inconspicuous; greenish white; pompoms of fragile stamens, held in clusters at leaf bases	
FRUIT	a legume, to 10 cm (4 in.); bright red; coiled, twisted dehiscent; black seeds	
USE	shade tree; street tree; living barrier; hedges; topiary; xerophytic	
ZONE	10–12	

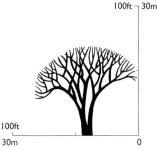

100ft ⌐ 30m
100ft
30m 0

(L.), Urban   37 spp.
Cojoba arborea
FABACEAE (Mimosoideae)

THIS HANDSOME EVERGREEN LEGUME is very popular as a street tree in many parts of the world because of its elegant, widespreading crown and gracefully sweeping limbs, which are lightly clad in fine, ferny foliage. *Pithecellobium arboreum* grows rapidly and withstands drought and high temperatures. The most striking feature of this species is the ornamental, brilliant red fruit, which is longer and narrower than *P. dulce* and coils and contorts as it matures and dehisces to expose its shiny, black seeds. The heartwood of *P. arboreum* is dark red or reddish brown. It is sometimes figured or has darkish streaks like mahogany and, being heavy, strong and durable, is used for construction, as well as for furniture and cabinetry. It is reported that Cojoba wood was used to make bobbins for the American cotton mills in the late 19th to early 20th century. Both are excellent honey trees. *** *P. dulce*, ([Roxb.] Benth.), C and S America, to 15 m (50 ft), MADRAS THORN or MANILA TAMARIND is popular throughout Asia for its xerophytic nature. This spiny species has paired, narrowly oblong leaves and small, creamy white, ball-like flowers. The curved or coiled, greenish red, white-lined pods split open to release shiny, black seeds, which are embedded in pink and whitish, sweet, spongy pulp (or aril). This is edible and may be made into a drink such as lemonade. In Hawaii, where the seeds are considered to resemble opium, *P. dulce* is known as Opiuma. The reddish wood is strong and durable but brittle and is mostly considered difficult to work. In Mexico, the bark (known as Guamuche in commerce) is high in tannin and provides a yellow dye. A useful adhesive, reddish brown gum exudes from the trunk. Livestock and wild animals browse on the pods. Cv. 'Variegata'; recently introduced to the trade as 'Snowflake Bush', is much smaller and bushier in form, with attractive, pink, white and green new growth. (10–12)

P. dulce; fr. has sweet, mealy, edible arils rather like *Inga paterno*.

P. dulce cv. 'Variegata'; known as Snowflake. This is a diminutive form with pretty pink, white and green lvs.

P. dulce; a group of trees displaying their vase-like habit of growth at the Jardin Nationale de Cuba in Havana.

P. arboreum; there is something almost comical about this startlingly attractive red fr., which contorts as it opens.

325

Pittosporum pentandrum

PHILIPPINE PITTOSPORUM

(Blanco) Merrill.   100 spp.

PITTOSPORACEAE

50ft ‒15m

60ft
18m   0

PITTOSPORUM are evergreen trees and shrubs of the humid forests of the Old World tropics and subtropics. They are grown for their elegant, glossy foliage and often honey-scented, waxy posies of flowers. Most of them have a sticky, resinous, glistening aril enclosing their seeds, which are contained in orange or yellow berry-like fruit. These compact bunches of brightly coloured berries, often held for many weeks and even months, may be as ornamental as the flowers. *Pittosporum pentandrum* has a neat, compact habit of growth, forming a classically airy crown of slender, polished leaves, which are whorled towards the tips of the many twigs. The small, greenish white flowers are quietly decorative; held in tight, little, posy-like panicles, they are sweetly fragrant and irresistible to bees. *P. pentandrum* strikes an almost flamboyant note with the formation of its turpentine-pungent fruit, which are held in small bunches, like orange 'grapes'. They are so bright, waxy and perfect that they look artificial and are pinned on for decoration. Luckily, these berries persist for a long time before ripening. They are 2- or 3-celled, with a persistent calyx at the tip; eventually they dry rather woody. On ripening, they dehisce to reveal a moist, glistening, bright golden interior, with 6 seeds clad in sealing wax red arils and lightly glued together by sticky sap.

*** *P. tobira*; (Ait.), China, Japan, to 5 m (16 ft). TOBIRA or MOCK ORANGE is, possibly, the most well-known *Pittosporum*. Although it does become a small tree, it is mostly grown as a shrub. It is more adapted to subtropical climates, although it does grow in the tropics. From late spring to summer, *P. tobira* carries little, umbellate clusters of fragrant, white flowers. These have an orange-blossom scent. (9–12) *Pittosporum* species are important honey plants.

ORIGIN	Philippine Is, endemic
HEIGHT	up to 10 m (33 ft)
TYPE	evergreen, small, foliage flowering and fruiting tree
STATUS	limited distribution
HABITAT	lowland evergreen woodland
GROWTH	moderate
FLOWG	winter
DRY TOL.	high
SALT TOL.	moderate
LIGHT	full sun or bright shade
SOIL	fertile, well-drained
NUTRIT.	balanced fertilizer annually; organic mulch
HAZARDS	none
PROBLEMS	none
ENVIRON.	bee nectar; wild fruit
PROPAG.	seeds; cuttings; layers
LEAVES	simple; dark green; to 9 cm (3.5 in.); ovate to oblong; whorled; margins wavy
FLOWERS	showy; milky white; held in brown, pubescent panicles; fragrant
FRUIT	a capsule, to 1 cm (0.4 in.); 2–3 valved, berry-like; seeds black, set in red, sticky arils
USE	small shade tree; hedging and screening; specimen; large planter; xerophytic; conservatory
ZONE	10–12

NOTE: this species is considered a noxious weed in Florida, USA.

P. pentandrum; with tight 'posies' of greenish white, fragrant, nectar-rich fls.

P. pentandrum; is attractive in bloom when its sweetly fragrant, nectar-rich fls attract many bees. It is even more flamboyant in fr. at Andromeda Botanic Gardens, Barbados.

P. pentandrum; the cheerful, tight bunches of bright orange berries seem pinned on for decoration.

P. tobira; embellished with little, umbellate clusters of fragrant white fls, which have an orange blossom scent.

Pittosporum hosmieri; (Rock), (syn. *P. amplectens*), Hawaiian endemic, to 10 m (33 ft). Ho'AWA or HUA KUKUI is very similar to *P. hawaiiense*. All parts are densely pale brown tomentose. Lvs to 60 cm (24 in), oblong, leathery, brown-hairy below, margins revolute. Infl. are axillary; fls are creamy white. Fr. to 5 cm (2 in.), globose, 2–4-valved, orange at maturity. Oily black sds are an important food of the Hawaiian crow, 'Alala. (**10–12**)

Pittosporum moluccanum; ([Lam.] Miq.); SE Asia to NT and W Australia, to 20 m (66 ft). A slender sp., native to coast. dry woods and seaside dunes. Narrowly elliptic lvs are spirally crowded at stem ends and have crimped margins. (Australian form is smoother, with more undulate leathery and glabrous lvs with a yellowish midrib.) In autumn, highly perfumed, little white fls attract insects. Fr. is bright orange and woody; it splits wide open when ripe. (**10–12**)

Pittosporum rhombifolium, (A, Cunn. ex Hook), E Australia and Qld, to 30 m (100 ft). QUEENSLAND PITTOSPORUM, or HOLLYWOOD at Royal Botanic Garden, Sydney. This is a large tree with long-petioled, glossy lvs, which are leathery and coarsely toothed. Fls are abundant and white in tight clusters, followed by large bunches of subglobose, orange fr. Blooming late autumn. (**9–11**) **NOTE:** *P. rhombifolium is now Auranticarpa rhombifolia.*

Pittosporum undulatum; (Vent.), E Australia, to 14 m (46 ft). Known as VICTORIAN BOX, MOCK ORANGE or CHEESEWOOD, this cold-hardy, popular sp. has bright green, polished, leathery lvs with undulate margins. The creamy white spring fls are fragrant; globose fr. is yellow, orange or brownish. The wood, which has a slightly 'cheesey' odour, is used in the manufacture of golf clubs. **NOTE: this sp. is naturalized in Hawaii. (8–10)**

(1) ***Pittosporum angustifolium***; (Lodd.), (*P. phylliraeoides*), Australia endemic, to 10 m (33 ft). This popular, ornamental sp., native to arid, inland areas throughout Australia, has many common names: WEEPING-PITTOSPORUM, DESERT WILLOW, BUTTERBUSH, or perhaps, more commonly, NATIVE APRICOT. This *Pittosporum* is an erect tree with willowy, pendulous twigs clad in narrow, aromatic, bright green or greyish lvs. Fls are pale yellow, tubular and scented, while the fr. is an orange, thick-walled, fleshy capsule, which splits open to reveal sds set in sticky red arils. It blooms in winter and spring, and has been popular in cultivation for many years in Australia,

SW USA and the Middle East. *P. angustifolium* is normally a slow-growing sp. which, given richer soils and adequate water, will develop more quickly. (9–11) (2 and 3) ***Pittosporum viridiflorum***; (Sims.), S Africa endemic, to 8 m (26 ft). CAPE PITTOSPORUM has a densely shrubby form of growth, resembling an oversized *P. tobira*, with obovate, deep green lvs that have revolute margins, held in dense spirals around the twigs. In late-spring, little, yellowy green, jasmine-scented fls are clustered tightly together and aree surrounded by small lvs. **NOTE: naturalized in Hawaii.** (9–11)

A late afternoon view of the superb Arboretum of Los Angeles at Pasadena, USA, where these 2 spp. were photographed.

ORIGIN	from C America to northern S America
HEIGHT	up to 20 m (66 ft)
TYPE	deciduous, flowering timber tree
STATUS	not common in the wild
HABITAT	mature rainforest, often on humid slopes and grassy savannahs
GROWTH	fairly fast
FLOWG	late spring
DRY TOL.	moderate to high
SALT TOL.	low
LIGHT	full sun
SOIL	deep, fertile, water-retentive
NUTRIT.	balanced fertilizer annually; deep, organic mulch
HAZARDS	none
PROBLEMS	none
ENVIRON.	nectar for bees and insects
PROPAG.	seeds; cuttings
LEAVES	pinnate; bright green; with 5–7 large, opposite leaflets
FLOWERS	showy; yellow; held in crowded, narrow racemes on old wood; sweetly violet-scented
FRUIT	a legume (samara); winged; with a single seed
USE	flowering tree; public open space; specimen; timber tree
ZONE	10–12

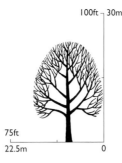

100ft — 30m

75ft
22.5m — 0

Platymiscium pinnatum

QUIRA

(Jacq.) Dugand.   20 spp.

P. polystachyum.

FABACEAE (Papilionoideae)

PLATYMISCIUM PINNATUM is a fairly rare, moderately tall forest tree, with a straight, cylindrical trunk that develops small buttresses at its base. The bark is light brown to grey and has vertical fissures, at least in larger trees. With long, slender petioles, the pinnate leaves have 5–7 large leaflets that are held in opposite pairs with 1 terminal leaflet. They are easily identified by the base of each petiole, which is swollen and cylindrical. When crushed, the leaves have a distinctive, bean-like smell. The stipules are white and fall readily, leaving a clear scar on the stem. Large trees are nearly, but not completely, deciduous. After a sudden shower of rain, towards the end of the dry season in mid to late spring, *P. pinnatum* bears abundant, narrow, crowded racemes of yellow flowers on year-old wood. Following the flowers, the green, indehiscent fruit forms. It is a large, thin, elongated winged samara with a single seed in the centre. As it ripens and turns brown, the fruit is eventually dispersed by wind from summer and the wet season. *P. pinnatum*, and other species of this genus, is prized for its hard, durable, finely grained reddish heartwood that is resistant to termites and is used regionally for making fine furniture and musical instruments. Some species of *Platymiscium* are known to act as hosts to colonies of ants.

*** *P. floribundum*; (Vog.) Brazil, 10–20 m (33–66 ft). SACAMBU is an elegant, sparsely branched tree with upwardly stretching branches and young growth weeping from their tips. Leaflets, to 6 cm (2.4 in.); racemes, to 10 cm (4 in.). (10–12)

*** *P. trinitatis*; (Benth.), Trinidad and Guyana, to 30 m (100 ft). ROBLE is considered one of the most beautiful native trees in Trinidad. It has rich orange, violet-fragrant blooms in early spring. Its hard, durable reddish brown timber is used for fine furniture, as well as for heavy constructional work such as bridges. (10–12) These are honey plants.

P. pinnatum; has abundant, violet-scented blooms in spring.

P. floribundum; an elegant, ornamental sp. of the Atlantic rainforests of Brazil, it is grown for its excellent timber.

P. floribundum; blooms are less dense than *P. pinnatum*.

P. trinitatis; bears abundant, narrow clusters of rich orange, violet-scented fls on year-old wood. Photographed at the Royal Botanic Gardens, Trinidad, W Indies.

329

Pleiogynium timorense

BURDEKIN PLUM

(DC) Leenh.   2–3 spp.

P. solandri

ANACARDIACEAE

100ft — 30m

75ft

22.5m   0

IN ITS NATURAL HABITAT in coastal rainforests from Malesia to New Guinea and south to N Qld, Australia, *Pleiogynium timorense* eventually becomes a forest giant, developing buttresses in old age. It is also found on sand dunes behind the mangroves and in dry, vine thickets. In cultivation, however, this species usually remains medium-sized, developing a thick, fissured trunk with peeling bark and an irregular, but buoyant, canopy. The pinnate leaves are large with 7–9 blunt, obliquely based ovate to elliptic leaflets; new growth is reddish. *P. timorense* is moneocious, with male and female flowers held separately on the same tree. Many tiny, creamy yellow flowers are borne in narrow panicles held at the leaf axils, the male clusters being much longer than those of the females. In late summer and autumn, flattened, globose fruits are formed. They resemble diminutive tomatoes in shape, but are dark red to purplish black, smooth and glabrous. A large, pumpkin-like stone is covered by a thin layer of plum-red, acrid, resinous flesh, sometimes eaten when fully ripe from trees selected for the size and flavour of its fruit, but mostly used in jams and jellies. Like Cashew Nut, Otaheiti Apple and Mango, the Burdekin Plum, or Queensland Hog Plum, is a member of the Anacardium family, which includes many very poisonous plants in its family tree. *P. timorense* is very closely related and similar to *Spondias* or the African species Marula (*Sclerocarya birrea*). In Tonga, this species is important as a timber tree and the hard seeds are strung together to create skirt-like garments for traditional dancing. In parts of Africa, this densely foliaged species is popularly planted as a street tree. Although tropical, *P. timorense* is a hardy species, and is cultivated in California and Florida, USA, and other frost-free regions. The seeds germinate slowly and erratically. This is a honey plant.

ORIGIN	from Malesia to Qld, Australia
HEIGHT	up to 45 m (148 ft)
TYPE	deciduous, large fruiting tree
STATUS	not threatened
HABITAT	dry monsoon rainforests
GROWTH	moderate
FLOWG	spring
DRY TOL.	moderate
SALT TOL.	low
LIGHT	full sun
SOIL	humid, fertile
NUTRIT.	high-potassium fertilizer; deep, organic mulch
HAZARDS	none
PROBLEMS	none
ENVIRON.	bee nectar; wild fruit for birds
PROPAG.	seeds; cuttings; layers
LEAVES	pinnate; deep green; 7–9 leaflets, blunt, obliquely ovate
FLOWERS	inconspicuous; creamy yellow; very small; held in large, airy panicles
FRUIT	a drupe, to 2 cm (0.8 in.); red to reddish brown; flattened globose; edible
USE	shade tree; backyard tree; specimen; street tree; public open space; xerophytic
ZONE	9–12

P. timorense; male and female fls are held on separate panicles on the same tree.

P. timorense; this Burdekin Plum tree was photographed at the Fruit and Spice Park, Homestead, S. Florida, USA.

P. timorense; flattened, globose fr., with claret-red pulp, resemble little tomatoes and are edible and used for jams and jellies.

P. timorense; in Tonga, this sp. is important as a timber tree. In Africa, it is popularly planted as a street tree.

The Royal Botanic Garden, Sydney, is situated on land farmed by the orginal European settlers. Located in the the heart of Sydney, yards from the sea, the Harbour Bridge, the Opera House and the Governor's Residence, these magnificent, historic gardens offer visitors and residents a recreation area, as well as functioning as an important centre for botanic research and display.

Plumeria rubra

FRANGIPANI

L.

P. acuminata

APOCYNACEAE

17 spp.

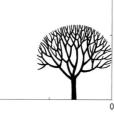

50ft ⌐15m

50ft
15m   0

ORIGIN	Mexico and C America
HEIGHT	up to 8 m (26 ft)
TYPE	deciduous, small flowering tree
STATUS	not threatened
HABITAT	dry, rocky lowland
GROWTH	slow
FLOW G	spring to summer
DRY TOL.	high
SALT TOL.	high
LIGHT	full sun
SOIL	fertile, well-drained
NUTRIT.	balanced fertilizer annually; organic mulch
HAZARDS	irritant latex
PROBLEMS	caterpillars; rust; red spider mite
ENVIRON.	moth nectar
PROPAG.	cuttings; layers
LEAVES	simple; rich green, paler below; to 40 cm (16 in.); obovate
FLOWERS	showy; white, yellow, rose-red to salmon; to 10 cm (4 in.) variable; very fragrant
FRUIT	a pair of follicles, to 30 cm (12 in.); dehiscent; seeds winged
USE	seaside; small flowering tree; accent; large planter; coastal median strip; bonsai subject; conservatory; xerophytic;
ZONE	10—12

PLUMERIA species are deciduous and slow growing, with swollen, succulent limbs that are charged with milky latex and dichotomously branched, in the manner of a candelabrum. Large, deeply veined leaves are whorled around the tips of the plump twigs. The latex is poisonous but not deadly, except when taken in large quantities. **Plumeria rubra** flowers secrete no nectar but are pollinated by moths that are attracted by their fragrance. The fruit is twinned, tough follicles. *P. rubra*, a revered tree of Trop. America, is found throughout tropical regions and planted near Asian temples, where its fragrant flowers are plucked daily as religious offerings. It is widely planted in W Indian graveyards, where it is said to be an emblem of immortality because of its ability to burst into flower even when taken out of the soil. On one island, it is said that a large branch was carried by the mourners to the cemetery and dug into the head of the grave. If it rooted, it was considered a sign that the body had been transported to paradise. There are so many superstitions surrounding this genus that in some communities *P. rubra* is never planted near a house. In Trop. America, *Plumeria* species are commonly infested and defoliated by the gigantic caterpillar of the Sphinx Moth, *Pseudosphinx tetrio*, which grows to 15 cm (6 in.) long. Despite this process being disturbing for gardeners, the tree actually suffers no permanent harm and quickly replaces its lost foliage. This colourful species has several forms. They grow easily from large limbs but before planting the cut edge must be left for about a week to dry completely and scar over.

✲✲✲ f. *acutifolia*; (Woods.), MEXICAN FRANGIPANI; the corolla is white and the throat golden.

f. *lutea*; (Woods.), the corolla is yellow, but the throat has a deep yellow exterior that is often suffused with pale red.

f. *tricolor*; (Woods.), the corolla is white, edged rose, and the throat yellow.

P. rubra; a slender pr of dehiscent follicles with winged sds.

P. rubra f. *acutifolia*; Frangipani is a very slow-growing, xerophytic sp. that may bloom all year in equatorial regions or in the summer in warmer areas of the subtropics.

P. rubra, being eaten by the gigantic caterpillar of a Sphinx Moth. The tree quickly renews its foliage.

P. rubra; with all its foliage, in full summer bloom. In drier regions, it will bloom without its lvs.

Plumeria rubra cv. 'Bridal White'

Plumeria rubra cv. 'Carmine Flush'

Plumeria rubra cv. 'Jean Moragne'

Plumeria rubra cv. 'June Bride'

Plumeria rubra cv. 'Kauka Wilder'

Plumeria rubra cv. 'Kimi Moragne'

Plumeria

Plumeria rubra cv. 'Maui Beauty'

Plumeria rubra cv. 'Pink Pearl'

Plumeria rubra cv. 'Royal Flush'

Plumeria rubra cv. 'Sally Moragne'

Plumeria rubra cv. 'Starlight'

Plumeria rubra cv. 'Sunbathed'

Plumeria alba; (L.), from P. Rico and Virgin Is to the Lesser Antilles, to 10 m (33 ft). Known as MILK TREE or PIGEONWOOD, this sp. is a common xerophyte of coast. thickets and woodlands. It has copious, milky latex and is specially designed for drought and seaside living. The distinctive, heavy, deeply veined lvs are tightly rolled inwards, leaving the blade very narrow and taut. The large, white fls are very fragrant, but have no nectar. (10–12)

Plumeria montana; (Britton and Wilson), Cuban endemic, to 10 m (33 ft). Named LIRIO or SUCHELI in Cuba, where it grows in the humid, mountainous forests of the Oriente region. This compact sp. has bright green, oblanceolate lvs that are particularly blunt-tipped and tightly whorled towards the ends of the erect twigs. The small, pure white blooms have a small, yellow eye and are held erect terminally. (10–12)

Plumeria obtusa; (L.), (syn. *P. marginata*; *P. bahamensis*), from Bahamas and Greater Antilles to Honduras, to 8 m (26 ft). SINGAPORE FRANJIPANI, WILD JASMINE or ELELI, this sp. varies greatly in its large region where it is found on rocky and sandy coast. scrub, often on poor soils. It has commonly, however, a neatly rounded crown, dense, erect, dark green foliage and huge, terminal panicles of white fls, with deep yellow eyes. (10–12)

Plumeria pudica; (Jacq.), from Colombia and Venezuela to Curacao, to 5 m (16 ft). Commonly called WHITE NOSEGAY, AMAPOLA or FLORON, this carefree *Plumeria* forms a slender, multi-stemmed shrub. It has curious, narrow, spathulate, very short-petioled lvs and large panicles of chalky white, funnel form fls. It was photographed at the Wild Fowl Trust, Trinidad, where it is a very popular garden plant. (10–12)

Podocarpus neriifolius

OLEANDER PODOCARP

D. Don.   94 spp.

PODOCARPACEAE

PODOCARPUS NERIIFOLIUS is known generally as Oleander Podocarp because of its dark green, leathery leaves that resemble those of *Nerium oleander*. A stately tree, which may attain a lofty height, *P. neriifolius* has its limbs whorled horizontally around a reddish trunk, with its bark exfoliating in strips. The spirally arranged leaves are narrow-lanceolate and very variable. In spring, the tree has spectacular flushes of pale pinkish new growth. Male or pollen-bearing cones are catkin-like; the female cones are composed of few to many bracts. The exposed embryo (or seed) sits on top of a swollen, fleshy stalk, and is reminiscent of the structure of a Cashew. This is designed to tempt birds, which will then distribute the seeds. Although *Podocarpus* is primarily a genus of the tropical mountains and highlands of the S hemisphere, there are a few species found from SE Asia to C and S America and the W Indies. It is a coniferous (or cone-bearing) genus, like the closely-related *Afrocarpus*, and is classed as a gymnosperm and linked with the cycads and conifers. *Podocarpus* species are without true flowers or fruit but have exposed or naked seeds. The sapwood of the *Podocarpus* genus is usually soft, moderately heavy, easily worked, much like pine and is particularly prized for cabinetwork and furniture.

*** *P. henklii*; (Stapf.), Tanzania to S Africa, to 35 m (115 ft). Known as FALCATE YELLOW-WOOD in the timber trade, this *Podocarpus* has charcoal-grey bark that also exfoliates in long strips. The pendent limbs sweep upwards towards their tips to form a symmetrical, conical crown, which is densely clad in narrow-lanceolate leaves of a bluish caste. The fruit is fleshy, with a greenish blue receptacle. The seed is sessile, ovoid to globose and yellow-green. The heartwood is yellow, of excellent quality but of very limited supply. (9–11)

ORIGIN	from SE Asia to W Pacific
HEIGHT	up to 40 m+ (131 ft +)
TYPE	evergreen, dioecious, large foliage tree
STATUS	not threatened
HABITAT	hot humid forests; coastal and lowland swamp forests, on volcanic soils
GROWTH	moderate
FLOWG	summer
DRY TOL.	moderate
SALT TOL.	moderate
LIGHT	full sun or bright shade
SOIL	fertile, slightly acid
NUTRIT.	regular fertilizer; deep, organic mulch
HAZARDS	none
PROBLEMS	scale; sooty mould
ENVIRON.	wild fruit for birds
PROPAG.	seeds; misted cuttings; layers
LEAVES	linear; dark green; to 18 cm (7 in.); thick, leathery; new growth pinkish
FLOWERS	inconspicuous; dioecious; males, pollen-bearing, catkin-like; females, cones, few to many bracts
FRUIT	a seed that is enveloped by an aril-like, red, fleshy structure
USE	accent; planter; specimen; screening; topiary; large planter; conservatory
ZONE	9–12

P. neriifolius; with a spectacular flush of new, pink spring foliage.

P. neriifolius; here can be seen the gymnosperm phenomenon: a naked embryo (or sd) is held at the tip of a swollen receptacle (modified stem), which turns red to attract birds.

P. neriifolius; a fine example in Singapore.

P. henklii; an African sp. photographed at the Arboretum of Los Angeles, USA, showing its attractive, compact, conical form.

(1) **Podocarpus macrophyllus**; ([Thunb.] D. Don.), S China and Japan, to 15 m (50 ft). This sp. is very popular in horticulture and is grown under many names: YEW PODOCARP, JAPANESE YEW, SOUTHERN YEW or BUDDHIST PINE, depending on the region. (In Japan it is known as KUSAMAKI.) This sp. has several forms but one of the most popular is the fastigiate form, cv. 'Maki', shown here. *P. macrophyllus* lends itself to topiary, formal screening and hedging, or is used as a strong accent. (2) *P.*

macrophyllus is distinguished by its broadly linear lvs, which are very thick and leathery, and by its small, glaucous-blue fr., which becomes red on ripening. (7–11) (3) **Podocarpus rumpii**; (Blume), (syn. *P. koordersii*), Malesia, has a fairly slender, open crown. This sp. was photographed at the Singapore Botanic Gardens where an excellent collection of Asian spp. of *Podocarpus* is represented. (4) Typical of its genus, the young fr. is pale, glaucous-blue. (10–12)

Pogonopus speciosus

GUANACASTE

(Jacq.) Schum.   3 spp.

RUBIACEAE

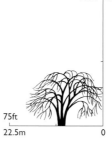

100ft – 30m

75ft
22.5m ― 0

SOME MEMBERS OF THE RUBIACEAE CLAN cheat a little to attract attention to their otherwise insignificant blooms, for example, the *Mussaeanda*, *Calycophyllum* or *Warszewiczia* species. ***Pogonopus speciosus*** is a fairly rare small species found in reasonably humid forests and has been described as one of the most beautiful trees of Panama. It is a loose-limbed, shrubby species with a fairly sparse crown of large, thin-textured, densely tomentose leaves. In dry regions, ***P. speciosus*** may be briefly deciduous during the dry season. In late spring or early summer, the tree is transformed by the spectacular, loose, terminal puberulous panicles of the flowers, which are small, tubular, 3 cm (1.3 in.) long and vary in colour from region to region, being red, purple or pink. These flowers would hardly be noticed if the bracts below had not been modified and enlarged into colourful, leaf-like banners to herald the blooms and so attract their pollinators. Each slender bloom has tiny, flaring lobes and is punctuated by an enlarged, leaf-like calyx. These extravagant lobes persist for several weeks after the flowers have aborted. The fruit are a cylindrical, flat-topped, thinly woody capsule with an apical rim formed by the calyx lobes; it is packed with many seeds. During his botanical survey in the Amazon Basin, Alfred Wallace, the renowned 19th-century biologist, was particularly impressed by the proliferation and exceptional beauty of the Rubiaceae species that he found there. A small genus of only 3 species, *Pogonopus* are native to the drier areas of this region, so renowned for its rainforests. They are closely associated with the *Rondeletia* genus. At Fairchild Tropical Gardens, in Miami, Florida, USA, the attractive ***P. speciosus*** flourishes as an understorey specimen, competing with larger trees in a fairly dry situation.

ORIGIN	C and S America and the W Indies
HEIGHT	up to 10 m (33 ft)
TYPE	evergreen, small flowering tree or tall shrub
STATUS	rare in wild
HABITAT	moist lowland forests
GROWTH	moderate
FLOWG	summer and winter
DRY TOL.	moderate
SALT TOL.	low
LIGHT	full sun or bright shade
SOIL	fertile, well-drained
NUTRIT.	organic fertilizer; deep, organic mulch
HAZARDS	none
PROBLEMS	none
ENVIRON.	nectar
PROPAG.	seeds; misted cuttings
LEAVES	simple; bright green; to 22 m (8.7 in.); obovate, thin-textured
FLOWERS	showy; purple, red or pink; calyx expanded to 5 cm (2 in.)
FRUIT	a capsule, to 7 cm (2.7 in.); 2-celled, woody; many fine seeds
USE	small flowering tree; shade garden; accent; screening; large planter; conservatory
ZONE	10—12

P. speciosus; large, soft lvs and fl. panicles.

P. speciosus; their small, tubular fls would hardly be noticed if the bracts below had not been modified and enlarged into colourful, leaf-like banners to signal the blooms.

P. speciosus; this is a slender-limbed, shrubby sp. with a fairly sparse crown.

P. speciosus; with tough, rugged bark.

338

ORIGIN	Dominica (Lesser Antilles), endemic
HEIGHT	up to 6 m (20 ft)
TYPE	deciduous, small flowering tree
STATUS	becoming very rare
HABITAT	moist or dry forest on limestone soils
GROWTH	slow
FLOWG	spring, after rain
DRY TOL.	high
SALT TOL.	low
LIGHT	full sun
SOIL	fertile, friable
NUTRIT.	balanced fertilizer annually; organic mulch
HAZARDS	none
PROBLEMS	none
ENVIRON.	insect nectar
PROPAG.	seeds
LEAVES	pinnate; light green; leaflets oblong, with 6–8 pairs; to 1.7 cm (0.7 in.)
FLOWERS	showy; crimson; pea-like, stalkless; in clusters of 3–5 along the length of the twigs
FRUIT	a legume, to 8 cm (3 in.); flat, linear, long-tipped
USE	small flowering tree; specimen; accent; large planter; xerophytic
ZONE	10–12

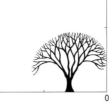

50ft – 15m

50ft
15m
0

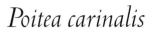

Poitea carinalis

SABINEA

(Griseb.) Lavin   12 spp.

Sabinea carinalis

FABACEAE (Papilionoideae)

WITH THE SWEEPING REVISIONS of long established nomenclature, the small genus of *Sabinea* has now been redefined and included in the small W Indian genus of *Poitea*. These species are mostly tall, woody shrubs or small trees of dry scrub and forest on limestone soils. Many of them are found in the Greater Antilles, in the Dominican Republic, Haiti, Puerto Rico and Cuba. *Poitea carinalis* is an endemic of Dominica, in the Lesser Antilles, an island known more for its magnificent rainforests than arid habitats. During the wet summers of its region, *P. carinalis*, known there as Bois Caribe, remains an undistinguished, diffusely branched, little, woody tree with pale grey to whitish, slightly fissured limbs and twigs. It has a spreading, arching habit, with little, imparapinnate leaves and tiny, oval leaflets that are green above and stained below with red or purple dots and dashes; they are shed during the dry, winter months. In early spring, while still leafless, its framework is suddenly encrusted with the pulsating brilliance of its tiny, crimson, pea-like flowers. This genus is characterized by a synchronicity in flowering, so that all individuals of *P. carinalis* in the same proximity burst into bloom in unison. It is reminiscent of the Cardinal Tree (*Phyllocarpus septentrionalis*) of C America, although that species develops into a substantial tree. The little Sabinea blooms are replaced by slender, flat, linear pods.

*** *P. florida*; ([Vahl.] Lavin), Puerto Rico and Virgin Is, to 6 m (20 ft). WATTAPAMA, RETAMA or SOLDIER WHIP is very similar to *P. carinalis*. The leaves are slightly thick and leathery, with inrolled margins. It grows slowly to form a sparse crown of pale, sturdy, whiplike limbs. In spring, when every little tree is leafless, each one is suddenly, and simultaneously, covered in bluish or pinkish lavender flowers, giving the hillsides a breathtakingly gauzy, but brief, splendour. (10–12)

P. carinalis; blooming when leafless in early spring.

P. carinalis; every sturdy, little, pale-coloured twig is encrusted with clusters of little, stalkless, brilliant crimson, pea fls.

P. florida; Wattapama is suddenly (and simultaneously) covered in bluish or pinkish lavender blooms.

P. carinalis; is completely transformed by its soft green, summer foliage.

Polyalthia longifolia

MAST TREE

(Sonn.) Thw.   100 spp.

ANNONIACEAE

THE MAST TREE is named for its broadly conical growth, accentuated by ascending limbs. *Polyalthia longifolia*, of the Annoniaceae clan, is a riparian species, with glandular, pellucid, dotted, oily leaves that are narrowly elongated and undulate along their edges. When crushed, they are pleasantly aromatic. In spring, the tree blooms briefly when, for 2 or 3 weeks, it is veiled in a profusion of tiny, starry flowers of the palest green, which gives the tree a misty appearance, as if it were swathed in moss. Each little, greenish white flower is borne on a slim, green stem, with a tiny calyx and 5 thin, waxy, spreading, spidery petals. In summer, small, reddish black, succulent fruit, resembling coffee berries, are clustered along the pendent stalks. When the fruit is ripe, bats and flying foxes swirl around the lollipop column, squealing and quarrelling, until dawn arrives to reveal the remains of their feasting strewn over a large area of the ground below. The wood is whitish yellow, light, very flexible and evenly grained. It is used to make small objects such as boxes and pencils and, in China, to make matches.
*** ***P. longifolia*** var. *pendula*; TEMPLE PIKA in Malaysia, is a stunning, narrowly fastigiate variety with short, pendulous limbs that sweep to the ground. Unfortunately, as the tree matures, it may list to one side, forming an unsightly diagonal shape. Editor Anton van der Schans comments, 'In my experience, the weeping form usually maintains its fastigate habit. Badly listing, storm-damaged trees, which have been severely pruned to a stump, quickly regrow their original shape.' He suggests that this variety may benefit from a more monsoonal climate, with a cooler, dry season to strengthen its wood. In Malaysia, traditionally it is grown in Christian cemeteries. (10–12)
*** ***P. suberosa***; ([Roxb.] Thwaites), from India and Sri Lanka to Malay Pen. CORKY DEBDAR is more shrub-like. The flowers are pale yellow; the fruit is reddish purple and edible. (10–12)

ORIGIN	India and Sri Lanka
HEIGHT	up to 20 m (66 ft)
TYPE	evergreen foliage tree
STATUS	not threatened
HABITAT	lowland rainforests, dry or humid
GROWTH	slow
FLOWG	spring
DRY TOL.	moderate to high
SALT TOL.	low
LIGHT	full sun
SOIL	fertile, deep, water-retentive
NUTRIT.	balanced fertilizer annually; deep, organic mulch
HAZARDS	none
PROBLEMS	none
ENVIRON.	insect nectar; wild fruit for bats
PROPAG.	seeds
LEAVES	simple; rich green; to 22 cm (8.7 in.); lanceolate; with wavy margins
FLOWERS	showy; pale green; waxy, star-like; held in large panicles; fragrant
FRUIT	a capsule, to 2 cm (0.8 in.) diameter; berry-like; reddish black, fleshy
USE	street tree; public open space; accent; specimen; large conservatory
ZONE	10–12

P. longifolia var. *pendula*; grows as a lean, lofty spire, with its short, closely pendulous branches sweeping to the ground. This is a very popular var. for street planting all over the tropics.

P. longifolia; with a profusion of tiny, starry pale green fls in spring.

P. longifolia; masses of berries will ripen reddish black to provide a tasty midnight snack for local bats.

P. longifolia; photographed in the huge arboretum at the Jardín Botánico de Cienfuegos, Cuba.

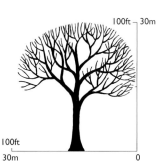

100ft — 30m
100ft
30m
0

Pometia pinnata

KASAI

Forst. & Forst. f. (Mal.)   2 spp

P. tomentosa

SAPINDACEAE

ORIGIN	from Malaysia to Polynesia
HEIGHT	up to 50 m (164 ft)
TYPE	evergreen, large foliage tree
STATUS	not threatened
HABITAT	river banks or humid woodlands and swamps
GROWTH	fast
FLOWG	spring
DRY TOL.	moderate
SALT TOL.	low
LIGHT	full sun or bright shade
SOIL	rich, humid, deep
NUTRIT.	balanced fertilizer annually; deep, organic mulch
HAZARDS	none
PROBLEMS	none
ENVIRON.	nectar; wild fruit for birds
PROPAG.	seeds
LEAVES	pinnate; bright green; up to 15 leaflets; to 35 cm (13.7 in.) long; with toothed margins
FLOWERS	showy; yellowish white or greenish; held in minute catkin-like, pendent clusters; to 60 cm (24 in.)
FRUIT	a capsule, to 5 cm (2 in.); subglobose; thick, shell-like skin, with gelatinous pulp; containing a single, large seed
USE	large shade tree; street tree; public open space
ZONE	10–12

NATIVE TO LOWLAND RIVERBANKS and swampy forests of SE Asia, this lofty evergreen is valued for both its timber and its fruit. Although *Pometia pinnata* does not have showy blooms, it is admired for its glowing, smooth, orange-brown bark and its glorious flushes of luminous-pink leaves that are covered with fine, golden brown hairs. Despite its great size, this is a graceful tree that becomes slightly buttressed in age, forming a buoyant crown of large, softly hairy, deeply veined, toothed, pinnate leaves. When seedlings first sprout, their juvenile leaves are enormous, but as the tree matures, the foliage become smaller, although no less handsome. Ants often use the lowest, stipule-like pair of leaflets for shelter or for making their nests. Minute, yellowish white or greenish flowers with bright, orange-red stamens are borne in ample, pendent, branched, catkin-like clusters that hang from the leaf axils. As the flowers are pollinated, their stalks thicken and large fruit the size of golf balls are formed, 1 or 2 per flower spike. Typical of the brittle-skinned, translucent-fleshed fruit of the Sapindaceae family (litchi, rambutan and Spanish lime), these heavy, smooth, thick-skinned, egg-shaped fruit vary in colour and quality of content. The skin turns red and then purple or blackish as it ripens. The jelly-like flesh is either yellow or transparent and in many parts of its range the fruit is eaten fresh. Within the flesh is a single, large seed, which is roasted and eaten like a chestnut. The inner bark yields an abundant, thin, red gum that is considered to have medicinal qualities. The heartwood of *P. pinnata* is hard and durable and has many uses, including construction, cabinetmaking, furniture and boatbuilding. Known as Kasai in Malaysia and Taun in Indonesia and New Guinea, this tree is very fast growing — as much as 1.7 m (5.6 ft) has been recorded in a year.

P. pinnata; with softly hairy, toothed lvs, which emerge rosy-red.

P. tomentosa; the heartwood is hard and durable. It is known as Kasai in Malaysia and Taun in Indonesia and N Guinea.

P. pinnata; typical of the brittle-skinned, translucent fleshed fr. of the Sapindaceae family.

P. pinnata; a young tree that is springing up above the surrounding growth to form its huge bole with narrow, plank-like buttresses.

Portlandia grandiflora

TREE LILY

L.   6 spp.

RUBIACEAE

PORTLANDIA ARE EXCEEDINGLY DESIRABLE, ranking in the top echelon of tropical flowering species, with their elegant, trumpet-shaped, white, ivory, rose or crimson, lily-like blooms. They are endemic to Jamaica and extremely rare in their natural environment. *Portlandia grandiflora* is the largest species and the only one that attains real tree status. Known as Tree Lily or Bell Flower, it grows in a regally restrained manner, to form a slender, multi-trunked, small tree with fissured, slightly corky bark. Typically Rubiaceae, *P. grandiflora* has large, handsome, leathery, polished, short-petioled leaves that are initially flushed rose pink. They greatly resemble the Christmas Lily (*Lilium regale*) but, if possible, are even more exquisite, with their slender, flaring form. In bud, they are deeply pleated and blushed pink. As the trumpet expands to open, its 5 triangular lobes flare backwards to reveal the slender throat and to expose the pistil and stamens. As if this was not of sufficient allure, these blooms are powerfully vanilla-scented in the evening to attract the moths that pollinate them. The plump, ridged, woody fruit pods are packed with seeds, which, surprisingly, are very easily germinated when fresh.

*** *P. coccinea*, var. *proctorii*; (Sw.), Jamaica, to 3 m (10 ft). PINK PORTLANDIA is a small understorey species from lowland crags and cliffs. It is distinguished by its small, slender, light or dark crimson, funnel-shaped flowers. Typically, these slender cones are deeply pleated at their base, flaring into 5-pointed, slightly curved petals. (10–12)

*** *P. domingensis*, (Britton, Bull.), (syn. *Cubanola domingensis*), Dominican Republic, to 2.5 m (7 ft). *Cubinella* is a shrub or small tree with elliptic or oblong leathery, deeply veined leaves. It has pendant, narrowly funnel-shaped, white or cream flowers with triangular lobes. (10–12)

NOTE: this genus remains under taxonomic review.

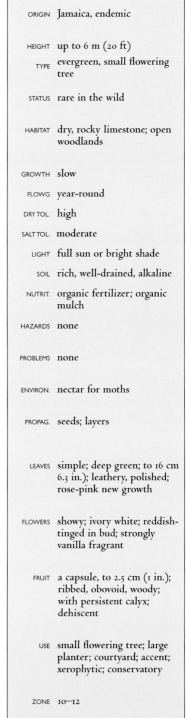

ORIGIN	Jamaica, endemic
HEIGHT	up to 6 m (20 ft)
TYPE	evergreen, small flowering tree
STATUS	rare in the wild
HABITAT	dry, rocky limestone; open woodlands
GROWTH	slow
FLOWG	year-round
DRY TOL.	high
SALT TOL.	moderate
LIGHT	full sun or bright shade
SOIL	rich, well-drained, alkaline
NUTRIT.	organic fertilizer; organic mulch
HAZARDS	none
PROBLEMS	none
ENVIRON.	nectar for moths
PROPAG.	seeds; layers
LEAVES	simple; deep green; to 16 cm 6.3 in.); leathery, polished; rose-pink new growth
FLOWERS	showy; ivory white; reddish-tinged in bud; strongly vanilla fragrant
FRUIT	a capsule, to 2.5 cm (1 in.); ribbed, obovoid, woody; with persistent calyx; dehiscent
USE	small flowering tree; large planter; courtyard; accent; xerophytic; conservatory
ZONE	10–12

P. grandiflora; large, lily-like, fragrant fls.

P. grandiflora; known as the Tree-Lily or Bell-Flower, it grows in a regally restrained manner, to form a slender, compact, multi-trunked, small tree with fissured, slightly corky bark.

P. grandiflora; plump, ridged, woody fr. pods are packed with sds, which are very easily germinated if fresh.

P. domingensis; is distinguished by its funnel-shaped, inflated trumpets with triangular lobes.

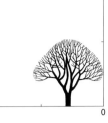

ORIGIN	from Mexico to S America
HEIGHT	up to 7 m (26 ft)
TYPE	evergreen, small flowering tree
STATUS	not threatened
HABITAT	humid forests on volcanic soils
GROWTH	fast
FLOWG.	autumn and spring
DRY TOL.	moderate to high
SALT TOL.	low
LIGHT	full sun to bright shade
SOIL	deep, rich, water-retentive
NUTRIT.	organic fertilizer; organic mulch
HAZARDS	none
PROBLEMS	none
ENVIRON.	moth nectar
PROPAG.	seeds; cuttings; layers
LEAVES	simple; dark green; to 20 cm (8 in.); elliptic to oblong, leathery
FLOWERS	showy; white; elongated, salverform; very fragrant
FRUIT	a berry, to 5 cm (2 in.); fleshy, globose, yellow; edible
USE	small flowering tree; courtyard; humid shade garden; large planter; conservatory
ZONE	10—12

THIS SMALL TREE could be mistaken for an *Ixora*. **Posoqueria latifolia** certainly displays all the classical beauty of its Rubiaceae clan, with its stiff form and its compact foliage composed of typically short-stalked, opposite, leathery leaves and dense heads of fragrant, elongated trumpet flowers that are as thin as quills. Although these blooms have the same basic structure (except this genus has 5 petals) as an *Ixora* flower, the actual tube is enormously long, hence this species being named Needle-Flower. Of all the *Posoqueria* species, *P. latifolia* is probably the most commonly grown. Like so many flowering trees of dry regions, the Needle-Flower Tree is triggered into bloom by heavy rain following a dry period. The blooms are held in dense, terminal corymbs, the flower tube being 17 cm (7 in.), ending in 5 little spreading petals. They are very fragrant to attract moths, which have proboscises long enough to reach the nectar at the base of the tube. The stamens are united into a cone and the pollen explodes on contact with the anthers, expelling the pollen grains. This is designed to deposit them on the pollinator. The fruit that follows is a round, fleshy, golden yellow 'apple' that is edible but not very tasty. The small calliper, finely grained dense wood (known as Brazilian Oak) is popularly used to make walking sticks. In some regions, powdered flowers are used to repel fleas. *P. latifolia* is valued regionally for its medicinal applications – the bark yields a blood-clotting agent that has been used in the Amazon for wounds caused by poison arrows and it has recently been tried as an AIDS vaccine.

*** *P. acutifolia*; (Mart.), endemic of Brazil, to 8 m (26 ft). All parts of this species are smaller. The leaves are leathery and rigid, to 15 cm (6 in.). The flowers are held erect; their tubes are to 18 cm (8 in.) long. The fruit are small, globose, to 2 cm (0.8 in.). (10–12)

P. latifolia; fr. has a large, brown calyx scar at its base.

P. acutifolia; this small Brazilian endemic is easily distinguished by its erect, abundant, short-tubed blooms.

P. latifolia; in full bloom at Jardin Botanico Nationale, Cuba, after heavy rain. The fragrance was quite fabulous.

P. latifolia; Needle-Flower blooms are strongly perfumed at night and have extended, narrow tubes specially designed for the long proboscises of moths.

Pouteria sapota

MAMEY SAPOTE

(Jacq.) Moore & Stearn   200 spp.

P. mammosa

SAPOTACEAE

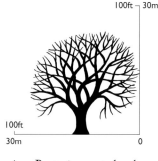

ONE OF THE BEST KNOWN fruiting trees of Trop. America, ***Pouteria sapota*** has been widely cultivated in all parts of the tropical world. Mamey Sapote (or Zapote), a majestic tree, is very closely related to the Sapodilla or Chicle, *Manilkara zapota*. It makes a fine shade tree in a large, humid or irrigated garden . (It is deciduous in prolonged drought conditions.) ***P. sapota*** is distinctive for its lush, dense, oval crown, stout trunk with reddish brown, shaggy bark, its milky latex and its rusty red, hairy, new growth. Small, pale yellow or whitish flowers are densely clustered along the tips of the branchlets. The fruit of ***P. sapota*** resembles a giant Sapodilla and contains the same milky sap in its soft, mellow-sweet, pinkish red or purplish flesh, which is eaten fresh, or made into preserves, marmalades, jellies, sherbets and ice cream. In its humid, forest habitats, this is an important food source for birds and mammals. The seeds, which are suspected of being toxic, are large, blackish brown and polished – resembling gigantic cockroaches – and have a smell of bitter almonds. In some parts of their region, they are ground and used for making confectionery and beverages and for flavouring chocolate. The seed-oil was popular as a hair dressing with the Aztec Indians. The heartwood is a light, reddish brown, moderately hard and heavy, strong and fairly durable and has been used regionally for cabinetmaking and for general carpentry. ***P. sapota*** may take 8–10 years to fruit from seed and 4–5 years from grafts. The fruit matures in 12–15 months. As there will be a great variation between the seedling trees, it is usually thought better to propogate by layering a reliable variety or by grafting onto a good rootstock.

*** *P. australis*; ([R. Br.] Baehni), (syn. *Planchonella australis*), Australian endemic. Black- or Brush-Apple is important for its timber. (10–12)

ORIGIN	Mexic and C America
HEIGHT	up to 30 m (100 ft)
TYPE	semi-deciduous, large fruiting tree
STATUS	not threatened
HABITAT	humid lowland woodland
GROWTH	moderate
FLOWG	late spring to year-round
DRY TOL.	moderate
SALT TOL.	moderate
LIGHT	full sun
SOIL	rich, deep, humid
NUTRIT.	regular, balanced fertilizer; deep, organic mulch
HAZARDS	seeds possibly toxic
PROBLEMS	red spider mite; fungus; twig borer
ENVIRON.	bee nectar; fruit for bats
PROPAG.	seeds; grafts
LEAVES	simple; deep green; to 36 cm (14.2 in.); oblanceolate, tapering; with prominent veins
FLOWERS	inconspicuous; pale yellow; in stalkless, terminal clusters
FRUIT	a berry, to 15 cm (6 in.); ovoid, with caramel-brown, sweet, soft, reddish flesh
USE	large shade tree; public open space; specimen; backyard tree
ZONE	10–12

P. sapota; tiny fls clasped along the tips of the twig.

P. sapota; a most delicious fr., especially if chilled before being eaten fresh. Mamey Sapote is a superb sp. worthy of planting for garden shade, as well as for its harvest.

P. sapota; Mamey Sapote resembles a giant Sapodilla and contains the same milky sap in its mellow pulp.

P. sapota; at a fr. farm in Savannah, Cayman Is.

Pouteria alniifolia; (Pierre), (syn. *Malacantha alniifolia*, *M. ferruginea-tomentosa*), Trop. W Africa, to 20 m (66 ft). This sp. is known in Kenya as Shimba Peach. Young growth (fls and fr.), densely rusty tomentose.This specimen was photographed at the Fruit and Spice Park, Homestead, Florida, USA, when it was showing off its brightly coloured autumnal foliage before losing its lvs in autumn. Note how beetles are attracted to the pungent, ripe fr. (10–12)

Pouteria campechiana, (Baehni), (syn. *Lucuma nervosa*), C and S America, to 30 m (100 ft). Canistel, Egg Fruit or Amarillo is probably the most showy of all the spp., and forms a hefty tree. After the tiny, white, fragrant fls come the egg-shaped fr., which are filled with mealy, slightly fibrous, musky-sweet flesh. These fr. are mostly eaten fresh, sometimes like Avocado, with salt and pepper or a squeeze of lime juice. (10–12). **Note: this sp. is listed as invasive in Florida, USA.**

Pouteria hypoglauca; [(Standl.) Baehni], (syn. *Lucuma hypoglauca*), Yucatan and El Salvador, to 20 m (66 ft). Cinnamon apple is eaten as famine food in its region, although it is said to cause stomach cramps and constipation if eaten in quantity. Of medium height, this sp. forms a lush canopy of large lvs and is tol. of calcareous soils. This specimen was photographed at the Fruit and Spice Park, Homestead, Florida. (9–11)

Pouteria lucuma; (Ruiz. and Pav.), (syn *Lucuma obovata*; *P. obovata*), highlands of Colombia and Peru to Chile. Known as Lucumo or Lucma, this subtrop. sp. is similar to *P. campechiana*. The yellow fr. has firm, dry flesh, which looks and tastes somewhat like sweet egg yolk, possibly, with overtones of Maple Syrup. It is used locally in milkshakes, ice creams and desserts. This is a heavy cropper but prone to fungus-related dieback and weak wood. (9–11)

345

Pseudobombax ellipticum

SHAVING BRUSH TREE

(Kunth) Dugand.   20 spp.

Bombax ellipticum; Pachira fastuosa

MALVACEAE (Formerly Bombacaceae)

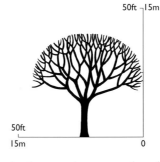

MOST OF THE YEAR, this small, sturdy tree with its smooth, plump, pale grey trunk and branches plays a quiet, anonymous role in the landscape, coping stoically with drought and adverse conditions. In the spring, *Pseudobombax ellipticum* suddenly takes centre stage and explodes with the most spectacular and original display of huge, deep, rose-pink flowers, with long, narrow, curling petals cupping a brush-like mass of silky, crimson stamens. Each day the individual flowers fall to carpet the ground, but the tree continues to bloom for many weeks. Just as this comes to an end, the red foliage bursts from its buds and unfolds as waxy, newborn, palmate leaves that cover the stubby tips of the stems. As the sun sinks in the sky and shines through the translucent new growth, it seems that the tree is on fire. Finally, the *P. ellipticum* settles down into the summer heat, cooling its roots with its sumptuous canopy of opulent, dull green, slightly folded, palmate leaves. The large, leathery fruit capsules enclose many seeds that are embedded in brownish, silky fibre. This species is used medicinally, with a decoction being used to treat toothache and to harden gums. *P. ellipticum*, var. *album*, has white flowers.

*** *P. grandiflorum*, (Robyns), Brazil endemic, to 25 m (82 ft). Known as IMBURUCU, this species has large, strap-like, staminous flowers that are dark, blackish purple externally, paler within and densely pubescent. The stamens are white and purple. The fruit capsule is to 30 cm (12 in.), narrow-oblong, glabrous, brown. With a long flowering period, from summer to autumn. (10–12)

*** *P. simplicifolium*; (A. Robyns), Brazil, to 7 m (23 ft), also known as IMBURUCU, this is a small, parasol-crowned species of rocky, alkaline slopes. Leaves are small, simple, densely pubescent, to 5 cm (2 in.). Flowers have narrow, strap-like, pinkish petals. (9–11)

ORIGIN	Mexico and C America
HEIGHT	up to 10 m (33 ft)
TYPE	deciduous flowering tree
STATUS	not threatened
HABITAT	dry, deciduous lowland forest and woodland
GROWTH	fast
FLOWG	spring
DRY TOL.	high
SALT TOL.	moderate to high
LIGHT	full sun
SOIL	fertile, well-drained
NUTRIT.	balanced fertilizer annually
HAZARDS	none
PROBLEMS	none
ENVIRON.	nectar for bats
PROPAG.	seeds; cuttings; layers
LEAVES	palmate; rich green; 3–6 leaflets, to 30 cm (12 in.); held on long, stout petioles
FLOWERS	showy; white or rich rose; coiled petals; staminal tube divided into bundles of crimson filaments
FRUIT	a capsule, to 15 cm (6 in.); woody, dehiscent; seeds embedded in silky fibre
USE	seaside; public open space; coastal specimen; xerophytic
ZONE	10–12

P. ellipticum; in early spring this little pink-washed seaside cottage in Cayman is embellished with the gorgeous, colour-coordinated blooms of this popular, sandy beach-tolerant sp.

P. ellipticum; with a huge 'brush' of crimson stamens.

P. ellipticum; the transparent, new, crimson foliage glows fiery-red in the setting sun. It quickly turns deep green.

P. ellipticum var *album*; with pure white stamens.

Psidium guajava

GUAVA

L.   100 spp.

MYRTACEAE

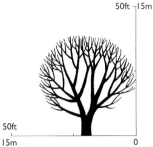

50ft ⌐15m
50ft
15m   0

ORIGIN	C and S America
HEIGHT	up to 10 m (33 ft)
TYPE	semi-deciduous, small fruiting tree
STATUS	not threatened
HABITAT	moist coastal limestone, in thickets
GROWTH	moderate
FLOWG	year-round
DRY TOL.	moderate
SALT TOL.	low
LIGHT	full sun
SOIL	fertile, water-retentive
NUTRIT.	balanced fertilizer twice yearly; deep, organic mulch
HAZARDS	none
PROBLEMS	scales; aphids; fruit fly
ENVIRON.	bee nectar; fruit for birds
PROPAG.	seeds; layers
LEAVES	simple; drab green; oblong or elliptic; heavily veined
FLOWERS	showy; creamy white; to 4 cm (1.5 in.); wavy petals; many white stamens; fragrant
FRUIT	a berry, to 8 cm (3 in.); skin white, yellow; with pinkish or white, sweet, pungently fragrant flesh; many woody, angular seeds
USE	backyard tree; courtyard; specimen; small shade tree; large, bright conservatory
ZONE	10—12

PSIDIUM GUAJAVA is so commonly cultivated throughout the tropics and so often naturalized that it appears to have a much wider habitat than it actually does. In the West Indies, where this species is not native, it is found growing in low-lying, seasonally flooded pastureland. *P. guajava*, typical of the Myrtaceae, has hard, heavy, fine-grained, sinewy limbs and pale, papery bark that peels off in long, irregular flakes, revealing the many hues of the inner wood. The charming, fragrant, simple pearly white flowers, with their bosses of sprightly, pure white stamens, attract honeybees. The flowers are followed by mellow, musky, aromatic, soft-fleshed fruit filled with many, small, angular, very woody seeds. The most common and attractive form has thin, very pale yellow skin and vibrant, salmon-pink pungent pulp in which is embedded many small, pale woody seeds. This fruit contains 2—5 times the vitamin C content of fresh orange juice and was used to fortify rations of the Allied troops during World War ll. Other varieties have white or yellow flesh that varies from insipid to sweet or tart; its pulp is eaten fresh or in fruit salad. *P. guajava* pulp is also preserved or canned or made into jellies or a paste known as 'Guava Butter'. The leaves are sometimes used for the treatment of diarrhoea, while extracts from the leaves, bark, roots and buds have served in folk medicines. In Malaysia, the leaves are pounded with coconut milk and other substances to make a dye to turn silk black. The brown or reddish heartwood is hard and heavy but, because of its small calliper, has mostly found use in the making of implements and handles. Cvs. include 'Beaumont', which is pink-fleshed, 'Detwiler', which is yellow-fleshed, and 'Pear', which has creamy white flesh. In Asia, the fruit is picked before it has ripened to avoid infestation from fruit fly. This is a honey plant.

NOTE: P. guajava has escaped cultivation in parts of the Pacific (incl. Galapagos).

P. guajava; fragrant, with many fragile, pale yellow stamens.

P. guajava; has hard, heavy, fine-grained, sinewy limbs and pale, papery bark, which peels off in long, irregular flakes.

P. guajava; sp. blooms and fruits all-year-round, making it a superb tree for a small trop. or subtrop. garden.

P. guajava; fr. varies from having whitish to pale or deep pink flesh. This pungent fr. is popular for making jelly or 'Guava Butter', a jelly-like paste, which is extremely sweet.

Psidium

(1) ***Psidium cattleianum***; (Sabine) (syn. *P. littorale*), Brazil endemic, to 7 m (23 ft). CATTLEY - or CHERRY-GUAVA is distinguished by its dense, bushy growth of leathery, glabrous lvs, small white, many stamened fls and sturdy, bronze-marbled, sinewy, forked limbs. There are 2 distinct forms: one is the RED- or PURPLE-STRAWBERRY GUAVA, which has purplish red, round, fr., to 2.5 cm (1 in), tasting somewhat of strawberries; it thrives in the subtropics, although it will grow in the tropics but probably not set fr. (9–11) (NOTE: this sp. has become a serious weed in Hawaii, as well as other Pacific islands.)

The other form (2) is var. *lucidum*; (Degener), known as the CHINESE GUAVA. It has little yellow fr., to 2.5 cm (1 in), and is grown in trop. regions. (3) ***Psidium longipes***; ([O. Berg.] McVaugh.) (syn. *Eugenia longipes*), Florida, USA, and W Indies, to 4 m (13 ft). BAHAMA STOPPER or WILD GUAVA is an erect, slow-growing, coast. shrub or small tree with slender-branching and small, erect, greyish green, ovate lvs with golden yellow petioles on dark brown twigs. Fls are white or pinkish, fr. is a bright red berry, to 10 mm (.4 in.). This is an excellent xerophytic or seaside sp. (9–11)

At the Botanical Ark, in a secluded valley near Mossman, N Qld, Australia, a couple live out a lifelong dream. From degraded farmland, they have nurtured rainforest regeneration, an important collection of rare fruits and many other ethnobotanically useful spp. threatened by trop. rainforest destruction. The husband, a true Renaissance man, has designed this paradise garden with a man-made lagoon that is overlooked by their home.

348

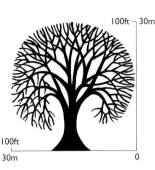

100ft – 30m

100ft

30m   0

Pterocarpus indicus

INDIAN PADAUK

Willd.   21 spp.

P. echinatus

LEGUMINOSAE (Papilionoideae)

ORIGIN	Trop. Asia
HEIGHT	up to 30 m (100 ft)
TYPE	deciduous, large flowering tree
STATUS	not threatened
HABITAT	rainforest; humid forests; seasonally flooded land
GROWTH	fast
FLOWG	spring
DRY TOL.	moderate to high
SALT TOL.	low
LIGHT	full sun
SOIL	fertile, water-retentive
NUTRIT.	balanced fertilizer annually; deep, organic mulch
HAZARDS	none
PROBLEMS	none
ENVIRON.	bee nectar
PROPAG.	seeds; large cuttings
LEAVES	pinnate; rich green; with 5–9 leaflets, to 10 cm (4 in.)
FLOWERS	showy; deep orange or yellow; with 4, crumpled petals in crowded panicles; short-lived; very fragrant
FRUIT	a legume (samara); to 5 cm (2 in.); orbicular, winged; seeds 1–2
USE	large flowering tree; shade tree; street tree; public open space
ZONE	10–12

PTEROCARPUS INDICUS has a shortish trunk and relatively few boughs supporting its elegantly, down-sweeping branches that carry profuse, deep, glossy green pinnate leaves. *P. indicus* is a species of rainforests, riverbanks and floodplains. In late spring or early summer, with the first rains, buds open for an extremely brief flush of bloom that lasts just up to 3 days and covers the tree with clusters of fragrant, deep gold blooms. These little, wrinkled and clawed pea-flowers are nectar-rich and attract honeybees. Characterized by synchronous flowering (all individuals in proximity bloom in unison, triggered by a drop in temperature during a storm), the tree flowers 3 times, but not before it forms masses of distinctive, circular, winged fruit (samaras). The rose-fragrant wood of *P. indicus* is highly valued and is known as Burmese Rosewood, Angsana or Naga. Its heartwood is streaked reddish brown and planks made from it may be wide enough to make a table-top. Indian Padauk is the Philippines' national tree and one of their most valuable timbers (Narra); it is used for construction and to make furniture and musical instruments. Infusions of wood are curiously flourescent; chips impart a blue and yellow hue to water. Bark of *P. indicus* yields a red dye and a sticky, bitter, oily, red latex used like kino gum for throat ailments.
  *** var. *burmanica*, WEEPING ROSEWOOD, is popular in Darwin, NT, Australia, for its smaller size, to 15 m (50 ft), finer foliage and pendulous branching.
*** *P. officinalis*; (Jacq.), Trop. America, to 30 m (100 ft), of humid sites. With red latex and buttressed roots. The flowers are bright yellow with crimson or brown stripes, and are longer lasting than the Asian species. The wood, however, is not as valued. (10–12)
*** *P. santalanus*; (L. f.), India, endemic. SANDERSWOOD or RED SANDALWOOD has red, fragrant heartwood used for cabinetwork. Wood paste is applied to boils or brewed as tea for dysentery. Powdered wood or chips have astringent, tonic properties and are used to treat inflammation. Extracted oil is used as a rejuvenating face cream. (10–12) These are important honey plants.

P. indicus; little pea-like blooms may be yellow or orange.

P. officinalis; grows to a great size with buttressed roots. Trunk and limbs have red latex, so typical of this genus.

P. indicus; dry, samara fr. will eventually glide down on their wings.

P. indicus; short-lived, the little, nectar-rich, pea-like fls are characterized by their synchronicity in blooming – all individuals in proximity fl. in unison 3 times during spring months.

349

Pterospermum acerifolium

MAPLE-LEAFED BAYUR

(L.) Willd.   25 spp.

MALVACEAE (formerly Sterculiaceae)

100ft – 30m

75ft
22.5m   0

ORIGIN	from India to Java
HEIGHT	up to 30 m (100 ft)
TYPE	evergreen, large flowering and foliage tree
STATUS	not threatened
HABITAT	humid lowland forests; swamps
GROWTH	fast
FLOWG	late spring
DRY TOL.	moderate
SALT TOL.	moderate
LIGHT	full sun
SOIL	fertile, water-retentive
NUTRIT.	balanced fertilizer annually; deep, organic mulch
HAZARDS	none
PROBLEMS	suckering roots
ENVIRON.	nectar for bats
PROPAG.	seeds; cuttings; layers
LEAVES	palmately lobed; deep green; to 35 cm (13.7 in.); silvery white below
FLOWERS	showy; white; silky petals and stamens; with long, velvety sepals; very fragrant
FRUIT	a capsule, to 15 cm (6 in.); woody, 5-angled; with many winged seeds
USE	large flowering tree; large shade tree; street tree; public open space
ZONE	10–12

PTEROSPERMUM ACERIFOLIUM is found along riverbanks and damp valleys where it grows rapidly to a great size. It forms an irregular crown over a crooked trunk and thick, steeply ascending limbs. The fruit, young growth and unopened flowers are all brown velvety. As the leaves first appear, they unfold into tiny, plush discs, increasing rapidly in size, especially on the younger shoots, until they reach 30 cm (12 in.) and unfurl. As they mature, these simple, heart-shaped leaves with rusty velvety petioles become leathery and jaggedly toothed at the apex, to resemble maple leaves. The upper surface is smooth and deep green, the lower surface is greyish tomentose. During the winter and the dry season, this grey undersurface becomes more intensely silvery white, causing the tree to glitter in the lightest breeze. The heavy, rusty tomentose flower buds split into 5 long, white-lined, velvety sepals, eventually reflexing to display pure white, silky, twisted petals that enclose a tassel of ivory filaments. Their fragrance is due to small, brown, hairy glands that cover the succulent sepals. It lingers for a long time, even when the flowers have become dry. In India, this species is much favoured as a shade tree, despite the fact that it suckers freely from its wide surface roots. *P. acerifolium* is also esteemed for its timber, which is hard, fine-grained and considered similar to teak and oak.

*** *P. lancifolium*; (Roxb.), SE Asia. A small tree, with slender limbs. Leaves are simple, shallowly lobed, dark green above, brilliant, silvery white below. The small, white flowers have narrow petals and long stamens. (10–12)

*** *P. suberifolium*; (Willd.), E Indies, to 10 m (33 ft). The CORKY-LEAFED BAYUR is a small tree with oblong, obliquely based, coarsely toothed leaves, which are pubescent below. White flowers are held in terminal or axillary racemes. (10–12)

P. acerifolium; faded fls remain fragrant, even when dry.

P. acerifolium; the bloom has heavy, velvety sepals, which enclose twisted, silky petals and a tassel of ivory filaments. These blooms are valued for their enduring fragrance.

P. acerifolium; is found along riverbanks and damp valleys where it grows rapidly to a great size with a somewhat slender form.

P. lancifolium; with small, sprightly fls and simple, leathery lvs, which are brightly tomentose below.

Punica granatum

POMEGRANATE

L.   2 spp

P. sempervirens

PUNICACEAE

ORIGIN	from SE Europe to the Himalayas
HEIGHT	up to 6 m (20 ft)
TYPE	deciduous, small fruiting tree
STATUS	not threatened
HABITAT	dry woodlands and open ground
GROWTH	moderate to fast
FLOWG	year-round
DRY TOL.	high
SALT TOL.	low
LIGHT	full sun
SOIL	fertile, well-drained
NUTRIT.	fertilizer twice yearly; possibly organic mulch
HAZARDS	spiny limbs
PROBLEMS	root rot; root suckers
ENVIRON.	insect nectar
PROPAG.	seeds; cuttings; suckers
LEAVES	simple; pale to bright green; obovate; to 8 cm (3 in.)
FLOWERS	showy; orange-red; set in heavy, campanulate calyx; petals funnelform-rotate, crumpled, sessile
FRUIT	a berry, to 12 cm (4.7 in.) diam.; globose; brown-yellow, blushed pink; flesh juicy; with many woody seeds
USE	small flowering tree; backyard tree; screening; large planter; bright conservatory; yxerophytic
ZONE	8—10

50ft 15m
50ft
15m
0

FROM THE EASTERN MEDITERRANEAN, across northern Africa, to the foothills of the Himalayas, this spiny, xerophytic, bushy small tree is native and renowned for its fruit, flowers and medicinal qualities. ***Punica granatum*** will grow but not thrive in the true tropics, where it is valued, perhaps, more for its superb, ornamental, double-flowered, sterile form, ***P. granatum*** var. ***flora-pleno*** or its dwarf cultivars. ***P. granatum*** originates in high, desert regions of scorching days, chilly nights and parched, infertile soils, where normal cultivation is difficult and vigorous, native species are treasured. The bright scarlet, crumpled flowers are contained in a thick calyx. The fruit has a thick, leathery, yellowish shell, flushed rich pink or red, with a persistent calyx at its tip. Within, the spongy, creamy pulp is packed with many woody seeds, each surrounded by a blood-red, astringent, sweet, juicy sac. It is these small sacs (or arils) that constitute the edible part of the fruit. For this reason, Pomegranate is usually eaten out-of-hand, or pressed for its delicious, refreshing juice. Grenadine cordial is made by fermenting the pulp. The fruit lasts so well after picking that it is carried by desert caravans as thirst-quenchers. Like acanthus and artichokes, Pomegranate flowers and fruit were the inspiration for design motifs in ancient times as a symbol of fertility, and the shape of the persistent calyx was adapted for King Solomon's crown. The pulverized bark was formerly official in medicine under the name Granatum (Pomegranate bark). The drug Pelletierine tannate is obtained from the same source. The fruit pulp has yielded oestrone and has proved to be effective against HIV. The rind has been employed in tanning and in the preparation of black ink. Seeds, dried with their aril, give the sour, Indian condiment, Anadana.

P. granatum; fls are held in very thick, bell-shaped calyxes.

var. *flora-pleno* cv. 'Andre le Roi' is an exquisite, sterile form.

P. granatum; fr. has a thick, leathery, yellowish shell, flushed rich pink or red with a persistent calyx at its base.

P. granatum; within its thick, leathery shell, it has cream, spongy pulp packed with sds with blood-red arils. It lasts so well that the fr. is carried by desert caravans as thirst-quenchers.

351

Quararibea cordata

CHUPA-CHUPA

(Bonpl.) Vischer   50 spp.

Matisia cordata

MALVACEAE (Formerly Bombacaceae)

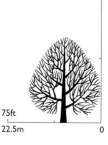

Quararibea cordata is a member of the Bombax clan and is the only one that is considered edible in the New World, unless the chestnut-like seeds of *Pachira aquatica* are taken into account. Known as Chupa-chupa, this species is native to northwestern S America around the Amazon Basin, where it grows in rainforest on fertile soils from fairly high altitudes to lowland, coastal regions. Of moderate height, *Q. cordata* forms a heavy canopy of stiff branches with large, coarse, long-petioled, broadly heart-shaped, heavily veined leaves clustered in rosettes towards the ends of the twigs. During cold weather, the leaves tend to thin out a little. This is one of several species known as the Hatrack Tree because its limbs are attached in regularly spaced whorls. Young bark, stems and twigs have copious, yellow, gummy latex. The cauliflorous flowers are most curious and resemble living coral; they are tiny and formed in random masses on the limbs; creamy or yellowish, they have 5 little cupped petals, which clasp bizarre, oversized, 5-fingered, 'hairy' stamens centred by a pistil. No less curious are the fruit, which look like little, nubile breasts with nipples. They are short-stalked and scurfy, brown-skinned, with the flesh within bright orange, juicy and sweet, but filled with large fibres; it is mostly eaten out-of-hand. The descriptions of its taste are surprisingly varied. One enthusiast has described it as tasting like a blend of mangoes, peaches and strawberries, other descriptions have highlighted its mango-melon qualities, while the least enthusiastic consider it to be bland.

*** *Q. funebris*; ([Llave] Vischer), Mexico, to 15 m (50 ft). Rosita de Cacao flowers are dried and added as a spice to flavour chocolate drinks in Mexico. (9–11)

ORIGIN	Trop. America
HEIGHT	up to 20 m (66 ft)
TYPE	semi-deciduous, fruiting tree
STATUS	not threatened
HABITAT	wet forests on fertile soils
GROWTH	fast
FLOWG.	late winter to early spring
DRY TOL.	low to moderate
SALT TOL.	moderate
LIGHT	full sun
SOIL	fertile, water-retentive
NUTRIT.	regular, balanced fertilizer; deep, organic mulch
HAZARDS	none
PROBLEMS	whitefly; scarab beetle
ENVIRON.	nectar and wild fruit for birds and mammals
PROPAG.	seeds
LEAVES	cordate; deep green; long-petioled; crowded at ends of twigs and branchlets
FLOWERS	curious; creamy yellow; single or in fascicles; with elongated, 'fingered', staminal column
FRUIT	a capsule, to 13 cm (5 in.); cauliflorous; orange; pulp fibrous, sweetish, edible
USE	sheltered seaside; backyard tree; public open space; large conservatory
ZONE	10–12

Q. cordata; with provocative, softly pubescent fr. crowded against the trunk and main branches. For all their eye-appeal, these S American beauties are not really renowned for their great taste.

Q. cordata; bizarre blooms with large, 5-fingered stamens.

Q. cordata; with large, coarse, long-petioled, broadly heart-shaped, heavily veined lvs clustered in rosettes.

Q. cordata ; a fairly slender, coarsely foliaged, fast-growing tree of moderate size, perfect for a small garden.

ORIGIN	Trop. S America
HEIGHT	up to 6 m (20 ft)
TYPE	evergreen, small flowering tree
STATUS	not threatened
HABITAT	understorey in rainforests and humid sites
GROWTH	slow
FLOWG	year-round
DRY TOL.	low
SALT TOL.	low
LIGHT	bright shade
SOIL	rich, water-retentive
NUTRIT.	organic fertilizer; deep, organic mulch
HAZARDS	none
PROBLEMS	none
ENVIRON.	hummingbird nectar
PROPAG.	seeds; semi-ripe cuttings
LEAVES	pinnate or simple; dark green; glossy; with broadly winged, red rachis; often flushed purple
FLOWERS	showy; bright red; in terminal, horizontal, branched racemes
FRUIT	a drupe, to 13 mm (0.5 in.); purple-black
USE	humid shade garden; large container; accent; botanic collection; conservatory
ZONE	10–12

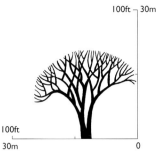

100ft – 30m
100ft
30m 0

Quassia amara

AMARGO BARK

L.   40 spp.

SIMAROUBACEAE

ALTHOUGH SMALL AND SLENDER, this tropical S American beauty is packed with more than 30 powerful phytochemicals in its tissues. *Quassia amara* was named in honour of a slave, Quasi, from Guyana, who showed Europeans the plant's fever-treating uses. A small, multi-stemmed tree, Amargo Bark forms a somewhat disorderly growth of wand-like, twiggy limbs. The pinnate, deeply veined, polished leaves are distinctive for their broadly winged rachis and reddish veins. Terminal, red-branched racemes of darting, vivid crimson, narrow flowers decorate the tips of each little limb and are perfectly presented for hummingbird pollination. Small, fleshy, purple-black drupes replace the flowers. All parts of *Q. amara* contain a bitter principle, Quassimarin, which has many medical uses, including anti-leukaemic, anti-tumour, astringent, digestive, febrifuge, vermifuge, insecticidal, laxative and tonic. Stems are ground into small chips, known as Amargo Bark, and employed commercially in medicines. It has also been found to stimulate the secretion of gastric juices, increase appetite and aid digestion, and has been successfully used to alleviate anorexia nervosa. A traditional, regional remedy taken popularly as a tonic or for malaria or fevers is a half a cup of shredded bark decoction twice daily. *Q. amara* is also the base for Angostura Bitters, which is famously added to gin-based drinks. In Brazil, a 'tea' of infused leaves is used to bathe measles patients or given as a mouthwash after tooth extractions. The bark of another genus of the Simaroubaceae, *Picrasma excelsa* ([Sw.] Planchon), of the W Indies, known commonly as Jamaica Bark, is a source of 'Quassia' chips and is often substituted for *Quassia* in commercially prepared medicines and insecticides.

NOTE: may be mildly invasive under ideal conditions.

Q. amara; fls have evolved to attract their pollinators – hummingbirds.

Q. amara; the stems are ground into small chips and employed commercially in medicines.

Q. amara; deeply veined, polished lvs are distinctive for their broadly winged axis and reddish petioles.

Q. amara; this trop., S American sp. is packed with more than 30 powerful phytochemicals in its tissues.

(1) *Quassia simarouba*; (L. f.), (syn *Simarouba glauca*), C America and W Indies, to 16 m, (52 ft), PARADISE TREE. Apart from its fr. and (2) deep, rosy red emergent foliage, this tree is otherwise quite anonymous (despite being called Paradise Tree). (3) The white fls are very small and held briefly in huge, yellow-stemmed, diffusely branched panicles. The fr. has a white pulp that is fairly juicy and slightly bitter. It is considered edible and contains 62% oil. In Salvador, the oil is extracted to make margarine and cooking oil, as well as being used in the manufacture of soap. Like *Q. amara*, the bark has medicinal qualities; a preparation is employed as a febrifuge and has also been used for malaria. The wood has little use apart from domestic fuel. This slow-growing sp. is very xerophytic and salt-tol. (10–12) **NOTE:** *Simarouba* **genus is now referred to as** *Quassia* **(thus,** *Simarouba glauca* = *Quassia simarouba***).**

Sprawling across the lower foothills of Table Mountain, the fabled Kirstenbosch Botanic Gardens of Capetown, South Africa, are particularly renowned for their splendid collections of the country's endemic flora. In spring, visitors flock from all over the world to enjoy the brilliant displays of wild veldt fls and shrubs.

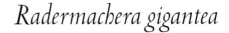
Radermachera gigantea

FOXGLOVE TREE

(Bl.) Miq.   15 spp.

R. amoena; R. triternata

BIGNONIACEAE

ORIGIN	from SE Asia to New Guinea
HEIGHT	6–40 m (20–131 ft)
TYPE	evergreen, small to large flowering tree
STATUS	not threatened
HABITAT	evergreen humid forest; along river banks
GROWTH	fast
FLOWG	year-round
DRY TOL.	low
SALT TOL.	low
LIGHT	sheltered sun
SOIL	fertile, humid soil
NUTRIT.	organic fertilizer; deep, organic mulch
HAZARDS	none
PROBLEMS	nematodes; scale
ENVIRON.	insect nectar
PROPAG.	seeds; cuttings
LEAVES	pinnate; deep green; 12–80 cm (5–31 in.); leaflets oblong to elliptic
FLOWERS	showy; pinkish mauve; to 6 cm (2.5 in.); arching trumpets, with yellow throats
FRUIT	a capsule, to 60 cm (24 in.); linear, terete; seeds winged
USE	flowering tree; small street tree; public open space; accent; large planter; civic centre; wind barrier
ZONE	10–12

RADERMACHERA are mostly native of humid forests of SE Asia to Malesia and are very closely related to *Stereospermum*; in fact, **Radermachera gigantea** is often confused with *S. chelonioides*. This is a family renowned for its handsome foliage and entrancing, trumpet flowers. **R. gigantea** is no exception, being a compact species with dense foliage that grows rapidly to a very grand 40 m (131 ft), or may remain as a tall shrub to 6 m (20 ft), depending on the depth and richness of the soil and the rainfall. The splendid, 2-parted, rich green, glabrous leaves, with oblong, or elliptic leaflets, vary greatly in length. The inflorescence is a huge, erect terminal thyrse to 40 cm (16 in), producing periodic flushes of pinkish-mauve (or creamy-white), trumpet-shaped blooms. Their throats are splashed with rich yellow or orange and are abruptly dilated above the tube, flaring into 5 unequal, crisped petals. **R. gigantea** is particularly renowned for its remarkable tolerance of high winds and is therefore planted as a wind barrier in some regions.

*** **R. glandulosa**; ([Bl.] Miq.), (syn. *Stereospermum glandulosum*), Burma to W Malaysia, to 15 m (50 ft). HILL FOXGLOVE TREE is a rather crooked tree, with pale, drab brown bark. Young, pinnate leaves are deep purple, and the heavy trumpet flowers pinkish purple outside, lined white inside, with white stamens. The fruit are straight capsules with winged seeds, to 30 × 0.7 cm (12 × 0.3 in.), held in clusters. (10–12)

*** **R. sinica**; ([Hance] Hemsl.), S and E Asia, to 7 m (23 ft). CHINA DOLL, an evergreen, small tree or shrub with attractive, lustrous, 2-pinnate leaves, is sold in supermarkets as a small container plant. From spring to summer in its native habitat, it has triangular-lobed, sulphur yellow or creamy white campanulate blooms. Carnation-scented in the evening, **R. sinica** suits being planted in cooler, frost-free climates. Flowers spring to summer. (9–11)

R. gigantea; group of trees with handsome crowns of glossy, pinnate foliage.

R. sinica; is an everg., small tree with attractive, lustrous, lvs and is widely sold in supermarkets as a house plant.

R. sinica; with large, white or yellow, carnation-scented, trumpet fls.

R. gigantea; the Foxglove Tree is a rainforest sp. The pinnate lvs may measure up to 80 cm (31 in.) in length, and the brilliant blooms are held in splendidly large thyrses.

Reevesia thyrsoidea

PERFUME TREE

Lindl. 4 spp

MALVACEAE (formerly Sterculiaceae)

ORIGIN	from S China to Java
HEIGHT	up to 8 m (26 ft)
TYPE	deciduous, small flowering tree
STATUS	not threatened
HABITAT	humid lowland forests
GROWTH	moderate
FLOWG	late spring and autumn
DRY TOL.	moderate
SALT TOL.	low
LIGHT	sheltered sun or part shade
SOIL	rich loam
NUTRIT.	organic fertilizers; deep, organic mulch
HAZARDS	none
PROBLEMS	none
ENVIRON.	insect nectar
PROPAG.	seeds
LEAVES	simple; dark green, to 25 cm (10 in.) long; glossy
FLOWERS	showy; white, with golden throat; with long staminal column tipped with knob of 15 anthers; fragrant
FRUIT	a capsule, a 2.5 cm (1 in.); obovoid, woody; 5-celled; seeds winged
USE	specimen; flowering border; accent; large planter; civic centre; bright conservatory
ZONE	9–12

THE *REEVESIA* GENUS was named in honour of John Reeves, FRS (died 1856), a tea inspector in Macao and Canton, and an avid horticulturalist who introduced many Chinese plants into English greenhouses. *Reevesia thyrsoidea* forms a slender, small tree with broadly oblong, glossy, elegant leaves, which are whorled around their stems, forming a sumptuous fan against which the terminal bouquets of long-stemmed blooms are nestled. Each little chalky white, 5-petalled flower has a reddish gold throat and a slender staminal tube tipped with a curious yellow knob, consisting of 15 anthers, hence it is often called the Matchstick Flower. In late spring, and again in early autumn, the fragrant, chalky white flowers are held in compact heads at the branch tips. With 40–50 blossoms in each posey, these blooms greatly resemble Viburnum 'snowballs'. As the flowers fade, they turn deep cream and then brownish, persisting until the ovaries are developed – a dangling, 5-celled, pear-shaped seed pod, with each of the cells containing 1 or 2 winged seeds that resemble the large seeds of a pine cone. *R. thyrsoidea* is an important and popular native of Hong Kong and Macao. This species is yet another example of the remarkable Sterculiaceae clan that is invariably innovative and unconventional.

*** *R. pubescens*; (Mast), Thailand endemic, to 8 m (26 ft). A rare, ornamental species with very furry, rusty tomentose parts and pink, hairy flowers. (10–12)

*** *R. wallichii*, (R. Br.), E Himalayas, to 15 m (50 ft). Leaves to 10 cm (3 in.), broadly ovate, thinly, stellate-pubescent, short-petioled. Flowers scented, petals white; staminal column exserted to 2 cm (0.8 in.). Fruit to 5 cm (2 in.), oblong, pendulous, woody, splitting into 5 sections with winged seeds. (9–11)

R. thyrsoidea; a small specimen in full bloom.

R. thysoidea; these little fls are unmistakable, with their elongated pistils tipped with a curious, round knob, giving it the common name, Matchstick Flower.

R. thyrsoidea; this slender specimen was photographed in the Singapore Botanic Gardens.

R. thyrsoidea; a small sp. with smoothish, grey bark.

ORIGIN	Trop. America
HEIGHT	up to 15 m (50 ft)
TYPE	evergreen fruiting tree
STATUS	threatened
HABITAT	lowland, humid limestone forest
GROWTH	fast
FLOW'G	winter and summer
DRY TOL.	moderate
SALT TOL.	low
LIGHT	full sun
SOIL	fertile, well-drained
NUTRIT.	organic fertilizer; deep, organic mulch
HAZARDS	none
PROBLEMS	none
ENVIRON.	nectar for beetles
PROPAG.	seeds; layers; grafting
LEAVES	simple; rich green, to 28 cm (11 in.); oblong-elliptic; pubescent below
FLOWERS	inconspicuous; yellow-green; to 2.5 cm (1 in.); with 3 thick, winged petals
FRUIT	a syncarp, to 15 cm+ (6 in.+); yellow skin; sweet, juicy, whitish pulp
USE	small shade tree; backyard tree; specimen
ZONE	10—12

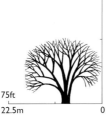

100ft — 30m
75ft
22.5m
0

(Jacq.) Baillon   60 spp.

R. deliciosa; R. pulchrinervis

ANNONIACEAE

ROLLINIA MUCOSA (previously known as *R. deliciosa*), a Trop. American species, is very closely related, and similar, to the genus *Annona*. It is a fast-growing, fairly small evergreen tree of moist lowland limestone, up to 600 m (2,000 ft) or more, and is said to be the most popular fruit in W Amazonia. *R. mucosa* forms a squat, grey-barked trunk and a coarse, open crown of rusty, silky hairy young growth, with its yellowish green leaves in 2 regular rows. These long, elliptic, slightly folded leaves have very small, yellowish petioles and many curved, sunken veins. It is the small blooms that really differentiate this genus from *Annona*. Like that genus, they are 3-petalled and yellowish green, but the petals are narrow, with laterally compressed wings and many stamens and pistils that are massed into a conical base. The rounded or heart-shaped, whitish green fruit that follows ripens rich yellow, with black-tipped points. It could easily be mistaken for *Annona cherimola* and may grow more than 15 cm (6 in.) across. Formed from the fusion of the pistils into a multiple fruit, it is composed of many crowded segments, each ending in a stout, spreading, wart-like point. Each segment has a brown, elliptic seed set in pleasantly sweet, juicy, mucilaginous, transparent, whitish pulp. *R. mucosa*, which varies greatly, with some types being sweeter and tastier than others (enthusiasts graft desirable varieties to ensure the best harvest), is eaten fresh as a dessert or squeezed as juice. The fruit matures in 90 days. *R. mucosa* is grown spasmodically as a domestic tree in some regions. In some parts of Brazil, however, the wild populations are threatened by accelerating deforestation by ranchers and farmers. The yellowish wood is hard, heavy and strong. Annonaceous fruit are especially rich in alkaloids and are currently the focus of research for biomedical applications as they may arrest the growth of certain cancers.

R. mucosa; it is the curious, 3-parted fls that define this sp.

R. mucosa; in some parts of Brazil, wild sp. are threatened by accelerating deforestation by ranchers and farmers.

R. mucosa; ripe fr. for sale at Tropical Fruit World, Duranabah, on the Gold Coast of Qld, Australia.

R. mucosa; photographed at the 'Bend-in-the-River', on the Gold Coast, Qld, Australia, where many growers specialize in rare trop. fr. This sp. is very like Cherimoya.

Salix chilensis

MEXICAN WILLOW

Molina   400 spp.

S. humboldtiana

SALICACEAE

THE COLUMNAR *S. chilensis* as introduced and established in many parts of the W Indies early in the 20th century as an ornamental. After the style of a small Lombardy Poplar, the branches are nearly erect, with ascending brushes of yellow-green twigs. Slender, papery thin, saw-toothed, light green leaves are also held erect and accentuates the tree's narrow form. Typical of the *Salix* family, *S chilensis* is dioecious, with male and female flowers on separate trees; male flowers form narrow, yellow catkins, while the less flamboyant females are green. The 2-valved fruit capsule has woolly seeds but, for some reason, this species has not been known to bloom in the W Indies. It is however, very easily propagated by fairly large cuttings. In Iran and other parts of the Persian Gulf, where it is known as Beed, *S. chilensis* is grown for fodder and green manure. The sapwood is whitish, while the heartwood is dull grey and reddish. Being soft, lightweight and easy to work, it is not, however, very durable, and is very susceptible to dry-wood termites. Like other willows, its slender, flexible young limbs are used to create wicker-type furniture and baskets and the bark has found use in ethnic medicine. *S. chilensis* is native to swamps or higher elevations of the tropics or in the subtropics and has been widely planted in S Qld, Australia, where it was popular for use as a boundary screen in the 1970s. It has since fallen from grace owing to its thirsty, invasive roots.

*** *S. babylonica*; (L.), China, to 13 m (43 ft). BABYLON WEEPING WILLOW is a temperate species. It will, however, grow in subtropical areas with deep, humid, rich soil but will never reach its full, billowing potential. (4–10)

NOTE: these spp. have invasive roots, which may clog underground water pipes.

ORIGIN	from W Mexico to S America
HEIGHT	up to 20 m (66 ft)
TYPE	deciduous, dioecious foliage tree
STATUS	not threatened
HABITAT	sheltered, humid lowland sites
GROWTH	fast
FLOWG	late winter to spring
DRY TOL.	moderate
SALT TOL.	low
LIGHT	full sun
SOIL	rich, humid, water-retentive
NUTRIT.	occasional fertilizer
HAZARDS	none
PROBLEMS	invasive roots
ENVIRON.	insect nectar
PROPAG.	large cuttings
LEAVES	simple; dullish green, to 15 × 1 cm, (6 × 0.4 in.); linear, with toothed margins
FLOWERS	inconspicuous; pale yellow, in catkins
FRUIT	a capsule; to 5 cm (2 in.); 2-valved, with woody seeds
USE	accent tree; pond or stream; screening; small avenue
ZONE	8–11

S. chilensis; the Mexican Willow is popular as a fast-growing accent tree, being narrow and fine-textured. It is often planted closely together as a windbreak, in Qld, Australia.

S. chilensis; with slender, yellow, catkin fls.

S. chilensis; with erect limbs and thin-textured, strap-like lvs. This sp. is very easy to grow from large cuttings.

S. chilensis; soft, lightweight wood is easy to work but not durable, and is very susceptible to dry-wood termites.

ORIGIN	Trop. America
HEIGHT	up to 21 m (70 ft)
TYPE	deciduous foliage (flowering) tree
STATUS	not threatened
HABITAT	dry lowland and coastal bushland and forest
GROWTH	fast
FLOWG	spring
DRY TOL	high
SALT TOL	moderate
LIGHT	full sun
SOIL	widely tolerant
NUTRIT.	balanced fertilizer annually
HAZARDS	none
PROBLEMS	invasive surface roots
ENVIRON.	bee nectar; wild fruit
PROPAG.	seeds
LEAVES	2-pinnate; mid green; pubescent; leaflets to 4 × 2 cm (1.5 × 0.8 in.), elliptic
FLOWERS	showy; pink; funnel-shaped flowers, comprising bundles of stamens
FRUIT	a legume, to 20 × 2 cm (8 × 0.8 in.); ribbed, dehiscent; seeds embedded in sweetish pulp
USE	street tree; public open space; xerophytic
ZONE	10–12

100ft – 30m
140ft
42m
0

Samanea saman

RAIN TREE

(Jacq.) F. Meull.   1 sp.

Albizia saman

FABACEAE (Mimosoideae)

SAMANEA SAMAN is a truly noble tropical tree. It has a sturdy, smooth, pale grey trunk mostly divided near its base into a few hefty branches that grow almost horizontally to support its monstrous parasol canopy. *S. saman* has large, pinnate leaves with blunt-tipped, diamond-shaped, asymmetric leaflets, which have the remarkable ability to open and close, responding to light or weather – their hinged stalks droop while the leaflets turn sideways and fold up. At night, they remain closed to reduce evaporation, while in sunlight they open fully to photosynthesise and shade the roots. A profusion of fluffy, greenish-tinged, pink pompoms spangle its colossal, soft green parasol in spring but gradually deepen to rose-pink as they age and are pollinated. The common name Rain Tree is due to a curious shower of moisture caused by thousands of tiny insects that suck on tender, juicy new growth. At the same time, they exude their bodily fluids that are said to 'fall as a gentle rain' to dampen the ground. *S. saman* is popular in all parts of the tropics, being planted for avenues or major shade trees in large parks and gardens. In areas of high rainfall, it could prove to be shallow-rooted and is better suited to drier regions where the tree will establish a deeper root system. The sapwood is thin and yellowish, while the freshly cut heartwood is a dark, chocolate-brown, turning golden brown as it dries; it is soft and lightweight but very durable against rot and termites. The nutritious pods are filled with sweet, caramel-like pulp tasting of licorice and are relished by cattle, hogs and goats. The pulp has been used to flavour chewing-tobacco. Probably the most celebrated *S. saman* is one in Tobago, which, in 1960, provided the frame for the treehouse in the film of the book, *The Swiss Family Robinson*. That tree measured 76 m (250 ft) wide × 60 m (120 ft) high.

NOTE: listed as undesirable in environmentally sensitive areas in Australia.

S. saman; a profusion of fluffy pink and white pompoms.

S. saman; glossy, blunt-tipped, leathery, pinnate lvs have the remarkable ability to open and close on their hinged stalks.

S. saman; sds are set in sticky, caramel-like pulp, which tastes of licorice.

S. saman; stretching its immense superstructure over the entrance to the magnificent Waimea Arboretum in Hawaii, this specimen demonstrates the typical growth habit of this sp.

A golden-leafed form of *Samanea saman* has been selected to form a glowing halo around the historic bandstand at the Singapore Botanic Gardens. This variety grows much smaller and less vigorously than the typical *Samanea*.

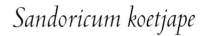

ORIGIN	SE Asia
HEIGHT	up to 50 m (164 ft)
TYPE	semi-deciduous, large fruiting tree
STATUS	not threatened
HABITAT	river banks, wet tropical lowlands, up to 300 m (1,000 ft)
GROWTH	fast
FLOWG	spring
DRY TOL.	low to moderate
SALT TOL.	low
LIGHT	full sun
SOIL	rich, well-drained
NUTRIT.	regular fertilizer
HAZARDS	none
PROBLEMS	galls; mites
ENVIRON.	insect nectar
PROPAG.	seeds; grafts; layers
LEAVES	3-foliate; deep green, aging deep red; leaflets to 25 cm (10 in.), leathery
FLOWERS	showy; yellowish or greenish; in panicles, to 20 cm (8 in.)
FRUIT	a capsule, to 7.5 cm (3 in.); round, velvety, dull to golden yellow; peach-like
USE	backyard tree; humid shade garden; specimen; accent
ZONE	10–12

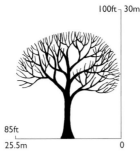

100ft — 30m
85ft
25.5m — 0

Sandoricum koetjape

SANTOL

(Burm.. f.) Merr.   5 spp.

S. indicum; S. nervosum

MELIACEAE

THIS NATIVE OF SE ASIA comes in 2 popular forms, as with *Lansium domesticum* (Langsat or Duku) of the same clan. **Sandoricum koetjape**, or Santol, as it is named in Malaysia, is a large, ornamental tree with a narrowly oval crown, found in humid habitats. It has brown or grey, slightly flaky bark and long-petioled, finely felty, 3-foliate, leathery leaves. In Sarawak, this species is often found along riverbanks, the deep roots holding the large trees precariously balanced over the rushing water. In spring, with a flush of new leaves, the outermost twigs bear small, erect, terminal panicles of whitish green flowers. By the summer, the fruits have formed; they are highly ornamental, being globose, velvety, yellow, sometimes flushed pink like exotic peaches, and dangled in great masses on long, robust stalks. Although they may smell like peach, these fruit are either thick- or thin-skinned, with pleasant, sweetish or sourish pulp, depending upon the variety. The pulp is pearly white translucent and contains thin, milky latex. Santols are eaten fresh, candied, preserved or made into chutney. In Malaya, an intoxicating drink is prepared from the fruit. Both the seeds and the stems are being studied for their anti-carcinogenic substances. A distinctive feature of *S. koetjape* is the manner in which the aging leaves change colour. In the Sentul type (syn. *S. indicum*), they become deep yellow, whereas in the Kechapi var. (*S. koetjape*), they turn bright red. These leaves are so brilliantly flame-coloured, as to resemble flowers at a distance. The timber, known as Katon, is valued highly in its native regions. At the Jardin Botanico de Cienfuegos, S Cuba, 2 30-year-old trees had never borne fruit until they were put under stress by pounding large, heavy stones into the narrow forks of the main limbs; the first crop followed.

S. koetjape; little fls in terminal panicles.

S. koetjape; the Santol or Wild Mangosteen, photographed at Montgomery Botanical Centre, Miami, Florida. The lvs of this sp. turn a startlingly brilliant red as they age.

S. koetjape; its timber, known as Katon, is valued highly in its native regions.

S. koetjape; with velvety, golden yellow, thick-skinned fr. filled with sweet, edible pulp and large sds.

361

Santalum album

INDIAN SANDALWOOD

L.

25 spp.

SANTALACEAE

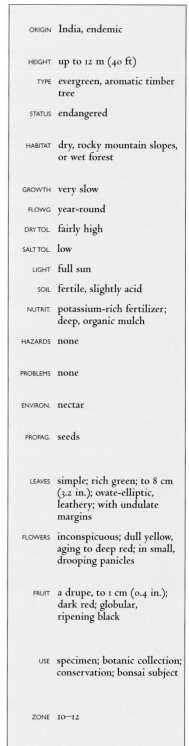

ORIGIN	India, endemic
HEIGHT	up to 12 m (40 ft)
TYPE	evergreen, aromatic timber tree
STATUS	endangered
HABITAT	dry, rocky mountain slopes, or wet forest
GROWTH	very slow
FLOWG	year-round
DRY TOL.	fairly high
SALT TOL.	low
LIGHT	full sun
SOIL	fertile, slightly acid
NUTRIT.	potassium-rich fertilizer; deep, organic mulch
HAZARDS	none
PROBLEMS	none
ENVIRON.	nectar
PROPAG.	seeds
LEAVES	simple; rich green; to 8 cm (3.2 in.); ovate-elliptic, leathery; with undulate margins
FLOWERS	inconspicuous; dull yellow, aging to deep red; in small, drooping panicles
FRUIT	a drupe, to 1 cm (0.4 in.); dark red; globular, ripening black
USE	specimen; botanic collection; conservation; bonsai subject
ZONE	10–12

SANTALUM ALBUM is a small, slow-growing, elegant tree of dry, rocky habitats. It has glabrous, evergreen foliage, small, dangling panicles of little dark-red, speckled flowers and bright red, cherry-like, oily, starchy fruit. *Santalum* species characteristically have entirely or partly parasitic roots that attach themselves to neighbouring plants to find nourishment, making Sandalwoods somewhat difficult to cultivate. Also, it often takes from 20–40 years for **S. album** to develop its heartwood fully. It is for these reasons that it has become rare and endangered in its region. For many centuries, *Santalum* wood has been renowned for its fragrant, reddish heartwood that produces timber and also a valuable, pale yellow, aromatic oil. Sandalwood oil is used in soaps, perfumes and medicine, as well as being used as an inhalant and a powerful antiseptic for lung and urinary tract infections. The tough heartwood is odourless when freshly cut but strongly aromatic as it becomes seasoned. It has been used to make small pieces of furniture, for lining chests (particularly teak chests from China), as incense in Buddhist temples and on funeral pyres in India.

*** **S. acuminatum**; ([R. Br.] A. DC), (*Eucarya acuminata*), Australia endemic, to 8 m (26 ft). NATIVE PEAR is a fairly rare, small, compact species with sickle-shaped leaves and tiny, creamy white, tubular flowers. Its red, fleshy, plum-like summer fruit is used for jam-making. They have oily, edible seeds known as Dong or Quandong. **S. acuminatum** has been important in the timber trade. (9–11)

*** **S. freycinetianum**; (Gaudich.), Hawaii endemic, to 13 m (43 ft). 'ILI-AHI, now rare, is found in 3 varieties and is 1 of 4 species of *Santalum* endemic to these islands. For many years, the fragrant wood was sold to China, being traded for tea and silk. (10–12)

S. album; this small, slow-growing and endangered parasitic sp. was photographed in a corner of the arboretum at Jardin Botanico de Cienfuegos, Cuba.

S. album; in small, compact panicles.

S. album; small, juicy, deep red berry fr. is, like the fl. panicle, dangled on long stalks.

S. album; Santalum wood has been renowned for its fragrant, reddish heartwood, which is odourless when fresh.

50ft ⌐15m

50ft
15m   0

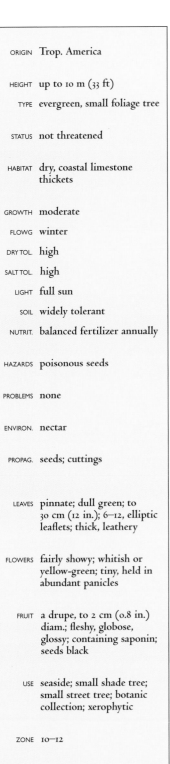
Sapindus saponaria

SOAPBERRY

L.   13 spp.

S. indicus

SAPINDACEAE

WHEN IT IS CUT UP AND SOAKED IN WATER, the fleshy fruit of **Sapindus saponaria**, which smells of strawberry, produces soapy suds. The husks of the drupes contain about 30% saponin, which is how Soapberry earned its Latin name. It is employed in some regions to wash wool and silk with remarkably rejuvenating results. **S. saponaria** is very closely related to the S American Spanish Lime, *Melicoccus bijugatus*. It has the same pinnate leaves, with winged petioles, and superficially similar fruit, but in reality, while the fruit of *Melicoccus* is sweet and delicious, that of the Soapberry is yellow, sticky and bitter. **S. saponaria** is actually very easily distinguished from *Melicoccus* as the Soapberry fruit has a strange, small, disc-like appendage at the base that is an abortive embryo. Insecticide and medicinal oil has been made from the crushed, toxic seeds, while in some parts of its region these ornamental, shiny, black seeds are used as beads and for making rosaries or buttons. They are also pounded and thrown into rivers and ponds to stun and catch fish in the same manner as *Gliricidia*. The sapwood is whitish, while the heartwood is light brown, hard, heavy and coarse-textured, but not durable when exposed. **S. saponaria** makes a handsome and interesting evergreen shade tree for the seaside, as well as in difficult, arid areas. This is a honey plant.

✳✳✳ **S. mukorossi**, (Gaertn.), from India to C. Japan, to 10 m (33 ft). CHINESE SOAPBERRY, or SOAP NUT, is also an evergreen species that has leaves to 40 cm (16 in.), with its leaflets to 15 cm (6 in); the rachis is slightly winged. It has large panicles of tiny white flowers. Fruit is slightly keeled, smooth, yellow to orange-brown, to 2 cm (0.8 in.). In Asia, fruit are gathered for their thick rinds that yield a lather and are used domestically as a shampoo or for washing clothes and jewellery. It is also used to eradicate head lice. (8–11)

S. saponaria; with panicles of tiny, whitish or yellowish green fls.

S. saponaria; the sapwood is whitish, while the heartwood is light brown, hard, heavy and coarse-textured.

S. mukorossi; Soap Nut is a native of China and Japan, and widely used domestically as a soap substitute.

S. saponaria; Soapberry has fr. that contains 30% saponin. It produces soapy suds when mixed with water. The poisonous sds are pounded and thrown in ponds or rivers to stun fish.

Saraca indica

ASOKA

L.

II spp.

S. arborescens

FABACEAE (Caesalpinioideae)

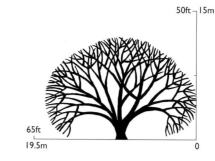

50ft — 15m

65ft

19.5m — 0

ORIGIN	from India and Thailand to Java
HEIGHT	up to 10 m (33 ft)
TYPE	evergreen, small flowering tree
STATUS	vulnerable
HABITAT	understorey in rainforest; along banks of streams
GROWTH	moderate to slow
FLOWG	spring and late summer
DRY TOL.	moderate
SALT TOL.	low
LIGHT	sheltered sun
SOIL	rich, humid, slightly acid
NUTRIT.	regular, high-potassium fertilizer; organic mulch
HAZARDS	none
PROBLEMS	none
ENVIRON.	moth and bat nectar; fruit for monkeys and squirrels
PROPAG.	seeds
LEAVES	pinnate; deep green; leaflets in 4–6 pairs, to 30 cm (12 in.); new leaves in flaccid 'handkerchiefs'
FLOWERS	showy; yellow-orange, then scarlet; in globose cymes; 4 calyx lobes (no petals); stamens exserted; fragrant
FRUIT	a legume, to 20 cm (8 in.); 2-valved, flattened, oblong, beaked; margins thickened; seeds to 4 cm (1.6 in.),
USE	courtyard; humid shade garden; specimen; large planter; large conservatory
ZONE	10–12

IT IS BELIEVED THAT BUDDHA was born under this sacred tree and for this reason it is planted near temples so that worshippers may use the blooms for votive offerings. *Saraca* are amongst the most lovely trees of SE Asia and challenge the *Brownea* of Tropical America (of the same family). **Saraca indica** is a plump, rounded species, sturdily branched with a neat, somewhat coarse-textured crown of large, drooping, pinnate leaves. Like the *Amherstia* and *Brownea*, new leaves are held within a conical stipule that splits open to release flaccid, pinkish, possibly spotted, 'handkerchiefs' of new foliage that hang limply until they gain their chlorophyll. With the first rush of blooms in early spring, **S. indica** has cauliflorous posies of small, yellow-orange flowers that deepen to red with age; massed on twigs and branches, they contrast richly with the dark foliage. At first glance, the blooms look like *Ixora*, but they have no petals, only a long-tubed, 4-lobed calyx clasping whiskery stamens. They are mostly males, with a few bisexuals, thus only a few fruit develop. Following the flowers, large, flat, sabre-like seed pods form. Those of *S. cauliflora* are almost as decorative as the blooms, being iridescent, burnished, purplish crimson, illuminating the tree as it stands in the forest shadows. In India, *Saraca* flowers are said to arouse passion and are considered a symbol of love. 'The eve of Basanti Puja is set apart for its special worship, when orthodox Hindu ladies drink the water in which have been immersed 6 Asoka blossoms, so as to guard their children from grief and trouble.' So wrote Miss Ida Colhurst in Calcutta in 1924. Both Buddhists and Hindus revere this tree, and Hindus have dedicated it to Kama, god of erotic love. Another popular Indian name is Sorrowless Tree. Although native of the rainforest understorey, cultivated *Saraca* will develop a fuller form, with lower branching and blooming, if planted in a spacious, humid, sunny but protected position.

S. declinata; new lvs emerge flaccid and reddish, taking time to become green.

S. indica; in early spring, with cauliflorous posies of small, petal-less, deep yellow fls, which deepen to red with age.

S. cauliflora; the young fr. are a luminous crimson are almost as decorative as fls.

S. indica; sturdily branched with a neat, somewhat coarsely textured crown of large, drooping lvs.

(1 and 3) **Saraca cauliflora**; (Baker), (syn. *S. thaipingensis*), Malaysia, to 10 m (33 ft). Yellow Saraca, the most hardy and vigorous of the clan, has very large, loose heads of whiskery, light yellow fls, which deepen to rich yellow with the eye becoming blood-red. (10–12) (2) **Saraca declinata**; ([Jack.] Miq.), of Malayasia, Java and Sumatra, to 30 m (100 ft). Red Saraca has a plethora of purplish-brown 'handerchiefs' as it flushes with new growth. The lvs and fr. of *S. declinata* have shorter stalks than either *S. indica* or *S. cauliflora*. The little 4-petalled, fragrant fls are like those of *S. indica*, emerging yellow, then gradually deepening to blood-red with a dark purple eye. As may be seen here, the fls may be held cauliflorously, low down on the trunk itself. (10–12)

S. cauliflora is easily distinguished by its ornamental young fr., which is luminous, dark red or purple, while the limp, new 'handkerchiefs' of foliage are pale lavender. Like the closely related *Brownea* clan, many *Saraca* have somewhat unattractive, disorganized growth, but of course both sp. more than make up for this shortcoming by the beauty of their blooms. This photograph was taken in the arboretum of the Jardin Botanico de Cienfuegos, S Cuba.

Sarcocephalus latifolius

AFRICAN PEACH

(Sm.) E.A. Bruce   2 spp.

S. esculentus; Nauclea latifolia

RUBIACEAE

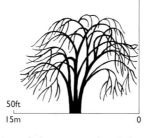

SARCOCEPHALUS LATIFOLIUS is a shrub or tree native of dry savannahs. It has a vigorous, arching, widely spreading habit, which may develop into semi-scandent growth. The large, lustrous, deeply veined leaves of the richest green add to the appearance of buoyant vigour of this ornamental species. In late spring or early summer, held on short, sturdy stalks, singular blooms emerge, which, like the closely related *Nauclea orientalis*, are known as Pincushion Flowers. Indeed, the 5 cm (2 in.) wide inflorescence is composed of a globular arrangement of slim, white, needle-like, extremely fragrant flowers set in little, slender, yellow calyxes and the whole composition resembles many sewing pins stuck into a diminutive pincushion. The stamens are concealed within the tube but the style and stigma are exserted, emphasizing the analogy of a pinhead. By late autumn or early winter, curious fruit have formed from a composite of all the ovaries. Held singly on stout stems, the warty, slightly lumpy and potato-shaped fruit recall the closely related *Morinda citrifolia* and its reddish brown skin is pitted like a golf ball with the pentagonal scars of the flowers. The pulp is deep red, watery, sweet and edible, with a taste of ripe apple. It contains many seeds and it is widely accepted that these germinate best when passed through a baboon. *S. latifolius* plays an important role in its region: in Zaire, it is used in the treatment of diabetes, while in Nigeria, small twigs are used as chewing sticks. The heartwood of *S. latifolius* is dark, red brown, hard and moderately heavy; it has found use for inlay work. These are important bee plants.

*** S. diderrichii; (Merrill), (*Nauclea diderrichii*), Trop. Africa, to 40 m (131 ft), has a clear bole and low buttresses. Young, sapling trees have very large leaves. (**10–12**)

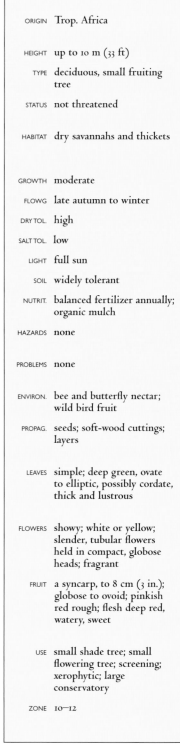

ORIGIN	Trop. Africa
HEIGHT	up to 10 m (33 ft)
TYPE	deciduous, small fruiting tree
STATUS	not threatened
HABITAT	dry savannahs and thickets
GROWTH	moderate
FLOWG	late autumn to winter
DRY TOL.	high
SALT TOL.	low
LIGHT	full sun
SOIL	widely tolerant
NUTRIT.	balanced fertilizer annually; organic mulch
HAZARDS	none
PROBLEMS	none
ENVIRON.	bee and butterfly nectar; wild bird fruit
PROPAG.	seeds; soft-wood cuttings; layers
LEAVES	simple; deep green, ovate to elliptic, possibly cordate, thick and lustrous
FLOWERS	showy; white or yellow; slender, tubular flowers held in compact, globose heads; fragrant
FRUIT	a syncarp, to 8 cm (3 in.); globose to ovoid; pinkish red rough; flesh deep red, watery, sweet
USE	small shade tree; small flowering tree; screening; xerophytic; large conservatory
ZONE	10–12

S. latifolius; with thick, lustrous lvs and curious fr.

S. latifolius; fls in summer and has its fr. in autumn before it loses it lvs during the dry season. Photographed at the Fruit and Spice Park, S Florida, USA.

S. latifolius; known as African Peach or Pincushion Fruit, this syncarp has deep red, watery, sweet pulp.

S. latifolius; with a vigorous, arching, wide-spreading habit, which may develop into semi-scandent growth.

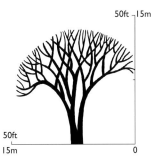

50ft — 15m

50ft

15m   0

Schefflera actinophylla

UMBRELLA TREE

(Endl.) Harms.   650 spp.

Brassaia actinophylla

ARALIACEAE

ORIGIN	from New Guinea to Australia
HEIGHT	up to 12 m (39 ft)
TYPE	evergreen foliage tree, (occasionally epiphytic)
STATUS	not threatened
HABITAT	lowland woodland and rainforest
GROWTH	moderate
FLOWG.	spring to summer
DRY TOL.	high
SALT TOL.	moderate
LIGHT	full sun to bright shade
SOIL	fertile, well-drained
NUTRIT.	occasional high-nitrogen fertilizer
HAZARDS	may be invasive
PROBLEMS	scales; sooty mould
ENVIRON.	insect nectar; wild fruit for birds
PROPAG.	seeds; cuttings
LEAVES	palmate; rich green; with 7–12 leaflets, oblong or elliptic; arranged in a rosette; glossy
FLOWERS	showy; pink or crimson; to 1 cm (0.4 in.); terminal, paniculate; flowers short-stalked in crowded heads
FRUIT	a berry, to 0.5 cm (0.2 in.); round or top shaped; fleshy, crimson; seeds dark purple
USE	shade garden; large accent; specimen; screening; large planter; xerophytic; large conservatory
ZONE	9–12

SCHEFFLERA ACTINOPHYLLA, with its sparse limbs and extravagantly leafed crown, looks more like an overgrown herb than a tree and forms several trunks that do not commonly divide. Each trunk supports a flattened, umbrella-like crown of very long-stemmed, enormous, digitately compound leaves that are oblong, long-petioled and form a cartwheel around the tip of the leaf stalk. *S. actinophylla* has a very vigorous root system, which makes it ideal for helping to bind soil prone to erosion but, for this reason, should not be planted near septic tanks, drain pipes or foundations. Older specimens may develop aerial roots. The nectar-rich blooms develop along the 60 cm (24 in.) axes of a huge, terminal, octopus-like, dark crimson umbel; the crowded, short-stalked, deep red flowers are ringed with golden stamens. As they are pollinated, they are replaced by tiny, clustered, fleshy, crimson berries that can be a nuisance as they stain masonry and parked cars. In some circumstances, in their native habitat, these berries may germinate in the crotch of other trees, sending their roots to the ground and growing like an epiphyte. With the burgeoning tourist industry around the Caribbean Sea, *S. actinophylla* has become an essential component of the landscaping of many holiday complexes. Unfortunately, aging originals have been flowering there for several years (they take about 10 years to come into bloom) and are beginning to volunteer in woodlands around developed areas, which is most disturbing to conservationists. Quite hardy, *S. actinophylla* has been found to tolerate a few degrees of frost.
*** *S. umbellifera*; ([Sond.] Baill.), S Africa, to 20 m (66 ft). BASTARD CABBAGE TREE with a dense, rounded crown. Flowers small, yellow-green, in umbels. (9–11)

NOTE: this species has escaped cultivation to become invasive in some regions.

S. actinophylla; short-stalked, showy fls.

S. umbellifera; Bastard Cabbage Tree with a dense, rounded crown at Kirstenbosch, S Africa.

S. actinophylla; crowded, fleshy, crimson berries with hard sds are beloved by birds, who distribute them far and wide.

S. actinophylla; in full bloom and draped in vines on the Atherton Tableland in N Qld, Australia. Fls develop along the axes of huge terminal, octopus-like, dark crimson umbels.

Schinus terebinthifolius

BRAZILIAN PEPPER TREE

Raddl.   27 spp.

ANACARDIACEAE

IT IS SAD THAT THIS LOVELY LITTLE TREE has a bad reputation in many tropical and subtropical regions, where it has gone out of control and become a noxious weed. The leaves of *S. terebithifolius* are handsome, being rich green, pinnate and leathery, with long, oval leaflets and a winged rachis. In early winter, branched panicles of tiny, short-stalked, white flowers are borne in the leaf axils. In female plants, they give way to profuse clusters of tiny, glossy, crimson berries. These sublimely decorative fruit are adored by birds, but seem to intoxicate them; they serve as distributors, nevertheless. However, it is not only because of its fecundity that this species has proved such a widespread pest. *S. terebithifolius* is also notorious for causing respiratory problems and dermatitis in people who are allergic to it, mostly because the male flowers, with their copiously charged pollen, produce a gaseous material. Despite the plant's problems and unpopularity, its holly-like winter fruit is very popular for Christmas decorations in Hawaii and other parts of the tropic of Cancer. In its native Brazil, however, *Schinus terebinthifolius* is very highly regarded for its wood, which is named Aroeira do Campo. It is dark yellow, turning red on exposure, very dense and hard and ideal for making fine furniture. A resin is collected from the trunk and sold locally as Mission Balsam.

*** var. *acutifolius*; (Engl.), S. Brazil to Argentina, Aroeira Mansa differs in having larger, broader leaflets. The fruit is pink.

*** *S. molle*; (L.), Subtropical America, to 15 m (50 ft). Pepper Tree, Peruvian Mastic Tree grows naturally in dry, sandy soils. This widely popular species has a slender, willowy habit and fern-like, leathery leaves. The aromatic leaves have a very high oil count. Rosy pink fruits are used to make an intoxicating drink. (8–10)

NOTE: listed as a pest in many regions, including S Florida, USA, and Hawaii.

ORIGIN	S America
HEIGHT	up to 7 m (23 ft)
TYPE	evergreen, dioecious, small fruiting tree
STATUS	not threatened
HABITAT	moist lowland scrub
GROWTH	fast
FLOWG	autumn
DRY TOL.	high
SALT TOL.	moderate
LIGHT	full sun or bright shade
SOIL	widely tolerant
NUTRIT.	not normally necessary
HAZARDS	none
PROBLEMS	invasive; pollen causes allergies
ENVIRON.	insect nectar; wild fruit for birds
PROPAG.	seeds; cuttings
LEAVES	pinnate; deep green; leaflets oblong, leathery, glossy; with toothed margins; rachis slightly winged
FLOWERS	inconspicuous; white; held in small, short-stalked panicles
FRUIT	a drupe, to 5 mm (0.2 in.); bright red or pinkish; glossy; held in large, abundant bunches
USE	small fruiting tree; accent; screening; large planter; xerophytic
ZONE	10–12

S. terebinthifolius; many people are allergic to these little gaseous, pollen-laden fls.

S. terebinthifolius; Brazilian Pepper loaded with its winter harvest. Birds love the fr., but it seems to intoxicate them. They are the main distributors of the sds, nevertheless.

S. terebinthifolius; in S Florida, this tree has infested the landscape and is considered a pest.

S. molle; with a slender, willowy habit and fern-like, aromatic, leathery lvs and rosy pink fr.

ORIGIN	from S Mexico to S Brazil
HEIGHT	up to 30 m (100 ft)
TYPE	deciduous, large flowering tree
STATUS	not threatened
HABITAT	wet to dry mixed forest
GROWTH	fast
FLOWG	spring
DRY TOL.	moderate
SALT TOL.	low
LIGHT	full sun
SOIL	rich, well-drained
NUTRIT.	balanced fertilizer when young
HAZARDS	none
PROBLEMS	brittle wood; shallow roots
ENVIRON.	insect nectar
PROPAG.	seeds
LEAVES	2-pinnate; greyish green; to 95 cm (38 in.) feathery; leaflets fern-like; young leaves extremely long
FLOWERS	showy; pale yellow; held in large, erect terminal panicles
FRUIT	a legume, to 12 × 5 cm (5 × 2 in.); compressed, spathulate, propellor-like; with 1 hard-coated, flat seed
USE	large flowering tree; public open space; humid shade garden
ZONE	10–12

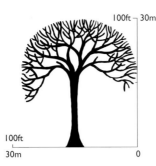

100ft – 30m

100ft

30m · · · · 0

Schizolobium parahyba

GUAPIRUVU

(Vell.) S.F. Bake   1–2 spp.

S. exselsum

FABACEAE (Caesalpinioideae)

IT IS DIFFICULT TO BELIEVE that this unique tree belongs to the legume clan. As a young, green-barked sapling, *Schizolobium parahyba* is disguised as a tree fern with a plump, bright green shooting stem and an outrageous parasol of elongated, silky, ferny leaves. As it develops branches and a wide-open crown, this pachycaul species takes on a more arboreal role, although it continues to have a lofty, slender, smooth, straight bole that has thin, red, peeling bark, and becomes wonderfully buttressed with age. As the limbs develop, they divide and re-divide in a classically dichotomous manner. The leaves are carried on top of long, naked limbs, however, and remain remarkably long and feathery. In its favoured habitat, it re-costumes itself in its new summer foliage, but not before it produces an extravaganza of stretching, billowing, erect panicles of large, lustrous, golden blooms around its great crown, becoming one mass of colour and visible from a great distance. The fruit that follows is also highly original and not at all like a legume; it is a flat, spathulate, 'tear-drop' wing, like an aeroplane propeller. When ripe, the wing splits open to shed a buff, papery, winged 'sealed envelope' that is broken down by rain to expose a single, hard flat seed resembling an oblong coin; if struck against a stone, it has a curious, metallic ring. Being light and soft, Guapiruvu timber is rarely used, although if overall growth is slower, it becomes significantly denser. The heartwood is pale brown or pinkish in colour, not very resistant to decay or insect attack and has a strong fecal odor when it is freshly cut. Nevertheless, foresters have considered the fast-growing, undemanding **S.** *parahyba* to be commercially suitable for use in the making of paper pulp. NOTE: **S.** *parahyba* is named for the river Parahyba and for this reason the specific name does not end, as usual, in 'um'.

S. parahyba; great candelabra of pale yellow panicles of spring blooms.

S. parahyba; greatly resembles a tree fern when young, with its huge, pinnate, frond-like lvs.

S. parahyba; beans shaped like propellor blades split to shed oblong, coin-like sds packaged in papery envelopes.

S. parahyba; this young specimen already demonstrates the sparse, wide-spreading, dichotomous branching of this very fast-growing Trop. American sp.

Schotia brachypetala

TREE FUCHSIA

Sonder.   4–5 spp.

FABACEAE (Caesalpinioideae)

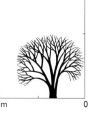

100ft – 30m

75ft
22.5m   0

THIS VOLUPTUOUS, LEGUMINOUS NATIVE of dry savannahs of the hot, southern regions of E and S Africa is well designed for arid life. **Schotia brachypetala** is often found perched on top of a red-earthed termite mound. Although it grows to be quite a large, stoutly trunked tree in parts of its habitat, forming a dense, slightly weeping crown, it may also develop a more shrubby growth. The leathery leaves are usually glossy but in some regions may be thinly pubescent. After a leafless winter, spring is heralded with a flush of new, waxy, rose and ruby foliage that mimics the vibrant display of summer flowers. In Africa, *S. brachypetala* has several descriptive names but probably the most common is Tree Fuchsia, referring to the resemblance of the blooms to those of *Fuchsia*, with their long-tubed, waxy, crimson 4-lobed calyx that conceals the true flowers, and long, sturdy, crimson stamens. The nectaries in the floral tubes are engorged with sweet nectar that drips from the tree, giving rise to its local name, Weeping Boerboom. Local sunbirds and insects are drawn to the blooms and ensure their pollination. During rain, the pollen ferments, making the birds, and possibly the insects, intoxicated. The seeds, contained in a heavy, woody pod, are edible but eaten only in times of famine. The heartwood is dark brown to almost black, hard, heavy and fine-textured. The bark is used for tanning, and Zulus make a decoction from the bark for heartburn or a hangover. *** *S. afra*; ([L.] Bodn.), (*S. speciosa*), S Africa endemic, to 6 m (20 ft). KAROO BOERBOON is a small, densely limbed tree with rigid branches. The inflorescence is terminal, with showy, bright red or pink flowers. The fruit is to 13×4 cm (5×1.5 in.), hard and woody, rusty and pink as it develops. The seeds are edible, either green or, if mature, roasted in the fire and ground to a meal. The leaves are browsed by stock. The S. African Butterfly, *Deudoris antalis*, breeds on this tree. (9–10)

ORIGIN	E and S Africa
HEIGHT	up to 15 m (50 ft)
TYPE	deciduous, small flowering tree
STATUS	not threatened
HABITAT	dry savannahs and along streams in semi-desert areas
GROWTH	slow
FLOWG	summer
DRY TOL.	high
SALT TOL.	moderate to high
LIGHT	full sun
SOIL	rich, well-drained
NUTRIT.	high-potassium fertilizer
HAZARDS	none
PROBLEMS	none
ENVIRON.	nectar for insects and birds
PROPAG.	seeds
LEAVES	pinnate; bright green; leaflets 2–5 pairs; leathery, with wavy margins; new growth red
FLOWERS	showy; claret-red; 4-lobed calyx; with long, exserted, crimson stamens; nectar-rich; fragrant
FRUIT	a legume, to 12 × 5 cm (4.7 × 2 in.), flat, oblong, woody, keeled; seeds edible
USE	small flowering tree; screening; accent; large planter; median strip; bonsai subject; xerophytic
ZONE	10–11

S. brachypetala; forming a dense, slightly weeping crown.

S. brachypetala; in spring, the little crimson fls are engorged with nectar, which sometimes ferments and intoxicates its pollinators, the sun-birds.

S. brachypetala; with heavy, keeled pods.

S. brachypetala; an elderly specimen in Cienfuegos, Cuba, showing its sturdy framework and billowing canopy.

ORIGIN	Trop. and S Africa
HEIGHT	up to 15 m (50 ft)
TYPE	deciduous, dioecious fruiting tree
STATUS	a protected species
HABITAT	sandy savannah soils; coastal scrublands
GROWTH	moderate
FLOWG.	spring
DRY TOL.	high
SALT TOL.	moderate
LIGHT	full sun
SOIL	fertile, well-drained
NUTRIT.	balanced fertilizer annually
HAZARDS	none
PROBLEMS	none
ENVIRON.	wild fruit for animals
PROPAG.	seeds; large cuttings in spring
LEAVES	pinnate; rich green; leaflets 7–13, to 10 cm (4 in); rachis pink, possibly winged
FLOWERS	showy (particularly males), in spiky racemes; sepals red, petals yellow
FRUIT	a drupe, to 5 cm (2 in.); pale yellow; plum-like; flesh whitish, sweet, edible
USE	fruiting tree; specimen; backyard tree; xerophytic
ZONE	10–12

100ft – 30m
75ft
22.5m — 0

Sclerocarya birrea ssp. caffra

DRUNKARD'S PLUM

(A. Rich.) Hochst.   4 spp.

ANACARDIACEAE

SCLEROCARYA BIRREA SUBSP. CAFFRA is a medium to large deciduous tree with an erect trunk and spreading, rounded crown. Dioecious, with male and female flowers on separate trees, this is a true provision tree, contributing many elements to everyday life. In spring, although the spiky racemes of little, male flowers are showy with their red sepals and yellow flowers, *S. birrea* is particularly esteemed for its fruit throughout its large range, from Ethiopia to S Africa. Borne during the autumn months, these pale yellow, plum-like fruit, with a stone that is difficult to separate from the flesh, tough, thick skin and juicy, mucilaginous, sweetly acid flesh, find many local uses. Known widely as Marula, it has been described by some as resembling a mango, by others a guava and by still others as being not tasty at all. Locally, in their arid habitats, they are popularly eaten out-of-hand, made into a refreshing juice and, in many regions, employed to make several beverages, including a popular, intoxicating beer and Marula liqueur, made from the fruit and available commercially. Humans, however, are not the only ones to enjoy these vitamin C-rich plums – they are relished by cattle and many species of game animals. The bark is often stripped off by elephants and it is said that animals may become intoxicated by overripe, fermenting fruit, thus earning the tree the name Drunkard's Plum in some parts. The seeds are rich in protein and oil and burn brightly like candles. The bark is widely used medicinally and is proven to contain antihistamine and to have antidiarrhoeal properties. The wood of *S. birrea* is a dirty white with reddish streaks, soft and coarse-grained; it provides drum wood for the Nyanga tribesmen, while other tribes use it to hollow out canoes. Several moths breed on the tree, including the beautiful green African Moon Moth, *Argema mimosae*.

S. birrea; fr. is whorled around the tips of heavy twigs on long, sturdy stalks.

S. birrea; with lively, attractive foliage.

S. birrea; the fr. have a delicious, rich, fruity scent and taste a little like a mango. They are rich in vitamin C.

S. birrea; known as Drunkard's Plum, this African sp. has a sparsely limbed crown of bright green, pinnate lvs that are pinkish on emergence.

371

Senna spectabilis

CALCEOLARIA SHOWER

(DC.) Irwin & Barneby   350 spp.

Cassia excelsa; C. spectabilis

FABACEAE (Caesalpinioideae)

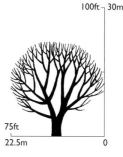

SENNA SPECTABILIS like many *Senna* species, was designated as a *Cassia* until recently. The *Senna* genus is distinguished by its flowers (usually yellow, rarely white), which have 5 unequal petals and curved stamens (*Cassia* stamens are S-shaped). *Senna* fruit are dehiscent while in *Cassia* they are indehiscent. This very fast-growing, deciduous *Senna* forms a pleasingly regular, spherical crown of softly pubescent, greyish green, pinnate leaves over a sturdy, small trunk with grey, smooth but warty bark. *S. spectabilis* is considered the Queen of Sennas for its superb foliage and flowers and is spectacular when it is in bloom. From late summer to early winter, the opulent, passion-fruit-fragrant yellow blooms weigh down the limbs and twigs with their abundance. Each ample, branched, erect inflorescence appears to be encircled by the feathery, greyish green leaves like a presentation bouquet. The individual flowers are considered to imitate *Calceolaria* blooms. They are composed of 5 rounded, cupped, hairy sepals and 5 slightly unequal, spreading yellow petals. *S. spectabilis* has blackish, long, narrow, cylindrical fruit pods packed in membranous, horizontal divisions, with many roundish, orange-tan seeds. The sapwood is whitish and fairly soft, while the brown heartwood is hard, heavy and durable. Easily the most ornamental of its genus, *S. spectabilis* is well named.
*** *S. spectabilis* var. *excelsa*; ([DC.] Irwin & Barneby), C and S America, to 9 m (30 ft). Canafistula-de-Besouro (Brazil) is weakly tree-like and often shrubby and very widespreading. The finely pinnate leaves have 10–20 pairs of elliptic leaflets to 4 cm (1.5 in.). This is a deciduous, xerophytic pioneer species and frequent in secondary woodland on deep, well-drained soils. It blooms from summer to autumn and fruits abundantly in winter. This variety is often planted to re-establish degraded soils.

NOTE: these spp. have escaped cultivation in many regions.

ORIGIN	C and S America
HEIGHT	up to 20 m (66 ft)
TYPE	deciduous flowering tree
STATUS	not threatened
HABITAT	dry, coastal regions
GROWTH	very fast
FLOWG	late spring to autumn
DRY TOL.	high
SALT TOL.	moderate
LIGHT	full sun
SOIL	widely tolerant
NUTRIT.	balanced fertilizer annually
HAZARDS	parts toxic to animals
PROBLEMS	brittle wood; scale
ENVIRON.	nectar
PROPAG.	seeds; cuttings
LEAVES	pinnate; dullish green; to 45 cm (18 in.); with 8–20 pairs of tiny, oval, leathery leaflets
FLOWERS	showy; light yellow; held in erect, densely packed racemes
FRUIT	a legume, to 30 cm (12 in.); cylindrical, compressed; packed with roundish, hard seeds
USE	small autumn-flowering tree; quick screening; specimen; large planter; civic centre; xerophytic
ZONE	9–12

S. spectabilis; a fine specimen near Danbulla, N Qld, Australia

S. spectabilis; considered to imitate *Calceolaria* blooms, the fls are composed of 5 rounded, cupped, hairy sepals and 5 slightly unequal, yellow petals.

S. spectabilis; each infl. appears to be encircled by the feathery greyish green lvs like a presentation bouquet.

S. spectabilis; long, narrow, cylindrical fruit pods are packed neatly in membranous, horizontal divisions, with many orange sds.

Senna alata; ([L.] Roxb.), (syn. *Cassia alata*), Trop. America, to 10 m (33 ft). EMPRESS CANDLESTICKS or CRAW-CRAW is a very common Senna, naturalized in most trop. regions. It grows as a bushy shrub or medium-sized tree with erect, candlelike infls most of the year. Lvs have been used traditionally in the treatment of ringworm. This sp. benefits from regular, severe pruning. (10–12) **NOTE: this sp. may be very invasive.**

Senna mexicana var. chapmanii; (Isley), (syn. *Cassia bahamensis*; *S. chapmanii*), Florida, Cuba and Bahamas, to 8 m (26 ft). STINKING PEA or BAHAMA SENNA is a vigorous shrub or small tree and is a native of dry, open land. This xerophytic sp., distinguished by a sessile, dome-shaped gland between the lower lfts, makes an excellent, small garden specimen with many uses. Photographed in farmland on the south coast of Cuba. (10–12)

Senna didymobotrya; ([Fres.] Irwin and Barn.), (syn. *Cassia didymobotrya*), Trop. Africa, naturalized in Asia and America, to 5 m (16 ft). POPCORN SENNA is very fast growing and easily confused with *S. alata*, but has denser, more compact growth and distinctive, glossy, dark brown fl. buds. In Kenya, where it is native, it is known as Mwenu or Kilao, it is has several medicinal uses. (10–12) **NOTE: this sp. may be invasive.**

Senna multijuga; ([Rich.] Irwin and Barn.), (syn. *Cassia multijuga*), W Indies and northern S America, to 25 m (82 ft) AUTUMN SENNA, a small, multi-trunked, decid. tree, may have a rather untidy appearance without its lvs. It compensates in early autumn when it blooms with foaming bubbles of bright yellow fls. This tree benefits from being well-pruned after blooming. Above, in its full glory at Sydney Botanic Garden in Australia. (9–12)

Senna nitida; ([Rich.] Irwin and Barn.), (syn. *Cassia nitida*; *Chamaefistula antlliana*), W Indies, to 7 m (23 ft). This small Senna may grow as a tall shrub or scrambler and is closely related to *S. quingquangulata* ([Rich] Irwin and Barn.) of S America and *S. viminea* ([L.] Rich and Barn.) of Jamaica. It differs in having only 5–6 fertile stamens. *S. nitida* makes a wonderful long-blooming screen or a specimen, even a large container plant. (10–12)

Senna polyphylla, ([Jacq.] Irwin and Barn.), (syn. *Cassia polyphylla*), from Puerto Rico to British Virgin Is, to 8 m (26 ft). This sp. is commonly known as W INDIAN SENNA or RETAMA. It is native to extremely dry habitats and is fairly slow growing, but flushes with bloom all year after a good shower of rain. This is a particularly lovely, but relatively rare, *Senna*, which deserves to be better known as it has many uses in the landscape. (10–12)

Senna siamea; ([Lam.] Irwin and Barn.), (syn *Cassia florida*; *Cassia siamea*) from Burma to Malaysia, to 13 m (43 ft). KASSOD TREE has glossy, dark green foliage and fairly sparse fl. panicles. The wood is very brittle and there is some die-back. It is used for coffee shade in some areas but has escaped cultivation. The pods and lvs are toxic to hogs, which relish the taste but die quickly after eating them. Blooming late spring to autumn. (9–12)

Senna surattensis; ([Burm. f.] Irwin and Barn.), (syn. *Cassia glauca*, *C. planisiliqua*), from Trop. Asia to Australia and the Pacific, to 7.5 m (25 ft). This sp. is known as GLAUCOUS CASSIA and SCRAMBLED EGG. (In Hawaii, it is KOLOMONA.) It blooms lavishly year-round on its widely arching, small crown and is deservedly popular for hedging, as well as a small specimen or accent. Seen growing at Queen Elizabeth II Botanic Park, Cayman Is, W Indies. (10–12)

ORIGIN	Trop. Asia
HEIGHT	up to 13 m (43 ft)
TYPE	semi-deciduous, small flowering tree
STATUS	not threatened
HABITAT	dry wasteland and roadsides
GROWTH	fast
FLOWG.	year-round
DRY TOL.	high
SALT TOL.	moderate
LIGHT	full sun
SOIL	widely tolerant
NUTRIT.	normally not necessary
HAZARDS	none
PROBLEMS	invasive; short-lived
ENVIRON.	hummingbird nectar
PROPAG.	seeds
LEAVES	pinnate; light green; to 16 cm (6.3 in.); leaflets held in 10–30 prs.
FLOWERS	showy; red, pink or white; very large, pea-like; held in loose racemes
FRUIT	a legume, to 51 cm (20 in.); slender, compressed, persistent; produced in abundance
USE	small flowering tree; specimen; large planter; xerophytic; conservatory
ZONE	9–12

50ft ⌐15m
50ft
15m   0

Sesbania grandiflora

VEGETABLE HUMMINGBIRD

(L.) Pers.   50 spp.

Agati grandiflora

FABACEAE (Papilionoideae)

WITH ITS LARGE, SOFTLY PUBESCENT, GREY-GREEN FOLIAGE and voluptuous, rosy red or creamy white, velvety, beaked flowers, ***Sesbania grandiflora*** is a beautiful specimen. The problem is that it grows too fast, resulting in brittle and weak limbs. The opulent, crested flowers are named Vegetable Hummingbird or Cockatoo Crest in some regions, but they are so quickly replaced by masses of ugly, long and stringy persistent seed pods that they seem an illusion. In Latin America, the pet names include Gallito, Cresta de Gallo, Cockscomb for the flowers or Baculo Walking Stick. the last presumably referring to the appearance of the seed pods. Those determined to grow this tree should try keeping it in a large container, trimming it into a standard and nipping it back after blooming, before the seeds have time to set. For all its faults, *S. grandiflora* is a provider. In India and other parts of Asia, the flowers are considered a delicacy and are often battered and fried, with the red blooms considered superior to the white. Tender leaves and green seed pods are eaten fresh in salads, added to soups or fried in curries. The leaves and young shoots are also fed to animals, especially in Java. The bark yields a fibre and gum, dyes are obtained from the pinkish white sap and extracts of leaves and flowers have been employed medicinally.

*** *S. formosa*; ([F. Meull.] N. Burb.), Trop. (monsoonal) Australia, to 12 m (40 ft). WHITE DRAGON TREE is common in swamps and flood plains. Fast growing, brittle, leggy; foliage is finer than *S. grandiflora*. Corky bark has medical uses. (10–12)

*** *S. tripetii*; ([Poit.] Hort. ex FT Hubb.), (syn. *Daubentonia tripetii*), N Argentina to Brazil, to 5 m (16 ft). SCARLET WISTERIA TREE has brilliant scarlet pea-flowers. (9–11)

NOTE: this species is considered a noxious weed in many regions.

S. grandiflora; the pink-flowered form.

S. tripetii, the Scarlet Wisteria Tree has soft, pinnate foliage and drooping racemes of scarlet fls.

S. grandiflora; fls are considered a culinary delicacy (red blooms are considered superior to white).

S. grandiflora; this over-ambitious sp. converts its large and lovely blooms into long, stringy fr. with tremendous rapidity and untidy results.

Sideroxylon foetidissimum

MASTIC

Jacq.   75 spp.

Mastichodendron foetidissimum

SAPOTACEAE

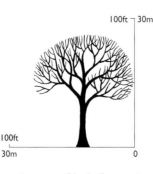

100ft ¬ 30m

100ft
30m   0

LIKE *CORDIA ALLIODORA*, **Sideroxylon foetidissimum** has a massive, mast-like bole carrying a high, dense, somewhat irregular crown of slightly wrinkled leaves. Typical of the Sapotaceae, all parts of the tree contain milky latex. The flowers of **S. foetidissimum** are clasped along the terminal twigs just below a clustered spiral of leaves. These minute, yellow blooms have a peculiar, musty, rather cheese-like odour – hence *foetidissimum*. This species is erratic in its blooming and may not flower every year in some regions, but when it does, it provides ample nectar for honeybees. The olive-shaped, yellow fruit, although edible, is unpleasantly gummy but eaten by birds and animals. **S. foetidissimum** is much respected in its region for its fine, thick, yellowish sapwood and its yellowish to orange heartwood that is hard, heavy, strong and durable. This valuable timber was quickly recognized as excellent for use in shipbuilding and construction. Consequently, it was extensively logged until, like mahogany, it became scarce in its natural habitat.

*** **S. salicifolium**; ([L.] Lam.), (*Bumelia salicifolia*), W Indies and C America, to 25 m (82 ft). WILLOW BUSTIC has a light, airy crown of willowy foliage clustered at its tips. In spring, minute, dull yellow flowers are massed tightly along the terminal shoots. The wood, although not as valuable as *S. foetidissimum*, is nevertheless important regionally. (10–12)

*** **S. sessiliflorum**; ([Poiret] Aubrév.), Mauritius endemic. This species rarely regenerates spontaneously, leading scientists to suspect that it was dispersed by Dodo birds, which have been extinct for some 300 years. To expedite germination, turkeys have been force-fed the fruit, although it has been observed that introduced monkeys also perform the task. (10–12) These species are important honey plants.

ORIGIN	W Indies and C America
HEIGHT	up to 25 m (82 ft)
TYPE	evergreen, large, foliage timber tree
STATUS	rare in some regions
HABITAT	dry coastal forests and woodlands
GROWTH	moderate
FLOWG.	intermittently, all year
DRY TOL.	high
SALT TOL.	high
LIGHT	full sun
SOIL	fertile, well-drained
NUTRIT.	balanced fertilizer annually
HAZARDS	none
PROBLEMS	none
ENVIRON.	bee nectar; wild bird fruit
PROPAG.	scarified seeds
LEAVES	simple; yellowish green; to 20 cm (8 in.) elliptic to oblong; lustrous
FLOWERS	inconspicuous; creamy yellow; clasped along twig ends; with pungent, cheese-like odour
FRUIT	a drupe, to 2.5 cm (1 in.); deep yellow, sour; with gummy latex
USE	seaside; street tree; public open space; xerophytic
ZONE	10–12

S. foetidissimum; sour fr. with gummy flesh is eaten by animals.

S. foetidissmum; a relatively young specimen at Fairchild Tropical Gardens, Miami, Florida, USA. It has still not formed the inevitable massive buttresses of an elderly tree.

S. salicifolium; minute, dull yellow fls are massed tightly along terminal shoots in spring.

S. salicifolium; a smaller, fast-growing sp. of dry woodlands. It is known as Willow Bustic for its willowy habit.

ORIGIN	S America
HEIGHT	up to 10 m (33 ft)
TYPE	evergreen, small flowering tree
STATUS	not threatened
HABITAT	dry and humid woodland
GROWTH	fast
FLOWG	year-round
DRY TOL.	high
SALT TOL.	low
LIGHT	full sun
SOIL	very well-drained
NUTRIT.	high-potassium fertilizer
HAZARDS	spiny
PROBLEMS	brittle; short-lived
ENVIRON.	insect nectar
PROPAG.	seeds; large cuttings
LEAVES	simple; dullish green; to 30 cm (12 in.); pinnately-lobed
FLOWERS	showy; dark changing to pale purple, then white; in large cymes
FRUIT	a berry, to 3.5 cm (1.3 in.); rounded; yellow to brownish; tomato-like
USE	small flowering tree; temporary shade tree; xerophytic
ZONE	10–12

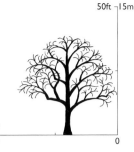

50ft ⌐ 15m

50ft
15m   0

Solanum wrightii

FLOWERING POTATO TREE

Benth.   1700 spp.

S. macranthum; S. grandiflorum

SOLANACEAE

THIS SUCCULENT, FAST-GROWING, overgrown Potato is rather shrubby and covered with yellowish brown prickles. The soft leaves vary a great deal in shape. They are sometimes narrow at the base to form a wing along the petiole and may be heart-shaped, egg-shaped or lance-shaped, with or without deeply cut angles or lobes, but they are invariably paler below with star-shaped hairs and small prickles. When young, *Solanum wrightii* has much larger leaves. The flowers are typical of the Solanaceae family and closely resemble those of the superb creeper *S. wendlandii* of the same genus, or, in fact, the bloom of the related Aubergine. Deep purple on opening, they fade through dark and pale lavenders and finally to white, creating a variegated effect on their sumptuous bouquets. The flowers are usually, but not always in some regions, followed by a fleshy, tomato-like, yellow to brownish fruit about the size of a golf ball. *S. wrightii* is easily propagated by seeds or by large cuttings. It is, unfortunately, quite short-lived, thriving for only 4–5 years before outgrowing itself. Nevertheless, *S. wrightii* is so easy to culture and blooms so extravagantly that it is well worth trying to grow it. Keep it well shaped on its new growth, to produce strong, stocky growth, and take cuttings every year or so to ensure a continuum. With its soft, succulent wood, *S. wrightii* is very drought-tolerant and best planted in a well-drained, sheltered, partially shaded position where it is not exposed to high winds.

*** *S. rantonnetii*; (Carr.); (syn. *Lycianthes rantonnetii*), S America, to 5 m (16 ft), PARAGUAY NIGHTSHADE, from marginal forests of Paraguay and Argentina. Usually grown as a long-blooming shrub, but it may become woody, but with a substantial trunk and a wide, bushy crown. cv. 'Royal Robe'; has deeper purple flowers. This species is subtropical. (9–11) **Note: this species is now *Lycianthes rantonnetii* (Bitter.).**

S. wrightii; large, soft lvs, which vary greatly from simple to deeply lobed.

S. rantonnetii; a subtrop. sp. with typical Solanaceae blooms.

S. wrightii; like a succulent, fast-growing, overgrown Potato, it is rather shrubby and covered with yellowish brown prickles.

S. wrightii; a fairly young specimen with deeply lobed lvs and a typically variegated infl. comprising newly emerged, deep purple blooms, which gradually fade lighter to pale lavender.

Spathodea campanulata

AFRICAN TULIP TREE

Beauv.   1 sp.

S. nilotica

BIGNONIACEAE

100ft – 30m

75ft

22.5m   0

THE DISTINGUISHED, world-renowned African native **Spathodea campanulata** grows tall and straight with a bushy, oval crown of large, coarse, pinnate leaves with large, leathery, dull olive-green leaflets that are smooth above and slightly hairy below. The new growth, including the inflorescence, is plush olive-green. At each leaf base there are extrafloral nectaries to attract bees. Most distinctive, the great, velvety, greenish gold, claw-like calyx-enfolded flower buds are held in massive, erect cones. As they mature, the unopened buds become engorged with liquid nectar. The local children love them because they make good water squirts. Beginning at the base, these buds swell until the 'claw' splits open to release its gaudy contents of sumptuous, crinkled, flaming scarlet goblets, gilt-edged and glowing deep yellow within. Like frilly tulips, they are held erect, cupping their copious nectar and attracting throngs of birds. In drier areas, *S. campanulata* will lose some of its leaves but seldom becomes completely leafless. In Africa, huntsmen boil the kernels of the long, boat-shaped, woody fruit to obtain a poisonous liquid for use on the tips of their arrows. The soft, brownish white wood has little practical use but, because it is difficult to burn, it has been used to make blacksmith's bellows. *S. campanulata* grows rapidly even in unfavourable conditions; however, it has a superficial root system that makes it unstable in high winds. Its limbs are fairly brittle and may become broken during storms. These trees should be trimmed as they may become hazardous. This will also encourage deep root growth. Sometimes, these trees produce vigorous suckers. For all these reasons, *S. campanulata* should not be planted near houses or pavements. It does best in dry regions and will thrive to 1,300 m (4,300 ft).

NOTE: this species has proved invasive in many regions.

ORIGIN	Trop. Africa
HEIGHT	up to 23 m (75 ft)
TYPE	evergreen flowering tree
STATUS	not threatened
HABITAT	dry and humid forest and dry scrubland
GROWTH	fast
FLOWG	spring to autumn
DRY TOL.	high
SALT TOL.	moderate to high
LIGHT	full sun
SOIL	rich, deep
NUTRIT.	high-potassium fertilizer
HAZARDS	poisonous fruit
PROBLEMS	possibly invasive; brittle wood
ENVIRON.	insect and bird nectar
PROPAG.	seeds
LEAVES	pinnate; deep, dull green; to 60 cm (24 in.); leaflets in 4–9 pairs, leathery, rough
FLOWERS	showy; scarlet-red (rarely yellow); to 12 cm (5 in.); campanulate
FRUIT	a capsule, to 21 cm (8.3 in.); oblong, tapered, dehiscent; stuffed with winged seeds
USE	large flowering tree; street tree; public open space; xerophytic
ZONE	10–12

S. campanulata; huge, cupped, gilt-edged blooms, which surround the velvety, clawed buds, hold copious nectar for birds to the amusement of children.

S. campanulata var. *flava*; is a fairly rare, charming yellow form.

S. campanulata; fairly brittle limbs can be broken in high winds and should be trimmed as they may be hazardous.

S. campanulata; huntsmen boil the kernels of the fr. to obtain a poisonous liquid for use on the tips of their arrows.

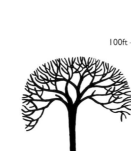

ORIGIN	Society Is, endemic
HEIGHT	up to 25 m (82 ft)
TYPE	deciduous, large fruiting tree
STATUS	not threatened
HABITAT	coastal or lowland limestone woodland
GROWTH	fast
FLOWG	summer to autumn
DRY TOL.	high
SALT TOL.	moderate
LIGHT	full sun
SOIL	widely tolerant
NUTRIT.	balanced fertilizer annually
HAZARDS	spiny seeds
PROBLEMS	phytophthora root rot
ENVIRON.	bee nectar; wild bird fruit
PROPAG.	seeds; large cuttings
LEAVES	pinnate; rich green, to 30 cm (12 in.); with up to 23 leaflets, lanceolate or oblong
FLOWERS	showy; whitish or yellowish; very small, held in erect panicles; fragrant
FRUIT	a drupe, to 8 cm (3 in.); elliptic to rounded; yellow skin and flesh; caulescent
USE	backyard tree; public open space; specimen; xerophytic
ZONE	10–12

Spondias cytherea

OTAHEITI APPLE

Sonn.   10 spp.

S. mangifera; S. dulcis

ANACARDIACEAE

OTAHEITI APPLE, FROM TAHITI in the Society Islands, is yet another edible fruit of the more often toxic Anacardiaceae family, which includes Cashew (*Anacardium occidentale*) and Mango (*Mangifera indica*) — in fact, **Spondias cytherea** was originally known as *S. mangifera*. *S. cytherea* has so many pet names as to cause great confusion from region to region. Indeed, it seems that every small island has a nom de plume for this popular fruit. It has a sturdy trunk and a few stout branches, and its smooth, grey bark exudes a resinous juice. The pinnate leaves' large, serrated, long-pointed leaflets are heavily veined, with their margins rolled under. Patches of foliage turn deep, butter yellow in the autumn. It is one of the few species to provide a reliable, but brief, colour display. Fragrant, yellowish male and female flowers are held on the same spikes (polygamous), small but fairly showy. They are held in large, terminal branched panicles and are haloed in bees during the summer. Borne in short-stalked clusters on old wood, the nectarine-sized fruit (much bigger than *S. mombin* and *S. purpurea*) is amber-yellow and thick-skinned, with an aromatic, juicy, sweet or slightly sour pulp with a pleasant, spicy odour suggestive of apples. H. R. MacMillan, in his book *Tropical Planting and Gardening*, describes *S. cytherea* as having a large stone, scanty, acid pulp and the flavour of an 'exceedingly bad' mango, but concedes that it makes excellent preserve, with some varieties being better for this than others. Inferior fruit such as this may even have a slight taste of turpentine, deserving the name 'Hog Plum'. Eating the fruit out-of-hand requires care as the seeds have very sharp spines. *S. cytherea* takes 4–5 years to bear from seed or 2–3 years from cuttings or grafts. The sapwood is whitish to light yellow in colour and the heartwood is a light brown. It is moderately soft and lightweight, but not durable. These are honey plants.

S. cytherea; this fr. has pleasantly aromatic, juicy pulp, not unlike the related Mango.

S. cytherea; crops heavily, with nectarine-sized fr. on sturdy stems, until autumn as its foliage colours.

S. cytherea; fragrant fls are held in widely branched panicles.

S. cytherea; in Qld, N. Australia, winter exposes its sturdy framework of straight trunk, whorled branches and grey bark. Related to Mango, this sp. was originally named *Spondias mangifera*.

Spondias mombin; (L.), (syn. *S. lutea*), Trop. America, to 30 m (98 ft). HOG PLUM, CAJA FRUIT or YELLOW MOMBIN, a huge, fast-growing sp., has a widespread but sparsely branched form. The fr. is bat dispersed and is deep yellow and sweetly pungent, but not very palatable. It is sometimes fed to pigs – hence its common name. Its wood is inferior, being perishable and susceptible to dry rot. This venerable specimen grows at Foster Gardens, Honolulu, Hawaii. (10–12)

Spondias purpurea; (L.), Trop. S America, to 10 m (33 ft). PURPLE or RED MOMBIN, SPANISH PLUM or CIRUELA, has pinkish red, little fls and thick-skinned, purplish red or yellowish 'plums'. Every part of this sp. is smaller than *S. cytherea*. Ripe fr. is popular regionally, especially in drier, less fertile areas. It is eaten out-of-hand, boiled or dried. A singular feature of this sp. is its low, sprawling habit. (see below) The wood is popular for domestic fuel. (10–12)

Spondias purpurea is a tree of arid regions, which seems to be especially designed for children to climb. It mostly spreads its stout, pale grey limbs in prostrate, lazy, languid loops, holding its sparse, wide-spreading canopy very low and far from its axis. This sp. is very easy to grow from fairly large cuttings of young or mature wood and is often planted to mark boundaries.

ORIGIN	SE Asia
HEIGHT	up to 20 m (66 ft)
TYPE	evergreen, monoecious fruiting tree
STATUS	rare and threatened
HABITAT	understorey of lowland evergreen forest and rainforest
GROWTH	slow
FLOWG	spring and mid-autumn
DRY TOL.	low
SALT TOL.	low
LIGHT	full sun to bright shade
SOIL	fertile, humid, acid
NUTRIT.	organic fertilizer; deep, organic mulch
HAZARDS	some parts toxic
PROBLEMS	phytophthora fungus
ENVIRON.	nectar; wild fruit for bats and birds
PROPAG.	seeds; softwood cuttings
LEAVES	simple; bright green; to 30 cm (12 in.); elliptic, deeply veined; glossy
FLOWERS	showy; pale yellow; females, slim, long-stalked, small trumpets; fragrant
FRUIT	a monocarp, to 7 cm (2.7 in.); oval, brownish, scurfy-skinned; sweet pulp
USE	shade tree; backyard tree; curiosity; specimen; botanic collection; conservatory
ZONE	10—12

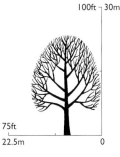

100ft — 30m

75ft
22.5m   0

Stelechocarpus burahol

KEPPEL

(Blume) Hook. f. & Thomson   5 spp.

ANNONACEAE

STELECHOCARPUS BURAHOL, a sturdy species of the humid, evergreen forests of SE Asia, is long-lived and forms a rough, gnarled, stout trunk. It has a neat, dense, conical crown of 2-ranked leaves that hang downwards; new growth emerges bright pink or wine-red. Secreted deeply within the deep green shadows of its canopy, its flowers and fruit are borne directly on the trunk and main limbs. *S. burahol* is monoecious and holds its fragrant, pale yellow, 4-parted male and female flowers separately on the same tree. The males are found on the branches while the females are held cauliflorously on the lower trunk where the fruit will form. Like most Annonaceae, these blooms are pollinated by insects. *S. burahol* fruit greatly resembles that of *Manilkara zapota*, being round, scurfy and brown-skinned, with juicy, aromatic yellowish or pinkish flesh enclosing large, brown seeds. The succulent pulp is mellow, with an aromatic sweetness, and is variously described as tasting of coconut or as having a flavour resembling papaya. It is this fruit that is the most extraordinary feature of this relative of the Custard Apple. Once the fruit is digested, all bodily excretions, including urine and perspiration, are said to smell strongly of violets. This phenomenon is temporary, of course. *S. burahol* was cultivated in the grounds of the Royal Palaces of Java, in Indonesia, where the fruit was reserved for the Sultans and their harems. Commoners were warned that bad luck would befall anyone who consumed the fruit. David Fairchild, the great American plant explorer, was delighted to find old trees scattered around the deserted grounds of the Water Palace in Jakarta. Fairchild admired the sensational, pinkish new growth but, to his chagrin, the trees were not in fruit.

S. burahol; little, pale yellow fls are growing directly from the trunk.

S. burahol; with sweet, aromatic, edible flesh. Once fr. is digested, bodily excretions are said to smell of violets.

S. burahol; fr. are held on sturdy stalks and borne directly on the trunk and limbs.

S. burahol; this small Keppel or Violet Tree is planted at the Waimea Aboretum, Ohau, Hawaii. This sp. is closely related to the Custard Apple and African Nutmeg.

Stemmadenia litoralis

LECHESO

(HBK) Allorge   10 spp

S. galeottiana

APOCYNACEAE

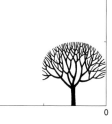

STEMMADENIA IS A TROPICAL AMERICAN GENUS that is very closely allied to *Tabernaemontana*. **Stemmadenia littoralis** is a small, evergreen tree with the typical dichotomous branching of the Apocynaceae. Also typical is its abundant, sticky, milky sap that, although poisonous, has found use medicinally with the indigenous people of the region. The Spanish named this species Lecheso for this white sap. **S. littoralis** is native of coastal forests and open bushland and is very tolerant as to soil, as long as it is well-drained and somewhat humid. It is cultivated for its showy, fragrant, long-tubed, bright yellow-throated, white flowers that are produced in loose corymbs most of the year. (It is worth noting that all *Stemmadenia* flower petals overlap to the left.) Following the blooms are small, twinned, leathery, arching fruit that are ribbed longitudinally and turn orange as they ripen. At this stage, they dehisce to reveal the seeds within, greatly resembling fruit of *Tabernaemontana* species. **S. littoralis** combines showy, fragrant blooms with vibrantly glossy foliage and salt-tolerance that makes this species a good choice for planting near the coast or anywhere in the tropics or subtropics, particularly in small gardens. It is quickly gaining popularity in south Florida, USA, as it performs so well in seaside gardens with alkaline soils.

*** **S. grandiflora**; ([Jacq.] Miq.), Guyana and Venezuela, to 8 m (26 ft). HUEVOS DE GATO has copious sap, unequal, sharply cuspidate leaves and large, wide-petalled flowers, to 6 cm (2.3 in.), that are soft yellow, orange or (sometimes) white. (10–12)

*** **S. obovata**, ([Hook. & Arn.] Schum.), (syn. *S. glabra*), Mexico to Ecuador, to 6 m (20 ft). HEUVOS DE CABALLO or COJONES DE BURRO is a small tree with large, inverted-ovate leaves. The flowers are pale or bright yellow or creamy white. The fruit is twice as large as *S. litoralis*. In Costa Rica, the sap is used medicinally. (10–12)

ORIGIN	from Mexico to Colombia
HEIGHT	up to 7 m (23 ft)
TYPE	evergreen, small flowering tree
STATUS	not threatened
HABITAT	understorey in humid coastal forest
GROWTH	moderate
FLOWG	all year
DRY TOL.	moderate
SALT TOL.	high
LIGHT	full sun to bright shade
SOIL	widely tolerant
NUTRIT.	balanced fertilizer annually; deep, organic mulch
HAZARDS	toxic sap
PROBLEMS	none
ENVIRON.	insect nectar
PROPAG.	seeds; cuttings; layers
LEAVES	simple; deep green; thin-textured, oval, short-stemmed, glossy
FLOWERS	showy; white with yellow throat; salverform; fragrant
FRUIT	a capsule, to 5 cm (2 in.) long; ovoid, orange-yellow; held in pairs
USE	seaside; specimen; large planter; accent; screening; coastal civic centre; conservatory
ZONE	10–12

S. littoralis; Lecheso is cultivated for its showy, fragrant, long-tubed, bright yellow-throated, white blooms.

S. littoralis; with twinned, ribbed, beaked fr.

S. littoralis; a small, everg. tree with the typical dichotomous branching of the Apocynaceae.

S. littoralis; contains abundant, sticky, milky white sap; for that reason, it is known as Lecheso in Mexico.

Stenocarpus sinuatus

FIREWHEEL TREE

Endl.   25 spp.

PROTEACEAE (GREVILLEOIDEAE – Embothrieae)

ORIGIN	E Australia, endemic
HEIGHT	up to 30 m (100 ft)
TYPE	evergreen, large flowering tree
STATUS	not threatened
HABITAT	slightly drier rainforest
GROWTH	slow
FLOWG	intermittently, all year
DRY TOL.	moderate
SALT TOL.	low
LIGHT	sheltered sun
SOIL	fertile; water-retentive; acid
NUTRIT.	organic fertilizer; deep, organic mulch
HAZARDS	dislikes phosphates
PROBLEMS	chlorosis
ENVIRON.	moth and bird nectar
PROPAG.	fresh seed; semi-ripe cuttings
LEAVES	very variable; olive-green; glossy; pinnately-lobed to obovate
FLOWERS	showy; red; held in terminal wheel-like umbels; allixary
FRUIT	a follicle, to 8 cm (3 in.); narrow, leathery, boat-shaped; seeds winged
USE	large flowering tree; street tree; public open space; specimen; large planter; large conservatory
ZONE	10—12

100ft 30m

75ft
22.5m   0

STENOCARPUS SINUATUS is a slow-growing species. Its trunk has wrinkled, brown or grey bark that is fissured and sometimes corky. The canopy is formed into a dense, narrow crown of lance-shaped, leathery leaves that vary from lanceolate with wavy margins to deeply lobed; new growth is soft, downy and bronze-coloured. *S. sinuatus* is a member of the eccentric Australian Protea family, distinguished for its extraordinary flowers that are attractive in bud and spectacular when open, often cupped in glossy, waxen bracts and sometimes conspicuously fringed. *S. sinuatus* has its improbable, short-stalked flowers arranged in a flat circle, mimicking a flaming wheel. The green flower buds turn yellow, then open red, with each slender, little, red floral spoke of the wheel tipped with an enlarged, globular apex resembling a golden yellow ball, reminiscent of a matchstick. *S. sinuatus* blooms intermittently throughout the year, usually with a peak display occurring in the heat of early autumn. These blooms may have a foetid smell, especially at night, when they attract their pollinators, the moths. They are particularly prized as cut flowers. Dry, boat-shaped, leathery follicles follow the flowers and contain winged seeds from which the tree is easily propagated. Like almost all the Protea clan, *S. sinuatus* prefers deep, rich, acid soil in which to thrive but is very sensitive to nitrates and phosphates, which may prove toxic and kill it. This species is also allergic to herbicides, which should not come into contact with any part of the tree.

*** *S. davallioides*; (Foreman & B. Hyland), NE Qld, Australia, to 40 m (131 ft). FERN-LEAF STENOCARPUS is a rare, slow-growing species found in high altitude rainforests. Its beautiful, ferny, juvenile leaves resemble those of *Grevillea robusta*. The small, spidery, cream flowers, set in rusty tomentose umbels, are fragrant. The fruit is a grey follicle. (9–10)

S. sinuatus; with dehiscent follicles full of winged sds.

S. davallioides; a rare, slow-growing sp. with masses of spidery, cream fls in rusty tomentose umbels.

S. sinuatus; this slow-growing sp. eventually forms a very large tree in the wild. In cultivation, it is much smaller.

S. sinuatus; these amazing fls, which seem more akin to exotic sea creatures than floral blooms, are known appropriately as Firewheels.

Sterculia foetida

POON TREE

L.   150 spp.

MALVACEAE (formerly Sterculiaceae)

SOARING ABOVE THE SURROUNDING TREES in its native woodland, the renowned *Sterculia foetida* is swathed in bright red in mid-spring, signalling its exuberant bloom. The Poon Tree is best admired from afar, however, since this specimen has a very offensive smell. The Sterculiaceae (now Malvaceae) clan is outstanding and original in its form and the noble Poon is no exception. *S. foetida* is a pachycaul species, typically tall, with a straight, clear, obese trunk that may eventually measure 2 m (6.5 ft) in girth. Horizontal limbs are whorled around its crown, with its branchlets gracefully curved upwards and crowded at their ends with large, digitate leaves. In spring, the tree reinvents itself, bursting into vigorous, new growth, its reddish twigs loaded with the waxy, crimson-brown or terracotta, emergent foliage. Without pause, these twigs soon hold sturdy, branched panicles of starry, waxy, bright-red blooms, which are, in fact, deeply lobed calyxes. Sadly, these beguiling blooms give off an incredible stench, a rank odour that is emitted also from many parts of the tree if it is bruised or cut. *Sterculia* species have sugar-secreting hairs within these calyxes, as well as their pungent smell, and both attract insects and cicadas – their pollinators. As the blooms fade, they are replaced rapidly with spectacular, huge, inflated, fluorescent scarlet fruit follicles comprising up to 5 egg-shaped, hard, woody pods that are held tightly together and contain large, blue-black seeds that are oily and considered pleasant tasting. Even though the seeds are well known to have a purgative effect, they are eaten raw or roasted, when they are said to taste like peanuts. They have also been used as a substitute for cocoa, although lacking a distinctive flavour. The soft wood is used in tea-growing regions to make tea chests.

ORIGIN	Old World tropics
HEIGHT	up to 20 m (33 ft)
TYPE	semi-deciduous flowering and foliage tree
STATUS	not threatened
HABITAT	lowland dry woodlands
GROWTH	moderate
FLOWG	spring
DRY TOL.	high
SALT TOL.	low
LIGHT	full sun
SOIL	deep, fertile, well-drained
NUTRIT.	balanced fertilizer annually
HAZARDS	none
PROBLEMS	all parts with a foetid odour
ENVIRON.	bat and insect nectar
PROPAG.	seeds
LEAVES	palmate; rich green; with 5–10 leaflets, to 30 cm (12 in.); long-petioled; new growth reddish
FLOWERS	showy; deep, rusty red; deeply cut into 5 lobes; in panicles, to 30 cm (12 in.); foetid-pungent
FRUIT	a follicle, to 10 cm (4 in.); rich red; ovoid; held in star-like clusters; seeds large, blue-black
USE	flowering tree; public open space; specimen; xerophytic
ZONE	10–12

100ft – 30m
75ft
22.5m   0

S. foetida; the Poon Tree, Indian Almond or Java Olives is fast growing, handsome and easy to grow. Sadly, although lovely, the little, fls are (like all parts of this tree) evil-smelling.

S. foetida; new lvs, blooms and fr. are all red.

S. foetida; the sds are oily and said to be pleasant tasting; they are eaten raw or roasted but have a purgative effect.

S. foetida; a tree in full, magnificent bloom in Port Douglas, N Qld, Australia.

Sterculia apetala; ([Jacq.] Karst.), C and S America, to 30 m (100 ft). BELLOTA, or PANAMA TREE, is the national tree of Panama. It is very large, forming a parasol crown over a naked, straight trunk with huge, slab-like buttresses that develop with age. Young, heart-shaped lvs are densely woolly and deeply 5-lobed. Fr. follicles are narrow and dark brown. Trunks were often hollowed out to make canoes. A honey plant. (10–12)

Sterculia monosperma; (Vent.) (syn *S. nobilis*), S. China endemic, to 30 m (100 ft), SEVEN SISTERS' FRUIT or CHINA CHESTNUT has broadly oblong to ovate, leathery, dark, dull green lvs. Curious little, spidery, pale pinkish, male and female fls are held in widely spreading, red-stalked, drooping panicles. Decorative follicles are held in groups of 3–5; they measure to 10 cm (4 in.) and contain 1–3 black sds. (9–12)

Sterculia shillinglawii; (F. Muell.), from E Malesia to Cape York Peninsula, Australia, to 29 m (95 ft). TULIP STERCULIA is native to lowland monsoon rainforest along river valleys. It has handsome, large, heavily veined lvs with stellate hairs on their undersides; they turn rich, amber-orange with age. The typical, 4-parted, scarlet fruit pods, which follow the little fls, are velvety hairy. (10–12).

Sterculia tragacantha; (Lindl.), from Trop. W Africa to the Congo Basin, to 25 m (82 ft). Known as GUM TRAGACANTH, it is sometimes buttressed and has dark grey, corky bark. The crown tends to be fairly small and sparsely branched. Tiny, yellowish fls are held in congested, catkin-like panicles. This sp. is a source of the valued Tragacanth Gum used in the textile, cosmetics and ice cream industries. (10–12)

385

Stereospermum kunthianum

PINK JACARANDA

Cham.   15 spp.

BIGNONIACEAE

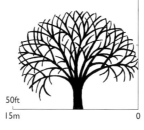

STEREOSPERMUM KUNTHIANUM is a charming, graceful tree of the dry, E African savannahs, growing from the coast up to 3,500 m (11,500 ft) on the slopes of Mount Kilimanjaro, in northern Tanzania. It is yet another member of the glorious Bignoniaceae family that provides so many of our most spectacular, tropical flowering trees and vines. This glorious genus could be considered Africa's challenge to the *Tabebuia* of the New World; *Stereospermum* wins over *Tabebuia* however, in that it has fragrant flowers. *S. kunthianum* has a short bole with thick, flaking bark and stocky branches forming a light, rounded crown clad in large, sturdy pinnate leaves. The wide, oval leaflets have prominent veins and pale undersides. At the end of the dry season, in the arid grasslands of the vast savannahs, the *Stereospermum* are the first to display their spring blooms of billowing, fragrant, pale pink or lilac blossoms that are borne in masses on old wood. Their sweet nectar is avidly imbibed by small, parched, nectar-loving insects and bees. The blooms are funnel-shaped, with crumpled, silken lobes streaked with red or violet 'bee' lines that are designed to lead the pollinators into their slender throats and to the nectaries within. The fruit is a typical Bignoniaceae capsule, filled with winged seeds. Locally, it is chewed with salt as a cough medicine. The wood of *S. kunthianum* is white, tinged yellow and pink; it is hard and heavy and valued as timber. This species is thought to be stimulated into bloom by veldt fires, typical of many plants of the African savannahs.

*** *S. fimbriatum*; ([Wall. ex G. Don.] A. DC.), from Indochina to Malaysia, to 35 m (115 ft). CHACHAH or SNAKE TREE is a briefly deciduous tree with a narrow crown and pale bark. The whitish, pink or pale lilac flowers have deeply fringed petals; the fruit to 60 cm (24 in) long, coiled like a snake. (10–12)

ORIGIN	Trop. E Africa
HEIGHT	up to 10 m (33 ft)
TYPE	deciduous, small flowering tree
STATUS	not common
HABITAT	rocky dry forests or savannahs
GROWTH	moderate
FLOWG	late winter to spring
DRY TOL.	high
SALT TOL.	moderate
LIGHT	full sun
SOIL	fertile, well-drained
NUTRIT.	high-potassium fertilizer
HAZARDS	none
PROBLEMS	none
ENVIRON.	nectar for bees and insects
PROPAG.	fresh seeds
LEAVES	pinnate; rich green; to 35 cm (14 in.); leaflets from 5–9, oblong, to 10 cm (4 in.)
FLOWERS	showy; pale to deep pink or lilac; to 5 cm (2 in.); held in large panicles; fragrant
FRUIT	a capsule, to 45 cm (18 in.); spirally twisted; with many winged seeds
USE	small flowering tree; small street tree; specimen; large planter; xerophytic
ZONE	10–12

S. kunthianum; is known as Pink Jacaranda because of its large, erect panicles of fragrant, pink, trumpet fls.

S. kunthianum; a sturdy specimen with its summer foliage at Cienfuegos in Cuba.

S. kunthianum; has a short bole with thick, flaking bark and stocky branches.

S. fimbriatum; with beguiling, deeply fringed pale pink fls.

ORIGIN	India and Burma
HEIGHT	up to 20 m (66 ft)
TYPE	evergreen, toxic fruiting tree
STATUS	not threatened
HABITAT	dry, sandy coastal woodlands
GROWTH	slow
FLOWG	spring to late summer
DRY TOL.	high
SALT TOL.	moderate
LIGHT	full sun
SOIL	widely tolerant
NUTRIT.	occasional general fertilizer
HAZARDS	extremely toxic seeds
PROBLEMS	none
ENVIRON.	fruit for monkeys and birds
PROPAG.	seeds
LEAVES	simple; dark green, paler below; with 5 longitudinal veins
FLOWERS	inconspicuous; greenish white; held in apical cymes; slightly fragrant
FRUIT	a berry, to 6 cm (2.4 in.); green; spherical; ripening reddish; with white, sticky, bitter pulp and 4–5 large, flat seeds
USE	collection; curiosity; barrier; xerophytic
ZONE	10–12

100ft — 30m

75ft
22.5m — 0

Strychnos nux-vomica

STRYCHNINE

L.   190 spp.

STRYCHNACEAE (Loganiaceae)

STRYCHNOS NUX-VOMICA surely has a suggestion of evil and sombre secrets in its name. Some even hold it to be the apple of the Garden of Eden. Certainly, this small, gaunt species does not effervesce with charm, although it would not be suspected that, like others of this large tribe, its seeds, bark and roots are highly toxic. *S. nux-vomica* is native to the dry coasts of S India and Burma and has greyish bark, a bushy, arching, twiggy growth and dark-green leaves, with longitudinal, prominent veins. Following tiny cymes of greenish white flowers, the pale, bony limbs hold green, globular fruit the size of a small orange, which turns reddish yellow as it ripens. At this stage, it is filled with white, sticky, bitter flesh, which is actually edible, and flat, ash-grey seeds. These contain alkaloids, the source of strychnine and brucine, both extremely powerful poisons. Traditionally, strychnine has been valued in medicine as a tonic and stimulant, or commercially has been processed for rodent poison. *Strychnos* species are distributed in both the Old and New World regions. Old World species usually carry alkaloids of the Strychnine group, while those of the New World contain curare-type poisons traditionally used to tip arrows.

*** *S. decussata*; (Lam.), S Africa endemic, to 8 m (26 ft). CAPE TEAK has teak-like heartwood that is used to make musical instruments. The bark and leaves have medicinal uses. The tough stems are used to protect buildings against lightning. The fruit is orange red. (9–10)

*** *S. spinosa*; (Lam.), Trop. and S Africa to Madagascar, to 8 m (26 ft). MTONGA, (Kenya) or GREEN MONKEY ORANGE (S Africa), is a diffusely limbed, small tree armed with vicious, black-tipped thorns. Greenish white flowers are held in short, dense, compound cymes. The fruit turns yellow orange when ripe and is filled with flat, round, toxic seeds, but the pulp is edible and may be sun-dried as a preserve. The leaves and roots are medicinal, and the leaves are browsed by game and stock. (9–11)

S. nux-vomica; is filled with white, sticky, bitter flesh and flat, ash grey sds.

S. decussata; bark and lvs have medicinal uses. Tough stems are used locally to protect against lightning.

S. lucida; Australian aborigines make an infusion from lvs, fr. and roots to be used as a bath for general illnesses..

S. spinosa; off-white wood is straight-grained and suitable for general carpentry. The hard shells of the dried fr. are sometimes painted and used to make ornaments.

Swietenia mahogani

MAHOGANY

(L.) Jacq.   3 spp.

MELIACEAE

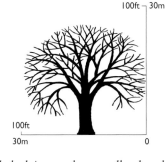

100ft – 30m

100ft

30m   0

SWIETENIA MAHOGANI is native to seasonally flooded plains or dry woodland and does well in calcareous, marl-filled, brackish land where little else will thrive. With a distinctive, deeply furrowed bark and robust, densely branched limbs, it forms a broad, rounded canopy made up of tough, pinnate leaves. In spring, panicles of little, cream, fragrant flowers are followed by striking, stout, 5-celled, woody capsules. These are held erect and split upwards from the base into 5 parts, like small parasols, to release their many flat, winged seeds that glide away on the winds. *S. mahogani* is renowned for its hard, rich, reddish brown, fine-grained wood. It has been fashioned into rare furniture, panelling and veneers through the centuries and is considered to be superior to the mahoganies. This was the species used by the great English cabinetmakers, such as Hepplewhite and Chippendale, for their fine furniture. It has also been used extensively for shipbuilding. Luckily, *S. mahogani* is fairly fast growing, as it has been widely cut throughout its region, very often without thought to replanting. The roots and stumps of large trees have been especially prized for their irregular, wavy grain that resembles walnut. *S. mahogani* has no peer for street planting or as a shade tree, for, although deciduous, it sheds its leaves and re-robes itself so rapidly in new, tender green as to appear evergreen.

*** *S. macrophylla*; (King,), (syn. *S. candollei*), C and S America, to 20 m (66 ft). Known as HONDURAS-, MEXICAN-, VENEZUELAN- or BRAZILIAN-MAHOGANY, it is more widely distributed than *S. mahogani* and therefore has been more important commercially. It is also larger in all its components. However, although the timber is considered excellent, to the real experts it is not as fine as that of *S. mahogani*. (10–12) These are important honey plants.

ORIGIN	S Florida and W Indies
HEIGHT	up to 25 m (82 ft)
TYPE	briefly deciduous foliage (timber) tree
STATUS	threatened
HABITAT	humid and dry lowland woodland
GROWTH	fast
FLOWG	spring
DRY TOL.	high
SALT TOL.	moderate
LIGHT	full sun
SOIL	fertile, deep
NUTRIT.	regular high-nitrogen fertilizer; organic mulch
HAZARDS	none
PROBLEMS	none
ENVIRON.	bee nectar
PROPAG.	seeds
LEAVES	pinnate; dark green; to 20 cm (8 in.); leaflets lanceolate, with an oblique base
FLOWERS	inconspicuous; yellowish green; in axillary panicles; fragrant
FRUIT	a capsule, to 12 cm (4.7 in.); erect, woody, dehiscent; seeds winged
USE	shade tree; street tree; public open space; xerophytic
ZONE	10–12

S. mahogani; planted as an avenue in Coconut Grove, Miami, Florida, USA, where they have, over the years, survived many hurricanes. This tree is fast growing despite its heavy, dense wood.

S. mahogani; with little whitish or yellowish, fragrant fls.

S. mahogani; opening into 5 sections like a parasol, fr. is a thick, woody, dehiscent capsule stuffed with flat, winged sds.

S. mahogani; is renowned for its hard, rich, reddish brown, fine-grained wood.

Swinglea glutinosa

TABOG

(Blanco) Merrill   1 sp.

RUTACEAE

ORIGIN	Philippines endemic
HEIGHT	up to 10 m (33 ft)
TYPE	evergreen small fruiting tree
STATUS	vulnerable
HABITAT	lowland evergreen woodland
GROWTH	slow
FLOWG	spring
DRY TOL.	moderate
SALT TOL.	moderate
LIGHT	full sun
SOIL	well-drained, sandy loam
NUTRIT.	nitrogen-rich fertilizer; deep, organic mulch
HAZARDS	spiny
PROBLEMS	citrus canker
ENVIRON.	insect nectar
PROPAG.	seeds
LEAVES	3-foliate; rich green; polished, gland-dotted; with winged petioles
FLOWERS	inconspicuous; white; with 5 linear, waxy petals; axillary; 1 to several, on slender stems
FRUIT	a berry, to 9 cm (3.5 in.); oblong, ribbed longitudinally; with aromatic pulp and leathery, woody seeds
USE	shade tree; specimen; botanic collection
ZONE	10–12

SWINGLEA GLUTINOSA honours Dr Walter T. Swingle, one of the early plant explorers of the United States Department of Agriculture. A renowned botanist, Swingle was an authority on *Citrus* and vitally interested in rootstocks for this crop, which was to become so important in America. *S. glutinosa* is a small to medium-sized tree, having angled twigs when young. Its aromatic, 3-foliate leaves, with narrowly winged petioles, are finely pubescent and covered in oil glands. The little, white flowers comprise 5 thick, waxy, linear petals. It is, however, the pungently aromatic fruit that is the most remarkable component of this species. Obovoid and longitudinally furrowed, it is divided into 10 faint segments. Each segment wall is thickened and contains aromatic, sour, glutinous pulp in which are set many seeds that have a woolly tuft at their tips. In cross-section, the pulp of *S. glutinosa* fruit resembles a pomegranate. The peel is leathery with radially arranged oil glands. Its juice is used like that of a lemon and is incorporated in soft drinks. Very closely related to *Aegle marmelos*, *S. glutinosa* differs in being an evergreen species. This is a monotypic genus found only on the main island of Luzon in the Philippine Is and is classed as a member of the Hard-shelled Citroid Fruit Trees (HSCFT) group of Rutaceae that comprises several genera that have leathery or hard-shelled fruit (including Bael Fruit, *Aegle marmelos*). There has long been much interest in *S. glutinosa*, or Tabog, as a rootstock for True Citrus as it has proved to be vigorous, although it requires fairly high temperatures during winter months. This species is used in its region in the treatment of skin disease. The wood, while not very large in calliper, is strong and durable and is used for the pillars of elevated, thatched village houses.

S. glutinosa; with aromatic, sour, glutinous sap.

S. glutinosa; sometimes with multiple trunks. The wood, while not very large in calliper, is strong and durable.

S. glutinosa; closely related to *Citrus*, this slow-growing, multi-trunked sp. has very deep green, glossy foliage.

S. glutinosa; an endemic of the Philippines, is very closely related to *Aegle marmelos*. The fr. contains aromatic, sour, glutinous, pulp with many sds and is mostly used in juices.

Syzygium malaccense

MALAY APPLE

(L.) Merrill & Perry   1000 spp.

Jambosa malaccensis; Eugenia malaccense

MYRTACEAE

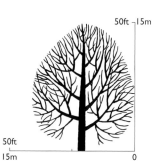

AN AMORPHOUS GENUS of the bountious Myrtle clan, *Syzygium* comprises 1,000 species. It is very closely related to the genus *Eugenia* (550 spp.), but *Syzygium* is confined exclusively to the Old World, while *Eugenia* belong to the New World. Characteristically, **Syzygium malaccense** forms a sombre, deep green, conical crown of slightly polished foliage. Its trunk, which becomes buttressed with age, has flaky, pale grey bark that exposes a pinkish brown inner bark. In spring, the tree becomes the most flamboyant of the SE Asian species, covered in rosy flowers that are almost stalkless and borne abundantly in short clusters at leaf axils along the stems. Because of the large leaves, they may be hidden from view. However, faded blooms carpet the ground below, witness to their abundance and ephemeral nature. The slightly sour stamens are added to salads in some regions. Early summer brings the squat, pear-shaped, short-stalked fruit that is crimson or rosy purple and abundant enough to illuminate the dark foliage, giving the tree a festive charm. While not as highly regarded in their region (which is spoilt for choice with wonderful fruit) as *S. cumini* and *S. samaragensis*, Malay Apples are nevertheless deliciously refreshing on a hot tropical day, with their transparent, crisply juicy, acid-sweet flesh and vaguely apple-like flavour. Great advantages of *S. malaccense* include its flourishing growth on low-lying islands with coralline soils, where many of the more desirable species do not thrive, and the ease with which young trees can successfully be transplanted. In some regions, this species is considered to have brittle wood and the young plants are liable to termite damage. *S. malaccense* was introduced into Jamaica by Captain Bligh in 1793. He brought this species, along with breadfruit and several other trees, to provide an inexpensive food for slaves. All species of this genus are honey plants.

ORIGIN	from Malay Archipelago to Australia
HEIGHT	up to 15 m (50 ft)
TYPE	evergreen, flowering fruiting tree
STATUS	not threatened
HABITAT	moist coastal areas
GROWTH	fast
FLOWG	late spring
DRY TOL.	moderate
SALT TOL.	moderate
LIGHT	full sun
SOIL	rich, well-drained
NUTRIT.	high-potassium fertilizer; deep, organic mulch
HAZARDS	none
PROBLEMS	scale
ENVIRON.	bee nectar; wild bird fruit
PROPAG.	seeds; layers; grafts
LEAVES	simple; dark green; to 30 cm (12 in.); paler below, oblong, curved upwards
FLOWERS	showy; crimson or rosy purple; cauliflorously clustered in axils; with many stamens
FRUIT	a berry, to 8 cm (3 in.); yellow, pink, red or purple; with crisply juicy, white pulp
USE	small shade tree; small flowering tree; backyard tree; street tree; large planter; large conservatory
ZONE	10–12

S. malaccense; with superb, many stamened, rosy blooms.

S. malaccense; fr. varies in colour from yellow, pink, red or purple. It has crisp, juicy, white flesh. It is held in abundance and lends the tree a festive charm.

S. malaccense; growing in the economic plant collection of Waimea Arboretum, Ohau, Hawaii.

S. malaccense; becomes buttressed with age. It has flaky, pale grey bark, which exposes a pinkish brown, inner bark.

Syzygium alliiligneum; (B. Hyland), NE Qld, Australia, to 30 m (100 ft). ONIONWOOD SATINASH, named not for any onion odour, but for its concentric rings of inner bark. Native of very wet, lowland rainforest, it is vigorous and popular for street planting. This sp. is very ornamental with red to cream, papery bark, flushes of pink new growth and large, white and fluffy fls. Abundant, edible fr. ripens rich red and is eaten by Cassowaries. (10–12)

Syzygium aqueum; ([Burm. f.] Alston.), S India to Australia, to 20 m (66 ft). WATER APPLE, (JAMBU CHILI in Malaysia) has a voluminous canopy and smooth, blunt, oblong lvs. White or pinkish, 4-parted fls and fr. tend to be hidden in the foliage. Top-shaped white or pink fr. have sweetish, crisp, watery flesh; strangely, these fr. turn bright yellow when bruised. *S. aqueum* grows vigorously on poor, alkaline soils but prefers better conditions. (10–12)

Syzygium aromaticum; ([L.] Merr. and Per.), (syn. *Eugenia caryophyllata*), Moluccas endemic, to 20 m (66 ft). The celebrated spice CLOVE, or sometimes ZANZIBAR REDHEAD, is a slow-growing sp. eventually forming a dense, conical cone. The slender, 4-parted, fragrant fls turn red-pink as they mature. They are harvested while unopened and are sun-dried to make cloves. Little purple fr. that are rose-scented are also harvested and used to flavour sweets and perfumes. (10–12)

Syzygium cumini; ([L.] Skeels.), (syn. *Eugenia cumini*; *E. jambolana*), India to Java, to 30 m (100 ft). JAMBOLAN or MALABAR PLUM, a fast-growing sp., has become a 'weed tree' in many humid trop. regions. Lvs have a smell of turpentine when crushed. Acid or fairly sweet, the abundant, little, watery fr. are deep purple; pre-soaking in salt water is recommended before eating. NOTE: this sp. is listed as an undesirable in Florida, USA. (10–12)

Syzygium forte subsp. *potamophilum*; ([F. Meull.] B. Hyland), N Qld, Australia, to 15 m (50 ft). FLAKY BARK SATINASH, a rheophytic sp. from riverbanks swept by monsoon floods, often grows with *Melaleuca leucadendra* and shares similar, ornamental white, papery bark. A hardy, cyclone-resistant tree used for street and copse planting. The subsp. differs in having narrower, duller green foliage, axillary fls and smaller, duller white fr. (10–12)

Syzygium grandis; ([Wight.] Walp.), (syn. *Eugenia grandis*), from Burma to Malaysia; to 35 m (115 ft). SEA APPLE or JAMBU LAUT (Malaysia) is a noble giant, found along the coasts in deep, humid soils. It blooms twice a year and is usually haloed with bees. The fr. is 4 cm (1.6 in.), oblong with a green, leathery rind when ripe; it is dry but edible. Photographed at the Fairchild Tropical Gardens, Miami, Florida, USA. (10–12)

Syzygium jambos; (Alston), (syn *Eugenia jambos*), SE Asia, to 10 m (33 ft). ROSE APPLE, POMA ROSA or JAMBU MAWA (Malay), a fast-growing, undemanding sp. with a neat, wide-spreading canopy. It tolerates poor, sandy and alkaline soils and will grow in dry areas, but requires humidity for better fr. Pale yellow or pink-blushed fr. retains its large calyx. Thin flesh is crisp, mealy, sweet (dry to juicy); tastes and smells of roses. Sds are toxic. (10–12)

Syzygium luehmannii; ([F. Meull.] LAS Johnson), E Australia endemic, to 15 m (50 ft). RIBERRY, CHERRY ALDER or SMALL-LEAFED LILLY-PILLY is one of the most outstanding of Australian *Syzygium*. Native of warm rainforests on sand or rich soil and found from high altitudes to within 20 m (66 ft) of the beach. New flushes of lvs are spectacular, as are the tumbling masses of deep, pinkish red fr. Timber of larger specimens is logged. (9–11)

Syzygium megacarpum; (syn. *Eugenia megacarpa*), from E India to Malaysia, is a shrub or tree with quadrangular twigs. White, many stamened fls measure to 2.5 cm (1 in.) diam. and are held at lf axils and branch tips. They are followed by highly ornamental, bright, pinkish red fr., to 8 cm (3 in.). Although very ornamental, this fruit's flavour is rather bland and only compares with *S. malaccense*. Fr. photographed at Lyon Arboretum, Honolulu, Hawaii. (10–12)

Syzygium papyraceum; (B. Hyland) N Qld, Australia endemic, to 20 m (66 ft). PAPERBARK SATINASH of highland rainforests forms a dense crown and buttressed trunk with superb, red-brown, flaky, papery bark. This is an ornamental sp. with stunning, citronella-scented, lavender fls and glossy, purple fr. Honeyeater birds and bees are attracted to the fls. Propagated by fresh, peeled sds. Fairly slow growing, this sp. requires humidity. (9–11)

Syzygium puberulum; (Merr. and LM Perry), NE Qld, Australia, to 8 m (26 ft). DOWNY SATINASH, so-called because of the downy calyx tube of its creamy white, whiskery fls, held in groups of 3–5 and mostly hang down on pendulous twigs below the foliage. Fr. is red or pink and edible. *S. puberulum* is a lowland, rainforest, understorey tree and has a weeping habit. Slow growing, with attractive, deep pinkish new growth, this sp. prefers shade. (10–12)

Syzygium pycnanthum; (Merrill and Perry). From Thailand to Java, to 16 m (52 ft). This full-bodied, densely foliaged sp. is known as WILD ROSE APPLE and is, indeed, a splendid sp., with its compact clusters of pink fls followed by pale pink or purple fr., which are fringed with persistent, enlarged, erect pink sepals. (10–12)

Syzygium samarangensis; ([Blume] Merr. and LM Perry), (syn. *Eugenia javanica*), Malesia, to 15 m (50 ft). JAVA APPLE or JAMBU AIR is a coast. sp. very closely related to *S. malaccensis*. It is fast growng and humidity-loving, developing a dense, very dark green crown that serves as an excellent windbreak. Its vigorous root system makes it valuable for soil control. The masses of fls attract nectar-loving birds and bees. Little, pear-shaped, abundant fr. may be white or pinkish. (9–11)

Syzygium wilsonii; ([F. Meull.] B. Hyland) subsp. *cryptophlebium* N Qld, Australia, to 30 m (100 ft); more usually a shrub. With an arching, willowy habit and sensational, red or pink new growth, white (rarely pink) fls and dull pink or purple fr. held in abundant bunches. This ornamental sp. is relatively unknown but most worthy of cultivation. Because it is an understorey sp. it requires a sheltered spot, protected from drying winds. (10–12)

Syzygium aromaticum; the tiny, yellow and pink fls are harvested before they open and are set out on mats to dry in the sun. As the days pass, they darken in colour until they become brown. When completely dry, but still pungent, they are used in pickles, sweets, cakes, and pomanders. An oil (eugenol) with analgesic properties is extracted and commonly used to relieve toothache. Cloves are an important crop in the Indian Ocean islands of Madagascar, Zanzibar and Réunion.

Schefflera actinophylla growing wild at Woopen Creek in N Qld, Australia.

Tabebuia heterophylla

WHITE CEDAR

(D.C.) Britton 100 spp.

Tabebuia lucida

BIGNONIACEAE

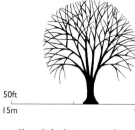

50ft⌐15m

50ft
15m   0

TABEBUIA HETEROPHYLLA thrives in dry, rocky woodland habitats, tolerating calcareous, coral-based soils and high, slightly brackish water tables, so often found on small, tropical islands. Known as White Cedar for its very pale grey, slender trunk and flaking bark that peels off in long, narrow strips, this species has slim, sinewy limbs and a fairly sparse, spreading canopy with tough, little 2–5-fingered, greyish green leaves. *T. heterophylla* celebrates an unexpected rain shower by erupting into masses of diaphanous, lavender-pink or blush white bloom. The delicate, tubular, frilly lobed, yellow-throated flowers are held in abundant clusters on slender stalks, eventually giving way to dark brown, cigar-like, dehiscent pods, stuffed with winged seeds. *T. heterophylla* is of very easy culture and is fast growing. It will transplant well, even when quite large, and because of this, several important plantations have been established for reafforestation in Puerto Rico and the British Virgin Is, where it is native. The seeds of *Tabebuia* are shortly viable and it is important to sow them soon after they are harvested. The light brown heartwood of this tree is moderately hard and strong, with a greyish or golden hue and fine, brown lines. The sapwood has been found to be difficult to separate from the heartwood, which takes a high polish and has been used widely in construction. Despite being susceptible to attack by termites, is has also been employed for boatbuilding, flooring and panelling. In prolonged drought, *T. heterophylla* is attacked by leafhoppers in some regions. NOTE: *Tabebuia* species have been found to hybridize quite freely. This has led to much confusion and, as a result, *T. heterophylla* and several other species of this genus are under taxonomic review. These are honey trees.

NOTE: this species may be invasive in some regions.

ORIGIN	W Indies
HEIGHT	up to 15 m (50 ft)
TYPE	semi-deciduous flowering tree
STATUS	not threatened
HABITAT	dry, rocky lowland woodland
GROWTH	fast
FLOWG.	intermittently, all year
DRY TOL.	high
SALT TOL.	high
LIGHT	full sun
SOIL	fertile, well-drained
NUTRIT.	balanced fertilizer annually
HAZARDS	none
PROBLEMS	leafhoppers
ENVIRON.	bee nectar
PROPAG.	seeds (fresh)
LEAVES	2–5 foliate; drab green; leathery, very variable; with long, yellow petioles
FLOWERS	showy; mauve to pale pink or white; to 8 cm (3 in.); flared trumpets, with yellow throat
FRUIT	a capsule, 20 cm (8 in.); ribbed, dehiscent; with many winged seeds
USE	seaside; small flowering tree; street tree; specimen; large planter; civic centre; xerophytic
ZONE	10–12

T. heterophylla; the frilly, nectar-filled trumpets are loved by bees.

T. heterophylla; this common sp. of the W Indies is quite variable in its form and in the colour of its fls; it flushes with glorious blooms when rain follows a dry period.

T. heterophylla; blooms range from deep to pale pink through to chalky white, but always with a yellow throat.

T. heterophylla; typical of the Bignoniaceae clan, it has long, dehiscent capsules stuffed with papery, thin, winged sds.

Tabebuia aurea; ([Manso] Benth. and Hook.), (syn. *T argentea*; *T. caraiba*), Paraguay, Argentina and Brazil, to 20–40 m (66–130 ft). SILVER- or PARAGUAYAN-TRUMPET TREE has sparse, rhythmic lines and deeply striated, corky bark and a heavy, coarse skeleton. With pewter-green, leathery foliage, this stalwart spring-flowg sp. is outstanding. Native of harsh conditions, it may develop 'rubbery' growth and become unstable in overly fertile, humid soil. (10–12)

Tabebuia bahamensis; ([North.] Britt.), Bahamas endemic, to 15 m (50 ft). A diffusely branched sp. known as BEEF BUSH and ABOVE-ALL or (as are many *Tabebuia* spp. in the W Indies) WHITEWOOD for its very pale timber. Typical of its genus, this sp. is triggered into abundant bloom by heavy rain throughout the year. The fls vary from white, pale to deep pink to mauve with a deep yellow throat. Very similar to *T. heterophylla*. (10–12)

Tabebuia chrysantha; ([Jacq.] Nichols.), (syn. *Tabebuia glomerata*), Trinidad, Tobago; Mexico to Peru, to 30 m (100 ft). GOLDEN TABEBUIA or ROBLE AMARILLO is a large, decid. *Tabebuia* and the most important sp. of coast. Ecuador. All trees of this sp. bloom synchronously (at the same time, in the same region) and are a splendid sight. This happens several times in late spring. (10–12)

Tabebuia chrysostricha; ([Mart. ex DC] Standl.), from Colombia to Brazil, to 10 m (33 ft). Known in Brazil as IPE-AMARELO or IPE-TABACO, it is a small tree of rainforests of the Atlantic coast of S America. The small, rounded lvs are densely rusty pubescent, as are the sd pods. It blooms late winter to spring, as this specimen shows in full bloom at the Arboretum of Los Angeles. (9–11)

Tabebuia guayacan; ([Seem.] Hemsl.), from Mexico to Colombia, to 60 m (197 ft). This young giant of the *Tabebuias*, native of coast. rainforests, is often buttressed in the wild. Lvs are 5–7-foliate, petioles to 17 cm (7 in.), scaly. Infls are rusty pubescence; fls are held in lax clusters, all opening together. This large, decid. specimen was photographed in full spring bloom at Foster Gardens, Honolulu, Hawaii. (10–12)

Tabebuia haemantha; ([Bert.] DC), Puerto Rico endemic, to 7 m (23 ft). The Puerto Ricans have given this rare beauty the names ROBLE CIMARRON or ROBLE COLORADO. It is native of dry forests and thickets, and grows in a distinctive, compact, fastigiate manner. Lvs are 3–5-foliate, margins slightly revolute. The slender, elongated, crimson fls, which never fully open, are specifically adapted for hummingbird pollination. (9–11)

Tabebuia impetignosa; ([DC] Standley), (syn. *T. ipe*; *T. avellanedae*; *T heptaphylla*; *T. palmeri*), Trop. S America, to 10 m (33 ft). This slow-growing, decid. sp. is mostly known as IPE or TOLEDO. It explodes into bloom in spring, when this specimen was photographed at the Arboretum of Los Angeles. Fls may be purple, to medium or deep pink. A sp. of high elevations, most suited to the subtropics. (9–11)

Tabebuia lepidota; ([Kunth.] Britt.), Bahamas and Cuba, to 5 m (16 ft). Known generally as BAHAMAS CEDAR, this small *Tabebuia* is restricted to damp scrublands or rock flats. It often does not achieve true tree status but remains as a small, diffusely branched, flowg shrub. Blooming from early to late spring, with whitish or purplish, funnel form fls. (10–12)

Tabebuia ochracea; ([Cham.] Standl.), (syn. *T. hypodidiction*), Brazil endemic, to 20 m (66 ft). Known in Brazil as Piuva or Taruma, this is a wide-spreading, xerophytic sp. of semi-decid. forests. *T. ochracea* is brownish yellow, velvety in all its parts, which, combined with deep yellow blooms, lends the tree an iridescent quality. It fls 3 times during the spring with all buds opening simultaneously. Blooms are very short-lived and easily damaged by the wind. (10–12)

Tabebuia pallida; ([Lindl.] Mers.), (syn. *T. heterophylla* subsp. *pallida*), W Indies (Lesser Antilles), to 35 m (115 ft). Mostly known as White Tabebuia or Roble Blanco, this is an opulent sp. found in dry, leeward, coast. forests and woodlands. It is only tenuously distinguished from *T. heterophylla*, that occurs on the same islands. *T. pallida* is much larger in every part and its blooms are paler, whitish pink or pure white. (10–12)

Tabebuia riparia; ([Raf.] Sandw.), (syn. *T. leucoxylon*), Jamaican endemic, to 20 m (66 ft). Known (like *T. heterophylla*) as White Cedar, referring to its white-coloured heartwood rather than the fls, which may be white, pink or light crimson. It is also known as White Poui. This is a sp. of dry thickets and open woodland on arid limestone and on sea cliffs, where it is often dwarfed to 6 m (20 ft) or less. (10–12)

Tabebuia rosea; ([Bertol.] DC), (syn. *T. pentaphylla*), Mexico to Venezuela, to 26 m (85 ft). The Pink Trumpet, Pink Tecoma or Pink Poui (plus innumerable other nicknames) is, without a doubt, one of the showiest of all the *Tabebuia*. Like *T. heterophylla* and *T. pallida*, this is a most vigorous sp. and may even prove invasive, but to see it displaying its bright, spring costume is unforgettable. (10–12)

Tabernaemontana arborea

COJON

Meull.   99 spp.

T. schippii

APOCYNACEAE

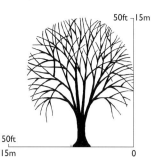

50ft – 15m

50ft
15m   0

FROM ITS NICHE IN THE DARKEST CORNER of the arboretum of Fairchild Tropical Gardens, in Miami, Florida, USA, *Tabernaemontana arborea* grows to form a classically spreading or rounded canopy of glossy, dark green leaves. The slender, light brown, scaly-barked trunk develops small buttresses in age. *T. arborea*, a quietly elegant tree, suddenly bursts into a glorious bloom of brilliant, snowy white posies and drenches the air with its sweet, orange-blossom fragrance. Although the flowers are much smaller than many of this grand, wide-spread family, they are produced in great abundance. The fruit of *T. arborea* is typically in the form of paired, deep yellow follicles that are filled with small, black seeds set in scarlet arils. In some species, the ripe fruit yields a dye. When cut, the trunk exudes a toxic, milky, protein-breaking latex that is being studied for its possible antibiotic properties. It is this latex that distinguishes *Tabernaemontana* from the look-alike jasmines. Cojon heartwood is yellowish or light, reddish brown, hard, heavy and fine-textured. In some species of this genus, the wood is burnt for incense. Various parts of the tree are employed medicinally. This obscure and largely unknown species from C America deserves a larger audience to experience its beautiful spring flowering.

*** *T. divaricata*; ([L.] R Br. ex Roem. & Schult.), (syn. *Nerium divaricatum*), NE India to N Thailand and S China, to 5 m (16.5 ft). COFFEE ROSE is a shrub or small tree and the most well-known of all *Tabernaemontana*. It is a twiggy, heavily foliaged species that resembles *Coffea*. The simple, white tubular flowers are scented in the evening. The fruit is narrowly ellipsoid. Var. 'Flora Plena' has double flowers that resemble a *Gardenia* but are only slightly fragrant in the evening. (10–12)

ORIGIN	from Mexico to C America
HEIGHT	up to 15 m (50 ft)
TYPE	evergreen flowering tree
STATUS	vulnerable
HABITAT	moist to wet thickets; mixed forest
GROWTH	moderate
FLOWG	late spring to summer
DRY TOL.	low to moderate
SALT TOL.	low
LIGHT	moderate to high
SOIL	rich, humid, well-drained
NUTRIT.	balanced fertilizer annually; deep, organic mulch
HAZARDS	toxic or irritant sap
PROBLEMS	none
ENVIRON.	moth nectar
PROPAG.	seeds; cuttings; layers
LEAVES	simple; deep green; to 18 cm (8 in.); ovate-elliptic, glabrous
FLOWERS	showy; white; held abundantly in branched cymes; nocturnally fragrant
FRUIT	a follicle, to 8 cm (3 in.); many seeds embedded in fleshy, orange-red arils
USE	shade tree; flowering tree; specimen; public open space; street tree
ZONE	10–12

T. arborea; with delightful, little posies of orange-fragrant blooms.

T. arborea; Cojon is a spring-blooming, arboreal sp. from Mexico and C America with a wide-spreading, vase-like shape. Like all *Tabernaemontana*, it is full of toxic, milky latex.

T. divaricata var. 'Flora Plena'; has double fls that resemble a *Gardenia*; they are only slightly fragrant.

T. divaricata; is a twiggy, heavily foliaged sp., which certainly resembles *Coffea* and is widely known as Coffee Rose.

Tabernaemontana cerifera; (Panch. and Seb.), endemic to New Caledonia, to 16 m (52 ft). Photographed at the Royal Botanic Garden, Sydney, which has a large collection of plants endemic to New Caledonia, (east of Australia in the Pacific Ocean). *T. cerifera* is found in bush or forest along river banks. Densely foliaged, it blooms all year. Strongly pinwheeled fls are fragrant at night to attract moths. Twinned fr. are green with bright red arils. (9–11)

Tabernaemontana elegans; (Stapf.), from E Africa to eastern S Africa. Toad Tree has a single-trunked, bushy crown; bark is thick and corky (latex white). Large glabrous lvs are crowded towards ends of limbs. Fls are white, fragrant, in terminal clusters. Distinctive, dark green fr. are held in prs on pendulous stalks, beaked, ridged and covered in pale grey, corky warts. Lvs are used to curdle milk, and latex is employed to stop bleeding. (9–11)

Tabernaemontana orientalis; there are 2 main vars. of this widespread sp.: var. *augustifolia*; (Benth.) New Guinea, Melanesia and Australia, and var *grandifolia*; (Val. in Bull.), Indonesia. The latter sp. (above), of coast. sites, is known as Iodine Plant for the medicinal use by Aborigines of its milky latex for treating sores and ulcers. This popular sp. has abundant, sweet-smelling fls and attractive, dehiscent fr. with shortly viable sds. (10–12)

Tabernaemontana pachysiphon; (Stapf), (*T. holstii*), Trop. E Africa, to 12 m (39 ft). Known as Adam's Apple (for the bulge in its throat). This is an understorey sp. of wet coast. and hill forests. It is heavily foliaged with much white latex. The fls vary in petal shape and are usually very fragrant. The toxic fr. is spherical and takes a full year to mature. The bark is a source of dodo cloth and the lvs yield a black dye that is used for hair colouring. (10–12)

Tamarindus indica

TAMARIND

L.   1 sp.

T. occidentalis; T. officinalis

FABACEAE (Caesalpinioideae)

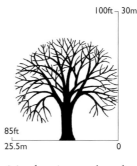

TAMARINDUS INDICA grows slowly but lives a long time, surviving hurricanes, droughts and fires. Its fine, billowing, bluish green foliage is ignited in spring by an abundance of sprightly, yellow and red butterfly blooms. In contrast, its heavy, lumpy, rusty velvety fruit have brittle, eggshell-like skin, with the hard seeds embedded in dark golden or rosy brown, sticky, fibrous pulp that is intensely sweet-and-sour. This pulp contains sucrose and acetic, tartaric and citric acids. It is used as a source of vitamin C and has long been used medicinally. It is also rich in minerals and B complex vitamins. *T. indica* also has many domestic and culinary uses: for flavourings, confectionery (Indian tamarind balls), drinks and sauces, especially English Worcester Sauce and Angostura Bitters, or in Sri Lanka, for preserving fish. When overripe, the pulp may be used to clean copper and brass. The seeds have also found value. After the brittle, shell-like skin and the pulp are removed, they are boiled or roasted for eating and are sometimes ground into flour. In some regions, the flowers and young leaves are eaten in salads, curries and soups, while the dried leaves have been found to yield a yellow dye. All parts of this venerable plant have been employed medicinally, particularly, as a 'tea' of young leaves that is remarkably effective, if applied in the early stages, for soothing and healing the irritations and skin eruptions of chickenpox and measles. The sapwood is light yellow and moderately soft, while the small area of heartwood is dark, purplish brown, very hard and heavy and takes a fine polish. In some regions, *T. indica* is used to make tool handles and walking sticks, but is more widely used for fuel and charcoal as it generates great heat. This is an important bee plant.

ORIGIN	Origin unkown, possibly Trop. Africa
HEIGHT	up to 24 m (80 ft)
TYPE	evergreen, large fruiting tree
STATUS	not threatened
HABITAT	dry coastal plains
GROWTH	slow
FLOWG	several times a year
DRY TOL.	high
SALT TOL.	high
LIGHT	full sun
SOIL	fertile, well-drained
NUTRIT.	balanced fertilizer annually
HAZARDS	none
PROBLEMS	scale; aphids
ENVIRON.	bee nectar
PROPAG.	seeds
LEAVES	pinnate; bluish green, to 11 cm (4.3 in.), paler below; 10–18 leaflets
FLOWERS	showy; pale yellow, tinged or spotted scarlet; held in pendent, branched racemes; fragrant
FRUIT	a legume, to 13 cm (5 in.); velvety brown, brittle shell; seeds set in sticky, dense, sweet-sour pulp
USE	seaside; large shade tree; street tree; public open space; bonsai subject; xerophytic
ZONE	10–12

T. indica; jaunty, yellow, orchid-like fls are held on branched panicles.

T. indica; velvety fr. is contained in a brittle, eggshell-like covering; inside is edible, sweetly-sour pulp and large sds. The thick, sticky pulp has many medical applications.

T. indica; the venerable Tamarind is an extremely slow-growing sp. It is also very drought-tol.

T. indica; used for tool handles and walking sticks, but more widely used for fuel and charcoal as it generates great heat.

ORIGIN	from NE Africa to W. Asia
HEIGHT	up to 10 m (33 ft)
TYPE	evergreen, small flowering tree
STATUS	not threatened
HABITAT	coastal scrubland, in saline soils
GROWTH	moderate
FLOWG	year-round
DRY TOL.	high
SALT TOL.	high
LIGHT	high
SOIL	humid, very well-drained
NUTRIT.	not normally necessary
HAZARDS	none
PROBLEMS	die-back
ENVIRON.	insect nectar
PROPAG.	seeds; semi-ripe cuttings
LEAVES	scales; greyish green; minute, clasping the wiry twigs
FLOWERS	showy; pink; in slender spikes; 5-petolled, with 5 stamens
FRUIT	a capsule, to 0.5 cm (0.2 in.); narrow, pointed, splitting into 8 parts
USE	seaside; small flowering tree; coastal screening; accent; median strip; large planter; xerophytic
ZONE	8–12

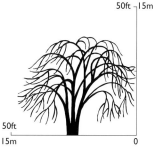

50ft ⌐ 15m
50ft
15m   0

Tamarix aphylla

ATHEL TAMARISK

(L.) Karst.   54 spp.

T. articulata

TAMARICACEAE

THERE IS NO MORE MEMORABLE and stunning sight than a well-grown *Tamarisk*. Finely, needle-like, grey-green foliage billows from a slender, arching frame of wiry, finely divided, spreading limbs that become deeply furrowed and ridged with age. As the foamy, delicate pink sprays of flowers develop, they veil the soft, silvery boughs to create a romantic impression. *Tamarix aphylla* has a superficial resemblance to *Casuarina*, but the foliage is much finer and more silvery. The many, spreading, greyish brown or reddish limbs form a rounded or irregular crown. As the tree grows, the smaller, wiry twigs become deciduous and, as they mostly fall off, it may be necessary to prune the older wood on a young tree during cooler months. The aim is to develop a balanced shape by removing dead wood and thus encourage plenty of fresh growth, on which the next season's flowers will develop. These rapidly growing trees are highly drought- and wind-resistant, as well as tolerant of alkaline and saline soil. Although this species is salt-tolerant and is widely planted as windbreaks and hedges in dry regions of the tropics and subtropics, they grow best when protected from strong, salty winds. The wood is light brown, hard and suitable for small articles.

✳✳✳ *T. dioica*; (Roxb. ex Roth.), Iran to India, to 3 m (10 ft). Small dioecious tree. The bark is red-brown; the leaves sheathing; the inflorescence simple or loosely compound. (8–11)

✳✳✳ *T. gallica*, (L.), (syn. *T. algeriensis*), Sicily and Canary Is, to 10 m (33 ft). MANNA PLANT is a slender tree with purplish bark. The leaves are sessile; the blooms, pink or white. (8–10)

✳✳✳ *T. mannifera*, (Ehrenb.), Iran to Arabia, GAZ or TARFA. A sweet, white powder is produced from the leaves when they are punctured by scale insects. This is the powdery substance that is known as manna to the Bedouin tribes and that is mentioned in the *Bible*. (10–12)

NOTE: these species are red-listed as undesirably invasive.

T. aphylla; the main trunk has deeply grooved, corky bark but young growth is smooth and reddish.

T. aphylla; with fine, needle-like, billowing foliage designed to withstand wind, salt and drought.

T. dioica; *Tamarisk* is both drought- and salt-tol. It has wiry, jointed, grey-green foliage and long-lived, slender spikes of tiny, lavender-pink flowers.

403

Taxodium mucronatum

MONTEZUMA CYPRESS

Ten.   2 spp

TAXODIACEAE

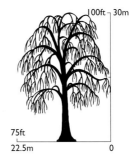

KIN TO THE FABLED *SEQUOIA* and almost as celebrated, the noble *Taxodium* is a worldwide favourite tree for public parks and botanic gardens. These moderately fast-growing, lofty monsters are surprisingly tolerant of soil pH and urban pollution. Native of the swamps and river valleys of the high Mexican plateaux, **Taxodium mucronatum** is known there as Ahuehueta, meaning, 'old man of the water.' It develops grand buttresses as its pole-like trunk soars upwards to support its voluminous, plume-like, weeping canopy. *Taxodium* have several curious characteristics. Firstly, they are found in swampy habitats where they grow with their roots in water. To facilitate their intake of oxygen, they grow pneumataphores, which look like knobbly knees, from their submerged roots. These act as breathing tubes, in the manner of many mangrove species. Secondly, they have 2 forms of growth, horizontal and vertical. The vertical limbs are persistent, but the horizontal shoots are deciduous and fall off in the autumn, with the leaves. However, before it loses its twigs and leaves, the tree turns a spectacular bright orange to rusty brown. With spring, the tree renews its foliage and produces masses of tiny, catkin-like male and female cones. **T. mucronatum** is one of the best-known trees of Mexico and is renowned for its longevity. A tree at Santa Maria del Tule in Oaxaca is said to be several thousand years old and its trunk has a girth of about 35.9 m (14 ft), although both its age and size are disputed. Scientists believe that the large trunk is actually the result of a fusion of several tree trunks and that the age is more likely to be 1,000 years. *Taxodium* species are valued for their timber and resins.

*** **T. distichum**; ([L.] Rich.), SE USA, to 40 m (131 ft). The BALD- or SWAMP-CYPRESS is very similar but less pendent than *T. muconatum* and usually has a single bole. It is also much more cold-tolerant. (6–10)

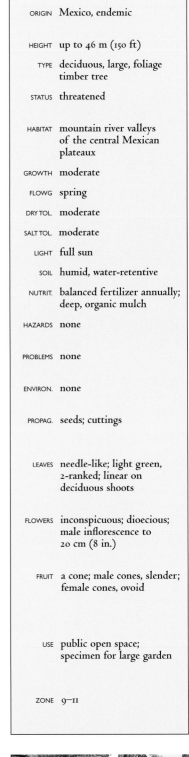

ORIGIN	Mexico, endemic
HEIGHT	up to 46 m (150 ft)
TYPE	deciduous, large, foliage timber tree
STATUS	threatened
HABITAT	mountain river valleys of the central Mexican plateaux
GROWTH	moderate
FLOW G	spring
DRY TOL.	moderate
SALT TOL.	moderate
LIGHT	full sun
SOIL	humid, water-retentive
NUTRIT.	balanced fertilizer annually; deep, organic mulch
HAZARDS	none
PROBLEMS	none
ENVIRON.	none
PROPAG.	seeds; cuttings
LEAVES	needle-like; light green, 2-ranked; linear on deciduous shoots
FLOWERS	inconspicuous; dioecious; male inflorescence to 20 cm (8 in.)
FRUIT	a cone; male cones, slender; female cones, ovoid
USE	public open space; specimen for large garden
ZONE	9–11

T. mucronatum; photographed at the Arboretum of Los Angeles, California, USA. Its foliage has turned rusty brown before the twigs and lvs are aborted.

T. mucronatum; terminal shoot with buds.

T. mucronatum, with *T. distichum*, to the right at the Arboretum of Los Angeles, California.

T. distichum; typically covered in Spanish Moss.

Taxodium mucronatum is native to river valleys at high altitudes, while *T. distichum* grows in flooding river-bottoms and coast. swamps (like the Everglades swamp of S Florida, USA). They are often buttressed and, in wet conditions, surrounded in aerial, conical roots or pneumataphores. In cultivation neither sp. needs waterside or flooding soils and both are frost-tol., but may be damaged below about -10 °C (14 °F). *T. distichum* is very tol. of city air and alkaline soils.

Tecoma stans

YELLOW ELDER

(L.) Kunth.   13 spp.

Stenolobium stans

BIGNONIACEAE

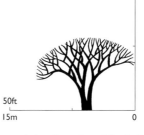

50ft ⌐15m

50ft
15m   0

TECOMA STANS is the national flower of both the Bahamas and the American Virgin Is. In Bahamas, it is known as Yellow Elder or Trumpet Flower, while the Virgin Islanders know it as Ginger Thomas. In the Cayman Is, however, where it is listed as a native plant but is doubtfully so, being found only in areas of habitation, it is known, strangely, as Shamrock. Popular and useful plants such as this tend to be endowed with a wealth of common names. Perhaps Yellow Elder makes most sense, as its foliage and cane-like new growth does greatly resemble that of *Sambucus*, the true Elder. *T. stans* is more commonly met as a shrub with a much-branched habit, dividing low on its trunk, although it may attain respectable tree size, with striated, shaggy bark. *T. stans* is a winter-flowering species with an extremely long blooming period. It responds to short day length (photoperiod), when the days are about 12 hours long, and produces billowing, slightly fragrant, golden *Tabebuia*-like blooms. Unfortunately, they are quickly replaced by bundles of ugly, green pods that, when ripe, release their winged seeds to germinate freely. For the patient gardener, these fruit may be cut away to promote new flushes of bloom. The sapwood is light brown and hard, but the wood is seldom available in a size large enough for practical use, although it is recorded as having been used in cabinetmaking, wood turning and construction. The bark, leaves and roots have been employed in home medicines, including use as a diuretic. This is a honey plant.

*** *T. stans* × 'Burchii'; (Will. Watts.), to 8 m (26 ft). Blooming non-stop without messy fruit, this form is most desirable. Otherwise, it is very similar to *T. stans*.

*** *T.* × *smithii*; (Will. Wats.) (*T. arequipensis* × *T. stans*), (syn *T. alata*), Australia and New Zealand, with golden trumpets with reflexed lobes, suffused deep orange. (10–12)

NOTE: this species may be very invasive in sandy soils.

ORIGIN	Trop. America
HEIGHT	up to 8 m (26 ft)
TYPE	deciduous, small flowering tree
STATUS	not threatened
HABITAT	sandy or rocky limestone thickets
GROWTH	fast
FLOWG	winter
DRY TOL.	high
SALT TOL.	high
LIGHT	full sun
SOIL	well-drained, fertile
NUTRIT.	apply fertilizer after pruning
HAZARDS	none
PROBLEMS	invasive
ENVIRON.	bee nectar
PROPAG.	seeds
LEAVES	pinnate; bright green; leaflets elliptic, to 10 cm (4 in.); with saw-toothed margins
FLOWERS	showy; bright yellow; funnelform, campanulate; slightly fragrant
FRUIT	a capsule, to 25 cm (10 in.); compressed, linear, dehiscent; seeds winged
USE	seaside; small flowering tree; screening; flowering border; large planter; bright conservatory; xerophytic
ZONE	10–12

T. stans; a sturdy specimen laden with winter bloom at Jardin Botanico de Cienfuegos, S Cuba.

T. stans; fls quickly change to bundles of ugly fr. pods.

T. stans × 'Burchii'; blooming non-stop without messy fr., this form is most desirable.

T. × *smithii*; a small hybrid sp. with small, golden yellow trumpets suffused with orange.

100ft ⌐ 30m

75ft
22.5m   0

Tectona grandis

TEAK

L. f.   4 spp.

VERBENACEAE

ORIGIN	SE Asia
HEIGHT	up to 50 m (164 ft)
TYPE	deciduous, large foliage tree
STATUS	threatened
HABITAT	well-drained, humid forests
GROWTH	moderate
FLOWG	summer to autumn
DRY TOL.	moderate
SALT TOL.	low
LIGHT	full sun
SOIL	deep, well-drained
NUTRIT.	balanced fertilizer annually; deep, organic mulch
HAZARDS	none
PROBLEMS	none
ENVIRON.	bee nectar
PROPAG.	scarified seeds; root suckers
LEAVES	simple; rich green; mature leaves to 75 cm (30 in.); tomentose below, broadly ovate; with long petioles
FLOWERS	showy; dull white; held in huge, erect, airy panicles
FRUIT	a drupe, to 1.5 cm (0.6 in.); light brown, hairy ball; contained in enlarged calyx
USE	public open space; specimen; botanic collection
ZONE	10—12

THE OPULENT AND PRESTIGIOUS TEAK of garden seats and salad bowls, of decks, blanket chests and grand yachts is one of the world's great timber trees and a native of the deep, equatorial lowland soils of SE Asia. *Tectona grandis* is a giant *Verbena*, with many of the familiar characteristics of that great family. There are not many trees in this clan of soft herbs, but the exception is exceptional. In its native forests, *T. grandis* grows a tall, straight, slender trunk that is deeply grooved and fluted, with soft bark that peels off. Square-stemmed, young growth supports a voluminous canopy of enormous, short-petioled, ovate, deeply veined, felted leaves that flap in the wind like elephant ears. (The leaves of a young sapling are many times larger.) From summer to autumn, terminal, erect, flowering branches hold huge panicles of starry white *Verbena*-like flowers above the foliage. As they fade, enlarged, thin, finely fuzzy, inflated calyxes about 2.5 cm (1 in.) across enclose the fruit, which is a light brown, hairy ball. Teak is the most important timber tree of the SE Asia monsoon region. It grows relatively fast at first, but slows down once established. *T. grandis* sapwood is yellowish or whitish, while the heartwood is olive-green when freshly cut, turning golden brown upon seasoning. The wood is moderately strongly aromatic, hard, heavy, strong and straight-grained (it contains silica, which dulls cutting blades), but it is only the heartwood that is useful; the sapwood, being susceptible to termites, is not durable. Celebrated for its indestructibility, the oily, aromatic Teak wood lends itself to outdoor use and to boatbuilding and is sought after around the world. It may be cut illegally in its regional habitats, causing a huge problem in the deforestation of SE Asia. *T. grandis* leaves are a source of a brown-red dye in Malesia. This is a honey tree.

T. grandis; large, airy panicles of fls and fr.

T. stans; Teak wood lends itself to outdoor use and boatbuilding and is sought-after around the world.

T. grandis; an enlarged, thin, egg-shaped calyx encloses the fr., which is a light brown, hairy ball.

T. grandis; Teak in full, glorious autumn bloom at Flecker Botanic Gardens in Cairns, N Qld, Australia.

Terminalia catappa

PACIFIC ALMOND

L.   150 spp.

T. latifolia; T. mauritiana

COMBRETACEAE

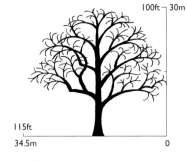

100ft — 30m

115ft

34.5m — 0

ORIGIN	from Trop. Asia to Australia and the Pacific
HEIGHT	up to 35 m (115 ft)
TYPE	deciduous, large foliage tree
STATUS	not threatened
HABITAT	dry, coastal scrub and woodland
GROWTH	fast
FLOWG	twice a year
DRY TOL.	high
SALT TOL.	high
LIGHT	full sun
SOIL	well-drained
NUTRIT.	not normally necessary
HAZARDS	none
PROBLEMS	invasive
ENVIRON.	insect nectar; wild fruit for birds and bats
PROPAG.	seeds
LEAVES	simple; rich green; to 23 cm (9 in.); glossy, spathulate, turning deep red with age
FLOWERS	inconspicuous; greenish white; in erect, narrow racemes; fragrant
FRUIT	a drupe, to 5 cm (2 in.); elliptic, flattened, beaked, fleshy; seeds with edible kernel
USE	seaside; public open space; xerophytic
ZONE	10—12

ALONG WITH *CASUARINA* AND COCONUTS, *Terminalia catappa* is one of the most common trees of many tropical coasts. It is immediately recognizable from its stiff, horizontal limbs and huge, spoon-shaped leaves set in rosettes at the tips of their stubby twigs. It is, in fact, superficially similar to *Barringtonia asiatica*, which is also a coastal species. *Terminalia* species are distinguished by their dichotomous branching – branches that divide repeatedly and regularly in pairs, with the 2 branches of each fork roughly equal. Twice a year, in early spring and late summer, the foliage of the *T. catappa* turns bright red and the tree suddenly sheds all its leaves. With the new foliage, every terminal rosette sprouts a fountain of long, slender spikes of tiny, star-like flowers that attract thousands of bees. In no time at all, these have spawned oblong, beaked, yellow, fleshy fruit. It is now the turn of the fruit bats that swoop around at night, leaving the ravages of their feast scattered below. These fruit have a sweetish, fibrous flesh that is palatable when very young and usually liked by children. The kernel of the fruit has a delicate, almond flavour, but is difficult to remove. As the last of the fruit fall, it is time for the cycle to begin again. This is definitely not a tree for a neat, ornamental garden. The sapwood of *T. catappa* is a light, reddish brown, while the heartwood, which is deep, red-brown with slightly darker stripes, is hard, moderately heavy and strong, tough and medium-textured, but is very susceptible to termites. In E Africa, a black dye that is used to make ink is extracted from the bark and fruit, while the leaves yield a yellow-green dye. Oil is pressed from the seeds and used in the treatment of abdominal swellings and scabies.

NOTE: *T. catappa* is an extremely invasive species in many parts of the tropical world.

T. catappa; with long, slender fl. spikes; fls are nectar-rich for bees.

T. catappa; twice a year, foliage turns bright red and the tree suddenly dumps all its lvs. Photographed in Homestead, S Florida, USA, renowned for its vast horticultural nursery industry.

T. catappa; beaked, short-stalked fr. quickly replaces fls to provide a larder for bats.

T. catappa; slightly sweet, white flesh of yellow or orange fr. is edible, while the fibrous interior contains an oily nut.

Terminalia arenicola; (Byrnes), NE Australia endemic, to 12 m (39 ft). Lvs are orbicular to 15 × 7 cm (6 × 2.8 in.), pubescent; fls are white and fragrant. The globular fr. are easily distinguished: they are sharply beaked and broadly winged, with the red, fleshy skin covered with a deep blue bloom. Lvs are bright red in autumn. This is a salt-resistant sp. and was photographed on Wonga Beach off the Great Barrier Reef, N Qld, Australia. (9–12)

Terminalia chebula; (Retz.), (*T. tomentella*), Indomal., to 20 m (66 ft). Young shoots densely, orange-brown hairy; mature lvs are smooth with a pr of glands near the top of the stalk or along the lf margins. Fls are green-white, in dense spikes. Fr. greenish yellow, ripening orange-brown, globose or oval; very high in tannins and widely used in the leather industry. Source of yellow and black dye, and with antibacterial and anti-fungal properties. Eaten in Pakistan. (10–12)

Terminalia ferdinandiana; (Exell.) northern Australia, to 10 m (33 ft), Billy Goat Plum, sturdy, decid., understorey tree with red latex and large, rounded, long-petioled lvs and profuse, cream fl. spikes. Fr., to 2.5 cm (1 in.), is edible, fleshy, beaked, yellow-green and exceptionally high in vitamin C (50 times more than oranges and possibly the highest in world). Currently researched for commercial potential. Gum has many medicinal applications. (9–11)

Terminalia grandiflora; (Benth.), W and N Australia endemic, to 15 m (50 ft). Slender, pendulous sp. demonstrates the enormous variation in this large genus. A common, understorey tree in open woodland, extending into dry regions. Narrow, willowy lvs are spiralled towards ends of branchlets; showy, long-stamened, scented, greenish cream fls. Fr. is a purple, oval, edible, drupe to 4 cm (1.6 in.); kernel is eaten by Aborigines. (10–12)

Terminalia

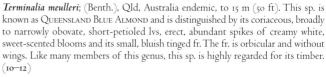

Terminalia kaernbachii; (Warb.), (syn *T. okari*) S New Guinea endemic, OKARI or OKARI NUT is a handsome, large tree with large, obovate lvs. It is renowned for its ovoid or obovoid fr., to 48 cm (19 in.) long, which turns deep, reddish purple when ripe. The large kernel, which is set in a fibrous pulp, has a dark brown testa and is relished by New Guineans who eat it raw or cooked. It has been described as one of the finest trop. nuts. (**10–12**)

Terminalia meulleri; (Benth.), Qld, Australia endemic, to 15 m (50 ft). This sp. is known as QUEENSLAND BLUE ALMOND and is distinguished by its coriaceous, broadly to narrowly obovate, short-petioled lvs, erect, abundant spikes of creamy white, sweet-scented blooms and its small, bluish tinged fr. The fr. is orbicular and without wings. Like many members of this genus, this sp. is highly regarded for its timber. (**10–12**)

Terminalia myriocarpa; (Heurk. and Meull.), SE Asia, to 15 m (50 ft). At first glance, this everg. tree would never be thought a member of *Terminalia* genus. It seems so untypical of its family and genus, with its apparently pinnate lvs and abundant, branched, rosy branched fl. clusters. Fr. is 4 × 2 mm (0.16 × 0.08 in.), ellipsoid, compressed, sericeous, 2-winged. (**10–12**)

Terminalia paniculata; (Roth.), India endemic. KINDAL is a decid. sp. of W Bombay and Madras states. It is easily recognized by its bundles of bright, rusty rose, papery, winged pods, which resemble dried Hydrangea fl. heads, which are formed in late summer or autumn. Its bark contains much tannin, but the wood, which is light brown and hard, is little used locally. (**10–12**)

Terminalia sericea; (Burchell.), S Africa, to 13 m (43 ft). SILVER CLUSTER-LEAF is a decid. tree with silvery grey, scurfy, leathery, short-petioled lvs in rosettes at the ends of branches. Spikes of creamy white fls are followed by bundles of ornamental, purplish red, broadly winged, flattened fr. Wood is yellow, hard and useful; roots are widely used medicinally. Photographed at Mt Coot-tha Botanic Gardens, Brisbane, Qld, Australia. (9–11)

Terminalia sericocarpa; (F. Muell.), N Australia endemic, to 30 m (100 ft). A large, fast-growing, decid. sp. of coast., humid vine-thickets or banks of lowland streams. It has a buttressed trunk and a widespread, layered, densely foliaged crown. Cream, strongly scented fls are held in narrow spikes; fr. are flattish, ovoid, fleshy, silky hairy, becoming smooth, slightly ridged, pink, purple or red, to 1.8 cm (0.7 in.), thin-fleshed and edible. (9–12)

Photographed on the banks of one of the small lakes at Fairchild Tropical Gardens, Miami, Florida, USA., QUEENSLAND BLUE ALMOND, *Terminalia muelleri*, an Australian endemic sp., demonstrates its kinship with *T. catappa* in its layered, sympodial growth and broadly spathulate (but smaller) lvs. The *Terminalia* spp. represented here give some idea of the amazing diversity of this widespread genus of 150 spp. trop. trees, which are valuable for their timber, dyes, tannin, medicinal properties, gums, nut kernels and edible fr. Sweetly fragrant fls are an important source of nectar for bees and the fr. attracts bats, parrots and other fruit-eating birds. *Terminalia* are widely grown for shade, timber, fruit, ornament and as street trees.

Theobroma cacao

COCOA

L.   20 spp

MALVACEAE (formerly Sterculiaceae)

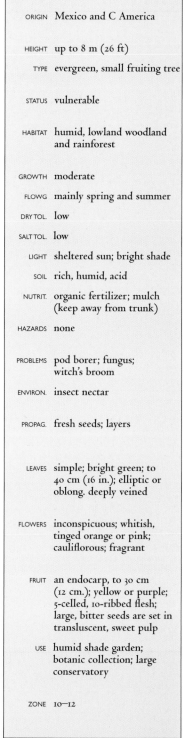

COCOA WAS CULTIVATED BY THE AZTECS AND MAYANS, who considered it divine. Linnaeus gave it the generic name of *Theobroma*, meaning, 'food of the gods'. **Theobroma cacao** is an understorey forest plant requiring rich soil, humidity, shade and shelter to thrive; it is therefore over-planted with fast-growing, light-canopied, evergreen trees. With a low-spreading, somewhat sparse, scruffy canopy, its thin, large leaves have a tendency to hang downwards in a languid, parched manner. New growth is flaccid and salmon-pink, like a mango. The tiny, long-stalked flowers are cauliflorous. As they are often self-sterile, several trees are planted to ensure fertilization. **T. cacao** fruit resemble large melons and may have yellow or reddish purple skin. When ripe, they glow like lanterns, illuminating the interior of the tree. The ripe fruit contains whitish, mucilaginous flesh in which are embedded large, bitter, brown or purplish seeds – or 'beans' – that are covered in a hard, brittle shell. The oily kernels within are pressed, fermented and dried, the cured beans then being roasted and ground into powder to make cocoa. A butter-like fat (cocoa butter) is also extracted from the beans and the sweet pulp surrounding the seeds has, historically, been enjoyed as a snack food by indigenous peoples. There are 3 main types of **T. cacao**: Criollo Cacaos (red-skinned, highest grade but low-yielding) originated in C America; Forastero Cacaos from the Amazon Basin, and Trinitario (high-grade) Cacaos arose in Trinidad. In Africa, the husks are burnt, pounded and made into a paste that has a soapy residue and is used for washing clothes. Early Aztecs and Mayans made a traditional, aromatic drink known as Kukuh from pounded cocoa beans mixed with maize and chilli pepper; it continues to be a popular drink in Guatemala and Belize.

ORIGIN	Mexico and C America
HEIGHT	up to 8 m (26 ft)
TYPE	evergreen, small fruiting tree
STATUS	vulnerable
HABITAT	humid, lowland woodland and rainforest
GROWTH	moderate
FLOWG	mainly spring and summer
DRY TOL.	low
SALT TOL.	low
LIGHT	sheltered sun; bright shade
SOIL	rich, humid, acid
NUTRIT.	organic fertilizer; mulch (keep away from trunk)
HAZARDS	none
PROBLEMS	pod borer; fungus; witch's broom
ENVIRON.	insect nectar
PROPAG.	fresh seeds; layers
LEAVES	simple; bright green; to 40 cm (16 in.); elliptic or oblong. deeply veined
FLOWERS	inconspicuous; whitish, tinged orange or pink; cauliflorous; fragrant
FRUIT	an endocarp, to 30 cm (12 cm.); yellow or purple; 5-celled, 10-ribbed flesh; large, bitter seeds are set in transluscent, sweet pulp
USE	humid shade garden; botanic collection; large conservatory
ZONE	10—12

T. cacao; tiny fls are often self-sterile.

T. cacao; ripe, swollen, melon-like fr. glow like golden lanterns in the shadowy interior of the Cocoa trees. The skin may be deep yellow or reddish purple.

T. cacao; large, 5-celled fr. have many large, bitter-tasting, pulpy sds. They are only shortly viable for planting.

T. cacao: large lvs have a tendency to hang downwards in a languid, parched manner. New lvs are salmon-pink.

(1) ***Theobroma grandiflorum***; ([Willd. ex Spreng.] Schum.); (syn. *Bruboma grandiflorum*), eastern and central Amazonia, to 8 m (26 ft), known in Brazil as CUPUAÇU, this small sp. has large, drooping, sub-coriaceous, dark green, elliptic, short-petioled lvs to 40 cm (16 in.), which are whitish below. (2) *T. grandiflorum* is distinguished by its bisexual, slightly scented fls, which are held in short-stalked, rusty pubescent clusters. Enclosed in a very thick, 5-parted, deeply lobed, persistent calyx, which holds small, dark red fls with 5 hooded, clawed petals. (3) Fr. measures to 25 cm (10 in.); it is rusty velvety, may weigh up to 1.5 kg (3.3 lbs) and contains 20– 50 large sds set in dense, slightly fibrous, delicately flavoured, milky white pulp, popular locally and eaten in sorbets, ice creams, desserts and for making aroma-rich drinks. The sds supply a substitute for cocoa and the tree is grown both domestically and commercially. Sds are shortly viable and must be sown immediately they are harvested.

A small grove of ***Theobroma cacao*** in Havanna, Cuba; they are over-planted with *Albizia lebbek* trees that provide light shade. This small plantation is sufficient to provide this farmer with chocolate for his large family.

Thespesia populnea

PORTIA TREE

(L.) Sol.   17 spp.

MALVACEAE

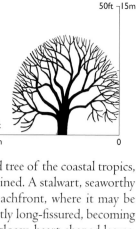

50ft ⌐15m

50ft
15m   0

THESPESIA POPULNEA, a languid, soft-wooded, loose-limbed tree of the coastal tropics, has a disorganized, even unruly growth; it is, however easily disciplined. A stalwart, seaworthy species, **T. populnea** is unparalleled for planting right on the beachfront, where it may be used for screening, hedging or shade. The pale grey trunk is distinctly long-fissured, becoming somewhat corky with age. It supports a globular crown of dark, glossy, heart-shaped leaves, but its succulent limbs have a tendency to criss-cross in a haphazard manner. Superficially, this species greatly resembles *Hernandia nymphaeifolia*. The flowers are sparse and mostly hidden in the foliage, but on close inspection are quite lovely, being pale yellow and bell-shaped, with frilled, spiralled petals. They gradually deepen to a luminous purplish pink during a 24-hour period, before being shed. **T. populnea** fruit are designed for sea voyages and have slightly wrinkled, waterproof skins for this purpose, explaining the pan-tropical distribution of this species. In the Pacific, the Portia Tree (or Milo, in Hawaii) has provided many elements for village life. The chocolate-brown and cream-coloured heartwood, known as Pacific Rosewood in some parts, is most handsome, like chocolate and vanilla swirled together; it is soft, durable and termite-proof. Traditional bowls, gunstocks and artifacts are fashioned from it. The tough, fibrous bark provides cordage, while the leaves and flowers are eaten fresh or cooked, or used as fodder. Tannin, dye, oil and gum are all found in this species, which has also been found to have medicinal properties. In many coastal regions, it is planted as a street tree. **T. populnea** is seldom seen without its little red, 'push-me-pull-you' cotton stainer beetles (*Dysdercus* sp.); this is one reason why this species has been eradicated in some cotton-growing regions.

NOTE: this species may prove invasive in some regions.

ORIGIN	pan-tropics
HEIGHT	up to 10 m (33 ft)
TYPE	evergreen foliage (flowering) tree
STATUS	not threatened
HABITAT	coastal scrub; mangrove swamps
GROWTH	fast
FLOWG.	year-round
DRY TOL.	high
SALT TOL.	high
LIGHT	full sun
SOIL	water-retentive
NUTRIT.	not normally necessary
HAZARDS	none
PROBLEMS	cotton stainer beetle
ENVIRON.	insect nectar
PROPAG.	seeds; large cuttings
LEAVES	simple; deep green; cordate, long-petioled; glossy
FLOWERS	showy; pale yellow, deepening to purple-pink; aborting in 24 hrs
FRUIT	a capsule, to 3.5 cm (1.3 in.); depressed-globose, obscurely 5-angled
USE	seaside; small shade tree; coastal screening; coastal street tree; hedging; xerophytic
ZONE	10–12

T. populnea; fr. with waterproof jackets.

T. populnea; the *Hibiscus*-like blooms open a pale yellow with a deep, purplish pink eye. Like the closely related *Hibiscus tiliaceus*, they deepen in colour as the day progresses.

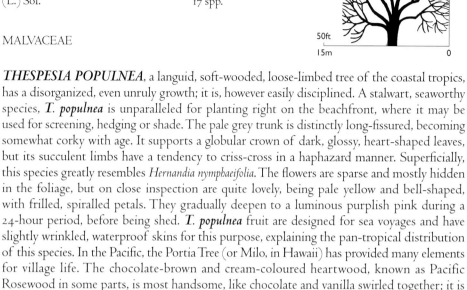

T. populnea; languidly looping, disorganized growth is quite easily tamed. Portia Tree is excellent for seaside planting.

T. populnea; this tree is seldom seen without its little red, 'push-me-pull-you' cotton stainer beetles.

Thevetia peruviana

LUCKY NUT

(Pers.) Schumann   8 spp.

T. neriifolia; Cascabela thevetia

APOCYNACEAE

ORIGIN	Trop. America
HEIGHT	up to 7 m (23 ft)
TYPE	evergreen, small flowering tree
STATUS	not threatened
HABITAT	dry, lowland thickets and scrubland
GROWTH	fast
FLOWG	year-round
DRY TOL.	high
SALT TOL.	high
LIGHT	full sun
SOIL	fertile, well-drained
NUTRIT.	balanced fertilizer annually
HAZARDS	very poisonous sap
PROBLEMS	caterpillars; possibly weedy
ENVIRON.	insect nectar
PROPAG.	seeds
LEAVES	simple; bright green; to 15 cm (6 in.); linear, glossy
FLOWERS	showy; lemon-yellow, salmon-pink or white; tubular-campanulate
FRUIT	a syncarp, to 3 cm (1.2 in.); triangular, with green flesh, ripening black; with 2 diamond-shaped, woody seeds
USE	seaside; small flowering tree; screening; hedging; accent; topiary; median strip; xerophytic
ZONE	10–11

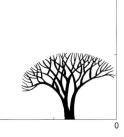

50ft ⌐15m

50ft
15m   0

THEVETIA PERUVIANA is often called Yellow Oleander – and for good reason. Without its flowers, this species could easily be mistaken for *Nerium oleander.* (In fact, the synonym for this species is *Thevetia neriifolia.*) This fast-growing Trop. American native species forms a fairly slender, supple, spreading shrub or small tree, with a sparse, light green crown of narrow, lustrous, crowded leaves. Every part of *T. peruviana* has extremely poisonous, milky latex. Despite this, it is widely popular for its attractive habit and constant, sweetly scented, bell-shaped, short-lived, apricot, yellow or white blooms, as well as for its stalwart tolerance of drought and salty conditions. The green (and later blackish), fleshy, triangular fruit contains 2 large seeds. These diamond-shaped, pale buff, woody seeds are worn as pendants or carried as good-luck charms in some parts of its region – hence the common name, Lucky Nut. It is, however, most unlucky for those who mistakenly eat any part of this extremely poisonous plant. The milky latex contains Thevetin (glucoside), a chemical like digitalis, that is a heart depressant and slows the pulse, causing vomiting and shock. In India, it is used as a means of committing suicide. In Mexico, however, it is administered as an extract against malaria and high fevers, while in Brazil, indigenous people throw chips of *Thevetia* wood into streams to paralyse and catch fish. In Australia, *T. peruviana* has been withdrawn from the nursery trade because several children have died after eating the fruit.

*** *T. thevetioides*; ([HBK] K. Schum.), (syn. *T. yccotli*), Mexico, to 7 m (23 ft). Yccotli differs from *T. peruviana* in having leaves that are downy below. The yellow flowers are larger, more showy and held in loose, terminal panicles. (9–11)

NOTE: in some lowland regions *T. peruviana* has escaped cultivation.

T. peruviana; ripe, diamond-shaped sds are used as charms in some regions.

T. thevetioides; with large, loose panicles of large, widely flaring blooms.

T. peruviana; although mostly clipped and grown as a screen or tall shrub, it does make an elegant small tree.

T. peruviana; both salmon-pink and yellow forms are commonly grown in dry, trop. and subtrop. regions. They are fast-growing, salt- and dry-tol. and of easy culture.

415

Tibouchina granulosa

PURPLE SPRAY TREE

Cogn.   243 spp.

Melastoma granulosa

MELASTOMACEAE

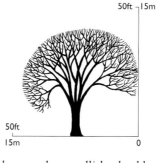

50ft ─ 15m

50ft
15m   0

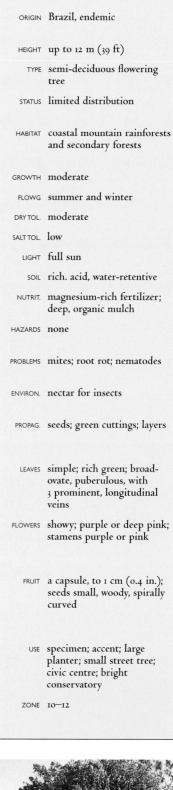

ORIGIN	Brazil, endemic
HEIGHT	up to 12 m (39 ft)
TYPE	semi-deciduous flowering tree
STATUS	limited distribution
HABITAT	coastal mountain rainforests and secondary forests
GROWTH	moderate
FLOWG	summer and winter
DRY TOL.	moderate
SALT TOL.	low
LIGHT	full sun
SOIL	rich. acid, water-retentive
NUTRIT.	magnesium-rich fertilizer; deep, organic mulch
HAZARDS	none
PROBLEMS	mites; root rot; nematodes
ENVIRON.	nectar for insects
PROPAG.	seeds; green cuttings; layers
LEAVES	simple; rich green; broad-ovate, puberulous, with 3 prominent, longitudinal veins
FLOWERS	showy; purple or deep pink; stamens purple or pink
FRUIT	a capsule, to 1 cm (0.4 in.); seeds small, woody, spirally curved
USE	specimen; accent; large planter; small street tree; civic centre; bright conservatory
ZONE	10–12

THE GLORY BUSH FAMILY of plants is mostly known by popular, smallish, shrubby species, especially *Tibouchina urvilleana* (syn. *T. semidecandra*). Of the 243 species, all are found in Trop. America – many from Brazil – where they are mostly found at middle to high elevations on freely draining, steep slopes and stream banks, often on the fringe of secondary forest. Many gardeners do not realize that this big family counts several splendid trees amongst its members, such as **Tibouchina granulosa,** which is native to Brazil, where it is known as Quaresmeira and grows to be a medium-sized tree with a sturdy trunk and wide, dense canopy. Typical of its family, the Melastomaceae, are its finely pubescent leaves, with their 3 strong, longitudinal veins impressed on the upper surface. Another feature is that the stamens and style are usually the same colour as the petals, in this case, purple on bright red stems. In Australia, where *Tibouchina* are very popular, many exciting new forms of this species have been developed, such as the superb, bright pink cultivar 'Kathleen'. Like most Melastomaceae, *Tibouchina* species require acid soil, although they may tolerate neutral soil if given amendments. In favourable conditions, they may bloom sporadically throughout the year.

*** **T. lepidota**; ([Bonpland.] Baillon), Colombia, to 6 m (20 ft), is a species of the high plains that forms a multi-stemmed, spreading canopy of large, 3-veined, puberulous leaves. Flowers are rich purple, held in congested clusters at branch tips. Summer flowering. Cv. 'Alstonville' is an outstanding Australian form of this species. (10–11)

*** **T. mutabilis**; (Cogn.), Brazil, to 12 m (39 ft), FLORA-DE-MAIO, a pioneer plant of coastal highland rainforest. This species has flowers that change colour: they open deep pink, gradually lighten to pale pink and, with age, they fade to pinkish white. The trunk and limbs are very pale. With flushes of bloom all year. (9–11)

NOTE: Tibouchina spp. has proved invasive in Hawaii.

T. mutabilis; the fls open pink and gradually fade to pinkish white.

T. granulosa; cv. 'Kathleen'; thrives in Sydney, Australia. Unlike the true form of this sp., Kathleen is bright pink with pink stamens; it fades to white in age.

T. lepidota; fls are rich purple held in congested clusters at branch tips.

T. lepidota cv. 'Alstonville'; an outstanding cv. originating in Dunstan's Nursery in Alstonville, NE NSW , Australia.

ORIGIN	Brazil, Argentina and Bolivia
HEIGHT	up to 35 m (115 ft)
TYPE	semi-evergreen, large flowering tree
STATUS	not threatened
HABITAT	inland river valleys
GROWTH	fast
FLOWG	spring to summer
DRY TOL.	moderate
SALT TOL.	low
LIGHT	full sun
SOIL	fertile, well-drained
NUTRIT.	balanced fertilizer annually; deep, organic mulch
HAZARDS	none
PROBLEMS	none
ENVIRON.	nectar for insects
PROPAG.	seeds
LEAVES	pinnate; greyish blue-green; leaflets oblanceolate, in 3–11 pairs, to 5.5 cm (2.2 in.); oval, thin-textured
FLOWERS	showy; deep yellow to apricot; held in pendulous panicles
FRUIT	a legume, to 6.5 cm (2.6 in.); samaroid, winged; seeds 1–3
USE	large flowering tree; shade tree; street tree; public open space
ZONE	9–11

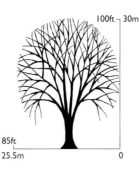

100ft — 30m
85ft
25.5m — 0

Tipuana tipu

PRIDE OF BOLIVIA

(Benth.) G. Kuntze   1 sp.

T. speciosa

FABACEAE (Papilionoideae)

TIPUANA TIPU derives its name from the Tipuani Valley in Bolivia, where it is a common tree, extending to adjacent areas of Brazil and Argentina. A monospecific, vigorous, flat-topped legume in the manner of a Delonix, it may be briefly deciduous in midwinter but is almost always crowned with bluish, grey-green, soft, ferny foliage on pale yellow, downy branchlets. In early summer, the great, buoyant parasol becomes covered in abundant, pendulous sprays of pea-shaped blossoms that jostle for space in the wide, crowded canopy. Each little flower has a widely reflexed standard petal that is deep yellow to apricot, lined rusty red. Following the flowers, winged, samara-like, 1–3-seeded fruits develop. In Florida and California, USA, *T. tipu* is virtually evergreen and grows quickly, but growers in Cairns, NE Australia, have found it short-lived in the humid, lowland, tropical regions; it prefers a drier, monsoonal climate. It certainly thrives in the cooler subtropics; in equatorial regions, it requires an elevation of 300 m (100 ft) or more to thrive. *T. tipu* responds well to pruning when young, if a shapely form is wanted. Its pliable limbs may be thinned to produce an extremely open structure, or shortened to achieve greater density. As it matures, the tree slows down and its limbs spread more horizontally to form a widespread, dense canopy. This species is very popular as a street tree and for parks in cooler parts of S America, particularly in Argentina. *T. tipu* timber is pale yellow to brown, sometimes with a rosy hue, and is finely striped with dark lines. It is moderately hard and strong, somewhat similar to maple, and much valued in its region. In Argentina, the wood is known as Tipa Blanca and is used in general carpentry. The leaves are used in tanning and the bark for dyeing.

T. tipu; is happiest in a subtrop. climate.

T. tipu; trees in full, early summer bloom at Yungaburra in N Qld, Australia.

T. tipu; with pale green, samara fr. that contrasts beautifully with the bluish green, pinnate lvs.

T. tipu; with abundant, pendulous sprays of deep yellow and apricot, pea-shaped blossoms that jostle for space in the tree's wide, crowded canopy.

Toona ciliata

TOONA

M. Roem.   4–5 spp.

Cedrela toona

MELIACEAE

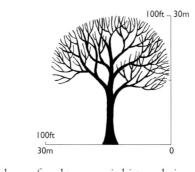

TOONA CILIATA, A.K.A. *CEDRELA TOONA*, has had a confused taxonomic history, being linked with the remarkable Cedrela, and divided into no fewer than 20 varieties by some authors. With a recent reassessment of the genus by taxonomists, **T. ciliata** now appears more secure in its identity. Lofty, with furrowed, scaly bark, this species has a buoyant canopy of long, graceful, pinnate leaves, which, when new, are flushed a luminous rosy crimson. Large clusters of small, fragrant, greenish white flowers develop in spring and are followed by brown, woody, 5-parted fruit, with 5-celled cores packed with lightweight, red, winged seeds. In Hawaii, where the fruit are known as Tree Wood Rose, Wood Jasmine or Wood Pikake, and where it has been planted for afforestation, they are prized for floral arrangements. *T. ciliata*, however, is celebrated for its timber. Lightweight, tough and resistant to insects and decay, the beautiful, reddish, fragrant Red Cedar is crafted into furniture and, more mundanely, used for construction, cigar boxes and fuel. In India, an infusion of Toona bark is used as a tonic. Unlike closely related *Swietenia* species, *T. ciliata* cannot endure drought or high winds.
*** *T. ciliata* var. *australis*; ([F. Meull.] C. DC.), Australia, to 50 m (164 ft). The AUSTRALIAN- or RED-CEDAR was extensively logged in rainforests along the east coast by timber-getters seeking the 'red-gold' and who rarely left large specimens. Sadly, this species is unsuited to monoculture plantations as its apical growth is severely damaged by the larvae of the Cedar Tip Moth, forcing excessive branching. Instead, it has been found that dispersed planting in small forest clearings safely protects young trees from the pest. (9–12)
*** *T. sureni*; (Bl.), Himalayan region. SUREN is very similar to the above species, but the seeds have 2 wings. Regionally, the bark is important medicinally. (9–12) These species are important honey trees.

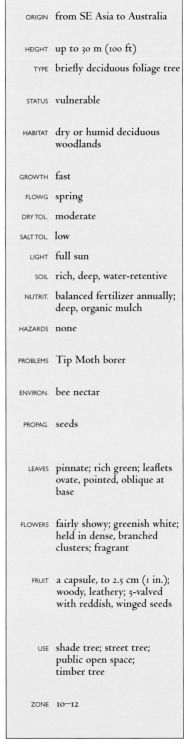

ORIGIN	from SE Asia to Australia
HEIGHT	up to 30 m (100 ft)
TYPE	briefly deciduous foliage tree
STATUS	vulnerable
HABITAT	dry or humid deciduous woodlands
GROWTH	fast
FLOWG	spring
DRY TOL.	moderate
SALT TOL.	low
LIGHT	full sun
SOIL	rich, deep, water-retentive
NUTRIT.	balanced fertilizer annually; deep, organic mulch
HAZARDS	none
PROBLEMS	Tip Moth borer
ENVIRON.	bee nectar
PROPAG.	seeds
LEAVES	pinnate; rich green; leaflets ovate, pointed, oblique at base
FLOWERS	fairly showy; greenish white; held in dense, branched clusters; fragrant
FRUIT	a capsule, to 2.5 cm (1 in.); woody, leathery; 5-valved with reddish, winged seeds
USE	shade tree; street tree; public open space; timber tree
ZONE	10–12

T. ciliata; var. *australis*; has white fls.

T. ciliata; a fine old specimen at the US Dept of Agriculture in Miami, Florida, where they have an historic arboretum of spp. that have been introduced to the USA.

T. ciliata; small, 5-valved dry fr. is known as 'Wood Rose' in Hawaii for the shape of its dried fr.

T. ciliata var. *australis*; this sp. has been extensively logged, leaving large trees like this one very rare.

ORIGIN	Trop. Africa and Madagascar
HEIGHT	up to 35 m (115 ft)
TYPE	evergreen, dioecious, large fruiting tree
STATUS	rare in some habitats
HABITAT	humid forests and rainforests
GROWTH	slow
FLOWG	year-round
DRY TOL.	moderate
SALT TOL.	low
LIGHT	part shade to full sun
SOIL	rich, deep, water-retentive
NUTRIT.	balanced fertilizer annually; deep, organic mulch
HAZARDS	toxic sap
PROBLEMS	none
ENVIRON.	insect nectar
PROPAG.	seeds; layers
LEAVES	simple, bright green; to 20 cm (8 in.); glabrous, oblong-ovate, leathery
FLOWERS	showy; males, green; held in globose, staminate heads, to 7 cm (2.7 in.); female flowers smaller
FRUIT	a syncarp, to 35 cm (13.7 in.); green, then yellow; rough skin; to 15 kg (33 lb); edible, with many seeds
USE	shade tree; fruiting tree; humid shade garden; botanic collection
ZONE	10—12

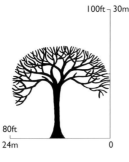

100ft – 30m

80ft
24m — 0

Treculia africana

AFRICAN BREADNUT

Decne. ex Trécul.   3 spp.

MORACEAE

IT IS EASY TO SEE THE KINSHIP between African Breadnut (*Treculia africana*) and fellow members of the great mulberry or fig tribe, Moraceae, such as jakfruit (jackfruit) or breadfruit (*Artocarpus* spp.), which differ only from *T. africana* in the number of stamens (2–3 instead of 1, respectively). In its native, rainforest habitat, it is found on the banks of rivers or in moist locations where it grows to a great height, with a mop of large, deep green, leathery leaves over a massive trunk, with a fluted bole up to 2.7 m (9 ft) in girth. The male flowers, to 7 cm (2.8 in.), of this dioecious species are globose, composed of tiny, tubular, greenish flowers, their stamens tipped with bright yellow pollen. The fertilized embryos of the smaller female flowers develop into a heavy, composite, fig-like fruit that may weigh up to 15 kg (33 lb). They begin green like a breadfruit and the finely knobbly skin turns yellow as it ripens, with abundant seeds buried in spongy, whitish pulp. These seeds are macerated before being dried and ground into a meal that is commonly used in soup, peeled and boiled or roasted and eaten as a dessert nut, or fried in oil as a savoury. In some regions, oil is extracted from ripe seeds, while in the Gold Coast they are used to make a beverage. The heartwood of *T. africana*, which is golden yellow or yellow-brown, very dense, flexible, heavy and finely grained, is known as African Boxwood and is suitable for furniture and fine carving. *Treculia* species exude abundant latex (or sap). The latex found in the male tree is caustic and toxic, but the bark of the female tree has several medicinal uses, particularly for coughs and as a laxative. In Guinea, W Africa, sap of *T. africana* is valued as a treatment for leprosy.
*** *T. obovoidea*; (NE Br.), Trop. W Africa, to 7 m (23 ft). A forest tree or shrub with copious latex. Fruit, like little hedgehogs, are borne on trunk and branches.

T. africana; male fls for a large, globular head.

T. africana; heartwood is golden yellow or yellow-brown, very dense, flexible, heavy and finely grained.

T. africana; a young tree at the Fruit and Spice Park, Homestead, Florida, USA.

T. africana; is a close relative of jakfruit (jackfruit) and breadfruit. The large, pulpy fr. may measure up to 35 cm (14 in.) and is packed with nutritious, oily sds with many local uses.

419

Trevesia burckii

GHOST'S FOOT

Boerl.   12 spp.

T. cheirantha; T. sanderi (hort.)

ARALIACEAE

THE ARALIA CLAN IS RENOWNED for its remarkable leaves rather than for flashy flowers — *Schefflera*, *Fatsia*, *Tetrapanax* and *Polyscias* are all clan members appreciated for their unusual, ornamental foliage. *Trevesia burckii* grows in humid lowland habitats along the banks of rivers and in rich valley forests as a tall shrub or small, single-trunked or sparsely branched pachychaul. These trees superficially resemble Papaya, but the trunk and limbs of *T. burckii* are armed with sharp thorns and are marked with large leaf scars. Like enormous snowflakes, the large, round leaves are deeply, palmately-lobed, with the 7 or more lobes pointed and elaborately toothed. Leaves are held out from the tree on metre-long, prickly or bristly stalks; young leaves emerge silvery tomentose, becoming deep, lustrous green as they mature. The red- or brown-hairy inflorescence may be up to 60 cm (24 in.) long and holds a whorl of long-stalked flower heads of either male or female flowers. Male flowers have white stamens set on an orange disc, females are yellow, with several green, sessile stigmas. They open morning and evening, when they smell faintly but sourly fragrant to appeal to their pollinators, bats, which also devour the succulent fruit. In Malaysia, there is a tale of a village which, on suffering a great defeat, took refuge in the forest where they ate, in desperation, the leaves of *T. burckii* and vanished.

*** *T. palmata*; (Roxb. ex Lindl.), India to S China, to 9 m (30 ft). SNOWFLAKE TREE may be either single-trunked or developing a coarse, wide crown. Stems are stout, thorny and hairy. Adult leaves are lustrous, palmately lobed and red pubescent below. The widely popular cv. 'Micholitzii' boasts lustrous, red-petioled, non-spiny leaves that are even more elaborately lobed than *T. burckii* and patched silver. The flowers are edible and the stems and leaves are believed to cure venereal disease. (10–12)

ORIGIN	SE Asia
HEIGHT	up to 10 m (33 ft)
TYPE	evergreen, small pachycaul foliage tree
STATUS	not threatened
HABITAT	humid forests or under-storey in rainforests
GROWTH	slow
FLOWG	spring
DRY TOL.	low to moderate
SALT TOL.	low
LIGHT	deep shade to part shade
SOIL	rich, water-retentive
NUTRIT.	organic fertilizer; deep, organic mulch
HAZARDS	spiny parts
PROBLEMS	none
ENVIRON.	insect nectar and fruit for bats
PROPAG.	seeds; cuttings
LEAVES	palmately lobed; dark green; with 7 or more deeply cut lobes, resembling snowflakes
FLOWERS	showy; creamy white; held in erect, sturdily stalked, hairy, red or brown, wheel-like panicles
FRUIT	a drupe or berry, to 1.5 cm (0.6 in.); fleshy, ovoid, yellow; with persistent style
USE	specimen; accent; humid shade garden; indoor plant; large container; large conservatory
ZONE	10–12

T. burckii; fls and fr. held in tight bundles.

T. burckii; a single-trunked specimen in the rainforest of Fairchild Tropical Gardens, Miami, Florida, USA.

T. burckii; like enormous snowflakes, the large, round lvs are deeply, palmately lobed.

T. burckii; may be single- or multi-trunked. These trunks and the lf petioles are protected by thorns.

ORIGIN	from Panama to N Peru
HEIGHT	up to 20 m (66 ft)
TYPE	evergreen, dioecious flowering tree
STATUS	not threatened
HABITAT	humid lowlands; seasonally-flooded plain
GROWTH	fast
FLOWG	late winter to spring
DRY TOL.	moderate
SALT TOL.	low
LIGHT	full sun
SOIL	rich, water-retentive
NUTRIT.	balanced fertilizer annually
HAZARDS	stinging ants
PROBLEMS	none
ENVIRON.	insect nectar
PROPAG.	seeds
LEAVES	simple; deep green; to 30 cm (12 in.); oblong, deeply veined
FLOWERS	showy; male flowers, inconspicuous; female flowers, 3-parted, bright, purplish red; abundant
FRUIT	an achene, to 4.5 cm (1.8 in.); with long, red, 3-parted, wing-like calyxes; in opulent panicles
USE	flowering tree; street tree; specimen; public open space
ZONE	10—12

Triplaris cumingiana

LONG JOHN

Fisch. & Mey. ex C.A. Mey   18 spp.

POLYGONACEAE

THIS IS 1 OF 3 very similar trees of Trop. America scientifically acclaimed for being *myrmecophytes*, i.e. inhabited by stinging ants that scrape away and consume the soft pithy medulla in the centre of the tree from its roots to the tips of its twigs. The ants enter the tree through tiny pinholes near the leaf stipules. Apart from having unsociable residents, ***Triplaris cumingiana*** is renowned for its elegance and grows in a tall, stately column with a straight, somewhat flattened or fluted trunk that is narrowly buttressed and clear of branches up to 15 m (50 ft) above the ground. The lofty trunk is beautifully mottled brown and light grey, with papery bark that peels in thin, rounded strips. Erect limbs hold the canopy in a narrow pyramid. *Triplaris* are dioecious trees and the spicate flowers of both sexes are quite inconspicuous; it is the females that eventually produce the remarkable 'floral' decorations. They comprise 3 tiny, velvety sepals that, on pollination, expand into 3 narrow wings to form a tiny shuttlecock-like parachute above the embryo. They change from green to white to rosy red, creating spectacular, plumey masses before each little fruit, equipped with its wings, is released to commence its spin earthwards. The sapwood of *T. cumingiana* is, of course, soft, but even so it is reported to have some use for construction in its native region. When used for firewood, it is coppiced and the stump resprouts several new, slender trunks.

NOTE: 2 other species, *T. americana*, (L.), Panama to S Brazil, to 30 m (100 ft), known as the ANT TREE, and *T. weigeltiana*, ([Rchb. f.] Kuntze.), (syn. *T. surinamensis*), Amazon Basin, Venezuela, Guiana, to 35 m (115 ft), known as LONG JACK, are very similar to *T. cumingiana*. They all require constant humidity.

NOTE: in Qld, Australia, *T. weigeltiana* has a reputation for being invasive.

T. cumingiana; plumey masses of 'fls.'

T. cumingiana; lofty trunk is beautifully mottled brown and light grey, with papery bark peeling in thin, rounded strips.

T. cumingiana; calyxes of the female fls expand into little shuttlecock-like parachutes.

T. cumingiana; in full, joyous, late winter bloom at Fairchild Tropical Gardens, Miami, Florida, USA.

Vitex agnus-castus

CHASTE TREE

L.   250 spp.

V. latifolia

LABIATAE (formerly Verbeneaceae)

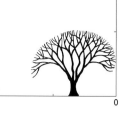

ORIGIN	S Europe
HEIGHT	up to 7 m (23 ft)
TYPE	deciduous, small flowering tree
STATUS	not threatened
HABITAT	dry deciduous woodland
GROWTH	fast
FLOWG	summer, or year-round
DRY TOL.	high
SALT TOL.	moderate
LIGHT	full sun
SOIL	fertile, well-drained
NUTRIT.	high-potassium fertilizer
HAZARDS	none
PROBLEMS	scales, fungus, nematodes
ENVIRON.	butterfly nectar; wild fruit for birds
PROPAG.	seeds; cuttings
LEAVES	digitate; greyish green, silvery below; pungently peppery aromatic
FLOWERS	showy; lilac or lavender; held in many-flowered terminal spikes; fragrant
FRUIT	a drupe, to 3 mm (0.1 in.); subglobose, black; held in abundant clusters
USE	small flowering tree; flowering border; large container; civic centre; xerophytic
ZONE	7–11

IT IS QUITE NATURAL THAT *Vitex agnus-castus* of S Europe should often be mistaken for *Buddleja davidii*: the flowers are strongly reminiscent of that genus and butterflies are frequent visitors. However, the intensely peppery-pungent, deep-green, 5–9 foliate leaves differentiate this genus; they are long-petioled and densely, silvery pubescent below. Tiny, lilac-blue or lavender, sweetly fragrant blooms are held in erect, slender panicles. They are quite long-lasting, decorating the tree with a spectacular display of nectar-rich, lavender candles. *V. agnus-castus*, like all *Vitex* species, produces masses of little fleshy drupes that provide a larder for fruit-eating birds. It was discovered by the Chinese several centuries ago and quickly became important in their traditional medicine. A preparation of the leaves, fruit and roots is used to prevent malaria and to treat colds, coughs and bacterial dysentery. In Indonesia, the leaves are used to treat abscesses and ulcers, while in Nepal, they are smoked for headaches, juice from the leaves is given for pneumonia, dried fruit is used as a de-wormer and roots used as a tonic. In Europe, the young, supple twigs are used to weave baskets and in some regions, the hot, spicy seeds act as a substitute for pepper. *V. agnus-castus* will grow and bloom in tropical regions, but is not really adapted to non-stop, tropical warmth. It tends to develop a pattern of dropping its leaves, regenerating new growth and blooming about once every 4 months. In tropical regions, where faded, old leaves become unsightly, it is better to cut back the plants severely after each flowering to encourage fresh growth.

*** *V. negundo*; (L.), Malaysia to Philippines, to 8.5 m (27 ft). HORSESHOE VITEX or LEGUNDI (Malaysia) and NIRGUNDI (India), is very like *V. trifolia* but differs in having its middle leaf stalked and in having smaller, paler blue flowers in widely branched panicles. Each tiny bloom has a yellow horseshoe mark on its lower lip – hence the common name. This species is often found near the sea and is considered fairly salt-resistant. (8–10)

V. trifolia; fleshy drupes with hot, spicy sds act as a substitute for pepper.

V. agnus-castus; is often mistaken for its cousin, *Buddleja davidii*: the fls are strongly reminiscent of that genus and butterflies are frequent visitors to the nectar-rich blooms.

V. agnus-castus; is a Mediterranean sp., which blooms most of the year in the tropics.

V. negundo; each tiny bloom has a yellow horseshoe mark on its lower lip – hence the common name, Horseshoe Vitex.

Vitex cofassus; (Reinw. ex Blume), from Malaysia to W Pacific, to 40 m (131 ft). This fast-growing sp. is highly valued for its timber, known as NEW GUINEA TEAK. It is used for carving drums and pestles (important domestically in Malaysia for grinding condiments). Its trunk to 2 m (6.5 ft) diam. and often buttressed. The fls may be blue, lilac, lavender or purple. Fr. is dark violet to black. (10–12) NOTE: this species is possibly invasive.

Vitex lucens; (D. Kirk.), New Zealand endemic, to 20 m (66 ft). PURIRI or KAUERE found from sea level to 750 m (2,461 ft). A massively trunked sp. with a large, twiggy, spreading canopy and abundant pink fls in winter, this sp. is one of N. Zealand's most valued hardwood timber trees. Because of its strength and durability, its timber was used extensively for bridges, wharf piles and railway sleepers and often compared to Italian walnut. (9–11)

Vitex parviflora; (Jusss.), from Malaysia, Philippines to Hawaii, to 16 m (52 ft). Known in Hawaii as MOLAVE or SMALL-FLOWERED VITEX, it is found in primary forest from sea level to 400 m (1,312 ft). Its tough, durable wood has proved invaluable for making agricultural implements. In Cuba, where this tree was photographed, it is very popular. In late spring, it enlivens the landscape with its clouds of soft, lilac-blue panicles. (10–12)

Vitex trifolia; (L.), from Asia to Australia; shrub or small tree, to 7 m (23 ft). COMMON BLUE VITEX or LEGUNDI has blackish bark, somewhat sprawling growth and 3-foliate, pungent lvs that are white tomentose below. Fls are held in a narrow, terminal panicle to 24 cm (9 in.), pale blue to purple, fragrant. Fr. is abundant, and black. This sp. is fairly salt-resistant. Both variegated and purple-tinged vars. exist. NOTE: all Vitex species are important honey plants. (9–12)

Wallaceodendron celebicum

BANUYO

Koord.   1 sp.

Pithecellobium williamsii

FABACEAE (Mimosoideae)

100ft ⌐ 30m

75ft
22.5m   0

WALLACEODENDRON CELEBICUM is found in low to medium elevations in seasonal (or monsoonal) deciduous forest that has a distinct wet and dry season. *W. celebicum* grows on thin limestone soil and is found in association with *Vitex parviflora*, *Pterocarpus indicus* and *Afzelia rhomboidea*. Even without its showy flowers, this leguminous mammoth of the Philippines is exceedingly elegant, its strong, lean form soaring upwards to create a stately framework for its voluptuous, little, 'pouffe-like' groupings of intensely green, polished foliage. Each pinnate leaf is composed of up to 7 pairs of glossy, leathery leaflets that hang neatly downwards and appear to have been sheared along their tips into a perfect, elongated shape. In early spring, each green, foliaged 'pillow' is accented by the deep rose of its reddish new growth. The inflorescence is bold and showy, being held erect in branched, velvety pyramids. The flowers have olive-brown, plush calyxes and white or yellow petals, opening to hold a mass of stamens typical of the Mimosaceae. The flowers are followed by large, oblong, leathery fruit that become dark brown and contain flat, circular seeds that are individually wrapped in a papery enclosure. The wood is moderately hard and in its native region is employed in the making of outriggers for canoes, household furniture and telegraph poles. Being a coastal species, *W. celebicum* is much used regionally as a street and shade tree in coastal settlements and towns. Despite being a legume, it bears a strong resemblance in its form and foliage to *Azadirachta indica*, the Neem Tree of the Mahogany (Meliaceae) family. *W. celebicum* is a monotypic species and is named in honour of the legendary naturalist, Alfred Russel Wallace (1823–1913). It is elegant, very salt-resistant and fast growing, and deserves to be more widely grown in tropical, coastal regions. This is a honey tree.

ORIGIN	Philippines, Sulawesi
HEIGHT	up to 70 m (230 ft)
TYPE	evergreen, very large foliage tree
STATUS	very limited distribution
HABITAT	coastal and inland humid forests
GROWTH	fast
FLOWG	early summer
DRY TOL.	moderate
SALT TOL.	high
LIGHT	full sun or bright shade
SOIL	rich, deep, water-retentive
NUTRIT.	high-nitrogen fertilizer; deep, organic mulch
HAZARDS	none
PROBLEMS	none
ENVIRON.	bat and moth nectar
PROPAG.	seeds
LEAVES	pinnate; bright green; to 7 pairs of leaflets, which are glossy, leathery and blunt-tipped
FLOWERS	showy; white or yellow; with long stamens; held in cone-like, ochre-tomentose heads; fragrant
FRUIT	a legume, to 15 cm (6 in.); oblong, thick, flat; with 1 circular seed
USE	seaside; large shade tree; street tree; public open space; xerophytic
ZONE	10–12

W. celebicum; the Banuyo is a lofty sp. that soars upwards in an elegant, lean, compact fashion. This is a coast. tree, making it most desirable for seaside planting.

W. celebicum; erect, olive-brown, velvety panicles of yellow fls in cone-like heads.

W. celebicum; the acutely pinnate lvs are held in little 'pouffes' at the ends of the twigs. The new growth is pale, rosy red.

W. celebicum; in its native region it is used in the making of outriggers for canoes, household furniture and telegraph poles.

424

ORIGIN	C and S America
HEIGHT	up to 8 m (26 ft)
TYPE	evergreen, small flowering tree
STATUS	not threatened
HABITAT	understorey in rainforest and humid river valleys
GROWTH	moderate
FLOWG	early summer
DRY TOL.	low
SALT TOL.	low
LIGHT	full sun to bright shade
SOIL	rich, humid, acid
NUTRIT.	magnesium-rich fertilizer; deep, organic mulch
HAZARDS	none
PROBLEMS	mealy bug; red spider mite
ENVIRON.	nectar for insects
PROPAG.	seeds; greenwood cuttings
LEAVES	simple; rich green, paler and densely pubescent below; new growth, red
FLOWERS	showy; orange-yellow; with 1 (or more) enlarged, scarlet calyxes
FRUIT	a capsule, to 5 mm (0.2 in.); oblong to subglobose, 2-celled; held in clusters
USE	small flowering tree; large planter; accent; humid shade garden; bright conservatory
ZONE	10–12

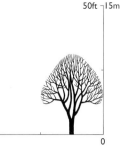

50ft ⌐15m

50ft
15m   0

Warszewiczia coccinea

CHACONIA

(Vahl.) Klotzsch.   4 spp.

Calycophyllum coccineum; Mussaenda coccineum

RUBIACEAE

NO COMPENDIUM OF TROPICAL TREES would be complete without this celebrated rainforest species. *Warszewiczia coccinea* is native of the Amazon River Basin and the humid forests from Costa Rica to Peru and Brazil, Trinidad and Venezuela. In Trinidad, it is commonly named Chaconia to commemorate the last Governor under Spanish rule, General Chacon. *W. coccinea* forms a slender, much-branched tree and is found abundantly in its region. Flowering in the early part of the rainy season, it brightens up its habitat with its long, narrow, darting sprays of scarlet flowers. The long, slender, rich green, deeply veined leaves are paler below. They have very short petioles and are held in bold whorls at the ends of the twigs; as they emerge, they are waxy red. Long, cymose flower spikes develop at the tips of the twigs. Minuscule, orange-yellow flowers are grouped in clustered heads along the length of the stem, with 1 bloom in each head being punctuated by a narrow, bright scarlet, leaf-like bract that is the decorative part of the bloom. The 2-celled, globose, dehiscent, fleshy fruit contains many very fine seeds. Although a most desirable ornamental, *W. coccinea* is not commonly planted as it requires high humidity and acid, volcanic soil. Sometimes called Jungle Poinsettia due to a resemblance to Poinsettia (*Euphorbia pulcherrima*) in the Euphorbiaceae family, it is, however, unrelated. Instead, it shares kinship and showy floral bracts with fellow Rubiaceae genera *Mussaenda*, *Pogonopus* and *Calycophyllum*.
*** cv. 'David Auyong' has a loose habit, with spreading branches. The leaves are large and waxy. The flowers are yellow on top of the rachis, circled by double, red calyx bracts. This double-flowered form lacks a functional pistil and does not produce fruit. Unfortunately, messy, dried, papery brown bracts persist on the plant when the blooms fade.

W. coccinea; orange-yellow fls are grouped along the stem with lf-like, red bracts.

W. coccinea; requires high humidity and acid, volcanic soil, which it finds in the volcanic islands of Trindad and Tobago.

W. coccinea; waxy new growth is reddish but, sadly, faded, papery blooms persist on the double cv.

W. coccinea; is native to Trinidad, where it was photographed at the Royal Botanic Gardens. It heralds the entrance with its regal blooms. This is cv. 'David Auyong'.

Wrightia arborea

DHUDHI

(Dennist.) Mabb.   24 spp.

Nerium tomentosum; W. tomentosa

APOCYNACEAE

100ft – 30m

75ft

22.5m   0

THE FIRST BOTANISTS considered this species an Oleander (*Nerium*), but eventually it was relegated to the *Wrightia* clan, which includes several other ornamental species. *Wrightia arborea* has thick, corky bark and slender limbs. The paired leaves are crowded on short stalks in 1 plane on either side of the twigs. Each elliptical leaf tapers to a long, blunt 'tail' at its apex and has prominent veins on its lower surface. Small, yellowish or orange flowers grow in cymes. Like Oleanders, they have a little, 2–3 lobed, whiskery coronet at the mouth of their flower tubes (*W. arborea* has an orange coronet). At its centre, stamens with short filaments and large, arrow-shaped anthers are fused into a cone around the style. *W. arborea* flowers have an unpleasant, pungently sweet odour of decaying fruit and are pollinated by flies. Unlike much of the Apocynaceae clan (which are paired), the fruit consists of a single follicle. These pods are packed with slender seeds that bear tufts of white hairs. The seeds and roots contain an indigo-yielding glucoside that is used in Nepal as a styptic to staunch bleeding. *W. arborea* is also used to treat colic, dysentery, earache, menstrual complaints, tumours and wounds. The wood is white, fairly hard and evenly grained in texture. In some instances, it is used as a substitute for ivory.

*** *W. pubescens*; (R. Br.), S China to Australia, to 10 m (33 ft). This is a large-foliaged species of coastal vine thickets, cliffs and sand dunes. The bark is slightly roughened and speckled cream. Slightly scented, summer-blooming flowers have white or pink, blunt-tipped lobes and a white coronet. The green fruit is speckled white. (10–12)

*** *W. religiosa*; (Benth. ex Kurz), Indochina to Malesia, to 5 m (16 ft). WILD WATER PLUM is a popular shrubby ornamental in Asia and Australia, especially for containers and bonsai. Its delicate white or purple-red tinged flowers nod on slender stems along the tips of the twiglets; they have no coronet. (10–12)

ORIGIN	from India and S. Lanka to Thailand
HEIGHT	up to 20 m (66 ft)
TYPE	deciduous, flowering large shrub or small tree
STATUS	not threatened
HABITAT	deciduous forests; river valleys
GROWTH	slow
FLOWG	spring
DRY TOL.	moderate
SALT TOL.	low
LIGHT	full sun to bright shade
SOIL	rich, humid, well-drained
NUTRIT.	organic fertilizer; deep, organic mulch
HAZARDS	sticky sap
PROBLEMS	none
ENVIRON.	nectar for insects
PROPAG.	seeds; cuttings; layers
LEAVES	simple; rich green, downy below; elliptic, with prominent veins
FLOWERS	showy; white, greenish white or orange; held in branched clusters
FRUIT	a follicle, to 34 cm (13.5 in.); brown with cream, warty dots; seeds with tufted hairs
USE	small flowering tree; courtyard; specimen; large planter; bonsai subject; conservatory
ZONE	10–12

W. arborea; with an unpleasant, pungently sweet odour of decaying fr.

W. pubescens; is a robust sp. of coast. habitats. The typical coronet and cone-shaped fusion of anthers is clearly seen here. This sp. was photographed in Cairns, N Qld, Australia.

W. arborea; the fr. consists of a follicles packed with slender sds that bear tufts of white hairs.

W. religiosa; delicate white, or purple-red-tinged fls nod on slender stems at tips of the twiglets. They have no coronet.

426

Xanthostemon chrysanthus

GOLDEN PENDA

F. v.M. ex Benth.   45 spp.

MYRTACEAE

ORIGIN	Australia, endemic
HEIGHT	up to 40 m (131 ft)
TYPE	evergreen, small flowering tree
STATUS	not threatened
HABITAT	in rainforests, along streams
GROWTH	moderate to fast
FLOWG	spring and summer
DRY TOL.	low
SALT TOL.	low
LIGHT	full sun
SOIL	preferably acid loam
NUTRIT.	magnesium-rich fertilizer; deep, organic mulch
HAZARDS	none
PROBLEMS	none
ENVIRON.	nectar for birds and bees
PROPAG.	seeds; layers
LEAVES	simple; bright green; glabrous, glossy; deep red on emergence
FLOWERS	showy; rich yellow; held in dense cymes; petal-less, with long, yellow stamens
FRUIT	a woody capsule, to 1.5 cm (0.6 in.); with smooth, persistent calyx; many wafer-like seeds
USE	small street tree; large planter; specimen; large, bright conservatory
ZONE	10–12

50ft — 15m
50ft
15m   0

XANTHOSTEMON, another of the Myrtle clan so important in Australia's flora, is closely allied to *Metrosideros* and *Lophostemon*; *Xanthostemon* is best represented in rainforests of Indonesia, New Guinea and New Caledonia. **Xanthostemon chrysanthus**, the most commonly grown species, is native to NE Qld's rainforests, typically as a riparian canopy tree. New foliage is burnished coppery red, maturing a deep, glossy green. The ovate leaves are crowded towards the ends of the branchlets, cupping large, terminal, crowded clusters of golden blooms. They lack petals but amply compensate with yellow sepals and starry circles of stiff, yellow stamens. Copious nectar is secreted in their centre and attracts little honeyeater birds. The woody seed capsules are tipped with persistent calyxes. Amongst boulders in flood-ravaged niches, **X. chrysanthus** remains quite small, as it does in open cultivation – often less than 10 m (33 ft). It requires full sun to bloom well, usually flowering while still young, often with several flushes following soaking summer rains. It is surprisingly easy to grow given rich, humid slightly acid soil. In Australia, **X. chrysanthus** is popular as a small street tree, windbreak or even as a hedge. Even without its sumptuous flowers, this small species is worthy for its superb, evergreen foliage, including newer variegated cultivars.

*** **X. graniticus**, (Peter G. Wilson), NE Qld, Australia, to 10 m (33 ft). MOUNTAIN PENDA, a slow-growing, wet highland rainforest tree, has deeply quilted leaves, bronze-tomentose new growth and terminal clusters of creamy white flowers. (9–12)

*** **X. youngii**, (C.T. White & W.D. Francis), N Qld, Australia, to 5 m (16 ft). RED PENDA is a very rare, small species found in remote beach rainforest along Cape York Peninsula. A desirable ornamental, this species requires full sun, well-drained soil and has proved difficult to propagate except from seed, and is often poor in form. (10–12) These species are important honey plants.

X. *chrysanthus*; a mature specimen shading a small church in Malanda, N Qld, Australia.

X. *chrysanthus*; like so many of the Myrtle clan, Golden Penda is rich in nectar and much sought after by bees and honeysuckers.

X. *youngii*; known as Red Penda, this is a rare coast. form.

X. *granaticus*; deeply veined, leathery lvs and terminal, rusty velvety, clusters of creamy white fls.

Zanthoxylum flavum

WEST INDIAN SATINWOOD

Vahl.   250 spp.

Fagara flava

RUTACEAE

100ft — 30m

75ft

22.5m   0

THE DISTINCTIVE, YELLOWISH HEARTWOOD of this W Indian species has long been prized as one of the most desirable of all Trop. American timbers. Closely allied to *Citrus*, *Zanthoxylum flavum* has ash-like, pinnate leaves covered in yellow, glandular dots. They are strongly aromatic when crushed. Flowering spikes have very fragrant, little nectar-rich flowers attracting honeybees in spring, making this an excellent honey tree. Named Satinwood (or Yellowheart) for its satiny, golden lustre and finely rippled grain, *Z. flavum* demanded the highest prices in the timber market early in the 20th century. It was widely employed for the fabrication of fine furniture and panelling, but more especially for intricate inlaid work and veneer. This has resulted in large trees becoming rare in their natural habitats. Puerto Rico and Jamaica were renowned for their Satinwood and, as late as 1920, logs were being exported even, it is said, to the extent of digging out the precious stumps. As with many hardwoods, this is a very slow-growing, dioecious species – factors that make wide reafforestation less economically attractive. In drier areas, *Z. flavum* may grow as a large shrub, with its limbs usually too small for use as timber.

*** *Z. coriaceum*; (A. Rich), W Indies, to 10 m (33 ft). PRICKLY-ASH is very slow growing. Young growth has sharp spines; leaves are thick, leathery, very dark green. Flowers are held in very dense corymbs. Known locally as Shake-hand. (10–12)

*** *Z. gillettii*; ([De Wild.] Waterm.), (*Z. macrophylla*), eastern highlands of Zimbabwe, to 30 m (100 ft). AFRICAN SATINWOOD is valued for its fine timber. (9–11)

*** *Z. martinicense*; ([Lam.] DC), W Indies, to 20 m (66 ft). YELLOW PRICKLE is a fast-growing, evergreen, dioecious tree of coastal limestone. It has a trunk and limbs with stout, corky thorns. The wood of this species is not durable. (10–12)

ORIGIN	Florida and W Indies
HEIGHT	up to 16 m (52 ft)
TYPE	deciduous, dioecious foliage and timber tree
STATUS	rare, threatened
HABITAT	dry, rocky limestone woodland and thickets
GROWTH	slow
FLOWG	spring
DRY TOL.	high
SALT TOL.	moderate
LIGHT	full sun or bright shade
SOIL	fertile, well-drained
NUTRIT.	balanced fertilizer annually
HAZARDS	none
PROBLEMS	none
ENVIRON.	bee nectar; wild bird fruit
PROPAG.	seeds
LEAVES	pinnate; dark green; to 30 cm (12 in.); leaflets elliptic, with wavy margins; strongly aromatic
FLOWERS	fairly showy; greenish yellow; held in axillary cymes; very fragrant
FRUIT	a capsule, to 0.5 cm (0.2 in.); 2-valved, dry
USE	conservation; specimen; botanic collection; xerophytic; large bright conservatory
ZONE	10–12

Z. flavum; with glossy, leathery, wavy, pinnate lvs.

Z. flavum; the satiny, golden lustre and fine, rippled grain was widely employed for the fabrication of fine furniture and panelling, but more especially for intricate inlaid work and veneer.

Z. coriaceum; is a slow-growing sp. with stiff lvs and little blooms in compact clusters. Young growth has sharp spines.

Z. martinicense; a fast-growing, everg. dioec. tree of coast. limestone. Its trunk has stout, corky spines.

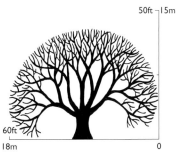

50ft ┐15m

60ft
18m   0

Ziziphus mauritiana

INDIAN JUJUBE

Lam.   86 spp.

RHAMNACEAE

ORIGIN	from India to SE Asia
HEIGHT	up to 13 m (43 ft)
TYPE	evergreen, small fruiting tree
STATUS	not threatened
HABITAT	coastal thickets; dry limestone woodlands
GROWTH	moderate
FLOWG	autumn
DRY TOL.	high
SALT TOL.	high
LIGHT	full sun
SOIL	widely tolerant
NUTRIT.	occasional general fertilizer
HAZARDS	spiny
PROBLEMS	rust; fruit fly; invasive
ENVIRON.	insect nectar; fruit for birds and bats
PROPAG.	seeds; root cuttings; grafts
LEAVES	simple; deep green, densely whitish below; to 6 cm (2.4 in.); broadly elliptic; with longitudinal veins
FLOWERS	inconspicuous; yellow; held in small, axillary cymes; fragrant
FRUIT	a drupe, to 2.5 cm (1 in.); deep yellow to orange-red; rounded; with edible, sweet whitish pulp
USE	seaside; backyard tree; specimen; coastal screening; living barrier; topiary; land stabilization; xerophytic
ZONE	10–12

IT MAY BE ASKED WHY THIS CHARMING, LITTLE XEROPHYTE is not more popular for planting in the landscape. Admittedly, it is rather thorny, but with its softly billowing, layered crown of tough little leaves that flicker their silver linings when stirred by a breeze *Ziziphus mauritiana* demonstrates a splendid worthiness. Indian Jujube leaves are small, spoon-shaped and finely toothed, with deep veins running longitudinally along the blades, and densely white, furry undersides. They are held alternately and regularly in 2 rows along the stems. Tiny, yellowish, fragrant flowers are crowded at the leaf bases and are followed by plum-like, golden or orange-red fruit with crisp, white pulp. Not as sweetly juicy as *Z. jujuba*, they are still popular as a backyard fruit in many dry parts of the tropics. Along the coast of E Africa, the timber is used to make beds, chairs and ribs for dhows. Before the development of plastics, *Z. mauritiana* was an important lac tree. The leaves are used for tanning.
*** *Z. jujuba*; (Mill.), (*Z. ziziphus*); SE Europe to China, to 12 m (39 ft). CHINESE JUJUBE is considered by the Chinese to be a 'kingly' herb and they use it as a general tonic with no harmful side effects. Very similar to *Z. mauritiana*, it is more cold-hardy and has glabrous foliage and larger, juicier fruit. In China, where it is traditionally cultivated, the fruit is enjoyed fresh, dried like dates, candied, preserved or made into a refreshing drink. The dried fruit is made into cough drops, taken as a heart tonic or to relieve poisons and, with the seeds, is prescribed for anxiety, insomnia and dizziness. The bark is used to treat diarrhoea and fever. *Z. jujube* is found in some Chinese anti-cancer formulae, and Japanese research suggests that it promotes immunity. Although these species may be invasive in some regions, in other parts of the dry tropics these are valuable provision trees. (7–10)

NOTE: in N Australia this species is invasive and is a serious problem.

Z. mauritiana; tough little lvs are stirred by breezes, which flicker their silver linings.

Z. mauritiana; an excellent, xerophytic shade tree with its finely textured, tumbling, layered canopy.

Z. mauritiana; fr. hang in long clusters; they will ripen orange-red.

Z. jujuba; fr. is larger and more desirable than *Z. mauritiana*, being crisply apple-like. This is a very important fr. in China.

PART 2

Quick Reference
Checklists

*These easy-to-use lists are designed to help
gardeners, designers and planners to
choose appropriate species
for specific use
and conditions.*

QUICK REFERENCE CHECKLISTS

The following checklists suggest trees, described in this book, which are suitable for growing in particular situations.

In Part 1, trees have been divided into drought-resistant (orange) salt-resistant (blue) and humid-loving species (green), as well as evergreen and deciduous. For further classification, species are divided into the following categories: fast-growing, slow-growing; suitable for shade, screening, hedges or living barriers; as accent specimens or for use in confined spaces, i.e. in planters or small, paved courtyards; or cultivated for their showy flowers or fruit.

Part 2 lists plant characteristics, special uses or problems.

PART I

I.
DROUGHT-TOLERANT, EVERGREEN TREES

★ = may be invasive

Major species

Aleurites moluccana, p. 19 ★
Andira inermis, p. 25
Annona muricata, p. 27
Araucaria heterophylla, p. 30 ★
Azadirachta indica, p. 40 ★
Blighia sapida, p. 53 ★
Brosimum alicastrum, p. 60
Brunfelsia americana, p. 65
Bucida buceras, p. 67
Bulnesia arborea, p. 70
Bunchosia argentea, p. 71 ★
Byrsonima crassifolia, p. 74
Caesalpinia echinata, p. 75
Calliandra surinamensis, p. 79
Calotropis gigantea, p. 84 ★
Canella winterana, p. 90
Casuarina equisitifolia, p. 98 ★
Ceratonia siliqua, p. 106
Cerbera manghas, p. 108
Chrysobalanus icaco, p. 111 ★
Clusia rosea, p. 121
Coccoloba uvifera, p. 122
Conocarpus erectus, p. 128
Cupaniopsis anacardioides, p. 137 ★
Cussonia spicata, p. 138
Dodonaea viscosa, p. 152 ★
Eriobotrya japonica, p. 165 ★
Eugenia uniflora, p. 174 ★
Euphorbia punicea, p. 176
Ficus benjamina, p. 182 ★
Geijera parviflora, p.199
Gnetum gnemone, p. 204
Greyia sutherlandii, p. 207
Guaiacum officinale, p. 208
Hamelia patens, p. 214
Hibiscus tiliaceus, p. 220
Hymenaea courbaril, p. 223

Inga jinicuil, p. 226
Ixora pavetta, p. 228
Jacquinia arborea, p. 231
Juniperus barbadensis, p. 233
Kleinhovia hospita, p. 236
Leptospermum madidum, p. 246
Leucadendron argenteum, p. 247
Lonchocarpus violaceus, p. 252
Lysiloma sabicu, p. 256
Malpighia glabra, p. 261
Manilkara zapota, p. 264
Melaleuca leucadendra, p. 268 ★
Melicoccus bijugatus, p. 272
Millingtonia hortensis, p. 278
Morinda citrifolia, p. 282
Moringa oleifera, p. 283 ★
Morus alba, p. 284 ★
Muntingia calabura, p. 285 ★
Murraya koenigii, p. 286 ★
Myrciaria cauliflora, p. 288
Myrica cerifera, p. 290
Newbouldia laevis, p. 96
Noronhia emarginata, p. 297
Ochrosia elliptica, p. 301
Parinari nonda, p. 309
Peltophorum pterocarpum, p. 314
Phytolacca dioica, p. 321
Pinus caribaea, p. 323
Pithecellobium arboreum, p. 325
Pittosporum pentandrum, p. 326 ★
Portlandia grandiflora, p. 342
Quassia simarouba, p. 354 ★
Santalum album, p. 362
Sapindus saponaria, p. 363
Sarcocephalus latifolius, p. 366
Schefflera actinophylla, p. 367 ★
Schinus terebinthifolius, p. 368 ★
Sideroxylon foetidissimum, p. 376
Solanum wrightii, p. 377
Spathodea campanulata, p. 378 ★
Strychnos nux-vomica, p. 387
Tamarindus indicus, p. 402
Tamarix aphylla, p. 403 ★
Thespesia populnea, p. 414 ★
Thevetia peruviana, p. 415 ★
Ziziphus mauritiana, p. 429 ★

Fast-growing species

Annona spp.
Araucaria spp.
Azadirachta indica
Blighia sapida
Brunfelsia spp.
Calotropis gigantea
Casuarina spp.
Cedrela odorata
Ficus spp. (several)
Hamelia spp.
Hibiscus tiliaceus
Inga spp.
Millingtonia hortensis
Moringa oleifera
Muntingia calabura
Newbouldia laevis
Peltophorum spp.
Phytolacca dioica
Pinus spp.
Pithecellobium spp.
Schinus terebinthifolius
Solanum wrightii
Spathodea campanulata
Tamarix spp.
Thespesia populnea
Thevetia peruviana

Slow-growing species

Bucida spinosa
Bulnesia arborea
Byrsonima spp.
Canella winterana
Ceratonia siliqua
Chrysobalanus icaco
Clusia spp.
Cussonia spp.
Dodonaea viscosa
Eugenia spp.
Euphorbia spp.
Guaiacum spp.
Hymenaea courbaril
Ixora pavetta
Juniperus spp.
Manilkara spp.
Melaleuca spp.
Myrciaria spp.

Noronhia emarginata
Parinari nonda
Portlandia spp.
Santalum album
Strychnos spp.
Tamarindus indica

To provide shade
○ = open ● = dense

Andira inermis ●
Azadirachta indica ●
Blighia sapida ○
Brosimum spp. ●
Bucida buceras ○
Bulnesia arborea ○
Canella winterana ●
Ceratonia siliqua ○
Coccoloba uvifera ○
Conocarpus erectus ○
Cupaniopsis anacardioides ●
Eriobotrya japonica ●
Ficus spp. (many) ●
Hibiscus tiliaceus ●
Hymenaea courbaril ○
Inga spp. ○
Kleinhovia hospita ○
Lonchocarpus spp. ○
Lysiloma spp. ○
Manilkara spp. ●
Melicoccus bijugatus ●
Moringa oleifera ○
Morus spp. ●
Murraya koenigii ○
Noronhia emarginata ●
Parinari nonda ●
Peltophorum spp. ○
Phytolacca dioica ●
Pithecellobium spp. ○
Pittosporum spp. ○
Quassia simarouba ●
Sapindus saponaria ○
Schinus molle ○
Sideroxylon spp. ○
Solanum wrightii ○
Tamarindus indica ○
Thespesia populnea ●
Ziziphus spp. ○

For screening & hedges

✚ = formal ✤ = infomal
★ = living barrier
✓ = wind break

Annona muricata ✤
Brunfelsia americana ✚
Byrsonima lucida ✚
Caesalpinia echinata ✚ ★
Casuarina equisitifolia ✚ ✤ ✓
Cerbera manghas ✤
Chrysobalanus icaco ✚
Clusia rosea ✤
Coccoloba uvifera ✤ ✓
Conocarpus erectus ✤ ✓
Dodonaea viscosa ✤
Eugenia uniflora ✤
Euphorbia spp. ★ ✤
Ficus benjamina ✚ ✓
Hamelia patens ✚ ✤
Hibiscus tiliaceus ✤ ✓
Ixora spp. ✚
Jacquinia spp. ✤
Malpighia glabra ✤
Morinda citrifolia ✤
Murraya paniculata ✚
Myrica cerifera ✤
Noronhia emarginata ✤ ✓
Ochrosia spp. ✤
Pittosporum spp. ✤
Schinus terebinthifolius ✤
Tamarix spp. ✤ ✓
Thespesia populnea ✚ ✤ ✓
Thevetia peruviana ✚ ✤
Zizyphus spp. ✚ ✤ ★

For accent & confined spaces

✠ = suitable for large planters
† = topiary

Aleurites moluccana
Annona spp. ✠
Araucaria spp.
Brunfelsia spp. ✠
Bucida spp. ✠ (some)
Byrsonima spp. ✠
Caesalpinia spp. ✠
Calliandra spp. ✠
Callistemon spp. ✠
Calotropis gigantea ✠
Canella winterana ✠ †
Casuarina equisitifolia †
Cerbera spp. ✠
Chrysobalanus icaco ✠
Clusia spp. ✠
Coccoloba spp. ✠ †
Conocarpus erectus var. *sericeus* ✠ †
Cussonia spp.
Dodonaea viscosa ✠
Eriobotrya japonica
Eugenia spp. ✠ †

Euphorbia spp. ✠
Ficus natalensis (& others) ✠
Geijera parviflora
Gnetum gnemon ✠
Greyia sutherlandii ✠
Guaiacum spp. ✠ †
Hamelia spp. ✠
Ixora spp. ✠
Jacquinia spp. ✠ †
Juniperus sinensis ✠
Leptospermum spp. (some) ✠
Leucospermum argenteum ✠
Lysiloma sabicu
Malpighia glabra ✠
Morinda citrifolia ✠
Murraya paniculata ✠ †
Myrciaria spp. ✠
Noronhia emarginata ✠
Ochrosia spp.
Parinari nonda
Pithecellobium dulce 'Variegata' ✠
Pittosporum pentandrum ✠ †
Portlandia spp. ✠
Quassia amara ✠
Schefflera actinophylla
Tamarix aphylla ✠
Thevetia peruviana ✠ †

With showy flowers

r = red : p = pink : b = blue :
m = mauve : v = violet :
y = yellow : o = orange :
w = white : g = green :
✳ = seasonal :
● = intermittently

Aleurites spp. (w) ●
Andira inermis (p/m) ✳
Brunfelsia spp. (w) ●
Bulnesia arborea (y) ✳
Bunchosia spp. (y) ✳
Byrsonima spp. (y/p) ✳
Caesalpinia spp. (y) ✳
Calliandra spp. (w/p & r) ●
Callistemon spp. (r) ✳
Calotropis spp. (p/m/v/w) ●
Canella winterana (r) ●
Catalpa longissima (p) ✳
Cerbera spp. (w) ●
Clusia spp. (w/p) ●
Cussonia spp. (g) ✳
Eriobotrya japonica (w) ✳
Euphorbia spp. (r/y) ●
Geijera parviflora (y) ✳
Greyia sutherlandii (r) ✳
Guaiacum spp. (b) ✳
Hamelia spp. (r/o/y) ●
Hibiscus spp. (y-r) ●
Ixora spp. (w) ✳
Jacquinia spp. (w/o) ✳
Kleinhovia hospita (p) ✳
Leptospermum spp. (w) ✳

Lonchocarpus spp. (m/v/b) ✳
Malpighia glabra (p) ●
Melaleuca spp. (w/r) ✳
Millingtonia hortensis (w) ✳
Moringa oleifera (w) ●
Murraya spp. (w) ✳
Myrciaria spp. (w-y) ✳
Newbouldia laevis (p/m) ✳
Ochrosia spp. (w) ✳
Peltophorum spp. (y) ✳
Phytolacca dioica (w) ✳
Pittosporum spp. (w) ✳
Portlandia spp. (w) ●
Quassia amara (r) ●
Sarcocephalus latifolius (y) ✳
Schefflera spp. (r) ✳
Solanum spp. (m) ●
Spathodea campanulata (o/y) ✳
Tamarindus indica (y) ✳
Tamarix spp. (p/m) ●
Thevetia peruviana (y/o/w) ●

With showy fruit

✕ = toxic ✓ = edible

Aleurites moluccana ✕
Annona spp. ✓
Araucaria spp.
Blighia sapida ✕ ✓
Brosimum alicastrum ✓
Brunfelsia spp. ✕
Bunchosia spp. ✓
Byrsonima spp. ✓
Caesalpinea vesicaria
Calotropis gigantea
Canella winterana ✓
Cerbera spp. ✕
Chrysobalanus icaco ✓
Clusia rosea ✕
Coccoloba uvifera ✓
Cupaniopsis anacardioides
Cussonia spp.
Dodonaea viscosa
Eriobotrya japonica ✓
Eugenia uniflora ✓
Geijera parviflora
Gnetum gnemon ✓
Guaiacum officinale
Hamelia spp.
Inga jinicuil ✓
Jacquinia spp. ✕
Kleinhovia hospita
Leucadendron argenteum
Lonchocarpus violaceus ✕
Manilkara zapota ✓
Malpighia glabra ✓
Melicoccus bijugatus ✓
Morinda citrifolia ✓
Morus spp. ✓
Muntingia calabura ✓
Murraya spp.
Myrciaria spp. ✓

Ochrosia spp. ✕
Parinari nonda
Peltophorum pterocarpum
Phytolacca dioica ✕
Pithecellobium arboreum
Pittosporum spp.
Quassia spp.
Sapindus saponaria ✕
Sarcocephalus latifolius ✓
Schefflera actinophylla
Schinus spp.
Tamarindus indicus ✓
Zizyphus spp. ✓

2.
MODERATELY DROUGHT-TOLERANT, EVERGREEN TREES

★ = may be invasive

Major species

Afrocarpus gracilior, p. 13
Agathis robusta, p. 14
Alstonia scholaris, p. 21 ★
Amphitecna latifolia, p. 23
Antidesma bunius, p. 28
Aphanamixis polystachya, p. 29
Archidendron lucyi, p. 32
Artocarpus altilis, p. 34
Argusia argentea, p. 33
Averrhoa carambola, p. 38
Backhousia citriodora, p. 41
Banksia dentata, p. 42
Barringtonia asiatica, p. 43 ★
Bischofia javanica, p. 51 ★
Bixa orellana, p. 52
Callistemon viminalis, p. 80
Calophyllum inophyllum, p. 82
Cananga odorata, p. 88 ★
Casimiroa edulis, p. 91
Cecropia peltata, p. 101
Ceratopetalum gummiferum, p. 107
Cestrum diurnum, p. 109 ★
Citrus sinensis, p. 116
Clausena lansium, p. 119
Cola acuminata, p. 119 ★
Crateva religiosa, p. 135
Deplanchea tetraphylla, p. 142
Dialium guineense, p. 143
Dolichandrone spathacea, p. 153
Dovyalis hebecarpa, p. 156 ★
Duabanga grandiflora, p. 157
Elaeocarpus augustifolius, p. 160
Eucalyptus deglupta, p. 170
Fagraea fragrans, p. 178
Fraxinus griffithii, p. 193
Filicium decipiens, p. 188 ★

Grevillea robusta, p. 205
Guettardia speciosa, p. 209
Gymnostoma rumphianum, p. 212
Intsia bijuga, p. 227
Khaya anthotheca, p. 234
Lagunaria patersonii, p. 242
Ligustrum lucidum, p. 249 ★
Litchi chinensis, p. 250
Lonchocarpus violaceus, p. 252
Lophostemon confertus, p. 255
Macadamia integrifolia, p. 257
Macaranga tanarius, p. 258 ★
Magnolia grandiflora, p. 259
Mammea americana, p. 262
Mangifera indica, p. 263 ★
Markhamia lutea, p. 267
Mesua ferrea, p. 273
Michelia champaca, p. 275
Mimusops elengi, p. 279
Montezuma speciosissima, p. 281
Nuxia congesta, p. 298
Nyctanthes arbor-tristes, p. 299
Ochroma pyramidale, p. 300
Ormosia ormondii, p. 303
Oxyanthus pyriformis, p. 305
Parmentiera cerifera, p. 313 ★
Pimenta dioica, p. 322
Pisonia grandis var. alba, p. 324
Pleiogynium timorense, p. 330
Podocarpus neriifolius, p. 336
Polyalthia longifolia, p. 340
Pometia pinnata, p. 341
Posoqueria latifolia, p. 343
Pterospermum acerifolium, p. 350
Rollinia mucosa, p. 357
Saraca indica, p. 364
Stemmadenia littoralis, p. 382
Stenocarpus sinuatus, p. 382
Swinglea glutinosa, p. 389
Syzygium malaccensis, p. 390
Tabernaemontana arborea, p. 400
Treculia africana, p. 419
Triplaris cumingiana, p. 421 ★
Wallaceodendron celebicum, p. 424

Fast-growing species

Alstonia spp.
Archidendron spp.
Artocarpus altilis
Bischofia javanica
Bixa orellana
Calophyllum spp.
Cananga odorata
Cecropia peltata
Cestrum spp.
Clausena lansium
Deplanchea tetraphylla
Dolichandrone spp.
Duabanga grandiflora
Eucalyptus spp.
Grevillea spp.

Hernandia spp.
Hymenosporum flavum
Intsia bijuga
Khaya spp.
Lagunaria patersonii
Ligustrum spp.
Lophostemon confertus
Macaranga spp.
Markhamia spp.
Michelia spp.
Ochroma pyramidale
Ormosia spp.
Pisonia spp.
Pometia spp.
Posoqueria spp.
Pterospermum spp.
Rollinia mucosa
Syzygium spp.
Triplaris spp.
Wallaceodendron celebicum

Slow-growing species

Agathis spp.
Argusia argentea
Averrhoa spp.
Backhousia citriodora
Pimenta spp.
Polyalthia spp.
Saraca spp.
Stenocarpus sinuatus
Swinglea glutinosa

To provide shade
○ = open   ● = dense

Antidesma bunius ●
Aphanamixis spp. ○
Archidendron spp. ○
Artocarpus spp. ●
Barringtonia asiatica ●
Bischofia javanica ●
Calophyllum spp. ●
Canaga odorata ○
Casimiroa edulis
Clausena lansium
Dialium guineense
Dolichandrone spp.
Elaeocarpus spp. ○
Fagraea racemosa ○
Filicium decipiens ●
Harpullia spp. ○
Heritiera spp.
Intsia bijuga ○
Kleinhovia hospita ○
Litchi chinensis ●
Lonchocarpus spp. ○
Lophostemon confertus ○
Macaranga spp. ●
Magnolia grandiflora ●
Mammea americana ●
Mangifera indica ●

Manilkara spp. ●
Mimusops elengi ●
Montezuma speciosissima ○
Nuxia spp. ○
Ormosia ormondii ○
Pleiogynium timorense ○
Pometia pinnata ○
Pterospermum acerifolium
Tabernaemontana arborea ○
Treculia africana
Wallaceodendron celebicum ○

For screening & hedges
✚ = formal   ✤ = infomal
★ = living barrier
✓ = windbreak

Afrocarpus spp.
Amphitecna latifolia ✤ ✓ (low)
Argusia argentea ✤ ✓ (low)
Bixa orellana
Calophyllum spp. ✓
Cestrum spp. ✚
Dovyalis spp. ✚ ★
Fraxinus griffithii ✤
Filicium decipiens ✤
Guettardia speciosa ✤ ✓ (low)
Ligustrum spp. ✚ ✓ (low)
Macaranga tanarius
Mimusops elengi ✓
Podocarpus spp. ✓
Tabernaemontana cerifera ✚ ✤

For accent & confined spaces
✠ = suitable for large planters
† = topiary

Amphitecna latifolia
Archidendron spp.
Argusia argentea ✠
Averrhoa spp. ✠
Backhousia citriodora (young) ✠
Banksia spp. ✠
Barringtonia spp. (not B. asiatica)
Bixa orellana ✠
Callistemon spp. ✠
Cananga odorata
Cecropia peltata
Cestrum spp. ✠ †
Citrus spp. ✠
Crateva spp. ✠
Deplanchea tetraphylla
Dovyalis spp. ✠ †
Fagraea beteriana ✠
Filicium decipiens
Fraxinus spp.
Grevillea spp. (some) ✠
Guettardia speciosa ✠
Hymenospermum flavum
Kopsia spp. ✠ †
Lagunaria patersonii

Ligustrum spp. ✠ †
Lophostemon confertus var. variegata
Magnolia spp.
Mammea americana
Markhamia spp. (some) ✠
Mesua ferrea
Michelia spp. ✠
Mimusops spp. †
Oxyanthus spp.
Parmentiera spp.
Pimenta spp. †
Pisonia grandis var. alba ✠
Podocarpus spp. (some) ✠ † †
Polyalthia longifolia var. pendula
Posoqueria spp. ✠
Saraca spp.
Stemmadenia littoralis
Stenocarpus sinuatus
Syzygium spp. (some) ✠ †
Tabernaemontana spp.
   (not T. arborea) ✠ †
Triplaris spp.

With showy flowers
r = red : p = pink : b = blue :
m = mauve : v = violet :
y = yellow : o = orange :
w = white : g = green :
✳ = seasonal :
● = intermittently

Alstonia spp. (w) ✳
Archidendron grandiflorum
   (w/r) ✳
Averrhoa carambola (p/r) ●
Backhousia citriodora (w) ✳
Banksia spp. (y/w) ●
Barringtonia spp. ✳ (r/p/w) ●
Bischofia javanica (y-g) ✳
Bixa orellana (p/w) ●
Callistemon spp. (r/p/w/g) ✳ ●
Calophyllum inophyllum (w) ✳
Cananga odorata (y) ●
Ceratopetalum spp. (r/w) ✳
Cestrum spp. (w) ●
Citrus spp. (w) ✳
Cola acuminata (y-r) ✳
Crateva spp. (w-y) ✳
Deplanchea tetraphylla (y) ✳ ●
Dolichandrone spp. (w) ✳ ●
Duabanga grandiflora (w) ●
Elaeocarpus spp. (w) ✳
Eucalyptus spp. (r/o/p/w) ●
Fagraea spp. ✳ (y/w) ✳
Fraxinus griffithii (w) ✳
Grevillea spp. (y-o/r/w) ✳
Guettardia speciosa (w) ✳ ●
Hernandia spp. (w-g) ●
Hymenospermum flavum (y) ✳
Intsia bijuga (y-w) ✳
Kleinhovia hospita (p) ●
Kopsia spp. (w/p) ✳

433

Lagunaria patersonii (p/m) ✳
Ligustrum spp. (w) ✳
Lonchocarpus spp. (b/m/v) ✳
Lophanthera lactescens (y) ✳
Macadamia spp. (w) ✳ ●
Macaranga spp. (p/r/w) ●
Magnolia spp. (w) ✳
Mammea americana (w) ✳
Mangifera indica (p/y/w) ✳
Markhamia spp. (y/r) ●
Mesua ferrea (w) ✳
Michelia spp. (y/w) ✳
Montezuma speciossima (r/p) ●
Nuxia spp. (w) ✳
Nyctanthes arbor-triste (w-o) ●
Ochroma pyramidale (w) ✳
Ormosia spp. (r/p/m/v) ✳
Oxyanthus spp. (w) ●
Pimenta spp. (w) ✳
Polyalthia spp. (g-w) ✳
Posoqueria spp. (w) ✳
Pterospermum spp. (y) ✳
Saraca spp. (r-o/y/y-o) ✳
Stemmadenia spp. (w) ●
Stenocarpus sinuatus (r) ●
Syzygium spp. (r/p/m/w) ✳
Tabernaemontana spp. (w) ✳

With showy fruit
× = toxic ✓ = edible

Antidesma bunius ✓
Aphanamixis spp. ×
Archidendron spp.
Artocarpus spp. ✓
Averrhoa spp. ✓
Backhousia spp.
Banksia spp.
Barringtonia spp. ×
Bischofia javanica
Bixa orellana
Casimiroa edulis ✓
Ceratopetalum spp.
Citrus spp. ✓
Clausena lansium ✓
Cola spp.
Crateva spp. ×
Dialium spp. ✓
Dovyalis spp. ✓
Elaeocarpus spp.
Fagraea spp.
Fraxinus spp.
Harpullia spp.
Hernandia spp.
Kopsia spp. ×
Ligustrum spp. ×
Litchi chinensis ✓
Magnolia spp.
Mammea americana ✓
Mangifera indica ✓
Markhamia spp.
Michelia spp.

Ochroma pyramidale
Ormosia ormondii
Parmentiera spp.
Pimenta spp. ✓
Pleiogynium timorensis ✓
Polyalthia spp.
Rollinia mucosa ✓
Saraca thaipingensis
Syzygium spp. ✓
Tabernaemontana spp. ×
Treculia africana ✓
Triplaris spp.

3.
DROUGHT-TOLERANT, DECIDUOUS TREES

★ = may be invasive
✳ = semi-deciduous

Major species

Acacia farnesiana, p. 1 ★
Acokanthera oppositifolia, p. 6
Adansonia digitata, p. 8
Adenanthera pavonina, p. 10 ★
Adenium obesum, p. 11
Albizia lebbeck, p. 18 ★
Anacardium occidentale, p. 24
Bauhinia variegata, p. 46 ★
Bolusanthus speciosus, p. 54
Bombax ceiba, p. 55
Brachychiton acerifolius, p. 56
Broussonetia papyrifera, p. 61 ★
Brya ebenus, p. 66 ✳
Bursera simaruba, p. 72 ★
Calycophyllum candidissimum, p. 85
Cassia fistula, p. 92 ✳
Catalpa longissima, p. 99 ✳
Cavanillesia platanifolia, p. 100
Cedrela odorata, p. 101
Ceiba pentandra, p. 104 ★
Chorisia speciosa, p. 110
Chrysophyllum cainito, p. 112 ✳
Cochlospermum vitifolium, p. 124
Cordia dodecandra, p. 131 ✳
Crescentia cujete, p. 136 ✳
Dalbergia sissoo, p. 139 ✳
Delonix regia, p. 140
Dombeya rotundifolia, p. 154
Duranta erecta, p. 158 ★ ✳
Enterolobium cyclocarpum, p. 163 ★
Erythrina variegata, p. 166 ★
Fernandoa magnifica, p. 181
Firmiana colorata, p. 189
Flacourtia indica, p. 190 ★
Flindersia brayleyana, p. 191 ✳
Genipa americana, p. 200 ✳
Gliricidia sepium, p. 201 ★
Gmelina arborea, p. 202

Haematoxylum campechianum, p. 213 ✳ ★
Hura crepitans, p. 222
Jacaranda mimosifolia, p. 229
Jatropha curcas, p. 232 ★
Khaya anthotheca, p. 234 ✳
Kigelia africana, p. 235 ✳
Koelreuteria elegans, p. 237 ★
Lawsonia inermis, p. 244
Leucaena leucocephala, p. 248 ★
Lophanthera lactescens, p. 254 ✳
Majidea zanguebarica, p. 260
Melia azedarach, p. 271 ★
Millettia pinnata, p. 276
Monodora myristica, p. 280
Myroxylon balsamum, p. 292 ✳
Oncoba spinosa, p. 302
Parkinsonia aculeata, p. 311 ✳ ★
Persea americana, p. 316 ✳
Petrea arborea, p. 317 ✳
Phyllanthus acidus, p. 318 ✳
Phyllocarpus septentrionalis, p. 320 ✳
Platymiscium pinnatum, p. 329
Plumeria rubra, p. 332
Poitea carinalis, p. 339
Pouteria sapota, p. 344 ✳
Pseudobombax ellipticum, p. 346
Psidium guajava, p. 347 ★
Pterocarpus indicus, p. 349
Punica granatum, p. 351
Samanea saman, p. 359 ★
Sarcocephalus latifolius, p. 366
Schotia brachypetala, p. 370
Sclerocarya birrea ssp. *caffra*, p. 371
Senna spectabilis, p. 372 ★
Sesbania grandiflora, p. 375 ★
Spondias cytherea, p. 379
Sterculia foetida, p. 384 ✳
Stereospermum kunthianum, p. 386
Swietenia mahogani, p. 388
Tabebuia heterophylla, p. 396 ★ ✳
Tecoma stans, p. 406 ★
Terminalia catappa, p. 408 ★
Vitex agnus-castus, p. 422
Zanthoxylum flavum, p. 428

Fast-growing species

Acacia spp.
Acrocarpus fraxinifolius
Adenanthera spp.
Albizia lebbek
Bauhinia spp. (most)
Broussonetia papyrifera
Bursera simaruba
Cavanillesia spp.
Cedrela odorata
Ceiba pentandra
Chorisia spp.
Cochlospermum spp.
Dalbergia sissoo

Duranta erecta
Enterolobium spp.
Erythrina spp.
Fernandoa magnifica
Firmiana spp.
Flindersia spp.
Gliricidia sepium
Gmelina spp.
Hura crepitans
Jacaranda spp.
Jatropha spp.
Khaya spp.
Kigelia africana
Lawsonia inermis
Leucaena leucocephala
Lophanthera lactescens
Melia azedarach
Millettia spp.
Parkinsonia spp.
Persea americana
Phyllocarpus septentrionalis
Platymiscium spp.
Pseudobombax spp.
Pterocarpus spp.
Samanea saman
Senna spp.
Sesbania spp.
Spondias spp.
Swietenia spp.
Tabebuia spp. (most)
Tecoma spp.
Terminalia spp. (most)
Vitex spp.

Slow-growing species

Adansonia spp.
Adenium spp.
Anacardium occidentale
Bolusanthus speciosus
Brachychiton rupestris
Brya ebenus
Crescentia spp.
Haematoxlum campechianum
Majidea zanguebarica
Oncoba spp.
Petrea spp.
Plumeria spp.
Poitea spp.
Schotia spp.
Zanthoxylum spp.

For summer shade
○ = open ● = dense

Acacia spp. (some) ○
Albizia lebbek ●
Cassia spp. (some) ○
Cedrela odorata ○
Chrysophyllum spp. ●
Dalbergia sissoo ○
Genipa americana ●

Jacaranda spp. (some) ○
Koelreuteria elegans
Melia azedarach ○
Millettia pinnata ●
Pterocarpus indicus ○
Senna spp. (some) ○
Swietenia spp.
Tabebuia spp. (some) ○

For screening & hedges

✚ = formal ✤ = infomal
★ = living barrier
√ = windbreak

Acacia acuifera (& others) ✚ ✤
Acokanthera spp. ✚ ✤
Bauhinia divaricata (& others) ✤
Duranta erecta ✚ ✤
Flacourtia spp. ★ ✚ ✤
Lawsonia inermis ✚
Oncoba spp. ★
Tecoma stans ✚ ✤
Zanthoxylum coriaceum ★

For accent & confined spaces

✠ = suitable for large planters
† = topiary

Acacia spp. (some) ✠
Acokanthera spp. ✠
Adenium spp. ✠
Bauhinia forficata (& others) ✠
Brachychiton acerifolius (& others)
Brya ebenus ✠ †
Bursera frenningae ✠
Cassia afrofistula (& others)
Ceiba acuminata
Cochlospermum spp. ✠
Cordia lutea (& others) ✠ †
Dombeya spp. ✠
Duranta erecta cv. 'Variegata' ✠ †
Erythrina crista-galli (& others)
Fernandoa magnifica (& others)
Firmiana simplex
Flacourtia jangomas ✠ †
Gmelina dalrympleana
Jacaranda jasminoides (& others)
Jatropha integerrima ✠
Koelreuteria spp.
Lawsonia inermis var. *rubra* ✠ †
Lophanthera lactescens
Parkinsonia spp.
Petrea spp. ✠
Phyllanthus angustifolia (& others) ✠ †
Plumeria spp.
Poitea spp. ✠
Psidium longipes (& others) ✠ †
Pterocarpus indicus var. *burmanica*
Punica granatum var. 'Flora Pleno' ✠ †

Schotia spp. ✠
Senna polyphylla (& others) ✠
Sesbania tripetti ✠
Tabebuia haemantha (& others) ✠ †
Tecoma stans x 'Burchii' (& others) ✠
Vitex agnus-castus (& others)
Zanthoxylum coriaceum ✠

With showy flowers

r = red : p = pink : b = blue :
m = mauve : v = violet :
y = yellow : o = orange :
w = white : g = green :
❊ = seasonal :
● = intermittently

Acacia spp. (y/w) ● ❊
Acokanthera spp. (w/p) ❊
Adansonia spp. (w/y) ❊
Adenium spp. (r/p/w) ❊
Bauhinia spp. (p/r/m/v/y/w)❊
Bolusanthus speciosa (b/v) ❊
Bombax ceiba (r/o) ❊
Brachychiton spp. (r/p/w) ❊
Brya ebenus (y) ●
Calycophyllum candidissimum (w) ❊
Cassia spp. (r/p/y/w) ❊
Catalpa spp. (p/y) ❊
Ceiba acuminata (p/y/w) ❊
Chorisia spp. (p/m/y/w) ❊
Cochlospermum spp. (y) ❊
Cordia spp. (o/y/w) ❊
Delonix spp. (r/o/y/w) ❊
Dombeya spp. (p/w) ❊
Duranta erecta (b/m/v/w) ●
Erythrina spp. (r/o/w) ❊
Fernandoa spp. (r/y) ❊
Firmiana spp. (r/w) ❊
Flindersia spp. (r/w) ❊
Genipa americana (w) ❊
Gliricidia sepium (m/p) ❊
Gmelina spp. (m/y/w) ❊
Haematoxylum campechianum (y) ❊
Jacaranda spp. (b/m/v/w) ❊
Jatropha integerrima (r/p) ●
Kigelia africana (r-y) ●
Koelreuteria spp. (y) ❊
Lawsonia inermis (w/p) ●
Lophanthera lactescens (y) ❊
Majidea zanguebarica (g-r) ❊
Melia azedarach (m-v) ❊
Millettia spp. (m) ❊
Monodora myristica (r-y) ❊
Oncoba spp. (w) ❊
Parkinsonia spp. (y) ❊
Petrea spp. (b/m/v/w) ●
Phyllocarpus septentrionalis (r) ❊
Platymiscium spp. (y) ❊

Plumeria spp. (r/p/o/y/w) ❊
Poitea spp. (r/m) ❊
Pseudobombax spp. (p/w) ❊
Psidium spp. (w) ●
Pterocarpus spp. (y) ❊
Sarcocephalus latifolius (y-w) ❊
Schotia spp. (r) ❊
Senna spp. (y) ❊
Sesbania spp. (r/o/w) ●
Sterculia spp. (r/w/g) ❊
Stereospermum spp. (p) ❊
Tabebuia spp. (r/p/w) ❊
Tecoma spp. (y/o) ❊
Terminalia myriocarpa (& others) (r/w) ●
Vitex spp. (b/m/v/p) ❊

With showy fruit

✕ = toxic ✓ = edible

Adansonia spp.
Adenanthera spp.
Albizia lebbek
Anacardium occidentalis ✓
Bauhinia var. *rubra*
Broussonetia papyrifera
Bursera simaruba
Cavanillesia spp.
Ceiba spp.
Chrysophyllum spp. ✓
Cochlospermum spp.
Cordia spp.
Crescentia spp. ✕
Duranta erecta ✕
Enterolobium spp.
Erythrina spp. (some spp.) ✕
Fernandoa spp.
Firmiana spp.
Flacourtia spp. ✓
Flindersia spp. (some)
Gmelina spp.
Hura crepitans ✕
Kigelia africana ✕
Koelreuteria spp.
Lophanthera lactescens
Majidea zanguebarica
Melia azedarach ✕
Monodora spp. ✓
Persea americana ✓
Phyllanthus spp. (several)
Pouteria spp. ✓
Psidium spp. ✓
Pterocarpus spp.
Punica granatum ✓
Sarcocephalus latifolius ✓
Sclerocarya birrea ✓
Spondias spp. ✓
Sterculia spp.
Swietenia spp.
Terminalia spp.
Vitex spp.

4.
SALT-TOLERANT, EVERGREEN TREES

★ = may be invasive
[1] = along beachside
[2] = sheltered from salt spray
[3] = salt air

Major species

Amphitecna latifolia, [2] p. 23
Araucaria heterophylla, [1] p. 30
Argusia argentea, [1] p. 33 ★
Azadirachta indica, [2] p. 40 ★
Barringtonia asiatica, [1] p. 43 ★
Byrsonima crassifolia, [3] p. 74
Caesalpinia echinata, [2] p. 75
Calophyllum inophyllum, [1] p. 82 ★
Calotropis gigantea, [1] p. 84 ★
Canella winterana, [2] p. 90
Casuarina equisitifolia, [1] p. 98 ★
Cerbera manghas, [2] p. 108
Chrysobalanus icaco, [1] p. 111 ★
Clusia rosea, [1] p. 121
Coccoloba uvifera, [1] p. 122
Conocarpus erectus, [1] p. 128
Cordia dodecandra, [2] p. 130
Cupaniopsis anacardioides, [3] p. 137
Cussonia spicata, [3] p. 138
Deplanchea tetraphylla, [3] p. 142
Dodonaea viscosa, [2] p. 152 ★
Dolichandrone spathacea, [1] p. 153
Euphorbia punicea, [2] p. 176
Guaiacum officinale, [3] p. 208
Guettardia speciosa, [1] p. 209
Harpullia pendula, [3] p. 215
Heritiera littoralis, [1] p. 217
Hernandia nymphaeifolia, [2] p. 218
Hibiscus tiliaceus, [3] p. 220
Hymenospermum flavum, [3] p. 224
Intsia bijuga, [2] p. 227
Jacquinia arborea, [1] p. 231
Kopsia arborea, [2] p. 238
Lagunaria patersonii, [3] p. 242
Lysiloma sabicu, [2] p. 256
Macaranga tanarius, [3] p. 258 ★
Manilkara zapota, [2] p. 264
Melicoccus bijugatus, [2] p. 272
Metrosideros polymorpha, [2] p. 274
Millettia pinnata, [3] p. 276 §
Morinda citrifolia, [1] p. 282
Myrica cerifera, [2] p. 290
Noronhia emarginata, [1] p. 297

Ochroma pyramidale, [**3**] p. 300
Ochrosia elliptica, [**1**] p. 301
Parkinsonia aculeata, [**2**] p. 311 ★
Pinus caribaea, [**2**] p. 323
Pisonia grandis var. *alba,* [**3**] p. 324
Sapindus saponaria, [**3**] p. 363
Sideroxylon foetidissimum, [**3**]
    p. 376
Stemmadenia littoralis, [**2**] p. 382
Tamarindus indica, [**2**] p. 402
Tamarix aphylla, [**2**] p. 403 ★
Thespesia populnea, [**1**] p. 414 ★
Thevetia peruviana, [**2**] p. 415 ★
Wallaceodendron celebicum, [**2**]
    p. 424
Ziziphus mauritiana, [**2**]
    p. 429 ★

Fast-growing species

Araucaria spp.
Azadirachta indica
Calophyllum spp.
Calotropis argentea
Casuarina spp.
Conocarpus erectus
Deplanchea tetraphylla
Dolichandrone spp.
Harpullia pendula
Hernandia spp.
Hibiscus tiliaceus
Hymenospermum flavum
Lagunaria patersonii
Macaranga spp.
Millettia pinnata
Ochroma pyramidale
Parkinsonia spp.
Pinus spp.
Pisonia spp.
Thespesia populnea
Wallaceodendron celebicum

Slow-growing species

Argusia argentea
Byrsonima spp.
Canella winterana
Chrysobalanus icaco
Clusia spp.
Coccoloba spp.
Cussonia spp.
Dodonaea viscosa
Euphorbia spp.
Guaiacum spp.
Heritiera spp.
Jacquinia spp.
Kopsia spp.
Manilkara spp.
Melicoccus bijugatus
Metrosideros spp.
Noronhia emarginata
Tamarindus indica

To provide shade
○ = open ● = dense

Azadirachta indica ●
Barringtonia asiatica ●
Byrsonima crassifolia
Calophyllum spp. ●
Clusia rosea ●
Coccoloba uvifera ○
Conocarpus erectus ○
Cordia spp. ○
Cupaniopsis anacardioides ○
Dolichandrone spp. ○
Harpullia pendula ○
Heritiera spp. ●
Hernandia spp. ○
Hibiscus tiliaceus ●
Intsia bijuga
Lysiloma sabicu ○
Macaranga spp. ●
Manilkara zapota ●
Melicoccus bijugatus ○
Millettia pinnata ●
Noronhia emarginata
Sapindus saponaria
Tamarindus indica ○
Thespesia populneus ○
Wallaceodendron celebicum
Ziziphus mauritiana ○

For screening & hedges
✚ = formal ❖ = infomal
★ = living barrier
✓ = windbreak

Amphitecna latifolia ✓
Araucaria heterophylla ✓
Argusia argentea ❖
Byrsonima lucida ✚
Caesalpinia echinata ★ (& others)
Calophyllum spp. ✓
Calotropis spp. ❖
Casuarina spp. ✚ ✓
Cerbera spp. ❖
Chrysobalanus icaco ✚
Clusia spp. ❖
Cocoloba spp. ❖
Conocarpus erectus ✚ ❖ ✓
Cordia spp. ❖ ✓
Guettardia speciosa ❖
Hernandia spp. ✓
Hibiscus tiliaceus ❖
Jacquinia spp. ✚ ❖
Kopsia spp. ❖ ✓
Manilkara jaimiqui ❖ ✓
Morinda citrifolia ❖
Myrica cerifera ❖
Noronhia emarginata ✓
Ochrosia spp. ❖ ✓
Tamarix spp.
Thespesia populnea ❖ ✓
Ziziphus spp. ❖ ★ ✓

For accent & confined spaces
⊞ = suitable for large planters
† = topiary

Araucaria spp.
Amphitecna latifolia
Argusia argentea ⊞
Barringtonia edulis (& others) ⊞
Byrsonima spp. ⊞
Caesalpinia echinata (& others)
    ⊞ †
Calotropis spp. ⊞
Canella winterana ⊞ †
Casuarina equisitifolia ⊞ †
Cerbera spp. ⊞
Chrysobalanus icaco ⊞ †
Clusia spp. ⊞
Cocoloba spp. ⊞ †
Conocarpus erectus ⊞ †
Cordia lutea (& others) ⊞
Cussonia spp. ⊞
Dodonaea viscosa ⊞
Euphorbia spp. ⊞
Guaiacum spp. ⊞ †
Guettardia spp. ⊞
Hibiscus tiliaceus cvs. ⊞
Hymenospermum flavum ⊞
Jacquinia spp. ⊞ †
Kopsia spp. ⊞
Macaranga grandifolia ⊞
Manilkara jaimiqui †
Metrosideros spp. ⊞ †
Morinda citrifolia ⊞
Myrica cerifera ⊞
Noronhia emarginata †
Ochrosia spp. ⊞
Pisonia grandis var. *alba* ⊞
Stemmadenia littoralis ⊞
Thespesia populnea †
Thevetia peruviana ⊞ †
Ziziphus spp. ⊞ †

With showy flowers
r = red : p = pink : b = blue :
m = mauve : v = violet :
y = yellow : o = orange :
w = white : g = green :
❋ = seasonal :
● = intermittently

Barringtonia spp. (r/p/w) ●
Byrsonima spp. (y-o/r-w) ❋
Caesalpinia spp. (y/r) ❋
Calophyllum inophyllum (w) ❋
Calotropis spp. (p/m/v/w) ●
Canella winterana (r) ●
Cerbera spp. (w-r) ●
Clusia rosea (p/w/y) ●
Cordia spp. (o/y/w) ●
Cussonia spp. (y-g) ❋
Deplanchea tetraphylla (y) ❋

Dolichandrone spp. (w) ❋
Euphorbia punicea (r) ●
Guaiacum spp. (b/v) ●
Guettardia speciosa (w) ●
Harpullia pendula (y-g/w) ●
Hernandia spp. (y-g) ●
Hibiscus spp. (y-r/r/w) ●
Hymenospermum flavum (y) ❋
Intsia bijuga (w-y) ❋
Jacquinia spp. (o/w) ❋
Kopsia spp. (w/p) ❋
Lagunaria patersonii (p) ❋
Macaranga spp. (r/w) ●
Metrosideros spp. (r) ❋
Milletia pinnata (m/p) ❋
Ochroma pyramidale (w) ❋
Ochrosia spp. (w) ❋
Parkinsonia spp. (y) ❋
Stemmadenia littoralis (w) ●
Tamarindus indica (y-r) ❋
Thespesia populnea (y-m) ●
Thevetia peruviana (o/y/w) ●

With showy fruit
✕ = toxic ✓ = edible

Araucaria spp.
Barringtonia spp. (some) ✕
Byrsonima crassifolia ✓
Caesalpinia echinata
Calotropis spp.
Canella winterana ✓
Cerbera spp. ✕
Chrysobalanus icaco ✓
Clusia spp. ✕
Coccoloba uvifera ✓
Cordia spp.
Cupaniopsis spp.
Cussonia spp.
Dodonaea viscosa
Guaiacum spp.
Harpullia spp.
Hernandia spp.
Jacquinia spp. ✕
Kopsia spp. ✕
Manilkara zapota ✓
Melicoccus bijugatus ✓
Morinda citrifolia ✓
Ochroma pyramidale
Sapindus saponaria ✕
Stemmadenia spp.
    (not recommended)
Tamarindus indica ✓
Thevetia peruviana ✕
Ziziphus spp. ✓

5.
MODERATELY SALT-TOLERANT, EVERGREEN TREES

★ = may be invasive

Major species

Afrocarpus gracilior p 13
Agathis robusta p 14
Aleurites moluccana p 19 ★
Alloxylon flammeum p 20
Andira inermis p 25
Annona murieata p 26
Artocarpus altilis p 34
Backhousia citriodora p 41
Blighia sapida p 53 ★
Brosimum alicastrum p 60
Brunfelsia americana p 65
Bucida buccras p 67
Bulnesia arborea p 70
Bunchosia argentea p 71 ★
Caesalpinia echinata p 75
Callistemon viminalis p 79
Calycophyllum candidiasimum p 85
Cananga odorata p 88 ★
Canella winterana p 90
Casimiroa edulis p 91
Catalpa longissima p 99
Ceratonia siliqua p 106
Ceratopetalum gummiferum p 107
Cestrum diuruum p 109 ★
Deplanchea tetraphylla p 142
Dialium guineense p 143
Elaeocarpus augustfolius p 160
Eriobotrya japonica p 165 ★
Eucalyptus deglupta p 170 ★
Eugenia uniflora p 174 ★
Fernandoa magnifica p 181
Ficus benjamina (many) p 182 ★
Filicium decipiens p 188 ★
Flacourtia indica p 190 ★
Fraxinus griffithii p 193
Gardenia taitensis p 198
Geijera parviflora p 199
Gnetum gnemone p 204
Grevillea robusta p 205
Gymnostoma spp. p 212
Hamelia patens p 214
Hymenaea courbaril p 223
Inga jinicuil p 226 ★
Juniperus burbadensis p 233
Khaya anthotheca p 234
Kleinhovia hospita p 236
Leptospermum madidum p 246
Lonchocarpus violaceus p 252
Malpighia glabra p 261
Mammea americana p 262
Mangifera indica p 263 ★

Melaleuca leucadendra p 268 ★
Mesua ferrea p 273
Metrosideros polymorpha p 274
Millingtonia hortensis p 278
Mimusops elengi p 279
Moringa oleifera p 283
Morus alba p 284 ★
Murraya koenigii p 286
Myrciaria floribunda p 288
Myristica fragans p 291
Newbouldia laevis p 296
Oxyanthus pyriformis p 305
Peltophorum pterocarpum p 314
Phyllocarpus septentrionalis p 320
Phytolacca dioica p 321
Pimenta dioica p 322
Pithecellobium arboreum p 325
Pittosporum pentandrum p 326 ★
Podocarpus neriifolius p 336
Portlandia grandiflora p 342
Pterospermum acerifolium p 350
Quassia simarouba p 354
Schefflera actinophylla p 367 ★
Schinus terebinthifolius p 368 ★
Senna siamea p 372 ★
Spathodea campanulata p 378 ★
Strychnos nux-vomica p 387
Swietenia mahogani p 388
Swinglea glutinosa p 389
Syzygium malaccense p 390
Ziyphus mauritiana p 429 ★

Fast-growing species

Backhousia spp.
Adenanthera spp.
Annona spp.
Artocarpus spp.
Bischofia javanica
Blighia sapida
Cananga odorata
Cestrum spp.
Deplanchea tetraphylla
Eucalyptus spp.
Grevillea spp.
Hamelia spp.
Inga spp.
Khaya spp.
Kigelia pinnata
Lawsonia inermis
Millingtonia hortensis
Moringa oleifera
Morus spp.
Newbouldia laevis
Peltophorum spp.
Persea americana
Phyllocarpus septentrionalis
Phytolacca dioica
Pithecellobium spp.
Pterospermum spp.
Schinus terebinthifolius

Senna spp.
Spathodea campanulata
Swietenia spp.
Syzygium spp.

Slow-growing species

Agathis spp.
Brunfelsia spp.
Bucida 'Shady Lady'
Bucida spinosa
Bulnesia arborea
Canella winterana
Catalpa longissima
Eugenia spp.
Filicium decipiens
Geijera spp.
Gnetum gnemone
Gymnostoma spp.
Hymenaea courbaril
Juniperus spp.
Leptospermum spp.
Majidea zanguebarica
Mammea americana
Manilkara spp.
Melaleuca spp.
Mesua ferrea
Metrosideros spp.
Murraya spp.
Myrciaria spp.
Myristica spp.
Oxyanthus spp.
Strychnos spp.
Pimenta spp.
Portlandia spp.
Quassia spp.

To provide shade
○ = open ● = dense

Afrocarpus spp. (some)
Andira inermis ●
Bischofia javanica ●
Blighia sapida ○
Brosimum spp. ●
Bucida buceras ●
Bulnesia arborea
Cananga odorata
Cassia spp. (most) ○
Catalpa longissima ○
Ceratonia siliqua ○
Dialium guineense
Elaeocarpus spp. ○
Eriobotrya spp.
Filicium decipiens ●
Ficus spp. (some)
Inga spp. ○
Mangifera indica ●
Moringa oleifera ○
Morus spp. ●
Peltophorum spp. ○

Phtyolacca dioica ●
Pterospermum acerifolim
Quassia simarouba ●
Swietenia spp.
Swinglea glutinosa
Syzygium spp. (some)

For screening & hedges
✚ = formal ❖ = infomal
★ = living barrier
✓ = windbreak

Andira inermis ✓
Afrocarpus spp. ✓
Bunchosia spp. ✓
Bucida spinosa ★
Cupressus spp. ✓ ❖
Caesalpinia sappan ★
Caesalpinia echinata ★ ✚ ❖
Cestrum spp. ✚
Eugenia spp. ✚
Flacourtia spp. ★
Fraxinus griffithii ❖
Gardenia taitensis ❖
Gymnostoma spp. ✓
Juniperus spp. ✓
Lawsonia inermis ★ (✚)
Malpighia glabra ❖
Mimusops elengi ✓
Murraya paniculata ✚
Pittosporum spp. (some) ✓
Podocarpus spp. ✓
Senna spp. (many) ❖
Ziyphus spp. ★

For accent & confined spaces
⊞ = suitable for large planters
† = topiary

Afrocarpus spp. (some) †
Aleurites spp.
Alloxylon spp. ⊞
Annona spp. ⊞
Backhousia spp.
Brunfelsia spp. ⊞
Bucida 'Shady lady' † ⊞
Bucida spinosa ⊞
Bunchosia spp. ⊞
Caesalpinia spp. ⊞
Callistemon spp. ⊞
Cananga odorata
Canella winterana †
Ceratopetalum spp. ⊞
Cestrum spp. † ⊞
Crescentia spp. ⊞
Deplanchea spp. ⊞
Elaeocarpus ferruginiflorus † ⊞
Eriobotrya spp.
Eucalyptus spp. (some)
Eugenia spp. †
Filicium decipiens ⊞

437

Flacourtia spp. †
Fraxinus griffithii ⌘
Gardenia spp. ⌘
Geijera spp. ⌘
Gnetum gnemone
Grevillea baileyana (& others)
Gymnostoma spp. † ⌘
Hamelia spp. ⌘
Juniperus spp. ⌘
Kleinhovia hospita
Lawsonia inermis † ⌘
Leptospermum spp.
Lonchocarpus violaceus ⌘
Malpighia spp. † ⌘
Melaleuca spp.
Mesua ferrea
Metrosiderpos spp. † ⌘
Moringa oleifera
Murraya paniculata †
Myrciaria spp. † ⌘
Newbouldia laevis
Oxyanthus spp. ⌘
Peltophorum africanum
Pimenta spp. † ⌘
Pittosporum spp.
Podocarpus spp. †
Portlandia spp. ⌘
Quassia amara ⌘
Schefflera spp.
Schinus spp.
Senna spp. (some) ⌘
Syzygium spp. (most) ⌘
Pterospermum lancifolium
Zizyphus spp. ⌘

With showy flowers

r = red : p = pink : b = blue :
m = mauve : v = violet :
y = yellow : o = orange :
w = white : g = green :
❋ = seasonal :
● = intermittently

Aleurites spp. (w) ●
Alloxylon spp. (r) ❋
Andira inermis (p/m/v) ❋
Backhousia spp. (w) ❋
Brunfelsia spp. (b/m/v/w) ❋
Bulnesia arborea (y) ❋
Bunchosia spp. (y) ❋
Caesalpinia spp. (y) ❋
Callistemon spp. (r/p/w) ●
Catalpa spp. (w/p/y) ❋ ●
Ceratopetalum spp. (w/p/r) ❋
Cestrum spp. (w/y) ●
Deplanchea spp. (y) ❋
Dialium guineense (y) ❋
Elaeocarpus spp. (w) ❋
Eriobotrya spp. (w) ❋
Eucalyptus spp. (most) (r/y/p/w) ●
438 *Fraxinus* spp. (w) ❋

Gardenia spp. (w/y) ❋
Geijera spp. (w-y) ❋
Grevillea spp. (o/p/r/y/w) ❋
Hamelia spp. (r/o/y) ●
Inga spp. (w) ●
Kigelia africana (r/y) ●
Kleinhovia hospita (p-w) ❋
Lawsonia inermis (w/p) ●
Lonchocarpus spp. (p/m/b) ❋
Malpighia spp. (p/m) ●
Mammea americana (w) ❋
Mangifera indica (p-w/y) ❋
Melaleuca spp. (w/r) ❋
Mesua ferrea (w) ❋
Metrosideros spp. (r) ❋
Millettia pinnata (m/v/p)
Millingtonia hortensis (w) ❋
Moringa oleifera (w) ●
Murraya spp. (w) ●
Myrciaria spp. (y/w) ❋
Newbouldia laevis (p/m) ❋
Oxyanthus spp. (w) ●
Peltophorum spp. (y) ❋
Phyllocarpus septentrionalis (r) ❋
Phytolacca dioica (w) ❋
Pimenta dioica (w) ❋
Pittosporum spp. (w/g) ❋
Portlandia spp. (w/r) ●
Pterospermum spp. (w) ❋
Quassia amara (r) ●
Schefflera spp. (r/y-g) ❋
Senna (y) ❋
Spathodea campanulata (r/o/y) ❋
Syzygium spp. (r/p/m/v/w) ❋

With showy fruit

✕ = toxic ✓ = edible

Afrocarpus spp.
Adenanthera spp.
Aleurites spp. ✕
Annona spp. ✓
Artocarpus spp. ✓
Backhousia spp.
Blighia sapida ✕
Brosimum spp. ✓
Brunfelsia spp.
Bunchosia spp. ✓
Caesalpinia echinata
Caesalpinia sappan
Cananga odorata
Canella winterana ✓
Ceratopetalum spp.
Cestrum spp. ✕
Crescentia spp. ✕
Dialium spp. ✓
Elaeocarpus spp.
Eriobotrya spp. ✓
Eugenia spp. ✓
Ficus spp. ✓ (some)
Filicium decipiens
Flacourtia spp. ✓

Fraxinus spp.
Geijera spp.
Gnetum gnemone ✓
Hamelia spp.
Hymenaea courbaril
Inga spp. ✓
Kigelia africana ✕
Kleinhovia hospita (not recommended)
Lonchocarpus violaceus
Majidea zanguebarica
Malpighia spp. ✓
Mammea americana ✓
Mangifera indica ✓
Mesua ferrea
Mimusops elengi
Moringa oleifera ✓
Murraya spp.
Myrciaria spp. ✓
Myristica spp. ✓
Peltophorum spp.
Persea americana ✓
Pimenta spp. ✓
Phytolacca dioica ✕
Pithecellobium arboreum
Pittosporum spp.
Podocarpus spp.
Pterocarpum spp.
Quassia simarouba
Schefflera spp.
Schinus spp.
Strychnos spp. ✕
Syzygium spp. ✓
Swietenia spp.
Swinglea glutinosa ✓
Ziziphus spp. ✓

6.
MODERATELY SALT-TOLERANT, DECIDUOUS TREES

★ = may be invasive
❋ = semi-deciduous

Major species

Acacia farnesiana p1 ★
Acokanthera ❋ p 6
Adansonia digitata p 8
Adenanthera pavonina p 10 ❋ ★
Albizia lebbek p 18 ★
Anacardium occidentale p 24 ❋
Bauhinia variegata p 46 ★
Bischofia javanica p 51 ❋ ★
Brya ebenus p 66 ❋
Bursera simaruba p 72 ★
Calycophyllum candidissimum p 85
Cassia fistula p 92 ❋

Cedrela odorata p 102
Ceiba pentandra p 104
Chorisia speciosa p 110
Chrysophyllum cainito p 112 ❋
Cochlospermum vitifolium p 124
Cordia dodecandra p 131 ❋
Crescentia cujete p 136
Dalbergia sissoo 139 ❋
Delonix regia p 140
Duranta erecta p 158 ❋ ★
Enterolobium cyclocarpum p 163 ★
Fernandoa magnifica p 181
Genipa americana p 200 ❋
Gliricidia sepium p 201 ★
Gmelina arborea p 202
Haemotoxylum campechianum p 213 ★
Hura crepitans p 22 ❋
Jacaranda mimosifolia p 229
Jatropha curcas p 232
Khaya anthotheca p 234 ❋
Kigelia africana p 235 ❋
Lawsonia inermis p 244 ❋
Majidea zanguebarica p 260 ❋
Melia azedarach p 271 ★
Millettia pinnata p 276 ❋
Myroxylon balsamum p 292 ❋
Pangium edule p 308
Parkinsonia aculeata p 311 ❋ ★
Persea americana p 316 ❋
Petrea arborea p 317 ❋
Phyllanthus acidus p 318
Phyllocapus septentrionalis p 320
Plumeria rubra p 332
Pouteria sapota p 344 ❋
Pseudobombax ellipticum p 346
Quararibea cordata p 352 ❋
Samanea saman p 359 ★
Schotia brachypetala p 370
Sclerocarya birrea p 371
Sesbania grandiflora p 375 ★
Spondias cytherea p 379
Stereospermum kunthianum p 386
Swietenia mahogani p 388
Tabebuia heterophylla p 396 ❋ ★
Taxodium mucronatum p 404
Tecoma stans p 406 ★
Tectona grandis p 407
Terminalia catappa p 408 ★
Vitex agnus-castus p 422
Zanthoxylum p 428

Fast-growing species

Acacia spp.
Adenanthera spp.
Albizia spp.
Bauhinia spp.
Bischofia javanica
Cedrela spp.

Ceiba spp.
Chorisia spp.
Cochlospermum spp.
Dalbergia spp.
Duranta erecta
Enterolobium spp.
Fernandoa spp. (fairly fast)
Gliricidia sepium
Gmelina spp.
Hura crepitans
Jacaranda spp.
Khaya spp.
Kigelia africana (when young)
Lawsonia inermis
Melia azedarach
Millettia spp.
Parkinsonia spp.
Persea americana
Phyllocarpus septentrionalis
Pseudobombax spp.
Quararibea cordata
Samanea saman
Sesbania spp.
Spondias spp.
Swietenia spp.
Tabebuia spp.
Tecoma stans
Terminalia spp.
Vitex spp.

Slow-growing species

Adansonia spp.
Adenium spp.
Anacardium occidentale
Brya ebenus
Cassia spp. (fairly slow)
Crescentia spp.
Haematoxylum campechianum
Majidea zanguebarica
Petrea spp.
Plumeria spp.
Schotia spp.
Zanthoxylum spp.

For summer shade
○ = open   ● = dense

Acacia (some) ○
Adenanthera spp. ●
Bischofia javanica ●
Bursera spp. ○
Cassia spp. (some) ○
Cedrela odorata ○
Chrysophyllum spp. ●
Cordia spp. (some) ○
Dalbergia sissoo ○
Genipa americana ●
Melia azedarach ○
Millettia spp.
Pangium edule ●
Persea americana

Pouteria spp. ●
Swietenia spp.
Tabebuia spp. (some) ○
Vitex parviflora ○

For screening & hedges
✚ = formal   ❖ = infomal
★ = living barrier
✓ = windbreak

Acacia spp. (some) ★
Acokanthera spp.
Bauhinia divaricata
Bauhinia forficata ★
Cordia boissieri
Cordia lutea
Duranta erecta ★
Jatropha integerrima ✓
Lawsonia inermis
Millettia pinnata ✓
Phyllanthus angustifolia
Schotia spp.
Tecoma stans
Terminalia sericea ✓

For accent & confined spaces
✠ = suitable for large planters
† = topiary

Acacia spp. (some) ✠
Acokanthera spp † ✠
Anacardium occidentale
Bauhinia divaricata † ✠
Bauhinia forficata ✠
Bauhinia monandra † ✠
Brya ebenus † ✠
Bursera frenningae ✠
Cassia afrofistula † ✠
Cassia 'Paluma Range' ✠
Cassia queenslandica ✠
Ceiba acuminata ✠
Cochlospermum spp. ✠
Cordia boissieri † ✠
Cordia lutea † ✠
Crescentia spp.
Duranta erecta † ✠
Fernandoa spp. ✠
Jacaranda jasminoides ✠
Jatropha integerrima † ✠
Lawsonia inermis † ✠
Majidea zanguebarica † ✠
Parkinsonia spp. ✠
Plumeria spp. ✠
Schotia spp. ✠
Tabebuia bahamensis ✠
Tabebuia haemantha † ✠
Tabebuia lepidota ✠
Tecoma stans † ✠
Vitev agnus-castus ✠
Vitex negundo ✠
Vitex trifolia 'Variegata' † ✠

With showy flowers
r = red : p = pink : b = blue :
m = mauve : v = violet :
y = yellow : o = orange :
w = white : g = green :
✳ = seasonal :
● = intermittently

Acacia spp. (y) ✳ ●
Acokanthera spp (w/p) ✳
Adansonia spp. (w/y/r) ✳
Bauhinia spp. (w/r/p/m/y) ✳
Brya ebenus (y) ●
Calycophyllum spp. (w) ✳
Cassia spp. (r/p/y/o) ✳
Ceiba spp. (p/y/w) ✳
Chorisia spp. (p/m/y/w) ✳
Cochlospermum spp. (y) ✳
Cordia spp. (y/o/w) ●
Delonix spp. (o/y/w) ✳
Duranta erecta (b/m/v/w) ●
Fernandoa spp. (o/y) ✳
Gliricidia sepium (p/m/w) ✳
Gmelina spp. (p/m/w) ✳
Jacaranda spp. (p/b/m/v/w) ✳
Kigelia africana (r/y) ●
Lawsonia inermis (p/w) ●
Majidea zanguebarica (w/y-g) ✳
Melia azedarach (m/p) ✳
Millettia spp. (m/v/p) ✳
Parkinsonia spp. (y-o) ✳
Persea americana (g-w) ✳
Petrea spp. (m/v/w) ●
Phyllocarpus septentrionalis (r) ●
Plumeria spp. (r/p/y/o/w) ✳
Pseudobombax spp. (p/w) ●
Schotia spp. (r/p) ●
Sesbania spp. (r/p/w) ●
Stereospermum spp. (p/m/v) ✳
Tabebuia spp. (r/p/y/w) ●
Tecoma spp. (y/o) ✳
Vitex spp. (p/m/v/w) ✳ ●

With showy fruit
✕ = toxic   ✓ = edible

Acokanthera spp. ✕
Adansonia spp. ✓
Adenanthera spp.
Albizia lebbek
Anacardium occidentale ✕ ✓
Bischofia javanica
Bursera spp.
Cedrela odorata
Ceiba spp.
Chorisia spp.
Chrysophyllum spp. ✓
Cordia spp.
Crescentia spp. ✕
Delonix spp.
Duranta erecta ✕
Enterolobium spp.

Fernandoa spp.
Genipa americana ✓
Gmelina spp.
Hura crepitans (not recommended)
Khaya spp.
Kigelia africana ✕
Majidea zanguebarica
Melia azedarach ✕
Millettia spp. ✕
Pangium edule ✕ ✓
Persea americana ✓
Phyllanthus spp. ✓ (some)
Pouteria spp. ✓
Quararibea cordata ✓
Schotia spp.
Sclerocarya birrea ✓
Sesbania grandiflorum
Spondias spp. ✓
Swietenia spp. ✓

PART 2

7.
TREES FOR HUMID SHADE

★ = may be invasive

Major species

439

Ficus benjamina (many spp.)
  p 182 ★
Filicium decipiens p 188 ★
Garcinia mangostana p 194
Gardenia carinata p 197
Genipa americana p 200
Gnetum gnemone p 204
Gustavia superba p 210
Heritiera littoralis p 217
Ilex paraguayensis p 225
Ixora pavetta p 228
Kopsia arborea p 238
Lansium domesticum p 243
Lecythis spp. p 245
Lophanthera lactescens p 254
Lophostemon confertus
  var. variegata p 255
Macaranga tanarius p 258
Magnolia grandiflora p 259
Mammea americana p 262
Maniltoa browneoides p 266
Markhamia lutea p 267
Mesua ferrea p 273
Michelia champaca p 275
Monodora myristica p 280
Morinda citrifolia p 282
Murraya paniculata p 287
Myristica fragrans p 291
Napoleonaea imperialis p 293
Nephelium lappaceum p 295
Nyctanthes arbor-tristes p 299
Oroxylon indicum p 304
Oxyanthus pynformis p 305
Pachira aquatica p 306
Parmentiera cerifera p 313 ★
Pimenta dioca p 322
Pisonia grandis var. alba p 324
Pogonopus speciosus p 338
Pometia pinnata p 341
Portlandia grandiflora p 342
Posqueria latifolia p 343
Quassia amara p 353
Radermachera gigantea p 355
Reevesia thyrsoidea p 356
Salix chilensis p 358
Sandoricum koetjape p 361
Saraca indica p 364
Schefflera actinophylla p 367 ★
Stelecocharpus burahol p 381
Stemmadenia littoralis p 382
Stenocarpus sinuatus p 383
Sterculia shillinglawii p 385
Tabernaemontana spp. p 400
Theobroma spp. p 412
Treculia africana p 419
Trevesia burckii p 420
Wallaceodendron celebicum p 424
Warszewizia coccinea p 425
Wrightia arborea p 426

440

Fast-growing species

Acrocarpus fraxinifolius
Alstonia spp.
Brugmansia spp.
Clerodendron spp.
Dolichandrone spp.
Ficus spp. (some)
Lophanthera lactescens (fairly fast)
Macaranga spp.
Michelia spp.
Nephelium lappaceum
Nyctanthes arbor-tristes
Oroxylon indicum
Pisonia grandis var. alba
Pisonia brunoniana var. variegata
Pometia pinnata
Radermachera spp.
Wallaceodendron celebicum

Slow-growing species

Alberta magna
Amherstia nobilis
Athertonia diversifolia (fairly slow)
Averrhoa spp.
Brownea spp.
Cinnamomum spp.
Clusia spp.
Crateva spp.
Fagraea spp.
Filicium decipiens
Garcinia spp.
Gnetum gnemone
Heritiera spp.
Ilex spp.
Ixora spp.
Kopsia spp. (fairly slow)
Lansium domesticum
Mammea americana
Magnolia spp.
Maniltoa spp. (fairly slow)
Mesua ferrea
Myristica spp.
Napoleonaea spp.
Oxyanthus spp.
Parmentiera spp.
Portlandia spp.
Quassia amara
Saraca spp. (fairly slow)
Stelecocarpus burahol
Stenocarpus spp.
Treculia africana
Trevesia spp.
Wrightia spp.

To provide shade
o = open ● = dense

Antidesma spp. ●
Aphanamixis spp. o
Barringtonia spp. (some)

Brosimum spp. ●
Dolichandrone spp. ●
Eperua spp. ●
Ficus (several spp.) ●
Genipa americana ●
Heritiera spp. ●
Mesua ferrea
Nephelium lappaceum
Pometia pinnata
Wallaceodendron celebicum ●

For screening & hedges
✚ = formal   ❖ = infomal
★ = living barrier
✓ = windbreak

Amphitecna latifolia ✓ ❖
Annona muricata ✓
Camellia sinensis ✚
Clerodendrum spp. ❖
Clusia spp. ✓
Coffea spp. ✚
Filicium decipiens ❖
Ilex spp. ❖
Ixora spp. ❖
Kopsia spp. ✓
Morinda citrifolia ❖
Murrraya paniculata ✚
Tabernaemontana spp. (some) ❖

For accent & confined
spaces
⊞ = suitable for large planters
† = topiary

Alberta magna ⊞
Amherstia nobilis
Archidendron spp.
Averrhoa spp. ⊞
Barringtonia spp. (some)
Brownea spp.
Camellia sinensis ⊞ †
Clerodendrum spp. ⊞
Clusia spp. ⊞
Coffea spp. ⊞ †
Crateva spp. ⊞
Dillenia spp. ⊞
Fagraea spp. (some)
Ficus spp. (some) †
Filicium decipiens
Garcinia spp.
Gardenia spp. (most) ⊞
Gnetum gnemone
Gustavia spp. ⊞
Ilex spp. ⊞ †
Ixora spp. ⊞ †
Kopsia spp. ⊞ †
Lophanthera lactescens
Macaranga tanarius
Magnolia liliifera
Markhamia lutea ⊞
Mesua ferrea

Michelia spp. ⊞
Morinda citrifolia ⊞
Murraya paniculata ⊞ †
Napoleonaea spp. ⊞
Nyctanthes arbor-tristes ⊞
Oroxylon indicum
Pachira quinata
Oxyanthus spp. ⊞
Parmentiera spp.
Pisonia grandis var. alba ⊞
Pogonopus speciosis ⊞
Portlandia spp. ⊞
Quassia amara
Radermachera spp. ⊞
Reevesia thyrsoidea ⊞ †
Salix chilensis
Saraca spp.
Schefflera spp.
Stemmadenia spp. ⊞ †
Stenocarpus spp.
Trevesia spp. ⊞
Warszewiczia coccinea ⊞
Wrightia spp. ⊞

With showy flowers
r = red : p = pink : b = blue :
m = mauve : v = violet :
y = yellow : o = orange :
w = white : g = green :
✳ = seasonal :
● = intermittently

Acrocarpus fraxinifolius (r/p) ✳
Alberta magna (o)
Alstonia scholaris (w) ✳
Amherstia nobilis (r) ●
Aphanamixis spp. (y) ✳
Archiodendron spp. (w/p)
Athertonia diversifolia (w) ✳
Averrhoa spp. (p/r/m) ●
Barringtonia spp. (r/p/w) ●
Brownea spp. (r/p) ✳
Brugmansia spp. (r/p/y/o/w) ●
Clerodendrum spp. (p/w) ✳
Coffea spp. (w) ✳
Crateva spp. (w/y) ✳
Dillenia spp. (w/y) ✳
Dolichandrone spp. (w) ✳ ●
Eperua spp. (r/p/m/v) ✳
Fagraea spp. (w/y) ✳
Gardenia spp. (w/y) ✳
Gustavia spp. (p/m/w) ●
Ixora spp. (w) ✳
Kopsia spp. (p/w) ✳
Lecythis spp. (m/y/w) ✳
Lophanthera lactescens (y) ✳
Macaranga spp. (r/w) ●
Magnolia spp. (p/w) ✳
Mammea spp. (w) ✳
Maniltoa spp. (w) ●
Markhamia spp. (r/y) ●
Mesua ferrea (w) ✳

Michelia spp. (p/y/w) ✳
Monodora myristica (y-r) ✳
Morinda reticulata (w) ●
Murraya spp. (w) ✳ ●
Napoleonaea spp. (v-y) ✳
Nyctanthes arbor-tristes (w-o) ●
Oroxylon indicum (r-v) ✳
Oxyanthes spp. (w) ●
Pachira spp. (w) ●
Pimenta dioica (w) ●
Pogonopus speciosus (r/v) ✳
Portlandia spp. (r/w) ●
Posqueria spp. (w) ✳
Quassia amara (r) ●
Radermachera spp. (p-y/p-v) ●
Reevesia thyrsoidea (w) ✳
Saraca spp. (r/o/y) ✳
Schefflera actinophylla (r/p) ✳
Stemmadenia spp. (w) ●
Stenocarpus sinuatus (r/w) ●
Sterculia foetida (r/p/y/w) ✳
Tabernaemontana spp. (w) ✳
Treculia africana (g) ●
Wallaceodendron celebicum (y/w) ✳
Warszewiczia coccinea (r) ✳
Wrightia spp. (o/y/w) ✳

With showy fruit

✕ = toxic ✓ = edible

Alberta magna
Amherstia nobilis
Amphitecna latifolia
Annona spp. ✓
Antidesma spp. ✓
Aphanamixis spp. ✕
Archidendron spp.
Athertonia diversifolia ✓
Averrhoa spp. ✓
Barringtonia spp. (some)
Cecropia spp. ✓
Clerodendrum spp.
Coffea spp. ✓
Crateva spp. ✕
Dillenia spp. ✓
Durio zebinthifolius ✓
Eperua spp.
Fagraea spp.
Ficus spp. (many)
Filicium decipiens
Garcinia spp. ✓
Gardenia spp.
Genipa americana ✓
Gnetum gnemone ✓
Gustavia spp. ✓
Heritiera spp.
Ilex spp.
Kopsia spp. ✕
Lansium domesticum ✓
Lecythis spp. ✓
Lophanthera lactescens
Magnolia spp.

Mammea americana ✓
Maniltoa spp.
Michelia spp.
Monodora spp. ✓
Morinda citrifolia ✓
Murraya spp.
Myristica spp. ✓
Nephelium lappaceum ✓
Oroxylon indicum
Oxyanthus spp.
Pachira spp. ✓
Parmentiera spp.
Pimenta dioica ✓
Pisonia spp.
Pometia spp. ✓
Posqueria spp.
Sandoricum koetjape ✓
Saraca cauliflora
Schefflera actinophylla
Stelecocarpus burahol ✓
Treculia africana ✓
Trevesia spp.

8.
TREES &
THEIR FLOWERS

♦ = one form of the the sp.
✚ = changes colour later

Trees with showy
white flowers

Acokanthera spp.
Adansonia spp. (most)
Aegle marmelos
Aleurites spp. (most)
Alstonia spp.
Archidendron lucyi
Athertonia diversifolia
Azadirachta indica
Backhousia spp.
Barringtonia calyptrata
Barringtonia edulis
Bauhinia spp. (some)
Bixa orellana var. *alba*
Blighia sapida
Brachychiton australe
Bravaisia integerrima
Brunfelsia americana ✚
Buckinghamia celsissima
Bulnesia sarmentoi
Bursera simaruba
Calliandra portoricensis
Callistemon salignus ♦
Callophyllum spp.
Calycophyllum candidissimum
Camellia sinensis
Casimiroa edulis
Castanospermum australe ✚

Cedrela odorata
Cerbera spp.
Cestrum spp.
Chorisia insignis
Citrus spp.
Clausena lansium
Clerodendrum minahasseae
Coffea spp.
Cordia boissieri (& others)
Crateva religiosa ✚
Delonix elata
Dialium guineensis
Dillenia philippensis
Dolichandrone spp.
Dombeya spp. (some) ✚ ♦
Duabanga grandiflora
Duranta erecta var. *alba*
Elaeocarpus spp.
Eriobotrya spp.
Erythrina variegata var. *alba*
Eucalyptus spp. (many)
Eugenia spp.
Fagraea spp. (several) ✚
Flindersia spp. (several)
Fraxinus griffithii
Gardenia spp. ✚
Geijera spp.
Grevillea baileyana (& others)
Guettardia speciosa
Hernandia spp.
Hibiscus waimea
Inga spp.
Intsia bijuga
Ixora spp. (several)
Kopsia spp.
Largerstroemia indica ♦
Lawsonia inermis
Lonchocarpus spp. ♦
Lysiloma latisliquum
Macadamia spp. (many)
Macaranga tanarius
Magnolia spp. (many)
Mangifera indica
Mammea americana
Maniltoa spp.
Melaleuca spp. (many)
Mesua ferrea
Michelia alba
Millingtonia hortensis
Moringa reticulata
Muntingia calabura
Murraya spp.
Nauclea spp.
Nuxia spp.
Nyctanthes abor-tristes
Ochroma pyramidale
Ochrosia spp.
Oncoba spp.
Oxyanthus spp.
Pachira spp.
Persea americana
Petrea volubilis var. *alba*

Phytolacca dioica
Pimenta spp.
Pittosporum spp.
Plumeria spp. (many)
Portlandia grandiflora
Posqueria spp.
Pseudobombax elliptica ♦
Pterospermum spp.
Radermachera sinica
Reevesia thyrsoidea
Sesbania grandiflora ♦
Spondias spp.
Stemmadenia spp.
Stenocarpus davallioides
Tabebuia spp. (some)
Tabernaemontana spp.
Tectona grandis
Thevetia peruviana ♦
Syzygium spp. (many)
Wrightia spp. (many)
Xanthostemon granaticus

Trees with showy,
yellow flowers

Acacia spp.
Adenanthera spp.
Aphanamixis spp.
Banksia dentata
Brya ebenus
Bucida spp.
Bulnesia arborea
Bunchosia spp.
Byrsonima spp. *
Caesalpinia spp. (most)
Cananga spp.
Canarium spp.
Cassia spp. (some)
Castillea elastica
Catalpa punctatus
Cecropia peltata
Ceiba pentandra
Cola acuminata
Cordia lutea (& others)
Crateva spp.
Delonix regia ♦
Deplanchea spp.
Dillenia spp. (many)
Dimocarpus longan
Fagraea berteriana
Fernandoa adenophylla
Gmelina arborea
Haematoxylon campechianun
Hamelia cuprea
Harpullia pendula
Hibiscus tiliaceus ✚
Hymenosporum flavum
Koelreuteria spp.
Lansium domesticum
Lophanthera lactescens
Mangifera indica
Markhamia lutea

441

Michelia champaca
Napoleonaea spp.
Parkia spp.
Parkinsonia spp.
Peltophorum spp.
Platymiscium spp.
Plumeria rubra vars.
Pterocarpus indicus
Sandoricum koetjape
Saraca cauliflora
Sarcocephalus latifolius
Schefflera umbellifera
Schizolobium parahyba
Senna spp.
Spathodea campanulata ♦
Stelecocarpus burahol
Tabebuia spp. (some)
Tamarindus indicus
Tecoma stans
Thespesia populnea ✚
Thevetia peruviana ♦
Tipuana tipu
Wallaceodendron celebicum
Zanthoxylum spp.

Trees with showy, red flowers

Acrocarpus fraxinifolius
Adenium obesum
Alberta magna
Alloxylon spp.
Amherstia nobilis
Anacardium occidentale
Archidendron grandiflorum
Averrhoa spp.
Barringtonia acutangula
Bauhinia variegata var. rubra
Bombax ceiba
Brachychiton spp. (some)
Brugmansia sanguinea
Brownea spp.
Butea monosperma
Caesalpinia cassioides
Calliandra haematocephala
Callistemon spp. (many)
Canella winterana
Cassia spp. (several)
Cavanillesia platanifolia
Ceratopetalum spp.
Couroupita guianensis
Delonix regia ♦
Erythrina spp. (many)
Euphorbia punicea
Fernandoa magnifica
Firmiana colorata
Flindersia spp. (a few)
Greyia spp.
Hibiscus kokio
Kigelia africana
Lawsonia inermis var rubra
Macaranga grandifolia

Markhamia acuminata
Melaleuca viridiflora ♦
Metrosideros spp.
Monodora myristica
Montezuma speciosissimum
Ormosia ormondii
Oroxylon indicum
Phyllocapus septentrionalis
Plumeria rubra ♦
Poitea carinalis
Pogonopus speciosus
Punica granatum
Quassia amara
Saraca indica ✚
Schefflera actinophylla
Schotia spp. (most)
Sesbania grandiflora
Stenocarpus sinuatus
Sterculia foetida
Syzygium malaccensis
Tabebuia haemantha
Tabebuia impetignosa ♦
Triplaris spp.
Warzewiczia coccinea
Xanthostemon youngii

Trees with showy, orange or salmon flowers

Bombax buonopozense
Broussonetia papyrifera
Byrsonima crassifolia ✚
Cassia brewsteri
Cassia grandis
Cassia moschata
Castanospermum australe ✚
Colvillea racemosa
Cordia spp. (several)
Delonix regia
Erythrina decora
Erythrina dominguezii (& others)
Euphorbia punicea ♦
Eucalyptus miniata
Eucalyptus phoenicia
Firmiana colorata ♦
Grevillea robusta
Hamelia patens
Jacquinia aurantiaca
Ormosia ormondii ♦
Plumeria rubra ♦
Pterocarpus indicus ♦
Punica granatum ♦
Saraca spp. ✚
Sesbania tripettii
Spathodea campanulata
Thevetia peruviana ♦
Wrightia aborea ♦

Trees with showy, pink or lavender flowers

Adenium obesum

Adenium multiflorum
Andira inermis
Bauhinia spp. (several)
Bixa orellana
Brachychiton spp. (some)
Calliandra surinamensis
Cassia bakeriana
Cassia javanica
Cassia nealii
Catalpa longissima
Ceiba acuminata
Chorisia speciosa
Clerodendrum quadriloculare
Callistemon salignus ♦
Calodendron capense
Dipterocarpus grandiflorus
Dombeya spp. (many)
Eperua falcata
Eucalyptus phytocarpa
Gliricidia sepium
Gmelina fasisculata
Gustavia spp.
Kleinhovia hospita
Kopsia fruticosa
Lagerstroemia spp. (many)
Lagunaria patersonii
Lawsonia inermis var. rubra ♦
Lecythis zabucajo
Lonchocarpus spp.
Malpighia glabra
Melia azedarach
Millettia pinnata
Newbouldia laevis
Plumeria rubra ♦
Pseudobombax ellipticum
Poitea florida
Punica granatum var. flora pleno
Radermachera gigantea
Samanea saman
Schotia afra ♦
Sesbania grandiflora ♦
Solanum wrightii ✚
Stereospermum kunthianum
Stereospermum frimbrosum
Tabebuia heterophylla
Tabebuia impetignosa ♦
Tabebuia lepidota
Tabebuia rosea (& others)
Tamarix spp.
Thevetia peruviana ♦
Tibouchina granulosa
Vitex spp. (some)

Trees with showy, blue or purple flowers

Andira inermis ♦
Averrhoa spp. ♦
Bauhinia purpurea
Bolusanthus speciosus
Brugmansia grandiflora ✚
Calotropis spp.

Canella winterana ♦
Duranta erecta
Eperua purpurea
Guaiacum spp.
Jacaranda spp.
Lagerstroemia spp. (several)
Lonchocarpus violaceus
Newbouldia laevis
Ormosia krugii
Petrea spp.
Solanum spp.
Syzygium malaccensis
Syzygium papyraceum
Tabebuia impetignosa ♦
Tibouchina lepidota
Vitex spp. (most)

9.
FLOWERING TREES & THEIR SEASONS

✚ = main (but not only) blooming period

Spring-flowering trees

Acacia spp (most)
Acrocarpus fraxinifolius
Adansonia spp.
Adenanthera spp.
Albizia lebbek
Alloxylon spp.
Alstonia spp.
Andira inermis
Archidendron spp.
Bauhinia binata
Bixa orellana
Bolusanthus speciosus
Bombax ceiba
Brachychiton spp.
Broussonetia papyrifera
Bulnesia spp.
Bunchosia spp.
Butea monosperma
Byrsonima spp.
Caesalpinia spp. (many)
Calliandra spp.
Calophyllum spp.
Cassia spp. (some)
Castanospermum australe
Catalpa spp.
Cavanillesia platanifolia
Ceiba spp.
Ceratopetalum spp.
Citrus spp.
Clerodendrum spp.
Cochlospermum spp.
Coffea spp.
Cola spp.
Crateva spp.

442

Delonix elata
Deplanchea tetraphylla
Dillenia spp.
Dombeya spp.
Eperua spp.
Eucalyptus spp. (many)
Eriobotrya deflexa
Eucalyptus spp. (many)
Erythrina spp. (many)
Fagraea spp. (many)
Fernandoa spp.
Firmiana spp.
Flindersia spp.
Fraxinus griffithii
Gardenia spp. (most)
Geijera spp.
Genipa americana
Gliricidia sepium
Gmelina spp.
Grevillea spp.
Greyia spp.
Haematoxylum campechianum
Hymenosporum flavum
Ixora pavetta
Jacaranda spp.
Jatropha integerrima ✚
Kleinhovia hospita
Kopsia spp.
Lagunaria patersonii
Lecythis spp.
Lonchocarpus spp. ✚
Macadamia spp. ✚
Mammea americana
Mangifera indica
Melia azedarach
Mesua ferrea
Michelia spp. ✚
Millettia spp. ✚
Millingtonia hortensis
Monodora myristica
Murraya koenigii
Napoleonaea spp.
Nuxia spp.
Ochroma pyramidale
Oncoba spp.
Parkinsonia spp.
Peltophorum spp.
Phytolacca dioica
Platymiscium spp.
Poitea spp.
Posoqueria spp.
Pterocarpus indicus
Pterospermum spp.
Quassia spp.
Reevesia spp.
Saraca spp.
Schefflera spp.
Schizolobium parahyba
Sclerocarya birrea
Senna spp.
Spathodea campanulata
Sterculia spp.

Syzygium spp. (most)
Tabebuia spp. (many)
Tabernaemontana spp. (many)
Tipuana tipu
Triplaris spp.
Wrightia spp.
Xanthostemon spp.

Summer-flowering trees

Adansonia spp.
Alloxylon spp.
Alstonia spp.
Andira inermis
Aphanamixis spp.
Archidendron spp.
Athertonia diversifolia
Backhousia spp.
Banksia spp. ✚
Bauhinia forficata
Bixa orellana
Bombax ceiba
Brachychiton spp.
Brownea spp.
Buckinghamia celsissima
Bulnesia spp.
Bunchosia spp.
Calliandra spp.
Calodendron capense
Cassia javanica x grandis
Citrus spp.
Clerodendrum spp.
Delonix regia
Dolichandrone spp. ✚
Dombeya spp.
Elaeocarpus spp.
Erythrina crista-gallii
Flindersia spp.
Genipa americana
Haematoxylum campechianum
Hymenosporum flavum
Intsia spp.
Kleinhovia hospita
Kopsia spp.
Lagunaria patersonii
Ligustrum spp.
Lophanthera lactescens
Magnolia spp.
Mammea americana
Melaleuca spp.
Mesua ferrea
Metrosideros spp.
Millettia spp.
Millingtonia hortensis
Monodora myristica
Newbouldia laevis
Nuxia spp.
Ochroma pyramidalis
Ormosia spp.
Ochrosia spp.
Oroxylon indicum
Parkia spp.

Parkinsonia spp.
Peltophorum spp.
Plumeria spp.
Pogonopus speciosus
Punica grantum
Reevesia thyrsoidea
Saraca spp.
Schefflera spp.
Schotia spp.
Spathodea campanulata
Tabernaemontana spp.
Tectona grandis
Tibouchina spp.
Tipuana tipu
Vitex spp.
Wallaceodendron celebicum
Warszewiczia coccinea
Xanthostemon spp.

Autumn-flowering trees

Acokanthera spp.
Caesalpinia echinata
Cassia brewsteri
Cassia roxburghii
Chorisia spp.

Winter-flowering trees
(in tropical regions)

Acokanthera spp.
Adenium spp.
Bombax ceiba
Bravasia integerrima
Calodendron capense
Calycophyllum spp.
Camellia sinensis
Colvillea racemosa
Eriobotrya spp.
Erythrina speciosa
Geijera spp.
Haematoxylum campechianum
Melaleuca argentea
Ochroma pyramidale
Phyllocarpus septentrionalis
Pittosporum spp.
Pogonopus speciosus
Sarcocephalus latifolius
Spathodea campanulata
Stereospermum spp.
Tamarindus indicus
Tecoma spp.
Tibouchina spp.
Tipuana tipu

Trees that bloom continuously
(in tropical regions)

Acacia farnesiana (& others)
Adenanthera spp.
Amphitecna latifolia

Barringtonia spp.
Bauhinia divaricata
Bertholletia excelsa
Calliandra spp.
Castillea elastica
Cerbera spp.
Cestrum spp.
Chrysobalanus icaco
Conocarpus erectus
Couroupita guianensis
Crescentia spp.
Deplanchea tetraphylla
Dolichandrone spp.
Duabanga grandiflora
Duranta erecta
Euphorbia punicea
Flacourtia spp.
Guettardia spp.
Gustavia spp.
Hamelia spp.
Hibiscus spp.
Ilex paraguayensis
Inga spp.
Jatropha integerrima
Lawsonia inermis
Leucaena leucocephala
Macaranga spp.
Markhamia spp.
Mimusops elengi
Montezuma speciossisima
Morinda citrifolia
Moringa oleifera
Muntingia calabura
Myrica cerifera
Myristica fragrans
Pachira spp.
Phyllanthus spp.
Pisonia spp.
Portlandia spp.
Psidium guajava
Punica granatum
Quassia amara
Radermachera gigantea
Santalum album
Solanum wrightii
Stemmadenia spp.
Thespesia populnea
Thevetia peruviana

Trees that bloom intermittently after rain
(in tropical regions)

Acacia spp. (many tropical spp.)
Aegle marmelos
Alberta magna
Aleurites spp.
Amherstia nobilis
Anacardium occidentale
Averrhoa spp.
Blighia sapida

443

Brosimum spp.
Brya ebenus
Bucida spp.
Bulnesia spp.
Bursera spp.
Callistemon spp.
Canella winterana
Catalpa longissima
Cecropia spp.
Clusia spp.
Cordia spp.
Eucalyptus spp.
    (many tropical spp.)
Eugenia spp.
Guaiacum spp.
Haematoxylum campechianum
Harpullia spp.
Hernandia spp.
Jatropha curcas
Kigelia africana
Macadamia spp.
Malpighia glabra
Manilkara spp.
Maniltoa spp.
Melia azaderach
    (in the tropics)
Murraya paniculata
Oxyanthus spp.
Petrea spp.
Posoqueria spp.
Rothmannia spp.
Sesbania grandiflora
Tabebuia spp. (several)
Tamarindus indicus
Tamarix aphylla
Vitex spp.

10.
TREES & THEIR
ORNAMENTAL
OR EDIBLE FRUIT

✓ = edible ✕ toxic

Trees with showy, yellow fruit

Aegle marmelos ✓
Anacardium occidentale (var.) ✓
Aphanamixis polystachya
Artocapus heterophyllus
    (& others) ✓
Averrhoa spp. ✓
Azadirachta indica
Byrsonima spp. ✓
Caesalpinia coraria
Caesalpinia sappan
Casimiroa edulis ✓
Cecropia spp. ✓
444 Citrus spp. (many) ✓

Clausena lansium ✓
Cordia dodecandra ✓
Cupaniopsis anacardioides
Dillenia indica (several) ✓
Dimocarpus longan ✓
Diospyros malabaricum .
Duranta erecta ✕
Durio zebethinus ✓
Eriobotrya spp. ✓
Garcinia spp. ✓
Genipa americana ✓
Gmelina arborea
Mammea americana (tawny) ✓
Mangifera indica ✓
Melia azedarach ✕
Mimusops elengi
Myrciaria (some) ✓
Myristica spp. ✓
Oxyanthus spp.
Parmentiera spp.
Phyllanthus spp. ✓
Phytolacca dioica
Posoqueria spp.
Pouteria spp. ✓
Psidium spp. ✓
Punica granatum ✓
Rollinia mucosa ✓
Sandoricum koetjape ✓
Sapindus saponaria
Sclerocarya birrea ✓
Sideroxylon spp.
Spondias cythera ✓
Spondias mombin ✓
Stemmadenia spp.
Swinglea glutinosa ✓
Tabernaemontana spp.
Terminalia catappa
    (& others) ✓
Theobroma cacao f . ✓
Treculia africana ✓
Vitex lucens
Ziziphus jujube ✓

Trees with showy, red fruit

Acokanthera spp. ✕
Alberta magna
Amherstia noblis
Anacardium occidentale f . ✓
Aphanamixis grandifolia ✕
Archidendron spp.
Bauhinia variegata var. rubra
Bixa orellana
Blighia sapida ✕ ✓
Bursera spp.
Canella winterana ✓
Cavanillesia platanifolia
Ceratopetalum spp.
Cerbera spp. ✕
Chrysobalanus f . ✓
Coffea ✓

Cordia laevigata
Dillenia suffruticosa ✓
Eperua falcata
Eugenia spp. ✓
Ficus spp.
Firmiana spp.
Flacourtia spp. ✓
Gmelina dalrympleana
Gnetum gnemone ✓
Hamelia patens (later black)
Ilex spp.
Jacquinia aborea ✕
Koelreuteria spp.
Litchi chinensis ✓
Malighia glabra ✓
Majidea zanguebarica
Mangifera indica ✓
Muntingia calabura ✓
Murraya spp.
Myrciaria spp. (some) ✓
Napoleonaea spp. (some)
Nephelium lappaceum ✓
Ochrosia spp. ✕
Terminalia kaernbachii ✓
Peltophorum pterocarpum
Pithecellobium arboreum
Podocarpus spp.
Polyalthia spp.
Santalum album
Saraca cauliflora
Sarcocephalus latiflorus ✓
Schefflera actinophylla
Schinus spp.
Spondias purpurea ✓
Sterculia spp. (several)
Strychnos spp. ✕
Syzygium malaccensis ✓
Syzygium jambos (& others) ✓
Triplaris cummingiana

Trees with showy, orange fruit

Bischofia javanica
Broussonetia papyrifera
Brunfelsia spp.
Bunchosia spp.
Castillea elastica
Citrus sinensis (& others) ✓
Cordia dichotoma
Cordia goldeiana
Cordia myxa
Diospyros kaki ✓
Dovyalis abyssinica ✓
Fagraea berteriana
Ficus spp. (many)
Gustavia spp ✓
Harpullia spp.
Napoleonea spp. (some)
Parinari nonda (tawny)
Pittosporum spp. (many)

Punica granatum f . ✓
Ziziphus mauritiana ✓

Trees with showy, purple fruit

Annona reticulata ✓
Athertonia diversifolia ✓
Barringtonia edulis
Chrysophyllum spp. ✓
Coccoloba uvifera ✓
Cussonia spp.
Filicium decipiens
Garcinia mangostana ✓
Gmelina leichhardtii
Kopsia spp. ✕
Myrciaria vexator ✓
Noronhia emarginata
Persea americana f . ✓
Pleiogynium timorensis ✓
Pometia pinnata ✓
Terminalia arenicola
Terminalia meulleri
Terminalia sericea
Theobroma cacao f . ✓

Trees with showy, blue fruit

Agathis spp.
Canarium ovatum (& others) ✓
Clerodenrum spp. (many)
Elaeocarpus spp. (several)
Juniperus barbadensis

Trees with showy, brown fruit

Acacia auriculiformis
Albizia lebbek
Amphitecna spp.
Araucaria spp.
Banksia spp.
Barringtonia asiatica
Bertholettia excelsa ✓
Brachychiton spp.
Bulnesia spp.
Butea monosperma
Caesalpinia echinata
Calodendron capense
Castanospermum australe
Ceratonia siliqua ✓
Clusia spp.
Couroupita guaianensis
Crescentia spp.
Delonia regia
Deplanchea tetraphylla
Dipterocarpus spp.
Duabanga grandiflora
Enterolobium spp.
Fernandoa spp.
Flindersia spp.

Gardenia spp.
Heritiera spp.
Hevea brasiliensis
Hura crepitans ×
Hymenaea courbaril
Inga spp.
Intsia bijuga
Jacaranda spp.
Jatropha curcus ×
Kigelia africana ×
Lecythis zabacajo ✓
Lansium domesticum ✓
Lonchocarpus violaceus ×
Macadamia spp. ✓
Manilkara zapato (tawny) ✓
Maniltoa spp. (tawny)
Michelia spp.
Magnolia spp.
Nauclea oeientalis (tawny)
Oncoba spp. ×
Ormosia spp.
Oroxylon indicum
Pinus spp.
Pterocarpus spp.
Schizolobium parahybum
Schotia spp.
Spathodea campanulata
Stelecocarpus burahol (scurfy) ✓
Stenocarpus spp.
Swietenia spp.
Toona spp.

Trees with showy, green fruit

Acacia nilotica
Aleurites spp. ×
Annona spp. (several) ✓
Artocarpus altilis ✓
Calotropis spp.
Cola acumuniata ✓
Diospyros dignya ✓
Dodonaea viscosa (later brown)
Hernandia spp.
Kleinhovia hospita ×
Melicoccus bijugatus ✓
Pachira glabra ✓
Parkia spp. ✓
Persea americana f. ✓
Pisonia spp.

Trees with showy, black fruit

Antidesma spp. ✓
Cananga odorata
Cestrum diurnum (& others) ×
Dialium spp. ✓
Dovyalis hebecarpa ✓
Enterolobium spp.
Ligustrum spp. ×
Morus spp. ✓

Myrciaria cauliflora ✓
Persea americana f. ✓
Pimenta dioica ✓
Thevetia peruviana ×
Vitex spp.

Trees with showy, white fruit

Cestrum nocturnum ×
Chrysobalanus icaco f. ✓
Cordia sebestena (& others)
Morinda citrifolia ✓
Syzygium forte ✓

Trees with showy, velvety fruit

Acacia nilotica subsp. *tomentosa*
Adansonia spp.
Brachychiton velutinosa (& others)
Ceiba spp.
Dialium spp. ✓
Diospyros ebenum ✓
Diospyros blancoi ✓
Dovyalis abyssinica ✓
Dovyalis hebecarpus ✓
Ficus aspera
Ochroma pyramidale
Pachira aquatica ✓
Pangium edule ✓-×
Pouteria alniifolia ✓
Quararibea cordata ✓
Sandoricum koetjape ✓
Tamarindus indica ✓
Theobroma grandiflora ✓

Trees with showy seeds

Adenanthera spp.
Anacardium occidentale ✓-×
Aphanamixis spp. ×
Archidendron spp.
Berthollettia excelsa ✓
Bixa orellana ✓
Blighia sapida ✓
Cola spp. ✓
Cupaniopsis spp.
Dillenia spp. ✓
Erythrina spp. ×
Guaiacum spp.
Harpullia spp.
Jatropha curcas ×
Hevea brasiliensis ×
Majidea zanguebarica
Michelia spp.
Magnolia spp.
Myristica spp. ✓
Ormosia spp.
Thevetia peruviana ×

II.
TREES VALUABLE FOR THE ENVIRONMENT

Trees with fruit for birds & bats

Anacardium spp.
Andira spp.
Antidesma spp.
Athertonia spp.
Azadirachta indica
Bischofia javanica
Blighia sapida
Broussonetia papyrifera
Brunfelsia spp.
Bunchosia spp.
Bursera spp.
Byrsonima spp.
Cananga odorata
Canella winterana
Casimiroa edulis
Castilla elastica
Cecropia spp.
Ceratonia siliqua
Cestrum spp.
Chrysobalanus icaco
Chrysophyllum spp.
Cinnamomum spp.
Clausena spp.
Clusia spp.
Coccoloba spp.
Cupaniopsis spp.
Dimocarpus longan
Diospyros spp.
Dovyalis spp.
Duranta erecta
Durio spp.
Elaeocarpus spp.
Eugenia spp.
Fagraea spp.
Ficus spp.
Filicium decipens
Flacourtia spp.
Genipa americana
Gnetum gnemone
Gustavia spp.
Hamelia spp.
Harpullia spp.
Ilex spp.
Jacquinia spp.
Kopsia spp.
Litchi chinensis
Ligustrum spp.
Mammea americana
Malpighia glabra
Mangifera indica
Manilkara spp.
Melaleuca spp.
Melia azedarach
Melicoccus bijugatus

Muntingia calabura
Murraya spp.
Morus spp.
Myrciaria spp.
Myrica cerifera
Nephelium lappaceum
Oncoba spinosa
Parinari nonda
Persea americana
Pimenta spp.
Pithecellobium spp.
Pittosporum spp.
Pleiogynium timorensis
Podocarpus spp.
Polyalthia spp.
Pometia spp.
Pouteria spp.
Psidium spp.
Quararibea cordata
Santalum spp.
Sarcocephalus latifolius
Schefflera spp.
Schinus spp.
Schlerocarya birrea
Sideroxylon spp.
Spondias spp.
Stelechocarpus burahol
Syzygium spp.
Terminalia spp.
Trevesia spp.
Vitex spp.
Zanthoxylum spp.
Ziziphus spp.

Trees with nectar for bats

Adansonia spp.
Amphitecna spp.
Barringtonia spp.
Ceiba spp.
Couroupita guaianensis
Crescentia spp.
Deplanchea spp.
Dolichandrone spp.
Duabanga grandflora
Durio spp.
Eperua spp.
Kigelia africana
Millingtonia hortensis
Monodora myristica
Ochroma pyramidale
Oroxylon indicum
Pachira spp.
Parkia spp.
Parmentiera spp.
Pseudobombax spp.
Pterospermum spp.
Saraca spp.
Sterculia spp.

Trees with nectar for birds

Acrocarpus fraxinifolius
Adansonia spp.
Alberta magna
Alloxylon spp.
Amherstia nobilis
Banksi spp.
Bauhinia spp.
Brownea spp.
Butea monosperma
Calliandra spp.
Callistemon spp.
Castanospermum australe
Chorisia spp.
Colvillea racemosa
Deplanchea spp.
Elaeocarpus spp.
Erythrina spp.
Grevillea spp.
Greyia spp.
Hamelia spp.
Kigelia africana
Leucadendron argenteum
Metrosideros spp.
Moringa spp.
Ormosia spp.
Phyllocarpus septentrionalis
Quararibea cordata
Quassia amara
Schotia spp.
Sesbania grandiflora
Spathodea campanulata
Stenocarpus spp.
Xanthostemon spp.

Trees with nectar for butterflies

Acrocarpus fraxinifolius
Alstonia spp.
Athertonia diversifolia
Averrhoa spp.
Brya ebenus
Buckinghamia celsissima
Calliandra spp.
Calotropis spp.
Calodendron capense
Cestrum spp.
Clerodendrum spp.
Dimocarpus longan
Dombeya spp.
Elaeocarpus spp.
Hymenosporum flavum
Ixora spp.
Nauclea orientalis
Nuxia spp.
Sarcocephalus spp.
Vitex spp.

Trees with nectar for moths

Brugmansia spp.
Brunfelsia spp.
Calliandra spp.
Cedrela spp.
Cestrum spp.
Dolichandrone spp.
Fagraea spp.
Gardenia spp.
Gmelina spp.
Guettardia spp.
Manilkara spp.
Michelia spp.
Millingtonia hortensis
Montezuma speciosissimum
Nyctanthes arbor-tristes
Oxyanthus spp.
Parmentiera spp.
Plumeria spp.
Portlandia spp.
Posoqueria spp.
Saraca spp.
Stenocarpus spp.
Tabernaemontana spp.
Wallaceodendron celebicum

Trees with nectar for bees

Acacia spp.
Adenanthera spp.
Aegle marmelos
Albizia spp.
Anacardium spp.
Andira spp.
Archidendron spp.
Averrhoa spp.
Azadirachta indica
Backhousia celsissima
Bertholettia excelsa
Bixa orellana
Blighia sapida
Brosimum spp.
Brya spp.
Bucida spp.
Bunchosia spp.
Bursera spp.
Byrsonima spp.
Caesalpinia spp.
Calycophyllum spp.
Canella winterana
Casimiroa spp.
Catalpa spp.
Cedrela spp.
Ceiba spp.
Ceratonia siliqua
Chrysobalanus spp.
Cinnamomum spp.
Citrus spp.
Clausena spp.
Coccoloba spp.

Cochlospermum spp.
Coffea spp.
Couroupita guaianensis
Dalbergia spp.
Dillenia spp.
Eriobotrya spp.
Eucalyptus spp.
Eugenia spp.
Flacourtia spp.
Fraxinus spp.
Genipa americana
Gliricidia sepium
Grevillea spp.
Guaiacum spp.
Gustavia spp.
Haematoxylum campechianum
Hymenaea courbaril
Hymenosporum flavum
Inga spp.
Jacaranda spp.
Jatropha spp.
Khaya spp.
Kleinhovia hospita
Leptospermum spp.
Lawsonia inermis
Litchi chinensis
Ligustrum spp.
Lonchocarpus spp.
Lophanthera lactescens
Lysiloma spp.
Macadamia spp.
Malpighia spp.
Mangifera spp.
Markhamia spp.
Melaleuca spp.
Melicoccus bijugatus
Mesua spp.
Millettia spp.
Mimusops spp.
Montezuma speciocissima
Muntingia calabura
Murraya spp.
Moringa spp.
Myrciaria spp.
Myrica spp.
Myroxylon spp.
Nuxia spp.
Oncoba spp.
Persea americana
Phyllanthus spp.
Pimenta spp.
Pithecellobium spp.
Pittosporum spp.
Platymiscium spp.
Pleiogynium timorensis
Pouteria spp.
Psidium spp.
Pterocarpus spp.
Samanea saman
Sarcocephalus spp.
Sideroxylon spp.
Spondias spp.

Stereospermum spp.
Swietenia spp.
Syzygium spp.
Tabebuia spp.
Tamarindus indicus
Tecoma spp.
Tectona grandis
Toona spp.
Wallaceodendron celebicum
Zanthoxylum spp.
Xanthostemon spp.

12.
TREES WITH SPECIAL QUALITIES

Trees with very fragrant flowers
✠ = nocturnal

Acacia farnesiana
Acokanthera spp.
Adansonia spp. ✠
Backhousia spp.
Barringtonia spp. ✠
Brugmansia spp. ✠
Brunfelsia spp. ✠
Callophylum spp.
Cananga odorata
Cestrum spp. ✠
Citrus spp.
Dolichandrone spp. ✠
Eperua spp. ✠
Eriobotrya spp.
Fagraea spp. ✠
Gardenia spp.
Gmelina arborea
Guettardia speciosa ✠
Gustavia spp. ✠
Hymenosporum flavum
Intsia spp.
Lawsonia inermis
Ligustrum spp.
Magnolia spp.
Mesua ferrea
Michelia spp.
Millingtonia hortensis ✠
Mimusops elengi
Murraya paniculata
Nuxia spp.
Nyctanthes arbor-tristes ✠
Oxyanthus spp. ✠
Pachira spp.
Pittosporum spp.
Plumeria spp.
Portlandia spp.
Posoqueria spp. ✠
Pterospermum spp.
Pterocarpus spp.
Tabernaemontana spp. ✠

Trees with aromatic parts

! = pungently unpleasant

Aegle marmelos (fruit & leaves)
Annona muricata (leaves)
Backhousia spp. (leaves)
Bursera simaruba (wood)
Caesalpinia echinata (leaves)
Callistemon spp. (leaves)
Canella winterana (fruit)
Cedrela odorata (wood)
Cinnamomum spp. (all parts)
Citrus spp. (all parts)
Coffea spp. (seeds)
Dalbergia spp. (wood)
Eucalyptus spp. (leaves)
Geijera spp. (leaves & fruit)
Gustavia spp. (wood) !
Leptospermum spp. (leaves)
Melaleuca spp. (leaves)
Monodora myristica (seeds)
Murraya koenigii (leaves & fruit)
Myroxylon (resin)
Myristica spp. (fruit)
Parmentiera spp. (fruit)
Persea americana (leaves)
Pimenta spp. (leaves & fruit)
Pinus spp. (leaves)
Pittosporum spp. (fruit)
Santalum spp. (wood)
Schinus molle (leaves)
Sideroxylon foetidissimum
   (flowers) !
Sterculia foetida (flowers) !
Swinglea glutinosa (leaves & fruit)
Syzygium aromaticum (flowers)
Syzygium cumini (leaves)
Vitex agnus-castus (leaves)
Zanthoxylum flavum (leaves)

Trees used to make dye

Acacia farnesiana (yellowish)
Adenanthera pavonina (red)
Aegle marmelos (yellow)
Aleurites moluccana
   (copper red)
Anancardium occidentale (black)
Artocarpus heterophylla (yellow)
Bischofia javanica (brown)
Bixa orellana (red)
Butea monosperma (orange-red)
Caesalpinia echinata (black)
Chrysobalanus icaco (black)
Coccoloba uvifera (reddish)
Garcinia dulcis (yellow)
Garcinia xanthochymus (yellow)
Gardenia spp. (yellow)
Genipa americana (blue)
Haematoxylum campechianum
   (black)
Lagerstroemia speciosa (yellow)

Lawsonia inermis (orange
   & black)
Ligustrum lucidum (yellow)
Mangifera indica (yellow)
Melia azedarach (red)
Mimusops elengi (brown)
Morinda citrifolia (red)
Nauclea orientalis (yellow)
Nephelium lappaceum (red)
Nyctanthes arbor-tristes (orange)
Wrightia arborea (indigo)

Trees used for timber

Acrocarpus fraxinifolius
Hibiscus elatus
Afrocarpus spp.
Agathis spp.
Alstonia spp.
Andira spp.
Aphanamixis spp.
Araucaria spp.
Bischofia javanica
Bulnesia arborea
Caesalpinia ferrea
Calophyllum spp.
Callitris spp.
Calycophyllum spp.
Canarium spp.
Castanospermum australe
Catalpa longissima
Cedrela odorata
Cordia alliodora
Cordia dodecandra
Dalbergia spp.
Diospyros ebenus
Dipterocarpus spp.
Eperua spp.
Genipa americana
Grevillea robusta
Guaiacum spp.
Harpullia spp.
Heritiera spp.
Hibiscus elata
Hymenaea courbaril
Khaya spp.
Kleinhovia hospita
Lagerstroemia spp.
Lophostemon confertus
Majidea spp.
Manilkara spp.
Mesua ferrea
Myroxylon balsamum
Nauclea orientalis
Pinus spp.
Platymiscium spp.
Podocarpus spp.
Santalum spp.
Sideroxylon spp.
Swietenia spp.
Tectona grandis
Toona ciliata

Tipuana tipu
Vitex lucens
Wrightia arborea
Zanthoxylum flavum

Trees important medicinally

Aegle marmelos
Annona muricata
Aphanamixis polystachya
Averrhoa carambola
Azadirachta indica
Calotropis spp.
Canarium spp.
Casimoroa spp.
Cassia javanica (& others)
Castanospermum australe
Cestrum spp.
Cola spp.
Dimocarpus longan
Dombeya rotundifolia
Flacourtia indica
Genipa americana
Gmelina aborea
Guaiacum officinale
Jatropha curcas
Lagerstroemia spp.
Leptospermum spp.
Lichi chinensis
Ligustrum lucidum
Mangifera indica
Melaleuca spp.
Melia azedarach
Mesua ferrea
Michelia champaca
Millettia pinnata
Mimusops elengi
Monodora myristica
Morinda citrifolia
Morus spp.
Myrciaria dubia
Myroxylon balsamum
Nauclea orientalis
Nephelium lappaceum
Newbouldia laevis
Pachira aquatica
Pangium edule
Parkia spp.
Parmentiera cerifera
Persea americana
Posoqueria latifolia
Psidium guajava
Pterocarpus spp.
Punica granatum
Quassia spp.
Rollinia mucosa
Sandoricum koetjape
Santalum album
Sapindus saponaria
Sarcocephalus latifolius
Sclerocarya birrea

Sesbania grandiflora
Sterculia foetida
Stereospermum kunthianum
Strychnos nux-vomica
Swinglea glutinosa
Tamarindus indica
Tecoma stans
Thevetia peruviana
Toona ciliata
Treculia africana
Vitex spp.
Wrightia arborea
Ziziphus spp.

13.
TREES WITH PROBLEMS

Trees with toxic parts

Acokanthera spp. (many parts)
Adenium spp.
Aleurites spp. (many parts)
Anancardium occidentale (nut)
Andira spp. (many parts)
Annona spp. (seeds)
Aphanamixis spp. (many parts)
Barringtonia spp. (seeds)
Blighia sapida (seeds)
Brugmansia spp. (many parts)
Brunfelsia spp. (fruit)
Canella winterana (leaves)
Casimiroa edulis (seeds)
Castanospermum australe (seeds)
Cerbera spp.
Cestrum spp. (many parts)
Clusia spp. (fruit)
Crateva spp. (fruit)
Crescentia spp. (seeds)
Duranta erecta (fruit)
Eriobotrya spp. (seeds)
Erythrina spp. (fruit)
Euphorbia spp. (latex)
Gliricidia sepium (roots & bark)
Hevea brasiliensis (seeds)
Hura crepitans (sap)
Jacquinia spp. (fruit)
Jatropha curcas (many parts)
Kigelia africana (fruit)
Kleinhovia hospita (bark & leaves)
Kopsia spp. (many parts)
Lecythis zabucajo (seeds)
Leucaena leucocephala (leaves
   & fruit)
Ligustrum spp. (fruit)
Lonchocarpus spp. (many parts)
Macaranga spp. (many parts)
Mammea americana (seeds)
Melia spp. (fruit)

447

Mesua ferrea (resin)
Millettia spp. (fruit)
Napoleonaea spp. (many parts)
Ochrosia spp. (fruit)
Pangium edule (many parts)
Phytolacca dioica (many parts)
Plumeria spp. (poss. latex)
Pouteria spp. (seeds)
Sapindus spp. (seeds)
Spathodea campanulata (fruit)
Stelecocarpus burahol (many parts)
Stemmadenia spp. (sap)
Strychnos nux-vomica (seeds)
Tabernaemontana spp. (sap)
Thevetia spp. (sap)
Treculia spp. (sap)

Trees with spines

Acacia spp. (many)
Aegle marmelos
Araucaria spp.
Bauhinia forficata
Bombax ceiba (trunk)
Bucida spinosa
Caesalpinia echinata
Caesalpinia sappan
Ceiba pentandra (trunk)
Chorisia spp. (trunk)
Citrus spp. (many)
Dovyalis spp. (several)
Duranta erecta
Erythrina (many)
Euphorbia candelabrum
Euphorbia ingens
Flacourtia spp. (most)
Haematoxylim campechianum
Hura crepitans (trunk)
Lagunaria patersonii (fruit)
Lawsonia inermis f.
Oncoba spp.
Pachira quinata (trunk)
Parkinsonia aculeata
Pithecellobium spp. (many)
Punica granatum
Solanum wrightii
Strychnos spp.
Swinglea glutinosa
Trevesia spp.
Zanthoxylum coriaceum
Zanthoxylum martinicense
Ziziphus spp.

Trees with weak wood

Albizia lebbek
Bischofia javanica
Brugmansia spp.
Bulnesia arborea
Bursera simaruba
Cananga odrata
Catalpa longissima

Duabanga grandiflora
Eucalyptus spp.
Firmiana colorata
Fraxinus spp.
Gliricidia sepium
Hura crepitans
Inga jinicuil
Melia azedarach
Millingtonia hortensis
Peltophorum spp.
Pithecellobium spp.
Schizolobium parahyba
Senna spp.
Sesbania grandiflora
Solanum wrightii
Spathodea campanulata

Trees that may prove invasive

Acacia spp. (many)
Adenanthera spp.
Albizia spp.
Aleurites moluccana
Alstonia spp.
Azadirachta indica
Barringtonia asiatica
Bauhinia variegata
Bischofia javanica
Blighia sapida
Broussonetia papyrifera
Bunchosia spp.
Calophyllum spp.
Calotropis spp.
Cananga odorata
Castillea elastica
Casuarina equisitifolia
Ceiba pentandra
Cestrum spp.
Chrysophyllum oliviforme
Coffea spp.
Cola spp.
Cupaniopsis anacardioides
Dodonaea viscosa
Dovyalis spp.
Duranta erecta
Enterolobium spp.
Eriobotrya japonica
Erythrina variegata
Eucalyptus spp. (some)
Eugenia uniflora
Ficus spp.
Filicium decipiens
Flacourtia spp.
Gliricidia sepium
Haematoxylum campechianum
Inga spp.
Jatropha curcas
Koelreuteria spp.
Leucaena leucocephala
Ligustrum spp.
Macaranga spp.

Mangifera indica
Melaleuca quinquinervia
Melia azedarach
Moringa oleifera
Morus spp.
Muntingia calabura
Parkinsonia aculeata
Peltophorum spp.
Phyllanthus acidus
Pittosporum pentandrum (& others)
Psidium guajava
Quassia amara
Samanea saman
Schefflera actinophylla
Spathodea campanulata
Syzygium cumini
Tabebuia heterophylla
Tabebuia pallida
Tabebuia rosea
Tamarix spp.
Tecoma stans
Terminalia catappa
Thespesia populnea
Thevetia peruviana
Triplaris spp.
Vitex cofassus (& others)
Ziziphus spp.

14.
TREES & THEIR SHAPES

Trees with a narrow form

Agathis spp.
Alloxylon spp.
Araucaria spp.
Brachychiton acerifolius
Bunchosia argentea
Byrsonima crassifolia
Callitris spp.
Casuarina cunninghamii
Coccoloba diversifolia
Duabanga grandiflora
Eucalyptus deglupta (& others)
Fagraea fragans (when young)
Firmiana colorata
Flindersia bourjotiana
Garcinia aristata
Garcinia cymosum
Garcinia dulcis
Gnetum gnemone
Grevillea baileyana
Grevillea robusta
Gymnostoma (some spp.)
Juniperus spp. (some)
Lagunaria petersonii
Lophanthera lactescens

Markhamia lutea
Melaleuca dealbata
Millingtonia hortensis
Newbouldia laevis
Oroxylon indicum
Pinus spp.
Pleiogynium timorensis
Podocarpus macrophyllus (& others)
Polyalthia longifolia
Polyalthia longifolia var. pendula
Salix chilensis
Spathodea campanulata
Tabebuia haemantha
Triplaris spp.
Wallaceodendron celebicum

Trees with a wide-spreading canopy

Albizia spp.
Barringtonia asiatica
Bischofia javanica
Calophyllum inophyllum
Castanospermum australe
Cedrela odorata
Cupaniopsis anacardioides
Delonix regia
Dolichandrone spathacea
Enterolobium spp.
Eperua falcata
Erythrina variegata
Ficus benjamina
Ficus benghalensis
Ficus elastica
Ficus macrophylla (& many others)
Garcinia xanthochymus
Harpullia arborea
Harpullia ramiflora
Heritiera littoralis
Hura crepitans
Hymenaea courbaril
Inga spp.
Jacaranda mimosifolia
Lagerstroemia speciosa
Leptospermum sativum
Macaranga tanarius
Mangifera indica f.
Manilkara spp.
Melicoccus bijugatus
Millettia pinnata
Monodora myristica
Morus spp.
Nauclea orientalis
Ochroma pyramidale
Pachira aquatica
Parinari nonda
Peltophorum pterocarpum
Peltophorum dubium
Persea americana
Phytolacca dioica

Pterocarpus indica
Quassia simarouba
Samanea saman
Schinus molle
Sclerocarya birrea
Sideroxylon foetidissimum
Sterculia foetida
Sterculia apetala
Swietenia spp.
Syzygium aqueum
Syzygium cumini
Tabebuia pallida
Tabernaemontana arborea
Tamarindus indica
Terminalia catappa
Tipuana tipu
Vitex parviflora
Zizyphus spp.

Trees with a compact form

Acacia confusa
Acokanthera spp.
Alberta magna
Aleurites montana
Alloxylon wickhamii
Amphitecna latifolia
Annona muricata
Argusia argentea
Backhousia citrifolia
Barringtonia calyptrata
Barringtonia racemosa
Bauhinia monandra
Bauhinia divaricata
Bauhinia tomentosa
Bixa orellana
Brachychiton rupestris
Brya ebenus
Bucida buceras var. Shady Lady
Buckinghamia celsissima
Bunchosia argentea
Caesalpinia mexicana
Callistemon salignus
Calodendrum capense
Camellia sinensis
Canella winterana
Cassia sp. var. 'Paluma Range'
Cassia roxburghii
Ceiba acuminata
Ceratopetalum gummiferum
Cerbera spp.
Citrus margarita
Clerodendrum quadriloculare
Coffea spp.
Cordia boissieri
Cordia laevigata
Dillenia indica
Dillenia philippensis
Diospyros blancoi
Diospyros malabarica
Dombeya x cayeuxii

Eribotrya spp.
Erythrina crista galli
Erythrina verspitillo
Eugenia uniflora
Euphorbia gymnota
Euphorbia ingens
Fagraea berteriana
Ficus cyathistipula
Ficus lyrata
Ficus pleurocarpa
Filicium decipiens
Flacourtia spp.
Fraxinus griffithii
Gardenia taitensis
Grevillea hilliana
Guaiacum spp.
Guettardia speciosa
Gymnostoma spp. (some)
Harpullia ramiflora
Ilex cassine
Ixora pavetta
Jacaranda caerulea
Jacquinia spp.
Jatropha integerrima
Juniperus chinensis
Kleinhovia hospita
Koelreuteria spp.
Kopsia spp.
Leucadendron argenteum
Ligustrum spp.
Litchi chinensis
Macadamia spp. (most)
Malpighia glabra
Mammea americana
Mangifera indica
Melaleuca bracteata
Melaleuca minutifolia
Mesua ferrea
Metrosideros spp.
Michelia spp.
Mimusops elengi
Montezuma speciosissima
Murraya koenigii
Murraya paniculata
Myrciaria spp.
Noronhia emarginata
Nuxia spp.
Ochrosia spp.
Peltophorum africanum
Phyllanthus angustifolia
Pittosporum tobira
Pittosporum undulatum
Pittosporum viridiflorum
Plumeria montana
Portlandia grandiflora
Pouteria hypoglauca
Psidium cattleianum
Radermachera sinica
Reevesia thyrsoidea
Senna spectabilis
Senna polyphylla
Senna surratensis

Syzygium forte
Syzygium pycnanthum
Tabebuia lepidota
Tabernaemontana cerifera
Thevetia peruviana
Tibouchina spp. (several)

Trees with a weeping form

Brosimum spp.
Brya ebenus
Callistemon viminalis
Cassia roxburghiana
Casuarina equisitifolia
Duabanga grandiflora
Ficus binnendijkii
Ficus celebica
Geijera parviflora
Leptospermum madidum ssp. sativum
Leptospermum madidum ssp. madidum
Melaleuca dealbata
Parinari nonda
Pittosporum angustifolium
Polyalthia longifolia var. pendula
Schinus molle
Taxodium spp.
Terminalia grandiflora
Zizyphus mauritiana

Trees with dramatic foliage

Amphitecna regalis
Aleurites moluccana
Alloxylon flammeum (young leaves)
Athertonia diversifolia (young leaves)
Artocarpus altilis
Barringtonia asiatica
Barringtonia edulis
Brownea spp. (young leaves)
Brugmansia spp.
Calophyllum sil (young leaves)
Calotropis spp.
Castillea elastica
Cecropia spp.
Chrysophyllum cainito
Chrysophyllum imperialis
Clerodendrom minahassae
Clerodendron quadriloculare
Clusia rosea
Coccoloba pubescens
Cussonia spp.
Deplanchea tetraphylla
Dillenia indica
Duabanga grandiflora
Fagraea crenulata
Ficus aspera

Ficus auriculata
Ficus dammaropsis
Ficus lyrata
Ficus pseudopalma (& others)
Filicium decipiens
Garcinia xanthochymus
Gardenia taitensis
Guettardia speciosa
Gustavia spp.
Harpullia ramiflora
Heritiera littoralis
Hernandia nymphaeifolia
Hibiscus tiliaceus cv Royal Flush
Hura crepitans
Leucadendron argenteum
Lophostemon confertus var. variegatus
Macaranga grandifolia
Magnolia grandiflora
Maniltoa spp. (young leaves)
Mesua ferrea
Monodora myristica
Pachira aquatica
Pouteria sapota
Quararibea cordata
Saraca spp. (young leaves)
Schefflera actinophylla
Schinus molle
Schizolobium parahyba (young leaves)
Sterculia shillinglawii (young leaves)
Syzygium leuhmanni (young leaves)
Syzygium megacarpum
Syzygium puberulum (young leaves)
Syzygium wilsonii (young leaves)
Tabernaemontana pachysiphon
Terminalia catappa
Terminalia kaernbachii
Trevesia spp.
Warszexiczia coccinea

Trees with interesting bark

Acacia seyal
Acacia xanthophloea
Adansonia spp.
Bertholettia excelsa
Bischofia javanica
Bolusanthus speciosus
Broussonetia papyrifera (young bark)
Bursera simaruba
Caesalpinia ferrea
Caesalpinia granadillo
Calycophyllum spp.
Casuarina equisitifolia
Chorisia speciosa (young)
Coccoloba uvifera

449

Colvillea racemosa (young bark)
Dillenia alata
Eucalyptus deglupta
Eucalyptus platyphylla
Eucalyptus miniata (young bark)
Leucadendron argenteum
Melaleuca quinquinervia
Melaleuca cajeputi
Montezuma speciossisima (old tree)
Myrciaria floribunda
Myrciaria vexator
Pangium edule
Parinari nonda
Pimenta dioica
Pogonopus speciosus
Stereospermum kunthianum
Syzygium papyraceum
Triplaris cummingiana
Tabebuia aurea

15.
TREES FOR SPECIFIC PLANTING

Large trees for public open space

Acrocarpus fraxinifolius
Adansonia spp.
Afrocarpus spp.
Agathis spp.
Aleurites moluccana
Alstonia spp.
Andira inermis
Antidesma spp.
Aphanamixis spp.
Araucaria spp.
Barringtonia asiatica
Bertholettia excelsa
Bischofia javanica
Bolusanthus speciosa
Bombax spp.
Brachychiton spp.
Brosimum spp.
Bucida spp.
Bulnesia spp.
Bursera simaruba
Butea monosperma
Calodendron capense
Calophyllum spp.
Cananga odorata
Canarium spp.
Cassia spp.
Castanospermum australe
Castilla elastica
Cavanillesia platanifolia
Catalpa longissima
Cedrela odorata
Ceiba pentandra

Chorisia spp.
Chrysophyllum spp.
Colvillea racemosa
Cordia alliodora
Couroupita guineense
Cupaniopsis anacardioides
Delonix regia
Dialium guineense
Dipterocarpus spp.
Dolichandrone spathacea
Duabanga grandiflora
Durio spp.
Elaeocarpus spp.
Enterolobium spp.
Eperua spp.
Erythrina spp.
Eucalyptus spp.
Fagraea spp.
Ficus spp.
Filicium decipiens
Flindersia spp.
Geijera spp.
Gmelina arborea
Grevillea robusta
Harpullia arborea
Hura crepitans
Hymenaea courbaril
Inga spp.
Jacaranda mimosifolia
Khaya spp.
Kigelia africana
Kleinhovia hospita
Largerstroemea spp.
Lecythis spp.
Leptospermum spp.
Lophostemon confertus
Mammea americana
Magnolia grandiflora
Mangifera indica
Manilkara spp.
Maniltoa spp.
Millingtonia hortensis
Mimusops spp.
Montezuma speciosissima
Myroxylon balsamum
Nauclea orientalis
Ochroma platanifolia
Peltophorum pterocarpum
Phyllocarpus septentrionalis

Trees for boulevard or street planting
♣ = boulevard

Afrocarpus spp.
Agathis spp. ♣
Alloxylon flammeum
Alstonia spp. ♣
Andira inermis
Antidesma spp.
Aphanamixis spp.
Athertonia diversifolia

Azadirachta indica
Barringtonia acutangular
Barringtonia calyptrata
Bauhinia spp.
Bolusanthus speciosa
Brachychiton spp.
Brosimum spp. ♣
Bucida buceras ♣
Buckinghamia celsissima
Bulnesia arborea
Bunchosia argentea
Bursera simaruba
Byrsonima crassifolia
Caesalpinia ferrea
Caesalpinia granidillo
Caesalpinia violacea
Callistemon salignus
Callitris spp. ♣
Calodendron capense
Calophyllum spp. ♣
Canarium spp. ♣
Cassia spp.
Castanospermum australe ♣
Cedrela odorata ♣
Ceratonia siliqua
Cerbera spp.
Chrysophyllum spp.
Cola spp.
Colvillea racemosa
Cordia spp. (some)
Cupaniopsis anacardioides
Dalbergia sissoo
Delonix regia
Deplanchea tetraphylla
Dialium guineense
Dillenia alata
Dolichandrone spathacea
Elaeocarpus spp.
Eperua spp. ♣
Erythrina ptychocarpa (& others)
Fagraea spp. ♣
Ficus spp. (many) ♣
Flindersia spp.
Fraxinus griffithii
Geijera spp.
Gnetum gnemone
Grevillea spp. ♣
Gymnostoma spp.
Harpullia spp.
Hernandia sonora
Hibiscus elata
Intsia bijuga
Jacaranda mimosifolia
Khaya spp. ♣
Kleinhovia hospita
Koelreuteria spp.
Lagerstroemia spp. (many)
Lagunaria patersonii
Lansium domesticum
Litchi chinensis
Lophanthera lactescens
Mammea americana

Magnolia spp.
Majidea zanguebarica
Mangifera indica
Manilkara kauki
Maniltoa browneoides
Melaleuca spp.
Melia azedarach
Mesua ferrea
Millettia pinnata
Millingtonia hortensis ♣
Mimusops elengi
Montezuma speciosissima
Moringa oleifera
Morus spp.
Noronhia emarginata
Nuxia spp.
Ormosia ormondii ♣
Parinari nonda
Peltophorum pterocarpum
Pimenta spp.
Pinus spp.
Pithecellobium spp.
Pleiogynium timorense
Polyalthia longifolia var. pendula
Pometia pinnata
Pterospermum acerifolium
Quassia simarouba
Radermachera gigantea
Samanea saman
Sapindus saponaria
Schinus molle
Sideroxylon spp.
Spathodea campanulata
Stenocarpus sinuatus
Stereospermum kunthianum
Syzygium spp. (some)
Tabebuia spp. (many)
Tamarindus indica
Terminalia sericea
Thespesia populnea
Tibouchina granulosa
Toona spp. ♣
Triplaris spp.
Vitex parviflora
Vitex cofassus
Xanthostemon chrysantha

Trees suitable for growing in conservatories
Note: trees grown in restricted, unnatural conditions may not bloom or fruit satisfactorily.

Acokanthera spp.
Adenium spp.
Alberta magna
Alloxylon spp.
Amhersita nobilis
Amphitecna spp.
Annona spp.

Archidendron spp.
Athertonia diversifolia
Averrhoa spp.
Banksia spp.
Barringtonia edulis (& others)
Bauhinia (some smaller spp.)
Bixa orellana
Brownea spp.
Brugmansia spp.
Brunfelsia spp.
Buckinghamia celsissima
Bunchosia spp.
Byrsonima lucida
Camellia sinensis
Cananga var. fruticosa
Canella winterana
Cecropia spp.
Ceratopetalum spp.
Cerbera spp.
Cestrum spp.
Chorisia spp.
Chrysophyllum spp.
Cinnamomum spp.
Citrus spp.
Clerodendrum spp.
Clusia spp.
Coccoloba pubescens
Coffea spp.
Cola acuminata
Crateva spp.
Crescentia spp.
Cussonia spp.
Deplanchea tetraphylla
Dillenia spp.
Diospyros ebenus
Duabanga grandiflora
Eriobotrya spp.
Ficus (smaller spp.)
Garcinia mangostana
Gardenia spp.
Gnetum gnemone
Greyia spp.
Gustavia spp.
Hamelia spp.
Hymenosporum flavum
Ilex spp.
Ixora spp.
Jacquinia spp.
Lecythis spp.
Litchi chinensis
Lophanthera lactescens
Lophostemon var. variegatus
Macadamia spp.
Macaranga grandifolia
Magnolia spp.
Maniltoa spp.
Markhamia spp.
Michelia spp.
Monodora myristica
Morinda citrifolia
Murraya spp.
Myristica spp.

Napoleonaea spp.
Nephelium lappaceum
Newbouldia laevis
Nyctanthes arbor-tristes
Oxyanthus spp.
Pachira spp.
Parmentiera spp.
Petrea spp.
Phyllanthus angustifolius
Pimenta spp.
Pisonia grandis var. alba
Pittosporum spp. (some)
Plumeria spp.
Podocarpus spp.
Pogonopus speciosus
Polyalthia spp.
Portlandia spp.
Posoqueria spp.
Psidium spp.
Punica granatum
Quararibea cordata
Quassia amara
Reevesia thyrsoidea
Radermachera sinica
Santalum spp.
Saraca spp.
Sarcocephalus latifolius
Stemmadenia spp.
Stenocarpus spp.
Syzygium spp.
Tabernaemontana (some)
Tecoma spp.
Terminalia kaernbachii
Tibouchina spp. (most)
Trevesia spp.
Warzsewiczia coccinea
Zanthoxylum spp.
Wrightia spp.
Xanthostemon spp.

Trees suitable for bonsai

Acokanthera spp.
Adansonia spp.
Adenium spp.
Backhousia citriodora
Brachychiton spp.
Brya ebenus
Bucida spinosa
Bulnesia spp.
Caesalpinia granidillo
Canella winterana
Citrus spp.
Delonix spp.
Diospyros ebenum
Eugenia spp.
Fagraea fragrans
Ficus (several spp.)
Geijera spp.
Guaiacum spp.
Ilex spp.
Ixora spp.

Jacquinia spp.
Leptospermum spp.
Malpighia spp.
Melaleuca minutiifolia (& others)
Mesua ferrea
Metrosideros spp.
Myrciaria spp.
Myristica spp.
Parinari spp.
Petrea spp.
Phytolacca dioica
Pimenta spp.
Plumeria spp.
Poitea spp.
Schotia spp.
Tamarindus spp.
Zanthoxylum coriaceum
Wrightia religiosa

Trees suitable for temperate, frost-free regions

Acacia baileyana
Acacia saligna
Acacia longifolia
Acokanthera spp.
Alberta magna
Annona cherimola
Brachychiton spp. (several)
Brugmansia sanguinea
Calodendron capense
Camellia sinensis
Casimiroa edulis
Ceratonia siliqua
Chorisia spp.
Citrus spp. (most)
Coffea arabica
Cussonia spp.
Diospyros kaki
Dodonaea viscosa
Dombeya x cayeuxii
Eriobotrya spp.
Erythrina caffra
Erythrina crista-galli
Erythrina x sykesii
Ficus elastica (& many others)
Euphorbia candelabrum
Euphorbia ingens (& many others)
Firmiana simplex
Fraxinus griffithii
Gardenia cornuta
Gardenia thunbergia
Geijera parviflora
Greyia spp.
Hymenosporum flavum
Ilex paraguayensis
Jacaranda mimosifolia
Juniperus chinensis
Koelreuteria spp. (most)
Lagunaria patersonii
Leptospermum scoparium

Leucadendron argenteum
Ligustrum spp.
Lophostemon confertus
Magnolia grandiflora
Melia azedarach
Metrosideros excelsus
Michelia figo
Mimusops caffra
Morus spp.
Murraya paniculata
Myica cerifera
Nuxia spp.
Oxyanthus pyriformis
Parinari curatellifolia
Peltophorum dubia
Persea americana f
Phytolacca dioica
Pinus patula
Pisonia brunoniana var variegata
Pittosporum angustifolia
Pittosporum tobira
Pittosporum undulatum
Pittosporum viridiflorum
Podocarpus henklii
Podocarpus neriifolius
Psidium cattleianum
Punica granatum
Radermachera sinica
Reevesia thyrsoidea
Salix chilensis
Schinus molle
Schotia afra

APPENDIX

Guide to the morphology of leaves, flowers and fruit
based on terms used in this book

PARTS OF A PLANT

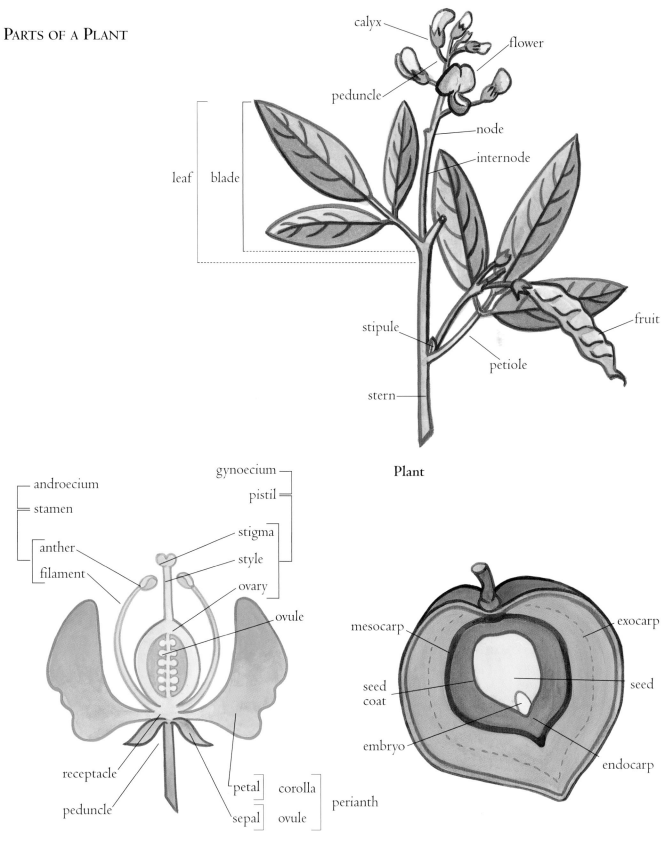

Plant

Flower

Drupe in cross section

LEAVES: their shapes, margins, apices and bases

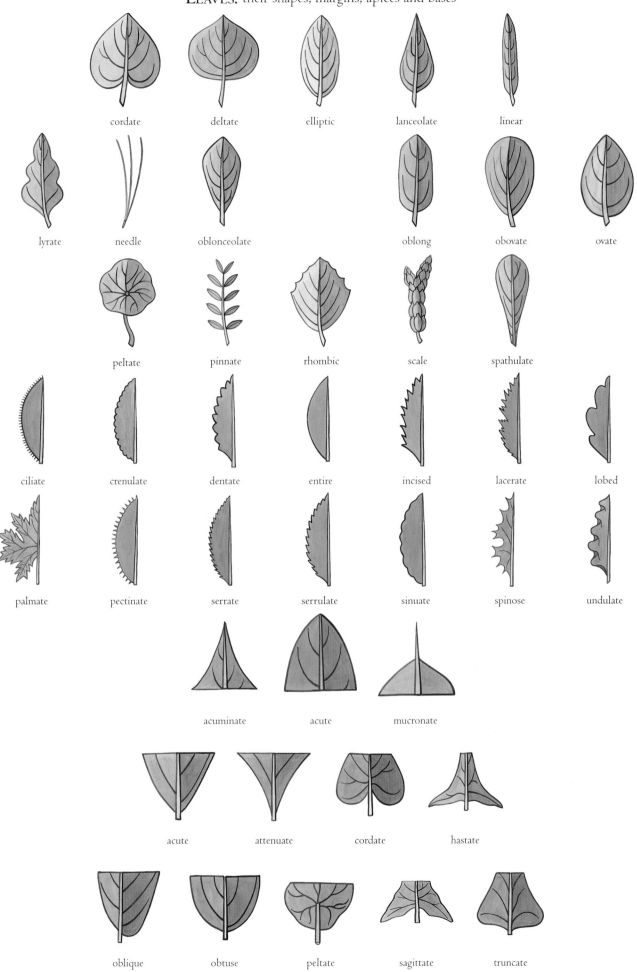

cordate   deltate   elliptic   lanceolate   linear

lyrate   needle   oblonceolate   oblong   obovate   ovate

peltate   pinnate   rhombic   scale   spathulate

ciliate   crenulate   dentate   entire   incised   lacerate   lobed

palmate   pectinate   serrate   serrulate   sinuate   spinose   undulate

acuminate   acute   mucronate

acute   attenuate   cordate   hastate

oblique   obtuse   peltate   sagittate   truncate

COMPOUND LEAVES

odd-pinnate

even-pinnate

2-pinnate

3-pinnate

3-foliate

digitate

LEAF ARRANGEMENT

opposite

alternate

whorled

LEAF LOBING

pinnately lobed

palmately lobed

pedately lobed

INFLORESCENCES: main types

raceme

cyme

panicle

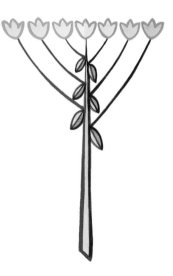

corymb

umbel

spike

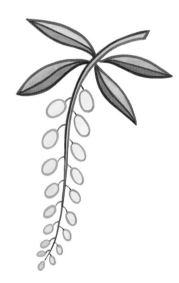

catkin

455

bilabiate

tubular

campanulate

composite

funnelform

salverform

staminous

papillionaceous

caesalpinaceous

TYPES OF FRUIT

aggregate

berry

(dehiscent) capsule

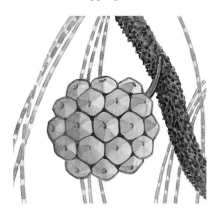

cone

drupe

fig

follicle

hesperidum

legume

nut

samara

swollen receptacle

GLOSSARY

of scientific terms used in this book

abaxial: situated facing away from the axis of the plant, as the undersurface of a leaf.

abortive: imperfectly developed.

acaulescent: stemless; having the stem very short and often underground, thus appearing stemless; opposite of caulescent.

achene: a small, dry, indehiscent, 1-seeded fruit that does not split to distribute its seed as, for example, *Pisonia* spp.

acuminate: tapering to an apex, the sides concave to the taper.

acute: tapering to a sharp apex, the sides straight along the apex.

adventitious: organs arising from unusual or irregular positions, as buds near a wound or roots from a stem or leaf; said of plants introduced to an area where they are not indigenous.

aerial: living above the surface of the ground or water.

aggregate fruit: a fruit developed from a single flower by fusion of many separate carpels (fruitlets), ripening into a mass (Magnoliaceae or Annonaceae family).

alkaline: having the ability to neut ralize acids; having a pH of more than 7; opposite of acid.

alkaloid: an organic compound produced by plants that has alkaline properties and that often forms the base of the active portion of many drugs and plant poisons.

alternate: any arrangement of leaves or other parts not opposite or whorled; placed singly at different heights along the axis or stem.

androphore: a stalk that supports stamens.

angiosperm: a plant with seeds enclosed in an ovary or pericarp.

annual: a plant of 1-year duration (or 1 growing season), completing its life cycle in that period.

anther: the pollen-producing part of a stamen.

apex: the tip of an organ; the extreme end or point farthest from the point of attachment; the growing point of a stem or root (Plural: apices).

apical: pertaining to the apex.

apiculate: terminating in a short, sharp, flexible point, not a spine.

appendage: an attached subsidiary or secondary part, as the hairs, prickles, or leaves of a stem.

appressed: flattened against underlying or adjacent tissues; pressed down or against.

approximate: close together but not united, as leaves along a stem; opposite of distans.

aquatic: living in water; growing naturally in water or under water.

arboreous: tree-like or pertaining to trees.

arborescent: tree-like.

arid: dry, having little rainfall.

aril: an extra covering of part, or all, a seed that may be more or less soft, fleshy and colourful, (*Podocarpus* spp.), or else dry and bony.

arillate: possessing an aril; more loosely, any outgrowth or appendage on the testa.

attenuate: gradually tapering.

axil: the angle beween the stem of a plant and the leaf stalk growing out of it.

axillary: pertaining to the axil; located in, or attached in, an axil.

axis: the whole main stem of a plant or the receptacle of a flower (Plural: axes).

berry: any simple fruit having a pulpy or fleshy pericarp, usually with several or many seeds n the pulp.

bipinnate: twice pinnately compound; doubly pinnate.

binomial: basic unit of naming a botany, comprising a generic name and a species, cultivar, group or hybrid epithet describing and distinguishing the individual belonging to that genus, e.g. *Cassia fistula*, *Cassia javanica* var. *indochinensis*, *Cassia javanica* x *grandis*.

bisexual: having both stamens and pistils in the same flower or inflorescence.

bract: a reduced, scale-like leaf arising from the stem of a flower and often apparently forming part of the flower head; usually in cases where the flower itself is insignificant. Sometimes resembling leaves.

buttress: a knee-like or plank-like outgrowth developing from the trunk-base of some kinds of trees, e.g. *Taxodium* spp. or *Ceiba pentandra*.

caffeine: a pharmecutical chemical; white, crystalline, bitter alkaloid usually derived from coffee or tea; used chiefly as a nervous system stimulant.

calliper: the diameter of a trunk of a tree or shrub.

calyx: group or cluster of modified leaves enclosing a flower bud, each segment being a sepal. In some plants, sepals partially replace the flower petals (*Brachychiton*) and are brightly coloured (Plural: calyxes or calyces).

cambium: the thin layer of formative tissue beneath the bark of gymnospermous and dicotyledonous trees and shrubs, from which new wood and bark originate; a sheath of generative tissue usually located between the xylem and the phloem; the tissue from which secondary growth arises in stems and roots.

campanulate: bell-shaped flowers (*Elaeodendron* spp.).

canescent: covered with greyish brown or greyish white pubescence.

capitate: borne in heads; dense clusters.

capitulum: a dense cluster of small, stalkless flowers.

capsule: dehiscent fruit, containing seeds, which dries and splits when ripe to discharge its contents.

carpel: plant's female reproductive organs, consisting of a pistil or ovary, stigma and style; the seed-bearing part of a flower.

catkin: mostly pendulous, stalkless flowers, often without petals and usually of individual sexes, the males being quite different from the females.

caudate: bearing a tail or tail-like appendage.

caudex: stem or trunk of a tree-fern or palm; the underground stem of a perennial herb from which the annual shoots arise.

caulescent: having an obvious main stem above the ground.

cauliflorous: flowering on the trunk of a woody plant, or on specialized spurs from it, or on the larger branches (see ramiflorous).

circumscissle: opening by means of a split around the circumference so that the top comes off like a lid, as in some seed capsules. The process is also known as equatorial dehiscence (also calyptra).

cladophyll; cladodes: 'stem leaf', a stem simulating a leaf; a flattened branch that takes on the form and function of a leaf (spp. of *Phyllanthus, Acacia*).

colony: a collection of organisms of the same kind growing together in close association.

column: the structure formed by the combination of the style and stamen (Hibiscus); a fused staminal tube.

columnar: shaped like a column.

compound: consisting of 2 or more similar parts, as a leaf divided into leaflets, or a fruit or pistil made up of several carpels.

cone: an inflorescence or fruit covered with overlapping scales.

contorted: twisted together; convoluted.

coppicing: the cutting back of trees to ground level in order to promote the growth of several new stems from the one rootstock.

cordate: heart-shaped, with a notch at the base; usually applied to leaves.

coriaceous: of a leathery texture; thick and tough as in the leaves of *Petrea*.

corolla: a general term usually applied to the inner whorl of a flower or floral leaves, as distinct from the sepals. It may be of several petals or sometimes in one piece.

corona: a crown or cup-like appendage, or ring of appendages (as in *Wrightia* spp.).

corymb: a more or less flat-topped flower clustering in which the flower stalks emanate from different parts of the main stem, as distinct from an umbel, where they radiate from a single point. The inner stalks are shorter than the outer ones, thus producing a flattish head.

corymbose: with flowers arranged in corymbs.

cotyledon: a primary leaf or seed leaf; quite different from the true leaves that develop later, they are usually dicotyledons (2-seed leaves) or monocotyledons (single-seed leaves); gymnosperm seedlings, such as *Pinus*, may have several cotyledons. In some plants, such as peas, the cotyledons remain underground.

crenate: having leaf-margins scalloped, with obtuse or rounded teeth.

crenulate: minutely crenate.

cusp: an abrupt, sharp point; a sharp point formed from the extended margin of a leaf; the thorns on some Holly (*Ilex*) leaves are cusps.

cuspidate: having a cusp; terminating in a point.

cyathia: an inflorescence-type characteristic of *Euphorbia*, it consists of a cupule (an involucre of small bracts, sometimes furnished with glands and subtended by petaloid bracts or appendages) enclosing several 'stamens', each one equivalent to a single male flower.

cyme: a flat-topped, usually few-flowered inflorescence in which the central, terminal flowers open in advance of the outer ones.

deciduous: falling off at certain seasons or stages of growth, such as leaves, petals, sepals flowers, etc. This term is commonly applied to trees that are not evergreen.

decussate: a term applied to leaves or branches arranged in pairs, with each successive pair at right angles to the next pair, or at least growing at a different angle.

deflexed: bent sharply downward or outward.

dehiscent: applied to fruits that split open to release their seeds when ripe, such as *Tabebuia* fruit; also applied to anthers that split to release their ripe pollen; cf. indehiscent.

deltate: triangular; term used in preference to 'deltoid' for flat structures such as leaves.

dentate: having a toothed margin, the teeth usually rather coarse and pointing outward.

denticulate: finely toothed, or minutely dentate.

dichogamy: producing mature male and female reproductive structures at different times, thus preventing self-pollination, as in *Brunfelsia* spp.

dichotomy: 1. division into two, especially in classification. 2. repeated branching and forking.

dichotomous: successively branched into more or less equal pairs; branching by repeatedly forking in pairs.

dicotyledon: a plant with 2 seed-leaves or cotyledons.

diffuse: loosely branching or spreading; widely or loosely spreading.

digitate: having parts that diverge from the same point like fingers of a hand; palmately divided as in *Tabebuia* spp.

dimorphic: occurring in 2 distinct forms, as in the adult and juvenile leaves, in many Proteaceae spp. (*Alloxylon flammeum* etc.).

dioecious: having male and female flowers on separate plants; for fertilization purposes, a male plant is usually set among a group of females, as in many Euphorbiaceae spp. c.f. Monoecious.

distichous: in 2 vertical ranks along an axis, producing leaves or flowers in 2 opposite rows.

diurnal: functioning during the day; said of flowers that open by day and close at night; the opposite of nocturnal.

dormant: 1. resting, as of a plant that has temporarily stopped growing, usually during winter or the dry season; 2. in a state of suspended growth, as of seeds.

drupe: a fleshy, 1-seeded, usually indehiscent fruit; a stone-fruit as Avocado or Mango.

druplet: a little drupe.

ecology: the branch of biology dealing with the relations and interactions between organisms and their environment, including other organisms.

ellipsoid: a solid or 3-dimensional body that is elliptic in section.

elliptic: oval, egg-shaped; mainly applied to leaves.

emarginate: with a shallow notch at the apex; usually applied to leaves or petals.

endemic: occurring in 1, limited locality or region only; confined to a particular area and found nowhere else.

endocarp: the stony part of a drupe or pome.

endosperm: a multicellular, usually starchy or oily nutritive tissue formed inside the seeds of many flowering plants, separate from the embryo.

entire: complete; not broken; of one piece; without indentations and the margins smooth.

epicarp: the outermost layer or skin of a fruit.

epidermis: the outermost layer of living

cells that forms a protective sheath for many plant organs, including leaves, petals and stems.

epiphytic: growing on other plants, not parasitically.

etiolate: drawn out and bleached or blanched by the exclusion of light.

evergreen: a plant having leaves that remain green and functional throughout the year; cf. deciduous.

exocarp: the outermost wall of a pericarp.

exotic: introduced from a foreign country; not native to a country: imported; sometimes used in the sense of showy or gaudy. cf. indigenous.

exserted: protuding or projecting organs, such as stamens or pistils, which protude beyond the rest of the flower; cf. included.

falcate: shaped like a sickle.

farinaceous: 1. starch-like or containing starch; 2. farinose.

farinose: covered with a mealy or floury coating as a means of protection, as the 'bloom' on new growth of *Aleurites moluccana*.

fascicle: a cluster or bundle of stems, leaves, flowers, racemes or roots almost always independent, but appearing to arise from a common point.

fastigiate: 1. having erect branches that are close to the stem; 2. becoming narrower at the top.

fertile: 1. capable of germinating; stamens carrying ripe pollen, flowers with receptive pistils or fruits containing seeds; 2. soil in good condition and capable of producing quality crops.

fertilization: pollination: impregnation. The fusion of the pollen of the male plant with the ovule of the female to form a seed.

fibrous: composed of, or covered with, tough, string-like fibres.

filament: the stalk of a stamen.

filiform: thread-like; hair-like.

flaccid: limp; lacking rigidity.

flagellate: with whip-like runners.

flagelliform: long and tapering; supple; whiplike.

flexuose: 1. pliable, easily bent; 2. bent alternately in opposite directions; zigzagged.

flora: 1. an aggregate term referring to all the plants occuring in a country or particular area; 2. a catalogue or descriptive account of the plants growing in a country or particular area.

fluted: marked by alternating ridges and groove-like depressions.

foetid: having an offensive smell.

follicle: a dry fruit formed from a single carpel containing several seeds, splitting along the ventral suture only; often pod-shaped with the seeds attached like peas to the seam.

funicle; **funiculus**: the stalk or thread sometimes bearing the ovule or seed and attaching it to the placenta.

gamopetalus: having petals joined at their edges in the form of a tube. Also known as **sympetalous**.

granulate: form into grains; roughen surface of.

generic: pertaining to genera.

genus: in classification, the principal subdivision of a family; a more or less closely related and definable group of plants comprising 1 or more species; the generic name is the first word of a binomial used to designate a particular kind of plant or animal; large genera are frequently divided for convenience into subgenera, but in such cases the same generic name is still used for all the species (Plural: genera).

geotropic: response of a plant to the force of gravity; the movement of shoots and roots of plants caused by gravity.

germination: the beginning of growth from a spore or a seed.

glabrate: nearly glabrous, bearing only a few scattered hairs; becoming glabrous at maturity.

glabrous: lacking hairs, bristles or scales.

gland: small structure, prominence, pit or appendage that usually secretes such substances as mucilage, oil or resin.

glandular: generally bearing glands (of hairs); bearing a gland, or gland-like prominence at the tip.

glaucescent: slightly glaucous.

glaucous: covered with an extremely fine, whitish or bluish, waxy substance that is easily rubbed off.

globose: round, spherical or nearly so; applied to plant organs, including fruits such as cherries, rounded shrubs or bushes and trees with a spherical type of crown.

glutinous: covered with a sticky exudation.

glycogen: a white polysaccharide, molecularly similar to starch, constituting the principal carbohydrate-storage material in animals, occurring in the liver, in muscle and in fungi and yeasts; also called animal starch.

granular: 1. small particles or granules; 2. covered with small granules.

gregarious: 1. species that tend to grow together in groups; 2. gregarious flowering; all trees of the same species flower simultaneously.

gymnosperm: plants whose seeds are not protected by enclosure in an ovary, i.e. conifer.

habitat: the kind of locality in which a plant grows.

haploid: having half of the diploid or full complement of chromosomes, as in mature gametes.

hastate: shaped like an arrowhead with divergent barbs.

herb: 1. a non-woody annual, biennial or perennial plant; 2. a plant valued for its aromatic, savoury or medicinal properties.

herbaceous: not woody; dying at the end of the growing season; having the characteristics of a herb.

herbivore: an animal or organism that feeds solely on plants.

hesperidium: a modified berry, with few seeds, a leathery rind, and membranous extensions of the endocarp dividing the pulp into chambers; an example is the orange.

heteromorphic: having several forms.

hilum: scar on a seed at the point at which the funiculus was attached.

hirsute: bearing long, coarse hairs.

hispid: having bristly or stiff hairs.

hybrid: the offspring of 2 different varieties, species or genera; a cross between 2 different kinds of related plants.

hypocotyl: the portion of the embryonic plant below the cotyledon.

imbricate: overlapping like shingles on a roof.

imparapinnate: where a pinnately compound leaf terminates in a single leaflet, pinna or tendril (see parapinnate).

incised: cut into; engraved.

indehiscent: said of a fruit that remains closed after it is ripe; not opening by any regular process; opposite of dehiscent.

indigenous: native to a country or area; not introduced.

inflorescence: an arrangement of flowers on a stem or axis; a cluster of flowers or a single flower.

involucre: whorl of bracts enclosing a number of flowers: as in the daisy family.

keel: 2 lower petals of pea-like, leguminous flowers (e.g. *Sesbania grandiflora*) united or partially joined to form a keel similar to that of a boat.

lacerate: irregularly cleft or cut; a margin having a torn appearance.

lacinate: cut into deep, narrow segments; cut into pointed lobes separated by deep, narrow, irregular incisions.

lanceolate: lance-shaped; usually applied to narrow leaves broadest below the middle and about 3 times longer than wide. The term is used, often in an abbreviated form, to denote shape intermediate between lanceolate and some other shape, a lance-oblong, lance-linear, etc.

latex: milky sap, as in *Ficus* or *Euphorbia*.

layer: method of vegetative propagation, usually of a wounded part, in which a branch or shoot is enclosed in a moist medium until roots develop; it is severed and cultivated as an independent plant.

leaf: a lateral appendage arising from the node of a stem and subtending a bud; it is usually of expanded shape and green in colour, being the chief organ of photosynthesis in most flowering plants.

leaflet: one of the subdivisions of a compound leaf.

legume: 1. a plant of the family Leguminosae; 2. a dry fruit formed from a single carpel opened by 2 sutures.

lenticel: a corky spot on young bark that serves as a path of gas exchange between the atmosphere and internal tissues of the stem.

lepidote: covered with minute, scurfy scales.

liane: a woody, climbing vine.

limb: 1. a main branch of a tree or shrub. 2 the free or expanded part of a petal, sepal or leaf.

linear: line-like; long and narrow, with parallel or nearly parallel margins.

lingulate: tongue-shaped.

littoral: of, or on, the shore; close to the sea.

locule: one of the compartments or 'cells' of an ovary, anther or fruit.

loculicidal: said of a fruit that dehisces along a suture about midway between the partitions separating the carpels.

lunate: in the shape of a half-moon; crescent-shaped.

lyrate: pinnatifid, with the terminal lobe much larger than the others; lyre-shaped.

malpighiaceous: describing hairs attached at, or near, the middle, with 2 horizontal points set in opposite directions (often stinging), especially characteristic of the Malpighiaceae.

margin: the edge of a leaf or a leaf-like structure.

marginate: having a margin of distinctive structure or colour, forming a well-defined border.

medial: located at, or near, the middle.

megafauna: the large animals of a particular region, habitat or geological period.

meristem: a region of plant tissue consisting of actively dividing cells.

mesocarp: the middle wall of a ripe ovary (fruit); the wall normally consists of 3 layers: 1. the exocarp, or outer layer; 2. the mesocarp and 3. the endocarp, or inner layer.

midrib, midvein: the main rib or central vein of a leaf or a leaf-like structure.

monocarpic (also **hapaxanthic**): applicable to plants that die after fruiting; not normally applied to annuals, but to those that grow for several years before fruiting and then dying, e.g. the *bromeliad* and *sempervirens*.

monoecious: having separate male and female flowers on the same plant. c.f. Dioecious.

monograph: an exhaustive, systematic account of a particular genus, family or group of organisms.

monotypic: said of a taxon containing, or composed of, but a single element, as a genus with but 1 species (*Amherstia nobilis*) or a family with only 1 genus.

montane: pertaining to mountains.

morphology: the study of form, structure and development; also used to designate the structure of an organism as contrasted with its physiology or classification.

morphological: pertaining to morphology.

mucilage: a gummy or gelatinous mixture of carbohydrates in plants; the slimy secretion of slugs and snails.

mucilaginous: composed of, or covered with, mucilage; slimy.

mucro: a short, sharp terminal point or tip.

mucronate: having a relatively blunt apex ending abruptly in a mucro.

naturalized: said of a plant or a species introduced from another region that becomes established, maintains itself and reproduces successfully in competition with the indigenous vegetation.

nectar: a sweet secretion produced in nectaries.

nectary: a nectar-secreting structure.

nocturnal: occurring, or functioning, during the night; opposite of diurnal.

node: the point on a stem where a leaf or leaves are normally borne; a joint.

nodule: a small, hard knot or rounded body, especially on the roots of legumes.

nomenclature: a set or system of names or terms used in a particular science or art by an individual or community, etc.

nut: a hard or bony, dry, indehiscent fruit derived from 2 or more carpels enclosed in a dense pericarp and usually containing 1 seed; the term is loosely used for any hard, dry, 1-seeded fruit.

nutlet: 1. a small nut; 2. a 1-seeded portion of a fruit that fragments as it matures, as in some Boraginaceae.

oblanceolate: roughly lanceolate, but with the distal end broader than the basal portion.

oblong: longer than broad, with the margins nearly parallel.

obovate: of a leaf, basically egg-shaped in outline, but with the maximum width away from the stalk. cf. ovate.

obsolete: not evident; rudimentary.

obtuse: of a leaf or petal that is blunt or rounded at the tip: obtusifolius.

ocrea, ochrea: a tubular or inflated sheath at the base of the petiole formed by a pair of stipules united around a stem (i.e. *Magnolia*).

461

odd-pinnate: said of a pinnate leaf with an odd number of leaflets, i.e. pinnate with a single terminal leaflet (see imparapinnate).

operculum: a cover, cap or lid, e.g. a circumscissle capsule or protective cap at the tip of a root.

operculate: having a lid or cap.

orbicular: circular in outline; round and flat; orbiculate.

oval: broadly elliptic, with the width greater than half the length.

ovary: the ovule-bearing part of the pistil.

ovate: egg-shaped and flat, with a broader end at the base.

ovule: the structure that becomes a seed after fertilization.

pachycaul: thick-stemmed; sometimes applied to tree-like herbs or shrubs with strong, erect stems, e.g. simple-stemmed trees like *Adansonia* spp. or *Moringa oleifera*.

palmate: with veins, lobes or divisions radiating from a common point.

palmatifid: of a leaf cut in a palmate manner more than halfway to the leaf stalk, as in a maple leaf.

panicle: a flower head with several branches, either opposite or alternate; a branched raceme.

paniculate: with flowers arranged in panicles.

pan-tropical: distributed throughout the tropical regions.

papilionaceous: reminiscent of a butterfly; applied to some leguminous subjects such as Sweet Peas, where the uppermost of the 5 petals (the standard) is the largest and erect, with a pair of laterals, or wings flanking it; also refers to the flowers of the Papilionoideae tribe of the Leguminosae family.

papilionate: with a pea-type (Papilionaceous) corolla.

parapinnate: where a pinnately compound leaf is not terminated by a single leaflet, pinna or tendril.

parasitic: deriving nourishment at the expense of another organism.

pathenogenesis: the development of seeds as in normal sexual reproduction but without fertilization. (i.e. *Garcinia mangostana*).

pedicel: the stalk of a flower.

pedicillate: having a pedicel; borne on a pedicel.

peduncle: a primary flower stalk supporting 2 or more flowers, or a solitary flower, if it is a remnant of a cluster.

pedunculate: pertaining to, or borne upon, a peduncle.

pellucid: wholly or partly transparent; translucent; applied especially to various dots or lines in leaves that contain internal oil glands that allow the passage of light.

peltate: of a leaf blade with the leaf stem joining the leaf at, or near, the centre on the underside, as in *Macaranga mappa*.

pendant, pendent, pendulous: drooping, hanging, dangling; suspended from the top.

perennial: continuing to live from year to year, as contrasted with an annual.

perfect: said of flowers having both stamens and carpels in functioning condition.

perianth: a collective term designating both the calyx and corolla considered together, especially if they are of a similar colour and texture.

pericarp: the wall of a mature ovary or fruit.

persistent: retaining its place, shape or structure; remaining attached after the growing period.

petal: a unit of the inner, floral envelope or corolla of a polypetalous (many-petalled) flower, usually white or variously coloured, seldom green.

petaloid: resembling a petal.

petiole: leaf stalk.

pH: a symbol denoting the relative concentration of hydrogen ions in a solution; a measure of the acidity or alkalinity. pH7 is neutral; less than 7 is acidic, greater than 7 is alkaline.

phloem: that part of the vascular bundle by which nutrients are transported within the plant; the softer part of the fibro-vascular tissue compared to the xylem or woody part.

photoperiodism: plants affected by day length; the response of plants to the relative length of day or night; also called day neutral.

photosynthesis: the process by which carbon dioxide is converted into carbohydrates by chlorophyll, under the influence of light.

phylloclade: a green, flattened or rounded stem functioning as a leaf; plants adapted to dry conditions are usually phylloclades, such as members of the Cactaceae.

phyllode: a petiole with the appearance and function of a leaf.

pilose: hairy; having soft, sparse and moderately long hairs, often covering the leaf surface.

pinna: one of the primary divisions of a compound leaf or frond, or (especially) of a compound fern frond (plural: pinnae).

pinnate: of a leaf, constructed in the manner of a feather with parts arranged on both sides of an axis in pairs, as in the leaves of *Tecoma stans*.

pinnatifid: pinnately cut more than halfway to the axis into segments.

pinnule: a secondary (or teriary, etc.) leaflet or pinna of a decompound leaf or frond; usually istinguished from a segment by being attached to the next higher axis only by the base of its own axis, the tissue margin being entirely free.

pistil: the female organ of a flower, consisting, when complete, of an ovary, style and stigma; a simple pistil consists of a single carpel; a compound pistil consists of 2 or more carpels; these are usually fused together.

pistillate: pertaining to a flower having a pistil but no stamens.

pith: the spongy tissue often occurring in the centre of a dicotyledonous stem; also found in some gymnosperms.

plicate: folded or plaited.

plumose: resembling a plume or a feather.

pollen: the male sex cells carried on the anthers of most flowering plants. When these are deposited on the stigma, the flower is said to be pollinated and fertilization of the ovule normally ensues. More than 1 pollen grain may grow a tube but only 1 will sucessfully fertilize a single egg.

pollination: the process by which pollen travels from the anther to a stigma, normally performed by insects, bats or birds. Flowers can also be hand-pollinated, or wind-pollinated.

polygamous: bearing unisexual and bisexual flowers on the same plant.

polymorphic: an organism that occurs in many forms, such as leaves of different shapes appearing on one plant.

polystichous: having leaves borne in many rows or series and spreading in many directions.

pome: a fruit constructed like an apple, with the enlarged, fleshy part enclosing the core formed from the carpels and enclosing the seed. Also applicable to some other members of the rose family (Rosaceae).

prop root: a root produced above the ground that serves as a prop or support to the plant, as in Mangroves or Pandanaceae.

pruinose: bearing a waxy-powdery, often bluish, secretion on the surface.

pseud- or **psuedo-**: a prefix meaning false or spurious.

pseudocarp: a false fruit; a fruit derived from parts other than the ovary, as in some Rosaceae, in which the 'fruit' is chiefly composed of the greatly enlarged receptacle.

puberulous: minutely pubescent.

pubescent: covered with soft, straight, short hairs.

punctate: marked with dots that they may be translucent or otherwise.

pyrene: a small, hard, stone-like seed in a drupe or similar fruit.

pyriform: pear-shaped.

raceme: a flower head on which individual flowers are carried on short stems of approximately equal length and are borne on an unbranched main stalk. In most cases, the flowers open from the base upwards, as in the *Colvillea racemosa*, but in others, they open almost simultaneously.

racemose: having flowers in racemes.

rachis: (rachises, rachides) axis of a compound leaf or inflorescence. Sometimes spelled rhacis.

radicle: the embryonic root of a germinating seed.

ramiflorous: bearing flowers directly on large branches and leafless twigs, but not on the trunk.

rank: a row, especially a vertical row, often used as a suffix, as 2-ranked, 3-ranked, etc.

receptacle: in flowering plants, the more or less enlarged or elongated apex of the pedicel; in Compositae, the enlarged apex of the peduncle.

recurved: bent backwards.

reflexed: abruptly curved or bent downwards or backwards.

regular: having flower parts of the same kind, all alike in size and shape; radially symmetrical.

remote: widely spaced; scattered; not close together.

reniform: kidney-shaped.

repand: undulate or wavy; having a slightly undulating or sinuous margin (as in some *Pittosporum*).

rhachis: See rachis.

rhizome: An underground stem that gives rise to roots and aerial stems, distinguished from a true root by the presence of nodes, buds or leaves, the latter sometimes reduced to scales.

rhizomatous: having rhizomes.

rhomboidal: parallelogram neither equilateral nor right-angled; diamond- or lozenge-shaped.

rind: a tough, outer layer, as on some fleshy fruits; sometimes used to designate any outer skin.

riparian: relating to the banks of a river.

root: the usually underground part of the plant that supplies it with water and dissolved mineral nutrients; in structure always lacking nodes and leaves; the absorptive, anchoring and storage organ of vascular plants.

rootstock: an underground stem or rhizome; sometimes applied especially to an erect rhizome, as in some ferns (See rhizome).

rosulate: in the form of a rosette.

rotate: wheel-shaped, with flat and spreading parts.

rotund: rounded in outline; nearly orbicular, but slightly inclined toward the oblong.

rugose: wrinkled in appearance, as a leaf-surface with sunken veins.

sagittate: shaped like an arrowhead, with prominent basal lobes pointing or curving downwards.

salverform: salver-shaped; said of a corolla composed of a slender tube abruptly expanding into a flat, rotund limb.

samara: a dry, indehiscent, 1-seeded, winged fruit.

saponin: group of soap-like compounds found in many plants, often toxic, but frequently used medicinally, as in *Sapindus saponaria*.

scabrid: referring to a surface that is rough, with a covering of very stiff, bristly hairs, scales or points.

scabrous: minutely roughened.

scale: 1. a small, usually dry leaf or bract. 2. an insect of the homopterus family Coccidae, which attaches itself to a plant and exudes a waxy, protective shield. 3. a small leaf arrached to, and protecting, a bud. 4. part of the cone of a coniferous tree.

scandent: climbing or scrambling over rocks or other plants without the aid of tendrils, but often with adherent roots or rootlets.

scarify: to roughen, slightly score or scrape the hard, outer coating of a seed before sowing, to aid the absorption of moisture and thus accelerate germination.

schizocarp: a dry fruit that separates at maturity into single-seeded, indehiscent carpels.

sclerophyll: plants composed of cells with thick walls that retain water; a common adaptation of plants at risk from drought, with hard, leathery or glassy leaf surfaces.

scrambling: said of a plant with weak, elongate stems that grow over other plants or any kind of support, but do not twine or have the aid of tendrils or aerial roots.

scrub: a type of vegetation composed of low and often densely packed bushes.

scurfy: covered with minute, bran-like scales.

self-fertile: a plant that does not need another to act as pollinator but is able to pollinate its own flowers.

sepal: one of the parts of the calyx.

sericeous: clothed with a silky pubescence; covered with closely appressed, fine, soft hairs.

serrate: having a saw-toothed margin, the teeth inclined toward the margin.

serration: a saw-like notch; a tooth of a serrate margin.

serrulate: minutely serrate.

sessile: lacking a stalk, as a leaf without a petiole.

seta: a bristle-like structure; needle-shaped process. (Plural: setae).

setaceous: bearing setae; covered with bristles.

setiform: bristle-shaped.

setose: covered with bristles.

sheath: a roughly tubular and close-fitting enclosure; a clasping leaf base or similar protective covering, usually around a stem.

shrub: a relatively low, usually several-stemmed, woody plant; a bush.

sinuate: having a deeply wavy margin.

sinus: the notch between 2 lobes or segments (Plural: sinuses).

solitary: single; only 1 in the same place.

spadix: a fleshy flower-spike usually partially enclosed by a spathe, as in Araceae family, etc. (Plural: spadices).

spathe: a leaf or bract, often brightly coloured, enclosing, or partially surrounding, a flower cluster such as a spadix.

spathulate or **spatulate**: shaped like a spatula, oblong with an attenuated base.

species: a term used in classification to denote a group or population of similar, mutually fertile individuals that show constant differences from allied groups that are more or less reproductively isolated (Plural: species).

specimen: a plant, or a portion of a plant, prepared and preserved for study; a preserved sample intended to show the characteristics of a species or other taxon.

spicate: spike-like; arranged in, or having, spikes.

spike: an unbranched, simple, elongate inflorescence bearing sessile or subsessile flowers.

spine: any sharp, rigid process or outgrowth, usually a modified branch, but also sometimes a modified stipule, petiole or other part; a thorn.

spinose: bearing a spine or spines.

stamen: the pollen-bearing organ of a flower, typically consisting of a filament and an anther, or the anther sometimes sessile.

staminate: having, producing or consisting of stamens; having stamens and no pistil, as the staminate flowers of dioecious plants.

standard: the upper, broad, often erect to recurved petal in many leguminous flowers.

stellate: star-shaped, having hairs or scales with branches or points radiating from a centre.

stem: the main axis of a plant bearing leaves and flowers, as contrasted with a root, which bears neither of these.

sterile: barren or non-reproductive, as a fern frond without sporangia or a flower lacking a pistil (see self-sterile).

stigma: the part of the pistil (usually the apex) that is receptive to pollen grains and on which they germinate (plural: stigmas or stigmata).

stipular: having stipules, or relating to them.

stipular spine: a spine representing a modified stipule, or having the position of a stipule.

stipule: a more or less leafy appendage at the base of the petiole in many plants.

stolon: an elongated, creeping stem (usually representing a modified basal branch) that roots at the nodes and often gives rise to new plants at some nodes, or at its tips, or both.

stoloniferous: producing stolons.

striate: marked with fine, linear, parallel lines.

style: that part of the reproductive system of a flower between the ovary and the stigma.

subspecies: a major subdivision of a species, between species and variety.

substrate: the material in, or on which, a plant is rooted.

subtropical: inhabiting or characterizing regions bordering on the tropics.

subtend: to be attached beneath and close to, as a bract below a flower.

succulent: juicy or fleshy; having tissues thickened to conserve moisture.

sucker: a shoot arising from underground, near the base of the parent plant; often directly from the rootstock.

superior: said of 1 organ when it is above another, such as a superior ovary, which has the perianth attached beneath.

suture: a seam or join, especially of carpels; a line along which dehiscence occurs.

symbiosis: the living together of dissimilar organisms, with benefit to one or both.

sympodial: a form of growth in which the terminal bud dies or terminates in an inflorescence, and growth is continued by successive, secondary axes growing from the lateral buds. cf. monopodial.

syncarp: a multiple or fleshy, aggregate fruit.

syncarpous: with 2 or more carpels fused or united in a compound pistil.

synchronicity: all individuals in proximity bloom in unison.

synonym: 1, 2 or more scientific names applied to the same taxon, one of which is correct and the others incorrect under the international rules of nomenclature. The term is commonly used to designate only the incorrect names.

taproot: a central or leading root that penetrates deeply into the ground without dividing; a prolonged and relatively thick, primary root.

taxon: a biological category or group (Plural: taxa).

taxonomy: the science of classification.

terete: circular in cross section.

terminal: pertaining to the end or apex.

terrestrial: growing on the ground.

tertiary: of the third order or rank, as tertiary veins, which are branches of secondary veins, which in turn arise from the primary or midvein.

testa: the outer coat of a seed, usually hard and brittle in texture.

theobromine: a white, crystalline, water-insoluble, poisonous powder; occurring in tea and obtained from the cacao bean; used chiefly as a diuretic, myocardial stimulant and vasodilator.

thyrse (or **thyrsus**): a dense panicle, especially one whose lateral branches are cymose.

thyrsoid: resembling a thyrse.

tissue: an aggregate of cells similar in structure or function.

tomentose: covered with matted, soft, woolly hairs.

tomentum: a covering of matted, soft, woolly hairs; wool-like pubescence.

torose: knobby; having a cylindrical body abruptly swollen at intervals.

torulose: the diminutive of torose.

torus; 1. the receptacle of a flower. 2. the disc-shaped structure in vessel segments, part of the water-conducting tissue of plants.

toxic; poisonous.

tribe: a taxon consisting of 1 or more genera, forming a natural group within a family.

trifoliate: having 3 leaves, or leaves in groups of 3.

truncate: ending abruptly; having a base or apex that is nearly straight across, as if it is cut off.

tuber: one of the swellings that form at the root of some plants and putting forth buds.

tubercle: a wart-like or knob-like projection.

turbinate: top-shaped.

umbel: an indeterminate, often flat-topped inflorescence, consisting of several or many pedicellate flowers arising from a common point of attachment.

umbellate: arranged in umbels, or pertaining to umbels.

umbelliform: in the shape of an umbel.

undulate: wavy; of leaves or petals with wavy surfaces or edges, usually applied to those that are wavy up and down; those that are wavy in and out are termed sinuate.

unisexual: having pistil or stamens, but not both.

urceolate: pitcher-shaped; hollow and contracted at the mouth.

urn-shaped: in the shape of a vase or pitcher; urceolate.

variety: a morphological variant or variant group within a species, differing from other variants of the same species by one or more minor characteristics.

variegated: marked with different colours or tints in spots, streaks or patches.

vascular: furnished with vessels or ducts through which liquid passes.

vascular plants: possessing, or pertaining to, tissues or vessels that conduct water, minerals, sugar and other organic substances. Vascular plants include ferns, gymnosperms and angiosperms.

vegetative reproduction: the method of propagation using pieces of living plants (cuttings) as apposed to seed. In vegetative propagation, the new plant will carry all the characteristics of the parent (a clone).

vein: a strand of vascular tissue in a leaf blade.

venation: pertaining to the arrangement or patterns of the veins.

ventricose: swollen on one side.

verrucose: covered with small wart-like projections.

villous: clothed with long, soft, weak (straight) hairs.

viscid: having a sticky coating or secretion.

whorl: cyclic arrangement of appendages at a node.

wing: 1. any thin, often dry and membranous, expansion attached to an organ, as on petioles or fruits. 2. a lateral petal of a leguminous flower.

xeromorphic: plants, or parts of plants, protected against excessive loss of moisture by hairs, thick cuticles or similar structural characteristics.

xerophyte: a plant adapted to life in areas where water supply is limited, or where water uptake is difficult owing to an excess of salts, e.g. on the seashore (*Tamarix* spp.) cf. Hydrophyte, Mesophyte.

xerophytic: a plant capable of survival under conditions of extreme drought, or one adapted to arid conditions, e.g. cacti.

xylem: a complex tissue in the vascular system of higher plants, functioning chiefly for the conduction of fluid upwards, but also for support and storage and typically making up the woody part of a plant stem.

zygomorphic: a flower divisible into 2 equal parts in 1 plane only such as *Gmelina arborea* or *Antirrhinum*.

BIBLIOGRAPHY

Adams, C.D.: *Flora of Jamaica*; University of the West Indies, Jamaica, 1972

Allaby, Michael: *The Concise Dictionary of Ecology*; OUP, UK, 1994

American Horticultural Society: *A-Z Encyclopedia of Garden Plants*; DK Publishing Inc., 1997

Anderson, W.R.: *Flora of the Lesser Antilles*

Anon.: *Arboles Maderables*; Instituto de Libro, La Habana, Cuba, 1970

Anon.: Centres of Plant Diversity (A Guide & Strategy for their Conservation): The World Wide Fund for Nature (WWF) & The World Conservation Union, (IUCN), Vols. 1–3; IUCN Publications Unit, Cambridge, UK, 1994–1997

Anon.: *Encyclopedia of the Biosphere*, Vols. 1–10; Fundacio Enciclopedia Catalana, Barcelona, 2000

Anon.: *Flowering Plants from Cuban Gardens*; Women's Club of Cuba; Criterion Books, New York, USA, 1952

Anon.: *Gardening in East Africa*; Kenya Garden Society; Longman's Green & Co., London, UK, 1950

Anon.: Hortus Third; *Liberty Hydes Bailey Hortorium*; Macmillan Press Ltd., 1977

Anon.: *L'Isle de la Réunion par ses Plantes*; Conservatoire Botanique de Mascarin; Solar, 1992

Anon.: *Neem, A Tree for Solving Global Problems*; National Academy Press, Washington, USA, 1992

Anon.: Huxley Anthony, editor-in-chief; *The New Royal Horticultural Society, Dictionary of Gardening*, Volumes 1–4; Macmillan Press Ltd., London, 1992

Anon.: Tropical Tree Fruits for Australia; Qld Dept of Primary Industries, Brisbane, Australia, 1984

Ansteguieta, Leando: Families & Generos de los Arboles de Venezuela;

Bannochie, I. & Light, M.: *Gardening in the Caribbean*; Macmillan Press, 1993

Bartels, Andrea: *Guide des Plantes Tropicales*; Editions Eugen Ulmer, Paris, France, 1993

Benthall, A.P.: *Trees of Calcutta & its Neighbourhood*; Thacker, Spink & Co. Ltd., Calcutta, India, 1933

Bisse, Johannes: *Arboles de Cuba*; Editorial Cientifico-Tecnica, La Habana, Cuba, 1981

Black, R.J. & Yuppert, K.: *Your Florida Landscape*; University of Florida, USA, 1995

Blatter, E., Milland, W.S. & Stearn, W.T.: *Some Beautiful Indian Trees*; Bombay Natural History Society, 1937; 1954; Thacker & Co. Ltd., Bombay, India 1950

Brandis, Sir Dietrich: *Forest Flora of North West & Central India*; Dehra Dun, India,

Britton, N.L. & Wilson, P.: *Botany of Porto Rico & the Virgin Islands*; (Scientific Survey. P.R. & V. Is.), N.Y. Academy of Science, New York, USA 1925–26, 1930

Brock John: *Native Plants of Northern Australia*; Reed, New Holland, Australia, 2001

Brooker, M.I.H. & Kleinig, D.A.: *Field Guide to Eucalypts*; Inkata Press, Sydney, Australia, 1994

Broschat & Meerow: *Betrock's Reference Guide to Florida Landscape Plants*; Betrock Information Systems Inc., USA, 1998

Bruggeman, L.: *Tropical Plants*; Thames & Hudson Ltd., London, 1957

Burton, F. & Clifford, P.: *Wild Trees in the Cayman Islands*; National Trust for the Cayman Islands, 1997

Cadet Th.: *Fleurs et Plantes de la Réunion et de l'Ile Maurice*; Les Editions du Pacific, Singapore, 1981

Campbell, G.D. & Hammond, H.D. (Editors): *Floristic Inventory of Tropical Countries*; The New York Botanical Gardens, Bronx, New York, 1989

Campbell, R.: *Guide to Mangos in Florida*; Fairchild Tropical Garden, Florida, USA, 1992

Castner, S.L. Timme & Duke, J.A.; *A Field Guide to Medicinal & Useful Plants of the Upper Amazon*; Feline Press, Gainesville. Florida, USA, 1998

Chin, H.F.: *Malaysian Flowers in Colour*; Tropical Press SDN. BHD. Kuala Lumpur, Malaysia, 1977

Chin, H.F. & Young, H.S.: *Malaysian Fruits in Colour*; Tropical Press, Malaysia, 1980

Chin, H.F. & Enoch, I.C.: *Malaysian Trees in Colour*; Tropical Press, Malaysia, 1988

Clay, H. & Golt: *The Hawaiian Garden*; Tropical Shrubs; University of Hawaii Press, Honolulu, Hawai'i, 1977

Corner, E.J.H.: *Wayside Trees of Malaya*; 2 Vols; Government Printing Office, Singapore, 1952

Coronel, R.E.: *Promising Fruits of the Philippines*; College of Agriculture, University of the Philippines at Los Banos, Philippines, 1983

Correll, D.S. & H.B.: *Flora of the Bahamas Archipelago*; J. Cramer, Vaduz, 1982

Cowen, D.V.: *Flowering Shrubs & Trees of India*; Thacker & Co. Ltd., Bombay, India, 1965

Cox, P.A. & Sandra A.B.; *Islands, Plants & Polynesians*; Dioscorides Press, Portland, Oregon, USA, 1991

Cribb A.B. & Cribb, J.W.: *Plant Life of the Great Barrier Reef & Adjacent Shores*; University of Queensland Press, St Lucia, Qld, Australia, 1985

Dale I.R. & Greenway, P.J.: *Kenya's Trees & Shrubs*; Buchanan's Kenya Estates Ltd, in association with Hatchards, London, 1961

Eliovsin, S.: *The Complete Gardening Book for South Africa*; Howard; Timmonds, Cape Town, S. Africa, 1960

Ellison, D.: *Cultivated Plants of the World (Trees, Shrubs & Climbers)*; Flora Publications International Pty Ltd; Brisbane, Australia, 1995

Enoch, I. & Holttum, R.E.: *Tropical Gardening*; Timber Press, Portland Oregon, USA, 1991

Elliot R. & Jones, D.: *Encyclopedia of Australian Plants – Suitable for Cultivation, Vols. 1–9*; Thomas C. Lothian Pty Ltd, Port Melbourne, Australia, 1997

Everard, B. & Morley, B.D.: *Wild Flowers of the World*; Ebury Press & Michael Joseph, London, 1970

Eyre, S.R.: *Vegetation & Soils – A World Picture*; Edward Arnold (Publishers) Ltd, London, 1968

Flannery T.: *The Future Eaters*; Reed New Holland, Sydney, 1994

Francis, W.D.: *Australian Rain Forest Trees*; Angus & Robertson; Sydney, Australia, 1951

Gardner S., Sidisunthorn, P. & Anusarnsunthorn, V.: *A Field Guide to Forest Trees of Northern Thailand*, funded by IUCN; The World Bank; Toyota Thailand Foundation; Kobfai Publishing Project, Thailand, 2000

Gentry, A.H.: *A Field Guide to the Familes & Genera of Woody Plants of Northwest South America (Colombia, Ecuador & Peru)*; The University of Chicago Press, USA, 1996

Gómez, E.S.; *Frutas en Colombia*; Ediciones Cultural
    Colombiana Ltda., Colombia, S. America, 1986

Graf: *Tropical Color Encyclopedia of Exotic Plants & Trees*;
    E Rutherford, USA, 1978

Groves, R.H.: *Australian Vegetation*; CSIRO, Cambridge
    University Press, Melbourne, Australia, 1981

Gymer, G.P.: *A Taxonomic Review of Brachychiton (Sterculiaceae)*;
    Queensland Herbarium, paper published in Australian
    Systematic Botany, 1988

Hall, Dr. D.W.: *Plants of Florida & the Coastal Plains*; Maupin
    House, Florida, USA, 1993

Hall, N., Johnston, R.D. & Chippendale, G.M.: *Forest Trees
    of Australia*; Australian Government Publishing Service,
    Canberra, Australia, 1975

Hanly, G. & Walker, J.: *The Subtropical Garden*; Timber Press,
    Oregon, USA, 1992

Herbert, D.A.: *Gardening in Warm Climates*; Angus & Robertson,
    Australia, 1952

Heywood, V.H.: *Flowering Plants of the World*; Oxford University
    Press, UK, 1993

Hodel D.R.: *Exceptional Trees of Los Angeles*; California Arboretum
    Foundation, California, USA, 1988

Holttum, R.E.: *Gardening in the Lowlands of Malaya*; Straits Times
    Press, Malaysia, 1953

Honeychurch, P.: *Caribbean Wild Plants & Their Uses*; Macmillan
    Ltd, London, 1980

Howard, R. (Editor-in-chief): *Flora of the Lesser Antilles Vols. 1–6*;
    Arnold Arboretum, Harvard University, Massachusetts,
    USA, 1974–1988

Huxley, A. (Editor); *The Macmillan World Guide to House Plants*;
    Macmillan Ltd, London, 1981

Hutchinson & Dalziel: *Flora of West Tropical Africa*; Crown
    Agents for Overseas Govts & Admin., London, 1963

Hyland, B.P.M., Whiffin, T., Christophel, D.C., Gray, B., Elick,
    R.W. & Ford, A.J.: *Australian Tropical Rainforest Trees &
    Shrubs*; CSIRO Publishing, Melbourne, Australia, 1999

Jackes B.R.: *Plants of the Tropics*; James Cook University,
    Townsville, Qld, Australia, 2001

Jennings, O.E.: *Botany of the Isle of Pines (Cuba)*; Carnegie
    Museum, Washington, USA, 1917

Jex-Blake, A.J.: *Gardening in East Africa*; Kenya Horticultural
    Society; Longman's, London, UK, 1950

Jones, D.L.: *Ornamental Rainforest Plants in Australia*; Reed,
    Sydney, Australia, 1986

Jones, D. & German, P.: *Flora of Malaysia Illustrated*; Oxford
    University Press, UK, 1993

Judd, Campbell, Kellog & Stevens: *Plant Systemics, a Phylogenic
    Approach*; Sinauer Associates, Inc., Massachusetts,
    USA, 1999

Keay, R.W.J.: *Trees of Nigeria*; Clarendon Press, Oxford &
    New York, 1989

Keppler & Mau: *Exotic Plants of Hawaii*; Mutual Publishing,
    Hawaii, 1989

Keppler, A.K.: *Trees of Hawai'i*; University of Hawai'i Press,
    Honolulu, Hawai'i, 1990

Lanzara, P. & Pizzetti, M.: *Simon & Schuster's Guide to Trees*;
    Simon & Schuster, New York, USA, 1978

Lear, R. & Turner, T.: *Mangroves of Australia*; University
    of Queensland Press, Brisbane, Australia, 1977

Leeuwenberg, A.J.M.: *Tabernaemontana: Old World Species*;
    Royal Botanic Gardens, Kew, London, UK, 1991

Leeuwenberg, A.J.M.: *Tabernaemontana: New World Species*;
    Royal Botanic Gardens, Kew, London, UK, 1991

Leon, Hno. & Alain, Hno.: *Flora de Cuba*; Museo de Historia
    Nat. de la Salle, Havana, Cuba, 1964

Lewis GP: Caesalpinia; Revision of the Poincianella –
    Erythrostemon Group; Royal Botanic Gardens, Kew,
    London, UK, 1998

Little, Wadsworth & Woodbury: *Common Trees of Puerto Rico &
    the Virgin Is.*; Dept. of Agriculture, Forest Service,
    Washington, USA, Part I, 1964 & Part II, 1974

Lorenzi, H.: *Avores Brasileiras: Brazilian Trees*; Instituto Plantarum
    de Estudos da Flora Ltda; Brazil, Vols 1 & 2; 1992 & 1998

Lotschert W. & Beese. G.: *Collins Guide to Tropical Plants*,
    translated by Clive King, Collins, London, 1983

Lovelock C.: *Field Guide to the Mangroves of Queensland*; Australian
    Institute of Marine Science, Australia, 1993

Macbride, J.F.: *Flora of Peru*; Field Museum Natural History,
    Chicago, USA, 1937

Macmillan, H.F.: *Tropical Planting & Gardening*; Macmillan & Co.
    Ltd., London, UK, 1912 (reprinted 1991)

Martin, Campbell & Ruberte: *Perennial Edible Fruits of the Tropics:
    An Inventory*; USDA Agricultural Handbook No. 642,
    USA, 1987

Martin, P.: *Botanica*; Random House Pty Ltd, Australia, 1997

Merrill, E.D.: *Flora of Manila*; Manila; Bureau of Printing,
    Philippines, 1912

Menninger, E.: *Fantastic Trees*; Timber Press, Portland Oregon,
    USA, 1995

Mabberly, D.J.: *The Plant Book*; Cambridge University Press,
    Cambridge, UK, 1997

Macubben, T. & Tasker, G.: *Florida Gardener's Guide*; Cool
    Springs Press, Tennessee, USA, 1997

Morton, J.F.: *Fruits of Warm Climates*; Morton, USA, 1987

Menninger, E.: *Flowering Trees of the World*; New York, USA, 1962

Minter S.: *The Greatest Glasshouse – Rainforests Recreated*; Royal
    Botanic Gardens, Kew, HMSO Publications, 1990

Morley, B.D. & Toelken, H.R.: *Flowering Plants in Australia*;
    Rigby Publishers, Sydney, Australia, 1983

Myers, N.: *The Primary Source, Tropical Forests & Our Future*;
    W.W. Norton & Co., New York & London, 1998

Neal, M.C.: *In Gardens in Hawaii*; Bishop Museum Press,
    Hawaii, 1965

Nellis, D.W.: *Seashore Plants of South Florida & the Caribbean*;
    Pineapple Press, Florida, USA, 1994

Nelson: *Trees of Florida, A Reference Field Guide*; Pineapple Press,
    Florida, USA, 1994

Nicholson, Nan & Hugh: *Australian Rainforest Plants*; Vols. ¾–v;
    Terania Rainforest Publishing, NS, Australia

Ortho Books editorial staff; *All About Citrus & Subtropical Fruits*;
    The Solaris Group, San Ramon, California, USA, 1985

Palgrave: *Trees of Central Africa*; National Publications Trust,
    Rhodesia & Nyasaland, 1956

Patterson, J. & Stevenson, G.: *Native Trees of The Bahamas*; 1977

Peck, S.: *Planning for Diversity; Issues & Examples*; Island Press,
    Washington, USA, 1998

Pennington, T.D.: *The Genera of Sapotaceae*; Royal Botanic
    Gardens, Kew, London, UK, 1991

Pittier, H.: *New or Noteworthy Plants from Colombia & Central
    America*; Washington G.P.O. USA, 1920–1922

Pittier, H.: *Plantas Usuales de Costa Rica*; University de Costa
    Rica, Costa Rica, 1957

Pittier, H.: *Manual de las Plantas Usuales de Venezuela*; Caracas; Litografia Comercio, Venezuela, S. America, 1926

Proctor, G.: *Flora of the Cayman Islands*; HMSO, London, UK, 1984

Project of the Science Education Centre: Plants of the Philippines; University of the Philippines, Manila, Philippines, 1971

Polunin, I.: *Plants & Flowers of Malaysia*; Times Editions, Singapore, 1988

Purseglove, J.W.: *Tropical Crop; Dicotyledons*; Volume 1; Longman, London, UK, 1969

Quesnel V. & Farrell, T.F.: The Trinidad & Tobago Field Naturalists' Club, Trinidad, 2000

Randall, J. & Marinelli, J.: *Invasive Plants*; Weeds of the Global Garden; Brooklyn Botanic Garden, New York, USA, 1996

Rauch F.D. & Weissich, P.R.: Plants for Tropical Landscapes – a Gardener's Guide; University of Hawai'i Press, 2000

Rauh, W.: *Succulent & Xerophytic Plants of Madagascar*, Vols. I & II; Strawberry Press, Mill Valley, California, USA, 1998

Research group: *Mangos, Guide to Mangos in Florida*; Fairchild Tropical Gardens, Miami, Florida, USA, 1992

Reyes; Philippine Woods; Manila; Bureau of Printing, Philippines, 1938

Riffle, R.L.; *The Tropical Look*; Timber Press, Oregon, USA, 1998

Robinson, L.: *Field Guide to the Native Plants of Sydney*; Kangaroo Press, Sydney, Australia, 1991

Rohwer, J.G.: *Tropical Plants of the World*, translated by Nicole Franke & Daniel Shea, Sterling Publishing Co., New York, 2002

Rubeli, K.: *Tropical Rain Forest in South East Asia*; Tropical Press SDN. BHD. Kuala Lumpur, Malaysia, 1986

Sahadevan, N.; *Green Fingers*; Sahadevan Publications SDN BHD, Negeri Sembilan, Malaysia, 1987

Sanchez, P. & Uranga, H.; *Plantas Indeseables de Cuba*; Instituto del Libro, Cuba, 1993

Sayer, J.A. et al, Editors; *The Conservation Atlas of Tropical Forests*; Macmillan Publishers Pty Ltd, 1992

Schmid, M,: *Fleurs et plantes de Nouvelle-Caledonie*; Nouvelle des Editions du Pacifique, 1981

Schuetz, F.: *Flowering Trees for Central & South Florida*; Gr. Outdoor Pub., Florida, USA, 1990

Scurlock, J.P.: *Native Trees & Shrubs of Florida Keys*; Laurel & Herbert Inc., Florida, USA, 1987

Smit & Hartog: *Tropical Gardens*; Flora in Focus; Smithmark, 1995

Smith, A.C.: *Flora Vitensis Nova*; A New Flora of Fiji

Smith, Earl E.: *The Forests of Cuba*; Cambridge, UK, 1954

Smith, Earl E.: Contributions I–III to *Coastal & Plain Flora of the Yucatan*; Field Colombian Museum, 1895–98

Smith, N.J.H., Williams, J.T., Plucknett, D.L., Talbot, J.P.: *Tropical Forests & their Crops*; Comstock Publishing Associates; Cornell University Press, Ithaca/London, 1992

Soepadmo, E. & Wong, K.M.: *Flora of Sabah & Sarawak*; Malaysia; Sabah Forest Research Institute, 1995

Sohmer, S.H. & Gustafson, R.: *Plants & Flowers of Hawaii*; Univ. of Hawaii, Honolulu, Hawaii, 1987

Specht, R.L. & Specht, A.; Australian Plant Communities (Dynamics of Structure, Growth & Biodiversity); Oxford University Press, South Melbourne, Australia, 1999

Standley, P.: Flora of Costa Rica; Field Museum of Natural History, Chicago, USA, 1938

Standley, P.: Flora of the Panama Canal Zone; Smithsonian Inst. Washington, USA, 1928

Standley, P.: Flora of the Yucatan; Field Museum of Natural History, Chicago, USA, 1930

Streets, R.J.: *Exotic Forest Trees in the British Commonwealth*; Clarendon Press, Oxford, UK, 1962

Tasker: *Enchanted Ground*: Andrews & McMeel, Kansas City, Kansas, USA, 1994

Teel, W.: *A Pocket Directory of Trees & Seeds in Kenya*; Kengo, Nairobi, Kenya, W. Africa, 1984

Tinggai, S.; *Brunei Darussalam Fruits in Colour*; University of Brunei, Darussalam, Brunei, 1992

Tomes & Mesa: *Diccionario Botanico de Nombres Vulgares Cubanos*; Volumes 1 & 2, Havana, Cuba, 1988

Tomlinson: *Trees Native to Tropical Florida*; Harvard Printing Office, USA, 1980

Tracey, J.G.: *The Vegetation of the Humid Tropical Region of North Queensland*; CSIRO, Melbourne, Australia, 1981

Turner I.M.: *The Ecology of Trees in the Tropical Rain Forest*; Cambridge University Press, Cambridge, UK, 2000

Valder, P.: *The Garden Plants of China*; Florilegium, Sydney, Australia, 1999

Van-Ollenbach, A.: *Planting Guide to the Middle East*: The Architectural Press Ltd, London, UK, 1978

Van Wyk, B. & Wyk, P. van: *Field Guide to Trees of South Africa*; Struik Publishers (Pty) Ltd, Capetown, S. Africa, 1997

Wagner, W.L., Herbst, D.R. & Sohmer, S.H.: *Manual of the Flowering Plants of Hawai'i*, Revised Edition, Vols. 1 & 2; University of Hawaii, Bishop Museum Press, Honolulu, Hawaii, 1997

Warren, W.: *Tropical Plants for Home & Garden*; Thames & Hudson Ltd, London, UK, 1997

Watkins & Sheehan: *Florida Landscape Plants*; University Press of Florida, Florida, USA, 1975

Webster, A.: *Caribbean Gardening*; United Coop. Printers, Jamaica, 1950

Whistler, W.A.: *Tropical Ornamentals*; Timber Press, Portland, Oregon, USA, 2000

White & Perchick: *Flowering Trees of the Caribbean*; Rinehart & Co. Inc., 1955

Whitman, W.F.: *Five Decades with Tropical Fruit*; Quisqualis Books, Engelwood, Florida, in cooperation with Fairchild Tropical Garden, Coral Gables, Florida, USA, 2001

Williams, K.A.W.: *Native Plants of Queensland*; Vols. 1–4, Brisbane, Australia, 1997, 1984, 1987, 1999

Williams, R.O.: *Flora of Trinidad & Tobago*; Parts 1&2, Government Printery, Trinidad, 1978–86

Williams, R.O.: *Useful & Ornamental Plants in Zanzibar & Pemba*; Gov. Printer, Zanzibar, E Africa, 1949

Williams, R.O. & R.O. Jnr.: *The Useful & Ornamental Plants of Trinidad & Tobago*; Guardian Commercial Printing, Trinidad, 1951

Wilson, E.O. (Editor): *Biodiversity*; National Academy Press, Washington D.C., USA, 1988

Wrigley, J.W. & Fagg, M.: *Banksias, Waratahs & Grevilleas, & all other plants in the Australian Proteaceae family*; Collins Publishers, Australia, Sydney, 1989

Wrigley, J. W. & Fagg, M.: *Bottlebrushes, Paperbacks & Tea Trees, & all other species of the Leptospermum alliance*; Angus & Robertson, Sydney, Australia, 1993

PHOTOGRAPHY CREDITS

All photographs taken by the author unless indicated below. The first number indicates the page number, the abbreviated letters used as follows: l = left; ul = upper left; ll = lower left; cl = centre left; c = centre; up = upper centre; lc = lower centre; r = right; ur = upper right; cr = centre right; lr = lower right; inset ul = inset upper left; inset ur = inset upper right; inset ll = inset lower left; inset lr = inset lower right; pan = panorama or large, lower photograph

Australian National Botanic Gardens: 37. uc; 282. r

Simon Barwick: 3. ll & inset; 5. ur & inset & pan; 6. lr; 22. r; 23. lr; 50. l, uc & r; 73. uc & r; 130. uc & lc; 138. r; 149. lr & inset; 163. uc & lc; 164. all; 167. ll & inset; 168. inset ur; 169. ul & inset; 177. lr; 187. ur & inset; 196; ul & inset; 234. lc; 235. r; 247. all; 293. lc; 312. pan; 329. r; 354. pan; 359. lc; 367. ll; 387. ll & lc; 401. ur & inset

Patricia Bradley: 208. r

Jane Brown: 89. ll; 159. lc; 341. lc

Gerald D. Carr: 403. uc &r

Andrea Kee Heng Choon: 115. ur & inset; 178. uc & lc

Collins-Bartholomew: xii. Climate map (© Collins-Bartholomew Ltd 2003. Reproduced by Permission of HarperCollins Publishers)

Maureen Emmett: 271. ll

Edward Flectcher: 8. l; 9. ul, ll &lr

Garden World Images: 145. no. 4 (© Ivan Polunin); 181. uc

Flecker Gardens: 286. lr; 310. l

Ross Hunter: 181. r

Hutchinson Library: 394. pan (© Hutchinson Library/ John Hatt)

Ali Ibrahim: 87. pan; 150. l & uc; 151. pan; 308. l

Daniel Luscombe: 14. uc

Mimi Merttens: 55. ll; 207. r

Hugh Nicholson: 20. lr; 32. r; 41. uc; 44. ll & ur; 57. ul; 93. lr & inset; 107. ll; 192. no. 4; 205. ll; 206. ul; 240. lr; 257. ll; 392. inset lr; 393. inset ll; 394. inset ur

Matt O'Riley: 24. lc

Oxford Scientific Films: 425. uc (© Michael Fogden)

Miranda Barwick-Philbin: 259. lc

Darrel Plowes: 386. l

Random House: viii–x. Zone map (Courtesy Random House, Australia, *Botanica; The Illustrated A-Z of Over 10,000 Garden Plants and How to Cultivate Them*)

Jerry Rogers: 30. l; 31. ur; 39. pan; 56. l; 81. uc & r; 115. pan; 358. l

Chris Rollins: 31. no. 3

Hermes Rodriguez Sanchez: 46. lc; 47. ul & inset; 48. ul & inset; 55. lc; 73. uc & r; 130. l & r; 167. ur & inset; 168. ll & inset; 329. ll, uc & lc; 369. uc; 370. r

Garry Sankowsky: 135. uc; 291. ll; 393. inset ur; 401. inse ll

Anton van der Schans: 3. ur & inset; lr & inset; 4. ll & inset; 7 all; 9. ur; 14. l, lc & r; 19. l; 20. l & lc; 21. l; 24. lc; 25. uc; 30. r; 31. pan; 37. ll & r; 42. all; 44.lr; 45. ul; 46. l & ur; 47. ur; 51. lc & r; 54. all; 55. uc & r; 57. ll & lr; 58. ll, ur & lr; 69. r; 71. ll; 77. pan & inset; 79. ll; 80. all; 82. r; 86. l; 92. l & uc; 93. ur & inset; 94. ur & inset; 95. ur & inset, ul & inset; ll & inset; 96. l & lc; 98. r; 107. uc, lc & r; 111. l; 114. lc; 118. ur; 121. lc; 124. r; 127. uc & lc; 134. lc; 135. ll; 137. ll & r; 140. lr; 142. l, lc & lr; 147. r; 149. inset ur; 152. l; 158. lr; 160. lc & lr; 161. ul, ll & lr; 162. all; 169. lr inset; 171. ul & l; 172. ul & ll; 173. all; 177. ul; 179. ul & inset; ur & inset; 182. r; 186. lr inset; 191. all; 192. nos 1, 2 & pan; 193; ll, uc & lc; 197. l & uc; 200. lc; 203. all; 205. uc & r; 206. ll; 209. r; 212. uc, lc & r; 215. uc & lc; 216. all; 217. ll; 224. l & lc; 227. lc; 228. l; 234. lr; 242. l; 246. all; 254. uc; 255. uc & r; 257. lc & r; 259. ll; 260. lr; 265. ul & ll; 267. uc, lc & r; 268. all; 269. all; 270. ul & inset; ur & inset; 277. all; 278. uc; 284. lc; 294. lc; 303. all; 309. ll & lc; 310. lr; 315. all; 330. lc; 340. l; 341. uc & rl; 345. lr inset; 349. uc & r; 352. uc; 355. lc; 356. uc; 367. r; 369. lc & r; 372. uc & lc; 373. ul; 374. l; 378. l & lr; 379. ll & r; 383. all; 384. lr; 385. ll; 391. ul & inset; 392. ul & inset, lr; 393. ul, ur & ll; 394. ur; 395. pan; 403. ll & lc; 408. lc; 409. ul, ur, ll & inset; 410 inset ul; 411. ur; 413. nos 1, 2 & 3; 416. uc & r; 417. ll, uc & r; 418. lc & lr; 427. all

Singapore Botanic Gardens: 266. lr

J. B. von Spix and C. F. P. von Martius: endpapers (Bird-hunting in the Brazilian forest. From *Atlas zur Reise Brasilien in den Jahren 1817 bis 1820*, by J. B. von Spix and C. F. P. von Martius, 1823–31)

Glenn Thomas: 42. uc

David Warmington: 147. pan; 159. uc

INDEX

Arranged as follows:

COMMON NAME

Botanical name of illustrated main species
    & subsiduary species

*Botanical name of species described but not
illustrated*
    (Botanical names – synonyms)

470

475

479

482

483